ENCYCLOPEDIA OF
Gardening

ENCYCLOPEDIA OF
Gardening

OCTOPUS BOOKS

Text by Č. Bōhm, A. Dolejši, A. Dvořák, K. Hieke, B. Jaša,
H. Kasparová, j. Mareček, V. Mōlzer, M. Opatrná, J. Soukup,
J. Šedivý, R. Šrot, V. Urban, J. Václavik, V. Vaněk and V. Valter.

617 colour photographs by V. Dolejši (4), I. Houser (46), P. Hron
(7), Z. Humpál (150), A. Koči (27), J. Krýsl (11), V. Plicka (35),
V. Pokorný (21), J. Tykač (136), V. Vaněk (172), R. Vitek (6),
M. Vokřál (2).
124 line drawings by M. Váňa

Translated by D. Coxon, N. Hronková, O. Kuthanová,
S. Pošustová and V. Sochor.
English edition first published in 1987 by
Octopus Books Limited
Michelin House, 81 Fulham Road
London SW3, 6RB, England
© 1987 Artia, Prague
Reprinted 1988

ISBN 0 7064 2858 7
Printed in Czechoslovakia by TSNP, Martin
3/99/51/51-02

Contents

Man and his garden   11
   Decorative and useful gardens   13
   Creating a garden   14
   The evolution of a garden   17
   A beautiful garden   19
   The artistic aspects of a garden   19
   Fundamental aesthetic principles in garden
     planning   21
   Types of gardens   25

Architectural features   **33**
   Paths   33
   Sitting-out areas and terraces   38
   Fences   41
   Summerhouses   42
   Water in the garden   43
   Steps   47
   Pergolas and arbours   50
   A children's corner   51
   A fireplace, barbecue or hearth   51
   Lighting   52
   Garden furniture   52
   Small architectural features   53
   Useful objects   53

The introduction of plants   **57**
   Plants and ecology   58
   Soil   60
   Irrigation   71

Basics of practical work   **74**
   Preparing the soil   74
   Sowing and planting   75
   Care of plants during the growing season   78
   Vegetative propagation   79
   Other work in the garden   82

Machinery, tools and garden accessories   **83**
   Basic tools   83
   Specialized tools   83
   A few words about mechanization   88

Diseases and pests in the garden   **89**
   Diseases   89
   Animal pests   97

Weeds   **113**
   Garden weeds   113
   Complex weed control in the garden   115

Fruit   **117**
   Division of fruit trees, bushes, etc.   118
   Parts of fruit trees and bushes   119
   The soil and climate requirements
     of fruit trees and bushes   120
   Shapes of fruit trees and stocks   120
   Planting fruit trees and bushes   121
   Care throughout the year   123
   Pruning fruit trees   125
   Budding and grafting   131
   Intensive methods of cultivation   133
   Picking and storing fruit   134
   The cultivation of various kinds of fruit   136
   Some lesser known species of fruit   160
   A few words in conclusion   161

Vegetables   **165**
   Conditions for the successful cultivation
     of vegetables   166
   Planning the planting of vegetables   167
   Crop rotation   168
   Growing vegetables by direct sowing   169
   Growing vegetables from pre-cultivated
     seedlings   170
   Caring for vegetables during the growing
     season   171
   Forcing vegetables   174
   Vegetables grown under cloches   176
   Harvesting and storage of vegetables   177
   Brassicas   178
   Fruit vegetables   184
   Onions and related vegetables   192
   Root vegetables   199
   Leaf vegetables   204
   Leguminous vegetables   210
   Herbs and aromatic vegetables   212
   Other vegetables   216
   Mushrooms in the garden   222

Lawn   **227**
   Sowing a lawn   227
   Laying turf   228
   Care of the lawn   228
   Other types of soil cover   231

Ornamental trees and shrubs   **233**
   Evergreen trees and shrubs   233
   Conifers in the garden   233

Evergreen broadleaved trees and shrubs   233
Deciduous broadleaved trees and shrubs   234
Climbing woody plants   234
Choosing conifers   235
Requirements of ornamental broadleaved trees
    and shrubs   244
Choosing evergreen broadleaved trees and
    shrubs   245
Choosing deciduous broadleaved trees and
    shrubs   246
Broadleaved trees and shrubs for the rock
    garden   249
Broadleaved trees and shrubs for the heath
    garden   250
Broadleaved trees and shrubs for miniature rock
    gardens and containers   252
Climbing woody plants   253
Hedges   256
General rules for planting ornamental trees and
    shrubs   259
Care of trees and shrubs in later years   262
Propagating ornamental trees and shrubs   264

Roses   273
Description of the plant   273
Biological properties of roses   274
Classification of roses   275
Soil and climatic conditions   275
Planting   278
Care of roses   281
Detrimental factors   291
Propagation of roses   292

Perennials   295
Importance of site   295
Selecting perennials for the garden   296
Cultivated varieties   297
Use of perennials   298
Two types of garden   298
From spring till autumn   299
Rules for siting perennials   300
Perennials for cutting   310
Specimen perennials   310
Prime sites for garden perennials   311
Preparing the soil   312
Planting   315
Care of perennials   316
Perennials in winter   318
Propagating perennials   319

Annuals and biennials   331
Origins of annuals   331
Use of annuals   332
Sowing, planting and care   342
Propagation   345

Bulbs and tubers   351
Use of bulbous and tuberous plants   352
Cultivation in the garden   360
Reproduction   366
Bulbs and tubers in pots   367

Rock plants   371
Rockeries and dry walls   371
Establishing a rock garden or a dry wall   372
Seasons in the rock garden   375
Planting rock garden plants   385
Basic care of rock plants   385
Miniature rock gardens   386
Rock garden plants in the greenhouse   389

Heath garden   397
Plants for the heath garden   397
Basic care   397
The heath garden throughout the year   398
Recommended plants   399

Grasses and ferns in the garden
Recommended ornamental perennial
    grasses   402
Shaded areas with ferns   404
Recommended ferns   404

Water in the garden   407
Plants in and by water   407
Planting and care of the plants   410

Flowers without a garden   415
Window-boxes   415
Plants for balconies   416
Roof gardens   417
Greenery in containers   419
Plants suitable for window-boxes, balconies,
    terraces and roof gardens   421

Index   434

Man and his garden

Man's close involvement in nature has been one of the most sympathetic features of the development of human society since time immemorial; not only on the level of economic needs but also cultural ones.

Economically, man has always depended on natural resources to provide food, shelter, clothing, furniture and furnishings. In terms of culture, natural elements have been an inexhaustible source of creative, artistic inspiration. The extent and quality of man's use of these resources has varied at different stages in his long history, but even in the most primitive human cultures we can find evidence of nature's influence. This is shown in the way questions of material existence were resolved and in the legacy of artistic expression, in which natural elements and motifs clearly played a very important part.

The deliberate cultivation of nature to create gardens, and the functional use made of these gardens, have also changed in the course of history.

The high expectations that the ancient Greeks and Romans had of their gardens grew from the already advanced culture of oriental gardens, one of the very foundation stones of the world culture of gardening. The ancient Greeks and Romans lived in their gardens just as often as in their houses. In summer, day and night, home life was lived in the courtyard. In hot, southern countries this area had to be cooled and moistened, and so the first cascades, pools and fountains, so typical of southern gardens, even today, were introduced.

In the 12th to 16th century Gothic conception of gardens, the trend was to move from naturalism; a characteristic feature being their geometrical division into regular shapes and a highly formal, mechanical planting of regular flowerbeds. This conception — of gardens as being simply collections of either decorative or useful plants — is also evident in their lack of relationship to the surrounding buildings: the garden did not form an integral artistic part of a building, but rather stood passively by.

The Renaissance period was of great importance in the development of gardens. In accord with the new trends of thought, the essence of which was the individual's longing for free self-realization and joy in earthly life, the idea of the garden also changed. Gardens became not only natural complements to the new-built homes of the nobility, but also took an important place in middle-class building. As comfortable mansions were built rather than inaccessible castles with their essentially confined, strictly limited gardens, the often extensive areas of manor gardens and parks became the fashion. The size of the gardens of the middle classes greatly increased, too.

Not only were Renaissance gardens designed on a grander scale, but great emphasis was placed on their social function. The garden became a status symbol, a pleasing and impressive place in which to receive and entertain guests. So beauty was of importance not only in the details of a garden, but in its whole composition. A characteristic feature of the

forms, and the masterly use of the natural terrain by building terraces from which even greater perspectives can be enjoyed.

At the height of the period of feudalism, the gardens of some big farms and smaller estates became more modest reflections of the magnificence of the noblemen's gardens and parks. These influences even appeared in vicarage or school gardens. A typical feature of these adaptations was the way in which they were sensitively linked with the rest of the village and its surrounding countryside.

The economic and social events of the end of the 18th century, as the long period of feudalism drew to a close, are reflected, among other things, in the critical view taken of the regular style that had thus far dominated baroque gardens. This new trend of thought basically represented the opinions of the French philosopher Rousseau, who advocated a return to nature. This was the beginning of a new trend in the evolution of the garden.

But the road to this new recognition of the beauties of nature was not a straight one. It was marked in the first place by romanticism, the early stages of which survived for a long time in many gardens in the form of buildings, such as hermitages, artificial ruins, follies, Egyptian pyramids or Turkish minarets, so that gardens became a collection of curiosities imposed at the expense of the overall plan.

The return to more natural gardens was partly influenced by the Chinese art of gardening, with its emphasis on unconfined nature. But this source of inspiration could not alone satisfy the needs of the newly forming society, as it was overweighted with symbolism of nature.

It was only when Europe became dominated by the influence of English landscape planning, which takes its inspiration from nature and develops it further according to the needs of the time and society, that a true relationship between modern man and nature could be formed. The basis of a garden is nature itself: the architecture merely underlines and seeks to enhance the effect of the natural environment. So the romantic landscape garden gradually gave way to the natural landscape garden. This, in turn, was changed by the Victorians, who introduced gravelled paths of white chippings intended to complement highly sentimental statues of coy young maidens and to offset garishly vivid flower beds. Fortunately, at the beginning of the present century, Miss Gertrude Jekyll and her esteemed colleague and friend, William Robinson, reintroduced a more subtle architecture and discarded everything 'jarring and displeasing'. Miss Jekyll strove always to create a harmonious whole in which plantings were subtly graded in colour. Her influence has endured even into the 1980s and no doubt will continue.

So the purpose and design of gardens have been through great changes in the past, according to the philosophy of each succeeding era. And we can hardly consider the present-day garden to be static in form. The extent of changes in its overall development undoubtedly corresponds, as it always has, to the changes that take place in our society.

planning of a Renaissance garden was an attempt to make it an aesthetically effective whole. Geometric divisions still applied — circles, semi-circles, rectangles and so on — but these were now linked by lawns, paths, well-spaced trees, open trellis fencing and elegant archways. Along with these tendencies, the first efforts were made to create a spatially functional link between the house and garden. Summerhouses, loggias, pools and so on were introduced in order to fulfil the social functions of the Renaissance garden. Chaucer's 14th century *Roumaunt de la rose* contains an illustration of one such garden.

One of the most important evolutionary contributions of 17th century baroque gardens was the way in which they penetrated into the landscape just beyond their own confines. This was achieved partly by forming vistas from the garden into purposely prepared landscapes, partly by actual penetration into this surrounding territory, for instance via approach drives. The buildings, too, formed a compositional whole with the garden. The variety of these excellently planned relationships between buildings and their natural surroundings is still a rich source of inspiration, as are many other aesthetic principles of planned gardens. For instance, variations of contrasts, ornaments, the geometrical shaping of bushes and hedges, the use of vistas, of water in various

Decorative and useful gardens

The relationship between the purely decorative value of a garden and its more down-to-earth economic use is often confused. People are apt to think that the two are incompatible, and this can lead to many mistakes in designing a garden layout.

The idea of obtaining beauty and usefulness in

a garden area should not be separated; each utilitarian element should also be a pleasure to look at. This is especially important in small gardens. We can hardly lay out two independent areas — one decorative and the other useful — when working with an area of 300 or 400 square metres, though such division might have been easier when gardens tended to be larger. So for modern life it is more practical to consider not separate decorative and useful parts, but rather a combined function.

However, the combination must be handled with care. It is not a matter simply of indiscriminately sowing vegetables and flowers next to one another, or placing strawberry plants in among the rock plants with little or no regard for the visual impact. It must be thoroughly worked out beforehand.

The main thing in planning the mutual relationships between the various elements is that their functions should not oppose one another. For instance, a direct view from the sitting-out area of the garden on to a well-kept fruit orchard is a good composition because it makes simultaneous use of both decorative and useful elements.

Cordons of fruit trees, besides being economically important, can make a very attractive and effective fence round a garden, or subdivide it into various sections. As cordons are of uniform size and shape they look good in an area of the garden that is regularly or geometrically designed; on the other hand, fruit trees growing singly look good in areas that are irregular or informal. Especially suitable for this sort of situation are types that do not need radical or regular pruning, or constructional cutting of their branches. For instance, hazels, walnuts, Morello cherries, cherries and currant bushes all fall into this easy category. These trees or bushes can be used in much the same way as ornamental shrubs. They can be planted irregularly or combined with decorative plants such as perennials. Other elements that make an effective contribution to garden composition are a well-designed pool which can also be used for watering the plants, a beehive, a small greenhouse and/or a cold frame, containers and garden furniture.

One of the most important considerations in garden planning is the relationship between decoration and usefulness in the case of a single element such as a hedge or a fence. Aesthetically, the basic failing of some hedges is that they make too abrupt an ending to a garden, a sudden and illogical full stop to the composition. Ideally, a hedge should, on the contrary, provide a fitting framework for the garden, a continuation of its architecture. The types of hedges chosen for various parts of the garden may be different, as required by the functions of the particular part, but they should be complementary.

Garden paths come into the same category. If they are of grass they can at the same time fulfil the aesthetic and useful functions of a lawn. Hard surface paths of brick, stone or gravel artistically divide up the ground plan, and at the same time form an architectural continuation of various garden buildings (for example a paved path of natural stone may con-

The horizontal plane of the surface of water is in harmonious contrast with the vertical axis formed by the aquatic plants and nearby conifers. Paving of natural stone is always preferred in proximity to water.

A roofed sitting-out area forms a natural link between the house and the patio.

A dense hedge protects the garden from dust and noise.

tinue the architectural effect of a terrace of the same stone). Another desirable function of paths is that if we site them carefully we can get good views of the whole garden when using them. Thus not even a path is merely a practical facility.

The cultivation of useful plants should also be aesthetically effective. Just as a well ploughed field is beautiful in its way, so the 'edible' plants in a garden should be visually appealing by virtue of their arrangement, cleanliness, and general state of health. Some of these plants — the globe artichoke or rhubarb, for example — also have good sculptural shape and colour. Visual impact can also be accomplished by, say, planting all the apple trees together, or all the plum trees together rather than mixing them arbitrarily.

The unity of purpose should also be one of the fundamental principles in arranging the garden as a whole. For instance, it would be insensitive to site a garden pergola or a laminated summerhouse containing massed, colourfull tall plants near to an old and tiny cottage. Here the layout should be in keeping with the age and style of the house. The main area of the garden might consist of a grassy courtyard with a period well; a widened threshold would serve the purpose of a small terrace; shade could be afforded by a lime tree or a chestnut. Vines, ivy or roses could be placed where they would climb the walls, and colour be supplied by sweet-scented lilacs, guelder-roses, snowball trees, geraniums or rosemary.

Creating a garden

Arranging a garden
The arrangement of a garden always depends on what is wanted of it. Broadly speaking, a garden may be said to have three main functions: economic, social and microclimatic. In practice, these functions are usually combined. Indeed they may be dependent upon one another.

The economic function of a garden is to provide space in which to cultivate fruit and vegetables. Here, the basic criterion is the maximum intensity of use of the available ground, and to achieve this, certain principles must be observed. One of these is the correct planning of light and shade, because the better the light that plants or trees have, the bigger and better the harvest that can be expected of them. A fundamental condition for the best use of sunlight is not only the correct spacing of the plants, but also their correct number and size. The extent of the area to be cultivated is decisive both for the number of plants grown and the species or varieties chosen. For example, if only a small area is available, we should cultivate dwarf fruit trees and quick-growing sorts of vegetables.

The economic utilization of a garden is also greatly influenced by the quality of the soil, the local climate, the amount of moisture and other natural conditions. Although measures can be taken to improve some of these conditions where necessary, they can seldom be changed completely. So cultivation plans should be based on existing conditions and be adapted to them.

One of the key ways in which a high cultivation intensity can be achieved is the rotation of crops. This is usually observed out of simple necessity in the case of annuals and biennials but with long-term plants it is often forgotten. A systematic rotation of fruit and vegetables should be thought out before the garden is laid out.

The system of rotation has other advantages besides being the most rational use of the soil. By confining short-season plants to areas neighbouring but not crowding one another, a whole formation of low growth occurs, so that sunlight and air can reach the innermost part of the crop. This allows the plants to develop properly and be less liable to attract diseases and pests.

The harmonious outlines of a flat rock garden are enlivened by the contrasting vertical lines of slender conifers.

An example of a garden serving as an extension of the house. The large terrace has become a part of the living space. The window offers a private view delineated by the nearby wall and by the screen of tall trees in the background.

the late summer and autumn, causing the fruit to fall prematurely. However, winds from all directions can be useful to gardens that lie in a valley, as they help to make it more airy. Air currents can be given the required direction by planting bushes as windscreens but remember that these are most effective if they slow down and filter the wind, rather than block it completely — in which event it will come over the top instead.

The atmosphere inside such green belts is also fresher, because foliage acts as a dust-filter. The larger the leaves the better filters they make. Because of the slowing down of the air current on impact with the green barrier, dust particles tend also to remain suspended in the atmosphere. This means that dustiness is increased in the direct proximity of the anti-dust plantings, so this is not a good site for a patio or terrace, or a recreation area.

Apart from its anti-dust function, vegetation has the effect of muffling sound, and here again it is the leaves which play the most important part. Most ef-

The microclimatic function of a garden is to improve the microclimatic and hygienic conditions of the environment. As a garden usually surrounds or adjoins a house, it also influences the microclimate of the home. Greenery has a cooling effect on its surroundings. It helps to regulate the microclimate's water system (humidity and formation of dew), by the very necessary slowing down of the natural cycle of water.

The planting of a garden can also exert a modifying influence on the air currents. Of course, a calculation must first be made of the potential harmfulness or usefulness of prevailing winds from different directions, and this depends on the use you plan to make of the given area. For instance, an apple orchard should be protected against winds that blow in

A green wall of broadleaved trees ensures privacy in the garden, ameliorates its microclimate and protects it from dust and noise.

fective of all are bushes with hairy leaves. When the leaves fall, of course, the trees become much less effective, but in winter this may be partly compensated for by a thick covering of snow or frost. Well-kept lawns also have this ability to muffle sound.

Greenery also has an influence on the content of micro-organisms in the atmosphere. Many plants exude volatile oils, resins and other substances that retard the development of microflora. Also, when micro-organisms settle on the leaves, they are held there by surface tension and adhesion, and thus can be better destroyed by solar radiation. Other plants repel insects. Another important function of green plants is their beneficial influence on the oxygen cycle.

Finally, there is their far from negligible effect on our mental well-being. The artistic aspect of creating a garden is very satisfying, and our physical state, too, can be improved — not least by the healthy exercise involved.

There are a few rules on garden-planning that should be stressed in connection with the principles already given to improve the microclimate:

The relationship between the house and the garden should be a direct one. Also, when planning what to plant, use should be made of the arrangement of plants at various levels. A combination of low-growing (and shade-loving) plants and taller bushes can be made. Or, one could combine low-growing perennial plants with fruit trees or bushes.

The planting of coniferous trees and evergreen shrubs can do much to improve the microclimatic conditions, and climbers, too, deserve special attention. By shading the walls of buildings they prevent these getting too hot on sunny summer days, and so decrease the possibility of unpleasant thermal radiation at night. It is thus very short-sighted to consider climbing plants as being merely decorative.

Lawns are in every respect a very effective form of greenery. They influence the maximum absorption of water, protect the environment from dust and noise, have a favourable effect on the microbes in the soil, make for a vast leafy area as compared with most other vegetation, and so exercise a considerable influence on many other microclimatic processes. Space is often a limiting factor, but there is no need to lay down single-purpose lawn areas. Other places can be made use of. For instance, little used paths, the sides of terraces, or the area just by the house can be grassed over. Maximum use should be made of the garden area from this aspect too.

The social function of a garden depends on the extent to which it is 'lived' in and on its aesthetic appeal. One of the things that make it pleasant to be in is its intimacy. Most people need at least part of their garden to afford privacy from being overlooked, if they are to achieve a feeling of complete, informal comfort. This means isolating the garden, at least optically, from its surroundings, and then creating intimate sitting-out areas.

In order to make the garden a nice, informal place to live in the mutual spatial links between garden and house are important. By this we mean direct connections between the various rooms and parts of the garden via garden doors or French windows which open out directly on to a terrace or patio area.

At least parts of these areas should always be covered, so that they can be used in any weather. As they are likely to be in constant use, they should also be strongly constructed. They may be joined on to

Key to symbols used in garden designs

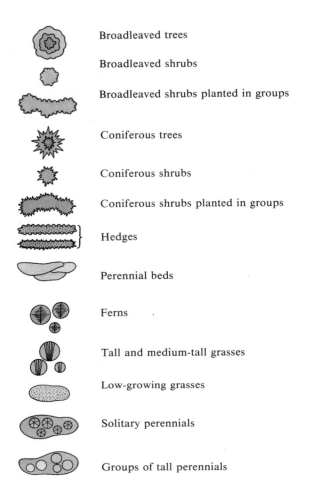

Broadleaved trees

Broadleaved shrubs

Broadleaved shrubs planted in groups

Coniferous trees

Coniferous shrubs

Coniferous shrubs planted in groups

Hedges

Perennial beds

Ferns

Tall and medium-tall grasses

Low-growing grasses

Solitary perennials

Groups of tall perennials

In a large garden, several pergolas can be linked to form a covered walk. In this plan, each section has been trained with a different climbing species, all in toning colours. The boundary wall is patly hidden by a hedge. The front garden features two focal points — *Corylus colurna* and a Douglas Fir. Colour is added by azaleas in spring and perennial groups in summer.

the house or they may be independent summer-houses strategically positioned in various parts of the garden.

Another important item in a garden that is lived in is durable and comfortable garden furniture: tables, chairs, hammocks, and also swings for children.

No garden should lack a grass play area for recreational sports and children's games; that is, for active leisure pursuits. A natural stream or a purpose-built pond or pool are also very desirable, as areas of water have a recreational, aesthetic and a micro-climatic function.

As the garden should also be for children, it should include a children's corner, and this should be in view of the house windows so that a watchful eye can be kept on very young children or toddlers.

To make the garden habitable as often as possible, it is important to plan places that will be in sunshine or shade for at least part of the day. The planting of flowers, foliage plants, shrubs and trees, and the siting of buildings so that they will throw a shade should all be thought out carefully so that, at any time of day, there should be both sunny and shady areas — particularly on a terrace, sitting-out area and lawn. This makes for a comfortable garden where people can always find just the place they want to be at any time of day or evening.

Night lighting increases still further the possibilities of using the garden. The lights should be sited not merely to make it easy to move about the garden safely at night, but to emphasize its most attractive features.

Another way to increase the use of the garden is to install some source of warmth. Mostly, one cannot sit out on the terrace for any length of time in the early spring or autumn, or indeed even on cool summer evenings, because it is too cold. This can be overcome by building a garden hearth or barbecue or some similar source of heat.

The evolution of a garden

No garden is ever completely finished; it is always at a certain stage of development. Its cultivation involves us in endless creative activity. We are constantly influencing its evolution towards what we want of the garden as a whole. So any plans for creating or altering a garden must take into account the aspects of space and time.

The first thing that is subject to change is the garden's economic yield. For instance, after planting apple trees we have to wait for several years before they bear much fruit. This time gap can be filled in by the cultivation of soft fruit, such as currants, gooseberries, raspberries and blackberries and, of course, strawberries. If space is at a premium, as the fruit trees reach mature size and give better crops, we can gradually decrease the cultivation of soft fruits over the years. In some circumstances too, the initial poor yields of apple trees can be increased by planting a greater number of young trees which can also be gradually reduced.

The decorative garden also changes from year to

This paved terrace with comfortable seating forms a pleasant connecting link between the house and the garden.

year. In the early stages, when especially the newly planted trees and shrubs are small, it is not very effective aesthetically. It sometimes takes many years for a garden to attain its full aesthetic effect. But this wait for the desired result can be compensated for by strategic short-term planting to create a 'temporary beauty'. These plants, too, will later be discarded or restricted according to the progress of those planted

Design for a plot located among tall buildings. A pergola with climbers shelters the sitting-out terrace and a part of the paved area behind the house, so that some privacy is provided for its inhabitants. The graduated, compact growth of mixed shrubs covers the neighbouring plot to such an extent that no fence is necessary. Next to the shrubs grows a group of tall spruces with an underplanting of low conifers. The vegetable garden is separated from the street by a group of woody plants which do not shade it too much. The kitchen garden has been located in the least frequented corner of the plot. The window-less wall of the neighbouring house is masked by climbers.

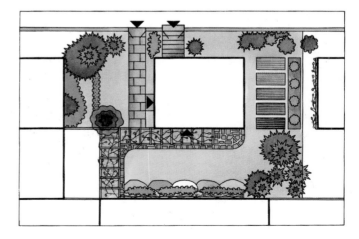

for more long-term effectiveness. With this in mind, don't get carried away by enthusiasm and spend disproportionate amounts on temporary 'fillers'.

These decorative short-term plantings may be of many kinds. In the first instance, use can be made of quick-growing shrubs, which provide a tall, thick screen in a relatively short time. However, care must be taken that they do not compete too strongly with other plants. It often happens that these 'temporary' plants push out or weaken those intended to be permanent, so that the original aim is never fulfilled, or at best becomes still more distant. To avoid such possibilities, plant temporary, quick-growing woody plants at some distance from those that you intend should remain permanently.

Another way is to plant long-term shrubs more closely together than usual, so that their foliage grows together more quickly and the desired overall effect is achieved sooner — a compact and pleasant mass of green. This kind of thick planting is suitable from the biological and technological point of view too. The thick growth of the shrubs makes for a more favourable microclimate, important for instance in dry sites. There is also less danger of infestation by weeds, and this favourable effect, in turn, improves the growth of the plants. Bushes make a good thick growth, but trees can also be used. These thick growths may be either permanent or temporary, but care must be taken if the two are mixed, because when endeavouring to thin out the temporary ones later there is considerable risk of damaging the permanent stock.

To guarantee the aesthetic effect of temporary groups of plants they must be chosen to group well together. For instance a young group of low, spreading junipers may be thickened with medium-high perennial grasses, the low-growing garden roses look well in a group of pine trees, and so on.

A large sitting-out area. A sandpit is placed on the right of the entrance, a barbecue is on the left. The barbecue area is screened by a hedge and planted with a Japanese Maple and junipers. Another maple, *Acer pseudoplatanus*, casts a pleasant shade in which another sitting-out area has been built. Genistas and tamarisks planted in front of the maple serve as a natural hedge sheltering the relaxation area. A group of perennials and a columnar juniper can be viewed from benches placed near the sandpit.

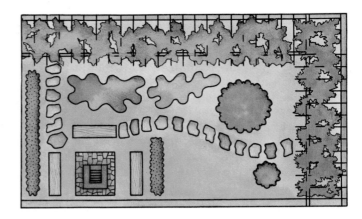

A sitting-out area equipped with a barbecue and garden furniture and screened from the neighbouring houses by a pergola covered with climbers. The main focal point is a Staghorn Sumach (*Rhus typhina*) with a group of hydrangeas as its counterpoint. The barbecue area is divided off from the rest of the garden by an evergreen hedge (*Ligustrum*). A mixture of medium-high perennials planted along the pergola adds colour and fragrance.

Flowers hold an important place among short-term plantings, because while shrubs and trees give an effect through their spatial mass, flowers give it by virtue of their colourfulness. So massed flowers may compensate beautifully for the smallness of young shrubs and fill any other temporary gap in a newly founded garden such as where a piece of statuary may eventually stand.

Climbing woody plants also hold a special place among temporary plantings. Within a very short time, they are able to cover various props and constructions and grow to a considerable height. So even a newly laid-out garden can quickly be provided with various isolating walls and divisions, lending the required intimacy or protection from dust and noise. A pergola covered with climbers can be an excellent source of shade until the time when the young trees grow tall.

Over the years the microclimatic conditions in the garden will also change and the choice of species and varieties to be cultivated may need to be altered, too. If the garden is not situated in a protected position, the planting of warmth-loving plants should be delayed until the microclimate improves with the growth of the surrounding vegetation. And in some cases, fully grown plants may complicate or prevent the cultivation of plants that formerly grew well on the site. For instance, a large number of birches or poplars radically reduces the choice of plants that will grow well in their close vicinity. This is because other plants can hardly compete with the extensive, shallow roots of such trees.

Changes in a garden according to space and time are inevitable, given the biological character of the material being used. The creation of a garden must reckon not only with the planting of plants, but also with uprooting some of them or, indeed, replacing old favourites.

A beautiful garden

People spend a great deal of time not only in their homes but also in their gardens; children grow up there and family relationships are formed. For these very good reasons, the artistic effect of this environment should not be a matter of indifference. If we think of a garden from this point of view we shall consider its beauty to be a vital feature — quite as important as its economic yield.

A beautiful garden does not come into being through a random collection of beautiful items. If, at the same time, we do not plan their mutual artistic relationships, the result — at best — will be a collection of beautiful items, but not a beautiful garden. No exact rules can be laid down for planning an artistic garden, because allowance must be made for individual tastes, but at least some generally valid aesthetic principles can be given.

The artistic aspects of a garden

The artistic planning of a garden is basically guided by the same generally valid rules that apply in other forms of artistic creation. In the first place it must be based on the aesthetic qualities of all the natural elements used, as these will always be the most essential components. Very important roles are played by the special function of planting, the effectiveness of the forms and textures of the green areas, and also the use of colour, light and shade and so on. Then, too, an artistic conception of a garden means that the economic and aesthetic aspects must be regarded as a whole, not separately.

A good scheme combining the utility and aesthetic functions of a garden. A sitting-out terrace with a pergola and a pool forms a link between the house and the garden. The grassy 'live-in' part of the garden features an old-fashioned well and a bench shaded by a stately tree (Walnut, Lime or Horse Chestnut). An orchard, with a perfectly kept lawn, is located behind this section. A wall covered with grapevines forms the boundary of the plot and at the rear end of the garden there is a clipped hedge. The kitchen garden, opposite to the orchard, has a group of broadleaved and coniferous shrubs separating it from the flower garden — which features statuary. The boundary between the terrace and the garden is marked by a group of dwarf shrubs which provides further visual interest without obstructing the view of the garden sculpture.

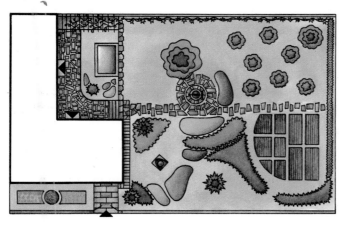

A chimney in the garden makes an attractive dominant in a rest area and enables a prolonged stay in this part of the garden late into the evening.

Natural elements in a garden

When considering the aesthetic conception of a garden we must assess the artistic values of the main groups of decorative plants. There are great differences between them, and not only with regard to their ability to fulfil an aesthetic function. Various species of decorative plants can call up very different impressions and ideas.

The use of water, artistic exploitation of the terrain, providing suitable conditions for birds to nest and so on, all come under the artistic planning of a garden.

The projection of an attractive garden entails the sensitive blending of the various pleasant qualities of the natural surroundings with the buildings, architectural details and with the landscape in general.

Grouping plants artistically

A beautiful garden does not take shape automatically, by the mere introduction of beautiful plants. Good results can only be achieved by respecting the relationships between the plants themselves, and between them and the garden as a whole. The beauty of many shrubs, for instance, can only be fully appreciated in certain combinations with other plants, buildings or spaces. There will be detailed guidance on suitable combinations of plants in later chapters devoted to the main groups.

Roughly speaking, there are two basic principles involved in the artistic planning of a decorative garden, i.e. two ways of combining decorative plants. The first groups them according to purely aesthetic rules and relationships, the second according to their natural occurrence in the wild.

Planting according to aesthetic rules

One of the basic principles here is to group the plants according to the colour of their flowers, either so that the colours harmonize or are in pleasing contrast. For instance, the mauve of the Chinese lilac combines well with the yellow of the laburnum, which flowers at the same time. Greyish or silver-leaved plants give the effect of white, and therefore have a linking, neutral effect. A contrasting effect may also be based on the proximity of plants with slender or rounded shapes, those with large leaves and small, or linking a light foreground of a lawn and flowers with a dark background of conifers.

Another aesthetic principle is to associate plants according to similar qualities. For instance maples, with their typical palmately lobed leaves, combine well with plane trees, which have similarly shaped leaves. In a small area of the garden there might be a group linked by the analogous qualities of the various species, for instance a corner of dwarf conifers or one composed of predominantly blue or red flowering plants.

The placing of decorative plants can also be planned with a view to their flowering time. For instance, the arrangement of a flowerbed that will be in flower from spring to autumn. Or one that has been timed to reach its maximum effect at a certain time — such as a grouping of annuals that will be in full flower during the holidays, or a group of shrubs that will give a spring or an autumn effect and so on.

In groupings of plants where the aesthetic effect is the decisive factor, the plants combined may often require different conditions. This frequently means different soil treatment, watering and general care, and is therefore apt to require hard work and specialized knowledge.

A colourful front garden with an irregular mixed planting of woody plants, perennials and annuals. The springy, green lawn crossed by a path of flat stones subtly links the various features of the composition.

Woody climbing plants serve many different purposes in the aesthetic design of a garden. One of their most important features is their ability to form a decorative link between the vegetation and the architectural elements. The material for supports must always be carefully chosen with a view to the final aesthetic effect.

This type of planting is suitable where the given green area is not in direct contact with the surrounding landscape, for instance when surrounded by buildings or high walls or fencing. This type of garden can successfully include all sorts of typical garden plants, often of foreign origin, that would not fit into a garden planned to look completely natural (for instance dahlias, tulips, gladioli, pansies, shrubs with variegated leaves, carpet-forming flowers etc).

Decorative planting as a stylized version of nature

Here, the artistic aim is not a mere harmonizing of colours, shapes and so on, as in the case given above, but an expression of the beauty of wild life.

The creation of this kind of stylization should always be based on the given local conditions, the aim being to make the garden blend with the natural landscape.

But this arrangement can also be chosen for a single, small part of the garden, where you can create, say, a miniature heath, a field of irises or a dry hillside. But there is a danger that in imitating nature in an artifical environment an originally good intention may turn into bad taste. For instance, a rocky slope built by piling up a heap of stones on level ground will look just as unconvincing as, say, a 'heath' right next to a brick wall or concrete steps. A large measure of sensitivity is essential in stylizing the characteristics of natural elements, and the overall conception of the garden must be constantly borne in mind. It can easily happen that enthusiasm takes over and by placing a number of such natural patches too close to one another, the garden becomes a series of small plots and its charm as a whole is destroyed.

However, even in such 'natural' parts there is no need always to use only the original native plants. Instead of the wild catchfly, its cultivated garden form can be used; instead of the common juniper its columnar garden form, or the numerous varieties of foreign junipers. A suitable combination of these garden forms and the corresponding foreign species with local ones enhances the natural 'wild' beauty of your carefully cultivated garden.

Other natural elements in garden planning

Plants apart, the character of the terrain is important in the aesthetic conception of a garden. The best conditions are formed by land that is rather undulated. This offers greater possibilities of creating different areas, even in a small garden, without upsetting the overall effect. For instance, a steep slope can be made into an alpine garden, a small level area into a lawn, and a deep, narrow depression is the ideal setting for a pond. The differing ground levels make these various areas look completely natural, not artificial and disconnected, as would be the case if they were contrived on flat ground. Hilly terrain also makes it possible to view the parts of the garden from varying heights, from above and below, and this further enhances the effect of the whole garden. These variations in the level of the land also usually indicate a variation in the soil composition, so that the growing of different kinds of plants looks very natural. Rocks or stones jutting out of the ground make a particularly favourable situation, improving the artistic effect.

On flat ground the garden cannot be so varied, but this does not mean that it cannot be equally effective. Here, for instance, larger uninterrupted areas of plants or stretches of grass or water will look well. With the distance of view that flat terrain affords, the effect of all sorts of dominants stands out. The lack of natural articulation can, to a certain extent, be compensated for by a few well chosen and strategically placed walls and partitions.

In forming an undulated terrain artificially, the most natural-looking result can usually be obtained by making the new formations quite obviously artificial — for instance, a regular shape for the lawn, which may have a depressed level, or geometrical shapes for terraces. Efforts to make such features look natural on completely flat ground seldom turn out well.

One of the natural elements that play an important role in a garden is water. The surroundings are mirrored on its surface, which multiplies and emphasizes the effects of their forms and colours. Also, on sunny days the water reflects sunshine, and a glistening pond makes an effective dominant. It is a pity therefore to make the water's surface invisible either by covering it completely with water plants or having too many tall plants growing on its banks.

Also the movement of water enlivens the garden — either through ripples on the surface caused by the wind, or actually moving water in the form of cascades, waterfalls and fountains, the latter being more usual in small gardens with limited space for features of this kind.

If you are lucky enough to have a stream running through the garden, then its natural curve should be stressed by open areas of grass on either side, or by sensitive planting. Every garden should have water in it in one form or another, situated near easily ac-

Conifers, deciduous broadleaved trees and annual as well as perennial plants, if chosen with taste, can offer attractive colour combinations.

cessible places such as by the edge of a terrace or sitting-out area, or alongside a path.

Another natural element that should not be forgotten is birds, which enliven a garden with their movement and their song. Good conditions should be provided to encourage them to nest in the garden. There might even be an aviary on the terrace or in some corner of the garden, set into the natural framework of trees.

Fundamental aesthetic principles in garden planning

Planning a garden is very similar to the work of an artist who transfers his spatial vision on to canvas

Design for a plot sloping towards the house. The garage is linked to the house by a pergola. The paved terrace has a perfect drainage of rainwater. An informal rocky slope opposite to the terrace is planted with rock garden plants and dwarf shrubs, while the top of the slope features a group of tall trees which heighten it optically when viewed from the house. The lawn is slightly inclined towards the slope to assist the drainage of water during heavy rain. The sloping terrain is made use of in a small rockery placed close to the pergola. Above it lies the vegetable garden and a free group of dwarf fruit trees.

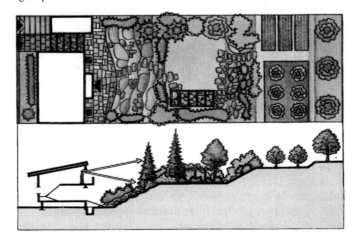

with the aid of various lines. From any given point of observation a garden also can be seen to evolve through a system of lines — axial, outlining and perspective. By means of well-planned planting and the use of suitable building materials the desired effect can be achieved.

A balanced composition

The composition of a garden, like that of a picture, should be well balanced, having on the left side roughly the same number of 'lines' as on the right. A garden may be balanced not only by the use of imaginary lines but also by judicious placement of various spatial objects — such as urns, tubs, statues and garden furniture.

The places where the greatest number of lines meet are called focal points. These require some inventive and interesting arrangement that draws attention to them, for instance a strikingly beautiful shrub or a charming or impressive statue. Not only the lines of the paths, but also the lines of the lawn edges and the outlines of shrubs should lead one's attention towards these focus points.

A dominant in garden composition

This is the element that awakens the observer's greatest interest. Looking from the street it is usually the house, but looking from the house on to the garden, it may be a summerhouse, a pergola, a barbecue area, a pool, a bridge over a stream and so on. The dominant of a garden arrangement may even be outside the garden itself, for instance a church tower or a remarkable group of trees or bushes in a neighbouring field. In a small garden, an interesting tree or an evergreen bush remarkable for its unusual growth, shape or colour may be chosen as the domi-

Various natural garden sections can be created in an undulated terrain. Water provides a dramatic accent to the scene.

nant — or a bed of roses or other flowers. As far as possible, the dominant element should be of a size proportional to the whole composition.

If the chosen dominant is really to stand out, there should be no competitor to it, nothing equally interesting. The most effective surroundings for a dominant is an arrangement of plants on either side of the

Design for a plot sloping from the house. The large paved terrace overlooking the garden offers a view of a perfect oval of lawn bordered by perennials, annuals, biennials, bulbs and tubers with a background of dark conifers. A paved path crosses the lawn towards a secluded summerhouse and a rocky slope next to the resting corner has been turned into a rockery. In the lowermost part of the plot lies the recreation lawn, framed by the surrounding vegetation.

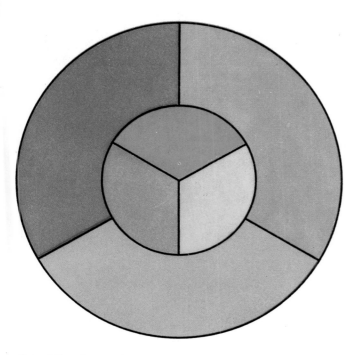

Ostwald's colour cycle.

vista so that the observer is not distracted from the dominant, but rather drawn to it. It should stand in a good light, and in front of it there should be an area of grass or water.

In more large-scale compositions there may sometimes be secondary dominants, subjected to the main one, but broadening and deepening the original idea with added points of interest.

Undesirable dominants, such as chimneys, telegraph poles, unsightly buildings and so on must be suppressed in the composition.

System in garden composition
A unifying link for the various elements used in composing a garden is vital to the success of a scheme,

whether it be of modest proportions or on a grand scale.

The simplest technique is to employ repetition. The repeated element in the composition may be, for instance, colour, shape, shade, the same species of plants, the same kind of stones or stretches of lawn. The repetition must not be so frequent that it becomes monotonous. But repeated use, for example, of the same species of shrub in the garden as grow in the near neighbourhood makes for a pleasant and harmonious link between garden and landscape.

Another system is succession. This, also, is basically repetition — but with a change in some quality of the repeated element, for instance in the colour, shape, size or distance from one another.

A system that is often used is balance: the right and left sides of the composition being so designed that they awaken the same interest in the observer.

Illusion in garden composition
Although the basic principle in the artistic arrangement of a garden is always truth, that is, a representation of nature itself, in many cases a certain deception is necessary in order to heighten the overall impression and effect of the composition.

A typical example of a useful illusion may be the way in which the garden boundaries may be disguised. Sometimes a fence can be so well masked by suitable shrub species that the impression is of an unfenced plot of land. Elsewhere, a fence can be masked by a grassy hillock, thus giving the impression that the garden merges with the landscape without interruption. In this way, the planner contrives the illusion of a large garden that continues into the landscape, of which there is an open view.

Harmony and contrast
The principles of harmony and contrast can be used in designing a garden either independently or combined. There can be harmony or contrast between groups of colours, light and shade, form and line.

Two warm colours placed next to each other (for example, yellow and red) often produce a disharmonious effect. In this case the disharmony has been reduced to a minimum by the pleasant green of the *Hemerocallis* leaves.

If you want to use climbers in the garden, even the slightest details, such as the relation of the plant's colour to that of the neighbouring walls or the size of the leaves in comparison with the scale of the object they are supposed to cover, must be taken into consideration in advance. The picture shows *Campsis radicans*.

A harmonious picture can most often be achieved by grouping together partially similar elements — in terms of colours or shapes, for instance, various shades of green or a repetition in various sizes of the same shape of plants. Basically harmony is repetition, but never exact repetition; it permits small changes.

Also, a harmonious picture may be formed by changing the grouping of identical elements, such as having one species of plants concentrated in thick compact groups in one part of the garden, but spaced out or even single specimens in another part. Harmonious compositions give an impression of calm because they are free of sudden changes, contrasts and tension.

Contrast can be attained by grouping opposites together, whether the opposite factor be one of size, shape, colour, structure, light and shade, the system of lines or whatever. Contrast is one of the most powerful means of expression, as it attracts attention and enlivens and brightens the composition. That is why shady areas should be alternated with well-lit ones, light-coloured statues placed in front of dark backgrounds and so on. It is also effective to combine contrasts of stillness and movement that show up best on close observation, such as the movement of a frothy waterfall descending on the calm surface of a pond.

The incorrect or excessive use of contrast, however, leads to disquiet, fragmentation and lack of truth. Both harmony and contrast must be used in reasonable measure. An excess of harmony makes the composition dull, an excess of contrast makes it confused and breaks up the view.

Ideal bioclimatic conditions for both house and garden are ensured by luxuriant greenery, together with an optimum supply of sunshine.

Light and shade

In arranging a garden, the alternation of light and shade is as important as the sensitive grouping of shapes and colours. The lightest element is always the sky, second place is taken by a surface of water, lawns are rather darker, followed by deciduous trees and shrubs, and lastly conifers — of which the darkest is the yew. Among these trees and shrubs, however, there are some with different-coloured leaves, for instance silver: the Silver-berry, Sea Buckthorn, and Silver Spruce are nearly as light as water.

The various shades of trees and shrubs can be used to stress or reinforce the character of certain parts of the garden. For instance, you can plant conifers in the dark, shady parts and light-coloured deciduous trees in the light places. The sunniest places are best reserved for the glowing colours of flowers, the shady spots being used for rest.

Of course light and shade change in the course of the day, so this must be taken into account both in choosing resting places and plant species to grow.

The role of colour

Colours heighten the effect of the composition, act on the emotions and evoke certain moods. The artistic effect of colours may depend on the use of just one, or on a variety of combinations.

The use of one colour is very effective in gardens planned in a more or less regular or ornamental

24

style, especially in large areas of grass, mirrored in ponds, or in carpets of flowers. However, this use of colour is mostly foreign to natural landscape compositions.

Colour combinations are much more frequent than the use of one colour and shades of it, but in a planned composition these cannot be left to chance. Though there is no hard and fast rule for making such combinations, there are a few principles that should be observed.

The traditional scheme of secondary or complementary colours can be seen on what is called Ostwald's colour cycle. Three sections of a circle are coloured with the primary colours — red, yellow and blue. By mixing two neighbouring colours we obtain orange, green and violet. The complementary colours are those that are opposite one another in the circle, i.e. red and green, yellow and violet and blue and orange. The combination of complementary colours is pleasing to the observer, provoking agreeable sensations. But, in some situations, even non-complementary colours may make an effective or dramatic colour combination.

Another factor that must be taken into account in grouping colours is their degree of luminosity. All of the warm colours, that is red, orange and yellow are glowing. Their opposites, that is, blue, green and violet, are cold. A combination of too glowing colours may be shocking, even if they are complementary.

For a harmonious relationship between two colours there must also be certain spatial conditions. For instance glowing yellow flowers scattered thinly against a dark background of conifers are harmonious in their contrast, but the yellow of the flowers loses its luminosity because they are not in a sufficiently concentrated planting.

In practice, garden compositions often combine not only two but more colours, and here disharmony may easily occur, especially if a third colour is added to two complementary ones with which it does not go well.

Types of gardens

The basic conception in planning a garden is usually decided by the type of buildings located within it, the environment or the shape of the terrain.

One principle that applies to all types of gardens results from its size. The smaller the garden is, the smaller should be the trees and shrubs planted in it, bearing in mind what their height will be when they are fully grown.

Large concrete or paved spaces can be 'softened' by containers generously planted with annuals, perennials and small woody plants.

Richness of shapes and texture offered by woody plants make them ideal for creating impressive contrasts in the garden.

The general aesthetic effect of a garden mostly depends on the sensitive blending of colours in individual garden sections.

A rock garden designed as a part of a mountain slope. This composition is particularly suitable for this part of a garden, providing a natural continuation of the surrounding rocky terrain.

Every garden should have well planned paths, a sitting-out corner, a recreation lawn or area and maybe a small pond. The rest can be filled in according to each person's own ideas. The purpose is to make a garden with pleasing variety without introducing so many elements that it becomes patchy, over-full and fragmented. The phrase 'sometimes less means more' applies to a garden too.

Front gardens

This area between the house and the street mostly serves as a decoration of the house, a pleasing intro-

Design for a country cottage garden. The roofed terrace continues into a paved path which, in turn, leads to a fireplace surrounded by benches. A grassy mound hides the fence at the rear end of the plot (at left). A low hedge on the opposite side of the plot forms a natural link between the front garden and the neighbouring forest. Three tall spruces planted next to the hedge close the plot from this side and the rest of this part of the garden is planted with woody plants characteristic of the surrounding landscape. The opposite side of the plot features shrubby conifers and a heath garden complemented with junipers and backed by a continuous wall of freely-standing yews. A small rocky slope planted with perennials inclines from the house towards the garden.

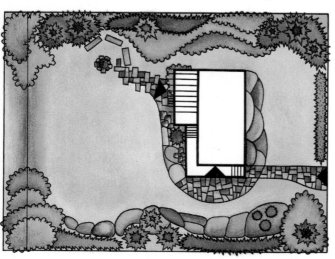

duction to it, and, furthermore, is often part of the public greenery, too.

A tiny front garden cannot be 'lived' in, both because of its restricted size and its lack of intimacy, and this is a basis for its planning.

It may be fenced — and in this case the fence should link aesthetically with the type of house and form a harmonious whole with the plants in the garden. If it is unfenced, at least optically, it becomes part of the public greenery. In this case it should be planned to harmonize with the street as well as the house.

If there is a busy street nearby, the front garden should primarily be a means of protecting the house and its occupants from noise and pollution. In this case, thick hedges should be planted.

There is an inexhaustible number of variations for planning a front garden but again, there are a few important principles that always apply.

The species and varieties of woody plants should be chosen carefully. Best are those that will not grow

The most natural effect can be achieved by following nature's design when planning a garden.

too large, so that the result is not an overgrown jungle with rampant climbers heavily shading windows. A front garden may be planted with groups of woody plants in an area of grass or with groups of perennials, or a combination of the two, but in no case should it be overfilled. Also, the choice of species must take into account the situation — that is, whether the garden faces north, south, east or west.

Usually a front garden is divided by a path or a drive, perhaps giving access to a garage, or steps leading to the house. The aim of the planting should be to tone down such divisions, not to stress them. If it is necessary to build further paths, stepping-stones do not decrease the optical space.

Often the shape of the terrain itself suggests the best solution for a garden design. This natural slope clearly offered an ideal site for a rock garden.

Apart from size, the arrangement of a front garden is influenced by the form of the terrain. Of course if it undulates, it affords more opportunities — for instance a rock garden or a low stone wall.

Larger front gardens can be used at least partially to be lived in, and in this case the general principles for garden planning apply.

Gardens adjoining detached family houses

This type of garden cannot be planned as a whole if

An attractive corner of a garden in which our eye is captured by the detail of aquatic vegetation.

— as is often the case — the house stands in the middle of it. So several sections need to be composed, within which the house is always the dominant factor.

This gives an opportunity for quite wide variation. One thing that is necessary is to create a secluded, private area that is not overlooked even from the neighbours' upstairs windows. This can be successfully done, for instance, by means of a pergola covered with climbing plants or groups of pyramid-shaped trees or shrubs. The ideal use of the garden area depends to some extent on agreement with the neighbours, as if the bordering areas can be planned in consultation, better use can be made of the other parts of the garden. For instance there may be a common evergreen hedge that could make a good background for the arrangements on both sides. Planning the groups of woody plants for the border areas together achieves a more effective composition, even though part of it belongs to the neighbouring garden. And such cooperation also nurtures a harmonious relationship with those neighbours — a considerable bonus.

When planning a garden there are no limits to the use of all elements of garden decoration, so long as the aesthetic aspect is borne in mind. Of course, it also depends on whether the house and garden are in a town or in the country amid fields or woods. In the latter case such species of plants should be chosen that look natural in the surroundings, forming a continuation of what nature herself has created.

Terracing. It is recommended to build retaining walls which not only contain the slope but also heighten the visual impact.

Gardens in a row of terraced houses

Usually, in the case of rows of family houses the plots of land are narrow — say, about 10 metres across — but several tens of metres long.

Here arises a problem in making the garden aesthetically effective as a whole. A long narrow garden may give the impression of being very confined, even tunnel-like; even so, an effective garden can be formed by observing certain principles of design and proportion.

In the first place, a certain proportion must be maintained between the height of the plants used and the width of the plot of land. If very tall trees or shrubs are planted along the sides of a narrow plot they will make it look still narrower, especially when they mature. On the other hand, a narrow garden benefits greatly if it is divided across its width into several less rectangular areas, either by hedges, decorative walls, shrubs cut into patterns, a trellis with creepers or a pergola. Also, increase the variety of the garden, for instance by suitable lighting and by altering the direction of the paths. These must not be straight or lead down the middle of the garden, as this would emphasize its length. A more meandering path, ideally part-concealed by shrubs or trees, lends an element of mystery and obscures the true overall size and shape.

Another thing that optically widens a narrow garden is light-coloured deciduous trees with an airy growth that can be seen through. Dark conifers or compact trees and shrubs, on the other hand, increase the impression of denseness and narrowness.

Housing estate or apartment block gardens

Usually, these gardens will be more for living in than for growing useful crops, owing to the very close links between the houses or flats and the gardens. In planning gardens of this type, one of the first needs is to make an intimate place that is private even from the upper windows of the surrounding houses. Another is to isolate it from environmental noise. Both aims can be achieved by using the woody species suitable for making hedges and climbers to create secluded nooks and corners.

Also, the specific microclimate of housing estate gardens must be respected. In view of the fact that there are buildings all round them and that they face different points of the compass, different conditions occur in each part of the garden, making it possible to cultivate both shade-loving and sun-loving species of plants. In choosing these, however, the changes in the conditions likely to occur in the course of the year should be remembered. These changes may be caused not only by the position of the sun, but also the lengths of the shadows thrown by nearby buildings. With some shrubs or plants, there is a greater chance, also, of using shrubs of the same species in both the sunny spots and shadier ones. They will thus flower sooner in the sunny spots than in the shady ones and the effective flowering period of the shrubs will be increased accordingly.

Water should not be missing in housing estate gardens, as it is an efficient regulator of microclimatic conditions. For instance, you could have a pool and fountain. Suitable paving material also helps to improve the microclimate — to give just one example, wood does not get heated to such high temperatures as concrete or stone.

An interesting group formed by an evergreen perennial (*Bergenia cordifolia*) and a clump of ornamental grasses, placed where they can spill over on to a path.

A bizarrely shaped knee-pine making a focal point of a natural rocky section stands out against the stark background provided by the house wall.

A large patch of brilliant, warm colour has an almost aggressive effect. The warmest colour in a theme is always dominant.

A simple but highly effective combination of complementary colours — red and green.

A wide range of climbing plants can be recommended for this type of garden, as they have both a bioclimatic and an aesthetic effect. A greater impression of space can be achieved by using pyramidal forms of trees and shrubs. Also, for practical reasons conifers and evergreens should be more numerous than deciduous species. They tend to be less demanding in terms of general care and provide foliage interest throughout the year.

Country gardens

As the traditional uses of the courtyards of farmhouses and farming estates are dying out, together with their extensive vegetable gardens, there is sometimes a problem of how to make use of this space. It can often gain a new value by being turned into a garden or gardens.

The areas are usually large, so that their planting with suitable shrubs and plants substantially improves the bioclimatic conditions in the house and nearby buildings. And the direct link between the house and garden is beneficial to the environment generally.

That is why a decorative garden is considered to be the most suitable for this type of space. There are many decorative shrubs that are not demanding in terms of work and time and that need no soil melioration, so a great effect can be achieved relatively quickly and cheaply. The planning of such a garden must take into consideration that it will be

An atrium garden, confined by the house in front and on the right and by a wall on the other two sides. The irregularly paved space in front of the door leading into the house serves as a sitting area. It features a circular pool with a simple fountain, and a path of flat stones leads across the lawn to the opposite corner of the garden where a small bench has been placed. Next to it grows a solitary specimen of *Robinia hispida*. The right-hand corner is planted with junipers and Mountain Pines. For a shaded part of the garden, rhododendrons and shade-loving perennials are a good choice. Irregular growths of annuals and grasses complement the picture. The centre of the plot is taken up by an irregularly shaped lawn.

An atrium garden with a pond. Two sides are contained by the house, the other two by a wall. The house door leads to a paved area neighbouring on to an irregularly shaped pond. A sitting area at the opposite end is sheltered by a pergola trained with climbers. The general depth of the pond is only 20—30 cm but there are several deeper compartments in the bottom for aquatic plants. A path of flat stones crosses the pond. Perennials with similar characteristics to aquatic plants grow along by the house and the pond. The largest portion of the garden is taken up by a lawn, framed on the wall sides by irregular groups of conifers and perennials, complemented by tall grasses and bulbs.

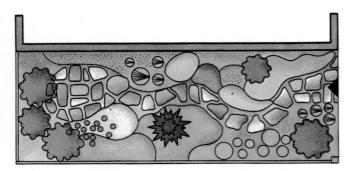

A front garden on the sunny side of the house. A solitary spiraea grows at the entrance to the narrow plot and a winding path of flat stones ends in a small paved area surrounded by more spiraeas. Large, irregular patches of creepers are interspersed with solitary trees and shrubs and taller perennials. In spring, the choice is enriched with bulbs. Grasses, an inseparable part of irregular plantings, are represented by low as well as taller species.

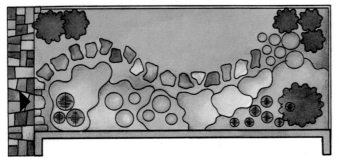

A north-facing front garden. An irregular path of flat stones runs through the narrow plot and the main planting is concentrated in the area between the path and the house. A solitary mezereon grows at right, close to the house, and is surrounded by patches of ferns and snowdrops. A group of mahonias with an underplanting of Christmas roses has been planted near the fence at right. The broad belt alongside the house features primulas, astilbes and ferns, while a group of rhododendrons grows left of the entrance. The area between the fence and the path can be covered with lawn or shade-tolerating low creepers.

not only a functional continuation of the house but will also link with the fields or the trees along the village street or some other public place.

Holiday cottage gardens

The main feature of these gardens is that usually they are set right in the country. So the creed of their arrangement is to attempt to be the peak of beauty within those surroundings, a concentration of their artistic effect.

Again, there are some important principles to be observed. There should be the same species of plants, especially trees and shrubs, in the garden as are growing in the surrounding country. The repetition of the same motif unifies the garden with its environment.

The details of the garden should be adapted to the dominant character of the landscape, so that the various parts of the garden are continuations of their natural surroundings.

In planning a country garden, some specific needs have to be met. For instance, it may well be necessary to create a windbreak to protect certain areas from harmful winds or again, a break to help prevent the formation of snowdrifts and so on.

Gardens on hilly sites

The artistic planning of a hilly garden must respect its exposure to the different points of the compass and the various height levels of the terrain. The southern slopes will be warm, protected and airy,

Design for two neighbouring plots, separated by a hedge continuing into a mixed group of woody plants which can be observed from both gardens. Pergolas provide intimacy for the sitting-out areas. Lawns are important components of both gardens and the paved areas render each accessible even in rainy weather. The front garden in the left-hand plot lies in a sloping terrain and has therefore been shaped into a rockery. The flower bed planted with perennials abuts a sheltered sitting-out area equipped with garden furniture. A hedge forms a background to the perennial bed in the left-hand plot. Water is an important decorative element in both gardens; the garden on the left has a small pond in the rockery while the neighbouring plot has a small pond placed among loose perennial groups with large boulders and a spacious swimming pool behind the house.

Two parts of a garden enclosing a family house, each with a different aesthetic approach. The small garden in front of the house has been designed as a decorative garden featuring cultivated varieties of plants and several small pieces of garden architecture. The large garden behind the house has been planned as a complement to the surrounding countryside.

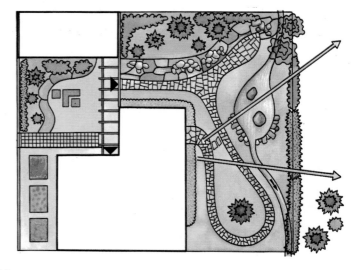

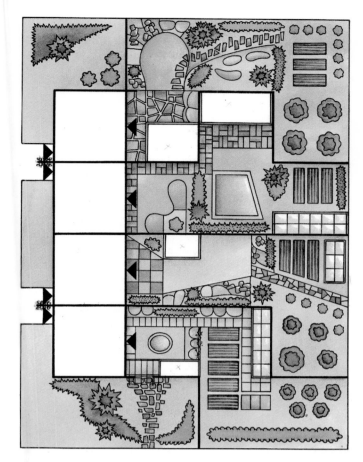

Design for a complex of four gardens surrounding a row of family houses. The plots are of unequal size and outline, which allows for more varied schemes. In all four gardens, the sections surrounding the houses are used as recreational, decorative or live-in areas. The details in each garden differ according to the inhabitants' needs. The public greenery at the sides and in front of the houses has been shaped in neat geometrics, in keeping with the character of the gardens.

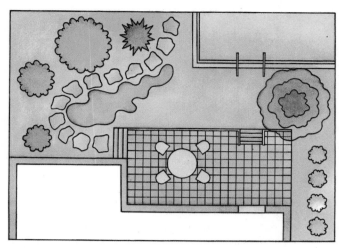

A well designed small garden with a terrace, a pool and a recreation lawn. The terrace is linked directly with the house.

A former yard, shaped into a very attractive garden. It is confined by the house on the left and in front, and by a wall on the two remaining sides. The secluded 'live-in' space is planted with evergreens. A small paved area close to the entrance continues into a path which leads to the sitting-out corner. This is sheltered by a pergola with climbing roses. An irregular planting of woody plants, perennials and grasses surrounds the area. The right-hand corner, next to the entrance, is planted with junipers and the opposite corner with firethorns. The shaded section close to the wall at the back features rhododendrons, mahonias, ferns and shade-loving perennials. A solitary yew grows in the right rear corner and the rest of the garden is covered with lawn.

thus enabling the planting of a wide selection of decorative plants and also some special useful ones.

The articulation of the terrain makes a wide variety of arrangements possible. To achieve these ends however, it will be necessary to introduce low walls, terraces, rock gardens, waterfalls and steps. The various levels will then provide conditions for an all-round, richer vision of the whole garden. They will also afford splendid views of the surrounding country, offering still further possibilities of composition.

But hilly sites also have their disadvantages. In the first place there will be a variety of soil conditions, so that uniform cultivation is apt to be a problem, if indeed, at all possible. This is why they are mostly used for decorative gardens. Another disadvantage is the cost of adapting the terrain, building those necessary supporting walls etc. Hilly areas are often dry, also; in consequence they often require the installation of an irrigation system and a systematic improvement of some qualities of the soil.

Architectural features

Paths

Garden paths are not merely functional, connecting the most frequented parts of the garden, they are also important artistic elements.

The placing of paths must be well thought out before you start to lay them down. All paths should be usable in all weathers, even during prolonged spells of rain or frost. Also, they should not need a great deal of care, but always look pleasing.

The path from the garden gate to the front door of a house usually takes the shortest route. All the other paths, between the house and the sitting-out place, the garage, pool or kitchen garden need not take the shortest route, but they should facilitate views of the prettiest parts of the garden.

In the kitchen garden straight paths are best (between the individual beds), and they should be at least 35 cm wide.

In all other cases the width of the path depends on its purpose. For example, the width of the front path from the gate to the house should be about 120—150 cm wide, so that two people can easily pass one another. A drive for cars should be 220—250 cm wide, or it suffices to have twin strips appropriate to the span of the car wheels. For other paths, usually used by one person at a time, 50—80 cm is enough. It should be remembered that shrubs planted along the paths must be sufficiently far from the paths not to hinder their use.

It is as well not to have a path or drive dividing a large area of lawn in front of the house. Particularly in narrow gardens, the path is better at the edge than in the middle, so as not to break up the space visually.

All paths need both a lengthwise and a transverse gradient, so that no water stands on them. On level ground the path must have a transverse gradient from the centre to both sides. If it leads along a slope the gradient should be to one side, following the slope. A lengthwise gradient should be half to one centimetre per linear metre. At the lowest point there should be an outlet, which can either lead to the drains or to a sump, so that no puddles form.

Identical building material — for instance one type of stone — serves as a unifying element. It is used here for paving the space immediately around the pool, for the path leading to the garage, and for the steps leading to other parts of the garden.

The highly aesthetic York paving is best for natural-style gardens. Here, it has been used for the path, steps and the terrace.

The best material for paths in the kitchen garden is pre-cast concrete slabs. They can be set into a concrete bed for better stability in more frequented places.

Sand paths, in spite of their many disadvantages, certainly look nice and are comfortable underfoot.

Hard-surface paths

These can be of various materials, from sand to pre-cast paving slabs. Each has its particular advantages, but always the aesthetic aspect must be considered.

Sand paths

These are cheap and their other main advantage is their porosity; the surface absorbs rain water and allows it to soak to the lower layers. However, there are some disadvantages, too. Puddles form when snow thaws in the spring, because the lower layers are still frozen and the water cannot seep through. During long spells of rain the surface becomes soft and impassable, whereas in periods of drought and strong winds they are very dusty. Sometimes weeds grow on them and will have to be removed. Sand paths also have to be raked and rolled, so all in all they need quite a lot of maintenance.

The way to build a sand path is as follows: first stake out both sides of the path with pegs, then between them dig out a strip 15—20 cm deep. Level and compress it. Lay a 10 cm deep foundation of coarse gravel, broken bricks or similar material and compress this too. Next lay 2—5 cm of fine gravel, cinders, ash or old plaster and water it thoroughly. Last comes the covering layer of sand, or better still a mixture of sand, grit and dry clay, which is levelled and rolled.

Any path wider than 120 cm should have a slightly arched centre and a 2 per cent gradient at either side.

So that earth from the flowerbeds does not spill on to the paths, these should be bordered with natural stones, concrete or bricks. However, these should not jut up more than 5 cm above the surface. Creeping rock-garden plants or annuals can be planted along these border stones, or you could use low-growing root vegetables.

Concrete paths

Although concrete lasts well and is relatively cheap and practical, its use in a garden is questionable from the aesthetic point of view. It must be regarded not only from the functional aspect, but the way the concrete surfaces are arranged.

The basic layers for a concrete path are made in the same way as for sand paths. Then line the future path with smooth boards about 3 cm wide, pegging them into the ground. Paint the boards with oil, so that the concrete will not stick to them. The upper edge of the boards must be horizontal, or have one edge slightly lower, in order to form a gradient to one side. Then lay a 6 cm layer of concrete (1 part cement, 2 parts sand and 4 parts fine gravel) on the compressed foundation layer. Cover this with another 6 cm of concrete mixture (this time 1 part cement, 3 parts sand) and level it with a smooth rod or board, making sure that it is compressed so that no cavities remain in which water could settle. Concrete should be laid over the whole surface at once. To prevent cracking, however, very large areas can be divided into 1 metre strips and the gaps later filled with asphalt. Concrete usually hardens in a day if allowed to do so, but it should be kept wet for at least a week to become sufficiently firm. A car can be driven over it after four weeks, when the board linings have been removed.

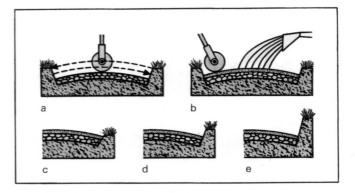

Laying a sand path. The layer of gravel has to be rolled (a), then comes a layer of sand, which is also rolled and watered (b). Too high and too deep-lying paths are shown in (c) and (e) respectively. The proper height is shown in figure (d).

Paths contribute considerably to the general design of the garden. They must be safe and comfortable, with a well-kept surface, and always in agreement with the character of the garden. Very important are the edges which keep out the surrounding vegetation. The edging stones or bricks should be laid before the layer of gravel. They must be set deeper than the bottom of the dug-out bed of the future path, and always below the level of the surrounding terrain. The measurements here are given in centimetres.

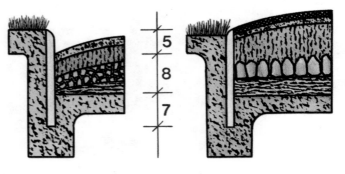

A carport is best built of pre-cast concrete blocks with spaces between them that can be filled with earth and sown with grass, so that a network of concrete and lawn results that looks well surrounded by grass. The width of the carport depends on the size of the car but it is usually 5×2.5 m.

The area in front of a garage, where the car can be washed, can be made with a concrete bed. The load-bearer is a prefab concrete slab on top of a 10—15 cm thick layer of gravel or gravel with sand, which is then covered with a 5 cm layer of peat and sand in a ratio of 2:1. The thickness of the paving slabs depends on the load anticipated, but 8 cm is a minimum. They should be laid level with the aid of a spirit level. The bottom of the foundation must have a slight gradient towards a drainage lead that is connected with an infiltration sump or the main drains. Fill the gaps between the paving slabs with a suitable soil substrate, laid in thin layers with the help of a trickle of water.

The paved area can then be sown with grass seed,

A flagstone path is particularly effective in the vicinity of flat areas such as lawns. It also goes well with brick curbing and flower containers.

Various paving materials and designs for laying them when building paths and paved areas.

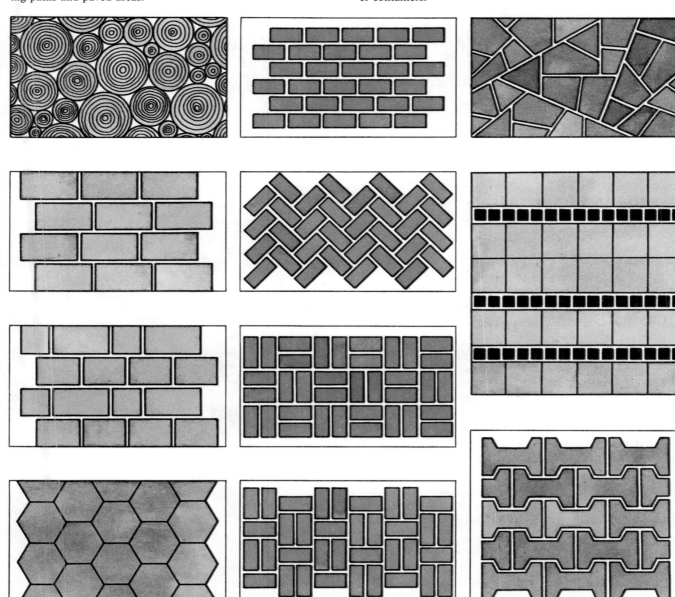

but it is best to wait a few weeks, to make sure that the soil substrate does not subside. If the paving slabs are laid on a level with the surrounding terrain it is easy to cut the grass, but this should be regularly watered in the summer, as it is apt to dry out easily in this sort of location.

Paths of concrete paving slabs

Paths are most often built of pre-cast slabs 50 × 50 cm large, but they look much more attractive if slabs of several different sizes are used, for instance 20 × 40 cm, 40 × 40 cm, 40 × 60 cm, 40 × 80 cm. They may have a smooth surface or various patterns.

If the path is not to be used very often, place the stones into a layer of sand 8 cm thick. If any of them sink later they can easily be taken out while more sand is put underneath them, and then be replaced.

The paving slabs are laid with the help of a taut string and a spirit level, to ensure that they are flat. They can be hammered into the sand if a piece of thick material (a wooden board for instance) is first placed over them. The gaps between the slabs should be as narrow as possible and long lengthwise gaps avoided completely. Finally, the gaps are filled with sand, which is watered sufficiently to wash the sand in as deep as possible.

Drives for cars need firmer foundations of large stones or a compressed layer of gravel at least 8—10 cm thick. Overlay this with 5 cm of lean concrete

Natural stone is the most appropriate paving material for informal gardens set in a rural landscape.

Paving made of wooden offcuts is quite impressive. Its natural colouring makes it complementary to any flowers planted close by.

(1 part cement and 6 parts sand). Then fill the gaps between the paving stones with thin cement mortar or with asphalt.

To avoid puddles forming, the path should have a 2° gradient.

The edges of the paths can be either straight or jagged, that is, with alternate slabs jutting into the grass. Border stones are unnecessary here and would make cutting the grass more difficult.

Natural stone paths

Best are blocks of natural stone about 5—6 cm thick. The type of stone should be chosen carefully, both from the aesthetic and practical points of view. Sand-yellow or ochre shades go well with a lawn. If the stones are too light they are inclined to dazzle in bright sunlight. Also, they should have a rough surface so that they do not become dangerously slippery in wet or frosty weather.

As small stones are difficult to lay firmly, they should not be less than 30 × 30 cm. They can be laid straight into sand or, for more frequented places, set into cement mortar on a 10—12 cm layer of gravel, with the smallest possible gaps, then hammered into place. Stones of different sizes should be used regularly over the whole area, putting the biggest at the edges. Check whether they lie flat with the help of long boards and a spirit level. Thin concrete, coloured if required, is then poured into the gaps. The surface should have a 2° gradient.

Asphalt paths

Nowadays, asphalt is often used for garden paths. Here again, the first thing to do is to make a firm foundation 10—25 cm thick. This can be covered with stone chips wrapped in asphalt, which are spread and rolled while still hot into a layer 3 cm thick; or coloured asphalts can be used, and these are laid cold.

Wood paving

A paving of wooden offcuts is very effective, but it is not suitable for damp situations. The offcuts should be at least 20 cm thick and can be of any kind of wood though, of course, hardwood lasts longer. To make this kind of paving more durable each piece should first be dipped into a preservative solution and left to dry. The part of the offcut to be inserted into the ground can also be immersed in liquid asphalt and then laid in a bed of sand, so that it does not rot. Take care in the distribution of offcuts of varying thickness with a view to achieving a regular effect, with the thickest at the sides. Then scatter the paving with sand and thoroughly water it in, so that sand reaches deep into all the cracks.

Brick paths

Paths with a variety of interesting patterns can be made of bricks. Use only well-fired bricks, or they will begin to break down in frosty weather. Lay them on a bed of sand and fill the gaps with sand, as above.

A path of flat stepping stones is the best solution for lawns. It looks very natural and if the stones are set level with the ground they make no obstacle when the lawn is being mown.

A dry wall forms a hanging garden below a terrace. The same type of stone was used as for the house. Once planted with rock plants, as here, large parts of the dry wall will soon be covered with greenery.

Paths of other materials

An interesting effect can also be achieved by mosaics of various sorts of paving material laid in concrete. The whole area can be laid irregularly with big paving blocks, stones or cobbles, or large stones with a mosaic of small ones set between them. This type of path can be pleasantly unusual, but the final effect must be thought of carefully when choosing the materials.

Where a path is not very much used, creeping and carpeting rock-garden plants that do not mind being trampled on, such as thyme, can be planted in the gaps between the stones. This results in a charming, flowering path that needs little maintenance once the plants have settled.

Stepping stones in grass

Stepping stones enable one to cross a lawn with dry feet even in very rainy weather. Most often, concrete slabs of 50 × 50 cm are used for this purpose, but

A quiet sitting-out area with York paving is equipped with simple garden furniture. Natural stones protruding from the wall serve as stands for flower containers. The climber *Campsis radicans*, evoking an intimate atmosphere, has flowers of the same colour as the *Pelargonium zonale* growing in the containers. Chair cushions also repeat this colour theme.

natural stone can be used too. The centres of the individual stones should be about 65 cm apart from one another, as this is the length of a step.

Before laying stepping stones, first plan the direction of the path and place the stones on the ground at the required distance apart. Cut round each stone with a spade and dig out the space beneath it to a depth of 8 cm. Scatter a thin layer of sand or easily crumbled earth into the hole, leaving a hollow in the middle so that the stone will lie mainly on the edges. Then lay the stone in place, hammer it in — first cover it with a thick plank — and use a spirit level to make sure it is lying correctly. If not, take it out, put in more sand and then replace the stone.

The surface of the stepping stones should be level with the lawn, so as not to hinder mowing or, indeed, damage the mower. It should by no means be lower, however, as dirt then accumulates at the edges and in time the stones become overgrown with grass.

Sitting-out areas and terraces

The sitting-out area in a garden must be chosen with due consideration for its possible use in all weathers. On cool days we need a resting place in the sun but sheltered from the wind; on hot days we may prefer to be in the shade and when it rains, under a covered terrace. In each case the area surrounding the resting place should be well planned and maintained, with a nice view of the garden. It should also be sheltered from the road by a hedge, a pergola covered with creepers or a wall.

Of course, the place for sitting out depends on the situation of the house in the plot. The prevailing direction of the wind is another point to consider. On the whole, the south side of the house is the best location for sitting out, but mostly the south-west and the south-east aspects also afford protection from cold winds.

If the sitting-out area is at the same level as the ground floor of the house there is an ideal connection between house and garden. On sloping ground, a terrace can either be built at house floor level, or steps can be made from the house to a sitting-out area at the level of the terrain. Height differences can be solved by building low supporting walls that prevent the terrace from subsiding.

A good size for a sitting-out area is 20—30 square metres. However, there is no need for the ground plan to be either square or oblong; it can be any shape you prefer. What is important is that it is set harmoniously into the garden space.

Where the sitting-out area links directly with the house there is usually an open view of the garden. But if it is situated at the opposite end of the garden we can see the house, sometimes from two sides, so that the garden gains in depth optically.

In time we may come to the conclusion that just one place in the garden for sitting out is not enough, and that really the whole garden should be for rest and amusement, both in sunshine and shade. Then we can gradually discover which place in the garden is most pleasantly cool in the summer heat, where the sun shines soonest in the spring and where it is warmest in autumn, where best to see the sunset and the house, and from where there is the most beautiful view of the garden and the landscape.

The sitting-out area should be arranged so that it can be used as soon as possible after rain. Even though garden furniture can be spread out on the lawn too, the most used areas of grass will soon become trampled and the lawn cease to be that much-admired green carpet. If, however, you do wish to

A sitting-out corner sheltered by concrete walls. Wood chairs of a contrasting colour are used to soften the rigid effect of the walls. The delicate fronds of surrounding grasses also pleasantly complement the quiet scene.

This resting place fulfils several important prerequisites: it is located in a quiet and pleasant corner of the garden, it offers interesting views of other parts, and it is sheltered by tall trees from wind and sun.

build a rest area on the lawn, proceed as follows:

Hollow out the earth on the desired site and spread a layer of gravel about 7 cm thick. Level it well and stamp it down, then cover with a 2 cm layer of good quality soil and sow this with grass seed. Then comes another thin layer of soil (about 1/2 cm) which is stamped down or rolled. An area made in this way will be firm, and the gravel will allow rain water to drain away to the lower layers of earth.

However, a more practical method of making an uncovered rest-area is to pave it with flat stones. The cracks between them should be as small as possible, and here and there carpeting perennials or low-growing shrubs can be planted in the cracks or in the corners. Or, if preferred, 10 cm gaps may be left between the stones, then filled with earth and sown with grass. But again, if the stones are uneven, this may cause difficulty in cutting the grass.

Covered sitting-out areas can also be paved, either with concrete paving slabs or imitations of natural stone. Their thickness depends on the material used and ranges between 4—6 cm. Pre-cast paving slabs are available in various sizes, colours and surface treatment.

Concrete or imitation stone paving slabs are usually laid in mortar, on a firm foundation, and thin concrete is poured over to prevent weeds growing in the cracks. They can also be laid in a 5 cm layer of sand, which has the advantage that if frost raises the slabs they afterwards settle back into the sand. The gaps between the slabs must be small so that high-heeled shoes or the legs of garden furniture do not become wedged into them. Also, weeds are apt to grow in wide gaps and are then hard to eradicate. To drain off rain water, the paving should have a 1—2° gradient, sloping away from the building.

Sitting-out areas are often surrounded on two or three sides by walls, both to form a quiet shelter and to give greater privacy.

The simplest and cheapest type of wall is one made of straw or rush matting. This not only protects the area from being overlooked but also from gusts of wind. However, it is not enough to fasten the mats on to a tight wire between metal posts. If it is not to be constantly in need of repairs, it is better to fix this wall to two horizontal slats or into a frame. A sitting-out area protected with mats on two sides can look very attractive.

A resting place can also be sheltered by a high or low wall. This is usually done to isolate it from the noise of the street. The wall can form a link between the house and other buildings (a garage, shed etc.), and it must have sufficiently deep foundations, preferably of concrete, reaching down to where the ground does not freeze in winter. According to the local climate, this varies from 80 to 120 cm. The width of the wall depends on its height: up to a height of 200 cm, a width of 24 cm is sufficient. The building material can be bricks, moulded blocks or natural stones. An insulating board should be placed on the levelled foundations to protect the wall from rising damp. As a finishing touch to the wall, a row of concrete or other slabs should be placed along the top to shield it from rain. In a wall of natural stones the gaps in between should be filled with cement mortar.

One of the prettiest ways of walling off a sitting-out area is with a wooden or metal construction covered with plants. This must be sufficiently firm to resist the wind and bear the weight of the plants. The overall effect depends not only on the material used and the efficiency of its treatment and erection, but also on the choice of plants used.

Here, by way of example, are instructions how to

The white colour of the house walls, the green lawn and the typical country-garden flower — *Althaea rosea* — offset by the simple, natural-looking picket fence evoke an atmosphere of undisturbed peace and cosiness.

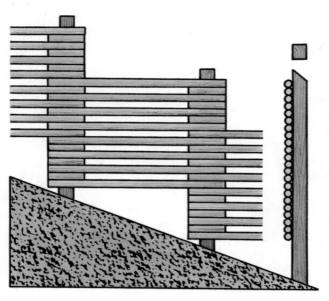

A graduated picket fence built in a slope can be very attractive, whether the pickets are barked or natural. The natural bark of trees felled in winter remains long on the wood, protecting it, whereas barked pickets have to be treated to check moulds and then coated with a colourless paint. The underground parts should also be soaked in a preservative.

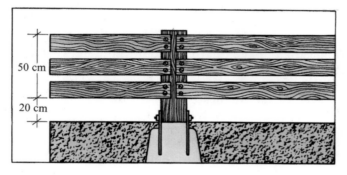

Timber fences are simple, practical and have a very natural effect. One of the basic conditions of their durability is the choice of appropriate building material. Besides pine, the best is larch timber but ash, mountain ash or elm can also be used. The picture shows a detail of a fence made of timber boards, fastened to posts treated with a preservative in their lower parts. The posts are set into concrete. Rustless screws, nails and other metal components must be used for better weather resistance.

A fence of unpretentious planks, if built with care and accuracy, is very decorative. Timber, however, is the most susceptible to decay of all building materials. To avoid various unwelcome deteriorations in its appearance, it must be properly dried, planed and preserved before it is used.

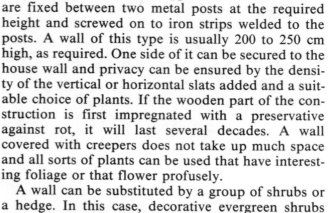

make a simple wall of this type. Two horizontal slats are fixed between two metal posts at the required height and screwed on to iron strips welded to the posts. A wall of this type is usually 200 to 250 cm high, as required. One side of it can be secured to the house wall and privacy can be ensured by the density of the vertical or horizontal slats added and a suitable choice of plants. If the wooden part of the construction is first impregnated with a preservative against rot, it will last several decades. A wall covered with creepers does not take up much space and all sorts of plants can be used that have interesting foliage or that flower profusely.

A wall can be substituted by a group of shrubs or a hedge. In this case, decorative evergreen shrubs can be used, especially those that do not have to be cut and yet will retain the appearance of a hedge.

Nowadays, sail cloth stretched between metal or bamboo posts is widely used for this purpose, as well as screens; or portable walls of various materials, some of which can be folded up. These are very mobile and therefore popular.

It is not always pleasant to sit in the sun. On hot sunny days shade is preferable. The simplest way to achieve this is to have a roof built over part of the sitting-out area, leaving the other part open. Or a tall tree can be planted nearby, that filters the sun's rays, making them bearable.

If you decide on a covered resting place or summerhouse, its form and the material used should be in harmony with the overall character of the house and garden. Apart from the traditional roofing materials, you can use canvas, straw matting or plastic — or some similar material that does not fade in sunlight.

Otherwise, protection from the sun can be afforded by a big garden sunshade or various canvas roofs that are either portable or can be fastened to the house.

A firm and decorative fence can be made of trellis-wise halved and barked pickets. It is particularly suitable for mountain and submountain regions in a flat terrain in combination with terracing walls. The supporting posts can be located 2—2.5 m apart and the pickets should jut up above them slightly. The top and bottom lines must be level, irrespective of the undulations of the terrain.

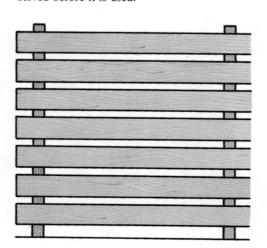

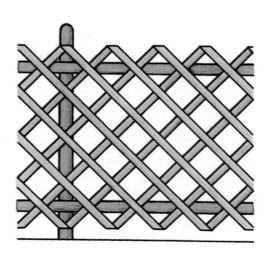
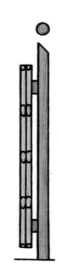

All elements of garden decoration and all architectural features should be carefully matched to make an impressive whole. A mosaic style paving in alternating bands of two different colours is nicely complemented by the sturdy wooden trellis.

Fences

The type of fence will depend on the type of the garden and the style of the house. In some cases, especially in a vegetable garden, wire netting can be used. Here the support posts are either of concrete or iron; whichever you choose, they must have struts at the ends of the fence and at the corners, in order to withstand the pull of the netting. A low concrete wall can be built between the poles, so that rabbits cannot get under the fence and it does not become overgrown with grass. Or, the netting can be painted with asphalt or some other protective coating and set into the ground to a depth of 20 cm. Galvanized wire netting of various dimensions is used, and the metal posts should have metal caps at the top.

However, this practical fence has rather a solid effect, so shrubs are often planted along it to soften its lines. When planting against these fences, remember to place the plants at some distance so that the fences can be painted or mended from time to time without the need to disturb the plants. Gates should be of corresponding material, and here framed wire netting looks better than sheet metal.

In the case of garden fences round family houses the base section is often of the same material as that of the house, surmounted by wire netting in a metal frame, or various types of wooden fences or trellis. As the wood should not alter in appearance under the influence of the weather, wood from freshly felled trees should not be used. To make a wooden fence last as long as possible it should be impregnated, stained or coated with preservative paint.

When building a picket fence, the support poles must be well impregnated with preservative, especially those parts that are to be below soil level. A very nice fence can be made of brick or concrete-covered pillars with stakes in between. Iron strips are then let into the pillars and the horizontal slats screwed on to them. A small space should be left between the pillar and the wood to allow for air insulation. When fastening on the stakes, the gaps between them should always be slightly less than the width of the stake. Interesting low fences can be made of thin stakes, suitable for front gardens, internal partitions etc.

Suitable gates for all of the fences described above are also made of stakes. They should be reinforced with slats in the shape of the letter Z, so that the gate does not sag.

High brick or stone walls overshadow a garden too much, so they should only be built to isolate it from a busy street. However, low walls surrounding front gardens or internal partitions of moulded bricks or bricks laid in ornamental patterns can look very good and heighten the general artistic effect.

Shrubs are often planted to divide off plots of land by serving as hedges. There are many advantages to this as they form a very effective protection against noise and dust and wind, they provide some privacy, forming a secluded area, they give birds places for nesting and help to improve the microclimate. If the garden is big enough, then hedges are the best way of defining its frontiers. The type of garden and its situation are decisive in choosing the kind of hedge. This subject is dealt with in greater detail in the chapter on ornamental shrubs.

Summerhouses

If your garden extends some distance from the house, you really need a summerhouse so that you can spend long periods in the garden, whatever the season. In a big garden, a summerhouse can also be a place to rest, or a shelter from which the garden can be observed even when it is raining. So it should always be situated in a spot with a good view of the landscape or in a pretty corner of the garden.

A summerhouse may house garden furniture and tools, or it can be fitted out with easily portable furniture and a cooking stove and so on, so that meals can be eaten there.

All kinds of material can be used to build a summerhouse, but the most suitable is timber, as this is likely to fit in best with the environment. However,

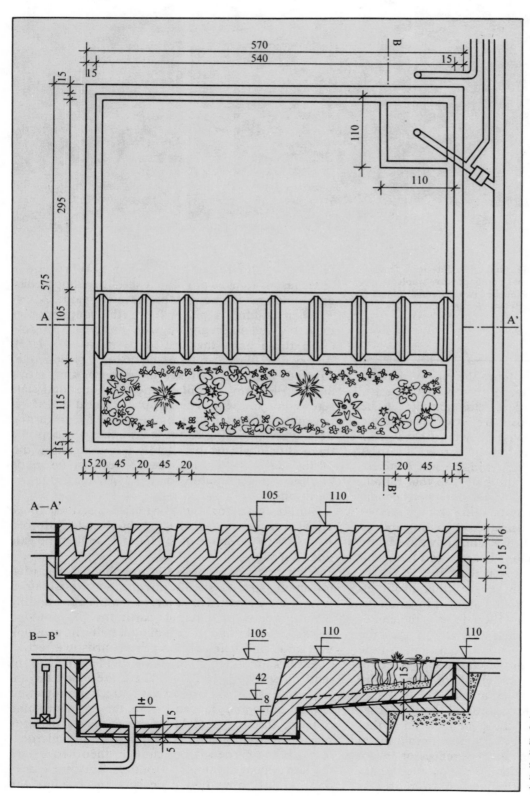

A children's paddling pool combined with a shallow water garden for aquatic plants is a good idea for larger sites. It should be built in a sunny spot and used only under supervision.

buildings of bricks or concrete blocks do last longer. White plaster combined with dark wood for the shutters or railings looks both nice and natural. Various types of assembled prefab summerhouses save the trouble of building, and the children can play there when the weather is too unsettled for them to play outdoors.

Whatever material is chosen, the main thing is that the summerhouse should not look out of place, but fit in tastefully with the rest of the garden. This can be achieved by planting climbing plants around the building so that it becomes a part of the surroundings.

A pool sited in an ornamental part of the garden needs a good-quality stone and large stone blocks. The final effect should be as natural as possible.

Various pools or ponds, either planted with vegetation or used for watering or swimming, can be very dangerous for very young children. They should therefore be built away from children's playing areas and furthermore covered with a grid.

Water in the garden

No garden can survive without water. It is necessary not only for watering the plants but as an important compositional element. In a modern garden water is used in all its forms. Sometimes it may be purely functional (barrels for watering, paddle pools), or elsewhere mainly for decoration (an ornamental pool perhaps, or a bird bath); sometimes it is both useful and beautiful. Whether the garden has its own well, or whether tap water is used for watering, it is a good thing to draw it off first into a reservoir, perhaps a concrete pool, and use it for the plants only when it has been warmed by the sun. Where there is no other source of water for this purpose, rain water can be collected from the gutter via a drainpipe leading into a tank. This tank is usually concealed by plants, a pergola with climbers etc., or on sloping

ground it can be let into the earth, with a tap set into the side.

A large garden can have a swimming pool or at least a paddling pool for younger children. Permanent paddle pools are usually oblong, square or, sometimes, round. Just 20—30 cm of water is sufficient, over an area of 2—3 square metres. It can be placed on an open lawn, the edges bordered with flat stones or concrete paving blocks, the bottom and side walls being well smoothed concrete. When dry they can be painted or tiled. The bottom must be slightly sloping with an outlet pipe at the lowest point.

Swimming pools

The best place for a swimming pool is some lovely but not very busy part of the garden. So that the water warms quickly, its surface should not be in the shade.

The pool should be sheltered from northerly winds, whether these be north-east or north-west. Also, as fallen leaves soil the pool and tree roots might disturb the concrete, a form of shelter better than trees is a wall, straw or rush matting, glass or plastic

A concrete-lined pool can either be sunk in a flat terrain or half-raised in an undulated or sloping terrain. In any case, the construction needs careful planning in advance and must include a properly arranged inlet and outlet of water. Having due regard for aesthetic aspects, the material used for the finish should be the same as that used for a neighbouring terrace or paved area.

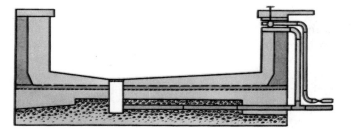

Important complements of decorative pools are not only the aquatic and bog plants growing directly in the water, but also all the neighbouring vegetation which should resemble that which grows near water in the wild. Some grasses are very good for this purpose — for example, *Avena sempervirens*.

An ingenious and natural-looking solution to providing an inlet of water for a small pool.

screen that will also protect the area of lawn used for sun-bathing.

The swimming pool should always be kept full of water, so that the surface consistently reflects the calm picture of the garden or landscape.

When considering the shape of the future pool, a principle to remember is that the simpler the shape, the cheaper it will be to build. An oval or oblong shape is more suitable than a round or square. The length should be roughly twice the width and the longitudinal axis should be in an east-westerly direction, so that the wind helps to clear any floating debris.

The minimum width recommended for a pool is 2.50 metres. It must be at least 80 cm deep for people to be able to swim in it, but 1.10 to 1.40 metres is preferable. A popular size for home swimming pools is $6 \times 3 \times 1.40$ m.

A swimming pool can have a sloping bottom, so that non-swimmers can bathe in it at the shallower end, but the incline should be slight, to avoid any danger of slipping and falling.

The pool can be entered by steps or by a ladder. The latter is both easier and usually cheaper. An aluminium ladder is most often fixed to the horizontal facing round the pool, but care must be taken not to pierce either the bottom or the walls. It should be done in a way that enables the ladder to be taken out of the water before the winter and stored for the following year.

An overflow opening ensures that, even with an increased in-flow, the level of water in the pool remains the same. The overflow should thus be placed immediately above the water level. The best solution is an overflow pipe round the walls, which at the

same time serves as a handle. The overflow is connected with the main drains.

At the deepest area of the bottom, there is an outlet pipe with a good plug. This again leads to the drains or to an infiltration sump, which should be able to take at least half the contents of the pool at once.

A strong nylon net should cover the water whenever its use cannot be supervised by an adult, to prevent children falling into the pool while playing in the garden; alternatively, a temporary fence can be erected.

The use of water in a garden has many different forms. Here, water ejected from a stone monolith cascades down and through a drainage layer of pebbles into a neighbouring brook.

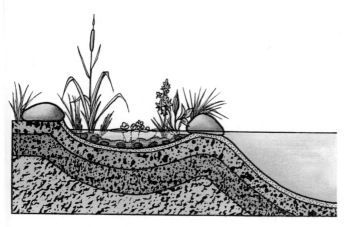

A pond in an informal rock garden looks better if irregularly shaped. A shelf on its margin allows a number of interesting bog plants to be planted there. A permanent overflow of water from the shelf into the pond must also be provided.

The inlet pipe feeding a pond in a rockery has been concealed beneath stones and the water falls on to a flat piece of rock, making a very natural-looking waterfall.

The bathing season can be prolonged by installing a heating system. If the pool is near to the house, the water inlet can be connected to the central heating hot water tank.

The worst problems arise in keeping the water clean. The debris that floats on the surface, such as dust, soot, dead insects and bits of plants, often

Two floor levels in a bird bath enable even the smallest birds to use it with safety.

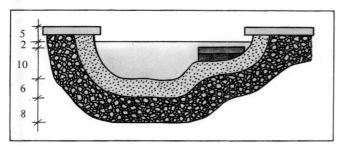

mixed with sun tan oils and creams, can be fairly easily removed by passing a strong current of water through the overflow. More troublesome are the fallen leaves, grass, soil and other dirt that falls to the bottom. This debris has to be drawn off by suction with a special tool, or removed by hand when the pool is drained.

Another problem is algae. These cloud the water in ten days to a fortnight at a temperature of 18° C, and they form even more readily at higher temperatures, given enough light and nourishment.

The formation of algae can be limited by placing a linen bag full of blue vitriol crystals in the water for one or two hours. The effect is increased by the addition of chloramine. This should be done every two or three days, but even so the pool must be emptied and refilled every so often.

If you do not want a permanent swimming or paddle pool in the garden, many types of portable pools are available, and these can be placed wherever it suits at any particular moment.

An ornamental pool

A pool designed for growing water plants can be made at some suitable spot — not directly under or close by trees. Water used as an aesthetic element enhances the charm of a garden. It is constantly alive, its surface reflects the sky and the nearest parts of the garden. Birds and useful insects fly down to it, and it can be enlivened still further not only with plants but also fish or small amphibious animals.

When building an ornamental pond not only must the site be well considered beforehand, but also the shape, size, depth, the way it is to be built and, of course, what to plant in it.

A simple stone sink makes a highly decorative complement to an ornamental garden. The bordering plants are mirrored in the water surface.

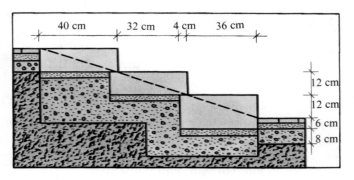

Steps are used to surmount slopes with a gradient of more than 15—20 per cent. Whatever their construction and design, steps must always be safe and comfortable to use in any weather. The treads should therefore overlap to a certain extent and be slightly inclined away from the slope in order not to retain rainwater.

A natural pool without a reinforced bottom is not very suitable, as the water level is variable and during a drought it may even dry up. Some plants, such as water-lilies, would not grow well in such a pool as they need a permanent water level. So a hard bottom, impenetrable to water, is recommended for every garden pond.

The most commonly used material is concrete. The shape and size can vary, the most usual area being 2—5 square metres. The site may be either open and surrounded by grass, or the pool can be within the sitting-out area, or by a flower-covered wall or a rock garden. A depth of 40 cm is enough for a pond, but if water-lilies are to be grown in it, one part should be hollowed out to 60—70 cm. The bottom should slope slightly, with an outlet pipe at the deepest part leading to an infiltration pit or sump, or to the main drains. Unless the pond is built to resist frost when it is full, it must be emptied before the first frosts set in. However, it is obviously best to build it so that water can remain throughout the winter, so that care of the water plants does not mean extra work.

Concrete for building the pond is a mixture of cement and river sand in a ratio of 1:4. If it is built in sandy soil it is as well to lay a foundation of coarse gravel and concrete first, so that the concrete layer is

not damaged by subsiding ground. First lay a 10 cm layer of concrete, then set a wire netting reinforcement into this, and on top of that another 10 cm layer of concrete. Border the edge of the pond with natural flat stones, fixed in situ with concrete so that they overlap the pool by some 3—5 cm and conceal the concrete edge. An overflow pipe fixed under this stone border will determine the level of the water. The edge of the pond should be of the same material as the path leading to it and link on to it naturally.

When the concrete hardens, smooth a cement slurry over it, so that no water can seep through. Water plants should be planted one or two weeks after the pond has been filled, so that water can first percolate the concrete.

A rubber or PVC liner can also be used for building a pond. First, the pond is hollowed out with gradually sloping walls and a marginal shelf, if required. Check that there are no sharp stones left in the cavity which could puncture the liner. A layer of sand in the base provides an extra safeguard. Then position the liner over the dug out pool and secure round the edges with bricks or paving. Then begin to pour water into the liner, smoothing out any wrinkles as they appear and gradually easing the liner into the pool under the water's weight, by moving the weights accordingly. When the pool is full, leave the weights in situ while you trim the overlap of liner to within 10—15 cm of the pool's edge. Then conceal this necessary, remaining overlap under grass turves or paving stones round the pool's edge.

Fountains. Of course, in a family garden you will not want to have the kind of large fountains that played in 19th-century castle parks. But even the most modest of fountains greatly enlivens the smallest area of water and its surroundings.

Today, with a view to saving water, we may not be able to link even the smallest fountain on to the main water supply and let the water run into the drains. If this is the case, a simple solution, which entails the minimum consumption of water, is to install submersible electric pumps. Almost all of the water then returns to the pool. (As a safety measure, get an electrician to install or check the installation of this type of equipment.)

Nowadays water reservoirs for fountains are most-

The material for the construction of steps should harmonize with the style of the garden. The individual steps must also be large enough to allow for safe and comfortable passage. The picture shows a well-constructed flight of steps leading to a path and bordered by a profusion of flowering plants.

A dead tree trunk can become a very decorative feature, particularly if combined with natural stone. In this instance, however, the stone wall is too massive; it would look better if planted with climbers.

ly made of monolith concrete, the surface of which can be variously decorated. But metal, wood or plastics can equally well be used for the purpose.

The size of the reservoir or pool for a fountain depends on the height to which the water is spouted and the place in which it stands. For classical fountains the principle used to be that the width of the pool or lake should be two to three times the height of the highest spout of water. But if the fountain is to be reflected on the surface of the water, the area should be much bigger.

The water from the reservoir is sucked up by the pump through the suction basket and shot back through the nozzle into the pool. A closed circuit is thus formed. The pool is filled in the spring, and the small quantities that evaporate or are blown off by the wind are replenished as required. For little fountains a submersible pump right in the pool is powerful enough.

The maintenance of a fountain consists mainly in seeing that there is a sufficient amount of water in the pool. Also, this will have to be changed periodically to avoid the growth of algae and prevent organic substances rotting in the water. The pool must be emptied before frosts set in.

A bird bath is not only much appreciated by the birds, but is a delightful ornamental element in the garden. It can be of all sorts of shapes and materials, the latter being most often carved or natural stone. The chief condition is that it should have a bowl-shaped hollow with a shallow edge, not deeper than 3—4 cm so that the birds do not drown. The water must be topped up regularly, because the birds splash a lot out, and furthermore, in such a shallow bowl it soon evaporates, especially on hot days. The bird bath should be placed in the open, so that the birds can bathe or drink safely without a predatory cat getting too close and so that they can be watched from the resting place.

Steps

Height differences great and small can be overcome by single steps or a whole flight of them. Even in a flat garden there is always scope for installing

A small wooden pergola linking the surrounding terrain with the group of tall trees. Being in semi-shade, it has been planted with the shade-loving climber *Aristolochia durior.*

steps — a few from the garden to the sitting-out area by the house, which is on the same level as the house floor etc. Steps can also be very welcome wherever the gradient of the path is more than 10 per cent.

Steps are an important element of garden architecture and can greatly influence the general picture of the garden. When a flight of steps in the right situation is supplemented by plants, troughs of flowers, even perhaps some special lighting, it can be most decorative and is a good way of dividing different parts of the garden.

The first criteria for steps is that they must be usable and safe at all seasons. Therefore, they should not be built in a screened place, such as directly beyond the entrance gate. Steps need not always keep to one direction however; while walking around the garden we want to see the most beautiful parts of it and at the same time enjoy every surprise that nature has prepared for us that day. Each garden is different and so, too, the placing and arrangement of steps will be different. The main thing is that the steps

Two types of pergolas sheltering a sitting-out area. In both cases, the building material is timber. The first one has been made of square posts, the other of pickets. They are trained with climbers which partly cover their sides, creating an intimate atmosphere.

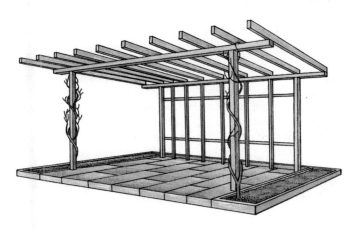

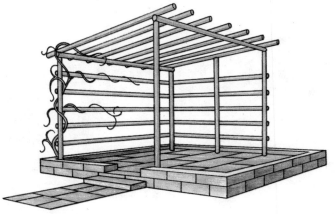

should contribute towards the garden's general harmony, not be a foreign element forced into it.

Before building a flight of steps, first decide on the right dimensions and proportions of each step and the whole flight. Here the general rule is: twice the height of the step + the width of the step = the length of the human step, i.e. 64 cm. Remember, too, that during an ascent the normal length of a human step is shortened. Steps built according to these proportions will make for easy use.

The height of the individual steps should be 12—15 cm, for instance (2 × 12 cm) + 40 = 64 cm, or (2 × 15 cm) + 34 = 64 cm etc. If there is a lack of space the steps must be steeper, for instance (2 × 17 cm) + 30 cm = 64 cm. That is, the higher the steps are the narrower they should be and vice versa.

After calculating the height and width of one step, the next thing is to decide on the space necessary for the whole flight. For example, to mount a height of 70 cm you will need 5 steps each 14 cm high and 36 cm wide, so that the finished length of the steps will be 180 cm.

Of course, all the steps must be of the same height. If this rule is not adhered to, it can lead to unnecessary accidents, as one automatically continues going up or down at the height or depth set by the first step.

Garden steps should never be too long, so if there is a greater distance to be mounted, a larger flat area is recommended after every few steps; this also offers an opportunity to change their direction. Especially if there is not much space to spare in the garden, it helps to have a flight of steps turn at any required angle. The number of steps between the flat areas need not be consistent.

If there is plenty of room, 3—5 steps is a good number between the flat areas — which also need not be of consistent length, as long as the basic measure of the human step or its multiple is respected.

A well-placed garden hearth on a terrace gives a characteristic touch to the facade of the house.

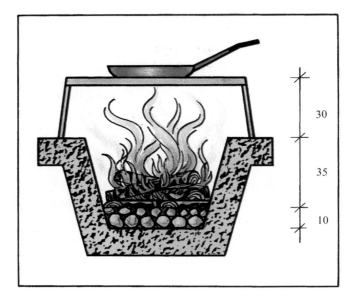

A sitting-out area can be equipped with a garden fireplace, sunk in the ground. Well-dried pine, fir or beech logs are the best fuel. Birch wood burns well even if slightly damp and leaves very little ash. Charcoal can also be used; it does not make a high flame but gives a good amount of heat.

Nor is the width of the flight of steps a matter of chance, but should be in accord with the path and the form of the terrain. On the whole, a wide flight of steps looks better than a narrow one.

The correct building technique is a condition of the stability of the steps. Having settled on the terrain, the next thing is to remove the turf and top layer of soil. Then start building from the bottom and work upwards.

If it is necessary to build a long, steep flight of steps, it should have a railing at least along one side, or a protective wall. The latter can be built only of stones or of stones in mortar. The beginning and end of the wall should be horizontal, the rest following the sloping line of the steps. Both the wall and the steps should be of the same material, and this should ideally be the same as the ground level of the house.

The steps can be let into the supporting wall or can jut out from it in various ways, and can be made of stone, concrete blocks, bricks, cast concrete or specially treated wood.

When each step is made of one block of stone, the steps both look and last well, but come rather expensive. They have to be cut exactly, so that all the steps are the same height and width. They are quite heavy and therefore sufficiently stable, so they can be laid directly on to a bed of sand, without mortar. A long flight of steps, however, needs a firm concrete foundation. The treading area should be rough and slope slightly forwards, so as not to trap rain water (a gradient of about 5 mm to a width of 40 cm). Crosswise, each step must be exactly horizontal, so a spirit level is essential when laying them.

A paving of natural stones is often used for garden steps, usually the same stone as that used for the paths and resting place. The paving blocks must have at least one straight side, be at least 5 cm thick, and have a treading area as large as possible. They should have a good concrete foundation and be joined with cement mortar. Each step overhangs the treading area of the one beneath it by a few centimetres to increase stability. If the treading slab overhangs its foundation stone by about 2 cm the steps look lighter. Usually slabs are only used for the treading area of the steps, the lower part being made of concrete or fragments of the slabs. The gaps between the paving blocks are filled with cement mortar and well smoothed.

If there is a lack of stones, steps can be built of cast concrete, which lasts well. These steps should also have a firm foundation, extending down to the level where the ground never freezes. The wooden boarding can be made on the site. The concrete mix (ratio 1:3) is well tamped down and smoothed. Any slight unevenness can be levelled with a thin cement slurry. The surface can be enlivened by the addition of small or large cobbles.

Nice garden steps can also be made of well-fired bricks. In this case the width and height of the steps will depend on the given dimensions of the bricks. They should be laid in mortar, usually with the nar-

rower, longer side down, and the cracks filled in with cement mortar.

Wooden steps are only suitable in such situations as in a country garden, or one near a forest etc. Timber from deciduous trees must be well rot-proofed before being used. Round sticks or cut stakes can also be used, indeed steps of sticks are both cheap and simple. The front of each step is formed by hammering two pegs some 40—60 cm long into the ground and laying three or four 4—6 cm thick sticks behind them horizontally. The space behind these is then filled with stones, gravel or cinders, and the treading area covered with a layer of pebbles. Large stones can be used to border the sides, or the banks can be sown with grass or planted with perennials.

Steps in less frequented parts of the garden can be made of large stones or blocks with low cushion-forming perennials or shrubs in the spaces between them. Good quality sieved soil should be used to fill in these spaces so that carpeting plants can spread in them and naturally soften the hard appearance of the stone.

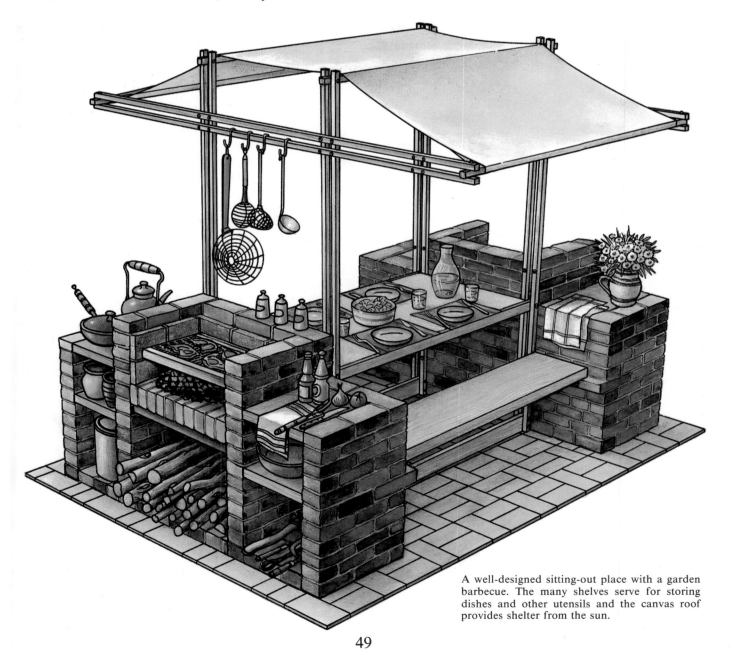

A well-designed sitting-out place with a garden barbecue. The many shelves serve for storing dishes and other utensils and the canvas roof provides shelter from the sun.

This garden hearth has been placed in the corner of a sitting-out area so as not to take up too much space. The low wooden benches may also serve as small tables.

A circular barbecue constructed of stone and metal. The windscreen is made of wicker; the garden furniture should be in the same style.

Pergolas and arbours

In modern gardens a pergola is not only intended to provide shade, it also contributes to making intimate, secluded places in the garden. It can serve both as an element of division (for instance separating the decorative part of the garden from the vegetable garden), or of unification, as it may link the garage, sitting-out area and other buildings with the

house into one organic whole. A small garden can be made to appear larger by a pergola. And it gives an opportunity for planting climbing plants, making for more greenery in the most frequented spots.

Usually, a pergola is connected with the sitting-out area. If it is already planned when the house is being built, it can be linked by having the roof or ceiling beams made long enough to extend over the sitting-out place. If the pergola is situated at the opposite end of the garden, however, it can be connected with the house by a pretty path.

When building a pergola, it is important to keep it in proportion. A good height is between 220—250 cm. Too low a construction looks confined, but one that is too high does not look well either. Remember that when the pergola is overgrown with climbers it will appear narrower and lower. A recommended width is 3 m, but this depends on the overall proportions of the garden.

The support posts and other parts of the pergola must be very firm, as they will have to withstand strong gusts of wind and bear the weight of the chosen climbers.

Monolithic pergolas

This is the original way in which pergolas were built, and in south Tyrolean vineyards they still are. The supporting pillars are cut out of a single piece of granite or sandstone and are from 20 × 20 to 20 × 40 cm thick and 240 cm high. There is a hole at the upper end, into which is placed a rod 10—12 cm thick. Laid across this at suitable distances are peeled poles of spruce, fir or pine wood. Nowadays, these massive pergolas are only used in large gardens or parks.

In a small garden the pillars can be made of bricks or stones. To provide perfect stability each pillar should be at least 40 × 40 cm in dimension. The amount of material required to build a pergola is rather large, but the most splendid effects can be achieved.

Wooden pergolas

Owing to its natural appearance, wood is the best material for a pergola. Pine or oak timber is used, and it must be healthy and dry so that it will not warp. It can be processed, but fir roundwood can also be used.

The supporting pillars are most often 12 × 12 or 12 × 24 cm wide. They are not let straight into the ground but screwed between two iron bands measuring 6 × 60 × 800 mm, which are let into concrete bases, leaving about 5 cm of space between the concrete and the wood.

The lower longitudinal beams are 10 × 12 or 10 × 14 cm wide and the upper ones 4 × 12 or 6 × 14 cm. They are nailed or, better still, screwed on with rust-proof screws. When joining the individual parts make sure that no gaps remain that might trap water, causing the wood to rot very quickly. With this in mind, before joining the parts they should be treated with a preservative, preferably one that leaves the structure of the wood visible.

This small barbecue with side shelves can be built on a terrace.

Metal pergolas

A metal construction for a pergola is long-lasting and looks nice, but plants cannot climb well on its smooth surface. Best is a combination of steel tubes as supporting pillars and a wooden horizontal construction. The diameter of the metal pillars depends on the size of the pergola and ranges from 4 to 10 cm. To increase the stability, thin metal tubes can be used double, that is, put two parallel supports at a distance of about 20 cm from one another, or place two tubes in a V-shape. The metal tubes are welded together and let about 50 cm deep into concrete bases, with a bit of flat iron welded across the lower ends.

Wooden longitudinal slats are either laid across the pillars or screwed on to either side of a welded strip of iron. In this way the tubes form a support, the wood being rather a decoration or filling.

Metal tubes with a square or oblong profile, bent into the form of the letter U and then stood up reversed also form an elegant support for cross bars.

All the metal parts of the pergola should be given an anti-corrosive coating. The lighter this is in colour, the airier will be the impression of the pergola.

Bamboo pergolas

A light pergola of bamboo canes is very original, but the pillars are wooden, as bamboo canes are too slender for the purpose. Also, bamboo cannot be nailed, so the canes are tied on with nylon thread, leather thongs or some other durable material.

A bamboo pergola looks natural and when covered with plants is most effective.

A children's corner

A children's corner can contain many elements, their number depending mainly on the size of the garden. The site of the play area should be clearly visible from the house, so that adults can keep an eye on the state of play.

A children's corner can hardly be imagined without a sandpit. This should be located in a sunny place, sheltered from the wind, if possible. The usual dimensions are about 200×150 cm, but of course it can be smaller or larger. First dig out a pit of the required size. Then make a frame of smooth planed boards with quarterings in the corners, and set it into the hollow. Pave the flat bottom of the sandpit with bricks, leaving rather wide gaps between them so that rainwater can drain away quickly and leave the sand dry. The brick bottom will also prevent earth from dirtying the sand. It is a good idea also to pave the surroundings of the sandpit, either with bricks or other material used elsewhere in the garden. Planed boards can also be fixed on to the frame round the pit so that the children can either use these as seating or as a worktable.

If there is sufficient space, a games area can be built next to the sandpit. Grass cannot flourish in such an area, so it is better to dig out a 15 cm layer of earth, fill the hollow with fine gravel and cover this again with a layer of sand, which can then be firmly tamped down or rolled.

Another essential for a children's corner is a swing. This can be built either of strong beams supported with struts, or of iron pipes welded or screwed together at the top. In any case the support must be set deep into the ground and strengthened with stones and concrete, to make it absolutely firm. Then a swing, rings or bars can be hung from the hooks in the crossbeam.

A fireplace, barbecue or hearth

A modern garden is more and more becoming an extension of the family's living space, so the above ele-

The style of the garden furniture depends on personal taste. It should, however, always be in agreement with the character of the garden, as here.

A simple but attractive garden bench made from a tree trunk.

ments are in ever greater demand. If the garden is used not only for rest but for entertaining guests, they become almost essential. In the evenings, particularly in early spring or late autumn, a hearth warms its surroundings and makes sitting out very pleasant.

A fireplace — which is best round or oblong — should be built in a sheltered spot, at some distance from any buildings and in the direction of the prevailing wind. If it is set into the ground, the base should be of concrete or, better still, paved with stones laid into cement mortar. An edging of flat stones looks very effective and at the same time makes it easy to keep the surround of the fireplace tidy. It also avoids the danger of fire spreading to the grass. When building the edge, short iron pipes should be set in concrete on either side at a suitable distance to hold a spike for grilling foods when having a barbecue.

An outdoor hearth is very practical; this is also built in a sheltered spot, usually on the paving of the sitting-out area and protected by a decorative wall of climbing plants. It can be made of carved stone or bricks, or a combination of the two. But it must have a proper hearth chimney, so it is best to have it built by an expert.

There is also a wide selection of portable barbecues available, and these can be taken out as required. They work just as well as a built-in one.

Lighting

Lighting in a garden is particularly useful in summerhouses, on terraces and other places intended for sitting out in the evening. It can also be put wherever it makes some corner accessible in the evening or lights up especially attractive or sculptural plants.

Lamps with wicker or straw shades look well in summerhouses that are mostly constructed of timber. Where the walls are of stone or brick, wrought iron, black painted chandelier-type fitments are better.

Lights placed in the garden to illuminate interest-

ing features should have a dull surface or a non-translucent shade, so they throw light only in the required direction. They may be made of metal or plastics, the important thing being that they should not be a disturbing or even unsightly element during the day. This can be resolved by placing them among plants that partially conceal them.

Electric wiring should be put underground, deep enough for it not to be damaged when digging the garden. A special cable covered in lead should be used for distribution, and bricks laid over it before the trench is filled in. If a surface cable is used, great care must be taken to avoid damaging it when digging or cutting the grass.

Garden furniture

So that the garden can be really lived in, it must be equipped with furniture. In choosing this, the basic requirements are that it should be comfortable, easily transportable, sufficiently stable, weather-proof, easy to store, and should fit in well with the character of the garden. Too bright colours and extreme variations of shape should be avoided.

There is a wide selection of various types of furniture on the market. The least resistant to weather is that made of wicker and bamboo. All sorts of swinging seats or loungers with canvas canopies are very popular, as are deck chairs and other folding chairs.

If you do not like what is on sale you can, with a little application and innovation, make your own furniture.

A thick board, at least 30 cm wide, for instance, makes a good bench when laid on a brick or stone base. The board can either be lifted off and stored away in the winter, or it can be permanently fixed to the footing, especially if it is sheltered by a high wall or a spreading tree. In either case, the wood should be painted with oil and varnished. Most people find that 40—50 cm is a comfortable height for sitting.

A convenient bench can also be made of wooden railway sleepers. One sleeper makes the seat, another, half as wide, the back. They can be fixed to a high wall by being strung on two to three metal pipes let into the wall. The bench may be cut to any required length.

A bench that looks well in a naturally designed garden can be made from a tree-trunk with a diameter of about 30 cm. Simply cut the trunk in two, lengthwise. A pedestal can be made at each end using either thinner trunks or large stones.

Simple portable seats can be made from logs cut into 40-cm pieces which can be placed wherever needed.

A set of table and chairs can be made of round wood offcuts. Best are maple ones with a diameter of 40—50 cm and about 10 cm high. These make the chairs when each has a 25 × 25 cm metal plate with a welded-on pipe in the middle screwed on to the underside. This is then fitted on to another, narrower pipe fixed into the ground with concrete and sticking up 35 cm above the surface. A table can be made in the same way, but the top of it should have a diameter of at least 80 cm and be 15 cm thick. The best height for the table is 75 cm. The seats should be positioned some 70 cm distant from the table. In winter they can be lifted from their pedestal stands and stored in a dry place.

Small architectural features

In the past, particularly in baroque times, many works of art were placed in parks and gardens. In a modern garden too, statues and other works of art can be used to increase its aesthetic value. The effect of any work of art is enhanced by certain surroundings, and there is no doubt that buildings, pieces of sculptural art and plants are all mutually complementary.

Of course, in the first instance, the choice of any work of art depends on personal taste. And not only statues, wall reliefs and ceramic pots can be used to beautify a garden, but also useful objects with a decorative element, such as bird baths, flower bowls and sundials. Even big stones with interesting shapes, found in their natural setting — say, when walking along a beach — can be very effective in a garden.

Not only the selection of a work of art but its placing in the garden needs sensitive handling. A simple statue can hold its own even when there are striking and multiform plants in its neighbourhood, but an elaborate or large-scale work of art can only be properly appreciated in calm surroundings, for instance against a background of evergreens.

An important role is played by the ratio of size between the artefact and the garden. It must be remembered that out of doors everything tends to look smaller than it does in a house. The pedestal should also be relatively big.

A garden must not be overcrowded with art objects, or it will look like a gallery or storehouse.

Useful objects

A garden frame
A frame is, in fact, a framed flowerbed, covered with a pane of glass. Simple ones tend to have one row of windows and a gradient to one side only. Double ones are usually twice as wide and the windows slope in both directions from a raised central beam.

In a vegetable plot or garden a frame of proportionate size is particularly useful. Firstly, it is good for growing the seedlings of early and warmth-loving vegetables until they can be planted out; it is also useful for forcing radishes, lettuces and kohlrabi, for cultivating delicate vegetables in the summer and keeping some late vegetables, for instance Brussels sprouts, Savoy cabbage, from autumn to spring. A deep piled-up frame can also be used for storing root vegetables over the winter.

A frame should be built in a sunny place, sheltered from the winds, especially from the north. Winds not only decrease the temperature in the frame, but may carry off the lids if they are not well

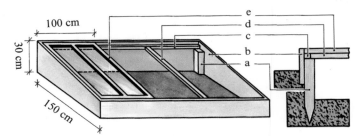

A simple cold frame is quite easy to make. Construction details: a) vertical batten, b) side panels, c) horizontal lath, d) ledge for glass, e) glass sheet.

secured, particularly if they are of framed polythene. The lids (lights) should slope towards the south.

Usually, frames are made of wood. The outside edge is made of thick pine or fir planks, nailed to pillars set in the ground at the corners. The length of the frame depends on the number and size of the lights. The sides can be reinforced with slats placed crosswise to prevent their buckling.

Single-bar frame lids may be, for instance, 150×100 cm large with two sheets of glass 4 mm thick and with an area of 144×45 cm. These glass lids are laid on support slats, nailed to the inside of the frame. All of the wooden components will last longer if they are soaked in linseed oil and then varnished.

Instead of glass the lights can be made of strong polythene sheets fixed to a light wooden framework. The outside edge of the frame can also be made of

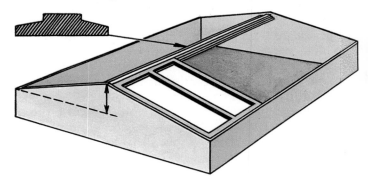

A double cold frame showing a detail of the cross section for the raised central beam.

A cross section of a garden frame made of bricks.

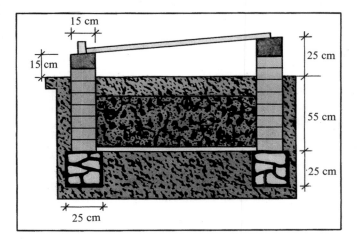

53

Two examples of easily transportable glass and plastic cloches.

bricks, concrete etc., but timber — though it does not last so well — retains warmth more efficiently.

Frame covers

Mats made of long rye straw or rushes can be used to cover the frame, especially at night during the early spring, to help the frame conserve its warmth.

In mountainous areas the frame may be covered not only with mats but also with boards, as a further protection against the weight of heavy falls of snow.

Frame shades

Shades are used to protect newly-sown seeds, young plants that have just been pricked out and freshly transplanted vegetables, from an excess of solar radiation. Cucumbers in particular are sensitive to very strong sunlight. A good practical shade can be made of coarsely-woven jute 150 cm wide, wound on to a round wooden stick. If need be, a coating of lime can be used for shading, but this washes off badly. Or you can use a yellowish-brown clay but this has to be renewed after heavy rain, and often special shading coats are used.

Ventilation pegs

These are wooden supports, about 40 cm high. If they are notched, the frame windows can be supported on them at various heights according to the required degree of ventilation. If the supports are without notches they can be stood under the windows upright, sideways or flat so as to regulate the temperature in the frame.

How to start a frame

Of course, a frame can be heated by hot waterpipes, electric radiators etc. But a small frame with a few lights is usually started with fresh stable manure as required from February to March. Horse manure is best, but if this is difficult to get, sheep or rabbit manure will serve the purpose.

For a warm frame, the manure has to be prepared several days ahead. To do this, first pile the manure up to a height of 150 cm. If it is dry or there is too much straw in it, pour warm water over it. As soon

as the manure is sufficiently heated it is piled up in the frame. If there is not enough of it, it can be supplemented with leaves, weeds, old hay or straw and other organic waste. This gives a semi-hot frame which is less warm, but retains its warmth longer.

After piling up the material it should be stamped down so that, after being covered with a layer of soil, there is a 15 cm space between its surface and the lid or roof of the frame; it subsides a bit after a time. For planting in pots, a layer of soil 10 cm thick is sufficient, for sowing vegetable seeds it should be about 15 cm and for planting early vegetables such as lettuces a layer of about 25 cm is needed. A good growing medium is well-matured compost, or topsoil enriched with peat. When the frame has been raked over, seeds can be sown at once. But it is better to wait one or two days before planting, to allow the frame time to warm up. As soon as it is prepared the frame is covered with its lights and these, in turn, are covered with straw mats for the night.

Portable cloches

Portable glass or polythene cloches have become very popular lately for the purpose of covering individual flower or vegetable beds to 'bring on' the plants. The side walls should be about 30 cm high, the frame being either of boards or wooden slats. For cultivating cucumbers the frame is 50 × 50 cm. When the plants grow, bricks are placed under the frame, so that the plants do not burn on contact with the sheeting. Polythene covered metal frames of various shapes are also widely used.

Greenhouses

In early spring many gardeners appreciate the advantages of a greenhouse. Different types and sizes of frames for greenhouses, to be glazed or covered with plastic sheets, can be bought readymade. For home vegetable growers who want to 'do it themselves', here are a few basic principles of construction and location.

A greenhouse should stand in a sunny place, sheltered from northerly winds. It should be easily acces-

A simple but very useful timber-framed greenhouse can be built even in a small garden.

A compact greenhouse such as the wooden one in the picture, is invaluable even in the smallest garden.

sible. If it is built out in the open, unprotected by other buildings, it is recommended that it be set partially into the ground, or else that the surrounding terrain should be raised by an embankment, especially where the ground soil tends to be particularly heavy and damp.

The question of heating must be thought out before you start building. The ideal way is to link the greenhouse to the central heating in the house — then the temperature can be regulated by the radiator. Some modern greenhouses are heated by electricity or gas. Coal and oil stoves can also be used but this, of course, means that the temperature is not uniform throughout the greenhouse.

When the matters of heating, building materials and size have all been determined, the building can begin. The greenhouse walls are mostly built on previously prepared foundations of concrete or smooth concrete bricks. They should be dug down to a depth of 100—120 cm and are best 250—350 cm wide, length as required. The foundations should be about 20 cm higher than the surrounding ground. A framework is then constructed of small beams, to which slats can be fixed to make the support for panes of glass or windows. Battens are fixed between these,

and the roof beam covered with tin or tarred paper. If the framework is metal, whether screwed or welded, it should be treated with an anti-corrosive before being glazed.

The door must be wide enough for a wheelbarrow containing compost or peat to pass through. If the greenhouse is to be long, it is useful to have a partition dividing off a little entrance hallway, so that when the external door is opened cold air does not get past the small entrance area. This hall is also useful for storing small items such as flowerpots, troughs, soil for seedlings etc. Or a large water tank can be kept here for ease of watering the plants in the greenhouse.

The shelves or counters for plants are best made of concrete slabs, and they must have a shallow rim at the front edge, so that earth does not fall on the path. This path should be paved with bricks or concrete slabs with a slight gradient to each side so that puddles do not form when the plants are watered.

To prevent the greenhouse from cooling too much in early spring and in the autumn months, it can be lined on the inside or covered on the outside with polythene sheets, fixed on to the slats with drawing pins. The space between the glass and the sheet will give the necessary thermal insulation, and the temperature inside the greenhouse will remain stable, even in windy weather and on cold nights.

The introduction of plants

Plants were the first living organisms to appear on this planet. Only plants are able to take up nutrients in the form of minerals and convert them into organic compounds which all animals can eat. Thus people, too, are in fact dependent on plants as the source of all food.

A **stem** is the aerial part of a plant which carries the leaves and flowers. It has a growing point at its tip and distributes nutrients to all parts of the plant body. Stalks are either herbaceous or woody. A herbaceous stalk is called 'caulis' if it carries both leaves and flowers (for example, a sunflower), 'scape' if it carries only flowers (for example, a tulip, hyacinth), or 'culm' if it has solid joint-like nodes between hollow internodes (for example, grass). Trees and shrubs have woody stems (trunks and branches).

Buds are germs of stems and have various functions. The narrow and pointed woody buds produce new twigs. The blunter leaf buds grow into leaves. The flower buds (bud eyes) are round and contain the germs of stamens, pistils and floral envelopes. Those hidden under bark are dormant buds which open when the tree loses its physiological balance — as when a thicker branch is broken, when the tree regenerates excessively or when the crown is damaged by severe frost and the like. The vigorous shoots which exuberantly grow from these buds are called 'suckers' or 'side shoots'.

Leaves usually have a blade, stalk (petiole) and sheath. Several layers of tissue appear on the cross section through the leaf blade. The outer layer is called the 'epidermis'. The epidermis on the underside of the leaf has tiny holes, called 'stomata', to control water evaporation from the plant. When there is a lack of water the stomata are closed to reduce evaporation. When the plant has enough moisture the stomata are kept open to get rid of any excess water.

Leaves are very important in the process of photosynthesis (assimilation). Photosynthesis can take place only in the green parts of plants because they contain chlorophyll, the green colouring matter essential for the formation of organic compounds. These are produced through a complex chain of reactions of carbon dioxide and water, with the assistance of solar energy. A plant takes carbon dioxide from the air and its stomata release the same amount of oxygen. We say that trees are the green lungs of the city because they remove carbon dioxide from the air and enrich it with oxygen.

However, plants do consume some oxygen in the process of respiration (dissimilation). The oxygen needed for respiration gets into the plant through the stomata and epidermis. The aerial parts of plants usually are well-supplied with oxygen.

Roots, on the other hand, may suffer from a lack of oxygen if the plant has to grow in muddy soil (for example, excess watering of a potted flower displaces air from the soil, hinders the breathing of the roots and eventually kills the plant). Plants generally produce much more oxygen than they need for respiration.

Mineral nutrients are carried from the roots to the leaves where they are converted into organic substances. Thus healthy foliage is the first prerequisite for a good crop of fruits in an orchard or nice flowers in a flower bed.

Roots. Besides the leaf, the root is another main organ responsible for nutrient uptake. Its task is to keep the plant firmly in the ground and to take up moisture and nutrients from the soil. The finest roots, called 'root hairs' (rhizoids), are the most important for plant nutrition. They grow and regenerate very quickly but cannot draw nutrients from the soil for more than a few hours; they quickly grow old and then serve only for the uptake of water. Their number is enormous. For instance, a year-old apple-tree seedling has up to 17 million root hairs with a total length of almost three kilometres. These finest roots are able to grow at comparatively low temperatures, close to 0° C. It is therefore best to plant trees in the autumn; by the following spring they will produce a large amount of root hairs which can then start drawing nutrients and water from the soil. A young tree planted late in spring is exhausted by having to draw nutrients and water from its own reserves at the beginning.

The roots also serve as a storing place where the tree keeps for the winter the substances it has produced during the growing season. In the following spring these substances are released and transported to the opening buds. Thus a good state and function of roots is the second prerequisite for good crops.

A **flower** is a very shortened stem whose leaves become transformed into reproductive organs. It usually has two main parts, i. e. stamens and pistils, and a third part, the floral envelope, which protects the

Although an unpleasant weed in the garden, the dandelion is an inseparable part of country meadows and one without which spring could hardly be imagined.

young flower and attracts insects for the purpose of pollination.

The leaves of the floral envelope are either all of the same kind, forming a perianth (for example, in the tulip, lily, lily-of-the-valley or snowdrop), or there is an outer green calyx and an inner corolla of bright-coloured petals (for example, the poppy, cherry, tomato or rose).

A stamen consists of a filament (stalk) and an anther containing four pollen sacs which in turn contain pollen grains, the male cells.

A pistil consists of an ovary (containing ovules, the female cells) and a stem (style) that ends in a stigma.

If a flower has both male and female parts, that is, stamens and pistil, it is bisexual (androgynous), as is the case with apple-trees and tulips. If it has only stamens it is called a 'staminate' (male) flower. If it has only a pistil it is called a 'pistillate' (female) flower. Monoecious species (such as the hazel, cucumber, spruce and maize) have both male and female flowers on the same plant. Dioecious species (hop, yew and willow) have only staminate flowers on some plants and only pistillate flowers on others.

Pollination is the transmission of pollen to the stigma of a flower. A pollen grain attaches to the stigma, grows through the style into the ovary to hit the ovule and produce a single cell with it. A seed develops from this cell. The unification of a pollen grain with the nucleus of an ovule is called 'fertilization'. Good conditions for good pollination are the third prerequisite for a good crop.

A plant takes food from its environment and increases its body mass. The plant body grows and its organs grow with it, changing their shape and chemistry: the plant develops. During their individual lives plants change their metabolism, develop new functions, form new leaves, flowers, fruits, seeds. New plants sprout from the seeds to develop again and produce new seeds. Thus metabolism, supporting the growth and development of an individual, is also involved in the formation of the germs of new individuals of the same species, that is, in the continuing process of reproduction.

Plants and ecology

All plants need a suitable environment in which to thrive. The environment, in turn, depends, in the essence, on climate, altitude and location.

Climate

Man cannot influence the climate but he can adjust the plants' environment by irrigation, protection against frost, shading, smoking and the like. These practices can be of considerable help in improving the microclimate of an orchard, a flower bed, a frame and so on.

All the seasons of the year are equally important for the healthy development of plants. In winter, plenty of snow, dry frost or ice coating, or on the other hand, abrupt warming, may be either favourable or very detrimental to the life of plants. In spring, the weather is particularly important. It is ideal if the snow melts slowly enough to let snow water seep into the soil; if, however, snow melts too quickly the water runs away and much of it is lost to plants. Plentiful rains in spring help to start a good water regime and encourage deep-rooting plants to grow vigorously.

Weather should warm up slowly in spring with no greater differences in temperature between the day and night. The trees and shrubs should not wake up too soon because if they do, late frosts will almost certainly kill their buds. In summer, rainfall and temperature should be balanced to ensure good development of the plants and good ripening of their fruits. In autumn, if temperatures fall too soon, too quickly to below the freezing point, the wood of trees and shrubs fails to ripen and becomes more susceptible to freezing and invasion by diseases. Abrupt frosts can kill sensitive species of vegetables and flowers.

Location

Location is one of the most decisive factors on which the use of a garden depends. Slopes (facing north or south) influence the action of, for instance, wind, changes in temperature, sunshine and shade. Sun is generous to southern slopes; as a rule, they are warm and dry and plants sited there are the first to start growing in spring. Eastern slopes also have plenty of sunshine and are usually even drier than those facing south because of the easterly wind. Western slopes are warm enough, too, and usually have more moisture than the southern ones. Northern slopes are the coldest. Their soil is the last to thaw and their plants are delayed in vegetation. Some plants grow poorly in gardens facing north, because they suffer from a lack of sunshine.

It is important, also, whether the garden is located in a sheltered or unsheltered place. Location in an open landscape exposes the garden to wind which usually dries the soil and often damages the plants. It is best to have a windbreak of trees or buildings on the northern side, or on the side from which the wind usually comes. Deep valleys and frost hollows are bad places to grow plants because cold air and fog tend to stay there a long time and the movement of air is generally poor.

Altitude

Altitude influences the temperature, sunshine, atmospheric humidity and rainfall. As a rule, the higher the altitude, the worse the weather and soil conditions and the shorter the growing season. Basically, we distinguish between lowland (up to 250 m above sea level), middle (from 250 to 450 m) and mountain altitudes (from 450 to 600 m or more above sea level).

We seldom have a chance to choose an ideal place (ideal location, climate and soil) when we are establishing a garden. We have to accept the reality and adapt to it as best as we can. First, the most suitable plants must be chosen from a very wide spectrum of plants with different requirements, ranging from utterly moisture-loving to drought-resistant species

By a sensitive intervention, man can create a most harmonious 'natural' environment.

and varieties, from those requiring light to those needing shade.

The choice of suitable plants helps us to make the best use of the given conditions. Wind can be controlled by suitable trees, screens or walls — which at the same time can be decorative features or visually divide the space. The soil can be drained to remove excess moisture or thoroughly watered if the place is dry. Certain plants can be relied upon to provide shade if the place is too sunny. Garden pools will improve the microclimate.

In short, the possible ways in which we can control undesirable local conditions are ample. If we use them wisely we shall have, even in the least favourable of sites, a garden where blossoms and fruits will offer an armful of beauty and bounty from spring through to winter.

Climatic factors

The sum of climatic factors makes the conditions either favourable or unfavourable for the life of a plant. The main climatic factors include light (intensity and length); temperature; moisture (rainfall rate and distribution) and atmospheric humidity, that is, the moisture content of the air.

Light

Different plants have different demands of light. Thus we distinguish light-demanding, semi-shade- and shade-demanding plants. The light-demanding plants have to be grown in sunny places, the semi-shade-loving plants need a partly shaded place or a 'temporary shade', and the shade-demanding plants prefer a shady site all of the time.

Different species also need different daily lengths of sunshine to set flowers and bear fruit. Thus there are short-day plants, for example, chrysanthemums, requiring a day shorter than 12 hours; medium-day plants, such as roses, which flower when the day length reaches about 12 hours; and long-day plants, such as carnations or radishes, which flower when daylight lasts for longer than 12 hours.

Light is very important to the growth, development and fertility of plants because it has a great influence on the intensity of their metabolic processes. Therefore, the gardener should give his plants as much light as they need, planting them at an appropriate spacing to prevent competition for light and pruning the crowns of trees to let light get in to help produce fine fruits.

Temperature

In western and central Europe the growing season of the majority of plants starts when the temperature rises to between 1 and 5° C, which is the 'threshold temperature' level. Plants die at temperatures above 40° C, which is therefore called the 'temperature maximum'. The best temperature or 'optimum temperature' for the majority of plants is between 20 and 30° C.

The early autumn and late spring frosts are the most dangerous to plants. If frost comes at the end of September or in the first half of October it often kills the susceptible plants, such as tomatoes. Late spring frosts damage vegetables and flowers. Fruit and ornamental woody species can be damaged if frost attacks them when they are in bloom. Danger to plants comes regularly with the 'Ice Saints' in the middle of May. It is only after these cold days that we can stop worrying and start planting vegetables such as tomatoes and sweet garden peppers, which need warmer temperatures in order to flourish. Fluctuations of temperature are particularly dangerous in early spring when, on sunny days, the temperature exceeds 10° C but can fall very low at night.

In fact, the hardiness of each plant species underlies its ability to grow under given conditions. Success of growing any garden plant therefore depends mainly on the choice of the site. Where the site conditions do not meet a plant's requirements it is better not to grow that plant there unless you are prepared to work to protect the site, to improve the conditions and try to meet the plant's needs. Plants can be protected by shelter walls or plastic or glass covers.

Moisture

Water means life. For plants, water is the direct source of oxygen and hydrogen and a medium in which other nutrients are dissolved so that they can be taken up through the roots. When the water supply is poor, the plant wilts. To live, every plant needs sufficient amounts of water from the onset of its development to the ripening of its fruits. According to the demands they make on water, we distinguish them as aquatic plants, moisture-loving plants (hygrophytes), plants with medium water requirement, and drought-loving plants (xerophytes).

The aquatic plants grow in water and root in the mud of the bottom (for example, water-lily). Hygrophytes need plenty of water in the soil and a high atmospheric humidity, so most of them can only be grown under glass. The majority of plants have medium water demands. Xerophytes are able to grow in dry and sunny places because they have fleshy, succulent leaves or stems where they store water for the dry periods (cacti, succulents and others).

The main source of moisture is atmospheric precipitation, falling to the ground in the form of rain, snow, hoar-frost or dew. Rain is the most important and richest source of moisture in the growing season. Snow covers the land in winter and protects plants against frost. In spring the snow thaws and the water is sucked into the soil where it is kept as the winter moisture. Hoar-frost consists of small crystals of ice produced from atmospheric moisture on soil or plant surface when the temperature decreases below 0° C. In the day-time, when it becomes warmer, hoarfrost thaws and runs down into the soil. Hoar-frost usually appears in the morning on the cold days of autumn and early spring. Dew is also an important natural source of moisture for plants because it provides moisture for the plants when the weather is dry. Like hoar-frost, dew is the product of the condensation of water vapour contained in the air: small drops of water appear on the surface of plants and soil which have cooled during the night.

Precipitation is not evenly distributed, however. The heaviest rains come in spring and autumn. To provide enough water for the plants whenever they need it we therefore have to use irrigation.

Air

Air is a mixture of gases and water vapour. For the plants, air is a source of oxygen and carbon dioxide, and for organisms able to fix atmospheric nitrogen it is also a source of nitrogen. Atmospheric humidity influences the evaporation of water: if the air is too dry evaporation is much more intensive and plants suffer from a lack of water. When there is too much moisture in the air the plants can become overheated and thus susceptible to fungal attack. Excess air moisture is usually encountered only when plants are grown under glass or plastic, which is why ventilation is so essential in such cases.

Polluted air is fatal to all living organisms: people, animals, plants. Dust and soot particles settle on plants, mainly on leaves where they block the pores, absorb solar radiation and hinder the important functions of the leaves. Sulphur dioxide contained in smoke is particularly dangerous because it breaks down chlorophyll. All this negatively affects the growth and development of plants.

A mild air flow — a breeze — is favourable for plants. A strong air flow — strong wind, gusty wind or a windstorm — is harmful because plants may be damaged, broken or even uprooted. Wind also increases the rate of evaporation of water from the soil and strong wind affects pollination by preventing bees from leaving the hive in the first instance and by drying the stigmas of flowers. Plants can be protected to some extent by planting suitable windbreaks — taller shrubs or trees able to break stronger winds, slowing down their speed and force. More delicate plants can also be planted close by a sheltering wall and the like. Fruit tree espaliers should be planted so that they allow the wind to pass along, not to stand in its path.

Soil

The yields of plants are influenced, besides climatic conditions, by a number of factors associated with the soil, including its physical, chemical and biological properties. These factors do not act separately: they interact with the climatic factors and combine their influence on the growth of plants. But the interaction of these factors also depends on:
— the plant species to be grown
— the given developmental stage of the plant
— the yields we want to achieve.

Many soil properties, particularly the soil structure, water and air content, organic matter content and the absorption capacity, are closely related with the reaction of nutrients in the soil and with plant nutrition and manuring.

If uncultivated soil is used these factors can be influenced only to a limited extent; this should be

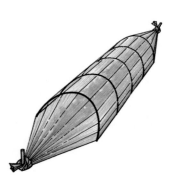

A polythene tunnel cloche, the arches of which are made of light metal tubes or strong wire with a light polythene sheet stretched over them. The sides can be weighted with laths. Short, about 1-m, sections can be jointed together to form tunnels of any length. Cloches shelter the plants from frost, ensuring an earlier and rich harvest. In spring, the cloche retains the warmth generated in the ground during the day.

known when manuring is planned. The soil should be treated with utmost care and all practices ought to be aimed at conserving and improving soil productivity.

Soil structure

Soil structure depends on the texture (granularity), humus content, root system of the plants, activity of the soil fauna, atmospheric precipitation and water seepage, and capillary elevation in the soil.

The best soils have a crumby structure with particles stuck together to form crumbs 1—10 mm in diameter. Crumby soils contain plenty of air, readily absorb water and are easily penetrated by the roots of plants. Water is easily drawn to the roots from the lower soil, supplying the plants with the nutrients they need. To give a soil the crumby structure, plenty of humus should be provided. Shading by plants and mulching help to keep the desired soil structure, once it has been achieved.

A puddled structure is less favourable for plants. It usually develops in soils of heavier texture with a large proportion of clay particles. Such soils are almost impenetrable to water and roots. The puddled structure is most frequently encountered after heavy rains or inexpert watering with a strong splash of water. Heavy water drops break the crumbs and the soil becomes muddy. When the mud dries a crust forms on the surface of the soil and has to be loosened as soon as possible.

Dusty soil structure is even worse because such soils fail to anchor the plants. The soil particles do not stick together to form crumbs and the soil is loose. Water quickly percolates, washing the nutrients down into the subsoil, so the plants also suffer from a lack of water and nutrients.

Various practices can be used with success to influence the soil structure. To obtain the desired crumby structure, humus should be regularly added to all soils, particularly to light, sandy soils of a dusty structure and heavy soils of a puddled structure. Light-textured soils need a regular supply of soil-fixing materials such as peat, carbonation scum from sugar production, mud and the like. Heavy soils, on the other hand, need texture-improving materials such as coarse sand, ash and peat — which is an invaluable soil amendment. The use of organic fertilizers, mainly compost, is essential in all soils.

Soil porosity

Another important soil property that can be controlled is the soil porosity. On this depends the soil's ability to keep, fix and exchange nutrients important for the plants. These nutrients can be bound physically, chemically or biologically.

Good humic soils of crumby structure with the best ability to keep nutrients available to plants have the highest absorption. Sandy soils have a low absorption and their nutrients leach to layers outside the reach of plants. In clayey soils, the movement of nutrients is limited and the soil conditions are not favourable for the plants to take up nutrients through the roots.

Water surfaces are calming and lively at the same time. Their often luxuriant vegetation adds a natural touch to the scene.

Soil pH

The pH of soil can be either acid, neutral or alkaline. The pH value of the highest-acidity soils is 4 or less. The neutral soils have a pH of 6.5 to 7.4 and the pH of the most alkaline soils is 7.4 or more. The pH is not fixed for all time however; it can be changed. The main factor that can influence soil pH is fertilization, both organic and mineral, followed by rainfall, products of the breakdown of the organic matter in the soil and the like.

The pH of garden soil ranges from 4 to 8. At pH values below 4 (for example, in peat bogs) the soil contains substances harmful to plants, and the same applies to soils of pH value above 8. Different plant species need specific pH soils and the existing soil should be adjusted as necessary to meet these requirements. Currant, gooseberry or apple-trees prefer somewhat acid soils. On the other hand, stone-fruit species (apricot, peach, cherry, plum) prefer soils of a higher alkalinity. However, it can be said that generally the majority of garden species require neutral to slightly acid soils (pH from 6.5 to 7.2).

We can have the soil pH exactly determined in an agrochemical laboratory. But we can also do some simple soil testing ourselves by pouring vinegar on to a lump of dry soil (alkaline soil effervesces). Or we can buy one of the inexpensive soil-testing kits readily available at most good gardening centres or department stores with a gardening section. The kits are easy to use and give a reliable analysis.

In nature, the soil pH can be judged from the occurence of some characteristic plants. For instance, sedge, cranberry, corn chamomile, plantain and other plants grow on acid soils, white charlock grows on neutral soils, wild chamomile, Dutch clover and white mustard prefer alkaline soils.

To reduce acidity, lime should be added to the soil. To reduce alkalinity, acid fertilizers (superphosphate, sulphates and the like) have to be applied. Different soils have different ability to keep their pH unchanged. The majority of soils tend towards gradual acidification. Sandy soils, unlike clayey soils, do not keep their pH easily, so sandy soils have to be frequently limed at small application rates whereas on heavier soils you can apply a larger amount in just one application.

Kinds of soil

The kind of soil is an important parameter of soil quality and productivity. A gardener must know, particularly when establishing a new garden, what kind of soil he has in his plot and whether substantial conditioning is needed.

Sandy soils contain a large amount of sand and little humus. Farmers call them 'light' or 'light-textured' soils. These soils are well-aerated and have a good permeability to water which, however, is not a good property because frequent watering is needed. Organic fertilizers should be applied as the main source of nutrients, but even these break down readily and the nutrients leach to the subsoil. Plenty of peat should be applied beside compost and commercial fertilizers — mainly the slow-release type (nitrates) — should be applied in frequent small doses.

Humus-rich soils are well-aerated, warm and easy to cultivate. After rain they quickly dry and form no crust on the surface. Commercial fertilizers are recommended to be frequently added to these soils at low application rates. Good results are obtained when peat and manure are used, mulching being a good method of application. Humus-rich soils are among the best garden soils because they retain water very well and are good fixers for mineral nutrients.

Clayey soils are very compact, adhesive, hard to cultivate. In farmers' terminology they are 'heavy' or 'heavy-textured'. They often form a crust on the surface and when ploughed they make large clods. Clayey soils crack when the weather is dry for long periods and grow muddy after long or heavy rains. However, they readily absorb nutrients. Plenty of manure should be applied to these soils.

Loamy soils stand halfway between sandy and clayey soils. They contain dust particles and enough humus and lime. The small crumbs forming their structure enable easy cultivation. Farmers call them 'medium-textured' soils. In the garden these soils are suitable to all purposes.

Marly soils contain plenty of lime. Their properties are similar to those of loamy soils but their productivity is usually greater.

Beside the basic kinds of soil mentioned above, some transient types can also be encountered in which some characteristics prevail and others are less apparent.

Hobby gardeners often cultivate soils unsuitable to normal large-scale farming. More effort may sometimes be needed but, in fact, a fine garden can be built anywhere.

Stony, flinty soils. Hillsides usually have stony soils, poor in humus which is washed down the slope. It is not easy to build a garden on such soil. Some earth work is first necessary. The biggest boulders should be removed and terraces should be built, adding a good garden soil to them. Hillside gardens are usually very attractive and almost everything can be grown there, especially on the southern slopes.

Waterlogged soils. Sometimes a waterlogged plot has to be reclaimed. Drainage is the first thing to be organized in such places, using drain pipes buried some 80 cm underground. If surface drainage is used, an additional decorative function can be contrived because the water in the ditches can be conducted into a small pool.

Soil quality

Books on gardening and farming often use terms such as 'soil fatigue', 'tired' or 'relaxed' soil, and soil in its 'old strength'.

Soil fatigue is a phenomenon frequently encountered in gardens where crops are not properly rotated. Soil usually becomes tired when the same vegetables are always planted in the same place. Every harvest removes great amounts of certain nutrients from the soil so that after several seasons of growing a crop in the same place these nutrients are exhausted. Soil fatigue may also be due to, or encourage, a dangerous overpopulation of some pests (for example, wireworms in root vegetables) in places where a crop is repeatedly grown for many seasons. Other factors also influencing soil fatigue still wait for scientific explanation.

To prevent soil fatigue, a garden can be divided into the flower and vegetable sections and a section for berry, stone- and pip-fruits. In the places from which old stone-fruit trees have been removed, berries and vegetables can be grown for several seasons before new stone fruits are planted. Other plants, mainly pip-fruits, should be regularly manured and inspected so that any lack of nutrients can be recognized and amended in time. Fruit-trees should be dressed with trace elements, mainly boron.

Sometimes it is advisable to leave the soil to rest for a while. For instance, after harvesting, a strawberry bed can be cleaned in readiness for a green-manure crop to be grown; this crop, still green, is then dug in. After copious autumn manuring the bed is thoroughly dug and the refreshed soil is ready to receive new strawberry transplants promising to give good results again.

Exhausted soil is a soil which is not regularly manured. Some of its nutrients have been consumed by plants, some have leached to the lower soil levels. Exhausted soil needs a generous supply of organic manure; mineral fertilizers should be added according to the requirements of the plants.

Soil in its old strength is a soil which was well-manured with dung the preceding year.

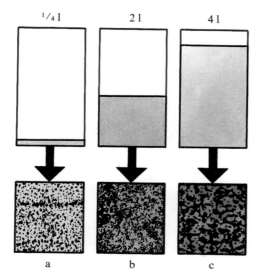

The water-absorbing capacity of various soil types per 1 kg of soil: a) sand, b) compost, c) peat.

Mechanical practices of soil improvement

Soil cultivation keeps the soil in good condition, though 'good condition' in this context does *not* mean that it cannot be better still. If mechanical practices are to be successful, each operation has to be carried out with adequate tools.

Primary and surface cultivation practices are distinguished. The primary practices of soil cultivation include spading, trenching and subsoiling. The surface practices include loosening and raking.

Digging turns the soil and mixes and crumbles it to an extent. After autumn spading the soil surface is left rough over the winter season, so that frosts and wind can help break it down. During spring digging the clods can be broken down, root-propagated weeds can be picked and the surface smoothed out.

Subsoiling is mainly practiced in shallow soils with only a thin layer of topsoil. To make the topsoil deeper, a thin layer of subsoil is lifted on the spade, turned over and mixed with the topsoil.

Trenching is a deep loosening of the soil to a depth of some 60—100 cm, using a spade, mattock and shovel. The purpose is to lift dead subsoil to the surface. Humus is also needed to give life to dead subsoil; manure or compost will do this job. This is particularly important when the plot is being prepared for the planting of grapevines.

Loosening is a shallow soil cultivation. The soil is aerated, not turned. The soil crust is broken. Sprouting weeds are controlled and root-propagated weeds are lifted to the surface. Frequent loosening prevents evaporation losses of the soil moisture. Rain water and irrigation water is easily infiltrated in loosened soil. Various loosening implements are used for this operation.

Raking means the smoothing of the soil surface. Any rhizomes of weeds can be pulled out with a wooden or iron rake.

Soil fertilization

Humus and micro-organisms have the greatest importance for the improvement of soil productivity. Humus is the product of the breakdown of organic substances such as manure and waste vegetable matter in which soil micro-organisms are involved. Without these microscopic organisms, stable manure, plant residues, peat and other kinds of organic matter would remain unused. The decomposition of organic matter into simple nutrients available to plants takes place mainly in the loosened upper layer of the topsoil where the micro-organisms have plenty of the oxygen they need for their work. During autumn digging, manure should therefore be left close to the surface, particularly in the medium-textured soils. On the other hand, sandy soils which are light have enough air even at the deeper levels so manure, too, can be placed deeper.

One kilogram of garden soil contains several hundred thousand micro-organisms, mostly bacteria.

Humus has a very great water-holding capacity. Soils with plenty of humus are therefore able to retain water more efficiently than low-humus soils.

Hence, the more humus in the soil, the higher its productivity. On the other hand, soils left longer without organic manuring lose their productivity. To add humus to the soil, apply manure, compost or peat, or a green-manure crop. The latter is grown to be spaded under before the crop can flower. Green manuring is described in detail on page 69.

Earthworms and the soil

Earthworms could well be called living ploughs. They aerate the soil and produce humus. In the process of eating plant residues in the soil, earthworms also ingest loam particles including algae, bacteria and protozoans. This heterogeneous material is mixed and crushed in their digestive tracts under the action of intestinal microflora. The undigested food residues are then ejected from the body. These worm

Content of air, water and various soil particles in different types of soil: 1) air, 2) water, 3) coarse sand, 4) fine sand, 5) clay particles; a) sandy soil, b) loamy soil, c) clayey soil.

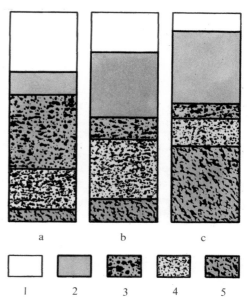

casts, appearing as large heaps, are left by the worms around the holes they make in the ground.

Air and water enter the earthworm holes and thus easily reach the roots of plants. The aerating and loosening work done by earthworms in the soil is far from negligible. A cubic metre of topsoil contains about 200 earthworms producing 7.5 to 10 kg of beneficial waste matter annually.

Garden substrates

The composition of garden earths has changed considerably over the past 30 years. The complex old formulae were first slightly adjusted to make up for the lack of some components. This was enough to revise traditional views concerning the preparation of earths. Growers saw that a certain component of the substrate could be replaced or even left out and still the plants thrived. Tendencies to simplification and standardization of substrates soon prevailed in all countries where gardening was advanced. Step by step, new types of garden substrates were produced.

Traditional garden earths

According to the basic materials used for the production of earth mixtures, the following groups of garden earths are distinguished:

a) earths with raw humus, usually containing humified material and undecomposed organic matter such as needle litter, leaf mould, peat, bog earth and heather mould;

b) high-nutrient humic earths such as hotbed earth, composted manure;

c) mineral earths such as topsoil and compost earths;

d) sand

Needle litter

Needle litter is basically the coarse raw humus of pine forests. Its main component is pine needles in various stages of decomposition. When it is fresh it has a high capacity for reducing compaction and improving aeration. Its pH is on the acid side. It is noted for a high permeability to water, associated with proneness to drying and nutrient leaching. Needle litter in itself is very poor in nutrients. Spruce needle litter is not suitable because its soil-loosening capacity is poor and its decomposition too quick.

Peat

Peat is a product of the decomposition of dead plants in the absence of air in permanently waterlogged places such as bogs. Depending on the con-

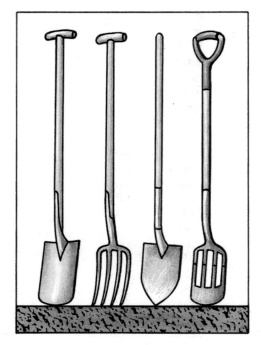

Various types of forks and spades with a D- or T-shaped handle can be bought.

ditions under which peat has developed in the bog, it is divided into:

a) high-moor peat — produced in spring areas of low-mineral water at high altitudes. Such peat is usually poor in nutrients and its pH is acid to very acid;

b) low-moor peat — produced in the spring areas of ground water of greater mineral content and in water reservoirs overgrown with plants to which minerals are supplied. This peat consequently contains more nutrients and its pH is slightly acid to neutral;

c) transition peat — standing halfway between the high- and low-moor peats; it develops under similar conditions, mainly where a high moor had a low-moor base. The composition of transition peat varies, being closer to either high- or low-moor peat. Its pH is usually slightly acid;

Hoes and rakes come in many different shapes, to cater for the various intensity and methods of cultivation.

d) peat earths — developing in peat bogs to which floods carry minerals. These earths usually have a large proportion of mineral components and much less undecomposed organic matter.

Since times immemorial, peat has been used to loosen garden earth and make it better-aerated. The specific trait of peat is its acid pH, implying a high resistance to bacterial decomposition. For this reason, peat keeps its good physical properties for a long time. The pH of pure (undecomposed) peat is 3.5 to 4.5. The addition of peat can, to some extent, also help to regulate the pH of the soil.

When deciding which kind of peat to choose, the main criterion is the purpose of use. The general rule is that plants that need a well-aerated substrate such as the heath-type species prefer untreated peat.

Heather mould
Its main component is raw humus produced by the decomposition of the remnants of plants of the heath family. Owing to its coarse structure it has a high aeration-improving capacity. Heather mould is acid, its pH being 4.0 to 5.5. It is low in nutrients and often contains a large amount of sand.

Heather mould is a suitable and, in fact, original earth for the growing of plants of the heath family, particularly rhododendrons and heaths.

Bog earth
Bog earth used in gardening is a brown-black amorphous matter. Its properties correspond with those of earthy, decomposed, high- or low-moor peat. Its pH may be acid or neutral, depending on the content of $CaCO_3$. Unlike high-quality peat, bog earth has little ability to improve soil texture.

Leaf mould
Leaf mould is a product of the decomposition of tree leaves. To decompose properly, leaves should be piled and the piles should be turned several times and sprinkled with water from time to time to keep them damp even in dry weather. The physical and chemical properties of leaf mould vary with the age of the mould and the species of the leaves. Beech leaf mould is considered to be the best and chestnut leaf mould the worst, even acting toxically if not mixed with other materials. The pH of leaf mould is usually neutral, except that of beech which has a pH between 5.5 and 6.5. The content of nutrients in leaf mould is low.

Frame earth
Frame earth is the product of composting partly decomposed manure which was used as the 'heat source' in a frame. The mixture of manure and frame topsoil is left to ripen on piles for two to three years, during which it is turned from time to time. Frame earth, usually loamy sand, is medium-textured to light and its pH is neutral.

Composted manure
Composted manure is added in small amounts to mixed earth as an organic fertilizer.

Sod earth
Sod earth is the compost of sod or sod slices. Sod earth is usually heavy loam or sandy loam. Its typical feature is a high content of organic matter. The pH is generally neutral or slightly alkaline.

Compost
Compost, used mainly as an organic soil amendment, is produced by the composting of various plant residues together with mineral earth and manure. Its composition and properties vary with the material composted. As a rule, it has a medium-heavy texture of sandy loam. The pH value of compost earth is usually neutral.

Sand
Sand, a common component of any soil mixture, is believed to improve soil looseness and aeration. River sand is best because it contains grains of various sizes. Fine sands are not suitable. However, recent studies have proved that sand simply increases the weight of the earth mixture and does not fulfil the functions ascribed to it.

Commercial substrates
Various standard substrates have been composed to simplify the preparation of the substrates used in the garden. The range of these ready-mixed soil supplements offered by local stores is wide. Each product has a label detailing the substrate components and properties and with detailed instructions for its use.

Plant nutrition and fertilization
All the substances needed for plant life get into the plant body in mineral form. Organic matter, humus or organic fertilizers must have been mineralized, that is, decomposed, before they can be taken up.

Plants' growth rate depends, among other factors, on the amount of mineral substances — nutrients — taken up. The amounts and ratios of nutrients with which to obtain the best results in terms of the quality and yield of a crop will depend on the state of growth of the plants and their developmental stage.

Nutrients
To grow and develop normally, a plant needs ten basic elements, referred to as 'biogenic', that is essential for life. These are oxygen (O), hydrogen (H), carbon (C), nitrogen (N), phosphorus (P), potassium (K), calcium (Ca), magnesium (Mg), sulphur (S), and iron (Fe). Were some of these elements lacking, a plant would only live until its reserves of those elements were exhausted. Then it would die.

Besides these basic elements, plants also contain others, called 'micronutrients', but these are present in very small (trace) quantities, for which reason they are called 'trace elements'. These are boron (B), sodium (Na), silicon (Si), zinc (Zn) and copper (Cu). Plants take some nutrients from the air (carbon, oxygen), others — the majority — from the soil: nitrogen, phosphorus, potassium, calcium and others. Nutrients are not taken up in their pure state but as various chemical compounds. For instance, phosphorus gets into the plant body as phosphoric acid, nitrogen as ammonia or nitric acid and so on. There should be a balance between all nutrients. Liebig's law of the minimum says that if the amount of one of the basic biogenic elements (N, P, K and Ca) in the soil is insufficient the remaining three nutrients can only be utilized by the plants to a limited extent, even though there may be a sufficient content of those three nutrients in the soil.

The role of the elements

Oxygen, carbon and hydrogen. These are the fundamental constituents upon which every plant body is built. Oxygen and carbon are taken from the air, so the grower has no practical chance to influence the supply of these elements. He can, however, keep the plants free from dust. Hydrogen is obtained through the decomposition of water during the process of photosynthesis.

Nitrogen. Nitrogen is one of the elements most important to plant nutrition. Most plants take it up as ammonia or nitric acid: only leguminous plants are able — with the aid of bacteria which live on their roots — to utilize the nitrogen from the air in pure form. Plants need plenty of nitrogen; for example, a fruiting apple-tree removes from the soil up to 7 kg of nitrogen annually.

Nitrogen should therefore be regularly added to plants but these additions should be correctly proportionate to the supply of other nutrients. High levels of nitrogen fertilization have the disadvantage of supporting vigorous vegetative growth (leaves) at the expense of flowers and fruits. Such plants are also more susceptible to disease. The fruits produced as a result of excess nitrogen fertilization are poor in colour and flavour and their storability is low. Trees to which excess of nitrogen is supplied remain green for too long and winter can catch them unprepared.

Plants draw nitrogen compounds from the leaves to the woody parts in the autumn to keep them in store for new growth in the following spring. At the onset of vegetation great amounts of nitrogen are needed for the production of new shoots, leaves and roots. The nitrogen stored in the woody parts is quickly consumed and has to be replenished with the fast-release nitrogen fertilizers (nitrates). Fruit-trees and berries therefore have to be fertilized as early in spring as possible. If nitrogen is lacking the plants will be stunted, the leaves will be pale green and they will be shed prematurely. Fruit trees need copious nitrogen fertilization, especially when the trees are still young and growing intensively while forming their root system and crown. Perennial plants (fruit and ornamental trees and shrubs, perennial flowers) should only be fertilized with nitrogen until the end of July. Then their wood should be left to ripen and get ready for the winter. Most leaf vegetables have to be supplied with nitrogen throughout the growing season. Root vegetables need plenty of nitrogen only at the beginning; nitrogen dressing applied later decreases their storability. In ornamental plants, excess nitrogen results in vigorous leaf growth but the flowers remain insignificant, with poor colour.

Phosphorus. Phosphorus is important for the formation of fruits and plants need it mainly in the period of intensive fruit setting. As a nutrient, phosphorus acts very differently from nitrogen: it actually shortens the growing season of the plants. There must be balance between the quantities of phosphorus and nitrogen since if phosphorus is lacking nitrogen behaves as if it were in excess. A lack of phosphorus re-

tards the growth of shoots in trees; the leaves are small and reddish in colour. In vegetables the flavour is reduced and carrots have a paler colour. Flowering plants have fewer flowers and their colour is dull.

Potassium. This element mainly influences resistance to frost and generally supports the health of plants. It is particularly valuable to plants grown for their fruits. Plants need plenty of potassium, especially when they are young, and the higher the uptake of nitrogen the higher should be the uptake of potassium. A potassium deficiency is not manifested so clearly in the plants as the lack of other essential nutrients. Plants lacking in potassium show brown markings on dark foliage and insignificant fruits. They are also less resistant to drought and frost and may die quickly if exposed to bad weather.

Calcium. Unlike other nutrients, calcium is stored in plants permanently. Plants need calcium as a building material and use most of it to develop woody tissues and roots. Stone fruits are among the greatest calcium consumers, using calcium and silicon to produce their pits. For instance, it often happens with apricots and peaches grown on low-calcium acid soil that no stones develop in the fruits, or the stone is so thin that it cracks, leaving the whole fruit open and usually decaying. In low-calcium soils the roots of plants grow slowly and there are few lateral roots and root hairs.

A lack of calcium often occurs in acid soils which are waterlogged and poorly aerated. Such soils have to be limed and, if necessary, drained and aerated. Excess calcium prevents the plants from taking up phosphorus, iron, magnesium and other elements. Peat should be added to the soil when it contains too much calcium. Excess calcium and calcium deficiency have the same effect on the appearance of the plants: chlorosis or the bleaching of leaf tissues.

Magnesium. Plants need magnesium mostly for the production of chlorophyll. Green plants lacking in magnesium have a pale or even yellow colour — this yellowing being particularly evident between the veins of older leaves. The amount of magnesium needed by plants is not so great as the required amounts of other nutrients and plants usually make do with the natural magnesium reserve in the soil. As a rule, magnesium deficiency occurs only when the soil contains too much calcium: excess calcium reduces the uptake of magnesium by plants. The typical sign is chlorosis. Brown spots occur on the leaves of affected apple-trees. If the calcium excess in the soil is reduced, the plants usually resume their normal uptake of magnesium. Magnesium is very important for flowering, fruiting and seed formation. Seeds contain a lot of magnesium and phosphorus; ripe seeds actually contain three times as much magnesium as calcium.

Sulphur. Different plants need different amounts of sulphur. Fruit trees require only tiny traces of sulphur whereas celery, onion, garlic or tomatoes need much larger amounts. These crops should be fertilized with sulphates which contain sulphur in addition to the macronutrients.

Iron. Iron is involved in chlorophyll synthesis and other vital processes taking place in plants. However, the amount required by plants is very small so that the natural soil reserve of this element will normally suffice. Because a lack of iron means there will be a lack of the green colouring matter in the leaves, the plants become pale. A lack of iron sometimes occurs when the soil contains too much calcium. Iron can be supplied, in particular to fruit plants, by watering with a one-per cent solution of green vitriol.

Trace elements. Among the trace elements, boron is particularly important, mainly for legumes and potatoes, though other plants also need boron for proper development. If a tree or shrub suffers from a lack of boron its growing points become dry, its flower-setting rate will be low and its leaves will be small and leathery. A boron deficiency also encourages diseases such as brown spot of apples. Silicon is important building material involved, like calcium, in the formation of woody parts. Some plants (e. g. celery) need chlorine while to others it is harmful, reducing their commercially valuable properties. Grapevines, berries and potatoes are the most sensitive. Aluminium is involved in the colouring of flowers. Copper plays a similar role to iron in plants: white patches on leaves are signs of copper deficiency. Molybdenum — a soft, flaky black mineral — is mostly needed in tiny quantities and its lack has almost no consequences except in cauliflowers, which fail to produce heads when grown in molybdenum-deficient soil.

Trace elements are needed by plants in such small amounts that their natural reserve in the soil is usually sufficient. Nevertheless, in a garden where intensive cultivation removes increased amounts of nutrients from the soil, it is helpful from time to time to replenish the soil reserve of trace elements with fertilizers containing these elements or with a trace element concentrate.

Reserve of nutrients in the soil

As a source of plant food, the soil or substrate must be able to supply plants with the needed nutrients throughout their growth. Physically, the soil must nurture a sound development of the roots which are needed if a plant is to have a sufficient nutrient-uptake capacity. Chemically, too, the soil must enable a maximum utilization of those nutrients.

To be able to purposefully regulate the amounts of nutrients in substrates, the grower has to know the optimum range of the content of each nutrient, i. e. the ideal levels between the minimum at which plants can starve on the one hand and the threshold of harmful excess on the other. It is often a difficult and lengthy process to determine the optimum soil nutrient level and the needed optimum fertilizer application rate. There are many factors influencing these values. The plant itself is the first to be considered: different species, and often different varieties, have different requirements for nutrients. The substrate, its pH, water and air content are all factors that influence the fixing of nutrients or their release

Compost heaps should always be located in some distant corner of the garden, and are best in semi-shade.

to the soil solution. Humus content, site and climate conditions are also involved.

The absolute amounts of the nutrients supplied are not the only factors underlying the results of the grower's effort. It is also important that the levels of the main nutrients be mutually balanced. The plants' requirement for nutrients varies according to which organs are developing in each particular stage of the growing season. Potassium and calcium dominate in the foliage, nitrogen and phosphorus in the flowers, and phosphorus and magnesium in the roots. The amounts of nutrients needed by the plants also vary according to their age. Generally it is the young plants that need plenty of nitrogen to produce their green matter. The uptake of potassium and calcium increases at every stage of growth until the vegetative phase is reached. The uptake of phosphorus is about the same throughout the growing season, with only a minor increase taking place during the period of flowering and fruiting.

Soil testing

The best way to learn the physical and chemical properties of a soil and to see whether it is suitable for growing garden plants is to have a soil sample professionally tested.

Basic information on the soil — its Ca, P, K, Mg, Mn, N levels — can be obtained with the aid of small home soil-testing kits which are now commercially available to gardeners.

Right method of turning a compost heap.

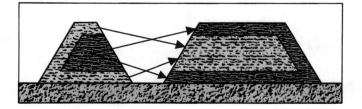

Fertilizers

We have already learned that plants grown in the garden remove nutrients from the soil and that consequently the soil reserve of nutrients has to be replenished. Soil tests will tell us which nutrients to add and which are already present in sufficient amounts. Any required nutrients can then be supplied to the soil as organic or inorganic fertilizers.

Organic fertilizers

Organic fertilizers improve and stabilize the soil structure, positively influence the water regime of the soil and improve the soil nutrient levels.

The natural organic fertilizers are divided into those of animal origin and those of plant origin. The organic fertilizers of animal origin help to influence the chemical properties of the soil whereas those of vegetable origin are mainly used for improving the physical properties of the soil.

Manure (dung), animal excrements, slaughterhouse waste and the like contain not only the main nutrients but also appreciable amounts of trace elements, usually in forms readily available to plants.

Organic fertilizers of animal origin need to be adjusted or composted in the majority of cases before use in the garden, in order to make them acceptable to the plants. Also, if they are not incorporated deep into the soil but are left on the surface, much nitrogen will be lost. The actual depth at which they will be most beneficial will depend on soil quality. Shallow placement is required in heavy and wet soils, deeper placement in light soils.

Organic fertilizers of vegetable origin are added to the soil to improve its physical properties. Excellent improvement is obtained when peat and bark of coniferous trees are added to a soil.

The best organic fertilizers of vegetable origin are pine and spruce bark, wood shavings, low- and high-moor peat, compost, straw, processed nettles, and seaweed. Straw improves aeration but this effect does not last long because its organic matter is quickly decomposed.

Soil crust can be expected to form everywhere as a result of long-continued use of the soil, and where weeds can be expected to grow vigorously, soil structure can be kept stable by mulching with organic materials or with black polythene sheeting.

Many organic fertilizers influence both physical and chemical properties of the soil. It is particularly advantageous to combine two or more organic fertilizers to intensify their effect and enhance the benefits to be gained from their use in plant growing.

To complete the picture, a survey can be given of the common organic fertilizers which every gardener will certainly want to use, since today it can already be objectively proved how adversely the quality of the soil and garden products can be affected by a long-continued use of commercially produced chemical fertilizers.

Manure — dung containing straw which was used as litter — is a high-quality fertilizer. Manure with peat litter is still better because peat has a better holding capacity for urine, solid excrements and ammonia. Litter of other materials is not so good. The average per cent levels of nutrients in stable manure are 0.5 per cent N, 0.25 per cent P_2O_5 and 0.6 per cent K_2O.

Horse manure is well-aerated; it readily decomposes while releasing a great quantity of heat. As such, it is mostly used for warming hotbeds. For straight manuring, it is perhaps suitable only in heavy soils where its decomposition is slow and where plants, particularly vegetables, grow better if the warm manure heats the cold soil. Horse manure is applied in larger quantities every other year. It is not suitable to use on light sandy soils. Similar in effect and application is goat, sheep and rabbit manure.

Cattle dung is suitable for straight application in all types of soil. On heavy and medium-textured soils cow dung is applied every three or four years, on light soils every other year, owing to faster decomposition.

Pig manure — this organic fertilizer is watery and decomposes slowly. Therefore, it is cold. It is not so good as other kinds of manure and should only be used on light sandy soils where it stays longer than other manures do. Heavy soils should never be manured with pig dung.

Pigeon and poultry manure — this manure is rich in nutrients: 1 per cent N, 1.5 per cent P_2O_5, 1 per cent K_2O. It is usually composted but straight application in fermented form is also possible: one part of dung is mixed with two parts of water and left to ferment, with occasional stirring, for 10—14 days. The final product is then diluted again at a 1:5—1:10 ratio.

Dung water — contains 0.25 per cent N, 0.013 per cent P_2O_5 and 0.4 per cent K_2O. It is left to ferment, then it is diluted 10—20 times and applied to serve a dual purpose: manuring and watering. The growth substances it contains also have a favourable effect.

Hoof and horn meal — contains 12—14 per cent organic N and 2—4 per cent P_2O_5. It is used for basic fertilization at a rate of 3—4 kg per m². Finely ground meals decompose more rapidly.

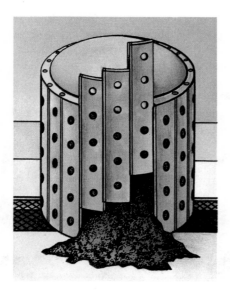

Transportable panel bins for the preparation of a quick compost can be obtained in various shapes, sizes and types.

Bone meal — it is noted for a high phosphorus content. Decomposed bone meal containing 10—12 per cent water-soluble P_2O_5 and 2—3 per cent N is used for fertilization. Otherwise bone meal acts very slowly and is therefore added to light-textured soils or compost and left there to break down.

Neutralized peat — high-moor and transition peat neutralized with finely ground limestone is added to heavy soils to enrich them with humus. Vegetables flourish on peat-enriched soils which enable them to develop a huge root system. Peat is also suitable for soil-surface mulching and composting. Neutral low-moor peat can be used in its natural form, without neutralization.

Conifer bark — peat sources are shrinking but composted spruce or pine bark, crushed to small pieces, is a good substitute. The bark compost needs from half a year up to a year to ripen. Bark compost usually contains 40—50 per cent bark, 10 per cent topsoil, 10—25 per cent manure or peat, 5—10 per cent dung water and 5—10 per cent loose ash. Two kilograms of quick lime are added to each cubic metre of compost material. The temperature under the compost surface should not exceed 60—70° C during ripening. Water must be sprinkled on to the compost if the temperature goes any higher. The material also has to be turned once or twice a year. Crushed bark is also used for mulching.

Straw — it is used for short-term improvement of soil structure. Straw degradation requires nitrogen, so nitrogen has to be applied together with straw.

Seaweed — traditional soil amendment of maritime areas, containing mainly potassium. It is also high in trace elements and some types of seaweed contain about 30 per cent calcium.

Green matter of some plants — used for green manuring. Full details are given in the next chapter. There is one plant, the foliage of which can be used for fertilizing in fermented form. This plant is the nettle, harvested before flower, fermented, and used in the same way as dung water. Nettle manuring encourages growth, supports chlorophyll production and has a curative effect.

Compost — an excellent organic fertilizer, or soil amendment, enriching the soil with humus and nutrients. Its actual nutrient content varies with the material composted. Full details are given in a separate chapter.

Ashes — wood ashes are the best, containing plenty of nutrients: 5—15 per cent P_2O_5, 8 per cent potash, 25—40 per cent Ca, Mg and sulphur compounds. Since potassium is contained in ashes as potassium carbonate which could damage young rootlets, ashes should be applied in autumn or winter, at the very latest this should be done 14 days before planting. Ashes contain no nitrogen so this has to be added when the ashes are applied.

Soot — can be added to both soil and compost. It is poor in nutrients (N, Ca) but its colour helps to enhance the warming capacity of the soil.

Green manuring

This method of fertilization is especially suitable when a new garden is being established because, by

The lawn needs regular watering if it is to look fresh.

adding humus to the soil, it improves the soil structure and helps to control weeds. Green manuring is also a good method of improving soils.

Plants with a large corolla are the best because, unlike other green-manure crops, they also enrich the soil with nitrogen and help to drain the soil with their deep roots. To grow green manure, 25 g of peas, horse beans, or lupin, 15—20 g of vetch or 2 g of clover, melilot and the like should be sown per a square metre. Other plants able to produce plenty of green matter in a short time can also be used, for example mustard, lucerne, rape, buckwheat and the like (2—3 g per m²). Mixtures of these crops can be used with advantage instead of single cultures. Lupin and buckwheat are normally grown on acid soils, other crops on neutral and alkaline soils.

It is advisable to grow green manure crops after early vegetables or early potatoes in beds which would otherwise remain unused for the rest of the year. They are usually sown in July or at the beginning of August so that the plants can produce enough green matter before winter. Plenty of moisture (watering is necessary if there is not enough rainfall), potassium, phosphorus and calcium in the soil are prerequisites for a good development of green matter.

The best crops to be grown after green manuring are potatoes and root vegetables.

In heavy soils, green manure should be incorporated early and to a shallow depth (about 10 cm) to afford plenty of oxygen to the soil micro-organisms for the conversion of green plants into humus and nutrients. In light soils this is done later and to a greater depth (15—20 cm). The plants should be juicy, not over-ripe or lignified.

Green manure crops can also be grown under fruit

69

trees to enrich the soil with humus. Field pea, vetch, white mustard, buckwheat, phacelia, Dutch clover, Italian ryegrass and annual ryegrass are the best; lupin is grown with success for green manure on sandy and acid soils.

The seeds are sown from the beginning of July to the beginning of August. The soil must be moist so watering is needed when the weather is dry. The green plants are dug in to a shallow depth. This operation should be carried out only in spring because in winter the stand provides thermal insulation of the soil and helps to retain snow.

Green manuring is not recommended in areas of low total annual rainfall (below 500 mm) and in young fruit orchards.

Compost

Every garden should have a pile of compost to replace manure and peat which are not so readily available now. Good-quality compost enriches the soil with humus, nutrients and the essential soil micro-organisms.

Among the materials which can be composted are various organic wastes and plant refuse which are layered or mixed with topsoil at a ratio of about 5:1. The topsoil contains the micro-organisms that facilitate the rotting of organic matter and its conversion into humus. This process is called humification. Manure and, particularly, peat are the ideal supplements to keep the compost damp. The material to be composted is gradually collected throughout the growing season, including the various residues of vegetables, leaves, grass cuttings, non-flowering weeds and the like. Weed plants which produce seeds should *never* be added to compost; the same applies to diseased plants, for example, brassicas suffering from root knot, tomato fruits attacked by late blight and the like. Perennial weeds such as couch grass or bindweed also do not belong on the compost pile. The addition of ground limestone helps to regulate the rotting down process and arrest the development of the causal agents of diseases. The recommended application rate of limestone is about 10 g per a cubic metre of compost.

Once the compost is established, heat is generated and the pile has to be sprinkled with water if its temperature exceeds 65° C. The ideal compost-ripening temperature, at which the greatest amount of humus is produced, is 35—40° C. Damp environments are the best for the rotting process and for the activity of micro-organisms; compost should therefore be piled in shady places and should be regularly sprinkled with water or dung water in dry weather. Cut grass or other mulching materials can be spread on the surface of the compost. The pile should be turned at least once a year to aerate and mix the composted material. Turning with a pitch-fork or hoe also speeds the ripening process. If proper care is to be given to the compost, the pile should not be wider than 2 m and no higher than 1 m (but there is no length limitation). Various practical compost bins are commercially available to enable easy compost handling.

Mineral fertilizers

Being industrially produced, mineral fertilizers are commonly called 'industrial fertilizers'. Unlike the majority of organic fertilizers, they usually contain nutrients at high concentrations.

It should be noted that there has been much opposition to the use of chemical fertilizers and a greater emphasis on organic gardening in recent years. If there is not an especially great lack of some nutrient in the soil we could certainly manage with organic fertilizers in the garden. As already mentioned, organic fertilizers can be combined to obtain a greater effect. However, it can happen that organic fertilizers do not suffice to make up for a serious nutrient deficiency, and once the nutrient balance is broken this has detrimental consequences to the plants. Their development is poor and their susceptibility to diseases is high. Mineral fertilizers will help in such cases. Their single application will not cause any problems. Some mineral fertilizers are nothing more than mechanically treated natural minerals so their use for improving the yields does not contradict the biological principles of organic gardening.

Single element fertilizers. The single element fertilizers are mineral salts containing only one of the main nutrients. The accompanying ingredients (filling materials) are, as a rule, utilized to a lesser extent by the plants so that they accumulate in the soil and may sometimes alter its chemical properties. For example, sulphates usually have a beneficial effect where-

Permanently damp soils need good drainage and a herringbone system of pipes can be constructed for this purpose. The lateral pipes are 5 cm in diameter, the main pipe can be 6.5—20 cm across. The depth of their location and the distance of lateral pipes depend on the character of the soil, the specific demands of the plants to be cultivated and on the underground water table. The pipes can lead the water to a ditch or to a soakaway.

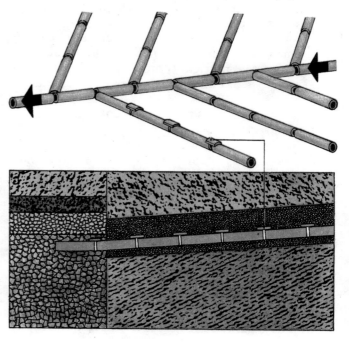

as chlorides and sodium act adversely. According to the main nutrient, single element fertilizers are divided into nitrogen, phosphorus, calcium, potassium and magnesium fertilizers.

Compound fertilizers. These fertilizers contain either two (double fertilizers — NP, NK, PK) or three (complete — NPK) major nutrients, usually fortified with Mg and Ca. Producers now add trace elements (Cu, B, Mn, Zn, Mo) to the compound fertilizers they produce.

The advantage of compound fertilizers is that their nutrient content is high in ratio to the filler materials. The laborious and often awkward preparation of appropriate mixtures of the single element fertilizers is avoided when the compound fertilizers are used.

Slow-release fertilizers. Some common mineral fertilizers such as slow-release phosphorus salts, some calcium fertilizers, granular formulations and the like, that is, materials expected to act longer than the fast-release fertilizers, used to be described as 'fertilizers for store dressing'.

However, by the modern conception the term 'store-dresser' is reserved for long-acting fertilizers specially formulated to release their nutrients slowly and for a longer time. The purpose is to reduce the leaching losses and to apply the fertilizer at higher rates without the risk of burning the plants. The release should be steady and uniform so that the plants do not starve.

Liquid and suspension fertilizers. Fertilizers in liquid and suspension form are among the modern fertilizer types. They are perfectly soluble, which is advantageous for sprayer application. When a solid fertilizer is dissolved for spraying, an amount of it always remains undissolved and tends to block the slots and nozzles of sprinklers. Like solid fertilizers, the liquid products are also either single-element or compound. The compound liquid fertilizers have a comparatively low NPK content, usually not above 25 per cent. Owing to their comparatively low fertilizing effectiveness these products are called 'physiological' or 'balancing' fertilizers.

Single element liquid fertilizers, on the other hand, are highly concentrated. Their fertilizing effect is good and their action fast. They can be used either alone or combined at appropriate ratios.

Trace element fertilizers. These special products are either mineral salts containing various trace elements or trace element concentrates.

A few words in conclusion

Various organic fertilizers are commercially available, ranging from processed straw to liquid guano (fish manure). Even an organic gardening enthusiast has much to choose from in the market, although he is able to produce organic fertilizers in his garden.

Naturally, the market also offers mineral fertilizers in various packages, always with instructions for use, with the statement of the quantities of each element and the recommended application rates. These should always be scrupulously observed — it is not a good idea to add more for 'good measure'.

For individual crops special fertilizers are avail-

A watering can is a must in every garden. The shape of the rose and the size of its holes greatly influence the quality of watering.

able, containing all the major nutrients and trace elements at optimum ratios.

Irrigation

Water is the main component of the plant body. Plants draw from water two of the main nutrients: oxygen and hydrogen. Water is essential, also for the uptake of other nutrients and for the transportation of the organic substances produced by the plants inside their bodies.

In many places the natural sources of water are scarce or unevenly distributed during the year so that efforts should be taken to retain in the soil as much moisture as possible (autumn digging, snow retention and snow gathering in winter, soil surface loosening during the growing season, supply of organic fertilizers to improve humus content, terracing of steep slopes will all be of benefit).

Water in the soil

One of the important functions of the soil is to supply enough water to the roots of plants. For this, good soil permeability is very important. If it is poor, rain water stays in the uppermost soil layer which becomes waterlogged and slushy. From there it evaporates, leaving a crust with cracks on the surface. On the other hand, in a highly permeable soil, water is quickly drained to the subsoil outside the root zone. What the gardener must do is to improve the soil to provide a medium permeability, thus ensuring uniform soil moisture distribution in the root zone.

Water for irrigation

Water used in the garden must be clean, with no turbidity or stagnant smell. Its salt content should be

Various types of sprinkler facilitate the gardener's work, supply the necessary moisture and furthermore improve the microclimate.

The fine stream of water is warmed by the surrounding air so that it reaches the plants at an optimum temperature.

low and its pH neutral to slightly acid. To a great extent, the properties of water depend on its source, according to which water is generally divided into four groups: rain water, tap water, well water and water from reservoirs and water courses.

Rain water has always been considered to be the best irrigation water and, in fact, it still remains so. It is usually soft and slightly acid. Its advantages include a high content of oxygen (about ten times higher than that of well water). Hence gathering rain water is not outdated: it is still a very wise practice.

However, it is suggested by the results of recent chemical studies that in some regions rain water absorbs air pollutants generated by the chemical industry, and the products of combustion of solid and liquid fuels such as soot, flue gases, exhaust gases and the like. Oil firing leaves fine droplets of oil on roofs and rain washes them down. In the vicinity of lime and cement works, lime or cement dust settles on the roofs and increases rain water hardness. It is problematic to use collected rain water for watering in such areas.

Tap water undergoes treatment and sterilization in water houses where impurities and pollutants are removed so that the water becomes drinkable. Tap water can usually be used for watering if it does not contain too many minerals. A high content of gaseous chlorine may also be a temporary defect.

Well water is usually high in minerals. The majority of the dissolved substances are called 'hardening salts'. Rain water seeps through the soil, dissolves the chemical compounds in the soil and parent rock and thus changes from clean water to well water. The content of minerals should not be higher than 1 g per litre of water, otherwise mineral water is obtained which may be safe for human consumption but not suitable for watering.

Water taken from a water course or reservoir may contain, besides the common minerals, various pollutants dangerous to plants, including mineral oils, modern cleaning and laundry agents and household wastes as well as waste waters from industrial estates and farms.

Water hardness

Hardness is a property of water which causes concern for many gardeners. The problems associated with water hardness had been recognized even before man was able to analyze water. Gardeners knew and practised various methods of water softening, that is, reduction of water hardness, even in antiquity. Water hardness is caused by dissolved mineral substances, mainly the salts of calcium and magnesium but sometimes iron also. Depending on the anion responsible for water hardness, the following water hardness types are distinguished:
1. Carbonate (temporary) hardness which can be removed by boiling or by leaving the water to stand for some time.
2. Non-carbonate hardness (caused by sulphates) which cannot be reduced by boiling.
3. Total hardness which, in fact, is the sum of all values of carbonate and non-carbonate hardness.

Non-carbonate hardness is usually harmless to plants and can even act favourably. Water of non-carbonate hardness is a good source of calcium and magnesium and has no influence on the pH of the substrate.

Carbonate hardness is also acceptable if it is low. A regular supply of low doses of calcium favourably influences plant nutrition, the biological activity of the soil and the formation of crumbly structure. Water of a higher carbonate hardness can act adversely mainly on the plants requiring acid soil: acid substrates are gradually made alkaline when irrigated with carbonate water. The affected plants suffer from chlorosis and their roots turn brown.

Excess water hardness can be reduced in several ways. The decision as to which method to choose will depend on the amount of water to be softened, on its degree of hardness and so on. Gardeners will prefer the simplest way: that is, mixing hard water with rain water. Hardness can also be reduced by the precipitation of the mineral substances with oxalic acid.

Methods of irrigation

Water can be applied in many ways; the choice depends on such considerations as the size of the area that is to be irrigated, the source of water and the crop to be grown.

Watering with a can is a good old practice still in use on smaller areas. However, the sprinkler head of the can must be so shaped that it allows water to fall lightly on to the plants from above.

Another old and popular method of irrigation is to use a hose connected to a water source. The water should be at least slightly warm before reaching the plants and fine nozzles are therefore used. These are available on the market in a variety of types. The fine droplets of water have enough time to warm in the air before falling on to the plants. The hose must be moved from one place to another and can damage the plants if not handled with care. Stakes and pulleys at the sides and corners of beds will protect the plants and help you to move the hose. A portable, winding drum is the best aid with which to move the hose about the garden. To stay with the hose on dry ground, the spraying should start from the farthest end.

Subsurface irrigation with drain pipes is a good technique in use primarily in kitchen gardens but can also be used to great advantage in a greenhouse. Drain pipes spaced closely throughout the area at a low gradient feed a trickle of water to the roots of the plants. The depths at which the pipes are placed vary, usually ranging between 20—40 cm. The main advantages of a subsurface irrigation system of this type are the elimination of evaporation and the conservation of soil structure.

Furrow irrigation can be used in gardens having their own water source. The beds should be located below the water source and should slope slightly. Water is conducted along an inlet canal to distributing canals, from which it is left to run through to furrows 10—15 cm deep, between the rows of plants.

Trickle irrigation is a very economical technique. The system has main lines sometimes as long as 100—150 m, with a pressure regulator. Short microtubes inserted into the main lines carry water to each plant. The advantages of this system are a low consumption of water (all water seeps into the soil) and irrigation of a comparatively large area.

Very many irrigation systems for small gardens have been developed in recent years. Suitable irrigation equipment can be chosen from specialist gardening catalogues to suit the conditions of every garden.

When and how to water

The art of correct watering is not so easy to learn as it might appear. Proper watering is beneficial, improper watering is a waste of water and can even be harmful to plants.

Sufficient amounts of water should be provided at each watering so that the water will reach the roots of all plants. It is useless simply to moisten the surface. The amount of irrigation water will of course depend on the species of the plants and the depth of their roots, but if watering is insufficient to reach deep-growing ones, they will be forced to come nearer to the surface, with great detriment to the plants.

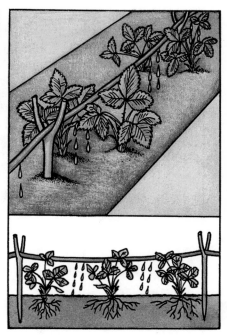

An economical method of watering strawberries is by trickle irrigation. With only a small amount of water, a relatively large strawberry bed can be kept sufficiently damp. Above: method of placing the irrigation hose. Below: how the water trickles from the hose.

Fruit trees have the bulk of their roots at the depth of 30—60 cm. They should be watered less frequently but more generously (at least five canfuls to every bearing tree). A fruit tree needs the greatest amount of water during budding and much water is also required when flowering is finished — in June when the shoots grow and in July when the flower buds differentiate. However, excessive watering towards the end of August may prolong the growing season and the wood of the trees may fail to ripen though some irrigation just before harvest is beneficial.

The irrigation requirements of vegetables are different. Brassicas have to be irrigated (preferably by spraying) every day if the weather is sunny. Warm-season vegetables, such as cucumbers and tomatoes, also have to be irrigated every day but never sprayed from above: the water must always go *under* the plants. It is best to make small furrows and let the water flow along them. Onions need watering only in periods of drought, otherwise no moistening is required. The same can be said of root vegetables such as carrot and parsley. On the other hand, celeriac needs plenty of water and could, in fact, be irrigated all the time. All young transplants of vegetables and newly sown crops need regular watering.

Flowers have various requirements on moisture. All have to be watered after transplanting or sowing. Annuals have to be watered frequently, perennials less frequently. Heaths and heathers require plenty of water on sunny days, but not while the sun is directly on them. Annuals need frequent application of small amounts of water, roses and ornamental shrubs require copious amounts but less frequently.

As in other parts of this book, the authors here wish to draw attention to the specific requirement of evergreen plants in the winter. All of these plants should receive a generous supply of water before the first frost comes.

Water evaporation from the green leaves of these plants does not stop in winter, particularly on sunny days. However, if the soil has been frozen for a long time, the plants are not able to make up for the water evaporated from their leaves and may die of thirst.

In summer, plants should always be watered in the evening when the evaporation is low. In the evening all water will get to the roots of the plants without unnecessary losses. This is particularly important on hot days when much water would evaporate if applied during the day. If, in summer, the watering cannot be done in the evening, early morning is the best alternative. In spring and autumn it is better to water in the forenoon or at noon but never while there is still direct sunshine.

Basics of practical work

Preparing the soil

Digging replaces ploughing when mechanical means cannot be used. When digging in autumn, the soil is left roughly turned through the winter to allow it to 'weather' and is levelled in the following spring. During spring and summer any lumps of soil are broken down, rootstocks of weeds removed and the surface of the plot prepared for planting.

Trenching involves turning and loosening of the soil to a depth of 60—100 cm. This can be done by using either a spade, pick or a shovel and is particularly important when you intend to cultivate vines.

Raking over the land levels the surface, helps to break up remaining lumps and prevents water from evaporating. This work can be started in spring, as soon as the ridges of the furrows are dry. The lines of harrowing should slant towards the direction of the furrows and rakes with a toothed finish prove the most efficient.

Rolling crushes clods in the soil, firms it up and levels its surface. Various types of rollers can be used for such work.

Loosening aerates without turning the soil. Sprouting weeds are destroyed and their rootstocks are pulled out. Various mechanical types of equipment can be used for this work, such as cultivators and hoes.

Hoeing levels the soil's surface and at the same time lifts out any remaining weed rootstocks; it also destroys sprouting weeds. This work is carried out manually, using a hoe.

Earthing up involves piling up soil around plants. The soil is also loosened and aerated in the process, its surface is increased and weeds are destroyed. Piled up soil warms through more effectively and plants grow additional roots from the base of their stems to receive water and nutrients. Some types of vegetables, such as tomatoes, peppers and cauliflowers, are earthed up to form a larger root system and to increase their intake of nutrients. Soil is earthed up about 10 cm high and this process is repeated after three weeks. Leeks, celery, Chinese cabbage and asparagus are earthed up to keep the bottom part of the plants white and crisp, a process called 'blanching'. Some ornamental shrubs and roses in particular, fruit trees, vines and others are earthed up in the autumn to protect them against winter frosts.

Amelioration substantially improves the quality of soil. Essentially, this includes drainage, irrigation and landscaping the surface, for example by terracing. All such improvements are relatively costly but have a real and lasting importance.

Drainage is provided by either open ditches or by drainage pipes, or both systems can be combined. Ditches divide the plot into small sections which makes mechanical cultivation more difficult. Drainage pipes are placed 80—120 cm below the surface. **Irrigation** is dealth with in detail in the chapter entitled *Plant irrigation.*

Terracing exploits the advantages and removes the disadvantages of gardens sited on slopes. Terracing is employed on plots with a gradient from 7—10° to 15—20°. Terraces should follow the direction of the land's contour lines so that they are as horizontal as possible. Terraces are usually made 3 m wide, but for soft fruit shrubs 1.5 m is sufficient. It is advisable to incline surfaces gently (5—10 per cent) towards the slope to retain all rainwater. When constructing terraces, work should start at the bottom of the slope and gradually progress upwards.

Sowing and planting

Preparing the seed

Seeds can be prepared in a number of ways. These include germination tests, disinfection, steeping and germination, stratification and, in some cases, the special preparation of the seeds.

Germination tests are carried out on a certain number of seeds and repeated four times, to discover the optimum conditions for germination in terms of temperature, humidity and light. After the completion of an average length of germination of one given type, the germinated seeds are counted, the average of the four repeated tests is calculated and germination data then given in percentages. This determines the minimum number of seeds to be sown, but this number is increased by a third when dealing with seeds which do not germinate easily, since it is likely that a percentage of seed will take longer to germinate or even fail to germinate.

Disinfection of seeds destroys the cells of fungous and bacteriological diseases which can infest seeds; the process can be carried out by using either a dry or a dissolved disinfectant. If only a small amount of seeds is involved, they can be disinfected with a dry disinfectant in a tin which has a lid, or in a linen bag, the contents of which are shaken together. Large quantities of seed are usually disinfected in a sterilizing drum. Whichever method is appropriate, the effectiveness of this process can be improved by adding a little talc to the disinfectant.

Liquid disinfection should be allowed 15—30 minutes to take effect. The disinfected seeds are then drained and left to dry. Liquid disinfection causes the seeds to swell and therefore also speeds up the germination. Disinfectants are usually poisonous so great care must be taken when using them.

Soaking accelerates the germination and the initial growth of plants. It is used for seeds or stones which take a long time to germinate, such as carrots, parsnips, onions, and peach or apricot stones. Seeds or stones can be steeped in drinking water in small plastic containers such as yoghurt cartons. The water should be 20—25° C warm and should be changed every 10—12 hours. The length of soaking necessary varies according to the type of plant involved. Peas, beans and lettuce seeds are left to soak for just 2—4

hours; brassicas, cucumbers and marrows 12—20 hours; tomatoes and peppers 24—40 hours; carrots, parsnips, onions and leeks 50—60 hours; seeds of flowering plants 12—24 hours. Pre-soaked seeds are left to drain and then should be sown without delay.

Germination is carried out at a temperature of 20—25° C in a room where a constant humidity is maintained. The seeds are scattered over a damp linen or jute cloth in a large container, then covered with another cloth which is kept damp. The germination process can be stopped when a half to three quarters of the seeds have germinated; they are then sown straight away.

Stratification is a process by which the hard casing of certain seeds is softened and then overwintered. Seeds are placed in layers with a mixture of coarse sand on a hard surface and then 'milled' to abrade the rough casing. Then the by now rather messy mixture of seed and sand is placed in a perforated tin and overwintered in a cold spot outdoors. Stratified seeds need to be checked and protected from rodents with wire mesh or netting round their container. If not prepared in this way, such seeds may not germinate for two or more years.

Of the other methods of the pre-sowing preparation of seeds **heating through** or **coating with nutrient-enriched humus** might also be mentioned. Heat treatment can be used on some bulbs and tubers after harvesting and during winter storage in order to speed up their growth later.

Sowing

The choice of location for sowing the seeds is determined by the requirements of individual species. Recognition of the most appropriate time for sowing, the methods of sowing and the depth at which the seeds are to be sown is critical.

Seeds can be scattered when the plants are preplanted in boxes and bowls. This method is also used when sowing a lawn or when growing seedlings in a frame or a seedbed. The seeds are scattered by hand and it is essential to maintain an even distribution. Very small seeds might be scattered by placing them on a sheet of paper, then gently shaking this over the prepared soil. Sown seeds are then pressed down, watered with a fine hose to avoid swamping them and, depending on the requirements of individual species, covered with a thin layer of sieved soil. Seeds which are left on the surface outdoors should be covered by a sheet of paper or glass to protect them from birds.

Sowing in rows is advisable when the plants are to be grown where they have been sown, without further transplanting. The sowing drills are made with a hoe to a depth of 5—7 cm and then seeds are sown evenly in these shallow drills. The distance between drills or rows is determined by the requirements of individual plants.

When sowing large areas, a multi-row seed drill can be used. The depth of sowing and the amount of seed released must be tried and adjusted.

Sowing in pinches, when compared with sowing in rows, allows an economical use of seed. When sowing by hand, depressions are prepared by a hoe in marked places, several seeds are put in each depression and covered with soil, using the hoe or a rake. This method can be used, for instance, with beans and cucumbers. The work can be simplified by using a cultivator if the plot is particularly large.

Sowing in bowls and boxes is used most frequently when growing flowers. Containers can be made of various materials and in a variety of sizes. They should always be disinfected before use.

Sowing in frames requires a well prepared, warm soil. Seeds are scattered or placed in rows by hand or by single row seed drill. The sown seeds are carefully pressed down, then covered or not by more soil, according to their type, marked by namecards and covered with sheets of glass or straw mats at night.

Sowing in seedbeds is used when cultivating late biennial members of the cabbage family and seeds of decorative and fruit tree stocks. Such seeds can be evenly scattered or sown in rows.

Sowing in beds is employed for plants which do not tolerate transplanting or when the labour involved in growing pre-cultivated stock needs to be minimized.

The time of sowing varies according to the requirements of individual plants. Seeds of winter species are sown in the autumn (including some types of spinach and stone-fruits), others in spring. The plants which germinate at low temperatures, such as brassicas and lettuce, can be sown as soon as the soil is prepared in spring. The plants requiring higher temperatures to germinate are sown in May or can be started under glass, as in the case of cucumbers and tomatoes.

The depth of sowing again depends on the size of seeds and the type of soil. Seeds are covered with a layer of soil which ensures sufficient moisture and warmth and which can be penetrated by the sprouting seeds. Usually, the depth of the soil layer is double the size of the seed. In dry areas and in light soil seeds are sown deeper; in damp regions and heavy soil, shallow sowing is preferable. Early in spring the seeds are sown shallowly while in summer a deeper sowing ensures a sufficient supply of water.

The preparation of soil before sowing is very important. It must first be loosened and made level; then a line is stretched out and a drill drawn along to the required depth. The seeds are sown evenly into it, lightly pressed in and covered with soil.

Planting out and pricking out

Planting out means placing the pre-cultivated seedling where the plant will continue to grow and develop until it reaches maturity and can be harvested. The chosen technique for planting out depends on which of the pre-cultivating methods was adopted, the extent of the root system and the location.

Planting out with a dibber involves using this stick-like tool to make a vertical hole and placing the plant's root system in it up to the root neck, then carefully pressing in the soil around the roots of the plant, before watering it with a fine hose.

Planting out using a trowel is best when planting stock with large root systems such as bulbs and tubers. When a hollow of the appropriate depth has been made with the trowel, the roots of the plant together with their ball of soil are placed in it; the small amount of soil that was removed is eased in around the bulb or tuber and pressed down. The same method is used when a hoe or a spade is being employed to cater for large root balls.

Planting out in furrows is appropriate when planting bulbs, some tubers and cuttings. These are spaced out in such prepared furrows, the distance between the plants being determined by the size of mature specimens and the distance between rows by the type of mechanised techniques which will need to be employed in further care for the plants.

Planting out in a frame usually involves a triangular layout, whereas **planting out in a bed** involves a quadratic or rectangular layout, individually or with several plants grouped together. This latter method is used when transplanting peppers and beans.

Planting out woody species involves making a hole in thoroughly prepared soil, big enough to accommodate the root ball. If a stake is needed this should be positioned in the hole before the plant is put in it, to

An even distribution of seeds sown into boxes can be secured by putting the seeds on a piece of stiff paper turned up at the outer edges to form a groove.

avoid possible damage to the roots. Finally, good quality soil improved by compost is eased in around the roots and then the remaining hole is filled in and the soil carefully firmed down around the plant.

Caring for sown seeds. Specific conditions are required for the sown seeds to ensure their successful development. Some species need light, others darkness, constant humidity and a certain temperature. These vegetative factors must be ensured, particularly for sensitive plants which are sown in greenhouses and frames. Greenhouses should provide a constant temperature and at night the glass can be covered with mats to prevent a marked drop in temperature. Watering should be carried out regularly and with care, using a fine nozzle or, for some plants, by watering them from below. On sunny days the greenhouse and frames need to be shaded to prevent the seedlings from flagging. After transplanting, the seedlings need to be regularly watered.

Pricking out of the seedlings is done as soon as they begin to develop in order to ensure a low broad growth and a good root system. Seedlings can be thinned out twice or even three times, as required.

When pricking out the plants, they are held by the basal leaves, then carefully lifted with the help of a small flat trowel or a dibber. If the soil is dry, it must be well watered a day in advance of the seedlings being pricked out into boxes, frames or beds.

Pricking out into boxes is most frequently done when growing flowers. A thin peg is required for this work. The smallest plants are pricked out using tweezers with blunt edges so that the seedlings are not damaged. The boxes should be 8—10 cm deep and filled with compost in the same way as when sowing seeds. Then the seedlings to be pricked out are placed on a sheet of glass. Tiny seedlings are pricked out in groups of 3—5. Well developed seedlings are pricked out individually, using a dibber. Transplanted seedlings are watered and placed in a shady, closed greenhouse until the roots are well established. Air is introduced gradually and shade is reduced. Watering is carried out as required.

Pricking out into frames is done by first marking out rows on a prepared surface. A peg is used to make

When sowing tiny seeds into boxes, a high-quality and well mixed seeding compost must be prepared. It has to be firmed (a) and the surface levelled with a flat wooden board (b). The seeds are sown (c), then covered with a thin layer of sieved soil (d) and watered with a fine spray so as not to wash them out (e).

holes in the soil into which the seedlings are inserted up to their basal leaves after the main root has been pinched. The soil is then carefully pressed down with the fingers to ensure close contact with all the roots, which must be directed vertically, straight down without being coiled.

Pricking out into a bed is the method used for the seedlings of fruit trees. Roots of these seedlings can be dipped first into a thin paste made of soil, manure and water with the possible addition of a disinfectant. The seedlings are inserted up to their basal leaves by using a peg, hoe or a spade.

Blocking involves pricking out the seedlings into small, square blocks of a firmly compressed mixture of damp growing medium. Seedlings planted in such blocks are then left until their roots are well established, at which stage the whole block, along with the plant, is transplanted. The advantage of this method is that the plant continues to grow without being disturbed. Blocks are made of peat, compost and frame soil. The mixture must be compact to

When sowing in a bed, sufficiently deep rows must be prepared in advance. To avoid disturbing the soil by treading on it, a wooden board or plank can be used to stand on.

When sowing small seeds into bowls you will need a fine-mesh sieve for the preparation of a fine compost and a flat piece of wood for firming up the substrate (a). A drainage layer at the bottom is necessary (b) and the hole in the bottom of the bowls must be covered with a crock to keep the compost in during watering (c).

avoid disintegration of the blocks when they are being planted out with the seedlings in situ.

Seed trays are available in various types and they can replace the blocks. They are usually made of plastic and consist of a base and a honeycombed mould. The mould is placed in the base of the tray and its holes are filled with soil, which is spread evenly with a flat piece of wood so that the holes are filled without being squashed. A hole is then made in each filled section and seedlings with developed basal leaves are placed in the holes, gently firmed in and watered. Three to four weeks later the mould is lifted out of the tray so that the plants in blocks are left on the base.

Peat and cellulose pots are arranged in a tray and filled with soil in the same way as seed trays. The plant roots first penetrate the soil and then the walls of the pots which, in addition to peat and cellulose, also contain necessary nutrients. When used, such pots must not be allowed to dry out as this would seriously inhibit the root growth of the seedlings. Finally, the plants are transplanted, in the pots.

Growing in pots is used for the production of forced vegetables, and flowers such as petunias and salvias. For this, containers made of clay or plastic are used. The bottom of the container is filled with a drainage material and the plants is then held upright in the middle while soil is poured in around it and pressed against the roots. The plants are then watered and placed in the shade. Ventilation is limited.

Hardening off of the seedlings involves the plants getting used to the conditions of their permanent habitat, in particular to external temperatures. Hardening off is required by early seedlings which are planted out in March and April as well as seedlings of thermophilous plants which are planted out in the second half of May. The process of hardening off begins a fortnight before planting out by gradually increasing ventilation within the frame. At first, the frame is ventilated for a short while at midday, then the time is gradually lengthened and ventilating

repeated more often. Finally, the sheets of glass can be removed from the frame during the day and at night a little air should be allowed in or the seedlings can be covered only by mats. For the last 3—4 nights before planting out, seedlings are left uncovered.

Care of plants during the growing season

Watering of the seedlings is done using tepid water which has the same temperature as the soil or is 2—3° C warmer. The plants must dry off as soon as possible after being watered and therefore a sufficient flow of air must be provided. This prevents the development of fungus diseases. In winter and early spring, watering is carried out in sunny weather between 8 and 9 o'clock in the morning or when it is cloudy between 11 a.m. and 1 p.m. In summer, the plants are watered towards the evening.

Mulching involves covering the surface of the soil with a 2—3 cm deep layer of organic material, such as thoroughly decomposed farmyard manure, leaves, grass, peat, weeds which have not flowered and the crushed bark of conifers. Mulching stops unnecessary evaporation of water, prevents the soil from developing a crust and inhibits weed growth. A similar effect can be obtained by covering the soil with sheets of black polythene.

Pinching removes the growing tips of plants in order to stimulate branching instead. Plants then become compact, bushy and low in growth. Plants which are nipped in this way include pelargoniums, some chrysanthemums, carnations, azaleas, and fuchsias.

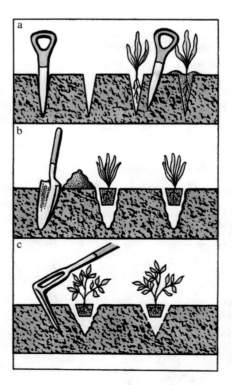

A special dibber (a) is used for planting out the seedlings. If, however, seedlings with a large root ball are planted, use a trowel (b) or a special hoe (c).

Disbudding is the process whereby all side shoots or buds are removed. In flowers this method is used when the development of a single stem with one large, well-coloured flower is required. This method is used in chrysanthemums, carnations and roses. In vegetable gardens, the side shoots of cordon tomatoes and the infertile shoots of greenhouse cucumbers are removed in the same way.

Supporting plants is absolutely essential in the case of species that grow to a height where they will flop without such support. This is required by some vegetables, fruit trees and some flowering plants such as the taller delphiniums.

Tomatoes should be supported by canes at least 1.5 m long and which have been impregnated with preservative in advance to prevent them from rotting in the ground. Runner beans, often reaching a length of 3 m, require a suitable support, for instance, in the shape of a tunnel constructed of canes tied together in twos at the top or alternatively a pyramid of canes. Metal stakes can also be used since plants can climb them easily. Basically, supports can be made of any type of suitable material which is strong enough to carry the weight of a mature plant. Such support must always be placed in situ *before* the plant to avoid possibly causing damage to the plant or its root system later.

A support is always required by fruit trees with tall stems or weak root systems until such time as the tree is strong enough to stand by itself. In the case of cordon-shaped, small, soft-fruit trees, supports are needed permanently. For fruit trees, the stake must not be as tall as the tree but should rather be about 10 cm shorter than the lowest branch. Conversely, for small soft-fruit species and standard roses such stakes must be of the same height as they are. Fruit grown on espaliers are dealt with in the later chapter on fruit growing.

Tying is used whenever a plant needs to be attached to its support. Herbaceous plants are fastened with a strong twine, as long as there is no danger that this might damage their fragile stems. Trees are initially tied to the stake loosely to enable them to drop

Pre-planted seedlings with fully developed roots have a better start in life. The photograph shows a set of plastic seed-pots.

slightly as they settle in; then they are resecured by a special strap with an adjustable girth. Rubber ties are unsuitable.

Vegetative propagation

Grafting and budding are indirect methods of vegetative reproduction which involve joining the graft (the scion) or the bud to the plant stock in order to reproduce species and cultivars which are difficult or cannot be reproduced in any other way.

Grafting is usually carried out on woody plants and involves joining the graft to the stock. This is usually done in early spring before the plant starts sprouting so that the stock has no sap. When both the graft and the stock are of the same thickness a method called 'whip and tongue' grafting is used. When the stock is thicker either 'splice', 'saddle' or 'crown' grafting are used. This method is mostly used for stone fruits. A more detailed description of individual methods can be found on page 132.

Principles of successful grafting

1. The cut surfaces of the stock and graft must be smooth, clean and of the same length. Grafts with longer cut surfaces take better than small ones.
2. Graft or scion is placed on the stock in such a way that the cambium (the layer between the woody element and the bark) of the graft and the stock come into the closest possible contact. If the cut on the stock *is* wider, the graft is placed so that tissue meets exactly at least on one side.
3. At the end of the stock and on its underside, opposite the cut surface, a bud is left in situ so that it can draw sap towards the graft. On the graft, a bud should again be left opposite the cut surface — on the top side of the graft.
4. Unite the graft with the stock, carefully matching the cut surfaces and tie them firmly together with raffia or tape, working from the middle of the

Pricking out seedlings must be done with care, for their quality influences the future development of the plants. The holes are made with a dibber or a similarly shaped object. Seedling are always handled by their seed leaves, never by the stem.

wound upwards and then downwards where a special knot is tied.

5. Then the cut surfaces, in particular those where the graft comes into contact with the stock, are carefully covered with a continuous layer of good quality grafting wax.

6. A sharp cutting knife must be used.

7. When the graft and the stock have grown together, the bast on the opposite side of the graft is loosed with a knife.

8. If shoots sprout out of all the buds, only the most suitable is retained and tied to a protective stick to protect it from breaking away; all of the other shoots are removed.

Grafts are taken from one-year shoots of fertile fruit-bearing and healthy trees, preferably from the southern side of the crown where they have matured well. Profusely growing shoots often develop vertically up the crown and these are not suitable for grafting. The same applies to any shoots older than one year.

Budding is carried out during the time of summer sap, when the cut bark can be easily detached from the wood. Some grafts can easily lose the sap and therefore budding has to be done earlier. Stone-fruit varieties such as greengages are grafted first, seed plants of plum trees, apricots and peaches follow, then kernel fruits and finally Cherry Plum and Perfumed Cherry. If the conditions are dry for some time before the graft is taken, the stocks need to be watered well in order to have enough sap. A fortnight before taking the graft the side shoots on the stem are removed up to a height of 20 cm. Shortly before budding the soil is eased away from the stock which is then cleaned with a soft cloth.

The buds are taken from mature current year's shoots of cultivated varieties. Only healthy and well-tested trees should be chosen. Beware particularly of virus diseases which can be spread by budding.

Grafting of terminal buds is sometimes carried out on Morello cherries. The terminal buds always develop into leaves. The annual shoot is cut close under the terminal bud and the cut is slanted as in grafting by whip and tongue method, then inserted into a T-cut on the stock and tied firmly.

Forkert's method of budding is used for kernel fruits, when the amount of sap is insufficient. A narrow, tongue-shaped flap is cut in the bark of the stock, the cut being directed from the top downwards and of the same length and width as the graft with a bud. The tongue of bark is then shortened to about a half and the graft with the bud is inserted behind it and tied securely in place.

Division is the simplest method of vegetative propagation. The mother plants of species which spontaneously form roots at the base of their shoots or form root runners can be lifted from the soil, divided simply by pulling them apart or cutting them into individual parts, which can then be planted out in their permanent location straight away.

Propagation from root suckers is used in species that produce offshoots from their roots or from the root neck. It is sufficient merely to remove or ease aside the soil from around the rooted shoots so that they, in turn, can be removed. The mother plant is then covered with soil again.

Earthing up. This is used for plants such as magnolias, which will not take root unless the stems are first blanched. It is carried out in spring, when the young shoots have reached the required height of 8 cm. Earth is then drawn up around the stem and this course of action is repeated once or twice over the ensuing months so that several layers of young roots are formed. In the following spring, the soil is cleared away from the shrub while the young plants

To ensure the best yields, tomato plants are fastened to tall stakes and their lateral shoots pinched out regularly.

are cut away. They can then be potted separately or planted out.

Layering is a method of propagation during which the branch or the shoot is left connected to the mother plant until it is well rooted. This is carried out in spring by pegging down one-year-old lateral shoots into shallow grooves made in the ground and then covering the shoots with soil when they start to produce new buds. These new plants are separated from the parent in the autumn.

Another method of layering is done by sinking arched annual shoots (exceptionally two-year-old ones) into the ground in the early spring. According to the length of the shoot, a wedge-like slanting groove 15—20 cm deep and 5—8 cm wide is made with a spade at an appropriate distance from the mother plant. The shoot is twisted in a circular motion about 180° around its axis, then it is inclined at a sharp angle and inserted into the prepared groove. The arch of the shoot should be as short and low as possible. The bent part is inserted into the soil in such a way that it allows the end of the shoot to lean against the far side of the groove and thereby be directed straight up. The shoot inserted in this way is carefully firmed down with the heel of the foot, then another shoot is sunk in the same way. Pegs are not needed; if the shoot does not stay in the soil without pegging, then the soil is not suitable for this method of propagation. The rooted shoots are cut away from the mother plant and dug up in autumn. Species which do not root easily, such as magnolias and witch-hazel, have to be left to root for two years.

Serpentine or Chinese layering is used to propagate woody species with long flexible shoots, which are sunk into the soil in a series of arches. They are later divided into as many new plants as they have rooted arches. This method is used mainly for climbing shrubs.

Cuttings. Taking cuttings is a direct method of vegetative propagation from healthy plants. Cuttings are sections of the vegetative parts of the plants, including soft spring shoots, leaves, rosettes of shoots which have become woody, mature shoots and roots. When prepared, these are inserted into potting compost or some other suitable substrate and there allowed to root.

When propagating by softwood and green cuttings, the material must not be allowed to wilt. It is washed in

Supports of various types can be used for runner beans.

clean water immediately after being taken away from the parent plant and prepared with a sharp knife by cutting the basal section at a slant. If it is from a plant which does not root easily, the cut surface is dipped in a rooting powder. Some of the lower leaves are stripped away. Using a peg or a dibber, holes are made in the propagating substrate, just a little larger than the diameter of the cutting — between 1 and 2.5 cm — then the prepared cutting is inserted and gently firmed in.

Propagation by hardwood cuttings is done by taking cuttings from the bottom part of the shoot and these are left to overwinter in a slightly damp substrate. In spring they are inserted into nursery beds where they take root and then are lifted in the autumn, stored for the winter and planted again in a nursery in spring.

Propagation by root cuttings is usually conducted in the autumn, before the frost, by cutting from the roots 5—8 cm long and 3 cm wide sections, which are then kept through the winter in a cellar, a frost-free room or a nursery. In February or March they are planted directly into pots and are kept in a slightly warm greenhouse until they begin to sprout. Alternatively they can be inserted into the soil in a warm frame. In spring, after hardening, the pots are placed out in beds.

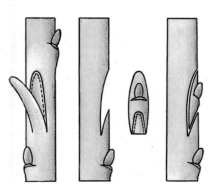

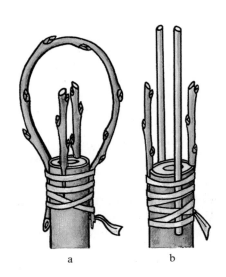

Forkert's method of budding. The strip of bark cut from the rootstock is of the same length and width as the slice with the bud. The strip of bark is then shortened to a half and the bud is inserted behind it.

a   b

To prevent birds from destroying a new graft, a bowed twig or two sticks can be fastened to the rootstock or the scion to protect it.

Grapes are harvested in warm, dry weather. They should be clipped off with secateurs or cut off with a sharp knife and transported in plastic or wooden vessels.

Propagating by cuttings taken from evergreen deciduous trees is carried out when the shoots, including their tips, have fully matured and hardened. Mature cuttings need a longer time to root and are therefore usually placed in propagative greenhouses where, in the autumn, rooting can be promoted by heating. Almost all evergreen woody species will root from cuttings, even in frames. However, it takes longer and the care and winter preparation is more labourious.

Propagating coniferous trees by cuttings is simplest when using young shoots which root easily. This can be done throughout the year with the possible exception of March and April. There are many methods and customs in the preparation of such cuttings. But basically it is the same as that used for deciduous trees. Once rooted, cuttings are planted in pots or planted out in their permanent sites.

Buildings and equipment suitable for rooting the cuttings include greenhouses, frames or elevated beds, depending on the conditions required by the given species. A small polythene greenhouse with a dug out path allowing good access and ventilation is sufficient for the needs of an average gardening enthusiast.

The propagating mixture is prepared from two parts of finely sifted moss peat, one part of fine river sand and one part of crushed polystyrene foam. This mixture is appropriate for propagating almost all perennials and woody species. The substrate is spread out in a 10 cm layer over the propagating bed and wetted with boiling water. You can propagate, even at home, using various boxes and bowls — these must be clean and disinfected. Fill them with the same substrate which is used in propagating beds. Propagating can be also done in pot trays made either of clay, plastic or peat and the propagating mixture can be substituted with other propagating materials.

Other work in the garden

Sifting of compost. According to the type of material used, the compost matures in 3—4 months if it is a quick compost made of green vegetable matter, farmyard manure, peat and crushed organic waste or in 2—3 years if it is a long-term compost from woody plants or animal waste. Maturation is promoted by periodically digging it over and watering. Quick composts are dug over only once, 3—6 weeks from the time of commencement. Long-term composts need to be dug over twice during the first year and once a year during the following years.

Taking care of soil. Garden soils require sifting, moistening, enriching with nutrients to regulate the soil chemistry or pH value and keeping them clean and free from weeds. Soil needed for young plants or plants with a low disease resistance should be disinfected for half an hour by steam at 90° C, before planting takes place.

Mixing soil. Flowering plants require substrates with specific qualities which can only be achieved by mixing together various types of soil. Soil should be mixed on a clean, swept and firm floor. The individual constituents are deposited in the correct quantities and sieved as many times as is needed to achieve a uniform mixture. If the soil is too dry, it should be sprayed during mixing so that the mixture becomes evenly moist. The finished mixture should then be left to rest for at least 2 weeks before planting.

Protecting plants from frost. Some plants which cannot stand low temperatures can be protected from frost, and in particular from dry frost, by mulching or covering the soil above the roots of a plant with a layer of organic matter such as peat, dry leaves etc. Plants can also be protected from frost by covering the ground with branches of coniferous trees. Spruce is best for this purpose. This cover must not be provided before it is needed and similarly, it must not be cleared away too early.

Protecting plants from dampness. Before planting warmth-loving plants, the permeability of the soil may need to be improved by introducing a good drainage system. Many plants are satisfied with that. However, there are some species which cannot stand higher levels of humidity, even in the late summer and autumn months. A variety of roofings can be positioned above such plants, to prevent too much water getting to the roots. Such coverings can be removed in spring.

Harvesting fruit. Fruit is gathered gradually, depending on ripeness. It is picked with stalks attached as it then lasts longer. Harvested fruit should never be left out in the sun.

Harvesting vegetables. Early and summer vegetables are harvested gradually as they are needed for consumption. They are picked at the times when they will not wilt; this means never around midday. They, too, should not be left in the sun. The most appropriate time for harvesting is early morning. The tops of carrots, radishes etc. should be removed immediately. Late vegetables which are to be stored are gathered as late as possible, but before the arrival of first frosts in October and November, to allow them to mature thoroughly. They are best collected during a spell of dry weather.

Storing fruit. Fruit is stored on the day of harvesting. Apples, carefully sorted, are stored with their stalks pointing downwards, pears with their stalks up. The storing place should be dark and a constant temperature should be maintained. In winter this should be 2—4° C and never below —2° C. The relative humidity of the air should be 85—90 per cent. Fruit should not be stored with vegetables, in particular not with potatoes.

Storing vegetables. The temperature of the storing place should be 1—4° C and have a relative moisture of 90 per cent, with the exception of onions which need only 70—80 per cent. The exchange of air should not be too fast but needs to be sufficient. No aromatic substances should be stored with vegetables; indeed the storage area must be kept free of strong smells — including those of mould and decay.

Harvesting and drying plant material. Harvesting takes place at different stages of development of individual crops, to ensure the longest possible durability. Flowering plants are cut usually when in full bloom but before they start to fade and drop. They are tied in small bunches and then suspended with their flowers down to ensure straight stalks. Individual everlasting flowers are picked before fully opened and with their stalks as long as possible. They, too, are tied together in small bunches. Fruit is picked in summer and is dried in the same way as grasses, that is, in its natural position. Cones are collected when ripe.

Machinery, tools and garden accessories

Basic tools

Basic tools are needed regardless of the type of garden. Basic equipment can be gradually added to as required but should definitely consist of a spade, border fork, shovel and hoe for the shallow and deep loosening of soil. One small and one large metal rake, and a scarifying rake will also be needed.

These can be supplemented by smaller tools, including a trowel which is used for planting out and a weeding hand-fork or similar tool for loosening and weeding dense growths in the beds, and sieves of varying mesh. Pegs, lines, a dibber, garden scissors, a knife for removing weeds and a universal gardening knife all come in handy. A pair of sharp secateurs are also invaluable.

Other indispensable tools are those needed for watering, fertilizing and protecting the plants. These include one or two watering cans with a choice of roses, sprays, a hose with a fine spray nozzle, and a small or larger insecticide sprayer.

Specialized tools

Apart from the basic tools mentioned above, different types of gardens require additional equipment and accessories, the most important of which are mentioned below.

For intensively cultivated vegetable gardens a hand soil cutter or a rotivator is useful for preparing large beds. These cultivators can be specifically modified for use by slightly built women or by the handicapped (for example, the semi-automatic cultivator, Terrex).

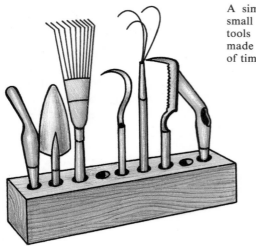

A simple stand for small gardening tools can easily be made from a block of timber.

In this type of garden other machinery that will come in useful includes seed and row drills with a distance adjuster and a sowing wheel. Some seed drills also enable control of the quantity of seeds released, cover up the seeds with soil, press them down and mark out another row. Such machines sow seeds in one or two rows.

Gardens with a predominance of fruit trees require specialized tools for the care of trees and for fruit harvesting. These include various types of saws and knives and specialized secateurs. If the trees are tall growing varieties, a platform ladder is also essential; you could buy a multi-purpose ladder.

No garden should be without a lawn and this also requires additional equipment. For maintenance of small areas of up to 50 m² a hand mower is sufficient, although a small electric lawn mower certainly makes work much easier. For larger expanses of grass electric or petrol lawn mowers can be chosen. The decision will be affected by the size of the garden and by the availability of a sufficient length of cable. The length of the cutting blade is determined by the type and quality of grass surface. In sloping gardens with an uneven surface this length should not exceed from 26 to a maximum of 32 cm.

Modern lawn mowers do not damage young grass so that the need for grass cutting by hand has been almost eliminated. If the lawn is to be maintained to a very high standard, the possession of a roller will be important as the true English lawn is rolled after each cutting. Special electric trimmers are also very useful for keeping the areas of lawn around paths and steps neat.

Another very useful lawn care item of equipment is a circular scarifying brush which removes cut and dead grass together with moss. The height of the brush can be adjusted and the scarified material is collected in a box which is emptied when full.

A lawn needs also to be aerated. This can be done with a special machine with a number of swinging blades, the height of which can be adjusted. It is especially used on surfaces infested with moss.

Gardeners will also need a storage place for smaller tools; this should contain pliers, drills, screwdrivers, chisels, an axe, a set of wrenches, various sizes of nails, screws and hooks, thin and thick wire and iron stakes. All the above will come in useful. Obviously, replacements and spares of hose extensions, seals, screw and connecting joints also need to be readily available.

Care of tools

Even the best quality gardening tools will rust and deteriorate without necessary care. It is quite obvious, therefore, that tools should never be left out among the beds after work or put away dirty. Each used piece of equipment needs to be thoroughly cleaned of soil, thoroughly dried and put in its place. It is a good idea to furnish the storage room or shed with stands or hooks for tools because this makes it easier to keep everything in order and allows a clear

Lawn shears can be used wherever mowers have difficulty of access.

Parrot-billed garden secateurs are useful in every garden.

A multipurpose collapsible ladder can be transported in the luggage space of your car. Stability of the joints is secured with a system of supports and rubber holders. A worktable can be constructed by adding a small board.

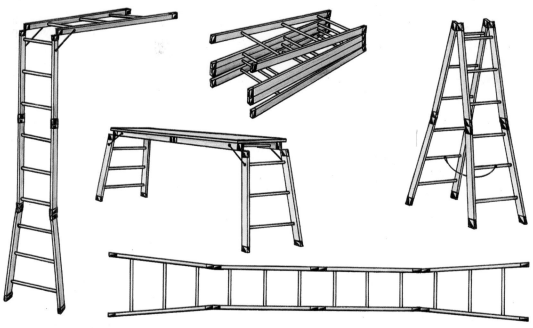

Various types of garden insecticide sprayers.

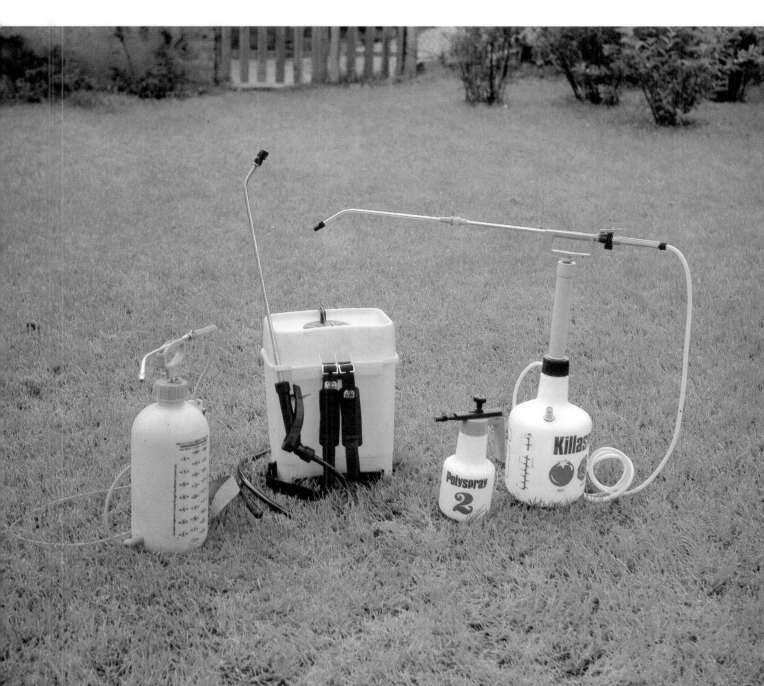

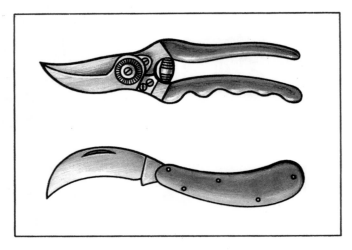

A universal knife and parrot-billed secateurs are indispensable for every gardener.

view of what is available. Before winter storage, all tools should be cleaned with particular care and any rusty patches treated with a special derusting agent or petroleum. Other metal parts should be wiped with industrial vaseline.

Miscellaneous garden accessories

Indispensable help is provided by a wheelbarrow, which can be used for moving heavy loads of soil, transporting harvested fruit and vegetables and many other garden jobs. Various well-designed types are available on the market. A small selection of garden troughs or baskets come in handy for carrying cut flowers.

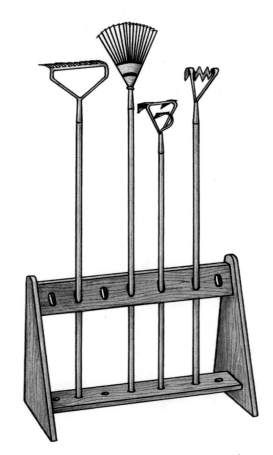

This large tool rack allows for easy handling of the tools. You simply incline them slightly backwards when lifting them out.

Clipped hedges need regular care. One of the most important tools for their maintenance is good shears.

Powered lawn mowers are available in various types. They not only save time and labour but guarantee a high-quality lawn.

A simple method of sieving soil directly into the wheelbarrow. Either the sieve can be fastened permanently or be detachable.

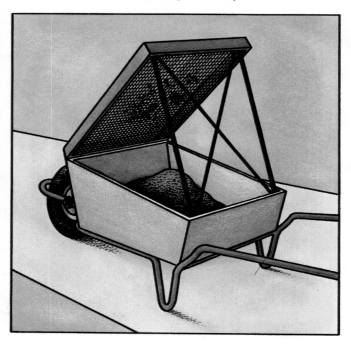

Gardeners should also remember various items for protecting their own health and safety. These should include gardening gloves, knee pads and a small mask for use when spraying insecticides.

A few words about mechanization

The problem of deciding whether to mechanize various garden tasks still persists. The decision will depend on whether physical activity in the garden is required to compensate for the lack of exercise resulting from modern life styles or if work in the garden needs to be done quickly in order to pursue other leisure activities. A final consideration is whether physical work is becoming too demanding, given the gardener's present or impending age.

Once the decision to mechanize is made, the type of energy to be used needs to be carefully selected. Both petrol and electricity have their advantages and disadvantages. The indisputable advantage of electricity is its comparative quietness but the inherent dangers of cables and plugs must be borne in mind. Motors driven by petrol draw on an independent source of energy and are easily mobile but at the same time make more noise and pollute the atmosphere. Batteries or two-stroke engines can be used for smaller, powered machines.

In this day and age multipurpose machines with a number of fitments prove the most popular. A universal device of this type can alternate as soil rotivator, lawn mower, pump, sprinkler and irrigation agent. The 'Kombi' is a mobile unit which can even be used for removing snow in the vicinity of the house and also can be adapted as a 100 cm roller or a mobile high-pressure spray with a 50 litre tank for pest-control sprays. The advantage of such equipment is that additional attachments can be bought gradually to suit one's need and experience.

Powered lawn mowers are particularly suitable for large stretches of lawn.

Electric hedge trimmers are also popular labour-saving devices. Similarly, an electric waste-disposal unit is not to be overlooked as by this means it is possible to dispose of all organic waste from the garden including lopped branches. This also substantially shortens the time needed for maturing of the compost. Since the mechanization of garden activities continues to develop, its adherents can look forward to the advent of new labour-saving devices.

Diseases and pests in the garden

A gardener who has several years' experience will undoubtedly have noticed an interesting thing: plant health problems seldom arise if the plants get all they need. Diseases will seldom attack a plant growing and developing in optimum conditions — and the animal pests are checked by the gardener himself. Assisted by his feathered insect-eating allies, the gardener can easily do without chemicals.

A wise gardener uses his winter rest time to study special literature and to learn new ways of preventing plant diseases and controlling pests. For instance, it has long been known that some plants repel certain pests. It is therefore a good control to grow insect-resistant plants next to the susceptible ones to repel potential pests. After all, Nature herself exerts such controls to keep her biological balance.

The main diseases and pests may sometimes cause problems but at the same time they tell us that mistakes have been made in the growing of plants.

Diseases

The diseases of garden plants (vegetables, fruit, flowers, ornamental trees and shrubs) are either non-parasitic (physiological) or parasitic, that is, caused by viruses, bacteria or fungi.

Physiological diseases

This category of plant diseases comprises all developmental disorders caused by environmental factors or various mistakes and shortcomings in our gardening techniques.

The most frequent mistake is failure to estimate what a plant can stand. Wishing to give the plants the best of everything, a gardener may vex them with too much water, fertilizer, sunshine, and is surprised to see that an adverse result is obtained. Excess is as harmful as deficiency.

The group of non-parasitic (physiological) dis-

Anthracnose of lettuce is manifested by aqueous, later browning spots on the leaves. No signs of mould occur, however. Most commonly attacked are plants sown in the autumn.

Dry spot of sweet peppers is of physiological origin. The spots start to form on semi-ripe fruits close to the tip. In damp conditions the fruits are secondarily attacked by micro-organisms which cause them to rot. Regular watering is the only prevention.

The causes of physiological diseases

Causal agent	Symptoms of disease	Control
Unsuitable soil pH (acidity/alkalinity)	Retarded growth, poor flower setting, leaf yellowing, chlorosis caused by lack of trace elements (iron, manganese and others) tied up in the soil in a form unavailable to plants; in potted plants excess acidity causes retarded growth, yellowing, failure to bloom	test soil pH from time to time; meet plants' requirements (e. g. azalea and rhododendron need acid soil); increase soil acidity by adding peat; reduce acidity by liming; treat chlorosis with acid fertilizers (superphosphate, ammonium sulphate) or by watering the plants with 1 per cent green vitriol
Unsuitable temperature a) too high or too low b) frost damage	leaf yellowing; chlorosis caused by cold or heat; reddening or curling of the leaves up to leaf tearing (e.g. lettuce, tulips); effect of low spring temperatures: watery spots, blisters on leaves, disintegration of leaf blades, softening of tissues	adjust temperature, choose a suitable site; for extreme sites, use suitable plant species and varieties
Unsuitable light conditions a) overexposure to sun b) underexposure to sun	in shade-loving plants, symptoms similar to yellows from lack of nutrients or to virus yellows; leaf rolling, browning, drying, shedding etiolation, i. e. bleaching of leaves, reduction of leaf area, abnormal elongation of stems, suppression of flowering	shade hotbeds and glasshouses; choose plants suitable to the site clean the glass of hotbed windows; reduce temperature if there is lack of light; in winter, use additional lighting on newly sown beds and young plants
Unsuitable water regime a) insufficient watering b) excess soil water content c) excess air humidity and excess soil moisture d) low air humidity e) abrupt changes in air humidity or soil moisture content	chlorosis—plant yellowing and withering, leaf shedding, flower drying root and root-neck rot, leaf shedding, plant dieback brownish corky swellings on leaves; increased susceptibility to bacterial and fungal diseases leaf drying and shedding in hygrophytes, increased susceptibility to attack by sucking insects (red spiders, thrips and others) leaf shedding, flower shedding, cracking of flower stalks and calyces	water the plants regularly grow every species in suitable soil; drain soil under vulnerable plants; reduce watering of slow-growing plants ventilate hotbeds and glasshouses; reduce watering sprinkle plants with water; wash the undersides of leaves apply proper amounts of water and adequate ventilation; use soils of adequate composition and structure
Damage by chemicals	leaf yellowing or browning, leaf rolling, spots of dead tissue on leaves, flower shedding	use only officially released chemicals, apply recommended doses and respect the protection terms after soil disinfection
Damage by industrial fumes and fly ashes	silvery appearance of leaves, mainly on underside, chlorosis up to browning and mummification of whole leaf; cauterizing fumes cause leaf burning and tissue death	grow more resistant plant species

A bad nutrient ratio in soil:
a) excess nutrients (overfertilization)
1. nitrogen
 	
2. potassium
3. phosphorus
4. calcium
 	
b) lack of nutrients
1. nitrogen
 	
2. potassium
 	
3. trace elements:
  molybdenum
  boron
 	
  magnesium
  manganese
 	
  iron
  copper
	excess foliage at the expense of flowers, stunted or deformed inflorescences, thin and watery leaf tissue (watery cauliflower heads), increased susceptibility to fungal diseases and frost damage; greening of the leaves of red-leaved ornamentals (begonia)
	growth disorders
	abnormal reddish or purplish leaf colour (lettuce)
	increased soil alkalinity, chlorosis from lack of trace elements (iron, manganese and others)
	
	stunted growth, irregularly developed and/or reddish leaves, flower shedding
	waviness of leaves, rolling and dying of leaf margins, stem winding, or chlorotic spots between the leaf nerves
	
	blindness of cauliflower
	a) corky pulp of apples
	b) vitreous cauliflower heads
	c) vitreous kohlrabi stems, dieback of growing point of seed plants
	d) heart rot of beets
	browning of margins in lettuce
	leaf spot, yellowing and slow dying (necrosis) of leaves in tomato
	
	chlorosis (effect of unsuitable soil pH)
	yellow-red or red blotches on tomato leaf margins
		reduce nitrogen fertilization, add potassium and phosphorus fertilizers
		
		reduce application of potassium fertilizers
		reduce application of phosphorus fertilizers
		avoid using lime-containing water for watering, use physiologically acid fertilizers and/or water the plants with green vitriol
		
		apply fertilizers at full and balanced rates
		
		apply fertilizers at full and balanced rates
		
		avoid using acid fertilizers, reduce soil acidity by liming
		use suitable fertilizers
		
		use suitable fertilizers
		fertilize with manganese sulphate at a rate of 600 g per 100 m³ or water the plants with a 1 per cent solution of this salt
		
		add copper sulphate at a rate of 200 to 600 g per 100 m³ or spray the plants with a 1 per cent solution of this salt

eases includes disorders caused by improper watering and fertilization and a bad soil structure, as well as damage due to overheating, frost, hail, industrial fumes and improper use of chemicals. These causes of damage and their consequences are given in the table on the opposite page.

Protection against physiological disorders derives from correct identification of the cause of the problem. An expert (professional gardener, phytopathologist or another specialist) should be asked to advise when necessary. Most of the physiological diseases can be prevented if proper cultural practices are applied to each crop.

Virus diseases

Viruses are responsible for great losses of ornamentals and vegetables. They live inside the cells of the host plants but the actual signs of infection depend on the kind of virus and the species and variety of the host plant.

The most frequent manifestations of a disease are various changes in the original green colour: whitish to yellowish spots irregularly scattered over leaves and stems. Their common name is 'mosaic'. For instance, cucumber mosaic virus (*Cucumis virus* 1) is a widespread organism responsible for mosaics of cucumbers but also other vegetables and a number of ornamentals (petunia, snapdragon, columbine, dahlia, lily, primrose, pansy and others).

More conspicuous spots of a characteristic type are symptoms of disorders included in the group of ring or ringspot mosaics and diseases, called 'white' or 'yellow' spot. Diseases of this type include, for instance, cucumber ringspot mosaic (*Nicotiana virus* 12), cherry ring mosaic and pear ringspot mosaic.

Another group of symptoms of virus diseases comprises dead spots on the leaves of lilacs, petunias, sweet peas and other plants, leading to various deformations if the healthy leaf tissue continues growing. Such spots are caused, for instance, by *Brassica virus* 1, the virus responsible for cabbage black ringspot. Virus leaf curl is a disease affecting phloxes and other plants.

Many virus diseases produce very conspicuous symptoms on the flowers. The colour breaking of tulips (*Tulipa virus* 1 and *Tulipa virus* 2) is a typical example. The affected plants, called 'Rembrandt's tulips', had long been regarded as very special and valuable until it was found that their special quality was, in fact, a disease accompanied by gradual degeneration of the plants. A similar breaking of the colour affects pansies, gladioli and other plants.

Many ornamentals, mainly perennials, suffer from a disease called 'false blossom', 'chloranthy', or 'green petal', usually combined with deformation of the inflorescence or sterility of the flowers. This disorder often accompanies yellowing or again, can be provoked by viruses of the stolbur group (for example, in potatoes and tomatoes). Another frequent disorder accompanying virus diseases is stunting or dwarfing, for example in dahlias.

How infection spreads

Sucking insects (aphids, thrips and leaf hoppers) are the common carriers of virus diseases. They spread viruses by moving from a virus-infested plant to a healthy plant for feeding. Viruses can also be spread via plant sap, for example, when flowers are cut or the plants are harvested or otherwise handled. Only a minor group of viruses can spread through the soil, for example, tobacco necrosis virus (*Nicotiana virus* 11); the attacked plants have dead spots on the leaves which are puckered and perforated. Plants

Mosaic virus causes irregular spots on the leaves and stems. It is usually spread by leaf beetles. The picture shows infested celeriac leaves.

Virus diseases of lettuce can be transmitted via the seeds. The contaminated plants are stunted and their leaves bear irregular mosaic-like patches. Autumn-grown plants are usually more prone to infection.

Plum pox virus is the most dangerous disease of plums. The fruits are completely spoilt; their surface puckered, the flesh hard and coloured reddish-brown. The content of sugar in infested plums is very low.

Diseases of the second group appear as spots on the leaves, spreading to affect other organs. Organs attacked in dry conditions wither; wet-attacked organs often excrete slimy bacterial matter. Most of the causal agents belong to the genus *Pseudomonas* which can also be spread via seeds. For instance, the halo blight of beans is caused by *P. phaseolicola*. Angular leaf spot of cucumbers, melons and gourds is induced by *P. lacrymans*. *P. pisi* is responsible for the bacterial blight of peas. One of the most conspicuous bacterial diseases, black spot of the leaves of the perennial delphiniums, is caused by *P. delphinii*. Brown stripes on the leaves of gladioli and later the characteristic brown glassy spots on the tubers (gladiolus scab) are due to *P. marginata*, a microorganism which also attacks freesias and saffrons.

The third group of bacterial diseases are systemic in-

are attacked when wounded. Soil pests (mainly eelworms) and soil fungi invading the roots are also involved in the attack. It should be added that, with no exception, all viruses can be spread by artificial vegetative propagation (grafting, budding or cutting) and by the plant parts involved in natural vegetative propagation: bulbs and tubers. Some viruses can be transmitted to the progeny via seeds or pollen.

Controlling virus diseases

Virus diseases of plants are difficult to control. Before choosing a method, the virus should be correctly identified and traced back to see how it has spread. The available controls include chemical sprays to kill sucking insects, disinfection of tools and hands, and disinfection of the soil and pots. The most practical cultural control is to pull out and burn all of the diseased plants so that healthy ones are left for further propagation.

Plant diseases caused by bacteria

Bacterial diseases are divided into several groups according to the signs observed on the plants.

The first group comprises the putrefaction of the soft sappy tissues. This takes the form of either soft rot or dry rot and its causal agents are usually bacteria of the genera *Pseudomonas* and *Erwinia*. Several examples can be given to illustrate their action.

Erwinia carotovora, for instance, is responsible for the rotting of roots and for soft rot of carrot. *E. arroideae*, a species attacking a number of ornamentals, causes the bacterial blight of tomatoes. The rotting of the shoots, leaves and inflorescences of lilac (lilac blight) is caused by *Pseudomonas syringae*. The rhizomes of irises are attacked by *E. carotovora*, *E. arroideae* and *P. iridis*.

The leaves of plum pox-attacked trees bear pale green or yellowish, indistinct spots.

fections. Bacteria of the genus *Xanthomonas* spread along the vascular bundles to affect, step by step, the whole plant — which turns brown, wilts and dies. For instance, *X. phaseoli* attacks kidney-beans. Brassicas are attacked by *X. campestris*, which spreads in harvested plants and often results in the rotting of stored heads. The causal agent of the dangerous hyacinth yellows is *X. hyacinthi*. The disease, appearing as stripes filled with yellow bacterial matter, can be seen on the cross section through the bulb. Begonias are attacked by *X. begoniae* which produces lesions called 'oil fleck' on the leaves in the early stages of infection. These bacteria are also transmitted via seeds.

The fourth group of bacterial diseases includes tumour (knot) diseases. Bacteria of the species *Agrobacterium tumefaciens* excrete into the plant tissues special growth substances which induce excess multiplication of cells. Tissues are hyper-trophied and tumours develop on either the roots or the basal part of the stem. The bacteria live in the soil and penetrate into the plant when the roots are wounded. They attack various species of fruit and ornamental woody species (mainly young trees and shrubs in nurseries) and flowering plants (roses, chrysanthemums, geraniums, dahlias and others). At first the tumours are tiny, soft and whitish but later they grow to be as large as a fist; they also become brown and woody. The attacked roots fail to fulfil their functions, the plant is weakened and may die.

The leaf galls forming on the basal parts of the stem in some ornamental species are also of bacterial origin. They are caused by *Corynebacterium fascians* (for example, on sweet peas and chrysanthemums).

How to control bacterial diseases of plants
Bacteria live either in the soil or in the plants they infect. In the majority of cases, they attack only damaged plants or plants weakened by growing in unsuitable conditions (heavy, damp, poorly aerated soil, high humidity combined with a high temperature and the like). The best method of control is prevention or localization of the disease by providing optimum growing conditions, removing any affected plants and rotating the crops.

Though bacterial diseases of animals can be chemically treated, no specific antibacterial preparations are available for the treatment of this kind of diseases in plants. To protect plants against soil-borne bacteria, the soil can be steamed or treated with formalin or mercury disinfectants. However, thorough control of soil pests such as wireworms and eelworms invading the roots is more effective in protection against bacterial diseases. Seeds and planting material can also be dressed with mercury disinfectants. Repeated copper-based fungicide sprays can be used if this is the only available control of bacterial diseases during the growing season.

Fungus diseases
The fungi responsible for this type of diseases reproduce by dust-like spores; the development, shape and appearance of the spores vary with fungus species and are therefore used as important diagnostic features in determining the causal agent of the disease. The spores are spread around by wind, water, insects and other organisms but can also spread by soil cultivation and plant handling. At a suitable temperature and humidity, a fungus spore settled on a host develops into a thread-like body which increases its size by cell division either on the surface or inside plant tissues. At maturity, if conditions are favourable, spores are produced, and the cycle of reproduction starts again. The majority of fungi pro-

duce two (or more) types of spores some of which are very resistant to adverse conditions and serve for the overwintering of the fungus. The spores are either produced directly by the mycelium or are hidden in various microscopic fruit-bodies.

Fungi can induce a wide variety of symptoms on the plants: ranging from conspicuous flour-like coatings of powdery mildew, brownish heaps of rusty spores and dusty coatings of grey mould, wilting of the plants with the fungus hidden inside the host tissue, up to fruit rot and root rot.

Some phytopathogenic fungi are bound to a single host species (as in rust on carnations); others attack several species. There are also many polyphagous fungi, able to parasitize various cultivated and wild plants. It will be useful, therefore, to classify fungi into groups according to the plant organs and parts they attack.

The common fungi responsible for diseases of plant roots and underground parts
These soil fungi occur practically everywhere and are spread through the soil or the attacked plant organs. They can occur individually or several fungi can associate to form complexes. The most frequent manifestation of the action of these fungi, or fungus complexes, is the damping off of seedlings in beds or cuttings in propagation houses. The tissue of the root neck and stem base blackens and softens, or shrinks, and the plant withers, damps off and dies. Gardeners call these signs 'damping off', 'black leg' and the like, and the causal agents are generally called 'propagation-house moulds'. When the infection occurs in a propagation house or a hotbed, plants are killed on a large scale. Brassicas, lettuce, tomatoes and ornamentals are among the plant groups attacked most frequently.

Club root is manifested by the formation of variously shaped tumours on the roots of cultivated and wild-growing members of the family Cruciferae. The aerial parts of diseased plants soon start to rot.

The control of propagation-house moulds and other soil fungi

The soil is preventively disinfected with steam or formalin. A suitable chemical can be used for spraying or watering the plants when the first signs of infection occur. Prompt action is vital.

The common parasitic fungi attacking the stems

This group also comprises soil fungi, including very dangerous parasites which cause great damage to garden crops and are difficult to control.

Fusarium diseases

Members of the genus *Fusarium* are among the most widespread soil fungi. They are responsible for the wilting and damping off of young plants in the propagation houses, for the yellowing and withering of mature plants, as well as for the store rot, found, for example, in bulbous ornamentals. The plants contract infection from the contaminated soil through root hairs or through a wound, usually occurring near the root neck.

The symptoms of infection include the browning or blackening of the basal parts of plants (black leg) which, however, may not always be clearly visible, and the browning of the vascular system inside the stems. A woolly or dry coating of mycelium and spores sometimes develops on the surface of the attacked plant parts in wet conditions. The mycelium penetrates into the vascular system of the plants and excretes toxins which kill the plant cells. This hinders the distribution of water and dissolved nutrients and the plant wilts. When the plant dies, the mycelium and spores stay on the residues and if a susceptible crop is repeatedly grown in the same place the soil becomes heavily contaminated. Fusarium diseases also spread with infected seeds and seedlings. The preventive methods include systematic crop rotation, reproduction of absolutely healthy plants and removal and burning of all attacked individuals.

Verticillium diseases (*Verticillium albo-atrum*)

This soil fungus, which commonly occurs in fields and gardens, attacks many cultivated and weed plants. If a plant is attacked its leaves abruptly turn yellow, the plant quickly withers and dies. The roots of attacked plants usually remain healthy and no signs of disease occur on the surface of the stem, as distinct from Fusarium diseases. The disease remains concealed inside: a longitudinal section through the plant will show that the vascular bundles are brown and dead.

Infection gets into the plants from the contaminated soil where the fungus survives on plant remnants. The mycelium grows through the conductive tissues of the plant, blocks them and produces toxins which kill the cells. The preventive measures are the same as those applied in the case of Fusarium diseases.

Sclerotinia sclerotiniorum

This is another common soil fungus, causing diseases called 'stalk break', 'root rot', 'drop' or 'cottony rot'. The attacked plant parts (such as dahlia stems) are covered by and filled with thick white cottony mycelium bearing hard oval tubercular formations called 'sclerotia' (these are up to 10 mm in size). The sclerotia are white when young and black at maturity. They get into the soil via plant remnants and live there 5—8 years. When conditions are favourable (a suitable host is found) they sprout again to produce mycelium and spores. Via the attacked plants, the disease often gets from the field or garden into stores where it appears as storage rot.

Protection against fungi inside plant stems

Protection against Verticillium and Fusarium diseases and all other fungus diseases of this group is based on the rotation of crops and sites. Susceptible plants should not be planted in a once contaminated bed for at least five years. It is also recommended that seedlings should then be planted farther apart. The attacked plants should be removed and burned as soon as the disease occurs. Only absolutely healthy plants can be used for propagation.

The available chemical measures include soil disinfection with formalin and treatment of seeds and seedlings with mercury-based disinfectants.

Main causal agents of leaf spots and other symptoms on leaves

The fungi of this group spread by spores during the growing season and survive winter as mycelium and spores on plant remnants. They are also transmitted

Brown rot is the most widespread disease of apple fruits. It is caused by *Sclerotinia fructigena*, which is the conidium stage of *Monilia fructigena*. The infection enters the fruits where they have been damaged. Contaminated apples should be removed immediately.

on the surface of seeds and on cuttings or other vegetatively propagated plant parts. Each group or genus of fungi causing leaf spot produces different spots of characteristic shape. The leaves of severely infected plants turn yellow and die, the plants are weakened, their growth is irregular, flowering poor and fruits are of bad quality.

From this largest group of fungi parasitizing green plants only those which occur most frequently, cause the greatest losses and require special control based on knowledge of their biology, are detailed below.

Powdery mildew (*Erysiphaceae*)

Powdery mildew is easy to recognize by the whitish powdery coating on the surface of the attacked plant organs. This coating is the mycelium on which spores are throttled off as if a chain were cut link by link. All species of powdery mildew are so-called 'obligate parasites' able to live only on living plant tissue. Each has its specific requirements. This even applies to polyphagous ('all-eating') species such as *Erysiphe polygoni*. If a powdery mildew species is specialized it does not attack any other host. As a result, there are considerable differences in susceptibility to powdery mildew between the species and even varieties of host plants, offering the possibility of controlling the fungus by the production of more resistant cultivars.

How to protect plants against powdery mildew

Fungicides based on sulphur are the oldest chemicals with specific anti-mildew action. However, their effect depends on temperature. The optimum temperature is 20—25° C. At lower temperatures, the active sulphur oxides are not released and treatment is not reliable. In greenhouses, good results are obtained when sulphur is left to evaporate from sulphurizers at an increased temperature.

Rusts (*Uredinales*)

Fungi of this group can be distinguished by the yellow, red, brown or black spores in the areas of infection. The reproduction of rusts is a very complex process. Rusts having a complete developmental cycle produce five types of spores. The summer spores are produced by the deposits of rust under the surface of the leaf which cracks and releases the spores to spread infection during the growing season. The winter spores develop in similar deposits in the autumn. Having overwintered, these winter spores extend special fungus threads bearing another type of spores on stalks. When these spores fall on to a host plant they renew the infection. Two other types of spores, the spermacia and sporidia, develop in the leaf tissues of the host plant, then unite to produce the summer spores again.

Rusts need more than one host to develop: their different spores are produced on different hosts. For instance, one phase of the development of pear rust takes place on pear trees and the other on savin (small, bushy evergreen shrubs). With these complicated relations it is extremely difficult to combat the disease because the hosts of rusts include both cultivated species and various weeds or wild herbs, shrubs and trees. On the other hand, summer spores are sometimes the only means to keep a rust perma-

Dry spot on the leaves, caused by *Corynespora melonis*. Preventive measures include meticulous observation of the basic principles of hygiene.

White spots on the leaves are caused by *Erysiphe polygoni*. They later merge into continuous patches and plants start to rot.

nently alive. In many rusts the other hosts are still unknown.

How to protect plants against rusts

Infested plants or parts of plants should be removed immediately. The plants to be used for propagation must be free from infection. The intermediate hosts should be destroyed.

Like powdery mildew, rusts have specific requirements on the host plants, and different varieties have different susceptibility to disease. Growing resistant varieties is therefore a good method of rust control.

Onion blight is the most dangerous disease of this vegetable. It is manifested at first on the leaves and flowering stems. Later, the attacked tissues die.

Downy mildew (*Peronospora*)

A plant attacked by downy mildew has light-coloured spots on the upper side of leaves; on the underside the leaves are coated with whitish or light violet mould consisting of spore-bearing fungus threads. Perennial (overwintering) spores are then formed in the dead tissues, shed leaves and plant remnants on the soil. Downy mildew sometimes causes a systemic infection: that is, the fungus attacks the whole plant so that it cannot grow normally and remains a dwarf.

Downy mildew thrives at a high humidity and at fluctuating temperatures. This is why its spreading is most fatal in spring and autumn when high daily temperatures alternate with cold nights or night frosts.

How to protect plants against peronospora
It is very important to thoroughly remove and burn the infected plant remnants — otherwise chemical control will be necessary. Infected plant parts should *never* be added to compost.

Moulds
The common grey mould (*Botrytis cinerea*) attacks plants in greenhouses or hotbeds and in outdoor cultures. It damages leaves, shoots, flower buds, flowers and fruits, as well as tubers and bulbs. On the green parts of plants the disease appears as small grey-brown spots, on the flowers as tiny pale or brown dots (depending on the colour of the flower), and on fruits as brown watery lesions. In damp weather the spots spread rapidly, take on a layer of powdery grey-brown spores, and the attacked organs decay. In dry conditions the spots dry and the leaf tissues crack. Later, the fungus produces *sclerotia* on the dead parts of plants. These small hard corpuscles, white when young and black when ripe, can endure adverse conditions and are able to infect susceptible hosts even after five years.

Grey mould attacks dying plant parts (such as shed petals), wounded plants or plants weakened by incorrect cultivation, and quickly spreads to healthy plants around. Excess humidity, dense spacing and nitrogen overfertilization all support the disease.

Common grey mould attacks various crops indiscriminately but other species of the *Botrytis* genus are narrowly specialized, each attacking just one or a few host plants (onion, lily, tulip, narcissus, peony, hyacinth).

How to protect plants against moulds
Correct growing practices are the best control. All plant remnants must be removed, greenhouses, hotbeds and all garden soil must be kept clean. Humidity inside hotbeds and greenhouses should be kept in check by ventilation. When it rains for long periods, a provisional shelter should be provided over the valuable crops on beds.

In conclusion, it will be useful to suggest several basic rules for the prevention of fungus diseases:
1. Reduce moisture in the plants' environment (space them wider apart, locate beds in airy places, keep above-ground parts dry during watering).
2. Avoid nitrogen overfertilization which supports the formation of soft watery tissue, prolongs the growing season and reduces the plant's resistance to low temperatures and parasitic micro-organisms. Potassium, conversely, usually increases resistance.
3. Provide plants with sufficient light and temperature, by choosing a suitable place for each crop.

4. Keep the soil clean in all beds, hotbeds and the like. Burn the remains of diseased plants, never add them to compost.
5. Rotate the crops and beds.
6. Use only healthy plants for propagation.
7. Meet the specific requirements of each plant (perfectly managed crops seldom suffer from diseases and usually have enough vigour to endure infection).

Animal pests

Plants grown in a garden can be attacked by animal pests. Some pests attack many cultivated plants, others only one or a few species. We shall only mention the most widespread pests of the first group.

Advice to use chemical control is given only in those cases where other methods fail. There is no general pattern of chemical control and the intensity and extent of attack must always be taken into account. Pests attacking fruits or those spreading virus diseases of plants are an exception: they require regular preventive measures according to the forecasts of their occurrence.

Soil pests
These pests live in the soil and damage the underground parts of plants. The pests living in the soil of newly established gardens are not the same as those in gardens cultivated for several years. Larvae of the click beetles (wireworms), caterpillars of the harmful noctuids and the larvae of cockchafers (white grubs) frequently occur in new gardens, whereas the common soil pests of established gardens are eelworms,

Grey mould (*Botrytis cinerea*) attacks the flowers and fruits of dense or insufficiently sun-lighted growths of strawberry. Moulds spread most rapidly in damp weather.

millipedes, larvae of bibionid flies and the like.

The caterpillars of noctuids do not stay in the new garden longer than the first year because thorough cultivation of the soil hinders their development. Wireworms and grubs will remain a problem for several seasons because their development lasts 3—5 years. The other soil pests are always more dangerous where the soil is too damp.

Cutworms

The cutworms most frequently occurring in gardens include the Turnip Moth (*Scotia segetum*), Common Silver Ypsilon Moth (*S. ypsilon*), the Heart and Dart Moth (*S. exclamationis*), Setaceous Hebrew-character Moth (*Amathes C-nigrum*) and some others. Their caterpillars damage the roots of all vegetables and ornamentals. In the early stages of development they live on the aerial parts of plants and chew round holes in the leaves. In the later growth stage they move to the soil and feed on the roots. They usually attack brassicas, lettuce, carrot and seedlings of ornamentals. Gardeners tend to overlook caterpillars feeding on the above-ground parts of plants and apply no control.

Larvae of click beetles — wireworms

Wireworms cause damage in newly established gardens or in dug grass plots. The Striped Elaterid Beetle (*Agriotes lineatus*) occurs most frequently, followed by another species of this group, *A. ustulatus*. Four other species also occur in some localities.

They attack the roots of vegetables, ornamentals and strawberries, eat the rootlets of seedlings, chew in or through the taproots of plants and bore tunnels in the roots of carrots and celeriac, in the bulbs of tulips and narcissi, and in the tubers of gladioli and dahlias. The damaged plants twist and wilt. The underground parts of attacked root vegetables are useless. Wireworms are most troublesome in March to June and in September and October when they stay in the surface layers of the soil.

In the dry summer period they hide deeper underground. Only the larvae of *Corymbites aeneus* do stay close to the soil surface and attack sap-filled parts of plants. The developmental cycle of wireworms lasts 3—5 years and for this period, plants growing in the contaminated beds are exposed to danger.

Larvae of cockchafers — white grubs

Most grubs found in a garden are the larvae of the European Click Beetle (*Melolontha melolontha*). They live in the soil and damage the underground organs of ornamentals, vegetables, strawberries and fruit trees. One or two grubs per square metre are enough to cause damage. The damaged seedlings of vegetables and ornamentals die. Fruit trees are endangered during the first two years after planting.

In the years of overpopulation the adult cockchafers cause clearly evident eating on cherries, apple-trees, plums and roses. The recommended method is to shake the beetles off and destroy them by treading on them.

Larvae of crane flies (*Tipulidae*)

Larvae of the crane flies can damage vegetables and ornamentals grown in wet places during the first years after the establishment of the garden. It is advisable when preparing a bed at a slightly water-logged site to check how many larvae are in the soil. To do this in an area of 1 m², the original plants are pulled out or cut and the soil is then soaked with a solution of cooking salt (1 kg per 5 litres of water). This will draw the larvae up to where they can be counted, on the soil surface. Once the infestation of the soil has been estimated, chemical control can be applied if necessary.

A garden cultivated for a long time is attacked by another group of pests. Again, the most common of these are described here.

Millipedes

Millipedes, particularly the Flat Millipede (*Polydesmus complanatus*) and Spotted Millipede (*Blaniulus guttulatus*) overpopulate in compost. In the dry years they cause damage to seedlings to which compost was added as a soil amendment. Millipedes also feed on the bulbs of ornamentals and ripening strawberries. It is recommended that ashes should be added to the infested soil to reduce its moisture. Excelsior or other such materials should be spread and regularly replaced under the strawberry fruits.

Earthworms (*Lumbricidae*)

Earthworms do useful work in the garden by aerating the soil and hastening the decomposition of or-

Sprayers of various types and sizes are available for applying pesticides and disease-combatting solutions.

98

Wireworms, the larvae of click beetles, attack underground parts of plants. They eat the rootlets of seedlings, chew in or through the main roots of established plants and make tunnels in the roots of carrots, celeriacs, the bulbs of tulips and narcissi and tubers of gladioli. They are particularly active in March—June and again in September—October. The picture shows the larva of *Athous hirtus*.

White grubs, the larvae of cockchafers, live in the soil and destroy the underground parts of ornamentals, vegetables, strawberries and fruit trees. Even 1—2 larvae to a square metre of soil can cause much damage.

ganic substances. However, when they overpopulate they loosen the roots of seedlings and the sprouting plants sink underground. Earthworms can be controlled by pouring warm water (40° C) into the soil, but they seldom have to be controlled.

Stem Nematode (*Ditylenchus dipsaci*)
The Stem Nematode is a dangerous pest of onion vegetables and many ornamentals (onion, garlic, narcissus, tulip, hyacinth, pink, carnation, oenothera, phlox, goldenrod). Its occurrence is high in wet years and in beds where the host plants have been grown for several years. The nematode lives in the tissues of plants and sucks their sap, causing growth changes typical of each plant species. The attacked plants remain stunted; they may also develop numerous shoots and some plant parts may swell. The leaves have dead spots and are puckered from the sucking nematodes' feeding on them. Dark (black or brown) rings appear on the cross section through an attacked onion. The eelworm also lives on many weeds and is hard to control. The attacked plants should be destroyed and the soil moisture content reduced. Chemical control will have to be resorted to if these cultural controls fail.

Larvae of bibionid flies (*Bibionidae*)
In some regions, larvae of bibionid flies cause damage in gardens. The female flies lay eggs in compost or in humus-rich soils. Beds and hotbeds where compost with these eggs was added swarm with larvae. In summer they live on the fine rootlets and the remains of decomposing plants. Having overwintered, they attack seedlings. The use of well-ripened compost will help to avoid a mass occurrence of these destructive larvae.

Mole Cricket (*Gryllotalpa gryllotalpa*)
The Mole Cricket is a troublesome soil pest. It cuts the roots or burrows close to the soil surface, thus loosening the young plants. Building its nest of clay at a depth of about 10 cm underground, it exposes the roots of plants above the nest. The location of the nest in the bed or hotbed can be recognized by the local wilting of plants.

The number of Mole Crickets in the garden can be reduced by catching them in smooth-walled containers buried in the soil with the opening on the soil surface. In June and July it is recommended to destroy the Mole Cricket nests.

Bulb Mite (*Rhizoglyphus echinopus*)
The Bulb Mite is a pest that damages the roots, rhizomes, bulbs and tubers of vegetables and ornamentals. It prefers wounded and rotting parts of plants. Bulb Mites bore small irregular tunnels where they leave their tiny brown droppings. Their occurrence is supported by a high humidity. Storing the plants in a dry, airy place provides some control. Chemicals are used when necessary.

Pests of the aerial parts of plants
The aerial parts of plants also have many common pests, each attacking a number of plant species.

Slugs and snails (*Gastropoda*)
The slugs and snails commonly occurring in gardens include the grey garden snails (*Deroceras agreste* and *D. reticulatum*), the Garden Slug (*Arion hortensis*)

Millipedes are active only in damp years, damaging seedlings to which the soil from a compost has been added. They also attack ripening strawberries, which should be protected from below with straw to keep them dry.

and the Grapevine Snail (*Helix pomatia*). The slug *Deroceras laeve* can also be encountered. Gastropods damage both the above- and underground parts of plants. They chew holes in the bulbs of tulips and narcissi, in the tubers of gladioli and other plants. Of the aerial parts, they damage mainly the leaves and stems. Young plants can be completely destroyed by these pests. On leaves their presence can be recognized by the holes chewed from above. Slugs and snails leave silvery trails of slime and dark and sticky faeces around the damaged places.

Slugs and snails can be destroyed mechanically. Lime, wood ashes, conifer needles or chemicals sprinkled on to the paths can also help.

Common Earwig (*Forficula auriculata*)
The Common Earwig is an omnivorous pest of the aerial parts of plants grown in gardens. It feeds on young leaves and stalks and chews flower buds and flowers of dahlias, carnations, roses and some other plants. The feed marks on the leaves have toothed margins. Earwigs also chew inside the ripening fruits of pears, plums, apricots and peaches.

The best control is to lure the earwigs to artificial shelters (straw, rags, bags, excelsior) and then destroy them together with this material.

Red spiders (*Tetranychidae*)
Several species of red spider are serious pests of fruit trees, various vegetables and ornamentals. Red spiders damage the leaves and whole plants by sucking juices from the surface cells. The first sign is yellowing, later the leaves turn white and are shed. In the following year the plants have less flowers and fruits. Red spiders are dangerous pests producing several generations in one year. Intensive chemical control is needed to combat them.

The Common Red Spider occurs most frequently. It feeds on more than 300 plant species. In the garden, it mainly attacks plums, currants, strawberries, raspberries, roses and cucumbers. If attacked, the developing leaves have yellow spots with irregular borders. Red spider mites are most troublesome in June and July, when the fruits ripen. The fruits of the attacked plants are delayed in ripening, their sugar content is reduced and the leaves are shed.

In heavily attacked trees the losses caused by red spiders may be as high as 30—70 per cent. Their flower-setting rate is reduced by up to 75 per cent. In spring the red spiders are not so active but one chemical treatment in spring is more effective than two sprays in summer. The greatest losses are registered when the weather is warm and dry.

Control should be applied before and after flowering. The spring spray against the Fruit-tree Red Spider Mite (*Panonychus ulmi*) should be applied when 60—80 per cent of the larvae are hatched and the chemical used should also kill the eggs.

If a gardener fails to reduce the red spider population below the tolerable level he will have much trouble with his garden in the growing season because during that period all the developmental stages of the pest occur on the leaves, each having a different sensitivity to chemicals. The majority of pesticides used for red spider control fail to kill the summer eggs. These hatch into larvae and the population is quickly restored.

The three principles of protection against red spiders are:
1. Apply the control according to the rate of occurrence of the pest, not at random.
2. Avoid, at least temporarily, using any chemicals that may support the development of the red spiders in gardens where this pest occurs regularly.
3. Use a different chemical for each spray to prevent the pest from developing resistance.

Aphids (*Aphidoidea*)
Many aphid species are harmful in the garden. For instance, vegetables are attacked by the Cabbage Aphid (*Brevicoryne brassicae*), Bulb and Potato Aphid (*Rhopalosiphoninus lathysiphon*), Bean Aphid (*Aphis fabae*), Carrot Aphid (*Cavaraiella aegopodii*) and others, fruit trees and shrubs by the Green Apple Aphid (*Aphis pomi*), Pear Bedstraw Aphid (*Sappaphis piri*), Peach Aphid (*Myzodes persicae*), Leaf-curling Plum Aphid (*Brachycandus helichrysi*), Mealy Plum Aphid (*Hyalopterus pruni*), Cherry Black Aphid (*Myzus cerasi*), Gooseberry Aphid (*Aphis grossulariae*), Red Currant Aphid (*Cryptomyzus ribis*), Raspberry Aphid (*Aphis idaei*), Hop Damson Aphid (*Phorodon humuli*), Woolly Apple Aphid (*Eriosoma lanigerum*) and many others. The best defence against aphids is to prepare a spray of tobacco extract in the following way: seep two packs of tobacco in 3 litres of rainwater for 24 hours, then add $1/2$ kg of washing up liquid, 2 decilitres of vinegar and 2 decilitres of diluted oil.

Thrips (*Thysanoptera*)
Thrips are sucking insects that damage many vegetables and ornamentals. They feed on plant juices. Damage is caused by both adults and larvae.

Butterflies (*Lepidoptera*)
The leaves and sometimes also fruits of fruit trees are attacked by the caterpillars of several species of butterflies. When clear eating marks appear on the trees, geometrids and the Gold-tailed Moth are usually the culprits.

Moths (*Geometridae*)
The caterpillars of the Winter Moth (*Operoptera brumata*) cause damage to cherries, apple-trees, pear-trees, apricots, plums and roses. In spring, they feed on the leaves and flower buds, and later on the fruits also. They chew round holes in the leaf, spread the holes until, step by step, they destroy the whole blade, leaving only the central nerve. In the young fruits the caterpillars make deep oval holes; in this way they can destroy a whole crop of cherries.

Similar damage is caused by the Mottled-umber Moth (*Erannis defoliaria*) but this species tends to be less common.

To control the moths, strips of paper treated with a special paste can be fastened to the trees to prevent the wingless females from creeping to the crowns and laying eggs there.

The Gold-tailed Moth, Gypsy Moth and Common Lackey Moth
In neglected gardens, clearly-visible eating marks on pear-trees, apple-trees and plums are caused by the caterpillars of the Gold-tailed Moth (*Euproctis chrysorrhoea*). At the end of autumn the caterpillars build nests of leaves high in the branches and overwinter there. Cutting and destroying these nests in winter will help to prevent spring damage to the trees. If not killed in winter, the caterpillars leave the nests during the first warm days of spring and chew the buds. Later they destroy the leaves and flowers. One nest per 3 m^2 of crown is enough to cause damage to trees.

Leaf roller moths (*Tortricidae*)
Fruit trees and some ornamental shrubs are hard to protect against leaf roller moths attacking leaves and buds. Apple-trees, pear-trees and plums suffer the greatest damage, apricots and roses are also damaged to an extent. The caterpillars feed on the buds

Slugs and snails destroy the aerial parts of cultivated plants. Their presence is easily betrayed by the silvery slimy paths they leave on the plant parts they have visited — and the gnawed leaves.

in spring, sometimes causing damage as great as 80 per cent to the young trees. Later, they roll the developing leaves, chew holes in leaf blades and feed on flower buds and flowers. The damaged leaves are small, deformed and puckered. The caterpillars of the following summer generation also skeletonize the leaves. They make small dense holes or shallow pits in fruit skin, usually in places where the fruit has been covered with a leaf and its surface could not ripen to full colour. Fruit damaged like this decay and cannot be stored. In some years, leaf roller moths can destroy up to 30 per cent of the fruit.

The most widespread moths of this family occurring in gardens are the Eye-spotted Bud Moth (*Spilonota ocellata*), Codling Moth (*Argyroploce variegata*), and the European Leaf Roller, also called Rose Twist Moth (*Cacoecia rosana*); the species *Pandemis heparana* and *Capua reticulata* can also be encountered.

Leaf mining moths

These moths often occur in large numbers in intensively cultivated gardens. Their caterpillars chew zig-zag tunnels in the leaves of plants. *Lithocolletis blancardella* and the Apple Leaf Miner (*Lyonetia clerkella*) occur at the highest rates. The caterpillars of the Apple Leaf Miner chew oval mines 1—2 cm long and 0.2—0.8 mm wide in the leaves of apple-trees and sometimes also pear-trees and Mountain Ash. Damage is caused when there are more than three such tunnels (mines) in a leaf. Severely attacked trees set far fewer flowers the following year. Chemical spraying two weeks after flowering is recommended to keep these moths in check. In the cases of mass attack, repeat the spray after 7-10 days.

The caterpillars of *Lithocolletis blancardella* make zig-zag tunnels 10—15 cm long in the leaves of apple-trees and cherries in the period from May to September. One leaf may have 10—15 such tunnels. The damaged leaves wilt, dry and fall. Chemical control is recommended only at severe infestation and should be applied during the flight of the second generation.

Nepticulid moths of the species *Stigmella mallela* and *S. mali,* and the Leaf Blotch Moth (*Ornix guttea*) of the family Gracilaridae, also sometimes occur on the leaves of apple-trees.

Wasps (*Rhynchitinae*)

In spring, the buds of apple-trees, cherries and plums are eaten by the adults of the Apple Fruit Wasp (*Coenorrhinus aequatus*) and some other related species. The Apple Fruit Wasp causes the greatest damage. It lays eggs in the fruits which grow irregularly and often decay.

Bark beetles and other bark damaging pests

The pests damaging the bark and wood of the trunk and branches of fruit-trees are not easy to control. The most dangerous are the Apricot Bark Tortrix (*Enarmonia formosana*), European Shot-hole Borer (*Xyleborus dispar*), Fruit Bark Beetle (*Scolytus rugulosus*) and Apple Bark Beetle (*Scolytus mali*).

The Apricot Bark Tortrix feeds on apricots, peaches, cherries and sometimes also plums, apple- and pear-trees. Its caterpillars chew tunnels in the lower layers of the bark. The damaged places can be

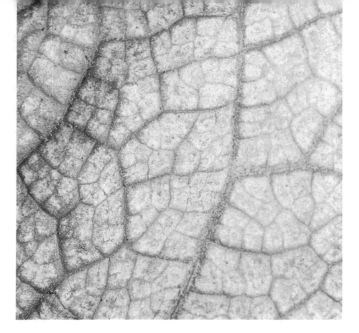

Red spiders suck the sap from the surface cells of plants. The damaged spots turn yellow at first and white later. This lowers the plant's metabolism, increases its transpiration and causes a premature shedding of the leaves. The picture shows an infested cucumber leaf.

recognized by the rusty heaps of droppings which the caterpillars remove from their tunnels.

Bark beetles prefer older trees and the females seek wounds on the trees where they can lay eggs. Mechanical cleaning of the attacked places would worsen the wounds and should therefore be avoided.

Protection against the European Shot-hole Borer which attacks weakened trees is particularly difficult. Prevention is the best control: the trees should be planted in suitable places and provided with adequate nutrition. The leaves of the attacked trees suddenly wilt and their branches become dry. Holes about 1 mm in diameter always appear on the at-

Many aphid species are the pests of garden plants — for instance the Cabbage Aphid, Bean Aphid, Bulb and Potato Aphid, which all destroy numerous vegetable species. The picture shows a damaged sweet pepper plant.

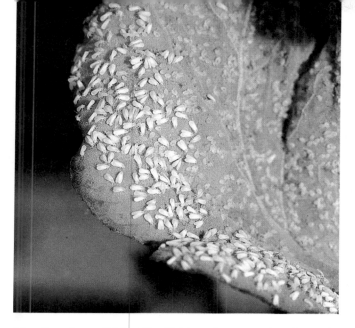

The Greenhouse White Fly (*Trialeurodes vaporariorum*) attacks many greenhouse ornamentals, as well as cucumbers and tomatoes, among other vegetables.

tacked branches. The bark beetles build systems of tunnels only under bark but the tunnels of the European Shot-hole Borer go deep into the wood.

Rodents

Rodents are troublesome pests of fruit trees. Hares and wild rabbits sometimes nibble the bark of trees and the shoots of ornamental shrubs in winter. The trunks of trees can be painted with a repellent for the winter season but wire or reed mats enclosing the trunks are much more effective.

The bark of fruit trees just above soil surface can be nibbled by the Common Vole (*Microtus arvalis*) in autumn and winter in the years of their overpopula-

Caterpillars of the Large White damage particularly members of the family Cruciferae, which they can destroy completely.

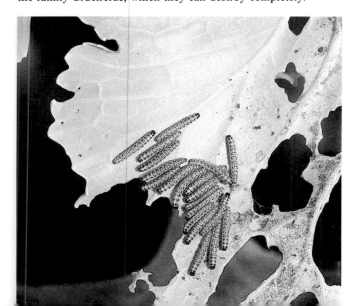

tion. Common Vole also feeds on the bulbs and tubers of ornamental plants. To prevent these damages voles can be killed in their underground holes with smoke or poisoned baits.

The Water Vole (*Arvicola terrestris*) causes damage in gardens next to water courses or waterlogged areas. It cuts the roots of fruit trees and destroys the underground parts of root vegetables and ornamentals. Chemical control mostly fails. It is recommended to put calcium carbide or smoke shells in the holes or to force the vole out with exhaust gases. All these practices should always be repeated after some time. It is advisable before a tree is planted to line the perimeter of the tree well with a galvanized wire net (up to 2 cm mesh) to keep the vole away from the roots.

Birds

Birds, mainly the Common Sparrow and Greenfinch, peck out the flower buds of currants, gooseberries, pear-trees, apricots and peaches in spring. Sparrows also destroy young seedlings of lettuce.

Birds cause greater damage to ripening fruits (mainly berries). Sparrows, Blackbirds, Thrushes and Starlings pick the ripening cherries and the berries of currants and vine grapes. They also peck into ripening pears, apricots, peaches and strawberries. Blackbirds and Thrushes also feast on ripening tomatoes.

Mechanical control is used for the protection of plants against birds. The trees and shrubs can be covered with fine nylon nets. Various noise-making devices or optical aids can be used to frighten the birds and keep them out.

Protection against animal pests

Like diseases, pests are also best controlled by prevention helping to check their occurrence.

The preventive measures include inspection of stored bulbs and tubers, reduction of relative humidity in greenhouses to curb the propagation of mites, ventilation of greenhouses and spraying of plants with water to control red spiders, use of planting material from healthy parent plants to keep down eelworms and the like.

The biology of plants varies and prevention varies with it. The occurrence of some pests can be reduced by the destruction of host plants (usually various weeds). Others can be controlled by the hand picking of the eggs, caterpillars and beetles or the physical removal of insects gathered on baits. Ant-hills in greenhouses can be destroyed with hot water. Reduced soil moisture, or wood ashes, lime, sand or charcoal scattered on the soil's surface will sometimes suffice to control springtails. Quicklime strewn over the paths will check the progress of slugs.

Natural predators can also be used with success in the pest-control efforts. For instance, the beneficial ladybirds and the larvae of hoverflies attack aphids, braconid flies can parasitize caterpillars and the like. Small birds are gardeners' great allies in combating insects. Effective botanical insecticides are available, for example, pyrethrum and nicotine. Chemicals are to be applied as a last resort or if they are the only available means of control.

Protection of stored products

The fruit, vegetables, and bulbs and tubers of ornamentals to be stored should be well-ripened and free of disease and damage. An injured place is an open invitation to fungal and bacterial infection.

Various decay-producing organisms usually penetrate the store via material already infested during the growing season. Therefore, as soon as fruit and vegetables are put in the store the conditions inside the store should be adjusted to hinder the penetration of fungi and bacteria. The majority of the products can be stored at a temperature of 2—5° C and relative humidity of 85—90 per cent. If humidity is below 80 per cent much water is lost from the roots and fleshy fruits. On the other hand, humidity above 90 per cent leads to a rapid spreading of fungi and, particularly, putrefactive bacteria. Ventilation and humidity control will help.

Before the bulbs, fruit and vegetables are stored, the store (usually a cellar) should be thoroughly disinfected, for example, by sulphurization (8 g of sulphur burned in a cubic metre of space). All door and window chinks or gaps must be blocked and metallic objects greased before sulphurization. The walls should be painted with lime or sprinkled with 5 per cent formalin. The shelves, internal window frames and inside of the door should be treated in the same way. The store should be ventilated thoroughly after 24 hours. The tubers and bulbs of ornamentals also have to be treated before storage.

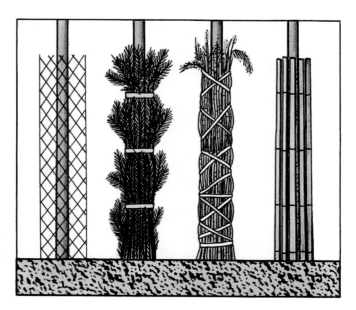

Where animals may damage fruit or ornamental trees and shrubs by feeding on them, it is necessary to take some preventive measures. The picture suggests several methods of trunk protection.

When selecting the healthy material to be stored, the greatest attention should be paid to root vegetables, onions, garlic, potatoes and pip-fruit because these cannot be chemically treated. Potatoes, fruit and onions should be stored in a thin layer; it is advisable to avoid piling them. Onions and garlic should be kept in a dry place where temperatures can fall even below 0° C.

It is important during storage to inspect regularly and remove all decaying or half-rotten fruit, bulbs or tubers. Also, avoid keeping them in store overlong; this will curb the propagation of the causal agents of store rots.

Flea beetles attack mostly young plants and, if the weather is dry and warm, can destroy them completely. Regular watering is the best prevention.

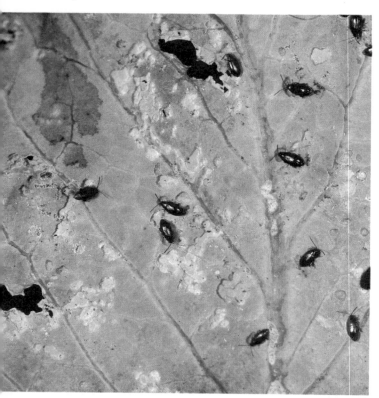

104

A survey of diseases and pests of the individual plant groups and genera

VEGETABLES

Disease, pest	Causal agent	Symptoms	Control
Brassicas (the same diseases and pests also attack radishes)			
Damping off of seedlings	parasitic fungi	tissue of root neck blackened or wrinkled, the plant dries and dies	soil disinfection, ventilation of glasshouses and hotbeds, proper spacing
Club root	*Plasmodiophora brassicae*	tumours of different sizes on roots, conspicuous dwarfing of above-ground parts	reduction of soil acidity, soil disinfection before sowing, destruction of attacked plants, removal of weedy brassicas
Downy mildew of cabbage	*Peronospora brassicae*	Light, irregular blotches of different sizes on leaves, a tinge of mould on the underside, leaves darken and die	thin spacing during pre-cultivation and/or suitable chemical control
Flea beetles	*Phyllotreta* sp.	feed marks, sometimes completely destroyed plants	timely chemical control
Large White Butterfly	*Pieris brassicae*	caterpillars eat leaf blades, leaving bare nerves	physical destruction of eggs, chemical control in cases of a mass occurrence of caterpillars
Diamond Back Moth	*Plutella maculipennis*	the caterpillars skeletonize leaves	mechanical destruction of eggs, chemical control during a high occurrence of caterpillars
Cabbage Maggot (Cabbage Root Fly)	*Phorbia brassicae*	larvae feed on young roots and epidermis of root neck, later destroy the whole root system	preparation of soil for pre-cultivation, chemical control at mass attack
Cabbage Aphid	*Brevicoryne brassicae*	leaves deformed by sucking, spread of virus diseases	spraying with tobacco extract
Root vegetables			
Celery leaf spot	*Septoria apiigraveolentis*	irregular yellow-brown spots, later the leaves die	appropriate crop rotation, soil disinfection for seedling pre-cultivation, seed disinfection
Browning of heart and inner tissue in celery stalks	boron deficiency in soil	grey-brown tissue portions inside the stalks	fertilization at a balanced nutrient ratio, addition of boron
Carrot Aphid	*Semiaphis dauci*	damage caused by larvae, heart leaves are curled, the plants stunted	spray with tobacco extract
Carrot blight	*Stemphylium radicinum*	infected places are dark and smelly, disease spreads deeper to kill whole roots	crop rotation, seed disinfection
Carrot Fly (Carrot Rusty Fly)	*Psila rosae*	larvae chew irregular tunnels in carrot and celery roots, pest also develops in stored roots, causing secondary rotting	chemical control after emergence of seedlings
Wireworms, grubs		wireworms chew tunnels, grubs nibble the surface of roots	baiting, mechanical killing
Leafy and salad vegetables			
Downy mildew of lettuce	*Bremia lactucae*	light-yellow patches on lettuce leaves, enlarging to cover whole leaves, white downy mould on the underside	soil disinfection, intensive ventilation of frames
Drop of lettuce	*Botrytis cinerea* and *Sclerotinia minor*	rotting of root neck	soil disinfection
Leaf mould of spinach	*Peronospora effusa*	yellow spots on leaves, greyish mouldy covering on the underside	appropriate crop rotation, thinner spacing
Wireworms	*Elateridae*	attack mainly lettuce	baiting, mechanical killing
Bulb vegetables			
Onion yellow dwarf	*Allium virus*	yellow stripes on onion leaves, later the leaves droop	the affected plants should be consumed first
Blight of onions (downy mildew of onions, mould of onions)	*Peronospora destructor*	pale yellow spots on onion leaves and flower stems, later a grey covering of mould, the attacked tissue dies	chemical control
White rot of onion	*Sclerotinia cepivorum*	attacks garlic, shallot and leek, gradual yellowing of leaves and dying of plants	avoid waterlogged soils, disinfect garlic before planting
Fruit vegetables			
Tomatoes			
Tomato mosaic	*Nicotiana virus* 1	irregular light green spots on leaves	destruction of attacked plants, soil disinfection, disinfection of hands and tools
Late blight of potato	*Phytophtora infestans*	the fungus affects leaves, stems and fruits, first small grey-green patches which quickly spread, the sick tissue is dark and brown, surface is wrinkled	chemical control

105

Disease, pest	Causal agent	Symptoms	Control
Tomato leaf spot	*Septoria lycopersici*	irregular grey spots with darker margin	chemical control
Aphids	*Aphidoidea*	damage by sucking	spraying with tobacco extract
Root knot nematode	*Meloidogyne hapla*		soil disinfection
Dry spot of capsicum	irregular water supply	yellowish spots on fruit, later the spots are darker with distinct margins, fruits are secondarily attacked by micro-organisms	regular and frequent watering

Cucumbers

Disease, pest	Causal agent	Symptoms	Control
Cucumber mosaic	*Cucumis virus* 1	irregular mosaic colouring of leaves, the plants are stunted	control the same as in other virus dieseases
Angular leaf spot of cucumber	*Pseudomonas lacrymans*	bacteria attack leaves, stems, flowers and fruits, oily spots and tear-like drops on leaf underside are formed, containing large amounts of bacteria	chemical control
Scab of cucurbits	*Cladosporium cucumerinum*	attacks fruits, leaves and stems, sunk necrotic spots with gummosis, fungus coating covers the spots in wet conditions	destruction of attacked parts, soil disinfection, seed disinfection
Powdery mildew	*Erysiphe polygoni*	white coatings, later becoming compact	chemical control
Wilting of cucumber plants	*Sclerotinia sclerotiniorum, Fusarium oxysporum, Fusarium solani, Verticillium albo-atrum*	fungi attack vascular bundles which turn brown, get choked, and the plants wilt	soil disinfection
Seed-corn Maggot	*Phorbia platura*	larvae attack sprouting seeds	seed disinfection
Red Spider Mite	*Tetranychus urticae*	sucks on the underside of leaves, attacked leaves yellow and dry	chemical control
White flies and aphids	*Aleurodoidea Aphidoidea*	curling and drying of attacked leaves, insects leave excrements on the underside of leaves, secondary infestation with saprophytic scab	spraying with tobacco extract

Pulses

Disease, pest	Causal agent	Symptoms	Control
Fusariosis—premature dying of plants	*Fusarium* sp.	Fusarium germs are both in and on seeds, the attacked plants die	seed disinfection
Leaf, stem and pod rot, Ascochyta blight	*Colletotrichum ascochyta*	the attacked above-ground parts of plants have numerous brown spots	seed disinfection
Seed-corn Maggot	*Phorbia platura*	larvae attack sprouting seeds	seed disinfection
Red spiders, Bean Aphid, Pea Aphid	*Tetranychidae, Aphis fabae, Acyrtosiphon pisum*	above-ground parts of plants damaged by sucking	spraying with tobacco extract
Pea and Bean Thrips	*Kakothrips pisivorus*	sucks sap from flowers, young shoots, pods, the flowers turn dry and fall, attacked pods are deformed	chemical control
Pea Midge	*Contrarinia pisi*	larvae eat inside soft grains, pods are deformed with cottony lining inside	chemical control applied at flowering time

Potatoes

Disease, pest	Causal agent	Symptoms	Control
Leaf roll, Mosaic, Streak of potatoes	*Viruses*	leaves rolling upwards into a boat-like shape, plants have broom-like appearance, leaves irregularly coloured, deformed, curled, necrotic spots on leaves, brown-black lines on leaves and petioles	timely removal of attacked plants, use of healthy potatoes for planting

FRUIT PLANTS

Strawberry

Disease, pest	Causal agent	Symptoms	Control
Common grey mould	*Botrytis cinerea*	brown spots on fruits, later whole fruits turn brown, with fructiferous covering	timely destruction of attacked fruits, chemical control
Strawberry Blossom Beetle	*Anthonomus rubi*	beetle lays eggs in flower bud, chews its stem, larvae develop in the flower buds which later drop	chemical control at opening time
Strawberry Mite	*Steneotarsonemus fragariae*	larvae and adults damage leaves and inflorescences, leaves turn olive-green, young leaves are stunted, some of them turn brown	runners taken only from healthy plants, burning of heavily attacked plants, rotation of sites, runners dipped 30 minutes in water at 43° C before planting
Strawberry Nematode	*Aphelenchoides fragariae*	delayed growth, a small number of fruits set	removal of attacked plants, exclusive use of healthy material for propagation, chemical control
Stem Nematode	*Ditylenchus dipsaci*	damages above-ground parts of plants and retards growth, leaves are curled, margins bent downwards	chemical control

Disease, pest	Causal agent	Symptoms	Control
Raspberry, bramble			
Raspberry rust	*Phragmidium rubi-idaei*	leaves yellow, later with browning spots, rusty brown dots of spores on the underside of leaves	picking of affected leaves, timely removal of old canes
Raspberry Stem Gall Midge	*Thomasiniana theobaldi*	larvae damage shoots up to 80 cm above ground, dark brown spots, loose bark, shoots turn dry, plant prone to infection	cutting of canes below the place of attack
Currant and gooseberry			
Anthracnose of currants	*Drepanopeziza ribis*	yellow, later blackening spots on leaves and flower stems at flowering time, fruit clusters are coarse, attacked leaves soon drop	thorough raking and destruction of leaves, cutting of old canes
	Incurvaria capitella	in spring, caterpillars feed inside currant buds	chemical control
Leaf Midge, Red Currant Aphid	*Dasyneura tetensi* *Cryptomyzus ribis*	damage by sucking the leaves on the tops of shoots, the number of flower buds set is low	spraying with tobacco extract
	Thomasiniana ribis	larvae live under the bark of branches; in attacked spots the bark is dark and dead, damaged shoots weaken and dry	cutting of attacked shoots
Apple-trees			
Twig blight of apple	*Erwinia amylovora*	petals turn brown to black, remain on branches, later the branches and whole tree turn brown	2 per cent formalin treatment, felling of trees, disinfection of soil around attacked tree with 2 per cent formalin
Powdery mildew of apple	*Podosphaera leucotricha*	flour-like coating of leaves and shoots, buds small, mycelium dies at —25°C	late winter pruning to remove all attacked shoots, chemical control
Nectria canker	*Nectria galligena*	canker wounds and swellings	cutting of affected branches, chemical control
Brown rot and spur canker of apple	*Sclerotinia fructigena*	concentric cushions of spore cases on fruits	control of insects (wasps, flies)
Green Apple Aphid and other aphids	*Aphis pomi,* *Rhopalosiphon incertum,* *Dysaphis plantaginea*	damage by sucking	spraying with tobacco extract
Pear-trees			
Pear scab	*Venturia pirina*	attacks all above-ground organs, fruits completely spoilt by spots, tree bark cracked	chemical control
Pear rust	*Gymnosporangium sabinae*	orange-red spots on leaves	destruction of intermediate hosts— savin, juniper
	Psylla pyri	larvae suck sap from leaf and flower buds, later from leaves, flowers and fruits, flowers drop	chemical control
Pear psyllid	*Psylla pyrisuga*	larvae and adults suck sap from leaves, greatest damage caused to the top parts of shoots	chemical control
Pear Leaf Curling Midge	*Contarinia pirivora*	larvae cause leaf rolling	chemical control
Pear Midge	*Dasyneura piri*	larvae feed inside the set fruits; after some time the pears blacken and crack	chemical control
Plums			
Plum pockets	*Taphrina pruni*	fruit deformation	removal of attacked fruits, chemical control
Plum witches' broom, Cherry witches' broom	*Taphrina insititiae,* *Taphrina cerasi*	unrestrained twiggy growth resembling a bird's nest	removal of the brooms, chemical control
Hop Aphid, Mealy Plum Aphid, Leaf-curling Plum Aphid	*Phorodon humuli,* *Hyalopterus pruni,* *Brachycaudus helichrysi*	the aphids suck on buds, leaves and young shoots, and spread virus diseases	spray with tobacco extract
Plum Sawfly	*Haplocampa minuta,* *H. flava*	larvae feed inside fruits	chemical control
Cherries			
shot-hole disease (gum spot disease)	*Clasterosporium carpophilum*	round spots on leaves with orange-red to red margin, turning black at the end; the tissue inside dies from above and falls out, brown-red spots on fruits, fruits completely spoilt	adjustment of soil pH (liming), chemical control
Cherry leaf scorch	*Gnomonia erythrostoma*	leaves covered with yellow to orange spots, dark fruiting bodies of the fungus on the underside of leaves, spots on fruits, fruits drop	adjustment of soil pH (liming), chemical control

Disease, pest	Causal agent	Symptoms	Control
Cherry Black Aphid	*Myzus cerasi*	aphids suck on shoots whose growth is then disordered; at mass attack the growing points dry	spray with tobacco extract

Apricots

Disease, pest	Causal agent	Symptoms	Control
Apricot Bark Tortrix	*Enarmonia formosana*	caterpillars chew the cambium of thicker branches and stem	chemical control

Peaches

Disease, pest	Causal agent	Symptoms	Control
Peach leaf curl	*Taphrina deformans*	first small blister-like spots on leaves, spreading to cover whole leaf blade; the whole leaf is curled and light red in colour, affected branches are delayed in growth	chemical control
Peach scab	*Venturia cerasi*	brownish spots on leaves, olive-green spots on fruits, fruits remain dwarf and drop	chemical control
Green Peach Aphid	*Myzodes persicae*	in spring it damages leaves and shoots by sucking, leaves turn yellow and are shed; the pest spreads virus diseases	spray with tobacco extract

Walnuts

Disease, pest	Causal agent	Symptoms	Control
Walnut blight	*Xanthomonas juglandis*	small brown spots on leaves, enlarging to merge, the leaves die and drop; dripping spots on fruits, later the inner tissue of the fruit is also destroyed	chemical control
Leaf blotch of walnut	*Gnomonia leptostyla*	yellow spots on leaves which enlarge and turn brown, the centre of the spots is lighter than the margins; young fruits are also attacked	removal of fallen leaves, chemical control
European Walnut Aphid, Dusky Veined Walnut Aphid	*Chromaphis juglandicola, Calaphis juglandis*	damage leaves and sometimes also green fruits by sucking; the leaves drop, fruit quality worsens	spray with tobacco extract

Hazels

Disease, pest	Causal agent	Symptoms	Control
Hazel-nut Gall Mite	*Phytoptus avellanae*	larvae and adults suck leaf and flower buds, flowers dry at flowering time; hazels grow irregularly and the number of fruits set is low	chemical control
Hazel-nut Weevil	*Curculio nucum*	larvae chew the kernel and cause 'worminess' of hazel-nuts	chemical control, picking and destruction of attacked fruits

Grapevines

Disease, pest	Causal agent	Symptoms	Control
Bacterial gall (crown gall)	*Agrobacterium tumefaciens*	leaves turn yellow (those of blue varieties turn red), starting in summer; root development is retarded	balanced nutrition, planting vines at uncontaminated sites, use of physiological fertilizers
Downy mildew of grape	*Plasmophora viticola*	first signs: 'oily' spots on leaves, sometimes the disease involves a whole leaf and also fruits; later the spots turn yellow and brown, fruits dry and brown and finally become completely mummified	chemical control
Grape mildew (Powdery mildew of grapevine)	*Uncinula necator*	whitish spots scattered on leaves, looking as if covered with flour; attacked grapes fail to ripen, berries break open, showing pulp with seeds	chemical control
Common grey mould	*Botrytis cinerea*	the attacked grapes turn brown, become soft and easily break; a grey coating appears on the surface	removal of leaves, timely cutting and destruction of affected shoots, chemical control
Grape Berry Moth, Vine Moth	*Conchylis ambignella, Polychrosis botrana*	first-generation caterpillars gnaw buds and inflorescences; second-generation caterpillars feed in the berries	chemical control

ORNAMENTALS

Genus	Disease, pest	Causal agent	Symptoms	Control
Perennials				
Alyssum	Finger-and-toe disease	*Plasmodiophora brassicae*	tumours of different size on root system, aerial parts wilt	destruction of attacked plants, soil disinfection
	Downy mildew	*Peronospora galligena*	pale spots on upper sides of leaves, whitish mouldy coating on the underside	destruction of attacked plants, chemical control
Aquilegia	Powdery mildew	*Erysiphe polygoni*	vhitish powdery coating on the surface of attacked organs	chemical control

Genus	Disease, pest	Causal agent	Symptoms	Control
	Aphids		above-ground organs are damaged by sucking	spray with tobacco extract
Aster	Verticilluim wilt	Verticillium albo-atrum	abrupt yellowing of leaves, wilting and death of plant	planting in uncontaminated soil, chemical control
	Powdery mildew of crucifers	Erysiphe cichoriacearum	whitish powdery coatings on the surface of attacked plants	chemical control
Campanula	Stalk break	Sclerotinia sclerotiniorum	rotting of the stems and wilting of the plants	soil disinfection, removal of affected parts, chemical control
Chrysanthemum	Wilting	Verticillium albo-atrum	Browning and necrosis of vascular bundles seen on longitudinal section, infection from contaminated soil	soil disinfection, chemical control
	Powdery mildew	Oidium chrysanthemi	Whitish coatings	chemical control
	Rust	Puccinia chrysanthemi	spots on the upper side of leaves; when tissue breaks, spores are released	removal of infected parts, destruction of intermediate hosts, chemical control
	Septoria leaf spot	Septoria chrysanthemella	first small yellowish spots; the spots spread, merge, turn brown to black	chemical control
	Ascochyta blight	Ascochyta chrysanthemi	attacks leaves, stems and flowers—dark spots	removal and burning of attacked plants, chemical control
	Common grey mould	Botrytis cinerea	damages leaves, shoots, buds, flowers, fruits—small grey-brown spots, later covered with powdery spores	good cultural conditions, chemical control
	Moths	Mamestra brassicae, Scotia sp.	caterpillars chew on the root neck and roots	chemical control
Delphinium	Bacterial leaf spot	Pseudomonas delphinii	irregular black glossy spots on leaves, petioles, stems and flowers	destruction of attacked plants, chemical control
	Powdery mildew	Erysiphe polygoni	whitish powdery coatings on the surface of attacked plants	destruction of attacked plants, chemical control
	Silver Moth	Plusia moneta	caterpillars feed on the top leaves	mechanical destruction, chemical control
Doronicum	Fern Nematode	Aphelenchoides olesistus	angular, translucent glass-like spots, gradually yellowing and blackening	destruction of attacked plants, chemical control, soil disinfection
Helenium	Septoria leaf spot	Septoria sp.	grey-brown spots with dark red or reddish margin on leaves, dark fruiting bodies inside the spots	chemical control
	Alternaria leaf spot	Alternaria sp.	small circular or irregular spots on leaf blades, sunken spots on stems, petioles and leaf nerves	seed disinfection, chemical protection of plants
Helianthus	Stalk break and plant wilt	Sclerotinia sclerotiniorum	rotting of the stalks and wilting of the plants	soil disinfection, removal of attacked parts, chemical control
	Powdery mildew of crucifers	Erysiphe cichoriacearum	whitish powdery coatings on attacked parts of plants	chemical control
	Sunflower rust	Puccinia helianthi	small spots on upper side of leaves, tissue breaks and powdery spores appear	removal of attacked parts, destruction of intermediate hosts, chemical control
Helleborus	Peronospora	Peronospora pulveracea	light-coloured spots on the upper side of leaves, whitish coating of mould on the underside	destruction of attacked parts, chemical control
Lupinus		Sitona griseus	semicircular feedmarks on the margin of leaves, almost clear eating at a high occurrence	chemical control
Paeonia	Bacterial gall (root knot)	Agrobacterium tumefaciens	tissue hypertrophy, tumours, the plant is weakened and dies	optimum growing conditions, chemical control
	Stem base rotting	Sclerotinia sclerotiniorum	stem rot and wilting of the plants	soil disinfection, disinfection of planting material, chemical control
	Wilting	Verticillium albo-atrum	Browning and necrosis of vascular bundles seen on longitudinal section, leaf yellowing, wilting	soil disinfection, disinfection of planting material, chemical control
	Stem and bud rot	Botrytis paeoniae	wilting of new shoots, browning and necrosis of buds, spots on leaves and stems in summer	good cultural conditions, chemical control
	Leaf mould	Cladosporium paeoniae	purple-brown spots	burning of old leaves
	Ring spot	Paeonia ring spot virus	irregular yellow spots and rings	removal and burning of infected plants, disinfection of tools

109

Genus	Disease, pest	Causal agent	Symptoms	Control
Phlox	Powdery mildew of crucifers	*Erysiphe cichoriacearum*	whitish powdery coatings on the surface of the attacked parts	chemical control
Primula	Root rot	*Thielaviopsis basicola*	blackening and rot of roots	removal of attacked plants, chemical control
	Common grey mould	*Botrytis cinerea*	damages leaves, shoots, flower buds, flowers and fruits, grey-brown spots covered with powdery spores	good growing conditions, chemical control
	Rusts	*Puccinia primulae, Uromyces primulae*	light-coloured spots full of shining spores, the attacked parts die	removal of attacked parts, removal of intermediate hosts, chemical control
	Leaf spot	*Ramularia primulae*	grey drying spots, hoary coating on the underside of leaves	chemical control
Rudbeckia	Powdery mildew of crucifers	*Erysiphe cichoriacearum*	whitish powdery coating on the surface of attacked parts	chemical control
	Peronospora	*Peronospora halstedii*	pale spots, whitish coating of mould on the underside of leaves	destruction of attacked parts of plants, chemical control
	Leaf spot	*Ramularia* sp., *Septoria rudbeckiae, Phyllosticta rudbeckiae*	spots on leaves	chemical control
Solidago	Powdery mildew of peas and clover	*Erysiphe polygoni*	whitish powdery coating on the surface of attacked organs	chemical control
Veronica	Peronospora	*Peronospora grisea*	pale spots, whitish mouldy coating on the underside of leaves	destruction of attacked parts, chemical control

Annuals and biennials

Genus	Disease, pest	Causal agent	Symptoms	Control
Callistephus chinensis	Wilting and damping off of plants, blackening of root necks	*Fusarium oxysporum, F. callistephi, F. culmorum, F. lateritium*	plants wilt, root necks and stem bases blacken	crop rotation, removal of attacked plants, soil disinfection, seed disinfection
Begonia semperflorens	Bacterial blight	*Xanthomonas begoniae*	yellowish translucent spots on leaves, leaves turn brown and die	soil disinfection, chemical control
	Common grey mould	*Botrytis cinerea*	grey-brown spots, in wet weather covered with grey-brown dusty coating, affects leaves, flowers, fruits	good growing conditions, chemical control
Zinnia	Stem rot	*Sclerotinia sclerotiniorum*	rot of stems and wilting of the plants	crop rotation, destruction of attacked plants, chemical control
	Alternaria spot disease	*Alternaria* sp.	spots on attacked organs	seed disinfection, chemical control
Cheiranthus	Bacterial wilt	*Xanthomonas campestris*	small yellowish spots ('oil fleck'), later wilting of the plants	chemical control
	Downy mildew	*Peronospora cheiranthi*	pale spots on the upper side, whitish coating of mould on the underside of leaves, the plant dies	chemical control
	Finger-and-toe disease	*Plasmodiophora brassicae*	plants stop growing and turn yellow; tumours on roots	removal of attacked plants, crop rotation, soil disinfection
	Large White Butterfly	*Pieris brassicae*	caterpillars feed on leaves	mechanical destruction of eggs
	Flea beetles	*Phyllotreta* sp.	beetles eat emerging and emerged plants	chemical control
Antirrhinum	Downy mildew	*Peronospora antirrhini*	light-coloured spots on upper side of leaves, whitish coating of mould on the underside	chemical control
	Rust	*Puccinia antirrhini*	small, pale green spots on leaves, stems, sepals and pods	removal of infected parts, destruction of intermediate hosts, chemical control
Lathyrus	Wilt	*Verticillium albo-atrum*	abrupt yellowing and wilting of leaves, the plants die (browning of vascular bundles is seen on longitudinal section)	appropriate growing methods, removal and destruction of attacked plants, soil disinfection
	Powdery mildew	*Erysiphe martii*	whitish dusty coatings on the surface of attacked plants	removal of attacked plant parts, good growing conditions
	Common grey mould	*Botrytis cinerea*	damages whole plants, small spots, quickly spreading and covered with a layer of powdery spores	good growing conditions, chemical control
Dianthus	Fusarium blight, Damping off, Black leg	*Fusarium oxysporum, F. dianthi, F. culmorum*	wilting, damping off of plants, blackening of stem bases	appropriate growing methods, removal and destruction of attacked plants, soil disinfection
	Rusts	*Puccinia arenariae, Puccinia dianthi*	pale green to yellowish spots on underside of leaves, tissue cracks to release spores	removal of infested plants, destruction of intermediate hosts, chemical control

Genus	Disease, pest	Causal agent	Symptoms	Control
	Carnation Maggot	*Phorbia brunescens*	leaves wilt and rot, shoots die, tunnels in the lower part of leaves and in stem	chemical control
Viola	Downy mildew	*Peronospora violacea*	pale spots on upper side of leaves, whitish mouldy covering on the underside; plants wilt and die	chemical control
	Rust	*Puccinia violae*	pale green to yellowish spots on upper leaf side, in the spots the tissue cracks to release spores	removal of infested parts, destruction of intermediate hosts, chemical control
Papaver	Downy mildew	*Peronospora arborescens*	pale spots on upper side of leaves, whitish mouldy covering on the underside	chemical control
Calendula	Leaf spot	*Entyloma calendulae*	circular yellow-green to grey-brown spots with dark margin, tissue drops out; leaves are perforated and die	chemical control
	Powdery mildew	*Sphaerotheca fuliginea*	whitish powdery covering on the surface of attacked organs	removal of attacked parts of plants, appropriate growing methods, chemical control
Myosotis	Downy mildew	*Peronospora myosotidis*	pale spots on upper side of leaves, whitish mouldy coating on the underside; plants wilt and die	chemical control
	Powdery mildew	*Erysiphe horridula*	whitish powdery coating on the upper side of attacked organs	removal of attacked parts of plants, appropriate growing methods, chemical control
Helichrysum	Common grey mould	*Botrytis cinerea*	small spots on leaves, dots on flowers; plant dies	good growing conditions, chemical control
Althaea	Hollyhock rust	*Puccinia malvacearum*	brown heaps of spores on leaves and stems; leaves die	removal of infested parts, destruction of intermediate hosts, chemical control
Salvia	Aphids and red spiders		plants damaged by sucking	spray with tobacco extract

Roses

Genus	Disease, pest	Causal agent	Symptoms	Control
	Bark necrosis	*Coniothyrium wernsdorffiae*	small reddish spots on bark which grow to form grey-brown bands of dead tissue; branches die	appropriate winter cover, its timely removal; chemical control
Stems and branches	Red Bud Borer	*Thomasiniana oculiperda*	larvae suck juice from tissues, chew tunnels in tissues; buds blacken and die	removal of attacked parts of plants with larvae, chemical control
Leaves	Non-parasitic chlorosis	excess liming, unbalanced fertilization, excessive salt concentration in soil	gradual yellowing of leaves	adjustment of soil conditions
	Rose mildew	*Sphaerotheca pannosa*	white powdery coatings on leaves	removal of attacked parts, chemical control, planting of resistant cultivars
	Black spot of roses	*Diplocarpon rosae*	dark brown to red-violet spots with fine radial margin, shoots and flowers can also be attacked	planting of resistant cultivars, chemical control
	Rose smut	*Phragmidium mucronatum*	yellowish or reddish spots, powdery heaps of spores on the underside	removal of infested parts, destruction of intermediate hosts, growing of resistant cultivars
Flowers	Common grey mould	*Botrytis cinerea*	damages flower stems, the parts above the attacked place wilt and die	proper growing conditions, chemical control

Weeds

Hearing this word, many a gardener feels pain in his back, remembering the many hours spent in a bent position, trying to rid his garden of invasive weeds. But the problem should be judged objectively. The plants called 'weeds' include many medicinal species, that is, plants which in fact serve man — or could serve, if they were used.

Weeds also add organic matter to compost and sometimes are the only available substitute for manure. The appearance of weeds in a garden can also tell us much about the quality of the soil.

If the principles of good gardening practices are respected, weeds can be kept under control without much effort. The siting and volume of the crops grown should realistically relate to the size of the garden, and should allow the gardener to remove weeds by hand.

However, sometimes it happens that a gardener is only able to manage weeds in spring but not in summer when he has a lot of other work to do. Neglected weeds then spread everywhere and their seeds get on to the beds and even into the compost heap. Coltsfoot occupies the rockery; roses, currant and fences are overgrown with Field Bindweed; the corners of the garden are full of Stinging Nettles. Paths and lawns harbour Couch-grass and weeds with creeping vegetative organs (Creeping Cinquefoil, Creeping Buttercup, Ground Ivy and others). Lawns are also a good environment for Common Dandelion and broadleaved docks to thrive.

Before resorting to the final solution — chemical control — a gardener must be sure that he has done his best to remove all weeds by other, less drastic means:
- Thorough hoeing and weeding.
- Efficient rotation of the crops (vegetables with legumes, lawn, sweetcorn, potatoes and the like).
- Reduction of the sources of weed infestation (the weed already settling into lawns, paths or beds).

Before a rockery is built, all perennial weeds should have been removed from the site (Field Thistle, Couch-grass and others) and before a compost is established, be sure that the site is free also from Common Horsetail, Field Thistle, Field Bindweed and all other deep-rooting weeds which can easily grow through the compost. Ensure also that there is no nearby source of Couch-grass which can easily send its rhizomes towards the compost.

If you apply systematic and regular mechanical weed control it really should be unnecessary to have to resort to chemicals.

Garden weeds

For thorough weed control in the garden it will be useful to classify weeds into biologically related groups, irrespective of the botanical system. Thus weeds can be divided into:

Annuals
—winter
—early spring
—late spring

Perennials
— with a prevailing generative (seed) reproduction pattern

The Dandelion (*Taraxacum officinale*) is one of the perennial weeds. It is an unwelcome visitor in gardens and particularly in lawns.
Preventive measures such as eradication of its sources, care of the purity of sowing material and rotation of crops must all be used if it is to be eliminated.

It pays to learn how to recognize weeds in their very early stages of development. Their timely elimination spares lots of future work. The picture shows a young Stinging Nettle (*Urtica urens*).

113

— with a prevailing vegetative reproduction pattern; these are subdivided into the shallow-rooting and deep-rooting species.

Annual winter weeds

This group comprises short-lived weeds (Ivy-leaved Speedwell, Early Speedwell, Whitlow-grass, Jagged Chickweed) which have a short growing season and ripen in the winter season or early in spring. It also includes species which have a very short growing season but are able to grow and finish their development in any season of the year. These are classified as the 'wintering species' (Shepherd's Purse, Field Penny-cress, Chickweed, Purple Deadnettle, Annual Meadow-grass, Persian Speedwell, Common Groundsel, Wild Pansy and others). The winter weeds also include species wintering as germinating plants and finishing their development only in summer, for example, Common Stork's-bill, Small-flowered Geranium, Canadian Fleabane, Common Fumitory, Fool's Parsley, Common Nipplewort and the like.

Winter weeds are troublesome in perennial and wintering crops (strawberries, lawns, perennial flowers), and wintering weeds also infest vegetables. To control such weeds, a gardener has to prevent them from fruiting and dispersing their seeds.

Annual early spring weeds

These weeds sprout very early in spring (weeds emerging in autumn are usually damaged by frost) and are not very dangerous in gardens. This applies to Wild Mustard, White Charlock, Hemp-nettle and Climbing Buckwheat, that is, typical field weeds which are seldom left to spread in gardens. More trouble is caused by the Comon Pimpernel, Knotgrass, Annual Nettle and some other weeds which are able to sprout all the year round.

Annual late spring weeds

Weeds of this group germinate at higher soil temperatures and occur typically in vegetable beds. Having a short growing season, they readily spread over the thinned rows of vegetables during vegetation. They produce large quantities of seeds or fruits on a plant. Their seeds remain viable for a long time and constitute, in fact, the largest proportion of the weed seeds in the soil. This group includes Annual Mercury, Yellow Foxtail, Green Foxtail, Barnyard Grass, Orache, Black Nightshade, Dungweed, Common Annual Sow-thistle, Sun Spurge, Persicaria and Redshank. A well coordinated series of gardening practices is needed to control the weeds of this group.

Perennial weeds with prevailing generative (seed) reproduction

These are typical weeds of lawns and paths, and beds where perennial crops are grown. They include

The Bindweed (*Convolvulus arvensis*) is a pretty but stubborn perennial weed, producing numerous root suckers. It is combated by deep digging and by cultivating other plants which form a dense ground cover.

Common Dandelion, Biennial Hawk's Beak, biennial Wild Carrot, Narrow-leaved Dock, Broad-leaved Dock and other dock species, White Campion, Lance-leaved Plantain and other weeds.

They usually get into the garden via poorly cleaned seeds of grasses or from the weed sources already present in and aroud the garden.

Prevention (clean seeds, destruction of weed sources), crop rotation and good gardening practices are the best controls.

Perennial shallow-rooting weeds with prevailing vegetative reproduction

This group comprises weeds with creeping rooting stems — Creeping Cinquefoil, Silver Cinquefoil, Ground Ivy, Creeping Buttercup, Creeping Wood-sorrel and the like.

Weeds of this group are troublesome in the garden because they have a comparatively high resistance to cultural control and even herbicides. They also have a high regenerating capacity throughout the growing season. They spread on to beds from the paths. To control them, the foci have to be localized and destroyed (both mechanically and chemically) and crops that have a short growing season and form dense stands should be grown.

The species with strong and hard offshoots include Couch-grass, Perennial Nettle, Velvet Bent-grass and German Velvet-grass. The most reliable control is hand weeding, with thorough removal of all roots.

The species with soft and crisp offshoots include Marsh Betony and Field Mint. They usually occur in damp places. Betony and mint cannot grow well in frequently loosened soil (mainly in drier weather); hence crop rotation and soil loosening are good practices to control weeds of this group.

Some of these weeds have bulbs or tubers, for example, Groundnut Peavine, Orpine and Creeping Bellflower. They prefer dry sites and are vulnerable to crop rotation.

Perennial deep-rooting weeds with prevailing vegetative reproduction

These are the hardiest weeds of all. They can only be controlled by deep soil cultivation and, particularly, by growing suitable crops (annuals that can be relied upon to form a dense group).

The rhizomatous weeds include Common Colts-foot, Common Horsetail and Lady's Thumb.

Among the weed species with root rhizomes are, for instance, Common Toadflax, Field Sow-thistle, Field Thistle and Field Bindweed.

This book does not and could not give a complete survey of the weed species that can infest a garden. A small daisy can in fact be also a weed, and even certain cultivated plants growing in the garden (tulips, poppies, dill, horseradish and the like) have to be removed from places where they are not wanted but have gradually strayed.

The Chickweed (*Stellaria media*), an overwintering annual weed, is best eliminated by a timely removal of its ripening seeds.

Complex weed control in the garden

Separate weed-killing operations will hardly suffice to keep weeds under control in a well-managed garden. Instead, a combination of preventive, straight and special measures must be used, based on good knowledge of the biology of the crops and biology of the weeds.

Principles of weed prevention

1. Use clean seed (this is very important in the case of broadcast crops such as grasses, clovers, pulses and the like).
2. Use weed-free organic fertilizers (compost may contain large amounts of weed seeds).
3. Do not leave weeds to shed seeds (this applies equally to beds and compost.) Even weeds that are still green can have viable seeds, or can ripen after they have been cut.
4. Kill weeds mechanically at their sources: they can be spread from that particular spot by wind (Dandelion, Field Thistle are examples) or vegetatively (from paths, lawns).
5. Use appropriate crop rotation schemes, cultivate the soil thoroughly and do not let weeds overpopulate, particularly before harvest and in the inter-cropping period.
6. Smother weeds with mulches of organic matter such as peat; or, lay black plastic sheeting between rows of vegetables.

Straight controls

Mechanical: weeding, hand hoeing, mechanical hoeing and other operations to remove weeds and encourage the growth of cultivated plants which form a dense canopy and prevent weed infestation.
Chemical: application of herbicides. Chemical control should be avoided whenever possible.

Fruit

The main importance of fruit nutritionally lies in their content of vitamins, minerals and other specific substances. Sugars give fruit their calorific value: various kinds of fruit contain on average 5—10 per cent sugar (grapes 17 per cent), but under very favourable conditions this may be as much as 50 per cent more. Apart from grapes, apples, pears and plums have the most natural sugar.

The organic acids in fruit are also of great importance from both the nutritional and taste points of view: malic and citric acids and, in grapes, tartaric acid. Berries have the greatest acid content and pears have the smallest.

There are relatively little amounts of proteins and fats in fruit. These are mostly found in walnuts, hazel-nuts and almonds, which are the richest fruit in terms of calories. Other fruit have a very low calorific value, so they are especially suitable for slimmers.

As for vitamins, the most carotene (vitamin A) is contained in apricots, much less in peaches, Morello and other cherries, still less in other kinds of fruit. There are most vitamins of the B complex in walnuts, hazel-nuts and almonds. Most vitamin C is contained in black currants, strawberries, edible rowanberries; the least amount is found in pears, grapes, plums and Reine Claude plums. The vitamin content often depends on the species, the method of cultivation, climatic and soil conditions, the ripeness of the fruit and its correct storage.

Fruit is also an important source of calcium (most in berries and peaches); phosphorus (black currants, Morello cherries, strawberries, raspberries); iron (plums, black currants, strawberries, Morello cherries) and various trace substances needed by the human body. In addition, fruit contains tannin, enzymes, aromatics and other substances important for the correct functioning of the human organism.

To sum up then, it can be said that from the nutritional point of view, fruits with berries are the most valuable (black currants, then strawberries, gooseberries, red currants, blackberries, raspberries); second place is taken by stone-fruit (apricots, plums, Morello cherries, peaches, cherries, yellow plums) and third, but still valuable are fruit with pips (apples, pears).

The optimal consumption of fruit per person per year is 100 to 120 kilograms, an amount that a gardener can easily grow himself.

Growing Morello cherries can be quite profitable if suitable varieties are chosen for the given climatic conditions. They are less risky than cherries as the danger of frost is usually over by the time that Morello cherries are in flower.

Division of fruit trees, bushes, etc.

These are sometimes divided according to the above-ground structure into four groups:

1. **Trees:** here, the above-ground part has a well-developed woody trunk. They include apples, pears, quinces, rowans, medlars, plums, Mirabelle plums, damsons, almonds, peaches, apricots, cherries and nuts.

2. **Bushes:** here the above-ground part is woody, but has no trunk; individual woody shoots grow straight from the ground. They include currants, gooseberries and hazels.

3. **Semi-bushes:** the above-ground part is semi-woody; individual shoots grow straight from the ground. They include raspberries and blackberries.

4. **Plants:** here, the above-ground part takes the form of a perennial plant. They include strawberries.

However, they are more often divided according to the fruit, that is, whether this is fleshy or dry.

Fleshy fruit is divided into three groups:

Fruit with pips — apples, pears, quinces, rowans and medlars.

Stone-fruit — cherries, Morello cherries, apricots, peaches, almonds, plums, greengages, damsons and walnuts.

Berries — currants and gooseberries.

The only **dry fruit** is hazel-nuts.

The size, shape and colour of the apple blossoms are among the characteristic features which distinguish individual varieties. In some of them, even the colour and shape of the buds is typical.

Parts of fruit trees and bushes

Roots

The root system of fruit trees may be deep or just below the surface. A root that extends from the trunk deep into the earth is called the 'main' or 'tap-root', and from this grow strong lateral roots. From these again root hairs grow, that absorb nourishment and water from the earth.

A suitable site for the fruit tree must be chosen according to the depth to which the root system penetrates to reach underground water. For a walnut tree this in 300 cm, for plums 140 cm, pears and cherries 250 cm, apricots and Morello cherries 200 cm, peaches 160 cm, apples 120 cm, gooseberries and currants 140 cm and strawberries 80 cm.

Above-ground parts

These consist of the trunk and the head, the latter being formed by the axis (the elongated trunk), the main skeletal branches, the terminal and lateral shoots and the new growth. The trunk forms the axis of the tree and links the head with the roots.

Trees and bushes have three types of buds: axillary, leaf and flower buds. New annual growth comes from the axillary buds, and these are usually terminal buds or those on upright shoots. Leaf buds sprout leaves and they usually appear on lateral shoots or new growth. Flower buds germinate into flowers and later fruit. In the case of fruit with pips, the flower buds can be distinguished easily because they are bigger than axillary or leaf buds. In the case of stone-fruit they are to be found on either side of the axillary or leaf buds.

Terminal, lateral, reserve, dormant and adventitious buds can be distinguished by their position on the shoot. The terminal bud is always at the top of the shoot. Lateral buds are placed beneath it along the whole length of the shoot. Little reserve buds can be found beside the lateral buds, and these only germinate if the lateral bud is destroyed. At the base of the branches there are little dormant buds, which only germinate if the shoot is cut off to where they are. Adventitious buds occur on thicker branches and on the trunk; they mostly germinate if the tree is harmed by frost or a deep cut, and form suckers.

The annual growth is divided according to its position into terminal, lateral and premature. Terminal annual growth comes from terminal buds and extends the branch. Lateral growth comes from lateral buds on the shoots and usually forms the new fruiting wood. Thick new branches sometimes form premature new shoots in the same year, but these are weak and immature, so they are frequently damaged by frost in winter.

During the tree's lifetime, fertile new growth is formed on the branches. This may be either long (15—30 cm) or short (10 cm) and may take one, two or more years to form.

The ability of the branches to bear fruit varies according to their position on the tree. Branches and shoots that grow straight upwards are the least fruitful: the more they lean out from the straight the more fruitful they are. Horizontal branches offer the most favourable conditions for fertility.

Flowers

In order that the fruit may form, the flowers of fruit trees and bushes must be properly pollinated and fructified. The flowers are pollinated either by insects or the wind. The growth of the pollen filament is greatly influenced by the temperature. In cold weather it grows slowly and fructification is therefore poor. Insufficient growth of the filament may also be due to genetic or chemical reasons, to drought or poor nutrition.

There are two types of pollination — cross-pollination and self-pollination. In the first type, the plant needs pollen from the flowers of a different variety. In the second type it needs pollen from another tree or plant of the same variety or even from the very same tree.

But pollen that germinates well does not in itself guarantee the success of pollination and fructification. In cross-pollinating species it is very important for the given variety to flower at the same time as the variety that pollinates it. When choosing which varieties to cultivate, this important factor should be borne in mind.

As soon as the flower has been fertilized, some of its parts start to decay: the pistil, stamens and petals dry up and fade and the fruit starts to form. In the case of fruit with pips (apples, pears), the actual seeds, formed after fertilization, are hidden in the core. In the case of stone-fruit they are in the stone. There are several distinct periods in the development of the fruit: the period of fertilization, after which the petals fall; the period of accelerated growth, and the period of maturing and coloration.

Shapes of fruit-tree saplings: a) one-year-old sapling, b) fan tree, c) dwarf, d) quarter-standard, e) half-standard, f) tall standard.

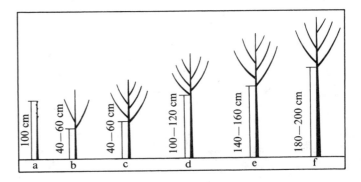

119

A simple polythene sheeting tunnel is effective for forcing strawberries or for speeding up their maturation in the autumn.

The growth of fruit during the summer varies in speed. For instance, pears grow slowly at first for about 3 weeks, then speed up until they reach the time of maturing, which begins — according to how early the species is — from 9 weeks after fertilization. Cherries also get off to a slow start, then grow quickly till they are ripe, some 8 to 12 weeks after fertilization has taken place.

The soil and climate requirements of fruit trees and bushes

The best situation for fruit cultivation is on gentle slopes rising from plains and on plateaus. Low country is less suitable. Areas exposed to strong winds are unsuitable, as are so-called 'frost hollows' as here the trees suffer from diseases, pests and especially early frosts at the time when they are in flower. Nor are sharp slopes suitable, particularly if they have shallow arable soil and rocky subsoil.

Southern slopes, which are warmest, are best for warmth-loving trees (almonds, peaches, apricots, nuts), for early species and, at greater heights above sea level, for all fruit trees. In warmer regions, on the other hand, it is better to cultivate apples and plums on northern or north-western slopes — so that the trees do not suffer so much from drought. Northern slopes at higher elevations are quite unsuitable for the cultivation of fruit trees.

Fruit trees do best in medium-heavy, loose soils with a sufficient content of humus and moisture. In warm, dry regions a heavy soil is best; in cool, wet regions a light soil. Dry, sandy soils, stony or very chalky ones, are unsuitable for fruit trees, and so are heavy, wet or acid soils.

On shallow land, where the underground water level is quite near the surface, it is a good idea to cultivate fruit with berries and small types of apples or pears grafted on to shallow-rooting stocks. On slopes with less moisture and less fertile soil the trees should be grafted on to more robust stocks with deeper roots.

Neutral soils or even slightly alkaline suit the main fruit species; neutral or slightly acid ones are good for berry fruit. Strawberries will tolerate a markedly acid soil, and blueberries even need it. But, on the whole, fruit trees adapt themselves well to the given soil conditions.

The minimum rainfall necessary for cherries is 450 mm per year, for other trees 500 mm per year. Of course, the crops can be greatly increased by watering at the right time.

The aerial parts of fruit trees can bear frost of as much as $-26°$ C in their dormant period without suffering damage — the exceptions being apricots ($-20°$ C) and peach trees ($-1°$ C). The roots of fruit trees are more sensitive to low temperatures. The roots of apples and currants freeze at a temperature of $-15.5°$ C, of pears at $-9°$ C, peaches at $-10°$ C. But even a thin layer of snow protects the temperature of the soil from dropping too low, and therefore prevents the roots from freezing.

Trees in wet soils or those over-fertilized with nitrogen are more sensitive to winter frosts, but all-round nourishment makes the trees more resistant.

Developed flower buds freeze at a temperature of $-4°$ C, the open flowers of apricots and peaches at $-3°$ C, other species at $-2°$ C. The young fruit of all species freeze at $-1°$ C. The moisture of the air and wind have a great influence on their resistance, very moist air decreasing it and aerial movement increasing it.

Shapes of fruit trees and stocks

In choosing fruit trees for the garden a good principle to keep to is: the smaller the garden, the smaller the overall shape of the tree. The advantages of small trees include early and regular fruiting, good quality fruit, easy care and picking. There can be quite a number of such trees even on a small area, and so more varieties that ripen in sucession, thus ensuring fruit practically throughout the year.

Apples and pears can be cultivated in the form of a wall, the trunks being 40—60 cm high, or as dwarfs with trunks 60—80 cm. This form is also suitable for Morello cherries and peaches. Other stone-fruit (apricots, plums, bullaces and cherries) are usually cultivated as quarter-standards, which means trunks 100—120 cm high. Walnut trees, unless grafted, are *not* suitable for small gardens.

In large gardens where space is no problem, and where plants are to be grown under the trees, half-standards (140—160 cm) may be planted, or even tall standards (180—220 cm high). The disadvantage of these is that they fruit later and both cultivation and harvesting are more difficult. So, even in a large garden, it is better to have some small trees.

The stocks of fruit trees have a great influence on the growth, fertility, age and resistance of grafted species to frosts and diseases.

Stocks grown from the seeds of wild or suitable cultivated species — the seedlings — have a stronger root system, so that trees grafted on to them grow well even in dry soil, if it is sufficiently deep. These stocks are mostly used for tall standards, for half-standards and quarter-standards. They start bearing fruit later, but live longer.

For smaller shapes, especially for apples and pears, vegetatively propagated type stocks are used, having their original known qualities. Trees grafted on to less strongly growing stocks fruit early and plentifully, but their life span is shorter.

In general, the principle applies that the taller the form required, the more fruitful and less quick-growing the species, and the less fertile the soil, the more robustly growing must be the stock used.

Planting fruit trees and bushes

Fruit trees and bushes should be planted during their dormant period. The best time, especially in regions with spring droughts, is the autumn (October and November). The saplings make good use of the

Apple branches laden with fruit bend almost to the ground. At this stage, it is advisable to use suitable supports to prevent them from breaking.

winter moisture, the earth settles well into the holes and the plants start to sprout earlier in the spring.

Bought saplings should be planted as soon as possible, care being taken that their roots do not dry. If the roots *are* dry, the trees should be immersed in water up to their tops for a day. If there is not time to plant the trees in the autumn, they should be placed in earth, well covered and protected. They can then be planted in their permanent site in the spring, as soon as the ground thaws and dries.

Peaches, as distinct from other trees, do not form root hairs in the autumn, so they cannot absorb water from the earth. Furthermore, water contained in the tree evaporates through the numerous pores in the trunk and branches, and they often dry up for lack of moisture. Therefore, autumn planting is only successful if the winter is mild and short; it is better to plant peaches in early spring. Even so, they should be planted at the latest within two days of being uprooted from the nursery. If the peach saplings have to be bought in the autumn, the best way is to lay them, slanting to half their height, in a trench dug in the ground where there is no danger of their getting wet over the winter. Apricots and walnuts are also best planted in early spring.

Strawberries are another matter. These should be planted in July or at the beginning of August, as in this way they give good crops even in the first harvest year. Strawberries should not be planted later than the middle of September.

Currants and gooseberries are best planted in the autumn, as they sprout early in the spring and, if planted in spring, the buds may be destroyed and growth slowed down. Raspberries, however, prefer a spring planting. If they are planted in the autumn, the shoots should be checked in spring and, if necessary, re-firmed into the ground.

Preparation of the soil

Before planting fruit trees, the soil must be properly prepared. The aim is to improve the quality of the soil to a depth of some 50—60 cm, especially to aerate it, enrich it with humus and nutrients and adjust its chemical composition. In the summer of the year when the fruit trees are to be planted the soil should be trenched or dug to a depth of 50—60 cm and a quantity of industrial fertilizers worked into it. If possible, the fruit trees should be planted into soil dug with stable manure. Before planting walls of fruit trees, a strip of soil should be prepared at least 1—1.5 metres wide.

Holes for the autumn planting of individual fruit trees should be dug at least a month beforehand; for spring planting, they should be dug in the autumn. In order to be able to plant the tree correctly in the centre of the hole, and therefore in line with any others, its position should first be marked with a peg and further pegs should indicate the perimeter of the hole. The hole should be 50—60 cm deep and 100—150 cm wide, especially in infertile or stony ground. In fertile ground it can be smaller. The bottom of the hole should be dug over, particularly if the soil is heavy and matted.

When digging the hole, put the upper fertile soil on one side and the less fertile subsoil on the other.

In measuring the distance between trees, if planting several, remember what they will look like when full-grown. Do not plant them too close together, or they will have insufficient light, will grow too tall in order to reach more light, have few flowers and fruit and be more vulnerable to diseases and pests. **Recommended distances** are: for apples on robust stocks and for cherries 8—10 m; for pears on seedlings and wild stocks 7—9 m; for walnut trees 10—15 m; for plums and Morello cherries 6—8 m; for apricots 6—7 m; for peaches 4—5 m; for apples and pears on dwarf stocks 4—6 m; for currants and gooseberries 2—3 m; for raspberries and blackberries 1—2 m and for hazels 4 m.

Fruit trees intended to form a wall should be planted 3—4 m apart, on flat ground in a north-south direction, and on slopes according to the inclination of the slope.

When planting the whole of a garden, or part of it, with trees of the same shape, a triangular form is best, as this makes the most efficient use of the whole area. When combining different shapes of trees, or species that live to different ages, for instance, apples and cherries or a combination of fruit trees and bushes, a square or oblong design is preferable, alternating trees with dwarf trees and bushes.

When planting fruit trees on land where old trees have been dug up, the ground should be left fallow for at least six months in between and dug over several times during that period, taking particular care to remove all the old roots. It is also useful to sow vegetables for a year on this ground, to renew its fertility, or dig in stable manure and industrial fertilizers. The new fruit trees should not be planted exactly where the old ones stood, and neither should they be the same species of fruit.

Preparation of the saplings

When purchased, the young fruit trees should be prepared for planting as follows: all damaged, dry or frozen roots should be cut off with a sharp knife or with good parrot-billed secateurs right back to the healthy tissue. Healthy roots are white; dried ones are brown, grey or even black. Roots that are too long or thin are also shortened, so that the root system has a fairly regular shape. The cut must be smooth, straight and as small as possible.

If the sapling has more than four side shoots, the surplus ones are cut off close to the trunk where they join. Also cut off all shoots from the lower part of the trunk or near the root (at the root neck). Neaten the cuts with a knife and smear with grafting wax. This is especially important in the case of peaches. All other shoots, even with autumn planting, should be shortened in the spring.

Before planting, the roots may be dipped into a paste of humus-rich soil and cow dung, to improve their rooting ability. Clay should not be used, as it is apt to dry hard and so prevent the roots from breathing and the root hairs from penetrating the earth.

If the young trees are tall or have a weak root system they should be staked, especially in windy positions. In the case of tall trees the stake remains till the trunk is sufficiently thick (5—8 years); in the case of shallow-rooting species, it is kept permanently. The stake must be of good material, shorter than the tree — standing about 10 cm below its lowest shoot. If the stake is wooden, the part that will be

The basic implements used in fruit-growing: parrot-billed secateurs, a set of pruning knives, raffia, a frame saw, horticultural wax and adhesive tape.

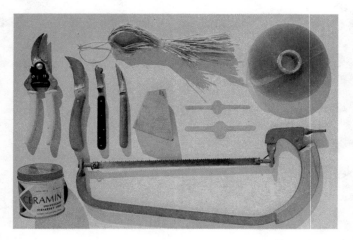

below ground should be treated by charring or by coating it with a protective paint. The stake is then driven into the ground before the tree is planted.

Planting

Next comes the actual planting, so long as the earth is not too wet or frozen. The hole with the stake in it is partially filled with the good quality surface earth that was put aside during digging. This is lightly stamped down round the edges. The soil may be enriched with a good compost, but never with fresh stable manure.

The earth should form a little mound beside the stake and the tree is placed on this mound. In windy situations, the stake should be some 10 cm from the tree on the side from which the wind usually blows. Otherwise, it should be to the south of the tree to protect the young trunk from the sun. The future development and fertility of the tree depends to a great extent on correct planting. Planting too deep is one of the causes of permanent infertility. The root neck should be 5—6 cm above the level of the surrounding soil. When it settles into the hole the tree will then be set as deep as it grew in the nursery.

In order that it should not settle too much, the earth is gently stamped down round the edge as the hole is filled. The correct depth is especially important in the case of small or dwarf fruit trees cultivated on slow-growing stocks. If they are set too deep they will push out their own fast-growing roots from the graft, and this weakens the influence of the slow-growing stock on early fertility and the size of the tree's head.

The saplings should be planted by two people, so that one person can hold the tree and spread out its roots while the other sprinkles them with crumbled, friable soil. The first person shakes the tree a little, so that the soil gets between the roots, leaving no air gaps in which the roots would moulder so that the tree would not 'take' well. This is also the reason why lumps or turfs are not placed on the roots. But the friable earth should adhere to the roots well, so it is trodden down carefully when the hole is filled.

The subsoil that was put on the other heap when dug out of the hole should only be used if there is not enough fertile soil, and even then it should be improved with compost and put on top of the hole.

The tree is then tied to the stake sufficiently loosely so that it can sink slightly as the soil around it settles. Only when the tree is finally settled is it firmly tied, and this is best done with textile fibres; never use rubber.

Before the planting, the site must be fertilized with industrial fertilizers: 1.5—2 kg of ground calcite, 1.5—2 kg of Thomas' powder and 0.2—0.3 kg of potassium sulphate per hole. Half this amount is dug into the soil already at the bottom of the hole, the other half mixed with the soil that will fill the lower half of the hole. The fertilizer should not come into direct contact with the roots.

Autumn-planted trees must be protected against being gnawed or bitten by animals such as rabbits or mice. They are therefore surrounded to a height of 130 cm by wire netting or other wrappings of rushes, sticks, fir bark or branches etc. In the spring these wrappings are burnt, so as to destroy any pests that hid in them during the winter. The roots are protected from frost by heaping up a mound of earth 25—30 cm high round the trunk; in the spring the earth is spread out again to form a bowl 1—1.5 m wide, to keep in the moisture.

Transplanting trees

Sometimes a fully grown fruit tree has to be transplanted, and here the condition for success is to preserve the root ball intact. So a year before transplanting, dig a trench round the tree 50—70 cm from the trunk. Then fill the trench with compost. The roots will take well in this layer during vegetation and the root ball will hold better during transplantation. If the tree is to be transported some distance after it has been dug up, the roots should be crated or wrapped in sacking. In the spring, the transplanted tree should be hard pruned and, to make it take root well, it should be secured against moving in the wind by three wires fixed to pegs in the ground. Sacking must be placed round the trunk under the wires, so they cannot cut into the trunk. Indeed, the whole trunk may be wrapped in sacking or straw to decrease the evaporation of water. Water the tree well during vegetation and when it has taken root apply some manure. The following year all the flowers and fruit should be removed from the transplanted tree, so that it does not waste its strength.

Care throughout the year

In early spring, the trunks of fruit trees should be painted with lime wash. This white coating will deflect the sun's rays, so the tree is not damaged by being overheated in intensive sunshine and then overcooled when the temperature drops below freezing point during the night.

In spring, the bowl round the tree that serves to keep in moisture can always be sprinkled with dry soil, compost, peat or plant cuttings, so that the water does not evaporate too quickly.

During vegetation, especially during a drought, fruit trees must be thoroughly watered. It is useless to water frequently in small quantities, as the water does not reach the roots but stays in the upper layers of the earth where it forms a hard crust. A good method of preserving moisture round the tree is to mulch it with a layer of peat, strawy manure or grass about 5—10 cm thick, before flowering.

If a young tree does not sprout in the spring, it should be carefully lifted out of the earth, the roots shortened and steeped in water, best in a shed, for several days, or the tree can be laid lengthways in damp soil. Only after sprouting is it replanted.

During vegetation, especially after rain, before a crust can form over the earth, the ground round the tree should be lightly dug over several times. Deep digging, however, damages the roots and increases the evaporation from the soil, so take care. This light digging should be done mainly between May and

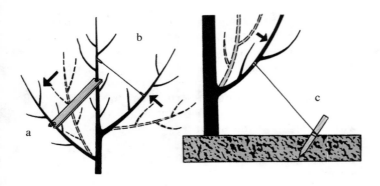

Shaping an irregular head: a) by braces and b) by tying.

July, when the annual growth and the fruit are developing. In August and September the earth should be left undisturbed, so that the fruit can ripen and colour better.

In the autumn, the earth should be dug round the trees to a maximum depth of 10 cm and between the rows to 15 cm. Do this with a fork or better still with a hoe, so as not to damage the roots. Summer digging is not recommended. As soon as the earth dries in the spring, it should be smoothed over with the wrong side of a rake, in order to prevent the water from evaporating.

To enrich the earth with humus various plants may be grown for green manure under the fruit trees. The best for this are the Field Pea, vetch, White Mustard, Buckwheat, California Bluebell, White Clover, ryegrass and, in sandy soils, Lupins. The seeds should be sown from the beginning of July to the beginning of August in rather damp soil, watered if dry. The plants are then forked into the soil in the spring, as their growth protects the soil from freezing in winter and makes the snow lie longer. The cultivation of plants for green manure, however, is not recommended in areas where the rainfall is less than 500 mm or in young fruit tree plantations.

Vegetables can be cultivated between the rows of newly planted trees, in the case of dwarf trees till they are 3 years old; and with tall trees, until their 8th year. The best vegetables for this purpose are beans, peas, lettuce, early cauliflower and kohlrabi, cucumbers, celeriac, tomatoes, carrots, and early potatoes. The vegetables should never be planted directly under the trees.

Manuring

The basic manure for fruit trees is organic manure. Best is well-composted stable manure, which is dug into the earth in the autumn to a depth of 10—15 cm, either over the whole cultivated area under the trees, or in rings under the heads. Light soils should be manured every year or at least every other year; heavier soils once every 3—4 years. Poorly growing trees should be given larger quantities. In spring and autumn, compost may be used instead of stable manure. Dry poultry dung is also suitable in quantities of 100—200 g to a square metre.

Industrial fertilizers can be applied at the same time as organic manure. If plants are cultivated for green manure under the trees, the amounts of manure or compost can be reduced to a half.

Each 2—3 year old tree should be given 12—15 kg of manure, and this amount is increased the older the tree, so that an 8—9 year old tree gets 40—50 kg of manure and older trees with a diameter of 6 m get 120—160 kg of manure.

Industrial fertilizers should be used according to the chemical composition of the soil and the age and fertility of the tree. During the autumn digging, phosphoric and potash fertilizers should be used, so that these substances reach the roots during the growing period. In early spring, nitrogen fertilizers are used. Or compound fertilizers can be used in both spring and autumn, if this is more convenient. Then nitrogen fertilizers can be added during the whole growing period, being dug in only to a shallow depth.

In years when the full quantity of compost or stable manure is used, the amounts of industrial fertilizers may be reduced to a half. If the trees grow too vigorously and the shoots do not mature well, the amounts of nitrogen fertilizer should be decreased and those of phosphoric and potash fertilizers increased. If vegetables are being grown under the trees, the amounts of fertilizers are increased according to their demands.

To promote the growth of poorly growing trees, manure solutions can be used, for instance, fermented poultry or rabbit dung diluted with 10 parts of water. A solution of well-dissolved compound fertilizers with water is another possibility. This is poured into a channel dug round the tree to a depth of 10—15 cm. When it sinks in, the channel is filled up again with soil, and this is firmed in.

Calcium is added according to the composition of the soil and the requirements of the individual species; apples and pears need the most, strawberries the least.

If there is a sudden lack of nutrients, or if their absorption from the soil is restricted say, by overwet soil or damaged roots a nourishing solution can be sprayed on the leaves. For 10 litres of solution use 40 g ammonia saltpeter with calcite or 50—60 g urea, 50—60 g potassium sulphate and the extract of 300—400 g superphosphate. The best time for spraying is after flowering. In cases of severe lack of nourishment the spraying can be repeated once or twice at intervals of 10—14 days. If necessary, these nourishing sprays can be combined with sprays to combat diseases and pests.

Protection against diseases and pests

The most effective protection is always prevention. If fruit trees and bushes are given good conditions and care their health will cause few problems.

If everything is done to make birds the gardener's allies, there will be still less to worry about. It is enough to put a suitable bird-table out in the garden over the winter and see that it is well supplied with food, and perhaps make a suitable place for useful bird species to nest, and the birds will repay this negligible care by keeping insect pests in check.

If problems do arise even then, the cause of the trouble must be quickly identified and corrected after consultation with an expert. Chemical preparations should be resorted to only in extreme cases.

Pruning fruit trees

No general rules can be given for pruning fruit trees. It must be done individually according to the species and variety, their growth and state of health, the shape required, the stock, the fertility of the soil and many other factors. The aim of pruning during the tree's early years is to produce a light, strong, firm system of branches and early and regular fruiting. In later years pruning maintains the correct relationship between the growth of the branches and fertili-

ty. Old trees may be rejuvenated by pruning, as it prevents their becoming exhausted, revises growth and improves fertility. Pruning also influences the number, size and quality of the fruit.

A great many theories and practical instructions about pruning have been put forward. Even though their authors may have achieved good results with them, many are now out-dated either because they are too laborious and time-consuming, or because other more suitable methods of cultivation and new species and rootstocks have been introduced.

Position of the branches
The laterals must be firmly joined to the trunk so that they do not break when weighed down with fruit. This is achieved by removing the crown shoots that grow from the trunk at an angle of less than

---

General terms

First of all, some general terms used in connection with pruning should be explained:

The central or terminal branch, also called the 'leader', is the one growing straight upwards, the leading shoot of a branch.

Laterals are the side shoots from the terminal branch. Laterals growing close together at the same height form a **floor.**

Extending shoots grow at the ends of laterals and branches.

Competitive shoots are those growing nearest to the extending shoots.

New growth are the shoots at the sides of the branches; they have either axillary buds or flower and fruit buds.

Annual growth is the growth formed during the growing period; in dormancy they are called shoots.

Buds can be seen on the shoots during dormancy, the slender ones being leaf or axillary buds, the rounder ones future flowers.

Dormant buds are located on the lowest parts of the shoots, visible as little notches. They only come into life if the whole shoot is cut off down to them.

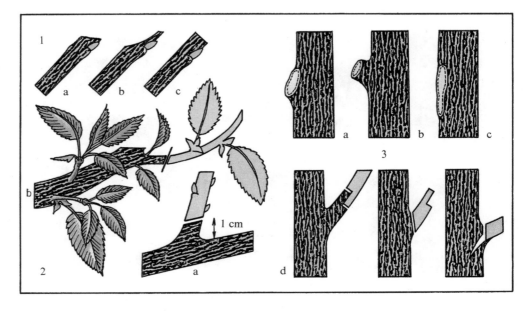

Methods of pruning the shoots and branches:
1 — cut above a 'waking' bud: a) right height and angle, b, c) wrong. 2 — cut to a heel: a) during winter, b) during the growing period. 3 — cut against the branch or trunk: a) right, b, c) wrong, d) course of cutting.

125

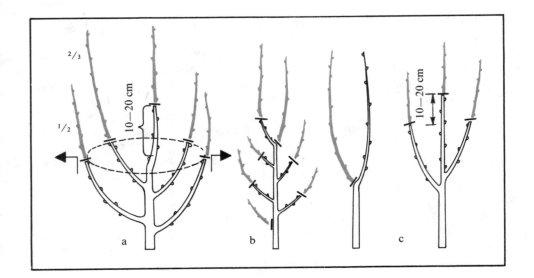

Pruning of fruit trees after planting: a) in a well-developed crown, b) in a poorly developed crown, c) in an irregularly developed crown.

40—60°, as they are apt to break. This is especially important in the case of stone-fruits. The firmest laterals are those that do not branch out at one level but have some distance between them on the trunk.

Growth, branching and fruitfulness are dependent on the position of the branches. Upright branches grow most vigorously, usually forking only at the top, and they produce little fruit. The more horizontal the lay of the branches, the greater the number of flower buds that sprout on their upper side. Therefore, when the tree is growing well, and only then, the shoots are tied into slanting or horizontal positions, to make them fruit more profusely. Premature tying immediately after planting, or tying the branches of trees on poorly growing rootstocks, may result in the tree being stunted. The branches should not be tied lower than to the horizontal position. Arched branches throw the most buds and flower best at the top of the arch.

Pruning

When pruning it is advisable not only to shorten the branches, but to remove whole branches where the growth is too dense. If the main branches are not shortened they remain weak and pliable. On the other hand, if they are shortened too much or too often they become too thick and stiff, the head becomes too thick and fruiting is delayed.

Pruning lets light and air into the head, which makes for better conditions for maintaining the health of the tree and for a more plentiful fruiting.

Winter cutting

Cutting and pruning in the dormant period supports the growth. Pruning affects the whole head of the tree, while cutting affects the individual branches. Winter cutting is done on trees with a poor growth, in order to encourage it. On the other hand trees that are growing too vigorously and throwing out long

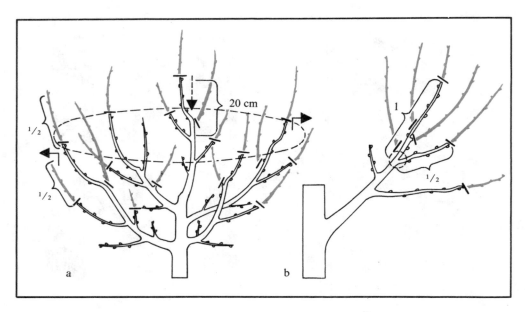

Pruning of the head and new growth one year after planting.

126

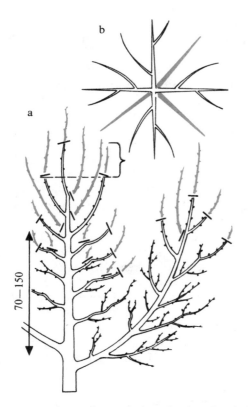

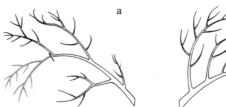

Care of the head in the years of alternating good and poor harvests. Slight rejuvenation: a) cutting back arching branches, b) cutting back forking branches.

Pruning in the 3rd to 5th year after planting, forming a second floor of laterals: a) two laterals are produced in one year, the third in the following year, b) a view from above of the distribution of laterals of the first and second floors.

shoots are cut in late spring, when they are sprouting or even flowering, to restrict growth. Severe winter cutting promotes the growth and restricts fruiting, which is why robustly growing young trees are cut less severely in the dormant period. Cutting should never be done at temperatures of less than —8° C, as the exposed parts would be damaged by frost.

Summer cutting

The cutting of green branches, called 'summer cutting', limits the growth of the tree. The results depend on the phase of growth at which it is done. The shortening of newly-grown tips weakens the growth most, whereas the surrounding annual growth that has not been pinched back will grow more vigorously. This can be made use of in shaping trees that otherwise grow irregularly.

Shortening the new growth in its strongest growing period (June to the beginning of July) promotes the formation of buds which, in the upper parts of the shortened new growth, grow into premature shoots. This is an advantage in the case of apricots, but in apples and pears no cutting should be done at this stage, as it makes for a poor crop.

In the case of apples and pears the annual growth should only be shortened in the final phase of growing and formation of the terminal bud (end of July to the middle of August). This cut allows the buds to develop better and cease sprouting. In some varieties it promotes the formation of flower buds.

To make a good crop

Correct nourishment and pruning maintain the bal-

Deep rejuvenating pruning of old heads: a) angle of cutting in apples, b) pears, c) an apple-tree after cutting. Extending twigs: 1 — at the end of a shortened branch, 2 — small horizontal fruiting twig on the upper branch, 3 — a weak twig slanting upwards from the lower branch.

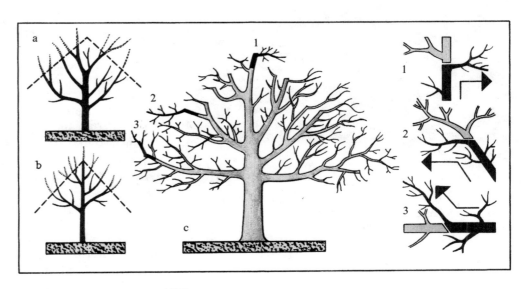

127

Grafting of fruit trees. The cut must be very smooth, so a sharp knife is a must. The longer the cut, the better the scions will take.

Budding. The bud is inserted into a T-shaped incision on the root-stock, then secured by being carefully tied with raffia or a special adhesive tape from the bottom upwards, and fastened with a special horticultural knot, but leaving the bud itself free.

ance between growing and fruiting. Poor growth and too many flowers are the reason for undesirable periodic fruiting in the case of apples and pears. The trees exhaust themselves by fruiting too much in one year and give no fruit the following year. To ensure even fruiting, regular, proportional, medium-heavy pruning and sufficient manuring, mainly with nitrogen fertilizers, are essential. However, excessive use of nitrogen-based fertilizers causes too lush growth at the expense of fruiting. On the other hand, when small doses of nitrogen fertilizers are applied the trees do not grow much and bear little fruit. Sufficient doses of phosphorus and potash fertilizers are also necessary.

Even fertile new growth must be cut. The annual growth that forms as a result of cutting and proper nutrition increases the tree's assimilation system, thus supporting the size and quality of the fruit.

Competitive shoots should be removed as they make the branch system too dense. They should either be cut off where they join the branch, or so that only a heel is left, that is, about 0.5—1 cm of the shoot, containing only dormant buds. Only weak annual growth of poor quality develops from these during the growing period.

Horizontal shoots or those slanting downwards are not usually shortened, or only if they are too long and in the lower part of the tree, as otherwise the fruit would touch the ground.

How to cut

In winter cutting, it is usual to cut down to the 'waking' bud. This means removing mostly the one-year shoots with a slightly slanting cut just above the bud, so there is no snag or a long wound as would occur if the cut is too slanted. In summer cutting, annual growth is shortened in the same way.

In summer or winter cutting of competitive and other thick shoots, the cut to a heel is used. The whole shoot is removed except for the lowest part, about 1 cm long, on which 2—3 small leaves can be seen in the summer and in winter only notches where they have fallen off. There should be no buds left on the heel. This kind of cut weakens the growth so that only a short, weak shoot grows from the dormant bud.

During pruning, when shoots or whole branches are removed, the cut should be made right against the branch or trunk. No snag should remain, but the cut should not be too deep either, leaving a long wound. Thick branches should be cut first from the bottom and only then should you finish by cutting through from the top, to avoid splitting or splintering the wood.

Cutting the head in the first years after planting

As a newly planted tree has only part of its original roots, not enough to supply the whole head with nourishment, the head must be shortened in proportion to the roots. In spring planting this is done before planting, in autumn planting the shoots are not

128

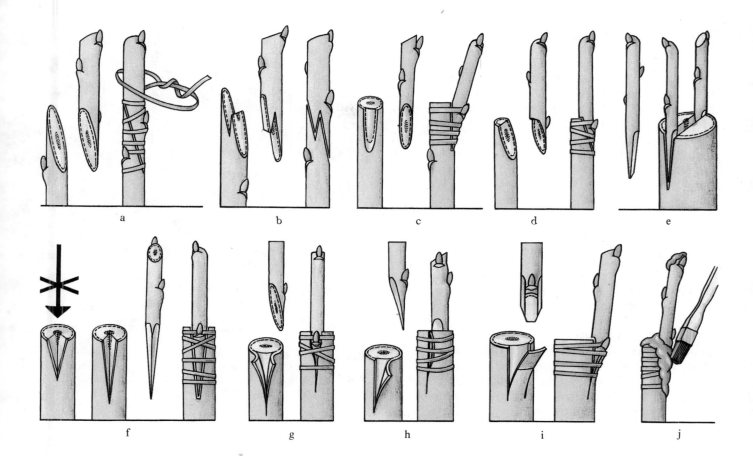

shortened (or only partially) until the following spring.

Cutting has another purpose besides making a balance between the roots and the head — it forms the head into the correct shape and promotes the formation of new lateral growth on the main branches. If the head is not shortened after planting the tree grows poorly and fruits prematurely, thus becoming exhausted. The uncut head is weak and often it will be stunted.

First cutting

First cutting after planting is the same for all shapes. Three or at most four lateral shoots are left besides the leader, and these should be of approximately the same thickness and placed regularly on either side of the trunk. In the case of apples and pears with short fruit-bearing new growth five laterals can be left. If the tree has more, the surplus ones should be cut off against the trunk. First the lateral shoots are shortened, then the competitive shoots growing straight upwards under the leader. In the case of autumn planted trees with normally developed roots, the highest lateral is shortened first by two thirds of its length, then the lower lateral by about half of its length. The terminal bud that is left should face outwards and the ends of the shortened laterals should be more or less level.

The leading shoot is shortened according to its thickness in such a way that the terminal bud left is above the scar left by the previous year's cut and some 10—20 cm above the level of the cut-off lateral. The leading shoot is cut the more deeply the

Methods of grafting: a) coupling — the rootstock and scion are tightly bound with raffia, b) English coupling, c) approach grafting, d) saddle grafting, e) whip and tongue grafting, f) cleft grafting, g) stub grafting — normal method, h) stub grafting — progressive method, i) Tittel's method, j) cut surfaces are carefully smeared with grafting wax.

thicker it is, the less vigorous is the variety and the weaker the lateral shoots.

In windy situations, the terminal bud on the leading shoot should be left on the windward side. The newly-grown shoot will then be straightened to the vertical position by the wind.

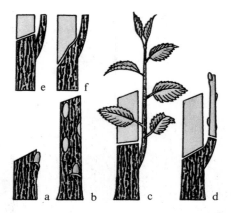

Cutting back the budded rootstock: a) above the bud, b) with a snag, c) above a sprouting twig, d) properly cut snag, e, f) wrongly cut snag.

129

The importance of the shape of the head

In the first 3—5 years after planting the aim is to form, by correct cutting, a firm, airy and light head with evenly placed basic branches and plenty of fertile new growth. Trees with properly shaped heads produce fruit early, regularly and plentifully, they are resistant to harmful influences — especially wind and fungus diseases — and live longer. When cutting the head the best principle is that varieties with a more vigorous growth and bearing fruit on long branches should be shortened less; varieties that grow poorly and bear fruit on short branches, as well as all trees that seem to have stopped growing, should be shortened more. This procedure is carried out with apples and pears for 4—5 years, with stone-fruit for 2—3 years, until the main branches have sufficient fertile growth. After that they should not be cut regularly, only trimmed according to need. Even after shortening, the extending shoots of the laterals should be twice as long as the new growth after cutting. In the case of apples with overhanging branches, the extending shoots should be cut to the inner bud in order to prevent the head from falling.

Vigorously growing trees should be cut both in winter and summer. Then in the spring they need not be cut so severely and are not encouraged into further lush growth. In the summer cutting, at the end of July, cut off the competitive shoots, that is, the ones growing straight upwards.

Every head should be formed into a regular shape. Laterals that grow too straight up can be encouraged to lie further from the trunk by means of braces or by being tied to pegs in the ground. Too horizontal branches, on the other hand, can be tied so they grow more towards the trunk.

Further care

In the third to fifth year after planting a further 'floor' may be made, provided that the laterals on the first 'floor' are well developed. The new laterals (usually 3) are made individually on the extended trunk, with some distance between them and 70—150 cm above the first 'floor'.

In the first years after the head has been formed,

Apple cordons either stand freely or are trained as espaliers along wire supports. Trained cordons are narrower and thinner and yield higher quality fruit. However, their cultivation is more painstaking.

Fruit walls and belts: a) Schlösser's fan tree three years after planting, b) Italian fan tree in its 3rd year, c) Schmitz-Hübsch's fan tree three years after planting, d) new growth in Debard's fan tree, e) three-year-old fan Hungaria, f) Duhan's fan tree, g) tree shapes recommended for pears (less for apples) — a two-tiered espalier, h) a fan shape suitable for pears with a well formed head, i) a freely growing fan at the time of bending the middle lateral.

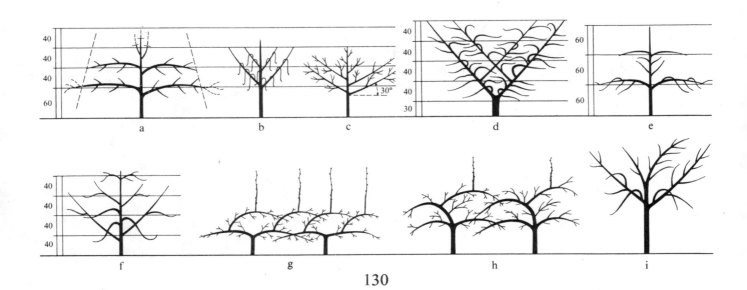

130

the tree should be pruned but the branches not shortened. This ensures that air and sun can get to the whole branch system. All superfluous branches are removed, that is, those that grow inwards, cross one another or grow close to each other in the same direction, and all branches that are dry, broken or diseased. If the heads are well cared for right from planting, pruning can be limited to the occasional removal of single branches.

In the case of early stone-fruit and fruit with pips, it is best to prune straight after the harvest, because if it is done in early spring the trees are impoverished of supplies stored in the wood. In later species the pruning can be done in early spring. Any wounds occurring during late autumn pruning would not heal by winter and the trees would suffer from frost. Thick branches should never be cut from the trunk in the autumn. Cutting during the growing period

Ripe pears are usually beautifully coloured. The proper time for picking is when the pear can be easily detached from the branch if turned and slightly lifted.

A spindle-shaped dwarf — tying the boughs to poles.

rather than in early spring makes it easier to recognize dry branches and judge the density of the head.

Later on, when good harvest years start to alternate with poor ones, the quality of the fruit decreases and the growth of one-year shoots is limited, the head should be gently rejuvenated. The bending and shadowed ends are cut off branches that arch down to the ground at the first or further branching. In varieties that do not form arches the laterals are shortened, or their thicker side branches, at the first or second fork from the end. At the same time the long fertile new growth is pruned.

Rejuvenating pruning

The heads of old trees need rejuvenating in early spring by cutting away the old wood. This cannot be done according to a general rule, but individually according to the variety, the state of the tree and the region where it is cultivated.

In rejuvenating pruning the head is cut first, taking out all dry and diseased branches. Then the main branches are cut from the highest to the lowest. Tall heads may be lowered by shortening the branches in the upper part of the head. The older the tree, the more shortening is needed, say by a quarter to a half. In the lower part the branches are shortened less, in order to achieve the required shape, typical of the given variety. The extending twigs at the ends of the cut branches should be left — the horizontal ones on the upper branches and the ones slanting upwards on the lower. Then the subsidiary branches are rejuvenated in the same way.

Correct all-round nourishment is a necessary complement to rejuvenation. Nitrogen fertilizers, that support growth and the formation of suckers, must be used carefully. The best way is to feed the tree one year before any planned rejuvenation.

If the garden contains healthy trees of an unsuitable variety, these can be grafted on to a better species. More information on this is to be found in the following section.

As cutting has its specific peculiarities in the different types of fruit, it will be mentioned in the respective sections that follow.

Budding and grafting

It is basically possible to grow fruit trees from seedlings in the garden, that is to get the rootstock from seeds or vegetatively and rear them in a nursery. Of course, this is a method requiring a great deal of work and time, and one that gardeners seldom use. They prefer to buy the saplings of fruit trees from an expert nurseryman.

However a knowledge of the cultivation of fruit trees can be useful if the gardener is dissatisfied with some variety and decides to graft it.

The essence of grafting is the joining of parts of two different plants in such a way that they then grow permanently as one plant. The new plant takes over the root system from the first plant (the stock) and the head from the second (the scion).

In early spring the head is cut off from the chosen tree, according to the species and type of the head, to form a top angle of 70—110°. A thin extending branch is left at the end of the shortened branch to draw up the sap so that the graft takes better. The cut branch should not be thicker than 15 cm in the case of pears, 10 cm in the case of apples and 8 cm in the case of stone-fruit.

Use scions from very fertile healthy trees of species that do well in the given region.

Preparation of the scions

Scions should be taken from one-year shoots, best from the south side of the head where they are well matured. Suckers are not suitable as scions.

They are cut during the dormant period, usually in December and January, especially in the case of cherries and Morello cherries. In apples and pears they can be taken as late as just before the beginning of sprouting. Over the winter lay them in damp sand in a cool cellar, or in grooves in the earth on the north side of the building. They should be half covered with earth, so that they do not dry.

The scion should have three buds and the upper cut should be just above a bud.

Methods of grafting

Grafting before the sap starts to rise is done by the whip and tongue method, and when the sap has risen by stub grafting. In the first case a three-sided wedge is cut in the stock, narrow and deep rather than broad and flat, and the scion, cut in exactly the same way, is inserted into this. Stub grafting can be done in two ways: according to the first method the bark cut lengthwise on the stock is inclined outwards on both sides and the scion inserted into the gaps. The second method is better, when the bark is inclined outwards on one side only and the scion from the opposite side is cut so that it fits better.

In grafting thinner branches coupling or saddling can be used. In ordinary coupling the scion is cut once slantwise and is joined on to the stock cut in the same way. In what is known as 'English coupling', both the stock and the scion have a double slantwise cut (see drawing). In saddling, a single slantwise cut is combined with a horizontal surface. These methods can only be used when the stock and the scion are of the same thickness.

For Morello cherries, scions from thick shoots are used with leaf buds from rejuvenated trees.

The variety 'Glockenapfel' is picked at the end of October, as late as possible, and it ripens in January. It can last until May or even later, is easily stored and does not suffer from rotting.

Branches are cut and grafted from the top downwards. On thin branches put 1—2 scions, on thicker ones up to 5. The scions are well bound with raffia and smeared with grafting wax. If a plastic band is used for binding, then the wax is unnecessary. The scions are protected with arched twigs, so that birds or wind cannot break them; or the scions can be tied to sticks fixed to the branches.

In the following year the best of the shoots grown from the scions are selected to become the basis for new branches. The others, with their extending twigs, are pared down to short snags and, when the wounds are healed, cut off. In the following years a head is shaped from the new shoots in the same way as after planting.

Budding

Peach trees cannot be grafted, but they can be budded after temporary rejuvenation in August. Also, young cherries can be budded or grafted in July and August.

The buds must be taken from the mature annual growth of well cultivated species. First prepare the scions, cut the day before. Remove the upper part of the leaves so that only about 1 cm of the lower part remains, wrap them in a damp cloth and lay them in a cool shady place. Cut away the buds from the central part of the scion. With a sharp budding knife cut out an oval sliver of bark about 3 cm long with a thin layer of wood and a bud. The wood can be carefully peeled off, but do not damage the bud in the process. A T-shaped incision is made in the bark of the stock, the cross-cut being about 1 cm long, the vertical one about 3 cm, and the prepared sliver is then placed behind the section of bark that has been prised open, so that the bud is 1 cm below the cross-cut. The wound is bound with raffia in such a way that the bud remains free. In about a fortnight the result can be checked. If the remaining lower part of the leaf falls off when touched lightly, the budding has been successful. The raffia is carefully removed after three weeks.

When choosing species for grafting their affinity must be taken into account. Strongly growing varieties grow best on strongly or less strongly growing stocks, late sprouting varieties on late sprouting stocks, and early sprouting varieties on early sprouting stocks. The grafting of poorly growing varieties on poorly growing stocks should be avoided, and also of early sprouting varieties on late sprouting stock or vice versa.

The variety 'Alkmene' is harvested in the first half of September. It ripens a week later and lasts until December. When overripe it quickly loses its taste and juiciness and falls.

The variety 'Starkrimson Delicious' is a mutation of 'Starking Delicious', first grown in 1952, in Oregon, USA. It needs warm, sheltered situations and a fertile, loamy soil.

The rows of trees in a plantation should run from north to south, as in this way they can make the best use of the sunshine. The distance between the rows is decided according to the estimated maximum height and width of the tree wall or belt. In this type of plantation the trees should generally not be taller than the distance between the rows, so as not to worsen the light conditions and in consequence suf-

The variety 'Ontario' is picked in the second half of October. The apples ripen in January and will last until May. It does best in sunny, sheltered situations and willingly adapts itself to the given soil conditions.

Intensive methods of cultivation

Intensive fruit planting should be done in deep fertile soils. Sunny situations are best. The saplings are planted in ground that has been well dug beforehand to a depth of 35—40 cm, well manured, and with all the underground roots of persistent weeds carefully removed. Regular and sufficient feeding with both organic and industrial fertilizers, and intensive protection against pests and diseases are very important.

The pear variety 'Fondante Thoriot' is collected in the first half of October. It ripens a fortnight later and lasts till mid-December. The trees start producing fruit in their fifth or sixth year. This variety is quite undemanding and does well even at higher altitudes.

fer a decrease in the quality and average weight of the fruit. A wall of trees should be at least 1.5 m from the border of the neighbouring plot.

As the number of saplings needed in this type of planting is large, it is cheaper to plant one-year cultivated trees and to form the required head later.

Espaliered trees are trained along wires. They are narrower and thinner than free-standing trees and give better quality fruit, but also require more work during shaping. A large number of types are cultivated in this way, and each of them has its rules, related to the wire support itself, the size of the plantation, the distance between the rows or, mainly, the methods of training and shaping. The wire should be zinc-coated, 2.5—3 mm thick; 2 mm thick raffia should be used for tying the boughs to it.

In freer wall formations the cutting and bending is restricted to the essential minimum. But here, too, there exist a number of fan forms that have their rules for training.

Mostly, it is apples and pears that are cultivated as walls, but this method can also be used for sweet and Morello cherries and for peaches. Dwarfs can be cultivated as belts or in the case of apples as spindle-shaped dwarfs where, in the first years cutting is combined with bending.

If you decide to go in for one of the intensive methods of cultivating fruit, more detailed information can be found in specialized reference books.

Picking and storing fruit

Fruit grown in light warm soils ripens earlier and has a better colour than that grown in heavy soils. On high ground fruit ripens later (4—8 days later for every 100 m above sea level) but it keeps better than fruit grown in the lowlands. Excessive feeding with nitrogen-based fertilizers (especially liquid manure at the later stages of vegetation) slows down the ripening, decreases the colour intensity of red fruits, and causes the fruit to rot more easily during winter storage. On the other hand, sufficient potash fertilization increases the sugar content of the fruit, and improves its colour and storage properties.

Fruit from small trees grafted on slow-growing stocks should be gathered ten or more days before that from tall trees on wild stock or vigorously growing types of stocks.

Extra large fruit store less well than medium-sized fruit of the same variety from trees at the height of their fruitfulness.

Rainy weather and watering towards the end of the ripening period have an unfavourable influence on the storage properties of fruit.

Fruit is best gathered by gradual selection according to species and ripening time, in dry and, if possible, cool weather. Soft fruit (especially strawberries) and fruit for storing are best gathered in the morning, after the dew has gone, or in the evening. Stone-fruit and summer apples and pears are gathered 4—6 days before full ripeness, as then they do not tend to rot so easily.

Autumn apples and pears should be picked when the pips are brown, winter varieties as late as possible, as they then keep longer. The right time for harvesting apples and pears can be recognized by the fact that, when slightly lifted and turned, the fruit comes away from the branch easily.

The following is a guide to the right moment for gathering various species:

Summer apples — The skin colours, green becoming yellow and white, the fruit is scented and comes away easily from the branch. Summer fruit falls from the tree even when the pips are white. Early harvesting prolongs the storage time, while fruit that is left to ripen fully on the tree keeps only a short time.

Autumn apples — Gather when the pips begin to turn brown. Leaving some of the fruit on the tree prolongs the storage time.

Winter apples — Most should be gathered as late as possible.

Pears — Gather on the same principles as apples, except for winter varieties. When gathered late these become edible sooner; when gathered early they need a longer time to ripen.

Cherries (geans) — Gather quite ripe, the softer hearts not yet quite ripe.

Morello cherries — Leave on the tree for as long as possible.

Peaches — Gather when the green of the skin starts to lighten, the fruit is scented and the surface gives a little under slight pressure.

134

Plums, Reine Claude and Mirabelle plums — For preserving, gather while the flesh is still rather tough; for eating, gather when the fruit gains its typical colour, the flesh is tender and the taste delicious.

Currants — As soon as they taste good.

Gooseberries — For preserving, these should not be quite ripe and the skin should be firm and springy to the touch; for eating, however, the fruit should be completely ripe.

A red skin is less common in pears. It is, however, by no means less attractive as can be judged from this picture, showing the variety 'Max Red Bartlett'.

Raspberries — Gather daily when the fruit comes away easily from the white pith.

Walnuts — Gather as soon as the green husks start to split and the nuts to fall out.

When picking fruit, work always from the lower branches upwards. Fruit should be picked with its stalks, as it lasts better (especially cherries and strawberries). When gathering fruit from low trees and bushes, place it straight in crates or suitable baskets. The softer the fruit, the thinner the layers in which it is placed. When gathering from tall trees a pannier lined with hessian should be used, so the fruit is not bruised. Picked fruit should never be left in the sun; store it immediately in a cool, dark place.

Fruit for the winter is best stored in a fruit cellar

The greengage 'Althana' is cultivated as a quarter-standard or half-standard. It needs favourable conditions and a good soil. The fruits ripen successively from the third week in August.

where it cannot freeze. It should be well ventilated, with an even, slow exchange of air throughout the cellar. Fruit can also be stored in other rooms, preferably facing north or north-east, where the temperature does not drop below freezing point. Ventilation should be of a type that can be closed in the winter, and holes should have a thick netting over them to keep out insects.

Before the fruit is ready to be put into storage, the cellar or shed should be well cleaned and whitewashed with a lime wash to which 3 per cent of blue vitriol has been added.

Fruit should be stored in the cellar on the day it is gathered. After discarding any damaged, diseased or sub-standard fruit, the rest should be laid according to species in a single layer in crates or on shelves that have been thoroughly washed and disinfected. Apples are laid with the stalks down, pears with the stalks up.

Check the fruit regularly and remove any that are damaged, however slightly. Apples keep longest into the spring if wrapped separately in paper.

The room where the fruit is stored should be dark and the temperature constant: in autumn and spring 6—8° C, in winter 2—4° C. It should not drop below —1° C, or the fruit will freeze. The air in the cellar should be relatively damp (85—90 per cent). If the room is dry there is a danger that the fruit will shrivel, so water should be sprinkled on the floor; alternatively damp moss or a wide-mouthed vessel of water can be put in the room. A room that is too damp, on the contrary, should contain calcium chloride, quick lime or dry moss, to absorb the excess moisture.

As fruit readily accepts other smells, it should not be stored together with potatoes or vegetables. Still less, of course, with other strong-smelling substances such as petrol, kerosene and so on.

Fruit can also be kept in an old well, a basket of it being hung on a rope above the water level — even plums or other soft fruit can be stored in this way.

If it is impossible to store the fruit in cool cellars, instead it can be kept in large crates, for instance, on a balcony that is protected from frosts. Or, in cellars with a winter temperature of about 10° C, in polythene bags with ventilation openings cut into them.

The cultivation of various kinds of fruit

Apples (genus *Malus*)

The original home of cultivated apple trees (genus *Malus*) is said to be beyond the Caucasus, in Iran and western Turkestan. From there, good quality apple trees spread into Asia Minor and on into Greece, Italy and other parts of Europe. The varieties of apples are classified according to the shape of the fruit and time of ripening.

It is difficult to define exactly the specific demands of apple trees on their living conditions. In general it can be said that they do better in loamy-sandy or sandy-loamy, loose, rather damp soils with a sufficient content of humus. Dry southern slopes are unsuitable. Apples are generally more demanding on soil fertility and moisture than pears, but they will tolerate colder situations.

Resistance to disease and frosts is specific for the individual varieties and often this is the decisive factor in selecting for planting in a certain place. The most feared diseases are mildew and scab.

Suitable shapes and stocks for the successful cultivation of individual varieties are given by their growing methods. For apples, use is made particularly of vegetatively grown stocks to influence the growth and fertility of species grafted on to them.

The shape and thus also the type of planting must be chosen on the basis of the growth and manner of fruiting of the species. The more strictly shaped types of fan- and spindle-shaped dwarfs are only suitable for species that will tolerate rejuvenating pruning. On the other hand, vigorously growing varieties are suitable for the freer, semi-natural shapes of dwarfs, quarter-standards and half-standards.

When pruning apple trees account must always be taken of the length of the new fertile growth and the speed of development according to the variety. New fertile growth usually forms on two-year-old and older wood. Flower buds are only formed on one-year shoots in some early-fruiting varieties, especially if they are grafted on to slow-growing stocks. Apples, particularly, require correct cutting; otherwise they are apt to form too dense heads.

When pruning species with short fruit-bearing growth, the branches should be shortened more. In species with long growth general pruning is usually used. Where the growth is medium long the two are combined.

Varieties that develop rapidly have poor growth, short new fertile growth, they bear early and plentifully, but soon get old. Therefore they need abundant nourishing, as well as regular trimming and early rejuvenating.

Damsons are a much-sought-after fruit. They are picked for eating when the fruits attain their typical coloration and the flesh is delicious in taste and scent.

Plums come immediately after raspberries and apricots in terms of nutritive value. Here are some Alsatian plums.

Varieties that develop slowly form large heads, produce fruit later and live longer. They are mostly cultivated as tall standards. These varieties require to be trained by pruning for 5—7 years, so that they develop strong, firm heads. Their later pruning is then much simpler.

Varieties with a medium rapid development come between these two. The training period is limited to 3—4 years, followed by simple pruning, shortening of the new fruiting growth and slight rejuvenation of the branches as necessary.

Pears (genus *Pyrus*)

Cultivated varieties of pear trees (*Pyrus communis*) originated through the multiple crossing of European and Asian species. The centre of their origin can again be placed beyond the Caucasus, from whence they eventually came by complicated routes to Europe. Many of the varieties that are still grown originated at the end of the 17th and beginning of the 18th centuries in Belgium and France. The varieties are classified according to the shape of the fruit and time of ripening.

As compared with apples, pears require a deeper and heavier but permeable soil, rich in humus and nutrients. They also need warmer and drier situations. They will not do well on soils with too much calcium or a high level of underground water. At higher elevations, pears need protection by walls.

The resistance of pears to disease depends very

Dark varieties of cherries also have a dark juice. According to their time of ripening, cherries are ranged into so-called cherry weeks that start when the earliest variety, 'Küpper's Frühkirsche', ripens.

The variety 'Royal of Querfurt' is quite undemanding in terms of soil requirements, although the fruits are smaller in dry conditions. It ripens at the beginning of the fifth cherry week (usually the first in July). The fruits remain relatively long on the tree.

much on the variety. Apart from scab, pears are subject to serious virus diseases, which again occur only in some varieties.

Shapes and stocks should be chosen to correspond with the natural growth of the given variety. Generally, pears form shorter new fertile growth and make less dense heads than apples. In the first years, efforts should be made by good training and pruning to prevent them forming high pyramid-shaped heads, which some varieties tend to do. When pruning, similar principles apply as in the case of apples, according to the rate of development, but the extending shoots should not be shortened so much.

The high pyramid-shaped head of pears should be lowered by a third. With young trees this should be done in August and for older ones in early spring.

Plums (genus *Prunus*)

Under the collective name 'plum', we group plums, damsons, bullaces, Reine Claude and Mirabelle plums of the genus *Prunus*. Plums have longish fruit, narrowing at both ends, and are usually dark purple with a remarkable bloom. Damsons are similar but rounder, and the consistency of the flesh is less firm. There are great differences between the individual varieties in both fruit and trees.

Reine Claude plums have larger fruit, rounded, oval or egg-shaped, with firm, tough flesh that is usually easily detached from the stone. The skin varies in colour, is sour in taste and peels well from the flesh. The stone is roundish.

Bullaces have more or less spherical or oval fruit, varying in size; the flesh is less firm and often sticks to the stone. The skin varies in colour and in the ease with which it can be detached from the flesh.

Mirabelle plums have smaller, spherical fruit, yellow to golden-yellow, with yellow flesh which usual-

ly comes away from the stone well. There are slight differences between the individual varieties, especially in their ripening time.

The individual plum varieties ripen from the middle of July to the end of September. On high ground, later-ripening plums often do not ripen completely.

Plums flower later than cherries. According to the time of flowering varieties are classified as 'early-flowering', 'medium early', 'medium late' and 'late-flowering'. Bullaces mostly flower early to medium late; Reine Claude plums, with a few exceptions, medium early; damsons and Mirabelle plums mostly medium early to medium late. Early ripening plums bloom medium early, later ripening ones late.

Some plums are self-pollinating, others are partially self-pollinating or require cross-pollinating. The partially self-pollinating and cross-pollinating species need a pollinator, so that a suitable variety, which will flower at the same time, must be planted near them.

Plum-trees grow best in loamy, medium-heavy to heavy, damp soils. Plums grown on vegetatively produced plum stocks can stand the wettest soil of any fruit trees. In drier soils and warmer climates, plums are cultivated by grafting on to *Prunus cerasifera*. They also require a good deal of calcium in the soil.

The production of fruit in plums depends on the situation and wind conditions. They are not so sensitive to frost when in flower as cherries are — but some species are more resistant than others.

Plums are mostly cultivated as half-standards, sometimes as quarter-standards, and in small gardens as dwarfs. They are grafted on to seedling or vegetative stocks. They are often subject to the dangerous plumpox virus.

Most important for plums is the correct forming of the head and maintaining sufficient light in it. Plums have brittle wood so, when starting the head, shoots

'Heimann' is a medium-late, self-pollinated variety. The fruit ripens successively but it lasts very long on the tree, so it can be collected when the last cherries have ripened.

'Morello Latest' belongs to the self-pollinated varieties.

should be chosen that lean out at a wide angle and with some distance between them. Heads where the laterals are not arranged in 'floors' live longer. Top cutting should be completed by the fourth year. Competitive shoots formed in the first years as a result of cutting should be removed in time.

Plums form flowers on one-year shoots only in varieties that fruit early and plentifully. Most flowers form on the short fruiting branches that grow on two-year-old wood. These are very fertile for 3 years and then gradually deteriorate, depending on the variety and the amount of light admitted to the new growth. The head must therefore be kept light and not too dense by systematic pruning and by timely rejuvenation of the branches by shortening them down to the old wood, especially in poor-growing varieties. The necessary pruning should be done at the end of the summer.

Intensive rejuvenation of old plum-trees is not often successful, as the wounds heal poorly. Grafting old trees is difficult too; it is better to graft them on to rejuvenated shoots.

Cherries

Cherries (*Prunus avium*) are divided according to the firmness of the flesh into 'firm flesh', 'semi-firm

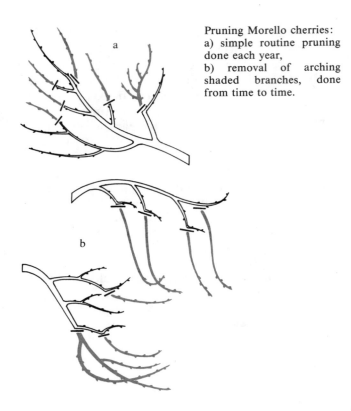

Pruning Morello cherries:
a) simple routine pruning done each year,
b) removal of arching shaded branches, done from time to time.

flesh' and 'soft flesh'. According to the colour of the skin, they are also ranged into 'dark', 'bright' and 'yellow' species. The juice of the bright and yellow fruits does not stain, but dark cherries have red juice that can leave lasting, deep stains.

Cherries belong to the early flowering fruit trees. They bloom after apricots and peaches, but before Morello cherries. They are distinguished according to their time of flowering as 'early-flowering', 'medium early', 'medium late' and 'late-flowering' varieties. All are cross-pollinating; the transfer of the pollen is done by insects, mainly bees. Some varieties do not fertilize each other.

Cherries do best on deep, permeable, light and gravelly soils that are sufficiently rich in calcium, well manured, cultivated and looked after. They grow poorly in dry situations and their fruit is small. In too damp places they tend to freeze in winter and suffer from sap dripping. The best position is a slope protected from the north. On flat ground, and especially in valleys, both the buds and the wood of cherries often freeze and they suffer badly from late spring frosts when they are developing buds, flowers and tiny fruit.

Fertility is greatly dependent on the weather, as cherries are more sensitive to frost than apples, and this applies not only to the buds and wood but especially to the flowers.

Cherries are cultivated in various shapes. The seedling trees of the wild Bird Cherry and Perfumed Cherry (*Prunus mahaleb*) are used as stocks. Vegetative stocks are also used.

Cherries do not need much pruning. They mostly form flower buds in clusters on flowering twigs on two-year and older wood. The one-year shoots usually bear axillary and leaf buds on the upper part and flower buds lower down. That is why when pruning once every 3 years the extending shoots should not be shortened by more than a half, so that buds which would form new shoots are not cut off.

The head is shaped by leaving 4 laterals at a wide enough angle from the leader and some distance between them. Laterals growing in a cluster from one place on the trunk give rise to sap dripping.

As cherries form sparse heads, pruning should be restricted — after the first 'floor' has been made — to removing badly growing or damaged branches. This is best done after gathering the fruit, when there is no danger of the sap dripping. In later years, if the annual growth is remarkably short, the leaves small and the fruit of poor quality, the head should be rejuvenated in the early spring or in the first half of August by cutting into the 3—5-year-old wood.

Some varieties of cherry form excessively tall heads on standard trees, so that harvesting is difficult. It is recommended that these heads be lowered either straight after the harvest or at the beginning of August by cutting the extended trunk to about 4 m from the ground above a thin horizontal branch.

Morello cherries

Morello cherries (*Prunus cerasus*) are divided into true Morello cherries and sweet sour cherries, and these are further divided into several varieties.

True Morello cherries are mostly grown in tree form, some varieties being dark to blackish red, with a sour and wine-like taste; others are bright red or even yellow.

The sweet sour cherries resemble sweet cherries in growth and, again, you can choose from dark and light coloured varieties.

Morello cherries bloom later than sweet ones, and again they are divided into early-flowering, medium early, medium late and late-flowering varieties.

Some Morello cherries are self-pollinating, some cross-pollinating. Some varieties can be pollinated by varieties of sweet cherries that are in bloom at the same time.

Morello cherries are less demanding in terms of soil requirements than sweet ones. They grow best in loamy soils, and are least successful in rough granular soils. They may even be cultivated with success on dry slopes, though here the Perfumed Cherry is recommended as stock. The best position is a slope protected from the north, as here there is no danger of the flowers freezing. Morello cherries are more resistant than sweet ones to frost in the wood and buds, even at flowering time.

Morello cherries are grown in various shapes, but the taller forms, standards and half-standards, are less frequently seen. The most commonly used stocks are Bird Cherry and Perfumed Cherry.

Morello cherries are cut according to their growth. They tend to form dense, overhanging heads, to age prematurely and have bare older branches. Competitive shoots should be removed in the first years after planting.

Poorly growing varieties form few lateral flowering twigs, mostly fruiting on one-year shoots that have the growth buds only at the ends. That is why the two-year-old and older wood becomes bare. This tendency is increased by the fruit being picked with stalks which bear the embryo flower and leaf buds. These varieties need regular cutting, the thick shoots at the end of the leaders being shortened by roughly a half, the lower thick shoots down to 2—6 buds. The terminal bud should always be a leaf bud. The new growth in the lower parts of the head is only pruned, the shoots that have fruited being cut away lower down. In detailed pruning all the one-year shoots are shortened in the spring by a fifth to a third and the older growth is slightly rejuvenated by being reduced to the young shoots near the laterals. After harvesting, excessive annual growth is pruned along with the shoots that have borne fruit. The least that can be done for these varieties is to remove some of the branches that are bent down.

The bareness of the branches can be restricted by cutting the stalks with secateurs when picking the fruit. Morello cherries can stand deep rejuvenation cuts quite well (to the 4—6-year-old wood). Excessive annual growth formed after rejuvenation can be pruned in August.

More vigorously growing varieties form more permanent fertile twigs. These should be pruned at fruiting time and, later, the older bent branches cut away. Pruning of the more vigorously growing sweet sour cherries is the same as for sweet cherries.

Apricots (genus *Armeniaca*)

The cultivated varieties of apricots (genus *Armeniaca*) do have different characteristics, but it is sometimes difficult to define the variety, as those most frequently grown are very uniform.

An important distinguishing feature is the time of ripening; also, in years with a late spring, the length of the vegetative period.

Another important sign is the early start of fruiting (that is, fruit appears in the third to fourth year after planting quarter-standards. A late start means that fruit only appears in the fifth year). Other indications are overall fertility, regular fruiting and resistance to disease.

Among the decisive factors for the successful cultivation of apricots are the conditions of the site. The apricot was formed genetically in regions with a continental climate, where there is a hard but short winter and spring comes quickly. It was here that the well-known quality of apricots developed — a short, deep winter sleep that is typical of most central European varieties. That is why varying temperatures in early spring have a very unfavourable effect.

The positions that suit apricots best are those near large stretches of water, on gentle slopes open to the west. They even like warm, dry winds in the second half of summer, and they prefer loamy and sandy-loamy soils.

The best shape for an apricot tree is quarter-standard, with the trunk 90—110 cm high. The most frequently used stocks are apricot seedling trees or the less suitable Cherry Plums.

With apricots, it is usual to form the head regularly only in the first 2—3 years after planting. As apricot wood is brittle, the head should be shaped so that the laterals lean out at a wide angle from the leader and do not grow from one place on the trunk. There should be a minimum allowance of 15—25 cm of space between them.

After planting, the laterals and the terminal shoot should be severely cut. As many varieties of apricot branch poorly and form too little fruiting growth, it is advisable in the early years of cultivation to pinch out the main shoots when some 12—15 leaves have formed on them at the beginning of June. This promotes the formation of fruiting growth in the lower part of the head and prevents over-abundant growth of the main branches. Summer cutting has the advantage that the flower buds formed on the shoots

Apricots are a favourite fruit. Individual varieties differ in the shape and colour of their fruit, the quality of the skin and the depth of the characteristic groove.

Warmth-loving peaches can be successfully cultivated only at altitudes of up to 350 m.

that grew after the summer pinching off sprout later in the spring, and therefore are not so likely to freeze.

In the spring, any fruiting growth longer than 50 cm should be shortened by one half to two thirds, so that clusters of flowering buds remain, but short growth should be left. In mid-June, annual growth longer than 20—25 cm can be shortened by a third to a half, which promotes the formation of flower buds.

After the training, pruning the head should be lightened, and is best during the growing period (August-September) or even in the spring. Strongly growing extending or lateral annual growth can be shortened by one third to a half at the beginning of June. Later, when the new growth is short (especially in summer after a good crop) the branches can be rejuvenated down to the two- to four-year-old wood, or even deeper if necessary. The robust shoots growing from the rejuvenated branches should again be shortened by summer cutting. Apricots do not tolerate deep rejuvenation down to the old wood.

Peaches

Economically important varieties of peach-trees (*Persica vulgaris*) are sometimes difficult to distinguish from one another. The greatest differences appear in the fruit and its characteristics: colour, shape and detachability of the flesh from the stone and the time of ripening. Also, whether the skin is felted or not. The time of ripening means the period when about a half of the fruit is ripe enough for picking.

Peaches require a lot of warmth, not only in terms of approximate yearly temperatures, but also the appropriate temperatures in the given season of the year, particularly in the growing period. In winter they can stand short periods of cold down to −25° C. Their resistance is mostly influenced by their state of nourishment, the weather during the previous year (mainly towards the end of their growing period), the level of the agrotechnology, how long ago they were planted and the quality of the previous crop. Their most sensitive parts, and those that freeze most often, are the flowers, then the leaf buds, the cambium cellular tissue, the wood and the roots. Peaches are less sensitive than apricots to drops in spring temperatures, but in this respect differences occur between individual varieties. Those with bowl-shaped flowers are damaged if the temperature drops to −3°C, whereas those with bell-shaped flowers can withstand temperatures down to

Peaches need much warmth for a good growth. Their blossoms are particularly sensitive to low temperatures. However, if the weather is favourable at the time of their flowering they can produce a high yield.

−4 or −5° C. Varying temperatures in winter and, particularly, early spring affect vegetative organs unfavourably.

Peaches also require a lot of light. If the heads are too dense and therefore shadowed, and if the trees are planted too close together, the fruitfulness and the quality of the fruit is unsatisfactory and the health of the tree rapidly declines. This must be borne in mind when choosing a site, planning the direction of the rows of trees and when pruning.

Pruning peaches: a) deep cutting of one-year-old grafted trees with premature growth, b) a kettle-shaped head in the 3rd year after cutting, c) a shoot with flower and leaf buds, d) cutting back new growth with flower buds, e) a short cut.

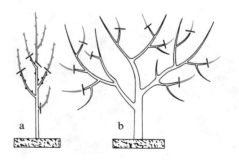

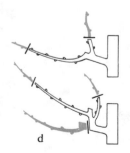
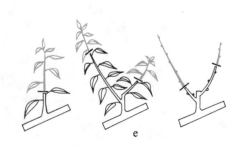

An essential condition for the growth and fertility of peaches is dampness of the soil. Optimum moisture conditions ensure correct nourishment, the growth of the vegetative organs, the efficiency of photosynthesis, the formation of flowers and fruit, as well as the maturing of the wood and the preparation of all the organs for the winter. Peaches especially need a great deal of water when the flowers are being formed, and even more after flowering but before the actual fall of the fruit, when it is growing most quickly.

The most suitable soil for peaches is medium loamy, with good water and air capacity and a neutral or slightly alkaline composition. Large quantities of calcium in the soil increase the danger of chlorosis. Slight slopes are suitable, where movement of the air decreases the damage caused by early spring frosts.

The best shape is dwarf trees with trunks 80 cm high, and the best stocks are those from cultivated seedlings; however, the vegetative type stocks are also used.

The pruning of peaches differs from that of other fruit trees. Peaches fruit mainly on one-year shoots, while older growth gradually dies off. So the aim of pruning is to cultivate firm head branches with plentiful fruiting growth.

Peaches are usually cultivated as free-standing dwarfs with widely branching heads (without central shoots). Cultivation of heads with a central shoot is unsuitable, as peaches are remarkable for their strong upward growth; they soon form a second 'floor', the first 'floor' becomes stunted and the fertile growth dies off in the shade.

For planting, one-year budded trees may be used, and these should be greatly shortened after planting. The trees take best if they have slender trunks and extensive root-hairs. The heads are pruned in the spring. If there are premature growths on the trunk, 3—4 shoots should be taken off where the head is to be. If they are pencil-thick, the upper ones should be shortened to 1—2 buds, the lower to at most 4 buds — cut to the outer bud. Any other growth and the leader should be cut above the highest side shoot.

If the side growth is weak, it should be shortened to the lowest bud close to the trunk. If there is no premature growth on the trunk where the head is intended to be, the head can be formed from the buds in these places.

When planting trees with branching heads that have been cultivated in the nursery, 3—4 shoots should be left and greatly shortened (the upper ones to 3, the lower ones to 5 buds at the most).

Summer cutting is important in the first year in the case of vigorously growing, irregular heads. This directs the growth of the heads and promotes the growth of fertile shoots in the lower parts.

In June, the annual growth made on the extending laterals should be slightly shortened to 20—30 cm, to a leaf pointing out from the head. But if the annual growth growing from a lower bud is in a good position it can be used for the further shaping of the head and the growth from an upper bud cut off instead. The ends of the growths should be even after cutting. The other annual growths are shortened more (behind the 5th or 6th leaf), so that they do not compete with the extending one.

In early spring of the second year after planting, the heads with short new growth should be shortened heavily — in the same way as in the previous

The presence or absence of felt on the skin, the colour of the pulp as well as the detachment of the stone from the pulp — these are the most important distinguishing features of peach varietes.

'Red Haven' is the most common peach variety. It adapts easily to various soil conditions, is undemanding, hardy and responds positively to watering. The fruits mature during the first 10 days of August.

year. Deep cutting promotes better formation of the annual growth, from which the basis of the head is formed by summer cutting.

Trees with well-developed heads should have the extending shoots of their laterals shortened in early spring to 30—40 cm (in vigorously growing varieties to 50 cm). If they have lush, strong new growth they are shortened less; if the growth is weak and thin, they are shortened more. Side growth pointing outwards from the head is shortened to two-bud snags, but strong shoots growing inwards are removed altogether. If the growth is dense it should be cut selectively to a distance of 10—15 cm.

At the beginning of June, thicker annual growth on the extending laterals should be shortened to 30 cm, but thinner growth should be left unshortened. The aim is to make each of the 3—4 main branches at a distance of 50—60 cm from the trunk form a fork, thus creating a head with 6—8 main branches. Annual growth near the extending main branches is shortened more, so as not to compete with the extending shoots.

In the third and following years the basis of the head is formed by the 6—8 main branches, widely and regularly branching outwards. In early spring, the extending shoots on the laterals should be shortened by one third to a half of their length, according to the growth capacity of the variety and of the fertile growth. The side annual growth on the laterals should be cut selectively, similarly to that in the second year.

The growth from the previous year's two-bud snags is shortened by cutting the shoot grown from the lower bud, again down to a two-bud snag. The shoot from the upper bud, if it has no flower buds, is cut off to the lower two-bud snag. If there are flower buds on it, it should be shortened above the 3—4 lowest flower buds or clusters of flower buds. There should always be an axillary bud at the end of the shortened shoot, as this forms the annual growth that ensures the nourishment of the fruit. The following spring, the shoot that has fruited is cut off. Shoots grown from the lower two-bud snag are shortened in the same way as in the previous year — the upper shoot to a fruitful snag, the lower one to a supply two-bud snag.

By about the 5th year the laterals, if they grow well, will reach a length of some 120—150 cm. They should not then be left to grow any longer, but all

The optimum soil pH for peaches is between 6.5 and 8. The best rootstock is a peach seedling.

the shoots at the ends should be shortened like the fertile growth, where 4—6 flower buds can be left. Only long, thick shoots are removed.

If the fertile growth in the lower part of the head starts to become dry and weak, rejuvenate the head down to the old wood.

June pruning is not usually done after the third year, though it is useful for rejuvenated trees, to suppress the formation of long shoots and promote that of fruitful growth.

In fruiting time it is important to prune at the end of the third week of August. This stops the annual growth and promotes the formation of flower buds. Longer shoots are shortened to 40 cm, shorter ones are not shortened.

Even with correct pruning of the fertile growth to 3 (later 4—6) flower buds, and with good pollination conditions, more fruit is sometimes formed than is desirable. If all of these fruits are left to develop, they will be small and of poor quality. Therefore small fruit, especially if in thick clusters, is removed soon after the flowers have faded, so that only 2—4 fruits remain on the branch at a regular, sufficient distance from one another.

Peaches have a great capacity for regeneration and stand this sort of pruning well. Peaches are rejuvenated when the heads have been neglected or frozen, or when the fertile growth in the lower parts of the laterals dies off. In dense heads with a large number of main branches, only 4—5 well-placed laterals should be left. If they have fertile growth, this is shortened by one third to a half, so that the ends are level. If possible, the fertile growth is not shortened, so that fruiting decreases excessive growth after rejuvenation. If the laterals in the lower parts are bare, they must be shortened more drastically, so that the dormant buds produce enough fertile growth.

Rejuvenated trees require treatment of the heads by June pruning. The extending laterals are shortened to 40 cm and the other shoots even more, so that they do not compete with the main branches.

Walnuts

Botanically, walnuts (*Juglans regia*) are divided into several varieties, which are:

tenera — with a thin papery shell

durissima — with a hard shell

maxima — with a large, deeply furrowed shell

racemosa — with smaller fruit in clusters of 8—12

serotina — a later sprouting tree

laciniata — a tree with imparipinnate leaves

fertilis — a shrubby tree (it sprouts late and fruits early)

The individual varieties differ from one another in habit, in size and in the number of leaves. Also, in their veining, the size of the catkins but, most of all, in the size, shape and shell of the fruit. There are differences in the sprouting time too.

Warm, open, gently sloping sites are the most suitable for walnuts. They require rather deep soil, rich in minerals and moisture, and do well on high plateaus with friable soil. Here they will not suffer from either hard winter frosts nor from lighter ones in

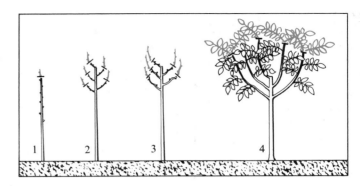

Pruning the head of a walnut after planting: 1—3) in the 1st-3rd year, in spring, 4) in the 4th year, in August.

spring and autumn. In lowlands, where they wake up earlier in the spring, they are most harmed by fluctuations in temperature. They cannot be grown in frost hollows or pockets where there is a high level of ground moisture.

The best shape for a walnut tree in the garden is half-standard or quarter-standard. Seedlings of the Stone Walnut (*Juglans regia* var. *durissima*) or the Black Walnut (*Juglans nigra*) are used as stocks.

Walnuts, too, require pruning of the heads after planting — particularly if the soil or climatic conditions are unfavourable. In the case of saplings with damaged roots cutting is essential, otherwise the trees become stunted.

Walnuts are best planted in the spring, as 2—3-year-old saplings — before the heads are trained — so that the roots do not freeze over the winter.

When the saplings are planted on their permanent site and the trunk is not tall enough, it can be prolonged from the terminal bud in the first year after planting. The other buds should be pinched out as soon as they sprout or, if the trunk is thin, they can be left as short lateral growth which is then removed in mid-August. The head should start being formed only in the second year.

This is done from the last 4—5 buds of the leader. The rest should be disbudded if the trunk is thick; if not, they can be left to form a strengthening growth which is removed in mid-August.

In the first year after planting, the sapling usually only makes short head shoots. These are cut down in the second year when they sprout (not earlier or the tree would lose too much sap) to 2 buds, one of which serves as a reserve; the growth from it is taken off at the beginning of the growing period, so that one new shoot is left on each branch.

If the new growth in the second year is not at least 60 cm long, it is shortened in the spring of the third year to 2 buds and the procedure is the same as in the second year. Then the head shoots usually reach the required length, so that they need not be shortened the following year. If the shoots are longer than 80 cm they are shortened by a few centimetres at the end of August. This better promotes their maturing and the forming of lateral fruit growth.

145

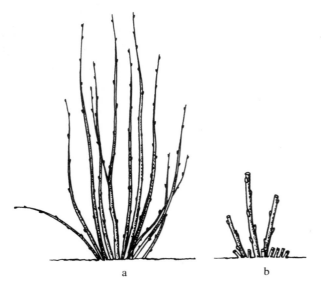

Pruning a hazel after planting: a) before cutting, b) after cutting.

Once the head of a walnut is formed it usually requires no further cutting. If some trimming is necessary later on such as the removal of certain branches, this should always be done in August, when the wounds heal better and the tree loses least sap. Walnuts should never be cut in their dormant period, as then they lose the most sap.

In less favourable conditions, when planting trees which already have a head, the shoots should be shortened to two buds. Only one new growth is left on each shortened shoot. If they do not reach the required length in the first year, repeat the cutting the following spring, again to two buds.

Under ideal site conditions the head shoots should only be shortened if the annual growth in the second and third years after planting is less than 20 cm.

The heads of walnuts that were not pruned after

Pruning a hazel: a) before cutting, b) after cutting.

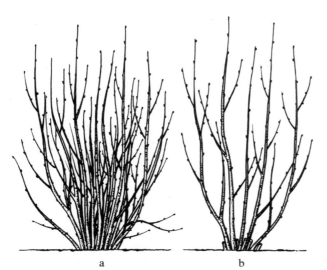

planting grow stunted after only a few years. But this can be corrected even later. The 3—4 best placed main branches are left in the head. The others are cut off at the end of August or in the spring when they sprout. The remaining branches are heavily cut back down to the 2nd or 3rd fork, during spring pruning. Only one new shoot is left on the extending main branch, the others being removed while green. If the shoots do not reach a length of 1 m in the first year, they are shortened the following spring to 1—2 buds. This second pruning is usually enough to promote a stronger growth of the head.

Otherwise, the dry or densely growing branches are pruned away every 2—3 years, to keep the head light. Old trees with short new growth at the ends of the branches (up to 10 cm) or those with drying heads, should be rejuvenated by shortening the branches at the end of the summer or after sprouting in the spring. It is best to rejuvenate gradually, say shortening 1—2 branches every year. If the tree is not too old and has a damaged trunk but healthy roots, it may be rejuvenated by cutting down to the ground. The trunk and head can then be cultivated from the new shoots.

Walnuts whose heads have been damaged by frost are rejuvenated in the spring of the following year, when it is evident where the branches have suffered. These are shortened down to healthy wood. The following spring, the remains of dead wood are removed from the ends of the shortened branches.

In less favourable soil conditions, walnuts can be cultivated from the nuts themselves. Some 5—6 nuts that have been treated against pests are sown to a depth of 10 cm on an area that has been well dug over. When they germinate only the best plant is left to grow on. This then forms a deep-reaching spherical root that can absorb the necessary moisture and nourishment from a considerable depth.

Hazels

Hazels grown in gardens today come from four botanical varieties: the common Old World Hazel (*Corylus avellana),* the Turkish Hazel (*Corylus colurna*), the Giant Hazel (*Corylus maxima*) and the Ponticus Hazel (*Corylus pontica*).

Cultivated varieties of hazel grow and fruit best in a mild, warm climate with a fair amount of rain. They need plenty of sunny days and a sufficiently long growing period. The best sites are submountain and hilly regions at medium elevations. Hazels like a sheltered position, preferably on western and south-western slopes. In southern regions they do well even on gentle northern slopes, if the soil is not heavy and cold. Frost hollows or pockets and windy situations are not suitable.

Hazels require warm, loamy to loamy-sandy, deep soils with sufficient humus. They will not do well in soils that are cold, heavy, layered or even too dry, however, as here they tend to be damaged by frost.

The natural shape of the hazel is a shrub, tapering at the top. 2—4-year-old saplings should be used for planting. For tree forms, the Turkish Hazel can be used as stock.

The advantage of the bush form is its rapid growth, though a slight disadvantage is poor fruiting inside the bush, and also hampered harvesting and cultivation of the soil. These are better in tree forms, but the trees age more quickly, a factor which makes itself evident in decreasing crops.

Most hazel varieties are cross-pollinated, so a mixture of varieties should be planted. The saplings are planted in the autumn, 4 m apart, then the shoots are shortened to 4—6 buds in the following spring. The bushes are kept light by pruning, which is done from the fourth year. Only 4—5 main branches are left and these, thanks to the improved light, then form plentiful lateral fertile branches, which can be shortened, if long, to 4—6 buds from June to July. Old branches are removed at 2—3 year intervals during the dormant period and, in the growing period, any

White currants are slightly less fertile than the red varieties; they are cultivated mostly in warmer, dry situations.

Shrubby form is the best for currants, which can last for as long as 40 years if tended properly. Several varieties of black currants should be planted together for better pollination, as most of them are poorly self-pollinated.

Currants

The modern currant varieties have been cultivated from a large number of botanical species of the genus *Ribes*, and so they have different ecological requirements.

Currants are divided according to the colour of

'Rondom' is a red-currant variety bearing dense clusters of scented, slightly sour fruits. It is a high-yielding, late currant that adapts willingly to all possible soil conditions. However, it suffers in frost pockets.

excessive new growth that will not be needed to take the place of old branches is cut off. The shrubs are rejuvenated in their 15th year, either all at once by cutting all the branches to 60—80 cm above the ground, or by gradually replacing them with strong new shoots.

The hazel usually starts fruiting in its fourth to fifth year. The nuts should be gathered when they are brown at the bottom and come out of the husks easily. During the growing period, the ground should be lightly dug over several times and kept free of weeds. Fully grown bushes are manured every 2—3 years with 20 kg of stable manure. A smaller amount of industrial fertilizers can be dug in every year. In dry soils hazels should be watered and mulched at least three times a year.

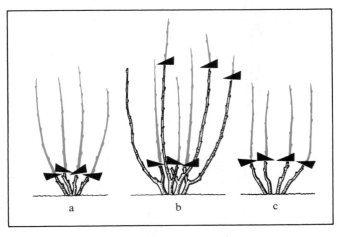

Pruning a currant bush after planting and in the second year: a) cutting back after planting, b) cutting back a strong bush in the second year, c) cutting back a weak bush in the second year.

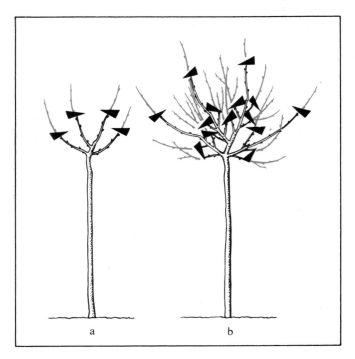

Formative pruning of a standard currant and gooseberry: a) cutting back the head after planting, b) cutting back the head in the first year after planting.

their fruit into red, white and black. The individual varieties can be identified according to their habit, their annual growth, buds, leaves, flowers, fruit, according to when they start to sprout and flower, the time the fruit ripens and their fruitfulness.

Currants should be planted where there is no danger of late spring frosts. Red and white currants do best at higher elevations, where there is plenty of moisture and an average annual temperature of 6—8° C. They require a high atmospheric moisture especially when flowering, and will tolerate even a slightly shaded situation. Black currants, on the other hand, need full light. They do best in lowland

'Jonkheer van Tets' is a fertile, very early variety with a slightly sour tasting fruit. It needs a humus-rich, nutritive and sufficiently humid soil.

regions with no frost, at most 350 m above sea level, with an average annual temperature of 7—9° C. Red and white currants are not so sensitive to frost in the wood as the black varieties.

As currants have shallow roots they require a fertile soil with a good humus content and great biological activity. Red and white currants need heavy, moist soils with a slightly acid composition; black currants can stand a drier, warm soil with a neutral to slightly alkaline composition. The soil must not be too wet, and the level of underground water should be 70—90 cm deep.

Most currant varieties are multiplied vegetatively, by either woody or soft green cuttings. Those that reproduce poorly are multiplied by dividing the plants, layering or grafting on to the Flowering Currant, which is also used to cultivate the tree forms.

Spring cuttings should be prepared from November to the beginning of February by taking cuttings 20 cm long with 4—5 buds from one-year shoots. These should be laid in bunches in slightly damp river sand and kept in a cellar. In early spring, they are put back in the bed with a light, humus-rich soil to which peat has been added. They are planted at a slant, so that the upper bud is above ground. Cuttings can also be taken in September, in which case they should be prepared and planted out in the bed straight away.

For layering, the mother plant is cut down to about 5 cm above ground the year before the layering is to be done, and the ground is well fertilized. The following spring, 5—10 strong new shoots are shortened by a third, then they are splayed out in ray

Gooseberries are relatively undemanding as regards soil and climate. Amateur gardeners usually prefer cultivating standard forms. The size, shape and colour of the fruits and their hairiness differ according to the variety.

Sunny, airy situations are the most favourable for gooseberries. They will tolerate slight shade but always produce better yields and larger fruit if grown in full sun.

Routine pruning of standard currants and gooseberries. Top: before cutting; bottom: after cutting.

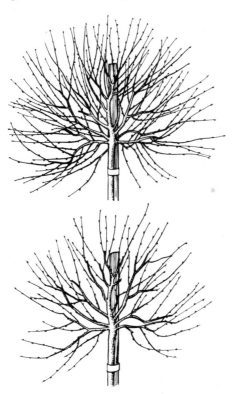

formation round the bush and pegged to the ground. As soon as the new growth from the buds reaches 25 cm they should be gradually covered over with a loose soil, so that they take root. When the growing period is over the rooted shoots are divided and planted out, and a year later planted out in the desired site.

Currants are best grown as bushes. In this form they can be rejuvenated easily and last longer; in good conditions and if well looked after, they survive as long as 40 years. Currants grown in the form of a standard are less suitable, as they age earlier.

Currants should be planted in rows 3 m apart. White and red varieties can be spaced 1.5—2 m from

Pruning gooseberry bushes: a) immediately after planting, b) in the second year.

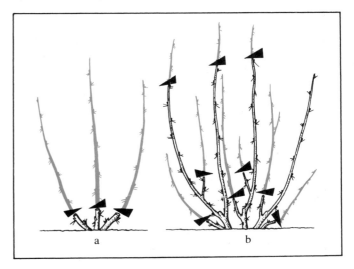

'Lloyd George' is the most widespread garden variety of raspberry. Several new hybrids have been cultivated from it. The fruit ripens at the end of June or the beginning of July. It produces a second, smaller crop at the end of September.

strong shoots can be left; the others, especially thin, immature or diseased ones, should be cut off.

In the ensuing years the long life and productivity of the currant bushes can be maintained by regular pruning. Early in the autumn or spring, 4—5-year-old ageing and poorly fruiting canes are cut off just above ground (age can be seen from the smaller leaves and fruit and darker bark) and all the branches lying on the ground (especially with black currants which rejuvenate inside the bushes), and any that are damaged or diseased. One-year shoots are left in their place. With regular care 2—3 shoots are thus replaced every year, and the bush is kept light with regular pruning. Then the one-year shoots are well covered and give good crops of high-quality fruit. Any large cut wounds are smeared with grafting wax, to protect the plants from fungus diseases, which otherwise penetrate the tissue through the wound and cause the branches to die off, especially in the case of black currants. At the end of May or the beginning of June, weak and excessive annual growth is cut off just above ground, leaving only those shoots necessary to round off the bush. Early removal of excessive annual growth encourages the

Methods of training raspberries and blackberries: a) box system, b) training along posts, c) training along wires.

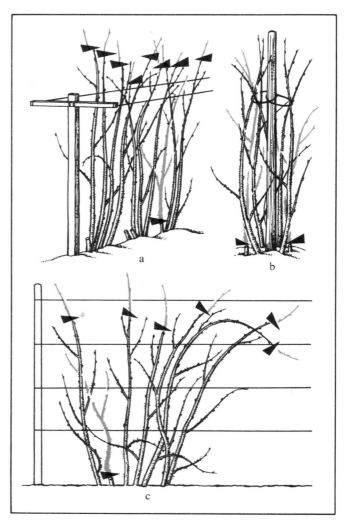

one another, black varieties 2—3 m apart. In the case of standards, the plants can be 1 m apart and 70 cm from the path.

Well-developed, fully-grown bushes should have 8—12 thick branches. This can be achieved through correct planting and care in the first few years.

As currants sprout early in the spring, 1—2-year-old saplings are planted in the autumn. Damaged or over-long roots are shortened so that 3—5 strong shoots are left on the aerial part, and the weak ones removed. Then the saplings are planted in holes with a diameter and depth of 40 cm, deep enough for them to be some 5 cm deeper than when they grew in the nursery. This enables all the shoots to be covered with earth, so that they make their own roots, which later makes rejuvenation of the bushes easier. Deep planting is also necessary in the case of species grafted on to the Flowering Currant, as otherwise the Flowering Currant forms shoots.

When planting, the holes should be filled with a well-ripened compost. Autumn-planted saplings need a hillock of soil round them and this is spread out in the spring, when the shoots are shortened to 2—3 buds so that they make strong shoots. The soil should be lightly dug over several times during the growing period, and weeded, watered or mulched, so that it does not dry out. In the autumn, the earth should again be built up round the roots.

In the second year after planting, the strong shoots should again be shortened in February to March to 2—3 buds, the thin ones either shortened to one bud or removed altogether. This forms big strong bushes on which, in the spring of the third year, 8—12

main branches to grow and makes them live longer. But shortening the one-year shoots of currants impairs their bearing, so this should never be done.

Standards can also be grown in the form of walls. The principle is the same as with bush currants, only the saplings are planted closer together and the rows run in a north-south direction.

For the belt form of cultivation the less vigorous varieties are planted 1 m apart and the more strong-growing 1.5 m. This form suits black currants and those varieties of red currants that have thick branches growing straight upwards. Shoots that grow between the rows should be eradicated, in order to keep the belts narrow.

When training currants along wires, the plants are planted in rows 1 m from each other and the bushes are trained flat. This is suitable especially for the less vigorous varieties. The shoots are either tied to two wires stretched at heights of 40—50 cm and 80—100 cm above ground or, to make the work easier, they are trained between two such wires.

Several varieties of black currants should be planted together to improve pollination, as some are poor self-pollinators and if grown alone the crops of fruit would be small.

Gooseberries

The varieties of gooseberry (*Ribes grossularia*) are divided according to the colour of the fruit into red, yellow, green and white. In addition, they differ in the shades of these four colours and in their intensity on those parts of the fruit that are in the sun.

Raspberries bear fruit on annual shoots produced by the previous year's canes. The two-year-old canes should therefore be removed after the fruit has been harvested.

Planting and first cutting of raspberries and blackberries: a) plant with shortened canes, b) plant in growing period.

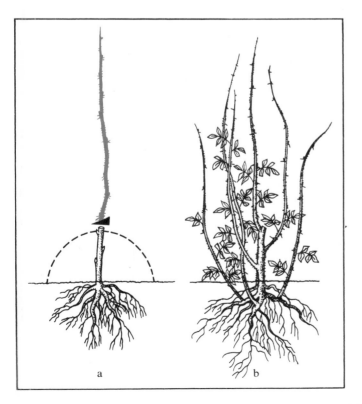

Pruning raspberries and blackberries in the following years. Weak canes can be removed during vegetation; 6—8 annual shoots are left to replace the fruited wood. Surplus new growths are removed and the remaining ones are cut back in early spring.

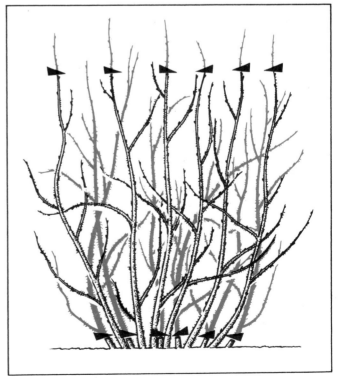

'Wilson's Early' is a blackberry variety with medium large, sweet fruit which matures from the end of July to the beginning of August. Its productivity is very good and regular and it has no special requirements with regard to climate and soil.

The individual varieties can be further identified according to the way they grow, the annual growth, leaves, flowers and fruit, and according to when they sprout and ripen.

The basic characteristics of the fruit are its size, form, colour, its hairiness, firmness of skin, the juiciness and taste of the flesh and, in table varieties, also in the number and size of the seeds.

The basic shape of the fruit varies from spherical to ovoid and ellipsoid. The evenness of shape is important and the resistance of the fruit to premature splitting; also, in table varieties, the delicacy of flavour of the flesh.

Gooseberries are not very exacting in terms of soil and climatic conditions. They do best in warm places at medium elevations and in medium heavy, loamy, damp soils with sufficient humus content. They can stand dry conditions well, though they do not fruit so well there, and they tolerate semi-shade. They need most moisture at the time of intensive growth and when the fruit is setting and ripening. As they are shallow-rooting they react immediately to any agrotechnical changes.

Gooseberries are best grown as standards. They multiply vegetatively very easily and have a good affinity with the Golden Currant, on to which they can be grafted.

Gooseberries are planted in the autumn (saplings with trunks 100 cm high) at distances of 2 × 1 m from each other, tied to firm stakes which, in contrast to the stakes for fruit trees, should reach higher than their heads. Later, when fruiting is plentiful, the individual branches are tied to the stake, too, preventing the heads being broken; 2.5—3 mm thick zinc-coated wire stretched at the height of the head can be used instead of stakes.

To make the best use of the space, the saplings can be planted alternatively with trunks 50—60 and 100—120 cm high, and at a distance of 75 cm from one another. In spring, after planting, the head shoots of standard gooseberries are shortened to 3 buds. The aim is to shape a strong, well-balanced head with at least 6 main branches. These are shortened every year by one-third to a half, the side growth by one- to two-thirds of its length. Shoots that make the head too dense are removed. In later years, ageing is prevented by rejuvenating the head through shortening the branches by about a third. Root suckers from the Golden Currant are carefully removed in time and at sufficient depth.

Saplings of bush gooseberries are planted 2 m apart, for belts 2 × 1 m. When planting, shorten the shoots to 1—2 buds. The following spring, shorten the 5—8 strongest shoots by a third, removing the weaker ones altogether. If side growth has already formed on the shoots during the first year, this should be shortened to 1—2 buds in the spring of the following year.

Further care should ensure that the bush does not become dense. To do this, all new growth not needed to round off the bush should be removed at the beginning of the summer (usually from the second year on). In early spring, shorten the lateral growth of the branches by one- to two-thirds, the extending branches by one-third to a half.

After 8—12 years, the bushes can be rejuvenated by cutting the old branches down to the ground, leaving strong new shoots to grow in their place.

Pendent branches of bush gooseberries grown in belts should be supported by a strong wire or stakes placed at a height of 25—30 cm on either side of the rows. More thinly planted bush gooseberries can be supplemented by alternating with standard forms.

Bush saplings of gooseberries can also be cultivated reliably by layering.

Raspberries

The cultivated varieties of raspberry (*Rubus idaeus* ssp. *vulgare*) can be divided into two groups: 'spring-fruiting' and 'spring- and autumn-fruiting'. They can be furthermore identified according to the amount and character of the growth, the formation of the shoots, buds, leaves and fruit. The fruits vary in size, shape, colour, taste, the aroma of the juice, yield and formation of the pith, according to the variety. Once-fruiting and double-fruiting kinds are cultivated in the same way.

Raspberries require a light soil, well supplied with nutrients and especially humus; they also prefer a rather damp situation with a slightly acid composition. They do particularly well in sheltered, sunny positions, where the shoots mature well, do not freeze and the canes bear plentiful and regular crops of very aromatic fruit. Shallow, poor, gravelly, dry soils and cold, shady positions are unsuitable.

Raspberries are grown either in belts between wires or trained on wire constructions. Canes obtained by division or root cuttings are planted in the autumn (in the spring only in heavy soils) in deep-dug soil that has been well fertilized with stable manure or compost. One-year canes are shortened, according to their thickness, to 3—5 buds and planted in rows 2 m apart and with 60—80 cm between the individual plants. The canes are earthed up to protect them from frost. In the following year, the soil is dug over in the growing period, weeded and watered and if necessary, mulched so that it doesn't dry out.

In further years, the raspberries are allowed to grow into belts 40—60 cm wide. The canes can be trained along two wires, one above the other, at heights of 80—120 cm.

Good pruning also promotes a good yield. The raspberry bears fruit on new shoots from the previous year. So after the harvest the two-year shoots that have fruited, as well as weak, damaged or diseased shoots from the current year, should be cut down to the ground. Only the strongest shoots from the current year are left, 6—12 per plant, according to the species. The following spring the canes are shortened again, according to the species, by one-fourth to one-third. If the canes are being trained on a wire construction, it is sufficient to shorten only the frozen or dried ends of the canes. Better branching of the canes and a better harvest can be attained by spring pruning.

With varieties that fruit in spring and autumn, it is an advantage to tie the canes to the wires in a loop immediately after the crop has been gathered.

Blackberries

The economically important cultivated varieties of blackberry (*Rubus fruticosus*) can be divided, according to their growth, into two groups: the upright brambles and the creeping brambles. These can then be sub-divided according to their growth, the formation of lateral growth on the shoots and the number of suckers. The varieties also differ in their time of ripening, size, shape, colour and taste.

The upright varieties can be considered the more highly cultivated blackberries. They are more exacting as regards growing conditions than the creeping ones. They also need a loose, clayey-sandy soil with plenty of humus and moisture. They are very sensitive to freezing in the wood. They require a sheltered, sunny position, as annual maturing of the wood is the first condition of their successful cultivation. Species that are frost-resistant have been cultivated from American brambles; there, they grow wild from New England to Carolina. Creeping brambles, apart from requiring a warm position, are not at all particular, and can rightly be called the most modest of all fruit species.

Saplings of blackberries (obtained in the same way as with raspberries), shortened to 2—3 buds, are usually planted in the spring in rows 2.5 m apart. Within the rows, the upright blackberries should be spaced 1—1.5 m apart from each other and the creeping ones 2—3 m.

The upright varieties can be grown in rows like raspberries. The two-year shoots that have fruited

Strawberries are among the most favourite fruits. They are the first to ripen in spring and the first fruit a newly founded garden will yield.

should be cut down to the ground after the harvest or in the spring, the thick one-year plants shortened in the spring by a third of their length, their new growth to 1—3 buds. Weak one-year shoots are removed in the summer. The creeping species is shortened in the spring to about 2 m and tied to a wire construction. The lateral growth is shortened in the summer to about 40 cm. As the creeping blackberries are less frost-resistant than the upright varieties, the shoots should be taken down from the wires in the winter in regions subject to frosts, and laid on the ground, so that they are covered with evergreen branches or with snow.

When planting strawberries in rows, the plants are spaced 25—50 cm apart in rows which are 60—80 cm distant. About 45—70 plants are needed for 10 square metres of soil.

Strawberries

Modern, cultivated varieties of strawberry are the result of a complex crossing, both by chance and intention, of many species of the genus *Fragaria*, from Europe, America and Asia. They are divided according to the number of crops per year into summer fruiters and perpetuals. The summer fruiters are again divided, according to their ripening season, into early, medium early, semi-late and late. Also, the size of the fruit differs according to the variety, and can be influenced by environmental conditions and cultivation. The flesh of the fruit differs in colour and so does coloration of the juice. Most varieties throw out runners, which are sometimes branched. These form leaf rosettes in the axils behind the stunted leaves, which take root on contact with the soil and form new plants. Only 2—3 runners should be left on each plant in order to obtain strong seedlings. Some perpetuals do not form runners but reproduce from seeds. There are great differences among the varieties in the intensity of the production of runners.

The best positions for the successful cultivation of strawberries are those with an annual average temperature around 7° C, best on flat land or gentle slopes open to the south-west. Unsheltered eastern slopes are less suitable, as are northern slopes. At higher elevations, strawberries bloom later, the flow-

Strawberries can be cultivated in any soil and at any altitude up to 700 m above sea level. A polythene sheeting tunnel or cloche protects the plants from low temperatures and ensures an earlier harvest.

One way to protect strawberries from moulds during rainy weather is to put a layer of straw or other suitable material under the fruits.

ers remain undamaged by late frosts and there is less occurrence of beemites. Of course, in warmer situations with sufficient moisture the crops are bigger.

In order to grow and fruit well strawberries must have plenty of water. The ideal amount is 600—700 mm a year. Enough rain in the ripening season has a beneficial influence on the crop, but excessive rain makes the fruit rot. The strawberry requires good heavy showers rather than frequent rain.

To ensure a good yield those varieties should be chosen that form their flowers below the leaves, so that they can better resist spring frosts. Windy positions are not suitable for the cultivation of strawberries, and neither are frost hollows.

The best type of soil is medium-quality, loamy-sandy to sandy-loamy, with a sufficient content of humus and nutrients. The composition of the soil should be slightly acid to neutral. Purely sandy soils are too drying, heavy clayey ones too cold. The level of ground water should be about 50 cm below the surface. Strawberries can be grown in raised beds in heavy, damp soils. The beds should contain at least 25 cm of fertile soil.

In the garden, strawberries can be grown in almost all positions and soils, because the soil and microclimatic conditions can easily be adapted to suit the plant's needs. In small quantities they can be grown up to a height of 700 m above sea level.

New plants should be set in July or the beginning of August; certainly never later than mid-September. Strawberries should never be planted on the same site twice without an interval of at least four years. They do well after beans, green peas, spring lettuce, early kohlrabi, spinach and onions.

The main mass of root hairs is at a depth of 20—25 cm, which is of importance for correct agrotechnology. Immediately after the preceding vegetables have been harvested, the ground should be dug to a depth of 20 cm. If the vegetables were not fertilized with stable manure, a good compost (at least 5—7 kg per 1 m²) or peat should be dug into the earth. Fresh stable manure is not suitable, but industrial fertilizers should be used at the same time (potash fertilizers containing chlorine are not suitable.

When preparing the soil, all the underground parts of persistent weeds must be removed. It is best to plant a week to a fortnight after the soil has been thoroughly prepared.

The plants can either be bought or grown from runners. These should be separated in cloudy weather from healthy, plentifully fruiting one- to two-year plants, which were marked for this purpose during harvesting. The most valuable are plants that grow on runners nearest to the mother plant. Strong seedlings should have at least 3—4 well-developed leaves, large leaf buds, a robust root neck and well-

154

formed roots. It is best if the seedlings can be taken out with a well-developed root ball and planted immediately in their new place. Before planting, the runner should be shortened to 1 cm. Also, the plants should be planted so that the root neck is level with the surrounding soil. If they are planted too deep they grow badly; if too shallow, with the roots exposed, they will suffer from drought. As soon as the strawberry plants have been planted, they should be thoroughly watered.

If there is no bed free for early summer planting, the seedlings can be pre-planted in a special bed. Here the soil should be enriched with peat (heavy soils with sand too), so that the plants form a large root system. The plants are put out in rows 20—25 cm apart, and at a distance of 10—15 cm from one another, then well watered. They are later transferred to their permanent place with a large root ball, so that their further development is interrupted as little as possible.

The traditional method of cultivation is to leave the strawberry plants in the same bed for three years. They are planted in rows 60—80 cm apart, according to the growing capacity of the species and its yield. The plants in the row should be 20—60 cm from each other. Also they can be planted over an area of 75 × 75 cm, 3—4 plants in groups 10 cm from each other. In the following year, after the harvest, all runners should be removed and only the original plants left. Care in the third year is similar. If the bed is kept for a fourth successive year, the crop will be considerably smaller.

Good crops can be obtained by growing the strawberries in sparsely planted belts. Several of the plants formed on the runners are left attached to the mother plants, planted in widely spaced rows, in the second and third years, so that a connected thin belt of strawberries is formed. This method prolongs the life of the plants, gives better crops and prevents the fruit getting soiled. But the plantation must not be allowed to grow too dense. So as not to exhaust the mother plants, the runners between them and the new plants are cut once they have taken root.

The most suitable for gardeners are dense, one-year or mixed one- and two-year plantings. Strong seedlings are planted close together, that is, in rows 35—40 cm apart, with the plants 15—20 cm apart. Fruit on the one-year plants ripen sooner, they are big and do not rot easily. After the harvest, the plants are taken out and planted in another bed. The former plantation is discontinued. The advantage of this method is that there is none of the laborious work of clearing the beds in the spring and in the autumn after the harvest. The disadvantage is the work connected with laying down a new bed every year.

If every other row of the plants is dug up after the harvest, a system of rows remains with a normal distance between them, and the young rooted plants are left in these rows, so that a narrow belt of two- and one-year plants is formed. The fruit of the two-year plants ripens rather later, so the harvest is spread over a longer time. The best plan is to have a dense one-year growth on half the area, and more sparsely grown, two-year plants on the other half.

The fruit can be forced to ripen earlier if a portable cloche of polythene sheeting is placed over the bed at the end of January.

Care of the strawberries during the year consists of hoeing and watering. For the winter, the soil should be earthed up round the plants a little, but the leaf buds must not be covered. On sites liable to hoarfrost, a covering of evergreen branches, straw or rushes is useful.

In spring the plants are cleaned, which means taking off any spotted or dry leaves, and fertilized with dung water diluted in a ratio 1:4 or fermented poultry manure diluted in six parts of water. Before flowering, the plants should be given industrial fertilizers — unless they are growing abundantly without it. Potash fertilizers should never be used from May to harvest time. Spraying microelements on the leaves increases resistance to botrytis and freezing.

Plentiful watering promotes the formation of flower buds for the following year. The ground may be covered with cut grass, strips of plastic foil or other aids, to prevent the soil from drying out and to protect the strawberries from getting dirty and rotting. Special care should be taken to water well when the flowers fade, after fruiting and at the end of summer.

When hoeing over the ground after the harvest, industrial fertilizers should be applied in the same way as before planting.

The use of black plastic sheeting protects the fruit from dirt, saves the work of weeding and digging over the soil, and speeds up the harvest by 3—4 days. The seedlings are either planted into holes cut in the sheeting, which covers the whole row, or strips of sheeting are laid between the rows.

Perpetual varieties are cultivated in the same way as summer-fruiters, but they can be planted closer to-

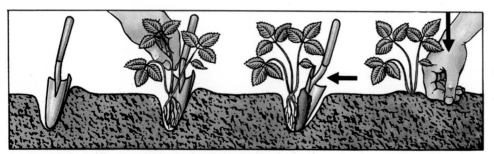

Planting strawberries. Mark out a row with a line, than use a trowel to make spacious holes, about 15 cm deep. The plants are placed into them with their roots evenly spread. Take care to have the crowns of the plants level with the soil; they should never be buried. Then cover the roots with the soil, press gently with the hand and smooth the surface of the soil around the plants.

The strawberry variety 'Rügen' produces almost no runners and has to be propagated from seed. It bears large amounts of sweet-sourish fruit regularly each year from the second week of June to mid-July, and again from August to October. It is suitable even for higher altitudes.

gether. After a fairly small crop in June, there is another crop after 6—8 weeks, which lasts until the first frosts. It is recommended that you pinch off the flowers and any small green strawberries at the beginning of October, so as to support the ripening of the remaining fruit. The ripening can also be speeded up by covering the plants with a portable frame or foil cloche. Fertilizing and watering after the first crop makes for a better harvest after the second growing period.

Alpine-type perpetuals are smaller and their taste is like that of wild strawberries. They reproduce by seed and can be grown in the garden as edging plants.

Strawberries picked on a hot day go soft and rot quickly. It is thus best to pick them in the early morning, as soon as the dew has partly dried, or in the evening. They should be picked carefully, with a short stalk, and placed in shallow baskets or crates. If picked without stalks they spoil easily. As soon as they are harvested the strawberries should be stored in a cool place. Any damaged or fallen fruit should be put aside during picking and then thrown on to the rubbish heap.

Vines

The original home of the oldest cultivated varieties of vines *Vitis vinifera* was in the western part of the Caucasus, in Asia Minor, Greece and, gradually, all over the Balkans. Although the varieties that originated in western Europe are well adapted in their biological qualities to the central European climate too, vines can only be cultivated in the warmest regions, where the average annual temperature is not less than 8° C. The average temperature in the vegetative period should be at least 15° C. The higher the temperature in this period, the better is the quality of the grapes. The nutritional value of grapes is given mainly by the high content of easily digestible sugars. Grapes also contain organic acids, micro-elements, vitamins and other substances.

One of the most important factors of a good site for the cultivation of vines, apart from warmth, is light. It has a great influence on the setting of flowers and buds, and consequently on fruiting in the following year.

Vines do well on southern, south-western and south-eastern slopes at a height of up to 300 m above sea level, or in warmer regions up to 400 m above sea level. Here they have plentiful sun and warmth in the summer, so the grapes are of good quality. But as steep plots of land suffer from erosion, they should be terraced.

At higher elevations, vines can be successfully cultivated only close by sunny walls, preferably painted white. They can also be grown under glass or under plastic foils by a wall.

Vines are not very exacting in terms of soil requirements. They can be cultivated in almost all types of soil, with the exception of wet or salty ones. The optimum soil reaction is pH 6.5—8. If the soil has a high calcium content, the varieties planted there must be grafted on specially chosen stocks, otherwise they will suffer from jaundice and die.

Vines need most water at the beginning of the growing period, after flowering and in the ripening

Planting strawberries through polythene sheeting. The sheet of polythene is spread over the bed and its margins covered with soil, then the plants are inserted through holes cut in the sheeting.

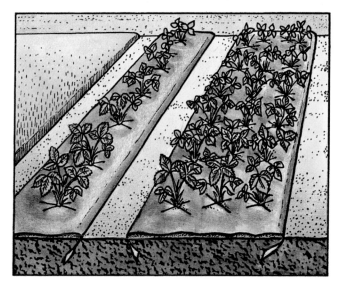

The grape variety 'Portugal Blue' ripens at the end of September. It has high, regular yields and is quite undemanding. It can be grown for the table as well as for wine-making.

season, when the grapes start to soften. Rain and cold weather are extremely unfavourable in the flowering season — the flowers pollinate poorly and the crop of grapes is small. To improve the chances of mutual cross-pollination several varieties should be planted close together.

Before planting the vines, the soil must be well trenched. Vines remain on one site for 30—50 years; so that their root system, which mainly spreads at a depth of 30—40 cm, has favourable conditions for development over such a long time (especially enough oxygen) the soil must be turned to a depth of at least 60 cm 2—3 months before planting. This means mixing the fertile soil with the subsoil. All large stones should be removed; however, small ones on the surface — on the contrary — help to keep the soil warm.

While trenching, sufficient quantities of phosphorus and potash fertilizers should be worked in, to a depth of 30—60 cm. If the soil is poor in calcium, this, too, should be added. Well-ripened manure or compost should also be dug into the top layer of the soil (10 kg to 1 m²).

New plants can be obtained from cuttings or by layering or grafting.

Strong 1- to 2-year-old plants should be used for planting, with root trunks (that is the parts from the roots to the base of the shoots) at least 30 cm long. The shoot should be at least 15 cm long, mature, with at least 4 developed buds on it and the roots at least 10 cm in length.

Vines are usually planted in spring, in March and April, or by mid-May at the latest, as soon as the soil is warm enough. First, the plants should be prepared as follows: the main roots, growing from the lower end of the plant, should be shortened to 10 cm, and any roots growing higher should be cut off. The shoot is shortened to 2 buds or, if there are two shoots, the second one is shortened to 1 bud. About 2 cm of wood should be left above the bud, so that it does not dry. It is a good practice to dip the roots into a paste of earth and cow dung before planting.

The vines are then planted in the well-prepared soil in holes slightly deeper than the length of the plant. A mound of fertile soil mixed with compost is made at the bottom of the hole, the plant put on it so that the upper bud is about 4 cm above the level of the surrounding soil, the roots spread out, and the hole half-filled with a mixture of fertile soil and compost, though never with manure. The earth is lightly trodden down and the hole filled up with water. When this has soaked in, the hole is filled with earth and a mound of light earth 3—5 cm high is heaped up over the top of the plant, to protect the young shoots from frosts and drying.

When planting by a wall, first put a stake in the ground beside the hole, so that the young shoots can later be tied to it. Then place the plants so that they slant slightly, with their roots away from the wall.

In the first year after planting, the ground should be lightly hoed several times during the growing period, to destroy the weeds and maintain the moisture in the soil. Special care must be taken in forking over the mound over the plants, so as not to break the sprouting shoots, which usually emerge in May or the beginning of June at the latest.

As soon as the shoots are 10 cm long, the plants should be treated for peronospora and mildew.

At the end of June, the earth should be carefully removed from the plant, any new upper roots removed and the plant earthed up again. This will encourage the growth of the main roots. In mid-August, the mound is spread out so that the parts of the shoots so far covered with earth can mature by the winter. Any shallow-growing upper roots are again cut off.

If the growing period is dry, the plants should be watered, and they may also be fertilized, but only until the end of July. New shoots are tied in to the stakes. In the autumn, mounds of earth are again made round the roots, so that they do not freeze. This completes the care of vines for the first year.

Even though vines can be cut from the middle of December, it is more usual to cut them in February and March, when there is no longer any danger of hard frosts. The temperature should not be less than −3° C. Sharp secateurs are used for cutting the one-year wood and a small saw for older wood. As distinct from the pruning of fruit trees, in pruning vines a snag of 2 cm should be left above the upper bud.

Table varieties give a rich harvest of big grapes if the cuts are short, leaving 1—3 buds. If more is left, the vine develops a larger number of clusters and is soon exhausted.

When cutting, each plant must be treated individually according to the variety, age, growth, state of nourishment and so on. It should be borne in mind that the shoots from the highest disbudded tip grow most vigorously.

From about mid-May to the beginning of June, when the new shoots attain a length of 20—25 cm and it can be seen that the flowers are setting, cut off all shoots from the highest buds that are not setting to flower, together with parts of the vine, to the nearest fertile annual growth.

During the growing period, the shoots are tied in to stakes or wires and all axillary shoots regularly broken off as they appear, so that the bushes do not become dense and will retain enough light. The axillary shoots are only left in the first two years after

'Müller Thurgau' is another variety cultivated both for the production of wine and for food. It has regular, high yields, needs airy situations and tolerates calcium in the soil. The grapes ripen in the second half of September. This variety is suitable even for more northerly regions.

planting, so that the bushes have a sufficient assimilation area and grow stronger.

At the end of June or in July, the fertile growth produced by the long rods is pinched off behind the 10th to 12th leaf, and non-fruiting growth is broken off. Axillary shoots are left behind the last three leaves of the shortened shoots. At the end of August, or when the grapes begin to soften, the ends of the shoots are cut back so that the grapes ripen better.

For gardeners, a good method of cultivating vines is in the form of a horizontal cordon with one or two laterals. These can be grown with trunks of various heights, according to conditions.

In places where there is a danger of hard winter frosts, slanting cordons are more suitable. The advantage is that they can be taken off the constructions in the winter, laid on the ground and covered with earth or with straw or evergreen branches. The laterals should be trained at an angle of 30—45° from the ground.

Irregularly trained cordons may also be used to cover a wall. Their laterals are tied to the construction in a fan formation, so that the vines cover the largest area of wall and the shoots do not overshadow one another. The laterals are formed gradually, one each year, so that they develop well. The growth on the laterals is cut to short (one-bud) and longer (four- to five-bud) lengths.

When a vine with a tall trunk ages, which can be judged from the lack of new growth, it should be rejuvenated. The old trunk is cut right down to the ground and the vines that have grown from the reserve snag at its foot cut to the height required to cultivate a new trunk. Only two shoots are left at the end of the trunk and one underneath it as a reserve. Other buds are pinched off soon after sprouting.

As the vines remain on one site for many years, regular supplies of nutrients must be ensured. In the autumn, the earth is dug deep, and every third year well-ripened stable manure is worked into it. If this is not available, compost or green manure is added in the spring. At the same time, phosphorus and potash fertilizers are put down: these are of great importance to vines. In spring, the ground is hoed to a depth of 15—20 cm and a nitrogen fertilizer applied. Or a compound fertilizer can be worked in to a depth of 25—30 cm.

In the following two years, when stable manure is not used for manuring, the amounts of industrial fertilizers should be proportionately increased.

During the growing period, the ground should be hoed several times and the weeds removed.

Table varieties of grapes should be picked gradually as they ripen and colour. The clusters of grapes should be cut off with secateurs or a sharp knife, taking care not to handle the grapes more than necessary, and laid in light baskets or crates so that they are not crushed. Spoiled berries should be removed.

To prolong the ripening season of grapes of table varieties, they can be hung up in individual clusters by hooks on a wire in a cool, dark cellar. Or even better, lay the grapes in thin layers in a crate or basket which is hung over the water in a deep well.

Some lesser known species of fruit

Mountain Ash

Some cultivated varieties of Mountain Ash (*Sorbus aucuparia* and *S. domestica*) have edible fruit, often called rowanberries. These trees are most undemanding as regards soil and climate requirements (they can be grown up to a height of 1200 m above sea level) and their fruit has a high content of carotene and especially vitamin C. Rowanberry compote is often served with game.

The Mountain Ash, in the form of a standard or half-standard, is usually planted at a distance of 8 m from the house and from other trees. After planting, the head shoots should be shortened in the same way as for other fruit trees. Later, the head should be kept light by sufficient pruning. Suckers growing from the trunk and the foot of the tree must be removed as they appear.

The fruit can be made into a juice with a high vitamin C content, in which case it should be picked at the end of August in the lowlands and in mid-September at higher elevations. If required for eating or making compotes, it is gathered later. If the stalks are left on the fruit, it can be kept in a cellar at a temperature of 2° C until March.

Chokeberry

This is also known as the Black Mountain Ash (*Aronia melanocarpa*), and its fruit has a high content of

Mountain Ash is quite undemanding in terms of soil and climate. It is grown in semi-standard as well as standard forms and is not only decorative but also very useful.

vitamins (especially vitamin C). It is very effective in cases of high blood pressure and sclerosis. It is grown either as a bush (reaching a height of about 2 m and a width of 1.5 m), or is grafted on to the ordinary Mountain Ash, on which it forms a small head. Saplings can be obtained from cuttings or by division, by layering and from seeds. As much as 10 kg of fruit can be harvested from a single bush, and keep for 2 months under suitable conditions.

The bush is also very decorative. It produces rich, flat clusters of white flowers in May, and in the autumn its leaves turn a beautiful red.

Quince

In central Europe, the Quince (*Cydonia oblonga*) is planted as an ornamental shrub, because even in the warmest regions its fruit never ripens enough for table use.

It requires a light, warm situation. The soil should be nourishing, medium heavy, rather damp and rich in calcium. The Quince is sometimes used as a stock for pear-trees.

The fruit is either pear- or apple-shaped, according to the variety. In south-eastern Europe varieties are cultivated that bear quinces weighing several kilograms. They keep very well if laid on a soft basis in a dry atmosphere.

The fruit is valued for its high content of pectin, and is used in making jams of other fruit and also in the production of medicaments. As the yellow skin is usually covered with greyish fur, it must be thoroughly wiped with a coarse linen cloth before being used in the kitchen. For cooking purposes, quinces should be picked as late as possible, in October or in November — before the frosts.

Medlar

The Medlar (*Mespilus germanica*) is a bush or a small tree reaching a height of 2—5 m. The fruits are oval or pear-shaped, about the size of walnuts and brownish-green.

It requires a warm, sheltered position with plenty of sun and a loose, nourishing soil. It is propagated by budding or grafting on to hawthorn trees, which makes it hardier than if grown from seedlings.

The Medlar reaches a great age, and gives as much as 15 kg of fruit or more a year. The fruits mostly have 2—5 stones with two kernels. They are gathered after the first frosts, which do them no harm; on the contrary, frosts make them softer. The raw fruit is not suitable for eating, but it is used in making wines and is added to jams.

Blueberry

The Blueberry (*Vaccinium corymbosum*) forms tall, sparse bushes with a very dense root system.

It likes a sunny place or a slight semi-shade. The soil must be loose, sandy-loamy, acid with plenty of humus and not too dry.

The Blueberry needs plenty of water throughout its growing period and, ideally, the level of ground water should be 60 cm below ground. Plants of several varieties (for better pollination) with well-

or suitable forest litter. They should not be fertilized with dung or industrial fertilizers containing calcium or chlorine, but with a suitable compound fertilizer, two thirds of which is put down in the autumn or early spring, and the rest at the beginning of June.

As the Blueberry gives the best fruit on strong one-year shoots (from the previous year), these are promoted by regular cutting in the dormant period. At the same time the bush is made lighter by pruning the weak or damaged shoots. A well developed shrub should have 5—8 thick branches.

Blueberries start to yield in the second or third year after planting. When the plants reach full fruiting, they give as much as 2.5—5 kg of fruit each, and the shrubs live up to 30 years. The berries can be eaten fresh or made into compotes.

A few words in conclusion

Apart from the species mentioned, use may also be made of the edible fruit of some ornamental shrubs. These include, for instance, the Cornelian Cherry (*Cornus mas*), which makes excellent compotes, the Barberry (*Berberis vulgaris*), which is added to compotes and jams. The juice has similar qualities to lemon juice. Haws have been gathered from the Common Hawthorn (*Crataegus oxyacantha*) ever since the late Stone Age. Today, they are made into juices and syrups and also dried. The fruit of the Japanese Quince (*Chaenomeles japonica*) — which only ripen in warm years — look similar to yellow quinces, and are excellent for making jellies, jams and sweets. Nor must hips be forgotten — the fruit of the rose, of which some species in particular take a leading place among edible fruits for their high content of vitamin C.

It would certainly be possible to find further plants that not only give pleasure by their beauty, but also the usefulness of their fruit, simply by researching into times past. Facts long forgotten can be re-discovered.

While on the one hand there are these old forgotten delicacies, there are on the other new species that are coming into being thanks to the tireless efforts of the cultivators. There are also hybrids formed by crossing, the fruit of which are or will in the future be a welcome enrichment of our meals. These include, for instance, the cross between the raspberry and the blackberry, and between the black currant and the gooseberry and others. We can only hope that there will be many more.

Blueberries, cultivated in many varieties, are both decorative and useful. To ensure better pollination, it is advisable to plant several varieties together. The fruits have a pale flesh, unlike the similar bilberries, but their taste is equally delicious.

developed root balls should be planted in autumn or early spring at distances of 3 × 1.5 m from each other. If the soil is lacking in humus or peat, the plants should be set in big holes, filled up with peat

Select list of fruit tree varieties

Variety	Size of fruit	Colour of fruit	Taste	Ripe for use	Other characteristics
APPLE					
Bleinhem Orange	medium to large	orange with slight russeting	nutty	November to January	dessert or cooking apple, does well on heavy soils
Bramley's Seedling	large	green, sometimes with red flushes	excelent when cooked	October to March	best all-purpose cooking apple, unsuitable for small gardens
Cox's Orange Pippin	medium	greenish, streaked and flushed with red	aromatic, juicy and sweet	November to January	best dessert apple, does best in frost-free areas
Egremont Russet	medium	russet with greenish-yellow flesh	distinctive nutty flavour	October to December	firm dessert apple, hardy, crops well
Ellison's Orange	medium	yellowish-green fruit with red streaks	aromatic with aniseed flavour	September to October	dessert apple, inclined to bear fruit biennially
George Cave	medium	red with greenish-yellow	juicy and sweet	mid to late August	firm dessert apple, regular cropper
James Grieve	medium	pale yellow with orange-red stripes	juicy and pleasantly spicy	September	crisp dessert apple, bruises easily but is resistant to frost
Laxton's Fortune	medium	yellow with red streaks or flushes, yellow flesh	juicy and pleasant	September to October	crisp dessert apple, inclined to crop biennially, frost-resistant
St. Edmund's Pipin	smallish	golden-russet	aromatic and juicy	September to October	tender dessert apple, heavy cropper
Sunset	medium	golden-yellow with red and russet markings	delicious Cox-like flavour	October to December	dessert apple, strong-growing and fertile
Worcester Pearmain	medium	red with fawn-coloured dots	juicy and sweet	August to September	crisp dessert apple, free-fruiting and hardy
APRICOT					
Moorpark	large	brown-orange with brown-red flush	juicy and sweet	August	regular cropper, good for a small garden
BLACKBERRY					
Bedford Giant	very large	shiny black	juicy and sweet	August	heavy, reliable cropper
Oregon Thornless	large	black	good 'bramble' flavour	August to September	no thorns
CHERRY					
Sweet cherry					
Bigarreau Napoleon	large	pale yellow, speckled with dark red	sweet	late July	fairly vigorous and spreading
Early Rivers	very large	deep crimson-black with pinky-red flesh	juicy and sweet	mid to late June	vigorous grower
Frogmore Early	large	pale yellow, mottled red	fine flavour	late June	vigorous and spreading
Merton Bigarreau	medium	reddish-black	rich	mid to late June	vigorous and spreading
White Heart	medium	pale yellow, flushed red	good flavour	late July	fairly vigorous and spreading
Sour cherry					
Morello	large	blackish-red, deep crimson flesh	slightly bitter	July to August	cooking cherry, hardy and excellent for north walls
CURRANTS					
Black currant					
Baldwin	medium to large	black	rather acid	August	ideal for cooking, dependable heavy cropper
Laxton's giant	very large	black	excellent and juicy	July	rather spreading
Wellington XXX	medium to large	black	sweet	July to August	vigorous and spreading
Red currant					
Laxton's No. 1	medium to large	bright red	juicy	early season	for dessert and cooking, heavy and reliable cropper
Red Lake	large	bright red	slightly aromatic	mid to late season	for dessert and cooking, heavy cropper, fruit is easily picked
White currant					
White Versailles	large	palest yellow, semi-transparent	rich flavour	early season	dessert currant, prolific and strong
GOOSEBERRY					
Careless	large	green to creamy-white	fine flavour	June to July	good for bottling and jam, heavy cropper
Leveller	very large	yellow-green	good flavour	July	one of the best dessert varieties, needs a fertile soil

Variety	Size of fruit	Colour of fruit	Taste	Ripe for use	Other characteristics
Whinham's Industry	medium to large	dark red	delicious	July	good for dessert or cooking, prolific cropper
Whitesmith	large	pale yellowish-green	delicious	June to July	good for dessert or cooking

GRAPES

Variety	Size of fruit	Colour of fruit	Taste	Ripe for use	Other characteristics
Black Hamburgh	large	blue-black	sweet	mid-season	greenhouse variety, hardy and prolific
Madresfield Court	medium	dark purple	rich and juicy	early	good indoor variety
Siegerrebe	large	golden	muscat flavour	October	outdoor variety, good dessert grape

PEACHES

Variety	Size of fruit	Colour of fruit	Taste	Ripe for use	Other characteristics
Duke of York	large	rich crimson with pale greenish-yellow flesh	rich	mid-July	easy to grow outdoors or under glass
Peregrine	large	crimson with almost-white flesh	good flavour	early August	favourite for outdoors
Rochester	large	yellow-fleshed	good flavour	mid-August	hardy and prolific, suitable for outdoors

PEARS

Variety	Size of fruit	Colour of fruit	Taste	Ripe for use	Other characteristics
Beurré Hardy	large	greenish-yellow with patches of russet	juicy and excellent	October	regular, heavy cropper
Bristol Cross	medium to large	clear yellow with golden russet, white flesh	good flavour	September to October	good cropper
Conference	medium to large	dark green covered with brown russet	sweet and juicy, fine flavour	October to November	reliable cropper, easy to grow, good for bottling and canning
Louise Bonne of Jersey	medium	greenish-yellow, flushed with deep red, white flesh	sweet and delicious	October	regular cropper
Packham's Triumph	medium	greenish-yellow, white flesh	sweet and very juicy	November to December	vigorous, good cropper
Williams Bon Chrétien	medium to large	golden-yellow with russet dots and faint red blush	juicy and sweet	September	good for bottling and canning, heavy reliable cropper
Winter Nelis	small to medium	dull green, with yellowish flesh	juicy and rich	December	one of the best late pears

PLUMS, DAMSONS AND GAGES

Damsons

Variety	Size of fruit	Colour of fruit	Taste	Ripe for use	Other characteristics
Farleigh	small	black with waxy bloom, greenish-yellow flesh	good flavour	mid-September	prolific cropper
Merryweather	large	black, greenish-yellow flesh	fine flavour	late August to September	good for dessert and bottling

Plums and gages

Variety	Size of fruit	Colour of fruit	Taste	Ripe for use	Other characteristics
Czar	medium	almost black, golden flesh	sweet and juicy	early August	good cooking plum
Deniston's Superb	medium	greenish-yellow with golden flesh	juicy and well flavoured	mid-August	dependable dessert plum for small gardens
Green Gage (Reine Claude)	medium	green with white bloom	excellent flavour	early September	fine for growing on walls or as a standard
Oullin's Golden Gage	large	pale yellow with red spots	sweet and juicy	mid-August	good for bottling
Pershore	medium	golden yellow, yellow flesh	poor flavour, but cooks well	late August	popular bottling plum
Victoria	large	pinkish-red with darker dots, golden flesh	good dessert flavour	late August	most reliable all-round plum

QUINCE

Variety	Size of fruit	Colour of fruit	Taste	Ripe for use	Other characteristics
Champion	large	yellow	acid and aromatic	October	pear-shaped

RASPBERRIES

Variety	Size of fruit	Colour of fruit	Taste	Ripe for use	Other characteristics
Glen Cova	medium to large	red	fine flavour	July to August	good all-rounder, heavy cropper over a long period
Lloyd George	large	rich red	juicy with good flavour	July	excellent for jams, desserts and freezing, heavy cropper
Malling Promise	large	medium red	moderate flavour	July	vigorous, heavy and early cropper
September	medium	bright red	fair flavour	September onwards	only moderately vigorous, needs regular feeding

STRAWBERRIES

Variety	Size of fruit	Colour of fruit	Taste	Ripe for use	Other characteristics
Baron Solemacher	smallish	bright crimson	aromatic and fragrant	June to October	alpine variety with a long cropping period
Cambridge Rival	large	crimson, red flesh	good flavour	June	prolific dessert variety
Red Gauntlet	large	scarlet-crimson	fair flavour	June to July	heavy cropping dessert variety, good for northern areas
Talisman	medium	deep scarlet	excellent flavour	June to July	dessert variety, needs fertile soil

Vegetables

Vegetables constitute a very important element of diet, being valuable sources of many nutrients. These include the very important vitamin C, provitamin A, vitamins B_1, B_2, PP, E and K. They also contain such minerals as calcium, phosphorus, magnesium, sulphur, iron and potassium. Medicinal principles found in them include antibiotics and diuretics. The importance of vegetables lies in the fact that they favourably influence the biological makeup of the intestinal microflora. They check the acidity of the internal organs caused by meat and sweet dishes. A further advantage is that they are an important source of digestive agents, such as enzymes, organic acids, digestible cellulose and many other minerals. Thus, the dietetic effect of fresh vegetables is considerable and their overall biological value exceeds even that of fruit. The desirability of vegetables is therefore obvious, as is the fact that they are the most important foods for people of all ages.

According to scientific and medical opinion we should individually consume at least 120 kg of vegetables every year. Ideally, this intake should include the widest possible range of vegetables, in order to benefit fully from their varied and complex content of the above substances. For example, a significant quantity of phosphorus — an element important in the growth of bones — is contained in parsnips and green peas. On the other hand, the greatest amount of calcium is present in onions, peas, cabbage and spinach. A high content of magnesium and iron — which influence pigment formation in the blood — is found in kohlrabies, cabbage, lettuce and spinach. The highest content of vitamin C, several times that of other vegetables, is found in peppers. Vitamin E is present in green vegetables, particularly in lettuce, peas and cabbage. Provitamin A can be found in carrots, parsnips and in spinach.

As the greatest shortage of vitamin C occurs in winter and spring, the consumption of vegetables during this period is of vital importance. The garden should therefore never be short of vegetables, which can then be harvested fresh, in the required quantity and with their fullest nutritional value. The latter should not be reduced by the unsuitable preparation of vegetables in the kitchen. To avoid this it is wise not to store them in unfavourable conditions for any length of time. Similarly, they should be cut or grated only with knives and utensils of stainless steel or plastic. They should not be cooked for long periods

Fully developed green peppers can be harvested from July until the first frosts. Mature fruits crack when pressed slightly between the thumb and forefinger.

in aluminium or iron containers, slowly fried or re-heated. In fact, the best method of cooking vegetables is to steam them.

Conditions for the successful cultivation of vegetables

Vegetables require a lot of looking after and this is usually very time consuming. If your time is limited, it is a good idea to grow only the least demanding species. These include chives, parsley, dill, caraway and lovage from the range of herbs available and radishes, peas, onions and possibly garlic from the traditional garden vegetables. A wider range — with any prospect of success — is, however, available only to those who possess sufficient spare time, a greenhouse and a cold frame. The latter can be employed not only for growing the seedlings of a range of species but also for forcing.

Heat and light

As temperature is a very important factor in the growth and maturation of vegetables, the siting of the vegetable plot, its height above sea level and its compass location, should all be borne in mind when selecting appropriate vegetable species for the garden. A plot facing north is some 30—40 per cent cooler than one located on flat ground, while plots facing south are about 10 per cent warmer than those on a level terrain. Gardens located high above sea level are colder, as the average temperature drops 1.5° C for every 300 m increase in elevation above sea level.

A frame should have its place even in the smallest garden. In spring it can be used for forcing and for preparing seedlings; in the autumn the growing period of some vegetables can be prolonged there. It can also be used to store vegetables during the winter.

An equally important growing factor is light. Shady areas are unsuitable for cultivating vegetables. Seedlings, in fact, suffer the most from a shortage of light. They develop slowly, flower late, are pale, weak, straggly and their tissue is thinner and finer. Frames and greenhouses must definitely not be sited in the shade. Apart from the amount of energy given off by the sun, the length of available light in the day is also significant. According to their requirements in terms of daylight hours, plants can be divided into short- and long-day categories with a third group being formed by plants that are not affected at all by the length of daylight. This specific characteristic of vegetables can be deliberately exploited in a number of ways. These include the speeding up of plant growth, the artificial shortening of daylight hours by means of blackout and their lengthening by providing some form of artificial light.

Soil

The majority of vegetables develop a deep root system during the growing season and therefore require a plentiful supply of minerals and moisture to ensure perfect development. They also need good soil. This should be at least 40 cm deep, with a drainage layer both to enable rainwater to seep in well and also the underground water table to rise. The optimum height of the underground water level is between 70—150 cm.

Although individual types of vegetables vary as to their soil requirements, it generally needs to be rich in humus as this contributes to the formation of its crumbly structure and provides a source of energy for its micro-organisms. A humus content also facilitates the warming up of the soil and its ability to retain both moisture and the necessary nutrients. The best soil for vegetables is a loamy sand or sandy loam. Clayey and marly soils are usually too wet and difficult to heat thoroughly and are therefore unsuitable. Similarly, light soils with a high content of sand, gravel and stones and those which dry out easily, are also less suitable for the successful cultivation of vegetables.

Planning the planting of vegetables

Individual vegetables or groups of vegetables vary considerably in terms of the length of their growing period, defined as the time between sowing and harvesting. As a result, it is often possible to grow two or more crops in the same bed simply by alternating the vegetables. However, this requires careful planning of the planting sequence in order to permutate early and late catch crops along with the main crop.
Early catch crops are vegetables with a short growing period, such as radishes, lettuce, early cabbage, early kohlrabies, spinach and peas. These are harvested at the end of spring, that is in May and June, before the main crop is sown or transplanted.
The main crop remains in the ground for the greater part of the growing season. Vegetables in this category include cucumbers, tomatoes, celeriac and sweet corn. They are sown or transplanted after the early catch crops. However, some main crops which take a long time to grow are sown without any pre-

A bed of onions with lettuce planted in between.

ceding catch crops early in the spring. These include carrots, scorzonera, parsnip and parsley. Main crops with a short growing season can be planted in succession after each other. Examples of this category include early potatoes and cauliflower, the latter being partly a late catch crop.
Late catch crops are sown or transplanted after the main crop has been harvested. Usually, they have a short period of growth and are frequently collected in autumn (early and late kohlrabies, lettuce, radishes, Chinese cabbage) or in the following spring (winter lettuce, leeks and spinach). The final choice between these times is usually related to the time when the main crop is harvested. For example, garlic can be planted with success after cucumbers have been gathered in the autumn and will then be ready for digging up in the following summer.

Some vegetables can be grown underneath fruit trees. These include early potatoes, lettuce and some members of the cabbage family.
Intercropping occurs alongside the growth of the main crop and the vegetables involved do not obstruct or compete with the development of the main crop. In fact, they usually have a short growing period and are harvested before the main crop proliferates. In such a combination, kohlrabies can be grown with tomatoes, lettuce with celeriac, carrots with leeks and so on. Gherkins are grown with success between tall, upright plants such as Brussels sprouts or sweetcorn.
Mixed vegetable culture involves growing two to three species in the same bed at the same time. Apart from maximizing the use of the surface area, such plants assist each other's growth and provide mutual protection against harmful pests. For example, lettuce planted alongside radishes or Chinese cabbage repels flea beetles and nitidulids. Similarly, tomatoes and garlic protect members of the cabbage family from the Cabbage White Butterfly. Rows of onions combined with rows of carrots protect each other from standard pests.

Many such possible combinations exist but it must also be remembered that some plants cannot stand each other. In fact, they can slow down each other's growth and transmit pests and diseases. This is the case, for example, when beans are associated with onions and peas, tomatoes with peas, and cabbage with onions. Equally, it is not advisable to plant tomatoes next to potatoes because of the easy transfer of potato blight. Tomatoes should not even be planted in places where potatoes were grown in the preceding year and vice versa.

The optimum use of the vegetable plot during the course of the year might be indicated by the following examples. Depending on the precise sequence, the first named vegetable is the early catch crop or the main crop, the second the main or the late catch crop, with possibly a late catch crop in third place.
Peas — Brussels sprouts; early lettuce — beetroot; early kohlrabies — carrots — spinach; early or winter lettuce from the preceding year — radishes — leeks; spring spinach — tomatoes — winter lettuce; radishes — gherkins — garlic; onions from seed or

Spinach is grown in rows spaced 20—25 cm apart. Either the individual leaves are cut off or whole plants can be harvested.

Cabbage contains the vitamins A, B and C and is rich in mineral substances. Lactic acid is produced during its fermentation; it stimulates the appetite and digestion and contains important antibiotic agents.

sets — Chinese cabbage; early potatoes — cauliflower; early lettuce — cauliflower — leeks; early kohlrabies — kos lettuce — white radishes.

Crop rotation

Vegetables demand a lot from the soil. In order to satisfy their needs it is necessary to rotate the crops around the individual beds. During the first year or phase, it is advisable to grow those plants which require a well fertilized soil enriched with farmyard manure. The following year less demanding plants

Cordon-type tomatoes are tied to canes or other similar supports. The sideshoots should be removed to allow the fruit to develop and ripen properly.

are then introduced. According to their requirements in terms of organic fertilizers, vegetables are divided into three categories, which are then used as the basis for the sowing plan, that is, the rotation of crops in a given plot on an annual basis.

Vegetables grown in the first year are members of the cabbage family; these include the cabbage, Chinese cabbage, Savoy cabbage, Brussels sprouts, cauliflower and broccoli. Kohlrabies also belong to this group but they do not tolerate being fertilized with farmyard manure. This group also contains fruit vegetables — tomatoes, peppers, aubergines, cucumbers, marrows and melons, and also celeriac, sweetcorn, leeks and early potatoes. The soil for the vegetables grown in the first year must be enriched with well composted farmyard manure at a rate of 6—10 kg per square metre. Alternatively, garden compost or possibly green manure can be used. Papilionaceous plants are the best for this purpose, as they tolerate liming and are a suitable early catch crop preceding the main crop of cabbages, leguminous plants, early potatoes and celeriac. Finally, a part of the growing season in the first year can be used for early lettuce and spring spinach.

The more fertilizers are added to the vegetables in this first phase, the more nutrients will remain in the soil for vegetables cultivated in the second year. This group requires a high humus content in the soil and is made up of root vegetables with the exception of celeriac; and of the onion family with the exception of leeks. It also includes such leaf vegetables as lettuce and spinach.

The third year, crops include leguminous plants such as peas and beans, along with herbs such as dill and marjoram. If the plot originally had a good quality humus-rich soil and is given a boost by the addi-

Kohlrabies are rich in calcium. Even the young leaves can be utilized in the kitchen; they contain three times more calcium and greater amounts of carotene and vitamin C than the thickened stems.

Onions contain valuable volatile oils with an antibiotic action that destroys bacteria, fungi and viruses.

tion of compost and industrial fertilizers, it can be used for growing carrots, onions, garlic, lettuce and spinach in the third year.

An entirely separate group is made up of perennial vegetables such as rhubarb, asparagus, horseradish, lovage and artichoke. They require the soil to be thoroughly prepared and substantially enriched by organic and industrial fertilizers. This builds up a reserve of nutrients before these vegetables are transplanted to their permanent place. In the following years, however, they also need a regular supply of fertilizers.

Growing vegetables by direct sowing

Hardy vegetables can usually be sown directly in the bed. They do not need to be transplanted or pre-cultivated in a frame or greenhouse. These include carrots, parsnip, parsley, beetroot, white radish, scorzonera and dill. Depending on the type of species being cultivated, the purpose of cultivation and the anticipated time of harvesting, such vegetables can be sown in spring, summer or autumn.

Less sensitive root vegetables and spinach are normally sown in early spring. Given favourable weather conditions this usually takes place about mid-March or, at higher elevations, towards the end of March. If they are sown in early spring the young plants first absorb the winter moisture, especially if the bed has been turned over in the autumn and then lightly loosened and raked before the spring sowing. More sensitive vegetables, such as beans, cucumbers, melons and marrows are sown in mid-May. Vegetables which were sown in early spring on to open soil usually do not require additional moisture.

During summer, especially in July and August, af-

ter the early vegetables have been harvested, the late catch crops are sown and are then harvested in the autumn (Chinese cabbage, beans, kohlrabies), or the following year in spring (leeks) or in summer (autumn onions). Chinese cabbage is sown in mid-July, autumn onions in mid-August and so on. These growths require regular watering, especially in dry and warm conditions.

The direct sowing method is particularly suitable for the later-growing members of the cabbage family. These have a compact root system, which is capable of drawing the maximum amount of moisture from the deepest layers of soil during the dry season. They are therefore not dependent on watering to the same extent as plants may be if they have been transplanted recently.

Sowing vegetables in the autumn is of benefit to those species which can spend the winter out in the open. These include spinach, winter lettuce, scorzonera, carrots and parsnips. The seeds are sown at the end of September and at the beginning of October; they then germinate and remain dormant as tiny seedlings. When the seeds are sown later, they do not germinate but simply swell during the winter and are therefore ready to germinate quickly early in the spring. The advantages of an autumn sowing can be best appreciated if the winter lasts a long time and the spring arrives late.

Sowing methods

Sowing in rows is the most common method of vegetable cultivation, in which the seed is sown directly outdoors. The rows are marked out beforehand at specific distances depending on the type of vegetable either along or across the bed. The beds are usually about 120 cm wide. The seeds are sown from the hand or by means of a funnelled sheet of paper into prepared drills. The depth of these seed drills is determined by the size of seed (larger seeds are sown deeper) and the type of soil (heavy soil requires shallow sowing). When sowing slow-germinating seeds, as in the case of carrots, it is a good idea to add to these seeds those of an indicator crop, such as lettuce, radish or spinach. These germinate faster and thus clearly delineate the rows before the carrots appear. Subsequent activities, such as hoeing between the rows, then become much easier.

Broadcast sowing is the method employed for seedbeds where seedlings are being prepared or where vegetables with short growth timespans are cultivated (for example, radishes, spinach, dill and onions for onion sets). The seeds are scattered by hand, then pressed in a little way into the soil surface, using the long handle of a rake or a piece of wood. They are then watered with a watering can, using a fine nozzle, and finally covered with a thin layer of sifted soil. Vegetables sown in this manner cover effectively the whole surface area of the seedbed, especially if the seeds have been scattered evenly. Such beds can only be weeded by hand, so only clean, weed-free areas are suitable for this sowing method.

Sowing in clusters involves putting the seeds in ring drills. This method is used for growing sweetcorn and cucumbers. When sowing in pinches, several seeds are placed in one spot. This is the practice with French and runner beans.

Preparation of seeds before sowing

To promote germination, particularly during the spring months when early plant growth is a precondition of a good harvest, several methods of pre-sowing preparation can be applied.

The steeping of seeds or spraying them with tepid water is perhaps one of the most common methods. This takes place before they are sown, with the objective of making them swell. They are then left to dry off slightly before sowing. The steeping of seeds is very effective because the water washes away various substances contained in the surface layers, which otherwise slow down or prevent germination. It is useful also to aerate the soaking seeds by shaking them in a closed container and to supply them with additional light — for which purpose a small table lamp is quite adequate. This is because seeds need oxygen for germination. During steeping it is important to change the water several times and maintain a temperature of 20—25° C. The longer the seeds are soaked the shorter the time required for germination.

The preliminary germination of seeds is similar to the above method. The steeped seeds are left in water until they begin to sprout. When the sprouting seeds are then sown, they must not be put into dry soil if subsequent adequate watering is going to be difficult. The young shoots would simply dry out and not develop further.

Steeping and preliminary seed germination significantly increases the percentage of seeds which will develop successfully. In fact, close observation has shown that — when compared to the dry seeds of the same plant — steeped and germinated seeds are twice as likely to develop as the dry ones.

Warming up the seeds before steeping and initial germination is carried out for a period of about two hours, at a room temperature of 40—50° C. Alternatively, the packet of seeds can be placed at a suitable distance from a lighted table lamp. This warming-up process should be repeated several times and is particularly useful for cucumber, melon and tomato seeds. It stimulates the growth of the plants and promotes the steady development of flowers and fruits.

Soaking. Seeds can also be forced by soaking them in a warm environment, followed by a cooling-off period in which the seeds are put in the refrigerator for one or two days. This method can improve the biological quality of some vegetable seeds such as tomatoes. In contrast, the seeds of onions, kohlrabies and celeriac, for example, must not be forced by this method as it causes them to flower too soon.

Coating. Seeds can also be coated to provide better nourishment for the young plants when they have germinated. This process involves dipping damp seeds in a pulverized organic fertilizer. Seeds treated in this way must then be sown as quickly as possible. The powder should contain basic minerals, trace elements and growth promoting agents, blended in such a way that they allow the germinating seeds to make the best possible use of them. The powder left over after the seeds have been coated can then be dissolved in water and used as a liquid fertilizer for plants growing in the cold frame.

Growing vegetables from pre-cultivated seedlings

The most important factor in the growing of vegetables is the thorough preparation of the bed. This should take place in spring, when the weather is still cold and the soil is not yet in an ideal state for planting. Growing conditions outdoors are usually much less favourable than the conditions in which seedlings have been grown, hence the care needed when planting them outdoors.

When the surface of the bed has been lightly loosened and raked, it can be marked out in the same way as for direct sowing, using a line or marker. This is easy to make by nailing evenly spaced large nails into a plank of wood. The plank should be the same length as the width of the bed (that is 120 cm); the nails should be 20 cm apart on one face of the plank and 30 cm apart on the other. Alternatively, hardwood pegs can be used instead of nails, these being hammered into prepared holes. The resulting rake can then be attached firmly to a handle.

The successful cultivation of vegetables is dependent on healthy, hardened off and adequately strong but not overgrown seedlings. The best results are achieved with plants which have had an uninterrupted growth from the time they were sown to the time of harvesting. Tough and stunted seedlings often stop growing prematurely; they flower but never produce quality vegetables, despite being given every care and attention. In particular, cauliflower seedlings can become tough and develop premature, small but tall rosettes if they have been growing for too long and too slowly. Low temperatures for any length of time can also adversely affect the growing rhythm of some plants. For example, kohlrabies — if forced too quickly — can form elongated, thickened stems and begin flowering even in the first year of cultivation. Celeriac seedlings are equally sensitive to low temperatures around the zero mark.

If seedlings are to be transported over long distances and are thus not going to be transplanted immediately, they need to be well watered and put into plastic bags. Similar treatment is required even for seedlings with a firm root system, especially if they are grown in peat pots, because these tend to dry out more quickly than other kinds.

The time and methods of planting out
The earliest vegetables are planted outdoors at the end of March. Under favourable weather conditions, these can be early lettuce and some members of the cabbage family. Warmth-loving vegetables, such as cucumbers, tomatoes, celeriac etc., are put out until the second half of May. Early varieties with a short growing season are planted out in July to be harvested in autumn. These late catch crops include cauliflowers, kohlrabies, Savoy cabbage and lettuce.

The best time for planting out is during cloudy weather prior to rain or after a substantial downpour, once the soil has had time to dry out a little. It is then possible to water the seedlings only slightly, as the ground will remain sufficiently damp until they take. It is not advisable to do the planting during windy weather or when it is warm and sunny. If the latter conditions prevail, it is best to plant the seedlings in the evening. The drop in temperature during the night and early morning allows the seedlings to settle and withstand the heat of the following day. Similarly, newly planted seedlings are best watered in the evening.

Seedlings grown freely in a frame or a seedbed can be planted using a dibber. Those grown in various types of pots are put out using a trowel or a hoe. Whatever the method, the roots should have sufficient room in the hole to avoid any damage being done to them. The soil is then pressed in firmly around the roots to ensure that the plant is well anchored and there are no pockets of air left around the root ball. Tomato and cucumber seedlings should be placed at an angle with about a third of their stalks covered with soil. Cabbage and leeks can also be set deep but, on the other hand, celeriac and lettuce must not be 'drowned' as celeriac then forms only small tubers with many roots and lettuce in such conditions 'hearts up' with difficulty and its lower leaves rot.

Depending on the vegetable species and the cultivation method to be employed later, the seedlings

The best yields of celeriac are obtained from individually potted seedlings.

are either placed in rows (onions, garlic, leeks), in clusters (tomatoes, peppers) or in a square, rectangular or triangular layout (lettuce, kohlrabies, cauliflower).

Caring for vegetables during the growing season

When growing vegetables all the agrobiological principles relevant to the given species must be observed. Vegetables need to be regularly watered and fertilized, hoed and weeded etc. Additionally, they

Potted celeriac seedlings have fully developed root balls and continue growing without interruption after they have been planted out.

might need to be thinned out if they have been grown directly outdoors or earthed up or mulched.

Thinning

Vegetables need to be thinned out if they have been sown too densely or if they require more space for successful and balanced growth. This applies to carrots, parsnips and parsley in particular. The seedlings are thinned out during the first phase of their growth so that only the stronger plants, regularly distanced from each other, are left while the remaining ones are pulled out. Some vegetables such as spinach, dill and chives, do not require this treatment.

Regular watering

Practically all vegetables need adequate and regular watering at a particular stage of their development. The most water is required by leaf and fruit vegetables, particularly if they have large root systems, designed to extract moisture from the greatest depths. Plants which are not particularly well rooted need to be given small amounts of water at short intervals.

In uncovered beds, the best time for watering is the late afternoon and early evening. Cloches, frames and greenhouses are best watered in the morning so that plants can dry out before the evening. Tomatoes, in particular, require plentiful watering of their roots. However, if the leaves and fruit are sprayed there is the danger of the spread of potato blight and other similar diseases. Onions only require abundant watering during the first half of their growing period. Indeed, some vegetables, such as onion sets, shallots, garlic and beetroot, do not need to be watered at all if there has been sufficient rainfall.

Fertilization during growth

Basic nutrition is added to the soil by means of fertilizers, before sowing or planting out. This is usually sufficient for vegetables with a short growing season but those which take longer to grow need to be given an extra portion of feed during growth. Vegetables sown outdoors are given further nourishment after they have been thinned out, whilst transplanted vegetables are fertilized again after two weeks. An adequate supply of nitrogen, which promotes plant growth, can be ensured by an application of ammonium nitrate with calcium or calcium nitrate or urea. Additional supplies of nitrogen can be given several times, at intervals of about three weeks. Nitrogen can be employed until the middle of the vegetative season and this ensures a good maturation of the crop. During the final growth period other minerals such as potassium and phosphorus can be added depending on the requirements of individual plants. For example, potassium sulphate is added to cabbage shortly before it starts forming the hearts; superphosphate is added to fruit vegetables to promote the formation of flowers and fruits. There are, of course, specific types of fertilizer for individual vegetable species.

The most effective method of applying a fertilizer is to deposit it in shallow grooves between the rows of plants or, alternatively, around the plants. It can be scattered in the grooves, or dissolved in water and applied by a watering can. The grooves are raked over afterwards. The fertilizer can also be scattered over the soil surface, either in the direction of the rows between the plants or in a circle around vegetables planted in wide clusters. It can also simply be broadcast if the vegetables have been planted in dense rows. Such methods are appropriate for quickly dissolving fertilizers which need not be worked into the soil. It is best employed before rain, particularly if the plants cannot be watered immediately afterwards. Without due care, the last method in particular could result in the fertilizer sticking to the plants and burning them.

The addition of fertilizers in the form of solutions is not only appropriate for soluble industrial fertilizers but also for organic fertilizers. The most suitable is poultry and pigeon manure. This should be added to water and occasionally stirred in a large container before being left for several days to ferment and then applied. The container should be about half filled with manure and then topped up with water. Before being used, the resulting solution should be diluted in the ratio of one part to ten parts water. A ten-litre watering can should then be used to fertilize 2 m² of the vegetable plot. Any remaining sediment at the bottom of the container can be emptied on to the compost heap.

Controlling weeds

Weeds deprive vegetables of much nourishment and moisture, they also facilitate the spread of diseases and harbour pests. They shade the cultivated plants and often suffocate them, to the detriment of the final crop yield.

In the battle against weeds there are a number of possible strategies to curb their growth. Above all, hoeing is important, employing hoes of various shapes and sizes. Gardeners commonly use the weeding or Dutch hoes, which are both suitable for small beds. Alternatively, a hand-weeding machine can be employed when treating long rows of vegetables in large plots. Hoeing also loosens and aerates the soil between the rows and breaks up the soil crust. Weeding is particularly effective in dry weather when the uprooted weeds soon dry out. In damp conditions, however, the dislocated weeds often continue to grow. Above all, weeding should be carried out well before weeds become too established.

Weeding and hoeing are often linked to other gardening strategies. For example, hoeing simultaneously loosens and aerates the soil, while the plants are thinned out and earthed up.

When the soil is loosened by a hoe or a hand fork this also inhibits the growth of weeds. Hand forks come in a variety of shapes: they may have one or more points, or several claws or a flat cutting edge. When employed for loosening the soil or making furrows, they are dragged along the soil surface. There are also various types of mechanical soil aerators for breaking up the soil crust.

The use of chemical herbicides for killing weeds is

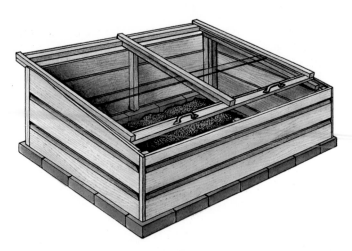

This light, transportable timber frame can either be left in one place or moved from one bed to another as needed. Glass or polythene sheets are used for cover. A row of bricks can be placed under the frame to protect the timber from rising damp.

not recommended. Herbicides should only be used in those situations where weed growth is so entrenched that weeding or hoeing will make little impact. The temporary destruction of weeds on paths or on compost heaps can be done by the use of herbicides with a short-term effect and which do not leave lasting traces in the soil.

In the fight against garden weeds periodic and routine interventions are inadequate. It is therefore necessary to develop an overall strategy, particularly designed to prevent their occurrence. First of all, weeds must not be allowed to reseed themselves either in the garden plot or on the adjacent paths, or on the compost heap. Their seeds usually mature during the summer, often after the parent plant has been cut down. The roots and shoots of perennial weeds are never put on the compost heap. In fact, all centres of weed infestation must be obliterated. To this end the rotation of cultivated crops is useful, particularly the introduction of root vegetables (early potatoes) and leguminous plants.

Earthing up

Plants that have been earthed up become much more firmly anchored in the soil and are not easily uprooted in rainy or windy weather. The earthed part of the plant usually forms roots and the enlarged root system is then able to draw more nutrients and moisture from the soil.

A cross section of a heated frame. The bottom layer, a 30-cm mixture of manure and leaves, is covered by a 15—20-cm layer of frame soil.

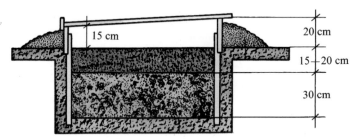

The soil is earthed up around tomatoes, cucumbers, sweetcorn and early potatoes. Besides hoes, various rotovating machines can be used when the vegetables are grown in rows. Celeriac, onions, kohlrabies and lettuce are not earthed up because they do not tolerate deep planting.

Earthing up is the process which stimulates etiolation (bleaching) of some vegetables. This takes place because the piled up soil stops light reaching the plants. As a result, the bleached section of the plant becomes finer, crisper and has a better flavour. The earthing up process is particularly employed for leeks, celery and asparagus.

Mulching

Mulching is the process which provides a protective covering for warmth-loving vegetables in particular. It promotes early ripening and positively influences the level of output of such plants. Traditional mulching materials such as manure mixed with straw, cut grass, peat and paper have now been replaced by more effective and practical sheets of plastic.

Mulching using sheets of plastic decreases significantly the evaporation of water from the soil. This conservation of soil moisture means that there is no need to water vegetables so frequently. Plastic sheets also prevent the soil from developing a hard crust, maintain its crumbly structure and by encouraging a more favourable environment, they also stimulate the activity of micro-organisms in the soil. However, the increased moisture and temperature underneath the sheeting can also provide equally favourable conditions for the development of moulds. Non-translucent sheeting impedes the growth of weeds better than translucent sheeting. The latter initially allows the fast growth of weeds but then, as the temperature underneath the sheeting rises, their growth is suppressed. Translucent sheeting increases the temperature of the soil surface by about 5° C.

Mulching is best conducted by using sheeting about 0.03—0.05 mm thick. This is either placed between rows of vegetables as close to the plants as possible or, more often, it covers the whole surface of the bed before plants are put out. If the latter is the case cross-shaped slits or circular holes are cut at regular intervals and plants or seeds are then placed in them. Mulching is especially recommended for warmth-loving plants such as the salad vegetables, tomatoes, peppers and cucumbers.

Protection against diseases and pests

In the course of the growing season many diseases and pests appear, damaging vegetables and reducing the crop. Natural preventive measures are often forgotten and replaced by chemical treatment, which is costly and demanding and must be applied in an experienced way. Often it also has little effect, particularly if it is applied late. If healthy nourishment is a prime consideration, the application of chemicals to protect vegetables in the garden should be undertaken as seldom as possible. In the case of vegetables in particular, the use of chemicals is inappropriate

and often harmful. In this respect, potatoes and root vegetables are the most vulnerable.

The principles of disease prevention and pest control are primarily based on the maintenance of a clean environment for the production of vegetables. In addition to the disinfection of seeds before they are sown, it is also important to ensure the thorough disinfection of the soil in which the seeds are to be sown or into which the seedlings are to be planted. The most suitable disinfection method is to steam the soil.

Another fundamental principle which should be routinely adopted for every garden, is never to put diseased plants on the compost. They should either be destroyed by burning or buried in a deep hole along with a sprinkling of quicklime. Plant remnants which remain after the vegetable has been harvested become a source of permanent infection for future crops. Such remnants include cabbage roots attacked by club root, carrot roots riddled with wireworms and tomatoes suffering from potato blight.

Simultaneously, the principles of correct crop rotation in the vegetable plot have to be observed. This means avoiding the successive cultivation of vegetables of the same species or group, or those susceptible to the same pests and diseases. Timely intervention can limit the spread of weeds which often carry fungus diseases (such as root deformities in weeds belonging to the mustard family) or act as hosts to pests such as the Colorado Beetle on nightshades and the Blackfly on many species of weeds.

Chemicals should only be used to fight large-scale infestations by pests and diseases. Even then, it is often better to remove and burn the entire plant or

A greenhouse makes it possible to grow vegetables even in winter and to prepare the most delicate seedlings.

group of plants which have been attacked, rather than embark upon the long, complicated and often problematic process of chemical treatment.

Forcing vegetables

Frames and greenhouses are invaluable for the pre-cultivation of seedlings, later to be set outdoors, and the forcing of some early vegetables.

Sowing in frames

Under favourable weather conditions, warm frames can be employed from the end of February. They are used for sowing the seeds of early varieties of cabbage and for lettuce to be transplanted outdoors in the middle of April. A part of the warm frame should be reserved for the sowing of warmth-loving vegetables, if these have not been pre-cultivated in the greenhouse. At the end of March and at the beginning of April tomatoes and peppers are sown there. They are followed in mid-April by cucumbers and melons, which are best sown directly into small pots. When the warmth-loving vegetables are put outdoors in the second half of May, as a result of which the frame becomes partly empty, some of the cucumbers and peppers can be transferred to it. By about mid-September, when these plants have been gathered, the frame can again be sown with lettuce, radishes or spinach. At this time it is also possible to sow dill, which — in a frame covered by sheets of glass — will mature by the end of October.

174

Semi-warm frames can be employed in a similar manner, the only difference being that the sowing should be started later, usually in mid-March if the weather permits. A part of the frame can again be reserved for forcing some vegetables such as lettuce. If the lettuce is planted sufficiently apart, radishes can be sown in between. After they have been harvested, cucumbers can be planted in the frame towards the end of April. When they have been collected at the end of August or in the first half of September, lettuce and radishes can again fill the space.

Sowing in a frame is done by broadcast sowing or in rows spaced some 8 cm apart. Sowing in rows is recommended for plants which are going to be grown in the frame for some time and will not be pricked out. This group includes leeks, chives and some members of the cabbage family. Sowing in rows also allows for easier weeding and aeration of the soil. A single sheet of glass is sufficient for an area sown with 10 g of common vegetable seeds. If the seeds have been sown more thinly and are not intended for pricking out, then 5 g of seeds would be sufficient.

The specific requirements of individual vegetable species determine their correct location. For example, it would be wrong to sow brassicas — which are hardy vegetables needing plenty of ventilation — under the same sheet of glass as warmth-loving cucumbers and peppers, which are sensitive to cold.

After sowing, the seeds are gently pressed down

A sowing box with electric heating allows you to prepare the seedlings of early vegetables at the very beginning of spring.

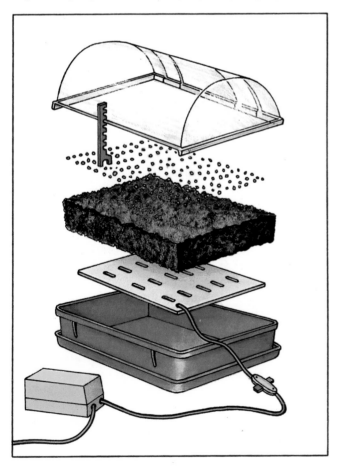

with a plank of wood, watered with tepid water and covered with a thin layer of sifted soil. As the majority of seeds germinate better in darkness, the frame can be left covered with sheets of glass and matting until the first shoots come through. The mats must then be removed and the frame covered only at night. At this time the young plants need as much light as possible, otherwise they will grow too tall and become weak.

If sowing is conducted later in the spring, the frame must be shaded to protect the seeds against too much sun. This is particularly the case if tiny seeds have been sown (for example, marjoram) as they are usually not covered with soil. In warm weather it is important to maintain an even soil humidity in the frame. Watering is carried out using only a fine spray. Higher, more spacious parts of the frame, which are dried out by the sun more, need to be watered regularly and more thoroughly.

Sowing in the greenhouse

Vegetables are sown in boxes, bowls and pots in the greenhouse. All such containers need to be thoroughly disinfected before use. This can be accomplished by wiping them out with a solution of lime or blue vitriol. The sifted soil to be used in the containers is best disinfected by steam. This destroys many pest embryos and, above all, fungus diseases. The soil to be used for sowing, often acquired from the frame or compost, can be improved by the addition of peat or sand.

The seeds are then sown by scattering them over the whole surface of the soil. This is then slightly depressed using a plank of wood, carefully watered and then a thin layer of soil is added, which should not exceed the diameter of the seeds. Some small seeds are not covered by soil at all but simply by, for example, a sheet of newspaper until they start to sprout. The boxes are normally used for sowing early species of the cabbage family, early lettuce, peppers, tomatoes, marjoram and others. In February, or even earlier, celeriac can be sown in boxes and bowls in the greenhouse. However, since the cultivation of celeriac seedlings is very difficult, less experienced gardeners would be well advised to purchase good quality seedlings.

Sowing directly into pots is only employed for fast-growing vegetables, to make the growing of their seedlings easier. It is an appropriate method for the cultivation of both frame and greenhouse cucumbers, melons and sweetcorn, when an early harvest is required. Sowing in pots is recommended only when small quantities of seedlings are being prepared, as pots take up too much space in the greenhouse. Later, when the harvesting of early lettuce and radishes has released some space, these seedlings can be transferred to the frame for hardening up.

Seedlings grown in the greenhouse require the same care as those cultivated in the frame. They are watered with tepid water through a fine nozzle or rose. In sunny weather the greenhouse has to be well ventilated and the seeds shaded as and when necessary. Early brassicas and lettuce require a temperature of about 16—18° C, while warmth-loving fruit vegetables, such as tomatoes, cucumbers and peppers, need 22—25° C.

Pricking out

Vegetable seedlings can be grown without being pricked out, but their quality will be impaired. Seedlings which have been pricked out are usually strong, well developed and, in contrast to those which have not been pricked out, they have a well-developed root system. Young seedlings are pricked out when they have formed their seed leaves or their first true leaves. They are first placed in deeper boxes but later are pricked out into the frame. The soil used for transplanting pricked-out seedlings can be improved with added peat or compost. This ensures that when such plants are finally put out in their permanent position, they have formed a firm and compact root ball. Brassicas are placed about 5 cm apart and tomatoes about 10 cm. During pricking out the seedlings' roots are shortened and straggly or diseased ones are removed. Some seedlings can be attacked at their base by a fungous necrosis. This first has a watery appearance but later becomes brown and black. The plant loses its firmness, becomes thinner and finally topples over. To avoid this, in addition to the preventative heat disinfection of the soil, tools and containers, healthy and well germinating seeds should be used. The correct density of sowing and the optimum temperature and humidity in the greenhouse are also important, and the seedlings have to be pricked out on time.

Vegetable seedlings can be potted in clay pots up to 10 cm in diameter. They can also be put in peat and cellulose jiffy pots or in plastic containers. The latter consist of a base and a honeycombed walling, which takes on the shape of a honeycomb when it is stretched. They can also be pre-cultivated in PVC pots that can be easily separated from each other. As such containers do not have a bottom they must be placed on a tray or crate.

Pots and other similar containers are filled with a humus-rich frame soil or a well-rotted and sifted compost. Pots are employed for the further growth of seedlings which have already been pricked out once. They might also be used for seedlings which

have been sown later and grown in rows in the frame or in the greenhouse.

Some vegetables, such as cucumbers and melons, are sown directly into pots which are half filled with soil. Seeds are gently pushed into the soil with the narrow, pointed end first and watered a little. It is a good idea to let the seeds steep in water for a few days before sowing so that they swell a little and start to germinate. Gradually, as the plants begin to develop, soil is added to the pots until it almost reaches the top. Seedlings grown in this way must have a good root system before they are transplanted outdoors. Before this, they need to be gradually hardened off in the frame.

It is desirable that the greenhouse is made use of throughout the year in the most economical and effective manner. In spring, it can be used for preparing all vegetable seedlings for later planting outdoors, into a frame (cucumbers, peppers) or even in the greenhouse itself (cucumbers, peppers and tomatoes) as it becomes available again in May. Apart from preparing the seedlings, a part of the greenhouse in spring can be used for growing early lettuce, radishes, kohlrabies, and to force the roots of parsnips. Chives can also be grown in pots to produce fresh leaves.

When the greenhouse becomes vacant, usually in May, after the outdoor beds have been planted with warmth-loving vegetables, then the whole greenhouse can be planted with peppers, cucumbers or tomatoes. These plants usually crop from mid-July to the end of August or mid-September. During September, the greenhouse can be further employed to grow vegetables with a short growing season, such as lettuce and radishes. Finally, in October both the greenhouse and the frame can be used for earthing up the root balls of vegetables such as Chinese cabbage and cauliflower, to allow them to mature.

Vegetables grown under cloches

Various types of plastic sheeting are available and most can be successfully adapted by small scale vegetable growers. Plastic sheeting is substantially cheaper than glass and it will easily cover various types of frame.

Low level cloches, shaped like small tunnels, can be made by arching strong willow or hazel twigs, reinforced with iron wire or polythene piping and positioning them in the ground about 1 m apart. Metal arches can also be soldered on to a frame which is partly anchored in the ground. It is important that the arches are firmly pushed into the ground or soldered together at the same angle and height above the soil surface. The arches are then covered with plastic sheeting, held down on both sides by wooden battens or covered with soil. Such low cloches are usually constructed to be portable and are used to force vegetables out on the open ground such as lettuce, kohlrabies and radishes. They also provide warmth-loving, fruit vegetables with sufficient protection against late frosts or low temperatures after they have been transplanted.

A transportable cloche of polythene sheeting protects tender vegetables (kohlrabi, lettuce, peppers, tomatoes atc.) from sudden drops in temperature.

Taller plastic-sheeting cloches can be put to the same use as standard greenhouses. They are built on a firm, arched or triangular framework which needs to be well anchored in the ground as it is more susceptible to damage by strong gusts of wind. The plastic sheeting should be strong and about 0.1 to 0.2 mm thick. Ordinary plastic sheeting lasts for only one season and therefore needs to be replaced every year; even so, its use is still very economical. It is possible to sow there radishes, carrots and spinach and plant lettuce as early as the end of February. Later, in mid-March, early brassicas can also be grown there. However, they will not be transferred to open ground until the beginning of April. The employment of plastic sheeting creates a large area of space with air at a favourable temperature, the correct light and humidity conditions; this is an excellent environment for cucumbers, peppers and tomatoes.

Harvesting and storage of vegetables

It must never be forgotten that a late harvest of vegetables can easily lead to a reduction of their nutritional value. For example radishes, if not harvested on time, become hollow or woody. Gherkins will grow too large and lettuce becomes bitter and starts to flower. Also, vegetables intended for storing, especially garlic and onions, need to be pulled out at the correct time. A timely harvest is similarly important for late vegetables, as autumn frosts can damage the less hardy species and crops damaged by frost will never last long.

Early vegetables and species which ripen slowly need to be harvested successively, as they mature. These include kohlrabies, gherkins, cauliflower, tomatoes and runner beans. Late vegetables to be stored during winter, such as parsnips, carrots, late cabbage, kohlrabies and garlic are harvested all at the same time. Some vegetables quickly fade and yellow after harvesting, particularly in warm weather. The most suitable time for cropping is thus in the early morning or possibly in the evening. In order to restrict the loss of colour in carrots, radishes and kohlrabies, the best method is to remove their foliage as soon as possible. Spinach and dill, which can only be expected to stay fresh for a short time, are best stored with their roots in water. Plastic bags are excellent for keeping chives and parsley fresh, especially if they are then placed in a cool cellar or in a refrigerator.

Storing vegetables

Vegetables are stored so that they can be used during the winter and in the early spring. This is the case particularly with root vegetables such as onions, garlic and some late brassicas. The best places for storing are a cellar, a frame or a pit. Some vegetables are even resistant to frosts and can be left out during the winter in their original beds.

Storage in a cellar

Before storing vegetables in a cellar, it needs to be aired and disinfected. This is best achieved by light-

Onion is harvested as soon as the leaves start to turn yellow and bend to the ground. The plants are pulled out and left to dry on the spot. In damp weather, however, they should be strung together and hung in a dry, airy place.

ing sulphur candles. It is also a good idea to whitewash the walls and ceiling with a solution of lime.

The cellar will store root vegetables, which are stacked in pyramids or piles, or sometimes put in wooden boxes or in a bed made of sand or peat. Cabbage heads should be stored in spacious wooden boxes made of laths or on shelves. It is also possible to stack them in pyramid formations with their roots intact and pointing outwards, sprinkled with sand. Kohlrabies can be stored in beds, in the same way as root vegetables.

Throughout the whole storage it is important to maintain and regulate a flow of air in the cellar, along with optimum temperature and humidity conditions. The replenishment of air can be ensured by properly located air vents and small windows. The temperature in the cellar is lowered by such ventilation, but during hard frosts the apertures must be kept closed. The optimum temperature for storing vegetables is 1—4° C, although frequently cellars have a slightly higher temperature. The relative humidity of the air should be about 90 per cent. It can be increased by damp peat, sacks soaked in water or by the occasional spraying of the floor.

If the cellar is permanently dry, as often is the case in modern, well-insulated houses, it is best to store healthy root vegetables in perforated polythene bags about 0.02 to 0.04 mm thick. Vegetables thus stored will not become limp and will stay fresh longer.

Vegetables and potatoes can also be stored with the help of lightweight sheets of polystyrene, which provide good protection against low temperatures and good insulation of the stored vegetables from their immediate surroundings. Protected by polystyrene vegetables can even be stored during winter on open balconies. The 10 cm thick sheets provide a protective wall as effective as one made of brick about 30 cm thick. Storage boxes for use on the balcony are best made of wooden boards, lined with polystyrene sheeting. This can be fastened by using a synthetic resin or staples. It is however most important to ensure that the joins in the sheeting are really tight. Root vegetables are then put freely in the box, or they may be placed in plastic bags, left partially open. The polystyrene sheeting must cover all of the walls, the bottom and the lid of the box.

Storing vegetables in a frame

A deep frame from which the soil is annually removed is also a suitable place for storing root vegetables and brassicas. Root vegetables are put between layers of soil or sand. Brassicas are stored with only their roots covered with soil. In the autumn the frame is left open as long as possible and is only covered with sheets of glass before the onset of severe frosts. Later, the frame can be insulated by covering it with a layer of straw or leaves.

Pit storage

Root vegetables, brassicas and potatoes can also be stored during the winter months in pits excavated in dry ground, where the underground water table is not too high and there is no danger of flooding.

A simple pit can be made by digging to a depth of about 20 cm; the hole should be about 2 m wide and as long as required. The perimeter of the base is then covered with dense rust-proof netting, inserted a fur-

ther 20 cm deeper than the bottom of the pit in order to ensure protection against mice. Root vegetables are then piled up in a pyramid in the pit and scattered with soil on all sides. Before the arrival of frosts, the vegetables are covered with a layer of old straw, followed by a 30 cm layer of soil. Ventilation is provided by the use of short pieces of piping or by a 'chimney' made of four wooden boards nailed together to form a rectangle. These are located on the ridge of the pit before the addition of the final layer of soil.

A more complex pit of a more permanent nature can also be quite easily constructed. The deeper the pit is, the thinner the layer of soil will be required to cover it.

Winter storage of vegetables in beds

Some vegetables can remain outside in the open air during the winter. These include scorzonera, parsley, parsnips, leeks, spinach, Savoy cabbage and others. Brussels sprouts harvested after the first frosts are in fact even tastier and more delicate. It is however more difficult to pull root vegetables and leeks from frozen ground.

Brassicas

Cultivated members of the cabbage family were originally developed from the wild species, *Brassica oleracea,* which comes from the Mediterranean, eastern Asia and eastern Europe. They are usually biennial plants, bearing their edible parts in the first year and developing their seeds in the second. In exceptional circumstances they flower in the third year. All brassicas, with the exception of kohlrabies, are grown in the first year after manuring, which is done either with a well rotted manure or compost. As all brassicas require a high level of potassium, this is best added to the soil in the form of potassium sulphate.

Preparing seedlings

The seedlings of kohlrabies, cabbage, cauliflower and other members of the cabbage family designed for planting in a frame or outdoors, are best grown from seed in a warm or semi-warm frame or in a greenhouse. If a heated greenhouse is available various early varieties of cabbage, cauliflower and kohlrabi can be sown as early as February and the seedlings planted into the frame at the beginning of March. Late varieties of white cabbage, Savoy cabbage and kohlrabi are best sown in mid-April in a cold frame or in a protected plot. Early varieties of cauliflower with a short growing season are sown in June for the autumn harvest.

Early spring seedlings grown in a warm frame or in a greenhouse are pricked out into deeper boxes when they have grown their basal leaves. If seedlings are pricked out in good time they can be prevented from becoming too straggly and weak. If they are not to be potted later on, they are best pricked out into seed trays or similar growing aids. About a fortnight before the planned time for transplanting the seedlings are gradually acclimatized by increasing the frequency of ventilation until the sheets of glass are

Cabbages are very demanding in terms of nutrients and humidity. They are also prone to pests and diseases.

removed altogether. Seedlings grown in the green-house are hardened off in a frame.

Round-headed and red cabbage

The round-headed or white cabbage (*Brassica olera-cea* var. *capitata*) is one of the most popular and widely grown vegetables. It can be eaten fresh, or pickled. It contains the vitamins C, B_1, vitamin A (carotene) and a number of minerals, in particular potassium and sulphur. The juice from raw cabbage and sauerkraut positively influences the intestinal microflora and has a marked antibiotic action.

Cabbage needs plenty of moisture and therefore grows well at higher elevations. It requires a high content of nutrients and prefers calcium-rich soils; it does not like acid soils. According to the duration of the growing season, which varies between 110 and 210 days, cabbage is classified as early, semi-early, semi-late and late varieties. Cabbage is normally grown from pre-cultivated seedlings; with the exception of the earlier varieties it can also be sown directly outdoors.

Early varieties, which are to be harvested at the end of May or in June, are sown in mid-February in the greenhouse or in a warm frame. Semi-early varieties are sown in the frame in March, semi-late and late varieties in the second half of April or at the beginning of May. Seedlings of the early varieties require adequate space when they are transplanted; they therefore need pricking out into larger pots. Later varieties need not be pricked out, especially if they have been sown thinly.

Depending upon the size of its root system, white cabbage is transplanted using a dibber, a trowel or a hoe. The plants should be placed about 50 cm apart and planted as deep as the height of their hearts. Cabbage is more resistant to low temperatures than, for example, kohlrabies. Early varieties are therefore sown as soon as the beginning of April. When the seedlings become well rooted they can be given additional fertilizer in the form of liquid manure, diluted at a ratio of 1:10. Or, ammonium saltpetre with calcium can also be added, at a ratio of 30 g per square metre. This is best applied before rainfall or watering. Early cabbage is particularly demanding in terms of watering, especially before it begins to heart up. Cabbage planted in rows needs to be hoed several times during the growing season and it is advisable to earth up the young plants.

Early and semi-early varieties are harvested successively as required, best pulled with several of their outer leaves intact, so that the hearts do not get bruised. If intended for storage, the plants are pulled out with their roots intact. After the outer leaves and any soil have been removed, the hearts are stored in a cellar or in a vacant bed.

Savoy cabbage

Savoy cabbage (*Brassica oleracea* var. *sabauda*) contains a large quantity of vitamin C and vitamin A along with several vitamins of the B group and minerals such as potassium, sulphur, phosphorus and calcium. It has a diuretic effect.

Late varieties of cabbage are harvested at the end of October and in November, before the first frosts. They should be stored in a cool cellar or in a frame together with the root ball.

Red cabbage is particularly well suited for summer and autumn harvest.

Savoy cabbage can easily be stored and keeps fresh throughout the winter. It has a higher content of vitamins than other cabbage.

Curly kale can be covered with evergreen twigs for the winter to protect the plants from winter sun. Individual leaves are picked successively, from the outer ones towards the centre. Even completely frozen plants can be used.

The requirements of Savoy cabbage are similar to those of white cabbage. However, Savoy cabbage is less demanding as regards the quality of the soil and fertilization. It also tolerates harsher climates and is hardier. Late varieties in particular survive the winter without serious damage, especially if the covering of snow during the most severe weather is adequate. In sheltered areas, early Savoy cabbage varieties can be planted in the autumn and harvested in spring. The seedlings are cultivated in the same way as those of white cabbage, except that they are planted out closer together. Early varieties are planted in a square layout 30 × 30 cm, later varieties some 60 cm apart. The depth of planting is the same as for white cabbage and the general care of the plants is also the same.

The early varieties of Savoy cabbage are harvested as they mature. Later varieties, suitable for storage, are gathered at the same time. Savoy cabbage is more difficult to store. If placed in a warm, damp or poorly ventilated environment it soon rots. It is

White, early varieties of kohlrabi provide the earliest yields. The seedlings are put out in mid-April, planted at the same height as they grew in the frame. The plants should grow quickly and without interruption.

White early varieties of kohlrabi do not tolerate high temperatures at the beginning of summer. Purple early varieties should be planted instead for harvesting at this time as they do not turn stringy so easily.

therefore better to pick the plants successively, leaving them in the beds as long as possible. A light covering of coniferous cuttings or straw allows this process to be continued well into the winter.

Curly kale

Curly kale (*Brassica oleracea* var. *acephala*) is grown in many forms and varieties, which differ from each other in shape, the extent to which they wrinkle, the colour of their leaves and the shape of their stalks. Curly kale has a high vitamin content and this, along with its mineral content, gives it a nutritional value in excess of Savoy cabbage. Furthermore, it can be consumed fresh throughout the winter as it survives without damage even the most severe winter frosts. In fact, its wrinkled, curled leaves are best gathered after the first frosts as they then have a better flavour. If an unheated greenhouse or light cellar is available it is a good idea to pull the plants from the ground with their roots intact and put them in plastic bags or large containers.

Curly kale is a modest vegetable in terms of its requirements with regard to soil, location, nutrients and moisture. It can even be grown in partial shade. It is sown in May, fairly thinly, in a nursery bed; the seedlings are then planted in June and July some 60 cm apart.

The growing season of most varieties is between 100 and 150 days.

Brussels sprouts

Brussels sprouts (*Brassica oleracea* var. *gemmifera*) are also tolerant of quite heavy frosts and are thus well suited for winter consumption. This valuable vegetable has a high content of vitamin C, vitamins B_1, B_2, K, provitamin A and minerals such as potassium, phosphorus and sulphur.

Brussels sprouts need a high content of nutrients in the soil. They grow well in damp conditions and at higher elevations. The growing period ranges between 160—180 days. The seed is sown in nursery

beds about mid-April and the seedlings are pricked out if growing too densely. They are planted out by mid-June at the latest, spaced 60—70 cm apart and as deep in the soil as possible. Another application of fertilizer is added during the growing season. Because of their upright growth they can provide good protection against the wind for other plants, such as cucumbers. The development of the sprouts at the axil point of the leaves is promoted by pinching out the top of the plants at the end of August. The leaves, however, should not be broken off as if this is done the sprouts will tend to open out prematurely.

The sprout 'buttons' are picked successively as they mature. Begin at the bottom and take a few from each plant. The plants are left in the beds for the winter as they can withstand frosts of up to —15° C. After exposure to frost they become very tender and acquire a better flavour. However, it is sometimes more convenient to gather the sprouts with their stalks and store them in a cellar or with their roots in a deep frame, particularly if the soil needs to be turned over after the crop has been gathered.

Kohlrabi

Kohlrabi (*Brassica oleracea* var. *gongylodes*) is one of the most favourite spring vegetables. When fresh it contains up to 50—60 mg of vitamin C in every 100 g. The young leaves contain several times more vitamin C than the thickened roots, three times as much calcium, along with provitamin A and a significant amount of iron. In some countries the young leaves of artificially forced kohlrabies are regularly used in cooking.

Kohlrabies are grown in a warm, damp soil as a first crop. They require humus- and nutrients-rich soils but do not tolerate direct fertilization with fresh farmyard manure. However, fertilizing the soil with compost before the seedlings are planted is very beneficial. As opposed to other brassicas, kohlrabies are very sensitive to a sudden and deep drop in temperature. In particular, forced kohlrabies — if subjected to repeated drops in temperature — are liable to speed up their growth and start to flower without forming tubers. Purple varieties are particularly susceptible to this. However, a brief drop in temperature to freezing point does not harm the seedlings. Kohlrabies require regular watering when young but not so much during the growing season. When they do not have sufficient moisture early on they become woody; on the other hand, after excessive watering they begin to crack.

They are usually grown from pre-cultivated seedlings and only rarely from direct sowing. Strong, well developed seedlings are raised in the same way as the seedlings of the white and Savoy cabbage. Early kohlrabies for early transplanting to outdoor beds are sown in a warm frame from the end of February to the beginning of March. Summer varieties are sown in March and late varieties in the first half of April. Early varieties which are grown as successive crops are sown in June. Kohlrabies are usually only thinned out; potting is not necessary for the fast development of their seedlings. Garden varieties take only 8—9 weeks from sowing. The seedlings should be planted fairly shallow in the beds, only as deep as they were in the frame. If planted too deep they tend to form elongated swellings. When they are being hoed later, care should be taken not to earth up their stalks. Early varieties are planted at the beginning of April and, with the help of cloches, their maturation can be speeded up by about a fortnight. Initially, regular and frequent watering is very important.

Because they do not store well, early kohlrabies are harvested successively as they mature and only a short time before they are to be used, in order to maintain their freshness. However, they must be harvested before they become woody. Late kohlrabies are usually all collected at the same time, before the advent of the first frosts. The healthy, undamaged plants with their roots intact are then placed in a deep frame or in sand in a cellar or in a pit.

Cauliflower

Cauliflower (*Brassica oleracea* var. *botrytis*) is one of the most valuable and popular vegetables. Its vitamin content is equal to that of Brussels sprouts although it has less vitamin A, and mineral content includes phosphorus, potassium and calcium. Because its florets contain less cellulose than other brassicas, cauliflower is also one of the most easily digested vegetables.

Of all the brassicas, cauliflower is the most demanding in terms of cultivation. It requires a rich, warm soil and a sunny but sheltered site. It does not grow in shade. Cauliflower is a typical first crop vegetable; it has the highest requirements on humus and nutrients content in soil. It needs frequent and regular watering during its growth and keeping free of weeds. Successful growth is also conditioned by the choice of the right variety and employment of the correct method of cultivation.

If forced, cauliflower needs a sufficiently deep and warm frame to which a layer of farmyard ma-

Cauliflower needs an open, sunny situation for good growth. Heading periods are subject to the locale.

nure has been applied. In the garden, it can only be successfully forced under large cloches. The seed should be sown in February in order to obtain strong seedlings ready for transplanting early in spring. These need pricking out once and then they are best grown in large seedling pots.

Pre-cultivated and hardened seedlings of early varieties, uninterrupted in their growth, are planted outdoors in the first half of April. They should be spaced about 50 cm apart and planted at a sufficient depth. Summer cauliflower is normally sown in April; the seedlings raised in a semi-warm frame are then planted out in May or June. Cauliflower is grown most successfully in the garden as a successional crop for autumn harvesting, following early potatoes, for example. It can be sown in mid-May and is then planted outdoors in mid-June or by the end of July at the latest. If planted later, the florets are late in forming. The plants, with roots intact, then have to be placed in a vacant cloche or frame sometime during October to mature.

During its growth, in addition to the basic organic fertilization with farmyard manure or good compost, cauliflower requires a supplementary feeding with industrial fertilizers. Prior to planting the beds

182

should be fertilized with ammonium sulphate, super-phosphate and potassium salt (60 per cent) at a rate of 50, 70 and 30 g respectively per square metre. If this is done it will then be sufficient, during the growing season, to add ammonium saltpetre and lime at a rate of 35 g per square metre. In place of initial preparation using ammonium sulphate, super-phosphate and potassium salt, a compound fertilizer can be employed at the rate of 100 g per square metre. Alternatively, a compound fertilizer containing molybdenum is often used. The absence of this chemical in the soil is responsible for the common problem of miniature florets. As can be seen, a well enriched soil is very important; only large plants with sizeable leaves can form large compact florets. Small and slowly growing plants, suffering from mineral deficiency and moisture shortage, start to develop their florets too soon and these remain small and of poor quality.

Cauliflower florets also need protection from the sun, to avoid their turning yellow. There are not as yet many varieties which have adequate foliage to protect the developing florets. During the final growing phase, the leaves should therefore be either tied or broken just above the florets and bent over to cover them. Cauliflower is harvested successively and, which is most important, on time. If this is not done the florets thin out and become straggly. The heads should be well-formed but compact when harvested; cut them early in the morning. Cauliflowers can only be stored for a short time. Hang them by the roots, with soil intact, and the heads lightly covered with tissue paper.

Broccoli

Broccoli (*Brassica oleracea* var. *italica*) is an intermediate form between the cauliflower and other brassicas. It has a stouter stalk which terminates in a medium small-sized head of florets, but is cooked in the same way as cauliflower or asparagus. It contains significantly more vitamins than cauliflower, particularly the vitamins C, E and A.

Being less demanding, broccoli is easier to grow than cauliflower. It grows well even at higher elevations in a damp atmosphere. It is usually sown in a nursery bed in June and planted in July, spaced 50—60 cm apart. Plants sown in June are then successively harvested in September. At first the main floret and about 15—20 cm of the fleshy stalk is cut away, followed by the gradual gathering of the florets developing on side branches. For an early crop, broccoli can be sown in a warm frame in February, the pre-cultivated seedlings then being planted out at the beginning of April. The spring harvest is however much shorter, as the plants soon start to flower.

Chinese cabbage

Chinese cabbage (*Brassica pekinensis*) is sometimes classified as a leaf vegetable as its leaves are eaten

Besides vitamins, broccoli contains important mineral substances. The heads are cut successively, while still compact. The main heads are harvested first, the lateral smaller curds over several following weeks.

Autumn is the only time when Chinese cabbage can be grown with success, as it needs short days in which to form the required heads. It should be watered abundantly to prevent its infestment by flea beetles and is best used fresh in salads.

raw just like lettuce. Nevertheless, it is a brassica species. The outer leaves are broken away and the elongated head is then sliced thinly. It can also be prepared in the same way as spinach, celery or cabbage. It has a high content of vitamin C, vitamin A and some mineral substances.

Chinese cabbage is quite undemanding in cultivation. It likes a moist soil and atmosphere and therefore grows well at higher elevations. Although it has a short growing season (2—3 months) it should be sown in summer, around mid-July. Plants sown in spring would not form sufficiently firm heads and would flower too soon. On the other hand, sowing in July must not be delayed any further if the plants are to mature before the first frosts.

Chinese cabbage is either sown directly outdoors, in rows about 40 cm apart or it can be grown from pre-cultivated seedlings. After germination the seedlings are thinned out at a distance of 25 cm. During their growth they need hoeing to keep weeds at bay and they need regular watering. Adequate moisture is of particular importance. Frequent spraying frees it from flea beetles which do not like a damp environment. A sufficiently nutritious soil is also a must to ensure a fast growth of the plants.

The plants are harvested successively as soon as they have formed heads, normally about two months after sowing. Although the Chinese cabbage is resistant to short periods of frost it is still a good idea to cover the bed with a transportable cloche. The plants can also be removed with their roots before the frosts arrive and should then be stored in soil in a deep frame or a cold cellar. They can then be har-

vested as required throughout the winter. (The dark environment does not harm the stored plants.)

Fruit vegetables

Fruit vegetables are mostly native to tropical and subtropical countries and therefore their major requirements are in terms of warmth and moisture. They are grown as a first crop and the soil for them must be well fertilized with farmyard manure, good compost, green manure or industrial fertilizers. Most fruit vegetables are members of the gourd family.

Cucumber

Cucumber (*Cucumis sativus*) is one of the most widespread vegetables, although its successful cultivation is dependent on many factors. The main requirement is warmth throughout its growing season. Its fruit is very popular for its refreshing qualities, being eaten raw in salads or sandwiches, or pickled. However, it contains a lot of water and very little vitamin C or mineral substances, the flesh having an even smaller value than the skin.

Cucumbers are very demanding as far as warmth is concerned — needing a minimum of 21° C. They are easily damaged by cold and are very sensitive to fluctuations of temperature. They need a warm, alkaline soil, rich in humus and nutrients. Above all, they benefit from being fertilized directly with farmyard manure. The plot for growing cucumbers should be in a sunny location, protected from wind. It is also advisable to grow cucumbers in among rows of taller plants such as sweetcorn, Brussels sprouts and tomatoes.

They are sometimes cultivated from direct sowing but more often from prepared seedlings. Plants sown directly outdoors have a higher resistance to less favourable climatic conditions but in cold or rainy weather they do not germinate well, or even not at all. Usually, it is better to pre-cultivate the seedlings as the plants then crop earlier. As fertility is increased with the age of the seeds, plants grown from young seeds therefore bearing less fruit, it is advisable only to sow older seeds (3—4 years old). As opposed to other vegetables, it is a good policy to buy cucumber seeds way ahead of time and then store them for at least two years.

The seeds can be sown outdoors in the second half of May, best in rows some 80—100 cm apart. Gherkins can be sown closer together, with the rows some 60—80 cm apart. A furrow, 30 cm wide and 20 cm deep, is dug out along the length of the bed. This is filled with well rotted farmyard manure or good compost. It is then filled up with soil. The seeds, preferably pre-germinated or swollen, are sown shallow. Before the cucumber plants mature and spread all over the surface of the bed, the space between the individual rows can be used for growing kohlrabies or lettuce.

If pre-cultivated seedlings are to be used, the seed should be sown directly into small pots or pot trays in the second half of April. These are then kept in the greenhouse or a frame to maintain their warmth.

The kitchen garden, too, should be attractive as well as functional. The paths between the beds are easy to keep clean if made of pre-cast concrete slabs.

Cucumbers have been grown by man since the 2nd—3rd millenium BC. They contain more water than any other vegetables and are the least rich in vitamins and nutrients. Nevertheless, they have a refreshing flavour and are much cultivated.

About 3—5 weeks later the hardened plants can then be put into the prepared bed outdoors or in a frame which has been emptied after a planting of lettuce has been harvested.

Forcing cucumbers in a warm frame usually takes place from mid-April; it can only be successful if the temperature in the frame is at least 18° C. The area covered by a single sheet of glass can be used to grow three seedlings. When at least five true leaves have been formed, the plants can be pinched out. They are planted shallow and at an angle so that the stalks can root easily. Cucumbers in the frame are watered with tepid water or water which has been allowed to stand. The soil between the plants must be hoed very carefully as cucumbers have shallow roots. In sunny weather the frame needs to be shaded and ventilated.

Cucumbers can be successfully grown in the protected and damp environment created by the tall cloches built by many gardeners. In these, greenhouse varieties of cucumbers are most frequently grown. The ground level beds must be well fertilized with farmyard manure or, at least, compost. The seedlings are pre-cultivated by the usual method of sowing directly into small pots. In order to obtain strong plants, these are then transplanted into larger pots about 10—12 cm in diameter. Expert gardeners can increase the resistance of young cucumber seedlings by grafting them on to the seedlings of a marrow. Pre-cultivated seedlings with a well developed root system are then planted, 60—80 cm apart, in piles of sifted compost.

In favourable conditions, cucumber seedlings grow quickly. Every plant needs to be trained gradually with the help of a string on to a frame made of laths or on to a horizontally stretched length of wire located about 180 cm above the ground. The string should be tied to the stalk very carefully, best under the seed leaves. It needs to be left fairly loose, too, so that it does not cut into the developing stalk. The same is true of the string which directs the plant towards the extended wire. As soon as the main shoots grow beyond the supporting wire, they need to be pinched behind the second leaf topping the wire. All side shoots on the main stalk are removed up to a height of 60 cm and then a single fruit is left to form after every leaf.

Meanwhile, above the supporting wire, two shoots will sprout from the axil points of the two leaves and these are allowed to hang towards the ground. They are finally shortened when they reach a height of about 60 cm above the ground. These hanging shoots are then allowed to form one fruit again after each leaf. This so-called 'parasol method' can be modified in a number of ways. There are also different ways of cutting the plant. During the second half of the growing season, surplus shoots and particularly those parts of the plant which are attacked by some virus or fungus disease should be removed. Sufficient humidity and temperature, between 20° —40 °C must be maintained. Faded male flowers, prone to rot in the damp environment, are also removed as they may infect neighbouring plants.

Outdoor-cultivated cucumbers should be afforded similar care. They need to be well watered at regular intervals. On a hot summer day, this is best under-

The earliest yields of cucumbers are obtained in a greenhouse. The fruits are formed without previous pollination of the flowers.

shape of a flat disc with a scalloped edge and are picked when their skin is still soft.

Courgettes

This delicate vegetable is most common in southern Europe but can be successfully grown even in our climate. Courgettes are a form of marrow (*Cucurbita pepo*) and have similar soil requirements. They grow well in warm sunny locations. The seeds are sown in pots in April and are put in the greenhouse, on a sunny window sill or in another protected location. The seedlings are transplanted outdoors in the second half of May, with a distance of 1 m between individual plants. Courgettes require a loosened soil and sufficient watering. The fruits are collected as they ripen when about 20 cm long. The harvest begins at the end of July or beginning of August and can continue until the first frosts. The plants can be protected from bad weather either in a frame or under a cloche.

Honeydew melon

Honeydew melon (*Cucumis melo*) is related to the cucumber but has much higher requirements in terms of warmth. It has small aromatic fruits with green, yellow or orange flesh, which contains about 5—8 per cent sugar and has excellent dietetic effects. The fruit also contains vitamin C, citric acid and malic acid.

Due to its high requirements in terms of warmth, this melon can only be grown outdoors in warm regions. In colder areas it can be grown in a frame or under a cloche. It needs a warm, humus-rich soil supplied with the necessary nutrients. It does not require a humid atmosphere but will not tolerate windy situations, extreme fluctuations in tempera-

taken in the morning. If watering cannot be carried out regularly, cucumbers should not be watered at all except for the short period of time after transplanting. They are hoed and weeded at surface level and can be slightly earthed up. The application of an industrial fertilizer during the growing season is very important. This can be a mixture of ammonium saltpetre and lime administered at a rate of 21 g per square metre.

Cucumbers grown outdoors are harvested from mid-July until mid-September, as they mature. Gherkins, in particular, must not be allowed to overripen. When overgrown, the fruits start to form seeds and the exhausted plants stop producing new fruits. The fruits should therefore be collected daily at the beginning of the fruiting season and every second or third day thereafter.

Marrow

Marrows can be divided into trailing (*Cucurbita maxima*) and bush species (*C. pepo*). The fruits contain vitamin C and have beneficial dietetic effects. Ripe fruits are used for preserving.

Marrow is a warmth-loving vegetable, favouring warm locations and a rich, moist and nourishing soil. It is more resistant to cold weather than is the cucumber.

The seed is usually sown directly outdoors, although at higher elevations and in cold areas it can be pre-cultivated in large pots in the same way as cucumbers. The sowing should be done in the second half of May, in clusters of 2—3 seeds, at least 1 m apart for bush varieties and 2 m apart for trailing types. Marrows are not suitable for growing on compost heaps. They shade the compost heap but their large roots deprive it of nutrients and moisture.

Bush marrows also include favourite custard marrows with short erect stalks. Their fruits have the

Custard marrow is sown in rows up to 2 m apart, and at a distance of 1—1.5 m between plants. The fruits are harvested successively, cut with the fruit stalk; otherwise they deteriorate very quickly.

Vegetable marrow needs a lot of warmth for a good growth. The first fruits can be harvested some 60—70 days after sowing. A regular harvesting of the fruits promotes further growth.

At the end of May, the strong hardened plants are put out about 80 cm apart. During the first phase of their growth the seedlings should be protected by cloches. These are removed at the end of June when the plants have grown stronger and begin to flower. At this stage, the plants are pinched to stimulate the formation of fruit. Each plant is left with no more than 2—4 fruits, to allow them to mature well.

At the beginning of the growing season, the surface soil is carefully loosened around the plants and they are frequently watered, especially during dry spells. Under normal conditions, watering in later phases of development is not necessary. Melons root deeper than cucumbers and therefore draw water from deeper layers of soil with much more ease.

Honeydew melons are harvested gradually as they ripen. Ripe melons can be easily recognized by their distinct aroma and the softening or cracking of the skin around the stalk. They cannot be stored for long; under normal conditions and temperatures they should only be kept for a week at the most after picking. Served fresh, chilled, the fleshy fruit is very refreshing.

Water melon

Water melon (*Citrullus lanatus*) forms stout plants with spherical, egg-shaped or oval fruit, which can weigh as much as 10—15 kg. They contain vitamin C, 3—5 per cent sugar and have the same dietetic virtues as honeydew melons.

Their growing period is between 130 and 150 days. They are cultivated in the same way as honeydew melons and their growth requirements also do not differ very much. They do, however, need more warmth than the honeydew melon. Pre-cultivated plants are also spaced out at greater distances, over an area of 80 × 150—200 cm.

The harvest can be started a little later than for the honeydew melon — from the end of August but mostly in September. The most reliable sign of ripeness is a hollow sound given off when the melon is lightly tapped. The stalk also becomes paler and begins to dry out. As opposed to the honeydew melon, the water melon has a tough, leathery skin and as a result can be stored much longer. In fact they keep for some 2—3 months after harvesting.

ture or prolonged rain. The length of its growing season is 120—130 days.

In warm regions, melons are sown during May directly into beds which have been generously supplied with compost or well rotted farmyard manure. The more common practice is to plant pre-cultivated seedlings, which are grown in a similar way to cucumbers — the seed is sown in small pots in April. Just as with cucumbers, it is better to use seed that is 3—4 years old. Pre-cultivated plants produce a first crop three weeks earlier than plants sown outdoors.

Melons can be grown only in the warmest regions. The honeydew melon is even more demanding as regards warmth than the vine. It does not tolerate prolonged rain, dampness and fluctuations of temperature.

Tomatoes are much favoured for their high content of carotene and vitamin C, particularly when grown in full sun.

Tomato

Tomato (*Lycopersicon esculentum*) is nowadays one of the most widely grown vegetables, although as late as the first half of the last century it was still regarded as unhealthy. Its fruit contains a large amount of vitamins C, B_1, PP and A as well as sugars and mineral substances. The vitamin and mineral balance in the fruit is excellent and therefore, even if eaten in large quantities, do not cause indigestion.

The main requirement of tomatoes is warmth. They grow best in years with an early spring, when the temperature in May does not drop to freezing point and the warm summer is followed by a dry autumn. Tomatoes, therefore, need a sunny, sheltered situation and a warm, humus- and nutrients-rich soil with plenty of moisture. They like a neutral or slightly acid soil. Tomatoes are never grown in the soil after potatoes as these can infect the soil with various diseases that can be transferred to tomatoes. Suitable

crops grown before tomatoes include winter leeks, autumn spinach or early lettuce.

In our climatic conditions, it is better to grow tomatoes from pre-cultivated seedlings rather than by direct sowing. They take a long time to grow (120—140 days) and are very sensitive to both late spring frosts and the first autumn frosts. If the grow-

Tomatoes are picked successively as they ripen. The remaining, fully developed green fruits are harvested before the first frost and stored in a warm, damp place.

Tomatoes come in various shapes — spherical, flattened, pear-shaped and so on.

ing season is prolonged by pre-cultivating the plants, larger crops can be obtained.

The seed is sown in mid-March in boxes or bowls. These are placed in a warm frame, in the greenhouse or in a light, warm room close to the window. After germination, when the seedlings have formed their seed leaves or their first true pair of leaves, they are pricked out into the frame, 8—10 cm apart. Small

Tomatoes grown under glass provide an earlier harvest. Two stems can be left to develop in greenhouse cultivation.

189

seedlings can also be planted in pots, filled with compost or soil. The pots are then sunk in the frame, level with the soil's surface. The plants must not get cold or freeze and they should have plenty of light so that they do not grow too tall or straggly. About 15 days before they are transplanted, the frame needs frequent ventilating. This ensures that the seedlings develop into healthy, robust and hardy plants when they are put out. It does not matter if before this the pre-cultivated plants have already started to form their flowers.

Tomato seedlings are transplanted at the end of May when the danger of late frosts has passed. They are planted deep so that a third of the stalk is in the ground, best at a slight angle, especially if the plants

Sweet peppers are particularly rich in vitamin C, an important agent increasing man's resistance to infection.

are tall and straggly. The parts sunk in the ground put out roots easily and the plants develop a more compact root system as a result. This will later prove useful in the resulting increase in crop.

The precise method of growing depends on the variety chosen. These are divided into tall, cordon varieties and low, bush ones.

The cordon varieties are characterized by a luxuriant growth from the main stem, which produces innumerable side branches from the leaf axils. Since the main stem can grow as high as 2 m or more, it must be supported so that the plant does not collapse. First, wooden poles or canes at least 150 cm tall, are hammered into the ground at a distance of 40—60 cm apart. Then, using a trowel or a hoe, a deep hollow is dug next to the pole and the seedlings are placed in them at an angle. Their roots are partly covered with soil and then they are watered. Only when the water has been absorbed is the hole filled completely. If a large number of plants is being planted and the requisite number of supports is not available, tomatoes can also be grown supported by a wire. This is stretched out between two stout posts at a height of about 1 m above the plants. The plants are arranged in a row. Pieces of string tied to the wire are then dropped to each plant and attached to each stem. This ensures that as the plants grow they can be brought towards the wire.

Cordon varieties are allowed to develop one to three shoots and the remaining side shoots are pinched out from the leaf axils as soon as possible. During the second half of August, the top of the plant above the last truss of developing fruit is cut away. This allows the rest of the fruit to ripen.

Bush varieties are characterized by a short main stem, which terminates in a cluster of flowers, and a number of quickly produced side shoots similarly ended by an inflorescence. As their growth is low and erect, they do not require supports. Additionally, they have a short vegetative season and their fruit ripens quickly and simultaneously. They are planted outdoors close together in a bed layout of 25 × 60 cm. It is a good idea to plant them in rows in deep grooves like potatoes and later they can be earthed up in a similar manner. The plants are allowed to develop naturally without being pinched.

During the period of their most intensive growth, both cordon and bush tomatoes need to be regularly watered. This is best done using a watering can without the rose and playing the water directly on to the roots so that the leaves and fruit are not sprayed. This is a good prevention against fungus diseases which spread in damp conditions. Tomatoes need an extra feed during the growing season; ammonium saltpetre with lime can be used, at a ratio of 22 g per square metre.

Early and rich harvest can be induced by forcing tomatoes using a large mobile polythene cloche or by directly planting them in such shelter. However, adequate ventilation should be ensured to prevent the water from condensing on the fruit as this encourages the spread of potato blight. If the atmosphere is very moist tomatoes have difficulty in forming their fruit. The flowers usually fall off as the pollen is not spread. Ventilation is therefore a must. A safer pollination can furthermore be achieved if the plants are slightly shaken.

A small garden hothouse provides a perfect environment for the creation of the right microclimatic conditions. This is a multi-purpose collapsible device, particularly suitable for tomatoes and peppers, and consisting of four plastic pipes, each 90 cm long,

The warmth-loving sweet peppers thrive in vine-growing regions. They should be planted in sun-warmed beds with a medium-heavy, warm and humus-rich soil. In colder regions they must be grown in protected places, best close to a wall facing south.

which are open at the top end and taper towards the bottom, where there are several side vents. The pipes are pushed into the ground in a square layout some 50 cm apart and covered with a foil sleeve. Every corner of the space thus provided is planted with one seedling. The construction is then covered with a lid and through this and the pipes water is led to the plant roots. In the last stages of growth, when the plants are outgrowing the hothouse cell, the lid is removed. Long willow rods can then be pushed into the pipes, joined at the top and the plants tied to them. Tomatoes planted at the end of April in such cells are already bearing fruit by mid-June. The average yield from a single plant is between 6 and 8 kg, so that a single cell can produce as much as 30 kg of fruit. The soil under the cells should be well fertilized in advance and the best tall hybrids chosen. Bush varieties are not suitable.

Before the arrival of the first frosts, all the green, well developed fruit should be collected. If they are not to be used to make green pickle, they should be spread out on a shelf in the greenhouse or in the frame on sheets of plastic to slowly ripen. It is also possible to pull out the whole plant with its fruit and hang it upside down in a warm room where they will also ripen. However, tomatoes ripened in this way do not have the same quality as those naturally ripening on the growing plant.

Pepper

Pepper (*Capsicum annuum*) is one of the most popular and valued vegetables. As far as the content of vitamin C is concerned, particularly present in unripe green fruit (up to 200 mg in 100 g), it occupies first place in the league table of vegetables. On the other hand ripe, well coloured fruit contain a high amount of vitamin A. Both in terms of the growing method and the use the fruit, peppers can be divided into two categories, namely: sweet, vegetable peppers and spicy, hot peppers.

The pepper is another warmth-loving plant and, indeed, requires much more warmth for its successful growth than cucumbers or tomatoes. Hot peppers in particular are much demanding on temperature. The pepper is one of the vegetables with a long growing season, of between 150 and 200 days. Apart from its high warmth requirements, the pepper also needs regular watering. It thrives in warm, sandy-loamy, humus-rich soils with a high content of nutrients, in protected places. The plants do not tolerate shade. Peppers should never be grown after tomatoes; they thrive best after well-fertilized brassicas.

The seed should be sown in the second half of March to the beginning of April in boxes or bowls, at a temperature of 18—25° C. Such conditions will ensure the growth of pre-cultivated seedlings on time. As soon as they have emerged, they are pricked out in twos into pots or the open ground of a frame. There the seedlings are gradually hardened off by frequent ventilation.

During the second half of May they are then put out into beds: two seedlings are planted together in a layout of 40×50 cm. It is important to stress that peppers can only be cultivated outdoors in warm areas. In colder regions, cultivation is only successful in frames or under cloches as these provide the plants with the necessary humidity. It is a good idea to water peppers with a spray sprinkler attachment; the traditional method of watering them only at their roots is no longer used.

When the plants start to flower, the frame or cloche should be ventilated more often so that the very high temperatures are lowered and falling of flowers limited. At this time, peppers are at their most sensitive to dry environments with high temperatures of 30° C or more. During growth, the plants are given additional feeding, either in the form of liquid manure diluted at a ratio of 1:10 with water or by ammonium saltpetre with lime, applied at a ratio of 20 g per square metre.

If peppers are grown for green fruit, the first crop will be ready in the frame or cloche by mid-July. Fully ripe fruits, whether red or yellow, are harvested gradually from the end of August through September. The last fruit under the cloche can be gathered as late as October and even later. Hot peppers are collected in the autumn. The red fruits are then hung up to dry in a warm room and the green are pickled.

Aubergine

Aubergine (*Solanum melongena*) has variously shaped fruits, usually purple in colour. There are, however, many other varieties with white, yellow, brown or black fruit. This fruit can be prepared in a number of ways, either by stewing, frying or marinating them.

The aubergine requires warm and sheltered sites with a humus-rich, nourishing soil. It is grown from pre-cultivated seedlings as its growing season is very long and it has the greatest temperature requirements of all fruit vegetables. In less favourable climatic conditions, aubergines need to be grown in a frame or under a cloche.

The seed is sown at the end of February or the beginning of March in boxes or bowls placed in a greenhouse or a warm frame. Seedlings are prepared in the same way as those of the tomato. They are put about 40 cm apart in the frame at the end of April and outdoors a month later. In open beds, mulching with a plastic sheet has proved to be a useful practice. During the growing season the plants should be given additional supplies of feed. Fertilizers can be liquid manure diluted at a ratio of 1:10 or ammonium saltpetre with lime scattered at a rate of 20 g per square metre. The plants should be regularly watered from mid-June until mid-August and the soil surface should be carefully loosened.

The fruit is gathered from about mid-August. Larger fruit can be obtained if only 5—6 fruits are left on each plant and the rest are pinched out. They must be harvested at the appropriate time and as soon as they have reached the correct colour, are well developed but still have soft seeds. Old fruit is usually bitter.

Onions and related vegetables

These are usually grown as a second crop after vegetables that have been freshly fertilized with farmyard manure or compost. In fact only leeks will tolerate fertilization with fresh farmyard manure and they are most demanding in terms of moisture throughout the growing period. All members of the genus *Allium* need a well prepared soil, free of weeds, best of all sandy-loamy, with an adequate content of lime and other nutrients.

Onion

Onion (*Allium cepa*) is one of the most commonly grown and important members of this group. It is an indispensable ingredient in the preparation of a wide range of dishes and is also well suited for drying and storing. The juice from onions contains substances with antibiotic properties and is often mixed with honey as a treatment for the common cold. Apart from volatile oils (allin, allicin), sugars and minerals, it contains the vitamins C, B_1, B_2 and E. The green tops of onions are rich in vitamin A. Onion, as with all vegetables, is most valuable if eaten raw.

Onions need a sunny position above all and a warm soil, if they are to attain a delicate, sweetish flavour. In heavy, acid and cold soils the onion forms a distinctively thick neck, ripens with difficulty and rots easily. It does not grow well at higher elevations with a damp climate and it ripens here with great difficulty. Of all the mineral substances, it particularly needs phosphorus and potassium. Nitrogen-based fertilizers should be used with care as, if they are applied in excessive amounts, the ripening

Growing onions by direct sowing is only possible in warm regions. The seeds are sown in the first half of March, in rows 25 cm apart. The resulting thick growth is thinned out to 8—10 cm between individual plants. Although the crops are generally smaller than those produced from sets, this method is much easier. If the seeds are sown in good time, the onions ripen and store well. This method is often referred to as 'single year cropping'.

Autumn varieties of onions can be sown in a similar manner in mid-August. Before winter arrives, these onions have usually achieved a height of 20 cm and winter well in the open ground. They are then thinned out in spring. They mature at approximately the same time as onions grown from sets.

Growing onions from sets is the most common practice. This two-year culture gives high yields of mature, high-quality onions. They are harvested about a month earlier than onions directly sown outdoors. The best onion sets are about 4—10 mm in diameter, although sets 10—15 mm across are still suitable. They are planted out in March and at the beginning of April in a 10 × 25 cm layout. They are planted shallow so that their ends slightly protrude above the surface of the soil. In light soil, planting can be a little deeper. During its growth, the onion has to be kept free of weeds and the soil between the rows needs to be well loosened. A small amount of water is required during prolonged drought.

The crop can be harvested at the end of July and early August. As soon as the leaves start to turn yellow and dry out and the whole plants start to tilt, they should be pulled out and left to dry on the bed if the weather is not rainy. Before the onions are cleaned and stored, they need to be dried out further in a dry place with good ventilation. Here, the bulbs

Onions are stored either hung in 'ropes' or laid in wooden crates in a dry, airy place where the temperature does not drop below 3° C. To avoid premature sprouting, the bulbs should be laid with their roots upwards.

If you want to produce your own onion seeds, plant spherical or slightly flattened bulbs that do not sprout in March or the first half of April. The flowering stalks are fastened to canes and cut off when they have turned white and the seeds are black on the surface.

process can be slowed down and the onions do not store very well. Onions are also very sensitive to chlorine and therefore only potassium sulphate, containing potassium in a sulphate form, can be used. A dosage of 25 g of potassium sulphate per square metre should be applied before sowing or planting onion sets.

Onions can be grown in three ways: by direct sowing, by using pre-cultivated seedlings or by onion sets. At higher elevations the use of pre-cultivated seedlings is preferred. The seed is sown very sparsely in the cold frame during the second half of March. Sufficiently robust seedlings are then transplanted without being further pricked out into beds with a 10 × 20 cm layout at the end of April or the beginning of May. It is a common practice to plant two plants together, especially during a dry spell, as not all of them take. In this stage of growth, constant watering is necessary.

For an amateur gardener, the best method of growing onions is from sets. These can be planted both in heavy, cold soils and in sandy ones, where growing from seed is usually less successful.

Onions contain more valuable substances than carrots or kohlrabi. They are most beneficial when eaten raw, as in salads.

can be stacked in shallow layers in trays or hung up in bunches.

The best place for growing the sets is a dry and sunny plot with a well worked and weed-free soil prepared in the preceding autumn. Seeds are then sown in spring as soon as soil conditions permit. The most suitable time for sowing is in March and April, as seeds sown in May suffer from lack of the water necessary for germination of the seed. Onions sown late, in May or even in June, as sometimes is quite wrongly recommended, create loose, unripe bulbs

194

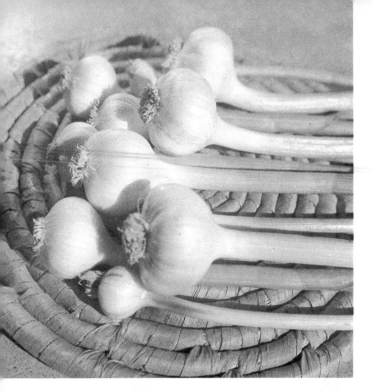

Garlic has been cultivated since ancient times. Its curative properties were already appreciated by the ancient cultures of India, Babylonia and Egypt.

of 10—15 mm make about 600—2.000 bulbs per 1 kg. Bulbs with a diameter of more than 20 mm are not used for planting, as they might start to flower and would not create large bulbs suitable for storage. These are better used for pickling.

Garlic

Garlic (*Allium sativum*) is one of the oldest cultivated plants and its curative properties have been known since ancient times. It contains even more antibiotic

with long necks. The seed is usually sown in wide, shallow rows made with a narrow hoe at a distance of 20—25 cm. Approximately 3—5 g of seed are used for a one metre long bed and about 15 g for a square metre bed. The optimum depth of sowing is 3—4 cm in a light soil and 2—3 cm in heavier soils. In the past, seeds used to be broadcast but this meant using about 30 g of seeds for one square metre. The basic prerequisite of this method is an entirely clean and weed-free plot. Late sowing can be speeded up by about a week if the seeds are pre-soaked in tepid water for about 24 hours. The sprouting plants are never thinned out but the soil is kept loose and weed-free. The plants formed in such a thick growth compete with each other and soon form small bulbs. During their growth onion sets are neither fertilized nor watered.

It is very important not to miss the right time for harvesting. This is approximately in mid-June when the tops are still green but the leaves start to droop. The plants are carefully pulled out and laid on the bed to dry out. The drying is then finished under the roof, the bulbs being spread out in thin layers on trays. Before they are stored in a dry place for the winter, the dry leaves and roots must be removed. If it is raining during the harvest period, the onions must not be left on the beds but should be placed in a covered, sheltered space.

One square metre of bed produces 1—2 kg of sets with the leaves. After they have been dried out and the bulbs cleaned, about 1 kg remains. Just 1 kg of first class sets with a diameter of 4—10 mm contains about 2.000—2.500 small bulbs. Sets with a diameter

Blue garlic has a bluish-purple skin and the cloves are streaked with purple. It forms flower heads. The bulbs are lifted when the lower part of the foliage starts to turn yellow.

White garlic has white skin and does not form flower heads. It is important to lift the bulbs at the proper time, otherwise the bulb disintegrates into individual cloves. This variety of garlic should be harvested as soon as the foliage becomes limp and bends.

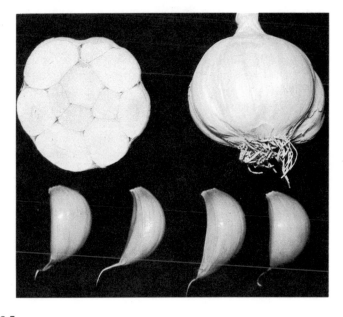

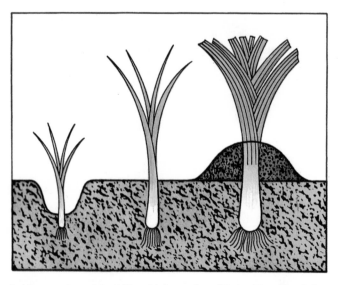

Leeks are planted in drills which are then filled with soil and the individual plants earthed up.

planting. The cloves are set out in rows some 25—30 cm apart, and within each row 8 cm apart. If planted in the autumn — at the end of September or in the first half of October — the cloves are placed deeper (6—8 cm). Spring-planted cloves (i. e. in March), are placed at a depth of 5—6 cm. Only the largest cloves from the outside of the heads are used for planting. Garlic needs regular hoeing and weeding during its growth. If it is very dry in May or June, watering is necessary. As they grow, the plants can be fertilized with a mixture of ammonium saltpetre and lime at a ratio of 18 mg per square metre. It is also important to remove any stunted and diseased plants from the bed.

The exact moment for harvesting must not be missed as the heads begin to disintegrate if the outside scales become overripe. Varieties which do not form inflorescences are taken out when the tops of their leaves begin to droop. In head-forming varieties it is more difficult to determine the right time for harvesting. Usually, the most reliable sign of ripening is when the curled stem at the end of which is the inflorescence with bulbils begins to straighten. At the same time the leaves and the stalk begin to turn yellow. After harvesting, the roots are shortened and the garlic is left to dry in the shade, best suspended under a roof in small bunches of 15—20 heads.

Leek

Leek (*Allium porrum*) tends to be grown on a smaller scale than onions and garlic but is nevertheless a very popular vegetable. Apart from the vitamins C, PP and some mineral substances, it also contains volatile oils which stimulate the gastric juices and

properties than onions and is also rich in vitamins. It can be used in the treatment of arteriosclerosis and high blood pressure, and is particularly effective in treating harmful intestinal bacteria. It is a valuable ingredient in some medicines and is almost indispensable in cooking.

Garlic requires a warm sunny position for its growth but is resistant to frost. It is one of the second crop vegetables and best cultivated after well fertilized brassicas and cucumbers. It should not be grown after potatoes, tomatoes, onions and leeks. The soil should be medium light to heavy; it should contain humus, be well limed and not freshly fertilized with farmyard manure. Heavy, wet soils are unsuitable. Under normal climatic conditions garlic does not require additional watering. This is only necessary after a lengthy drought, especially if the garlic has been planted in spring.

From the botanical point of view garlic can be subdivided into varieties which form flower heads and those which do not. The head-forming varieties have an inflorescence which contains many bulbils and a large purplish head with purple-tinged cloves. The bulbils, which are usually in a better condition than the cloves, can be used for propagation. Varieties which do not form flower heads usually have large white bulbs composed of many cloves.

From the grower's point of view it is possible to differentiate winter and spring varieties. Winter varieties are planted in the autumn and produce a higher yield but are more difficult to store. If they were planted in spring, their crop would be markedly smaller (by approximately 30 per cent). Spring varieties, which are planted in spring, store better but yield less. If the spring variety is planted in the autumn the yield may increase by as much as 20 per cent but the storage qualities are not as good.

Garlic is grown from cloves or possibly from small bulbils, either of which should be disinfected before

Chives can be forced for harvesting in winter. Dig healthy two-year-old clumps from the bed in October, plant into pots and add soil. During winter, the pots should be kept in a warm room until harvested. Clumps can be put out again when winter is over.

The short, roundish varieties of carrot are the earliest. They have a delicious taste and are very juicy. However, they are not very suitable for storing.

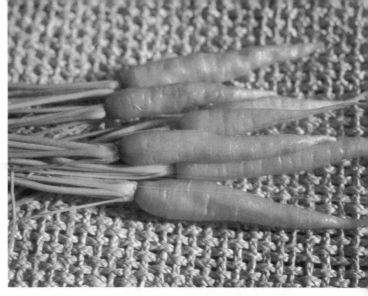

Carrots are particularly rich in carotene, which positively influences the metabolism and increases resistance to infectious diseases.

aid digestion. For cooking, the leek can be used in a large number of ways. It has the additional advantage of being hardy, so that it can be harvested throughout the winter and into the spring.

As opposed to other related vegetables, the leek has specific requirements in terms of soil. It needs damper, medium heavy and deep soils with an adequate moisture and nutrients content. It tolerates being fertilized directly with rotted farmyard manure. It is often grown after early brassicas, particularly cauliflower, and thrives even at higher elevations with a harsh climate. Leeks are divided into winter and summer varieties. The winter leek has a longer growing season, is shorter and stouter, is long lasting and frost resistant. Summer varieties are rarely grown in our climate. They develop earlier, their growth rate is quicker, the edible part is taller, it is less resistant to frost and may even freeze completely.

Leeks are either sown directly into an outdoor bed or they can be grown from pre-cultivated seedlings. The latter method can be more recommended for the garden, as the plants can be put deeper. Plants from direct sowing need thinning and earthing up to ensure as long and white a stem as possible.

The seeds should be sown in a nursery bed or a frame from March until May, depending on whether the crops are intended for autumn, winter or spring. As soon as the plants are ready for transplanting, that is when they are about as thick as a pencil, the tops and roots are shortened and they are replanted in 10 cm deep furrows, in a layout of 10 × 20 cm. When the soil is later loosened the leeks are systematically earthed up until the end of summer, when they are taller and stronger; they are finally banked up in the same way as potatoes.

They need to be kept well watered throughout the growing period, especially if conditions are dry. It is also a good idea to add some feed in the form of diluted liquid manure or superphosphate at an approximate ratio of 45 g to a square metre. Finally, the leeks are gradually dug up as they mature, that is, from early autumn until spring.

Shallots

Shallots (*Allium ascalonicum*) a form of onion, produce a cluster of similarly sized bulbs from one parent bulb during a short growing season. Some varieties flower. They are widely used in the kitchen in the same way as common onions. However, they have a more delicate, sweetish flavour and are very popular for pickling in vinegar. The shallot tops are a spring delicacy as valued as chives.

Shallots can be grown everywhere, even at higher elevations with a less favourable climate. Here they will grow even more reliably than the onion.

The bulbs are planted in early spring just beneath the surface of the soil, usually in a layout of 10 × 20 cm. Autumn planting is also possible, but in this case the bulbs must be placed at least 5 cm below the soil surface. However, if they are planted in the autumn they often start to flower the following year. Shallots should be weeded and the soil aerated during the growing period but watering is not necessary.

Shallots are harvested when the leaves start to droop. With plants put out in early spring this is usually at the beginning of July. The harvesting and drying method is similar to that of onions. Shallots even ripen better and remain in good condition during storage. They can be stored for long periods and, as opposed to onions, do not begin to sprout at the end of the winter. They can still be used some two years after being gathered.

In winter, smaller bulbs can be densely planted in a bowl and if kept at room temperature and occasionally watered, will grow fine green tops which can be used in the same way as chives.

Winter onion

Winter onion (*Allium fistulosum*) is a frost-resistant perennial which has the great advantage that it

197

Curly-leaved parsley tolerates semi-shade. It can be harvested successively throughout the whole year.

Parsley roots contain much vitamin A, B and C and the leaves are rich in vitamin C. The roots should be lifted before the frosts.

sprouts early in spring, well before chives. It is mostly cultivated for its crisp, delicate leaves, which are larger and therefore yield more green matter than chives. Its small, elongated bulbs growing in clusters also have a delicious flavour.

They are not very demanding in terms of soil or situation. They are easily propagated by the division of their clusters or grown from seed. This can be easily obtained from plants which flower every year. They are sown in spring or in August in rows. The young plants are not thinned out but are transplanted to their permanent place sometime during autumn or spring.

Non-flowering varieties of winter onion form small bulbs on their stalks instead of flowers. This is reminiscent of garlic, although in this instance they occur in several layers, one above the other. As a result of this feature the onion is called multitiered.

Pearl, spring or salad onion

The salad onion (*Allium sativum* ssp. *ophioscorodon*) is a perennial onion with leaves resembling those of the leek. It forms small, white, silvery-scaled bulbs with a delicate, spicy, aromatic flavour. It can be pickled in the same way as shallots and is used in vegetable salads. These onions do not last very long after they have been pulled and so cannot be stored for any length of time. They are propagated only vegetatively from small bulbs at the end of July or in August, when the ripening onions are being harvested. Smaller bulbs are then planted in a layout measuring 5 × 20 cm.

Substitute salad onions can be grown from leeks which have been wintered and are then not pulled in

the spring. They are not allowed to flower, the flowering stems being cut away in time. This leads to the formation of small, white bulbs, which can then be replanted and grown. Their flavour is indistinguishable from real pearl or salad onions.

Parsnips develop thick, white, sweetish-tasting roots. They can be stored in the same way as carrots.

Chives

Chives (*Allium schoenoprasum*) are a frost-resistant perennial forming dense clusters of fine, tubular leaves, containing a high quantity of the vitamins C and B_2. Chives are most valuable for the winter and spring, when they can be forced.

Chives require a heavier, loamy and humus-rich soil, with a sufficient amount of nutrients. They have no special requirements as to situation but will not grow in a light dry soil.

Chives are propagated by the division of their clusters or they can be grown from seed. This is usually sown during March in a nursery bed or in a frame. Shallow, circular impressions are made in the loosened soil, about 10 cm apart. This is best done by using the base of a small pot. A pinch of seed taken in three fingers is then deposited and lightly covered with soil. The chives then grow in groups, are easy to weed and to transplant at a later stage. This method removes the problem of having to divide plants growing densely all over the bed, which is particularly painstaking if transplanting has been delayed and the chives have been allowed to develop too much.

The tufts are then taken out from the frame or nursery bed sometime during May. A part is transplanted to its permanent, weed-free place and the rest, intended for forcing later in winter, is planted in another bed and allowed to mature in a layout of 25×25 cm. The plants are watered, hoed and given additional supplies of feed, usually ammonium saltpetre with lime at a rate of 15 g per square metre.

The tops of chives intended for winter forcing are not cut away in summer, to ensure that the plants do not lose their strength through the formation of new leaves. The clusters are taken out of the ground in September and put in an empty frame or in a cellar, where they gradually stop growing and die back. They must be left in the dormant state for a certain time. Individual clusters can then be gradually transplanted into pots from the beginning of winter through to spring. They are brought inside and placed close to a window, where they soon start to sprout. When spring comes, they are again transplanted outdoors.

Root vegetables

Apart from celeriac, root vegetables do not tolerate direct application of farmyard manure. In a freshly fertilized soil, they will produce an excess quantity of green tops and very small roots. Manure can also negatively influence their taste. If farmyard manure is used for fertilizing, it is better to grow root vegetables as a second crop.

Carrots

Carrots (*Daucus carota* ssp. *sativus*) is one of the most common and popular vegetables. It is valued for its high content of vitamins A, B_1, B_2, PP and many mineral substances. Just like other vegetables, it is most valuable in its raw state. From the grower's point of view, carrots are divided into early, semi-late and late varieties. Early varieties usually have shorter roots and blunt ends. Their nutritional value is greater, they contain more sugars and have a more delicate flavour. Semi-late and late varieties of carrots have longer, spindle-shaped roots but produce greater yields.

Carrots need a deep, humus-rich, light soil with a sufficient content of lime. They do not tolerate being fertilized with fresh farmyard manure, which causes their roots to branch and split, particularly if the nitrogen content of the manure is high. Acid soils need treating with lime in the autumn.

Carrots are sown as early as possible in spring, in rows some 25 cm apart and about 1.5 cm deep. It is advisable to use some other plants, such as radish, spinach or dill as markers for the rows, because carrots often take as much as three weeks to germinate and the soil between the rows needs to be loosened on time. Emerging carrots are very susceptible to the formation of soil crust and to weeds. The soil crust can be easily broken up by using a rotary cultivator, a hoe or a weeding frame. The young plants need to be thinned out as soon as possible to a distance of 4—5 cm in early varieties and to some 7—10 cm in later ones. Immediately after being thinned out they should be fertilized with ammonium saltpetre and lime at a ratio of 15 g to a square metre. Subsequent fertilization is unnecessary, although watering in dry weather is advisable. However, during the period of the most intensive growth, watering directly on to the roots should be limited, to avoid them cracking as a result of too much moisture. Cracks in the roots

Scorzonera is sown in rows 25—30 cm apart. Later, the seedlings are thinned out to a distance of 10 cm. If any flowering stems appear they should be cut off.

may also occur if there is a sudden change from dry summer weather to damp autumn conditions.

Early varieties of carrot are sown gradually from March until June. They can be sown in a cold frame as early as the end of February. If they have been sown thinly, they will not require thinning out and after some three months will have achieved a size ready for eating. The roots are then pulled out gradually as they mature.

Carrots for winter storage are gathered in the autumn before the advent of the first frosts. They are best dug out with a garden fork. The roots are cleaned and the green tops carefully twisted and broken off. Healthy, undamaged roots are then stored in a deep frame, in a pit or in a cold cellar in layers of sand.

Hamburg parsley

Hamburg parsley (*Petroselinum crispum*) is a much valued vegetable, especially when it is fresh. Its roots contain the highest quantity of vitamin A, next to those of carrots. They also contain many minerals, in particular manganese. The leaves are very rich in vitamin C. If the objective is to grow parsley leaves, then there are varieties with curled leaves which develop only a short, branched root system.

Parsley has similar soil requirements to carrots. It needs plenty of light, and regular watering in dry conditions. It grows in all areas. Like carrots, it is intolerant of fresh farmyard manure, which causes rusty patches to appear on its roots. Its cultivation is also similar to that of the carrot. The seed is sown as early as possible in spring. The young plants need thinning out at relatively great distances (8—12 cm). They are harvested later than carrots but can withstand frosts if they are provided with some light cover. The roots will survive in the bed until spring.

Apart from the specific varieties grown only for the leaves, there are also root varieties which can be cultivated for their green tops as well. The leaves can be dried but their value is far greater when they are fresh. Parsley can be forced in winter in the same way as chives, that is in a warm room on the windowsill. Parsley roots are first planted in several pots and placed in a frame or a cold cellar. Then, as they are needed, they are taken indoors and left to sprout.

Parsnip

Parsnip (*Pastinaca sativa*) is a favourite vegetable, quite undemanding and easy to grow. It is primarily grown for its roots, which resemble those of carrots both in appearance and flavour. In the kitchen it can be used as a substitute for carrots and for celeriac. When compared with carrots, it contains more vitamin C and less vitamin A.

Parsnip likes damp conditions and grows well even at higher elevations. Its requirements are identical to those of parsley but it will grow in much worse conditions and even in partial shade.

It is grown in the same way as parsley. It has a long vegetative period; the seeds take 3—4 weeks to germinate and it therefore needs to be sown as early as possible in spring, in rows some 30 cm apart.

At the appropriate time it needs thinning out to a distance of 10—12 cm. As it is frost resistant, only a part of the crop needs to be harvested and the rest can be left in the bed for use in the following spring. Alternatively, all the roots can be stored for the winter in a frame, to allow the bed to be turned over in the autumn.

Scorzonera

Scorzonera (*Scorzonera hispanica*) is a very nourishing and valuable vegetable. Its biological and dietetic qualities make it one of the best vegetables for cooking. When its roots are damaged they produce a white juice which contains inulin. Because of this substance, scorzonera is most suitable for consumption by diabetics. The roots are easily digested and, when fresh, have a taste reminiscent of walnuts. In winter and spring they are prepared in the same way as asparagus.

Scorzonera has few demands in terms of climate and grows well almost everywhere. However, it needs a well worked loamy-sandy soil, free of weeds and rich in humus and nutrients. It does not like an acid soil or the direct application of farmyard manure. Excessive amounts of nitrogen cause it to become bitter and soft.

Scorzonera has a long growth period and therefore needs to be sown as early as possible in spring. It can also be sown at the end of summer to be ready for harvesting the following year. Plants kept through the winter, however, sometimes start flowering prematurely. The seeds are sown in rows some 25—30 cm apart and the seedlings are later thinned out to 5—8 cm.

The roots are harvested late in the autumn or in

Celeriac should be watered in drills as permanent wetness of the aerial parts may lead to rot.

200

spring, as it is a frost resistant vegetable. When the roots are dug up, great care must be taken as they are very fragile and break easily. Since they are very long, it is a good idea to dig a deep furrow alongside the row of plants and then lever the roots from the other side into this trench using a garden fork or a spade. The roots are then stored as soon as possible in the frame or cellar in damp sand as they dry out easily.

Celeriac

Celeriac (*Apium graveolens* var. *rapaceum*) is an important vegetable used in the preparation of various dishes. The thickened roots contain protein and minerals and the leaves have a high vitamin content. Apart from its general medical properties, it activates the gastric juices and stimulates the appetite.

Celeriac is a warmth-loving vegetable with a long growing season of between 180—240 days. It is quite demanding in terms of nutrients in the soil. But it needs frequent watering particularly when grown in light sandy-loamy soils. During the growing season it needs generous feeding with farmyard manure, compost and industrial fertilizers. It tolerates the presence of chlorine in the soil, thus allowing the use of fertilizers containing that chemical.

In beds on open ground, celeriac is only grown from pre-cultivated seedlings. This process is a very demanding one and only the most experienced gardeners are successful. Celeriac must be sown as early as January or at the beginning of February in bowls or boxes best located in a warm greenhouse. The seeds germinate very slowly. When the seedlings emerge, they are pricked out in the usual way and put into boxes 3 cm apart. Several weeks later, when they have grown a little more than their seed leaves, they are transplanted again, this time about 8 cm apart in deeper boxes or in a frame outside. At each stage of transplanting the roots are shortened by about a third to a half. The seedlings are sensitive to cold and thus their hardening should not begin before the beginning of May.

In the second half of May the pre-cultivated plants are transplanted into a well fertilized soil. The roots are once again shortened along with the leaves and the plants are put very shallow at the same height they were in the frame. They are spaced 30 × 30 cm apart and are then regularly watered until they take.

Celeriac requires a lot of care during the growing season. Apart from watering and regular loosening of the soil, an additional application of feed, best in the form of liquid manure diluted at a ratio of 1:8 is necessary. Until the end of July, ammonium saltpetre with lime is added each fortnight at a rate of 30 g per square metre, along with a combined fertilizer at a rate of 100 g per one square metre. The leaves should not be removed from the plants as that would decrease both the assimilative surface area of the plant and the yield. Similarly, it is not necessary to remove the soil around the thickening roots, or clear away or even cut away small roots to make the main tuber smooth. Modern celeriac varieties form small

Celeriac should be lifted before the first frosts. The leaves are removed by hand, leaving only the tuft in the centre. The roots are then stored in boxes filled with sand or soil.

roots at the bottom of their thickened main root. The removal of soil would be of importance only if the plant was planted too deep.

Celeriac must be harvested before the arrival of the first frosts in autumn. It can be dug out with a garden spade or fork. The tops are twisted away except for the heart and the soil between the roots — which should be slightly shortened — is shaken away. It is then stored in a storage pit or in a cellar in damp sand; otherwise the bulbous roots dry out very easily.

Red radish

Red radish (*Raphanus sativus* var. *radicula*) is one of the most healthy and popular of the spring vegetables. The fleshy, swollen roots contain plenty of vitamin C and mineral substances, mostly sulphur, iron, magnesium and calcium. Its typical spicy, slightly pungent flavour is due to the content of a volatile oil.

The red radish has a short growing season and, contrary to other vegetables, it is shallow rooting. It is relatively resistant to cold but the late spring frosts can damage it. It needs a humus-rich soil, supplied with readily available nutrients. It also requires plenty of moisture throughout its growing period. A lack of water causes its roots to become elongated, soft

201

and acquire an unpleasantly pungent aroma. In the summer months the radish easily forms flowers. Early varieties are sown in a warm frame in February and forced to crop by the second half of March. Sowing in a cold frame can be started in mid-March; rows of radishes can be combined with those of early carrots, which are then harvested a little later. Radishes are also grown outdoors in open ground from March until mid-June. The seed should be sown thinly in rows 10—15 cm apart. If winter growth and cropping is required the seed must be sown from mid-August until mid-September. Radishes are not usually sown during the summer although, if the conditions are damp and there is partial shade and if they are well watered, they can grow quite well.

Radishes are harvested successively as they mature. Overdeveloped roots become hollow, soft or woody. To achieve the best results, it is a good idea to sow radishes gradually, at two week intervals.

White radish

The white radish (*Raphanus sativus* var. *major*) is one of the oldest cultivated plants but is not so widespread as it deserves. It has a more pungent flavour than the red radish and larger roots. If grated in the same way as horseradish it goes well with meat dishes. However, it surpasses the horseradish in its dietetic qualities. It contains vitamin C, volatile oils and various mineral substances.

White radish requires similar soil and climatic conditions to the red radish. It prefers lighter soils with plenty of humus, although the winter varieties also grow in heavier soils. It is intolerant of fresh farmyard manure. Spring varieties are sown at the end of March and at the beginning of April, directly into open ground in rows about 20 cm apart. When the seedlings emerge they are thinned out to some 10 cm apart. Late winter varieties are sown from the end of July until mid-August, in rows about 30 cm apart; later, they are thinned out to distances of 10—15 cm. While spring varieties require regular watering, winter ones can do without it, although they have a better flavour if they are watered.

Spring white radishes are harvested in succession, as they reach the required size. Winter varieties are pulled out from the end of September until the beginning of November. They should be collected and stored in bulk before the arrival of the first frosts. The tops are carefully twisted off and the roots placed as soon as possible in sand in the cellar or a storage pit, otherwise they quickly wilt.

Horseradish

Horseradish (*Armoracia rusticana*) is a very popular vegetable. It is used as a condiment with meat dishes and in the preserving of some vegetables (for example, beetroot and gherkins). It contains a large amount of vitamin C, aids digestion, helps to loosen phlegm and alleviates pains during rheumatism and sciatica. Volatile oils present in the horseradish also have a bacteriological action.

Horseradish is a frost and drought resistant perennial. It needs a deep, humus-rich, not too heavy soil.

Radishes are harvested in succession, as soon as the thickened roots have developed properly.

It is not suited for wet soils which have a tendency to become compacted.

At present, horseradish is still traditionally cultivated as a perennial. Root cuttings about 10 cm long and 2—3 cm in diameter are planted some 30 cm deep in a well-prepared soil, fertilized with about 5 kg of farmyard manure, 40 g of superphosphate and 40 g of ammonium sulphate per square metre. The cuttings are placed in the soil horizontally and about 70 cm apart. In the first year the sprouting buds develop shoots which show above the surface of the soil. The first harvest can then take place in the spring of the following year. The soil is carefully moved away from the plant with a hoe, as far as the original part. The new roots are cut away, leaving only one or two to develop. The plant is then again covered with soil. During the growing season, the horseradish is given some additional supplies of feed. The soil surface is kept loose around the plants and watered if conditions are dry. In the second year, the remaining roots have grown stronger and reach a size for eating. This method of cultivation is then repeated every year. It is very important to thin the growth of shoots regularly; otherwise the horseradish would spread out of control and become a very unpleasant weed.

A more modern method limits cultivation to one year. In March or April, longer cuttings are planted more shallowly and positioned in the soil at an angle so that the bottom part of the cutting is about 10 cm below the surface of the soil and its uppermost portion just below the surface. The cuttings should be at least 20—25 cm long, with a diameter of 1—2 cm.

Before the cuttings are planted, their middle section needs to be rubbed with a coarse fabric so that all buds and roots are removed. The terminal parts, however, must not be damaged. Individual cuttings are planted some 10—15 cm apart. During the growing season the soil around them is kept loose and free of weeds. It is also advisable to add ammonium saltpetre at an optimum ratio of 30 g and a compound fertilizer at a ratio of 65 g per square metre. At the end of June, the main roots can be unearthed and the small roots at the top and in the centre removed. The plants are then covered up with soil again.

Horseradish is harvested as late as possible in the autumn but before the arrival of severe frosts. The roots are dug up, cleaned and put into sand in a cellar or in a deep frame. The thinner roots are retained and prepared with a knife as fresh cuttings to be planted in the spring. They are also stored for the winter in a frame or in a bed outdoors. In order to be able to recognize the top and bottom ends of the cuttings in spring, the bottom parts are cut at a slight angle and the top parts shortened vertically. After excavating the roots, it is important to remove all remaining cuttings and root pieces so that they do not infest the bed the following year. The best vegetable to follow the horseradish is the potato, as the constant digging and earthing up of the rows and later the compact growth of the potato completely destroy the last remnants of the horseradish in the soil.

Beetroot

Beetroot (*Beta vulgaris* var. *conditiva* f. *rubra*) has a low vitamin content but is valued for its high concentration of organic acids and pectins. Apart from alkaline mineral substances, it also contains lipotropic substances which are especially effective in treating the hardening of the arteries and liver diseases. However, it should not be consumed during kidney and gall bladder problems.

Beetroot has average requirements in terms of soil and grows at all elevations. It does not like fertiliza-tion with fresh farmyard manure and is therefore grown as a second crop or as a successional one. It is less resistant to cold weather and frosts and if it is sown too early in spring, the plants form flowers prematurely. These need to be removed or the roots then become smaller and woody.

The seed is sown outdoors from April to June, in rows 30 cm apart. The newly emerged seedlings are thinned out to a distance of 10—15 cm. During growth the plants are hoed and weeded and also given additional supplies of feed in the form of ammonium saltpetre with lime at a ratio of 30 g and a compound fertilizer at a ratio of 65 g per square metre. Watering is required only if the summer is really dry.

The growing season lasts between 90 and 140 days, so that the roots can be gradually harvested for immediate use from the end of summer. Before the frosts arrive the remaining crop is taken out completely and the roots, from which the leaves have been carefully twisted off, are preserved or stored in damp sand in a cellar. In dry conditions the roots can easily wilt.

Turnip or white beet

Turnip (*Brassica rapa* var. *rapa*) is a very popular vegetable, its fine taste resembling that of kohlrabi.

It has a short growing period of 60—100 days and is not a very demanding plant. It grows well at higher elevations in a damp atmosphere and favourable soil conditions. In dry weather it can be infested with flea beetles just as radish or Chinese cabbage. The plants are well tolerant to autumn frosts.

The seeds are usually sown in July, after the early crop of potatoes has been harvested, in rows some 30 cm apart. When the seedlings appear they are thinned out to about 15 cm. Routine care during the growing season consists of regular hoeing and weeding. The spring sowing from March to May produces crops in summer. Turnip for winter storage should be sown in summer. If stored properly, it may last until spring.

Black radish should be harvested in dry weather. The leaves are carefully twisted off and the roots stored in a cool, frost-free cellar or other similar location.

Beetroots are carefully lifted from the bed, the leaves twisted off and the cleaned roots are stored in the same way as black radish.

Swede or Swedish turnip

Swede (*Brassica napus* var. *napobrassica*), is grown for its thickened roots which have a distinctive, slightly pungent flavour.

It has similar soil requirements to those of the turnip. The plants like damp conditions and therefore grow well at higher, mountain elevations. The growing season lasts some 130—140 days. The seed is sown either directly outdoors or the plants are grown from seedlings pre-cultivated in a nursery bed. With direct sowing the rows should be about 40 cm apart and the seedlings thinned as soon as they emerge. Seedlings can also be prepared by sowing the seed in a nursery bed from the end of April until the end of May. Thinly sown plants need not be pricked out; at the end of May or in June, they are put out at a distance of about 40 × 40 cm. The beds are regularly weeded, the soil loosened around the plants and in dry weather they are well watered.

The swede is collected successively, as its thickened roots mature. If they are to be stored for the winter, they are harvested in the late autumn before the onset of severe frosts, and put in a cellar or storage pit. Swedes will then keep until spring, although from February their quality begins to deteriorate.

Leaf vegetables

The majority of leaf vegetables are characterized by their short growing season. They are therefore not grown as main crops but as catch crops before and after the main crop. They are also suitable for intercropping. For their good growth, they require adequate light, a rich soil with easily absorbed nutrients and regular and plentiful watering.

Lettuce

Lettuce (*Lactuca sativa* var. *capitata*) is the most popular and commonly grown leaf vegetable. It contains a large quantity of vitamin A, vitamins of the B group, PP and E, and a small amount of vitamin C. Its mineral content includes iron and calcium. Most important of all is the early lettuce, as this — along with the radishes — is a main source of vitamins when other vegetables are in short supply at the end of winter and in early spring.

Lettuce requires sunny, warm places and a light, humus-rich soil with a neutral or slightly alkaline reaction. It does not tolerate acid soils and requires a continuous supply of nutrients in the soil. Besides a good application of compost before the lettuce is planted, ammonium sulphate at a rate of 30 g and superphosphate at a rate of 60 g per square metre should be added. During the growing season, an addition of ammonium saltpetre with lime and a compound fertilizer at rates of 15 and 60 g per square metre is also advisable. The soil surface must be regularly loosened and it is also necessary to water the plants regularly as their hearts develop with difficulty in a dry soil and the plants flower prematurely.

Lettuce can be grown in the same location for several years without causing an imbalance of miner-

Lettuce is one of the few crops that can be grown for several seasons in the same bed without negatively influencing the quality of the soil or encouraging the spread of diseases and pests.

Lettuce contains a considerable amount of carotene, vitamins of the B group and other effective principles. It promotes the appetite, digestion and formation of blood cells.

Crisp cabbage lettuce varieties form large, very crisp heads with curly leaves. It is grown for summer and early autumn harvest.

als in the soil or the spread of pests and diseases. Lettuce is resistant to low temperatures and even slight frosts do not harm well hardened seedlings. However, it is important to plant lettuce shallow, otherwise it forms funnel-shaped heads of poor quality and in damp conditions its outside leaves rot. Pre-cultivated seedlings are used for the production of forced lettuce, early lettuce grown outdoors, and even summer lettuce. Winter lettuce is usually sown directly into the bed or frame. Lettuce seedlings are prepared in the same way as brassicas. It is recommended that you sow small amounts of seed, gradually, from the beginning of May until late autumn in order to achieve a continuous supply of fresh lettuce. The winter lettuce can be harvested from a covered frame by the end of March. It is always necessary to choose suitable varieties for the summer crop. Spring lettuce grown in summer does not heart up easily or else has poor quality hearts that soon start to flower.

Early lettuce intended for a warm frame and harvesting at the end of April and in May is sown in boxes from February through to March by simply scattering the seeds. When the seedlings have formed the seed leaves, they are pricked out into deeper boxes, trays or pots. They are then transplanted into a warm frame around mid-March, set 20 cm apart. Early lettuce sown in March is planted outdoors in beds during the second half of April, spaced 25 × 25 cm. In favourable conditions this might even be at the beginning of April.

Summer lettuce is grown gradually from April to May, the seed being thinly scattered on a nursery bed. Well developed seedlings are then planted in outdoor beds at least 30 × 30 cm apart. The reason for this is that the summer varieties, and in particular the cabbage head lettuce, grow to large proportions. If sown gradually they can be harvested at fortnightly intervals from July to September.

Early varieties are most suitable for autumn cropping between September and October. These are sown from July until mid-August in a nursery bed and transplanted to an outdoor bed in August or into a frame during the first half of September. Here they can be grown until November.

Winter lettuce is either sown directly in a sheltered bed with a humus-rich soil, or pre-cultivated seedlings are planted there. The sowing is done in August and at the beginning of September. The young plants are then transplanted in September or at the beginning of October at the latest. Some growers recommend that winter lettuce is planted in ridges to protect the plants against the frost but this is not a good idea. In wet weather and when the snow is melting, water begins to accumulate, particularly in heavier soil. It is only slowly absorbed and can freeze at night. Plants suffer more from this covering of ice than from frosts when there is no snow. A sufficiently humus-rich soil provides winter lettuce with the best protection against freezing. It can be recommended to put some of the plants in a frame or in some similar place which can be covered in spring with sheets of glass or plastic for forcing. This method will produce the first lettuce by the end of March,

Early varieties of lettuce are forced in cold or semi-heated frames or under a transportable frame, a cloche or in a cold greenhouse. They need much light, a sufficient soil and atmospheric moisture and a temperature of about 15° C.

Lettuce can easily be forced under a light tunnel cloche of polythene sheeting.

Lettuce is harvested as soon as it has formed closed, firm heads; best time for lifting is in the morning or evening.

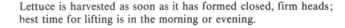

Loose-leaved lettuce is grown either from transplanted seedlings or from direct sowing. The leaves are picked successively as required or the whole plants can be cut off.

while the plants in uncovered ground cannot be harvested until the middle of April at the earliest.

The lettuce is harvested gradually throughout the growing season as it develops well formed and firm heads. As it loses its freshness easily, it should be cut just before it is to be used, best done early in the morning or in the evening. Loose-leaved lettuce (*Lactuca sativa* var. *secalina*) differs from head-forming varieties in that it does not form heads but just large rosettes of pale green, yellow or even reddish-brown, curled leaves. Not the whole plants, but only the outside leaves are usually cut away gradually as required. The leaves are very crisp, delicately flavoured and can even be picked in summer. It is also possible to use the whole rosette in one picking.

The cultivation is very simple. It is sown systematically from March through to the end of August, usually directly into open ground in rows some 10—20 cm apart. It is thinned only if it has been sown too densely, at a distance of some 10 cm.

Endive

Endive (*Cichorium endivia* var. *latifolium*) is cultivated and sown in the same way as lettuce. Apart from the early endives with their slightly bitter rosettes of richly curled leaves, there are also the broad-leaved varieties called 'escaroles'.

Endive requires a deep, warm soil in a sheltered place and sufficient moisture; in a dry soil it soon forms flowers. It needs the same nourishment as that provided for the lettuce.

Wavy endive is used in summer, when it often replaces other salad vegetables. It is sown in April, in rows about 30 cm apart, and is harvested in the same way as loose-leaved lettuce.

Broad-leaved varieties are grown as an autumn and winter crop, either by direct sowing or from young plants that have been pre-cultivated in a nursery bed. The plants sown in July are thinned out or transplanted at a distance of about 30 cm. Gradually, at least three weeks before the planned time for harvesting, the leaf rosettes are tied together so that they become white. The blanched leaves are less bitter, more crisp and have an excellent flavour. They are harvested from October to November. The last plants are taken out before the arrival of severe frosts and placed with their roots in damp sand in a cellar or deep frame, where they will keep until Christmas or even longer.

Chicory

Chicory (*Cichorium intybus* var. *foliosum*) is grown for its blanched, fleshy leaves, which provide a very welcome supplement to winter and early spring salads. The delicate chicory leaves contain the vitamin C, vitamins of the B group and minerals. They have valuable dietetic qualities, stimulate the appetite and assist digestion.

Chicory needs a medium heavy, deep, humus-rich soil with an average content of nutrients. In poor soils it forms small roots and in excessively fertilized soils large roots with several tops. The most appropriate roots for forcing are about 3 cm in diameter at their uppermost part.

The seeds are sown in April directly in the bed, in rows about 30 cm apart. When the seedlings appear

Chicory is grown in rows 25—30 cm apart and with 25 cm between the plants. Its requirements and care are as for lettuce.

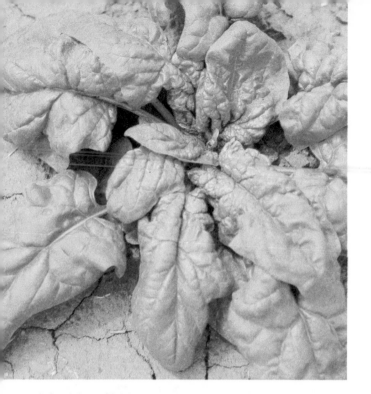

Spinach has a high content of carotene and vitamin C. It also contains vitamins of the B group, vitamin E and K and many important mineral substances.

they are thinned out to about 30 cm. During the growing season usually routine care is sufficient, i.e. loosening of the soil and removing weeds between the rows. Watering in dry weather is necessary. The plants are taken out at the end of October, the leaves cut away about 2 cm above the heart and this is placed in a frame or sand in a cool cellar.

The roots can be gradually forced from December to February in a deep box with a humus-rich soil. A space of at least 20 cm is left in the box above the roots and this is then filled with wood shavings and sand. The box is left in a warm room at an optimum temperature of 12—15° C. In order to keep the roots constantly moist, the box is covered with a sheet of plastic. In 3—4 weeks the chicory tops reach the appropriate size and can be harvested. The roots are taken out, the tops cut away and rinsed under running water, and immediately used in a salad.

A proportion of the chicory roots can be left to overwinter in a covered frame. Alternatively, they can be composted and covered with a 30 cm layer of soil. During winter in low temperatures the roots will slowly start to sprout, reaching full size by the spring when they are ready to take in some time during the first half of April.

Lamb's lettuce

Lamb's lettuce (*Valerianella locusta*) is a salad vegetable. The edible parts are its elongated, juicy leaves which have a sweetish flavour. These are collected gradually from the developing ground rosettes. The leaves contain a large amount of vitamin C, vitamin A and a number of mineral substances.

Lamb's lettuce is an undemanding plant in terms of climate and soil. It is usually sown in July or August for harvesting in the autumn or at the beginning of September for winter storage. The sowing is done in rows some 20 cm apart.

The crop is harvested gradually from October until late winter. Plants which have been kept throughout the winter can be used until the end of March, when they start to flower. Individual leaves or the entire plants can be collected in the same way as spinach.

Cress

Cress (*Lepidium sativum*) is a leaf vegetable which is grown for its piquant and pleasantly pungent aerial parts. Just like chives, it is a popular ingredient in salads and various spreads, and is particularly welcome in the winter and spring months.

Cress can be sown in March, directly into a bed, in rows about 15 cm apart. It has a short growing season and is harvested within 2—3 weeks of being sown. The growing stalks are cut as necessary. It cannot be kept long as it soon fades.

More frequently, cress is forced in the winter months. It is sown in bowls or in other shallow containers with any type of substrate at the bottom. This can be whatever is available; for example, you can use sand, wood shavings or a little peat. Cotton wool which is kept permanently damp all the time is equally suitable. The seeds sown on the surface of the substrate begin to germinate at a temperature of

During its growing season, spinach should be kept free of weeds and the soil aerated regularly. The supply of water must be increased some 3—4 weeks before harvesting.

16—18° C. This is usually within some three days, and the delicate stalks can be cut in succession after a further week.

Spinach

Spinach (*Spinacea oleracea*) is a widely grown vegetable, used fresh in the spring and autumn but available in a frozen form throughout the year. Apart from vitamin A, it contains large quantities of the vitamins C, E, B_1, B_2 and K and also many mineral substances including iodine, calcium and iron. However, it should be eaten with restraint as it also contains oxalic acid, which bonds calcium and which, if consumed in large quantities, deprives the body of this important element. Spinach however stimulates the activity of the thyroid gland and aids digestion but is not recommended for people suffering from kidney diseases.

Growing spinach is easy. Because of its short growing season (30—45 days, except in winter months), it is grown as a first crop prior to the main crop or as a successional crop. It requires a humus-rich alkaline soil with a large amount of nutrients, in particular nitrogen. It can endure cold weather and if there are no severe frosts without snow it will keep well during the winter.

Swiss chard does best in medium-heavy, nutritious soils. The leaves are picked successively — after two months of growing for the leaves and after three months for the mid-ribs.

Spinach is sown early in spring, in the first half of March, for harvesting in May, and in August for an autumn harvest. If sown in summer it would soon start to flower. Spinach for overwintering should be sown between mid-September and mid-October in order to be harvested in April. The seeds are sown in rows some 25 cm apart. The spring sowing should be very thin, but for the winter the seeds should be sown more densely to ensure that the plants survive the cold. Spinach benefits from watering and weeding shortly after the plants begin to appear. It also needs additional supplies of feed in the form of ammonium saltpetre applied at a rate of 22 g per square metre.

The harvest begins about five weeks after sowing. Well developed leaves can be picked individually but it is better to cut out gradually the most mature plants along with a short part of their root. In this way the plants are thinned out and weaker plants

208

given a chance to develop. The crop from the first sowing will thus be extended by up to three weeks. Spinach should not be picked in wet or hot weather as it soon overheats and fades.

New Zealand spinach

New Zealand spinach (*Tetragonia expansa*) is a good summer substitute for ordinary spinach, which is not grown in summer because it soon produces flowers and becomes bitter. New Zealand spinach, on the contrary, can be eaten even if in flower.

It is, however, more demanding, needing much warmth, a sheltered location and a deep humus-rich soil. It is also sensitive to frost and needs plenty of nitrogen. It is usually grown from pre-cultivated seedlings rather than from direct sowing in April. The seed can be sown in pots in March with an optimum of two seeds per pot. The young plants are left in a frame or in the greenhouse until they are put out in mid-May, when the danger of late frosts is over. They are then planted in a layout of 50 × 80 cm.

As opposed to ordinary spinach, only the individual leaves and young shoots are harvested.

Swiss chard

Swiss chard (*Beta vulgaris* var. *cicla*) is a relatively less well known vegetable, although it deserves a wider reputation and cultivation. It is similar to sugar beet in apperance but is grown only for its aerial parts. The curly leaf blades are used in the same way as spinach and the thick fleshy stalks are prepared like celery or asparagus. It is, in fact, a very valuable vegetable with proven benefit in the treatment of sclerosis. It contains much vitamin C, vitamin A, proteins and minerals.

It can tolerate cold weather and prefers humus-rich, damp soils enriched with nutrients, especially nitrogen. The seeds are sown directly outdoors in clusters of three, in rows placed about 50 cm apart. In the first half of May the plants are thinned to about 30 cm. During the growing season the soil is hoed around the plants, to keep weeds at bay, and the plants are watered in dry weather.

The leaf blades can be harvested at the beginning of summer while they are still young, the stalks being broken off later — commencing in mid-August through to the autumn.

The plants are dug up with their roots before the arrival of severe frosts and kept in a deep frame or placed in containers in a cellar. The gradually growing leaves can then be collected throughout the winter. Some of the plants can also be left in the bed to overwinter, protected by a layer of soil, straw manure or leaves. In March, this protective layer is removed and in April the new young shoots harvested until the plants begin to flower.

Orache

Orache (*Atriplex hortensis*) is used in the kitchen in the same way as spinach, containing less oxalic acid than the latter. Orache can be grown almost everywhere, having no special soil requirements, although

Peas can be grown in all types of soils, except too dry or too damp ones. The best yields are from medium-heavy, calcium-rich soils.

Pea pods are picked when the peas are fully developed and the pods still have their fresh green colour.

Green bean pods are cropped in succession, when still young and smooth.

Runner beans need some support for good growth. A wire fence can be used for this purpose.

it prefers a warm location. It is best grown during the spring or autumn months, but it soon starts to flower in dry summer conditions. The seeds are sown either in April or at the end of August and in September, very thinly, in rows 25 cm apart. As soon as the plants emerge, they should be thinned to about 20 cm.

The leaves or parts of the plant are harvested when the plants are about 40 cm tall. As in spinach, the leaves soon fade after being cut.

Leguminous vegetables

Legumes belong to vegetables grown as a third crop. They do not require organic manure, being satisfied with industrial fertilizers with a calcium content. They enrich the soil with nitrogen which they absorb from the air through the bacteria present in their roots. Because of this, they can be grown before some vegetables needing nitrogen for their growth.

Garden pea

Garden pea (*Pisum sativum* ssp. *hortense*) is grown in vegetable gardens for its green pods and sweet peas. The latter have a high calorific value. It contains significant amounts of vitamins C and E, proteins and minerals (phosphorus and calcium).

Garden peas can be divided into three categories, wrinkled-seeded, round-seeded and sugar varieties.

The wrinkled-seeded peas are the most widespread, and are grown essentially for their unripe pods. These are either consumed whole or else the unripe seeds are removed from them and eaten fresh or boiled. When ripe and dry the seeds are wrinkled and remain tough even after boiling.

Round-seeded peas are grown above all to produce a crop of unripe, sweet and round seeds. The pods have a tough interior. The yellow or green ripe seeds can be boiled and are round and smooth even when dry.

Sugar peas are cultivated for the green, crisp, fleshy, flat pods without the inside tough layer. They are eaten raw or boiled. Their seeds are round, sweet and slightly wrinkled.

The growing season of the pea lasts between 65 and 85 days. It has no significant demands in terms of soil or climate, though it prefers a damp soil with an adequate amount of lime. It is always sown directly outdoors *in situ* and the plants are not transplanted. The hardier, round-seeded varieties are sown first at the end of March and the wrinkled-seeded and sugar peas are sown in mid-April, about 5 cm deep and in rows about 25 cm apart, individual seeds being placed about 2 cm apart. During the growing season the beds are hoed and weeded and in dry weather the plants need watering well. Although low growing varieties, which grow unsupported, are now in existence, the taller, climbing varieties need a support. Peas can be supported by having a thinly sown row of oats placed alongside. Alternatively, a strip of zinc-coated wire mesh can be stretched between two rows of peas. If an autumn cropping is needed then the wrinkled-seeded varie-

Marjoram is harvested before flowering, for the first time usually at the end of July. The plants are cut back to about 5 cm above ground. They will then sprout anew and the second harvest can take place in September.

Dill is a relatively undemanding plant, best grown in spring or in the autumn. Summer-grown plants tend to form flowering stems too soon.

ties, which have a shorter growing season, need to be sown in the middle of July at the latest.

Bean

Beans (*Phaseolus vulgaris*) are very popular and grown mostly for the unripe green or yellow pods, which contain much protein, many sugars and a range of B vitamins. They have a diuretic effect and decrease the sugar content in the blood.

Beans are divided into French and runner varieties. French beans yield less than the runner beans, do not need to be supported and have a shorter growing season. The runner beans have a longer growing season and therefore the harvest is spread over a longer period; in addition, the yield is greater. They require firm supports in the form of frames of wire or poles.

Beans are warmth-loving plants and need a medium-heavy to light, humus-rich soil with a sufficient quantity of lime. They do best in a sheltered position, prefer a damp climate and do not grow well in dry weather. However, if the weather is too wet they suffer from millipedes. Because they need warmth, they are sown at the end of May when the danger of late frosts has passed. French beans are sown in rows 40—50 cm apart, at a distance of 20 cm, or in clusters of 3—4 seeds, 30×40 cm apart. Runner beans are sown in groups around pyramid frames, constructed from canes at least 250 cm long. These are best positioned some 60×100 cm apart.

The green beans are harvested successively, de-pending on the time of sowing. This is usually between July and mid-September. The ripeness of the beans can easily be determined by breaking them in half. If they are truly ripe the break is smooth, vertical and has no filaments or parchment scales.

Broad bean

Broad beans (*Vicia faba* var. *major*) are an excellent vegetable. They must, however, be harvested while the pods are still green and soft, before they start to get tough.

Unlike other legumes, they require a damp, humus-rich and well fertilized soil, best supplied by farmyard manure or compost. They also like a sunny, warm situation.

Broad beans are sown in mid-March, in the same way as French beans, that is, in clusters some 40×60 cm apart. The plants need to be watered in dry weather. Harvesting can begin in June.

Lentil

Lentil (*Lens culinaris*) is a very popular pulse and in the opinion of many gourmets it ranks as a delicacy.

As a member of the pea family, the lentils are not particularly demanding. They need more warmth than peas but less than beans. They like light, loamy-sandy soil with a sufficient amount of nutrients and, above all, a weed-free site. A compound fertilizer can be applied before sowing at a ratio of 50 g per square metre. During the growing season the young plants can then be given an additional supply of ammonium saltpetre with lime at a ratio of

8 g per square metre. Lentils do not tolerate being fertilized with farmyard manure.

The seeds are sown in rows, 15 cm apart and about 3 cm deep, during April. The beds must be kept free of weeds, particularly when the young plants start to emerge.

Lentils are harvested when the bottom pods start to turn brown. The plants are then pulled out or scythed. They are then dried, tied together and suspended from the roof void. When they have dried the seeds are rubbed clear or better still thrashed out on a large sheet, using a piece of wood.

Herbs and aromatic vegetables

These are grown in the garden to add flavour and aroma to various dishes. Their nutritional value is therefore minor, but many herbs have outstanding medicinal properties. The main active principles are volatile oils, tannis, glycosides and resins. This chapter covers only the most common herbs, which can easily be grown in the garden.

Marjoram
Marjoram (*Majorana hortensis*) is used fresh or dry in the preparation of sausages, burgers, soups and

Dill seed is obtained from spring-sown plants. It should be collected as soon as the umbels start to turn brown as the seeds tend to fall out soon afterwards.

many other dishes. It contains volatile oil, bitters and tannins. It aids digestion, increasing the secretion of digestive juices. It helps to combat flatulence, intestinal colic and is recommended as a treatment of conditions arising from the common cold.

Marjoram grows well in light humus-rich soils in a sunny position. It is generally grown from pre-cultivated seedlings and is only individually sown directly into the bed. Its small seeds are scattered in a frame or in boxes in the greenhouse during March. The seeds are not covered with soil but simply lightly pressed into its surface. This is then kept damp until the seeds start to germinate. It is recommended that the seeds be covered with a sheet of paper or plastic until they germinate. The seedlings are transplanted outdoors in the second half of May, 3—4 plants being put together in rows 20—30 cm apart, and at a distance of 15 cm within the row.

The aerial parts are cut twice or three times in the year to a height of about 5 cm above the ground. This is always done before the plant has started to flower, to ensure the highest quality. The first cropping is usually the best. The leaves and stalks are then dried in a mildly warm atmosphere, in shade. If they are dried artificially the temperature should not exceed 35° C, otherwise valuable constituents are lost. After the dry leaves and stalks have been crushed, the herbs should be stored in air-tight, opaque containers and kept out of direct sunlight.

Dill
Dill (*Anethum graveolens*) is mostly cultivated for its young stalks and leaves, which are used fresh, dried or pickled. When the plant produces its umbels, they and the seeds are used in pickling gherkins. Dill contains vitamin C and oils. It stimulates the appetite, has a mild diuretic effect and also helps to combat flatulence.

Dill does not have any specific requirements as far as cultivation is concerned but it does not grow in dry soil. It is often grown as an intercropping plant and sown along with other vegetables. As it germinates very quickly, it also fulfils the function of a marking crop, for example, in rows of carrots and parsnips. If grown by itself the seeds should be sown in rows spaced some 25 cm apart, gradually from April on, to ensure a permanent supply of fresh leaves. For an autumn harvest, dill is sown at the end of August in beds, and well into September, under a frame.

Caraway
Caraway (*Carum carvi*) is commonly used in cooking. Its seeds are used in baking and meat dishes, in the production of liquors, oils etc.

Caraway is a biennial plant forming a rosette of basal leaves in its first year of growth and only flowering and producing seeds in the second year. It grows well in damp humus-rich soils which are sufficiently rich in lime. It has modest demands in terms of position and grows well even at higher, submountain elevations. It is sometimes sown alongside poppy as an intercropping plant to save space.

Lovage is propagated either from seed or by the division of older plants. Leaves can be picked during the whole growing season.

In the garden, however, caraway is usually grown on its own, the seeds being sown from April until June in rows 30 cm apart. The plants growing in rows can be slightly earthed up in the autumn so that they overwinter more easily. In the following year the seeds are harvested when the umbels and fruit begin to turn brown, usually at the end of June or in July. The plants are then tied in bundles and left to dry, and the dried seeds are then ready to be threshed out and cleaned.

Mint

The dried leaves of mint (*Mentha* × *piperita*) are used in the preparation of numerous dishes. Mint stimulates the appetite, relieves flatulence, calms the digestive tract and has a favourable influence on nervous stomach conditions. It is also used in herbal teas, particularly for the treatment of liver and gall bladder diseases. The leaves contain oils with menthol, bitter principles and tannis.

Mint is a perennial plant which grows well in warm, sunny places with a light calcareous soil. It spreads easily by its underground rhizomes. The new varieties in particular do not form seeds and can therefore only be propagated vegetatively. The young divisions are planted in spring or autumn, at a depth of 6 cm and in a layout 20 × 50 cm.

The stalks and leaves are gathered before the plant has started to flower and then a second time when the plant has regenerated later in the growing season. The leaves are dried in semi-shade as quickly as possible. This plant is left in the same spot for a maximum of four years. Its great disadvantage is that its continuously growing rootstock spreads like a weed, unless contained by being planted in an old tin bucket or similar vessel, with a number of drainage holes punctured in the base.

Anise

Anise (*Pimpinella anisum*) has been used in medicine for several thousand years. Its seeds and ethereal oils

213

obtained from them are used as components of medicines for treating coughs and colds. Aniseed is used in larger quantities in the food industry for confectionary and pastry making, in the preservation of vegetables and in the production of liqueurs. Fennel has similar properties but is easier to grow and is an almost perfect substitute for aniseed.

Anise is a very demanding plant. It grows only in warm, sunny and sheltered places, otherwise it might suffer from late frosts. It also needs a well prepared, humus-rich soil. The seeds are sown in April in rows 30—40 cm apart. When the seedlings emerge they are thinned out to 5 cm between individual plants. The plants are harvested when the seeds start to turn brown. They are then left to dry under the roof void and the seeds are then threshed out.

Tarragon

Tarragon (*Artemisia dracunculus*) is a traditional herb with a bitter-sweet flavour used in the pickling of vegetables, as an ingredient in sauces, mayonnaise, vinegar, mustard, and tarragon butter. It stimulates the appetite and increases the secretion of bile and digestive juices. Its leaves also contain oils which are used in the production of perfumes.

Tarragon is a perennial plant that needs a dry, warm and sunny position, but has few demands in terms of soil. The plants are usually propagated by underground stolons, planted in a layout of 30 × 50 cm (growing from seed is a lengthy and tedious process). The plants are left in one site for a period of four years. The leaves and stalks are harvested usually before the plant has started to flower and this can be repeated several times a year. It is then dried in partial shade.

Thyme

Thyme (*Thymus vulgaris*) is equally important in cooking and as a herbal remedy. It is used in cooking to flavour game, poultry, smoked meats, soups and sauces and it is also added to pickled gherkins. It has disinfective properties in the treatment of intestinal parasites and helps relieve flatulence and diarrhoea. It contains ethereal oils with thymol, cymol, carvacrol and tannins.

Thyme is a perennial plant and can be left in the same spot for 4—5 years. It is easily propagated by the division of clumps or by seeds, sown in a frame in the second half of March. The seedlings are pricked out and then, in May, they are planted in groups placed some 30 × 40 cm apart. The stalks and leaves are harvested between May and July, just before they begin to flower. The plants are then cut down to about 5 cm above the ground and the crop is dried in a shady, airy place.

Sage

Sage (*Salvia officinalis*) goes well with roast meat and fish and is also used as an additive to stuffings and minced meat. Its grey-green leaves contain ethereal oils, tannins and bitter principles. In small quantities, sage can be used as a gargle to treat mouth infections. It is also said to reduce excessive sweating,

aid digestion and have a beneficial influence on liver and gall bladder conditions.

This undemanding plant grows well in sunny and sheltered locations, and prefers an alkaline soil. It is propagated by the division of its clumps or from seeds (round, black and rather large for such a small plant) sown in a frame during March. The well developed seedlings are planted outdoors in beds 40 × 50 cm apart at the beginning of the summer. The tops of the aerial parts are then gathered just before they begin to flower. In their first year of growth the plants are cut once and then twice in successive years. The stalks and leaves are dried in the shade, but they do not retain their flavour as well as most dried herbs, so use the fresh leaves while you can.

Fennel

Fennel (*Foeniculum vulgare*) is a very popular herb. Besides being used for home cooking, it also has a general application in the food industries, confectionary and for pastry making. Fennel oils are useful in the treatment of flatulence and for loosening phlegm. Indeed, the substances present in fennel are used in the production of many medicines.

This perennial herb needs a sunny, warm yet slightly damp situation and grows well in vine-growing areas. It can be propagated from root cuttings, but it is better to grow it from seeds, which are sown at the end of April in rows 40 cm apart. If exposed to winds, the plants may need staking. Fennel is either sown thinly in the first place or the seedlings are subsequently thinned out. In the autumn the plants are dug up, their tops cut away, their roots cleaned and stored for the winter in an empty frame or in sand in the cellar. In the spring of the following year the roots are then planted 60—80 cm apart. The fruit in the umbels gradually ripens from the centre outwards. The entire umbel is then cut off and dried,

Dry coriander seeds are used mainly for pickling vegetables, but also for cooking.

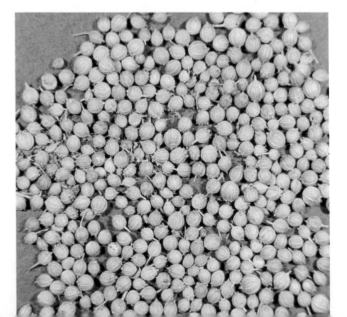

spread out on trays in the shade. When dry they are threshed or rubbed free of seed and fully cleaned. When baking, sprinkle fennel seeds on the top of bread or rolls before placing them in the oven, for a delicious aniseed flavour.

Chervil

Chervil (*Anthriscus cerefolium*) is an annual plant with very fine, profusely curled leaves, much reminiscent of parsley. Varieties with more sparse and less curly leaves also exist. Chervil is used to flavour omelettes and egg dishes, meat dishes, soups and sauces and to decorate open sandwiches. It is also an ingredient in various pastes. Its fresh leaves contain vitamin C. Chervil stimulates the appetite; it also has diuretic properties.

It grows well in both sunny or semi-shaded situations. The seeds are sown gradually from April to September, to ensure a constant supply of fresh stalks and leaves, which can be gathered as early as a month after sowing. It does not transplant very well, so leave it where sown. Plants sown in late September winter well outdoors and early in spring develop rich rosettes of leaves, from which sweet, slightly pungent and aromatic leaves can be harvested. Do this with a pair of scissors as chervil is so delicate you may pull up the whole plant if you try to pull off a few leaves.

Coriander

Coriander (*Coriandrum sativum*) is an annual herb. Its fresh, ray-like leaves and ripe seeds are used in the preserving of vegetables, for spicing various dishes, and to flavour breads. Coriander also contains aromatic oils which aid digestion.

This slim, erect herb requires a medium heavy, permeable soil. The seeds are sown in April, in rows some 30 cm apart. The plants are harvested when their umbels and fruit turn brown, usually at the end of August. The umbels are left to dry and seeds are then easily rubbed away. They are very aromatic with a pleasant, sweetish, slightly pungent flavour.

Lovage

Lovage (*Levisticum officinale*) is a tall-growing, perennial, aromatic plant with leaves resembling those of celeriac. Apart from vitamins, resinous substances and acids, it also contains enzymes. Lovage has a wide use in cooking. Fresh or dried it can be added to potato and pea soups, to boiled potatoes, beef stock, burgers and sauces. As a medicinal herb, lovage is used in the treatment of sclerosis; it also reduces flatulence and stimulates the secretion of chlorides. It is also a diuretic.

Lovage is quite a difficult herb in its initial stages of growth, but grows well in damper soils in full sun or partial shade. It can be propagated either from cuttings taken from established plants or from seed. The seeds have a low germination rate and therefore are sown as soon as possible, often immediately after the autumn crop, directly into a bed or in a frame. The one-year-old plants are planted out at the end of summer or in autumn at distances of 40 × 50 cm.

The leaves can then be harvested as early as the first year after initial sowing but the roots, intended for medicinal purposes, are only taken from two-year or older plants. It takes about four years to reach its full height.

Basil

Sweet basil (*Ocimum basilicum*) has pleasantly aromatic leaves, reminiscent of cloves in their smell. It is used to flavour sauces and soups, and in the cooking of game, liver and pulses; it is also a suitable pickling spice for beetroot. It relieves flatulence and stimulates the appetite.

Basil is an annual plant thriving only in warm, sunny and sheltered situations. The seeds are sown in a frame or in boxes, in March. Its small seedlings should then be pricked out into small pots and the seedlings then put out about 30 cm apart.

As the plant grows, pinch out the main stem to encourage side shoots, keeping the plant bushy.

The stalks and leaves are harvested for the first time when the plants begin to flower and then a second time in September, before the seeds ripen. The first cutting should be done to about 10 cm above the ground, so that the plants are not damaged. The stalks and leaves are then dried in the shade.

Savory

Savory (*Satureja hortensis*) is an annual herb with a pleasant aroma and a pungent, spicy flavour. Its dried or fresh leaves are often used instead of pepper. It is an excellent flavouring for pulse soups, pickled gherkins, sausages, sauces and game. Its stalks and leaves contain ethereal oils (carvacrol and cymol) and also tannins which alleviate diarrhoea. Savory also improves the appetite, treats inflammations and has a diuretic effect.

The plant requires light soil and above all a sunny and warm situation. It is cultivated in the same way as sweet basil or marjoram. Young plants, pre-cultivated in a frame or box, are put outdoors during the second half of May, some 20 × 30 cm apart. In warmer regions the seeds can be sown in April, directly into a bed in rows 30 cm apart. The stalks are cut away about 5 cm above the ground when the plants start to flower and the leaves are stripped away, then dried in a thin layer in a shaded place, where there is a slight flow of air.

Purslane

Purslane (*Portulaca oleracea* ssp. *sativa*) is an annual plant with fleshy, branching stalks and fleshy spatulate leaves. For centuries it has been used in the kitchen along with vinegar, pepper and oil, in the preparation of salads. Its leaves can be cooked in the same way as spinach.

It has specific environmental requirements. It grows well in a lighter soil and in a warm spot. Because of its sensitivity to low temperatures, it is sown in a frame in March and then the young plants are put outdoors at the end of April. Alternatively, it can be sown directly into the bed in May and June, in rows 30—40 cm apart. The young shoots and leaves are then gathered gradually from July until mid-October, depending on the time of sowing. It is advisable to sow gradually, at monthly intervals.

Hyssop

The fresh and dried leaves of hyssop (*Hyssopus officinalis*) have a distinct spicy flavour, reminiscent of camphor. They are used in cooking, in soups, meat sauces, stuffings and in vegetable salads. As with sage, the stalks are used to reduce excessive perspiration. The plant also contains oil (pinene), tannins and glycosides.

Hyssop is a hardy perennial — a compact plant that grows well in warm, sunny and sheltered spots, where there is a plentiful supply of lime. It can be propagated by the division of its clusters or from seeds. These are sown at the end of March in a frame or in boxes. The pre-cultivated plants are then put out in the second half of May, some 40×40 cm apart. In favourable weather conditions, hyssop can be sown in the bed some time during April.

The tops of the plant are cut off about 10 cm above the ground when they begin to bear their attractive blue flowers and are harvested twice a year. They are then dried in the shade.

Balm

The lemon-like aroma and flavour of balm (*Melissa officinalis*) renders this perennial herb suitable whenever lemon rind or juice is recommended. Balm contains in its leaves ethereal oils (citral, geraniol) and tannins. It lends its fragrant aroma to vinegars, mayonnaise, meat dishes, salads, soups and sauces. It also has similar medicinal properties to those of mint, reducing flatulence, blood pressure and soothing migraines. The fresh or dried aromatic leaves are also used for the preparation of an excellent and most refreshing tea.

Balm has specific requirements on temperature and is therefore grown in warm, sunny and sheltered places. It grows particularly well in light, humus-rich soils. It is propagated by the division of large clusters in spring or autumn or from seed. It can be left in one place for five years or longer, but in winter the plants need to be protected by earthing them up with soil and leaves. The seeds are sown in a frame in March. The germinated seedlings are then pricked out in order to develop a better root system. They are planted out in May in a 40×40 cm layout.

The leaves and stalks are harvested in dry weather, best before the formation of inflorescences. Alternatively they can be gathered when the plant starts to flower, as at this time the leaves have their best aroma. The tops of the plant are cut off twice a year, dried carefully in the shade and stored in air-tight containers so that the aromatic oils do not escape. Despite these precautions, however, the quality of the dried herb only lasts until the next harvesting.

Rue

Rue (*Ruta graveolens*) is a perennial semi-shrub with aromatic leaves and young shoots that have a slightly bitter, sharp taste that many people actually dislike. It is therefore used only in very small quantities to flavour salads, meat dishes and sauces. Rue contains ethereal oils, bitter principles and the glycoside rutin. It improves the appetite, lessens tension and has a diuretic effect.

It requires a medium heavy to lighter calcareous soil and a warm, sunny situation. It is propagated by the division of large clumps in spring or from seeds which are sown at the end of March or in April in a frame. The young plants are put out at the end of May, spaced about 30 cm apart.

The stalks and leaves are best harvested before the plant has started to flower. The handling of the fresh plants can sometimes cause an unpleasant rash in susceptible people and therefore it is advisable to put on gloves beforehand. After the cut parts of the plant have been dried in the shade, the leaves can be rubbed away from the stalks and, as in the case of balm, stored in air-tight containers where they keep for about a year.

Borage

Borage (*Borago officinalis*) is an easy-to-grow annual plant, currently cultivated on a much smaller scale than it used to be. Its young, smooth, hairless leaves are used, finely cut, as an excellent ingredient in vegetable salads, sauces and vegetable soups. When they are sliced or crushed the leaves give off a pleasant cucumber aroma. The dried leaves are a popular remedy for the treatment of rheumatism and inflammation of the urinary tract.

Borage is sown in spring or in autumn. It has few demands in terms of place or soil and does not require any special attention during the growing season. Borage is often left to seed itself out and is thus propagated naturally. The ripe seeds that have thus fallen germinate in the autumn or during the following spring in the same place in which the plant has been growing during the preceding year. The grey-green leaves are hairy and liable to sting, so this is another herb to harvest when wearing gloves.

Other vegetables

Rhubarb

Rhubarb (*Rheum rhabarbarum*) is grown for its long, fleshy leaf-stalks. They contain vitamin C, vitamin A and minerals such as phosphorus, potassium and magnesium. Their piquant, sour flavour is due to the content of malic and oxalic acids. The leaf-stalks are stewed and used for desserts.

This perennial is best grown in a deep, medium heavy and relatively damp soil. Wet, acid soils are not suitable. Before planting, the bed needs to be well fertilized with farmyard manure at a rate of about 8 kg per square metre. At the same time it is advisable to add superphosphate, ammonium sulphate and potassium salt (40 per cent) at a rate of 60, 40 and 25 g per square metre or an application of a combined fertilizer at 80 g per square metre.

Rhubarb has few demands in terms of situation and grows well in all regions. It is resistant to frost and tolerates semi-shade, but it benefits from occa-

Rhubarb stalks should not be pulled in the first year after planting. In the second year, some stalks can be pulled successively from the first half of April to mid- or end of July.

sional watering during the growing season especially if the soil is light. Every three to four years, usually in the autumn, the soil around the plant should be treated with lime. It is not advisable to grow rhubarb from seed as it is not self-pollinating and the new plants would probably not have the correct balance. They are therefore best propagated vegetatively by the division of clumps. The cuttings, with one or two buds, are planted in spring or in the autumn, during October, some 80 cm apart. The autumn planting is the more reliable and the plants develop sooner. When the cuttings are being planted, care must be taken to ensure that their buds are about 5 cm below the surface of the soil. In winter, the plants are protected with a thin layer of compost, peat or straw manure. In the first year after planting, the stalks are not harvested, to ensure that the plants do not lose their strength. During the growing season the plants are fertilized with ammonium saltpetre and lime at a rate of 22 g per square metre.

The stalks can then be pulled from the second year of growth, gradually from April to the end of June. They must be gently pulled out, never cut away, and several young leaves should be left on each plant. The leaf blades are removed from the stalks immediately to ensure that they do not fade. The inflorescences should be removed as they appear so that the plant is not weakened by the development of seeds.

Asparagus

Asparagus (*Asparagus officinalis*) is grown for its young fleshy spears, which are usually blanched but sometimes green. In spring, when early vegetables are in short supply, they are a favourite vegetable delicacy. However, the nutritional value of asparagus is rather low. It contains a small amount of vitamin C, minerals, fats, sugars, protein and the ethereal oil asparagine. Asparagus used to be widely grown for its medicinal properties. It helps to regulate high blood pressure, lessens tiredness and supports the functioning of the heart and kidneys.

Asparagus grows well in all areas where vegetables in general grow well. It likes a sunny, warm position in dry loamy-sandy soils, where the underground water table is relatively low. It does not grow well in heavy cold soils and is intolerant of chlorine. Since asparagus is grown in the same spot for many years, often up to 20, the soil needs to be particularly well prepared before it is planted. Dig down to a depth of at least 50 cm and fertilize with farmyard manure at a rate of 8 kg per square metre. Of the industrial fertilizers, superphosphate can be employed as a basic fertilizer along with potassium salt (40 per

Globe artichokes can be grown in the open only in very warm localities. Only 2—3 flower buds should be left to a stem.

The young spears are ready for harvesting from the third year onwards. Early in that spring the soil is earthed up some 30 cm above the plants. The surface of the soil is made firm with a shovel and the resulting crust will be lifted by the growing spears. They are harvested regularly, several times a week, by cutting away the spears revealed as the soil is pushed aside. At first, only a small portion of the spears are cut away to prevent the plants becoming too weak. However, in the following years — when the plants are being regularly and frequently fertilized in the autumn and through the growing season — some two thirds of the spears, often up to 20—25 cm long, can be harvested.

The harvesting of the so-called 'green' asparagus is much simpler. The plants are earthed up with only a thin layer of soil and then the green, unblanched spears are harvested. They contain more vitamin C than the blanched ones and vitamin A.

Globe artichoke

Globe artichoke (*Cynara scolymus*) is a vegetable delicacy, plants being cultivated for their fleshy recept-

Artichoke seedlings are grown in a frame or a greenhouse. They are put out into holes 20—30 cm deep, partly filled with compost so that the roots are some 10 cm below the surface of the bed. The plants should be 80 × 80 or 100 × 100 cm apart.

cent) and ammonium sulphate at a rate of 60, 50 and 30 g respectively per square metre.

The seedlings can be grown at home. In April, the seeds are soaked in water for three days. The water must be changed regularly. Then the seeds are sown in a nursery bed in rows about 30 cm apart. When the seedlings develop they are thinned out to about 10 cm. The soil is kept loose around them and well watered. In June, the young plants are fertilized with ammonium saltpetre and lime at a rate of 15 g per square metre. If the one-year-old plants are sufficiently strong, they can be planted outdoors in the spring of the second year. More often, however, they are kept in the nursery bed for a further year.

Strong, one- or two-year-old plants are put outdoors during April and May in prepared, 40 cm deep ridges. The bottom is covered with a layer of compost on which the plants are placed some 50 cm apart. They are then covered with a layer of compost and, after watering, the remaining soil is added. If a large number of plants are to be grown, the ridges need to be made 120 cm apart from each other. Given normal care and attention, that is, weeding, watering and feeding, the plants will mature after some two years of growth. The space between the rows of asparagus can be employed for growing shallow rooting plants with a short vegetative season, such as lettuce, radishes and spinach. In the autumn the branched above-ground parts are cut away and the rest is covered with compost.

218

Sweetcorn can be grown for kernels only in fertile, warm regions. The cobs are harvested when the kernels are fully ripe, tough and glossy, and the sheaths are yellow.

leaf-stalks are strong and fleshy; these are blanched and cooked in the same way as asparagus or green beans. Celery can be added to burgers in the same way as leeks. It is a valuable and tasty vegetable with dietetic properties.

It has the same requirements in terms of soil and weather as celeriac. Its seedlings are also precultivated, using a similar method.

Formerly, many varieties used to be artificially blanched by earthing them up, by tying the plants together or by lifting whole plants from the beds and placing them in a dark cellar or covered frame. New varieties with whitish to yellow-green leaves are self-blanching. However, this desirable quality can be increased by planting them closer together in the row, 20 × 20 cm apart, or in the short term by covering the bed with a dark sheet of plastic or similar material until the leaf-stalks become white. The method of harvesting is to cut them away with part of their rootstock intact, to prevent them disintegrating.

Sweetcorn

Sweetcorn (*Zea mays* var. *saccharata*) when it is ripe, exudes a creamy liquid and is an excellent delicacy. The cobs can be eaten raw, boiled in salty water or even roasted. Very young cobs, 3—10 cm long, can be preserved in the same way as gherkins. The nutritional value of sweetcorn in its raw state is equal to that of green peas. The seeds contain easily digested proteins, sugars and starch.

As opposed to corn grown for fodder purposes, sweetcorn has a small, often bushy growth. It likes warmth and can therefore only be cultivated in warm locations. In order to germinate it requires a minimum temperature of 8—10° C. It has great demands in terms of the humus and nutrient content of the soil. Apart from the use of a good compost or farmyard manure, the bed also needs fertilizing with standard industrial fertilizers. The most suitable is a compound fertilizer applied at a rate of 80 g per square metre. The best crops to be used before the planting of sweetcorn are early lettuce, radish or autumn-sown spinach. Sweetcorn is sensitive to frost and is therefore not suitable for cultivation at higher altitudes or in frost pockets.

Sweetcorn is usually sown at the beginning of May and in vine growing regions at the end of April. If an early crop is required, the plants can be precultivated in a frame or in the greenhouse by sowing seed straight into large, compost filled pots. They are then planted outdoors, spaced 40 × 80 cm apart, in mid-May.

Alternatively, sweetcorn can be sown directly in prepared rows and in pinches of 3—4 seeds at a depth of 6 cm. As the seedlings emerge only two plants are left in each cluster. Sweetcorn sown in rows also provides shelter for vegetables that cannot withstand a windy location, for example, cucumbers. In their first stages of growth, when the plants are being hoed for the first time, it is a good idea to add 30 g of ammonium saltpetre per square metre. Similarly, in the later stages — as the cobs start to develop their silky sheaths — it is advisable to add

acles, which can be as much as 10 cm in diameter. They are cooked in a similar way to asparagus, and contain vitamin B, provitamin A, sugars and inulin.

Artichokes are perennial warm-loving plants, sensitive to frost. They need a deep humus-rich soil with a high nutritional content, and adequate watering.

They are propagated from suckers thrown off by the older plants and also from seed. They are sown in March in small pots. Until the end of May, when they are transplanted outdoors, they are cultivated in the greenhouse or in the frame. The plants are put 80 × 100 cm apart and left in the same place for 5 years. They usually flower in the second or third year after sowing. However, plants sown in February can flower in the same year. In winter, the plants need to be covered with leaves or a layer of straw and during the most severe frosts with a sheet of plastic weighed down by soil.

To ensure the harvest of well-developed flower buds, each plant is left with three at the most. These need to be collected on time before the flowers open, that is, when the fleshy receptacle and bracts are well developed.

Celery

Celery (*Apium graveolens* var. *dulce*), when compared with celeriac, forms much larger tops and has a small root which is unsuitable for consumption. Its

Potatoes need a lot of water when in flower. This is the time when the new tubers are starting to form.

a diluted liquid manure along with 200 g of super-phosphate per 100 litres of water. When the plants reach a height of 40 cm, they then need to be earthed up. Apart from regular hoeing they also need abundant watering, although this will be regulated by the requirements of other vegetables growing nearby. As a matter of principle, herbicides are not used in the garden, although they are commonly employed when sweetcorn is grown on a large scale.

The cobs are harvested gradually as they ripen. The individual seeds should be soft and, when pressed, should exude a creamy, yellowish juice.

Another variety which is occasionally cultivated is popcorn. This is collected when the seeds are fully ripe and when the outer sheaths are dry. They are then peeled back and the cobs left hanging in the shade to dry out. When they are dry, the hard kernels are rubbed away and stored in a dry place. They are prepared by slow-roasting them.

Poppy

Poppy (*Papaver somniferum*) conjures up images of poppy seed tarts, strudels, cakes and other pastries. Apart from being used in the food industries, for example in the production of oil pressed from the seed, the poppy is also used in pharmacology. The seeds themselves and the empty capsules contain dozens of alcaloids.

Poppies can be divided into two groups. The first variety has capsules which, when ripe, develop openings through which the seeds fall out. The second variety's capsules remain closed, even when ripe.

The poppy requires a humus-rich soil with a sufficient content of calcium. Wet and heavy soils in windy locations are unsuitable, and the poppy is also sensitive to the presence of weeds. Recommended plants to be grown immediately before the poppy are fruit vegetables, brassicas, and early potatoes fertilized with farmyard manure. Good quality, healthy plants are obtained if sowing is done early and the seedlings are thinned out on time. Poppies can be grown in the same plot once every five years.

The seeds are sown as early as possible in spring, in rows 30 cm apart. When the seedlings emerge, the soil is weeded and the surface kept loose. When the young plants have developed 3—4 leaves, they are thinned out to 10—15 cm. They can also be left in clusters of 2—3 plants some 25 cm apart. Throughout the growing season they should be hoed and kept free of weeds.

The poppy is harvested gradually as the capsules mature and reach the required size, that is, when they begin to dry out and the seeds inside them rustle when the capsules are shaken. This is usually at the end of July and in August, but at higher elevations or as a result of a late sowing, the harvest can take place at the beginning of September. The capsules are best removed along with some 10—15 cm of the stalk and then dried off in suspended bunches. When dry, the tops of the capsules are cut off and the seeds shaken out. Manually shaken poppy seed is of the highest quality, as it is not likely to be damaged and therefore lasts a long time when stored; also, it does not become bitter.

Early potatoes

There is little doubt about the importance of early potatoes (*Solanum tuberosum*) in the vegetable garden. Along with other vegetables, they are an indispensable part of our diet. In fact, their nutritional and dietetic value makes them one of the premier vegetables and every year a small plot in the garden should be apportioned for their growth. Early potatoes are particularly useful as they can be gradually collected as early as three months after planting.

They require light to medium heavy humus-rich soils, the best being sandy or loamy-sandy ones. They prefer sheltered positions at low elevations, up to 300 m above sea level. Heavy, wet soils are unsuitable. In terms of nutrients, potatoes have a particular need for potassium. The soil in which they are to be grown should be prepared in the autumn. When the ground is being turned over, 6 kg of farmyard manure per square metre or twice that amount of compost is worked in. In spring, industrial fertilizers such as ammonium sulphate, superphosphate and potassium sulphate at a ratio of 30, 50 and 40 g per square metre are applied. During the growing season, best in May, the potato plot is given an addition of ammonium saltpetre at 20 g per square metre.

Potatoes require regular watering. A lack of moisture retards their growth and considerably reduces the yield. They need plenty of moisture, particularly when they are forming their buds and then start to flower, as this is the time when their tubers begin to form. They require a temperature of 15—20° C for an optimum growth. If the temperature is lower than 7° C their growth comes to a halt and frosts below —3° C damage the entire plant.

One of the most important preconditions for the growth of an early crop is the preparation of a pregerminated or even rooted culture. At about the end of February or at the beginning of March, the selected tubers are laid out in trays with most of the eyes pointing upwards. The trays are then placed in a light room where they are pregerminated at a temperature of 12—15° C until the time when they are planted outdoors. During this period they should form strong sprouts, about 2 cm long. An earlier crop can also be achieved by the initial rooting of the potatoes. They are covered with compost or peat in trays about 10 days before planting. It is a good idea to plant a small number of tubers in peat pots or pot trays. The roots then form a firm ball and when transplanted these tubers do not stop growing.

Depending on the weather, early potatoes are planted out about mid-April. As a rule, the pregerminated or rooted tubers are capable of continued growth outdoors even at lower temperatures — of about 5° C. Tubers which have not been germinated in advance remain dormant in the ground in these conditions and take a long time to germinate. The young shoots start to appear at the beginning of May but can be damaged by late frosts. It is therefore better to delay the planting outdoors in regions where late frosts occur. The tubers are planted in shallow ridges, 8—10 cm deep and about 60 cm apart. Within the ridges they are put with their shoot ends uppermost, 25—30 cm apart. They are then earthed up and the soil is made firm with a shovel. The plot is then hoed and earthed up again when the plants are about 10 cm tall and a third time when they are 20 cm tall. Watering is necessary in dry weather.

The first tubers are harvested as early as the second half of June, when the plants begin to flower, especially if a pregerminated or rooted culture has been used. Initially, some plants can be dug up from the side of the ridge, so that only the largest tubers are extracted. If this is done, the smaller tubers will continue to grow undisturbed. The whole plant is then dug up during the second half of July or in August, depending on the variety and the moment when the tops turn yellow and dry up.

The mushroom *Pleurotus ostreatus* is collected by cutting or breaking off the individual fruit bodies or whole clumps.

Healthy, undamaged potatoes are stored in dry, well ventilated and cold cellars. Alternatively, potato clamps can be used, where the potatoes are placed in shallow wooden boxes or trays. Tubers for later use should be stored in the dark; if they are not, they turn green and begin to form the poison solanine. Tubers intended for planting can be stored in dispersed light as this usually limits the onset and spread of rot and slows down germination in the same way as low temperatures. Seed potatoes with a greenish skin are more healthy and usually have more vitality. The optimum temperature for storage is 3—5° C.

Jerusalem artichoke

Jerusalem artichoke (*Helianthus tuberosus*) is not as yet fully appreciated as a vegetable. It is grown as fodder, but can be prepared in a similar way to potatoes and can even be eaten raw. The tubers do not contain starch, but they do contain inulin and therefore are a good vegetable for diabetics.

The Jerusalem artichoke is an undemanding perennial which can be grown almost everywhere. It does not require watering, is frost-resistant and can grow in shaded locations. However, places exposed to wind are less suitable as the 2—3 m-tall plants are easily broken and uprooted. It has few demands in terms of nutrients. If the soil is fertilized in the same way as for potatoes, a higher yield of tubers will result and the green tops, which are an excellent fodder, will grow larger.

The tubers are planted outdoors as soon as possible, at a depth of 15 cm and 50 × 100 cm apart. During growth the soil between the rows should be loosened and the plants earthed up in the same way as for potatoes.

The tubers are harvested in spring or in late autumn, or even during the winter as long as the ground is not frozen. They do not freeze in the ground but could be damaged if they are more exposed. If a part of the crop has been left in the ground after the harvest, new plants will develop from them. Jerusalem artichokes can be grown in the same bed for up to 5 years.

In winter, the tubers are stored in a cold cellar, in a clamp or in a frame. It is useful to put them in sand to prevent them from drying out. Their skin colour varies but is most often whitish or reddish.

Mushrooms in the garden

Field mushroom

Field mushroom (*Agaricus hortensis*) has become a very popular delicacy. The fruit-bodies can be prepared as a supplement to various dishes or they can be fried as a main course, or used in sauces or sterilized and pickled. Fresh mushrooms are most sought after in winter and in spring.

Field mushrooms can be grown anywhere. In summer, on a bed in a sheltered corner of the garden, in a frame or even underneath the benches in the greenhouse. In winter, they can be grown in boxes in the house. During growth they need a constant temperature. The optimum temperature for the growth of the mycelium in the chosen substrate is between 18 and 20° C; for the subsequent development of the fruit-bodies a temperature of 11° C is sufficient.

The basic precondition for a successful cultivation is the nature of the substrate. This is fresh horse manure if available, and can be prepared at home. If the amount of manure available is inadequate, then cut straw, bran etc. can be added. The horse manure should be piled up about 120 cm high in a suitable, sheltered, draught-free position and made up of several layers. Each successive layer needs to be watered well and trodden down. After a few days the temperature of the manure reaches about 60° C and the mound is then dug over, the original outer walls now being placed in the centre of the pile. Five days later, when it has warmed through again, the pile is once again turned over and after a further digging some 15—20 days later, a well fermented substrate will have been prepared. This should be brown and crumbly, and no longer have an unpleasant smell as the ammonia content will have evaporated during the fermentation.

The substrate prepared in this way is put in the cellar or in the frame, to form a bed about 20 cm high. When it has been slightly compacted, it is then thinly scattered with a granulated culture and this is covered with a further 3 cm deep layer of the substrate. Alternatively, bits of mycelium can be pressed into the substrate to a depth of about 4 cm and about 20 cm apart. To keep the bed dry, it is covered with a layer of damp sacking or with a perforated sheet of plastic. In about three weeks, when it is clear that the mycelium has taken and started to grow, the substrate is once again covered with a 3-cm layer of soil, made up of one part frame soil, one part river sand and one part peat. This soil covering has to be prepared several weeks in advance and disinfected with formaldehyde. A wheelbarrow load of this is then mixed with 1.5 kg of ground limestone. Quick lime must not be used.

After about 4—5 weeks, the first fruit-bodies will appear and these are gathered when their caps are about 3 cm in diameter. They are carefully removed from the substrate by a slow turning movement. One square metre can yield up to 4 kg of fruit-bodies. In the course of the harvest period, which can last 3—4 months, the bed has to be watered and the cellar or frame periodically ventilated.

Stropharia rugosoannulata
The flesh of the fruit-bodies is white, slightly spicy and has an excellent flavour. In cooking, this mushroom is used in soups and meat sauces or fried. It can be used fresh or dried.

It can easily be grown in a frame, in a layer of any type of straw. This should be watered and trodden down regularly over several days to form a layer some 20—30 cm deep.

The best time for preparing the substrate is mid-May. After about a week, small pieces of the culture are planted about 5—7 cm below the surface and about 15 cm apart. The substrate is then covered by a sheet of plastic or glass. The temperature of the substrate should be around 20—25° C. It should be watered occasionally, as required, with tepid water. In about a month the white mycelium will begin to break through the substrate. This should then be covered by a 5-cm layer of sterile soil mixed with peat and sand so that the substrate retains its moisture and the fruit-bodies do not become uprooted later. The frame needs protection from direct sun with a sheet of polythene or a straw mat.

Harvesting of the gradually maturing fruit-bodies lasts from about mid-July to mid-September. From an area of one square metre it is possible to collect about 3 kg of fruit-bodies and under cloches this might be 8 kg or more.

If the substrate with its mycelium content is kept through the winter in a cellar or if it is covered with a sufficient layer of compost or manure to prevent it freezing through, it can be used again for the cultivation of fruit-bodies in the following year.

Oyster fungus
Oyster fungus (*Pleurotus ostreatus*) is one of the most tasty mushrooms. It has a strong mushroom flavour and is more aromatic than the field mushroom. Although it is rather tougher and requires longer cooking, it can be prepared in a number of ways and is particularly suitable for pickling in vinegar. It grows on rotten wood and therefore cannot be grown in beds. In the garden it can be grown on the stumps of various trees, best of all poplar, beech or walnut. These should be cut into pieces 30—40 cm long and with a diameter of 10—20 cm. However, it must first be ascertained that the wood has not been infected by any other wood fungus. The purchased mycelium is introduced into the prepared logs through holes that have ben drilled in the middle. The mycelium is pressed into these and the logs are then sunk into the ground so that the mycelium is buried about 3 cm below the ground surface and a part of the log is protruding out above the ground level. A shaded, sheltered spot is the most suitable and it is recommended to cover the wood with a sheet of polythene. The mycelium grows through the logs in about three months and the first clusters of fruit-bodies begin to appear.

As the oyster fungus is an autumn species, it starts to form its fruit-bodies when the temperature has dropped at night to about 8—10° C. If you want to pick the first fruit-bodies in the first year of growth, the culture needs to be started in spring or in summer. Once started, the prolific oyster fungus continues to produce its fruit on the same logs for four or more years.

The autumn harvest can easily be extended into December by covering the logs with sheets of polythene or glass. A short frost will not harm them. The method of collecting this mushroom is by carefully breaking off or cutting off the individual fruit-bodies or by removing the entire clusters.

Schedule for sowing, planting outdoors and harvesting vegetables

Vegetable species	Sowing in frame	Sowing in bed	Depth of sowing in cm	Thinning	Planting outdoors	Planting layout in cm	Harvest
cabbage, early	end February	—	0.5	March	beginning of April	50 × 50	May—June
cabbage, summer	April	April	0.5	May	May	50 × 50	June—October
cabbage, winter	—	May	0.5	July	—	50 × 50	November—January
Savoy cabbage	March—April	April	0.5	May	July	60 × 60	gradually
Brussels sprouts	—	April	0.5	May—June	June	60 × 60	October—March
kohlrabi	—	March—July	0.5	as needed	—	30 × 30	June—October
cauliflower, summer	February	—	0.5	—	April	50 × 50	May—July
cauliflower, winter	—	April	0.5	—	June—July	50 × 50	August—November
broccoli	February, early varieties	June, late varieties	0.5	—	April, early June, late varieties	50 × 50	from July
Chinese cabbage	—	mid—July	2	as required	—	25 × 40	from September
cucumber	April—May	—	2—3	—	June	80 × 40	August—September
marrow	—	May	3—4	June	June	100 × 200	September—October
melon	May	May	3—4	—	June	80 × 80	August—September
tomato	from mid-March	—	3—4	—	from mid-May	60 × 80	July—November
pepper	March—April	—	1	—	from mid-May	40 × 50	August—October
onion	—	autumn or spring	3	April	—	25 × 10	July—September
garlic	—	—	4—5	—	October or March	25 × 8	when leaves turn yellow
leek	March—May	April—May	0.5	—	May—June	10 × 20	October—March
shallot	—	—	just below soil surface	—	February—March	10 × 20	July—September
chives	—	March	2—3	—	—	25 × 25 (clusters)	May—September
carrot	—	March—June	3	as needed	—	25 × 7	gradually
parsley	—	March	2—3	as needed	—	25 × 10	also in winter
parsnip	—	February—March	2—3	April	—	25 × 10	October—December
scorzonera	—	March, September	2—3	as needed	—	25 × 8	October, March
celeriac	January—February	—	2—3	—	mid-May	30 × 30	October—November
radish	February	March—June August—September	2	—	—	thinly	May—October
beetroot	—	April—June	3	when seedlings appear	—	30 × 15	August—October
lettuce	from February	from March	2—3	—	from April	25 × 25	April—October
lettuce for cutting	—	March—August	2—3	as needed	—	10 × 10	gradually
endive	—	April, July	2	as needed	—	30 × 30	July, October
lamb's lettuce	—	July—August	2—3	—	—	in rows 20 cm apart	October—December
spinach, summer	—	mid-March	4	—	—	in rows 25 cm apart	May
spinach, winter	—	August	4	—	—	in rows 25 cm apart	September—October
peas for shelling	—	March	4—5	—	—	in rows 25 cm apart	June—July
sugar peas	—	April	4—5	—	—	in rows 25 cm apart	July—September
beans, French	—	May—June	2—3	—	—	30 × 40	July—September
beans, runner	—	May—June	2—3	—	—	60 × 100	July—September
sweetcorn	April	May	6—8	—	mid—May	40 × 80	gradually as ripens
potatoes	—	—	8—10	—	April	60 × 25	July—August

A selection of vegetable varieties

Vegetable species		Variety
artichoke, globe		Vert de Laon
artichoke, Jerusalem		Fuseau
asparagus		Martha Washington
		Lorella
aubergine		Black Prince
bean, broad		Aquadulce
		Imperial Green Longpod
		Green Windsor
bean, French		Tendergreen
		Chevrier Vert
		Kinghorn Wax
		Purple-podded Climbing
bean, runner		Achievement
		Enorma
		Streamline
		Scarlet Emperor
		Hammond's Dwarf Scarlet
beetroot		Boltardy
		Detroit-Little Ball
		Cheltenham Green Top
broccoli		Purple Sprouting
		Late White Sprouting
Brussels sprouts	early	Peer Gynt
	medium early	Citadel
	late	Achilles
cabbage, Chinese		Sampan
		Pe-Tsai
cabbage, red		Ruby Ball
		Stockley's Giant Red
cabbage, Savoy		Best of All
		Ormskirk Late
		Savoy King
cabbage, spring		Durham Early
		April
		Harbinger
cabbage, summer		Greyhound
		Primo (Golden Acre)
		Winnigstadt
cabbage, winter		Christmas Drumhead
		January King
capsicum		Worldbeater
		Gypsy
carrot	early	Amsterdam Forcing
		Early Nantes
		Early French Frame
	maincrop	Chantenay Red Cored
		Autumn King
		New Red Intermediate
cauliflower	summer	Snowball
		Alpha
	autumn	Canberra
		Barrier Reef
	winter	English Winter
		St Agnes
celery		Giant White
		Golden Self-Blanching
chicory		Witloof
		Sugar Loaf
courgette		Zucchini
		Gold Rush
cucumber	outdoor/ridge	King of the Ridge
		Burpless Tasty Green
		Crystal Apple
	greenhouse	Telegraph
		Conqueror
endive		Batavian Green
kale		Hungry Gap
		Pentland Brig
kohlrabi		Green Vienna
leek	early	The Lyon-Prizetaker
	mid-season	Musselburgh
	late	Giant Winter-Royal
		Favourite
lettuce, cabbage: butterhead		All the Year Round
		Tom Thumb
		Avondefiance
lettuce, cabbage: crisphead		Vebb's Wonderful
		Windermere
		Iceberg
lettuce, cos		Lobjoit's Green
		Little Gem
marrow		Long Green Trailing
		Green Bush
onion	sets	Stuttgarter Giant
		Sturon
	seeds	Ailsa Craig
		Rijnsburger
		Paris Silver Skin
onion, spring		White Lisbon
		Ishikura
parsnip		Tender and True
		Hollow Crown Improved
		White Gem
pea	round-seeded	Feltham First
		Meteor
		Pilot
	wrinkled-seeded	Kelvedon Wonder
		Hurst Green Shaft
		Onward
	mangetout	Sugar Snap
	petit pois	Waverex
potato	first early	Duke of York
		Pentland Javelin
	second early	Red Craig's Royal
	maincrop	Maris Piper
		Majestic
		Desirée
		King Edward
radish	summer	Cherry Belle
		Scarlet Globe
		French Breakfast
	winter	Black Spanish Round
		Russian Giant
scorzonera		Hative de Niort
shallot		King of Denmark
spinach	summer	Sigmaleaf
	winter	Broad-leaved Prickly
		Long-standing Prickly
swede		Marian
		Purple Top
sweetcorn		First of All
		Kelvedon Glory
tomato	greenhouse	Moneymaker
		Ailsa Craig
		Eurocross
		Shirley
		Big Boy
		Golden Sunrise
	outdoor	Gardener's Delight
		Sigmabush
turnip	early	Snowball
		Purple-top Milan
	maincrop	Green-top White

Lawn

A nice, bright green lawn is an indispensable part of any garden. Its colour is pleasing to the eye and its smooth texture invites relaxation. A well kept, dense lawn also improves the microclimate. Apart from these functions it also fulfils an architectural role by forming a handsome green frame for flower beds, clusters of roses, specimen plants and groups of decorative shrubs. It is a natural complement to the warm colours of all flowering plants.

It must be pointed out that neither laying the foundations of a lawn nor its subsequent maintenance are simple. However, since the lawn will give years of pleasure, it makes sense to make whatever effort is necessary and such work will be amply and quickly rewarded.

The lawn is best located in a sunny or slightly shaded place, one that is well protected from constant wind. Excessively damp locations or places where snow lingers for a long time in spring are not suitable. Damp plots will need to be drained and the quality of heavy soil improved.

Sowing a lawn

The soil must be well prepared in advance. It should be dug over to a depth of 25—40 cm but the lower layer of soil must not become the topsoil as is the case when making furrows. After digging, scatter a humus-rich substrate, such as a good quality compost, over the surface to form a layer at least 15 cm deep. The entire area of the future lawn should have all weeds and stones removed. Make sure that they really are all removed; otherwise they will later make the maintenance of the lawn difficult. Then rake over the whole area until it is absolutely level — checking this with a spirit level and a flat board.

It is best to carry out this preparatory work in autumn; the soil being turned over and left to be further broken down by the elements, then levelled in the spring. Alternatively, it might be prepared in early spring when the late frosts and rain will break up the clods. If the preparatory work has to be carried out just before sowing, the soil should then be left at least for several days, to allow it to settle.

The choice of lawn seed depends on the purpose the lawn is going to serve (an English-type lawn —

It is difficult to imagine a garden without a stretch of lawn which enhances the effect of each and every section.

A well-kept lawn attracts the eye by its pleasing, fresh colour.

an area for leisure and sporting activities — or a lawn for semi-shaded places etc.) The finer the quality of the grasses, the more care will be necessary and the less wear the finished lawn will stand. The seed is usually sown in mid-April or mid-September as the weather permits. Obviously, sowing can be done throughout the summer but only if it is possible to water the sown area regularly. On horizontal surfaces 20—25 g of grass seed per square metre are sufficient. On slopes and along the edges of the lawn-to-be seed should be sown a little denser.

In the garden, seed is usually evenly scattered by hand. Then the ground is lightly raked over with a metal rake to cover the seed pressed down with the aid of stepping boards, that is, wide planks that can be systematically moved from place to place. Alternatively, the surface can be lightly rolled. It is also advisable to protect the newly-sown lawn against birds eating the seed by criss-crossing the area with black cotton about 10—15 cm above ground level.

Even germination of the seeds is achieved by keeping the soil evenly damp. For this purpose, a spray with a fine nozzle is used to prevent the seeds and the soil from being washed away as would be likely with a fiercer jet. The most suitable time for watering is early morning or late evening.

The first green shoots start to appear about 10 days after sowing and as soon as these reach a palm's height, the new lawn must be cut. The first cutting is preferably done with hand shears rather

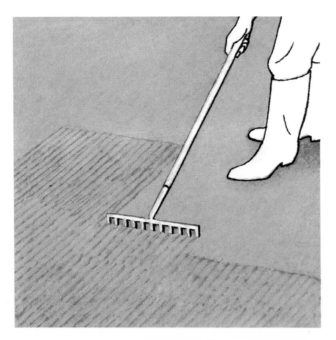

When sowing grass seed during dry weather, the soil must be well firmed in advance. Two wooden boards fastened to your feet will do if only a small stretch of lawn is to be sown.

than with a mower, which might pull the young plants out by their roots. After cutting, the lawn should be rolled again. If the grass is sown some time between April and the end of June it needs to be cut initially every week.

Laying turf

A faster, but more expensive method of creating a lawn is to lay a ready-made one in the form of grass turf bought in strips or squares. By this method the time taken to acquire a thick growth is reduced to a minimum. Such pre-grown turf should always be laid on dry soil.

Initially, the place where the turf will be laid needs to be prepared. The surface is levelled out and enriched with a 2- to 3-cm layer of crumbly humus-rich and nutritive soil. Then the turves are carefully laid edge-to-edge and pressed down so that the root system immediately penetrates the soil and is joined to it. Any slight gaps between the individual turves should then be completely filled in with a trickle of compost so that the grassy surface does not lose any moisture through evaporation. The laid out turf is then watered thoroughly and must not be allowed to dry out.

There is a choice of grasses available even when acquiring ready-made turf. Various firms supply samples which allow customers to choose the required type. If laying turf seems too problematic, it can of course be left to a specialist, but if you set about it methodically it is a fairly simple job.

Care of the lawn

Grassy surfaces are maintained by cutting, watering,

Sowing a lawn. The soil is firmed shortly before sowing, either with wooden boards or with a roller. The sowing is done by hand; if you want it to be more regular, sow twice, the second time moving vertically in the direction of the first sowing. The quantity of seed depends on the type of mixture and ranges between 15 and 50 g to a square metre. The edges are sown separately to ensure the required thickness of grass. The seed is then pressed down so that it is some 1—1.5 cm deep into the ground and the surface is again hardened with wooden boards or with a roller. The whole lawn-to-be is then watered with a fine spray. The grass will emerge within some 8—14 days.

weeding, raking, aerating as necessary and fertilizing. Weeds have to be controlled in lawns just as they are in the flower and vegetable beds. Persistent weeds are carefully levered out along with their roots, using a sharp knife or a special tool which prevents damage to the surrounding area of growth. After weeding the surface is firmed down again. Large areas of lawn where it would be difficult to pull weeds by hand may need to be treated with herbicides. However, annual weeds are easily controlled by regular mowing.

The lawn is mowed as necessary every 5—14 days until the autumn; the grass should not be long when the first frosts arrive. Regular mowing keeps the lawn in an optimum condition and to a certain extent reduces excessive evaporation of water so that it is not necessary to water it too often. However, after every mowing, especially during dry spells in summer, the lawn should be thoroughly watered. Apart from watering the lawn needs to be regularly fed while it is growing strongly. Some chemicals for lawn care contain both herbicides and a suitable fertilizer so that when applied they provide both protection and fertilization at the same time.

At the end of summer, fertilizers containing nitrogen are discontinued to stop the grass growing so quickly as otherwise it would be more susceptible to frost in winter. Poor soils, in particular those from which nutrients have been washed out by heavy rains, need to be fertilized after the last mowing at a rate of 150 g of PK and 1 kg of compost per 10 square metres. If the last mowing does not produce

Variously coloured conifers are in a pleasant contrast with the lush green of the lawn.

The lawn forms a neutral and harmonious link between the various sections of a garden.

a

c

e

b

d

f

much green matter and if this is evenly distributed, it can be left on the lawn as a protective covering.

From time to time, the lawn needs to be raked with a metal rake, especially if growing on heavy soils which tend to become compressed. This loosen-

Squares or bands of turf are cut with a spade and laid on the prepared soil, arranged in a brick-like pattern, with the cracks between them being left as small as possible. At the end, when all the turves are in place, fill in the cracks with soil.

A wide range of sprayers and sprinklers are available. Those shown are particularly suitable for watering a lawn.

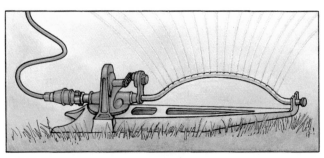

ing of the soil prevents the growth of moss which is a very unwelcome feature. It usually appears in places which are not properly looked after. Its growth is stimulated by permanent shade, by cutting the grass too short, by permanent dampness and long periods of nutrient deficiency. It is therefore advisable at least once a year, before winter sets in, to rake the lawn, fertilize it and apply lime.

It is also important to aerate the lawn from time to time. This can be done with a hollow fork or by using a normal fork sunk to a depth of about 10—15 cm deep. Aerating promotes a stronger growth and aids the better drainage of heavy soils prone to compacting.

Another important part of lawn care is maintenance during early spring. At this time the surface needs to be raked to remove dead grass, moss, fallen leaves and other debris. At the same time the lawn needs fertilizing. In April, uneven or damaged sections of the surface can be supplied with compost, levelled with a besom or short-tined rake and resown with the appropriate grass seed.

Even a sloping surface can be covered with lawn. For this purpose it is best to use turf which must be securely laid to prevent possible slipping.

The lawn can provide an attractive complement to the colour of the house walls.

Other types of soil cover

A green ground cover for areas in deep shadow can be provided by some species and cultivars of perennials which form a thick, low carpet. Alternatively, low-growing evergreen woody species can be employed. The most suitable for this purpose is the undemanding periwinkle (*Vinca*) which forms thick growths and has a profusion of blue flowers. Other species which can be recommended include cotula (*Cotula*), New Zealand burr (*Acaena*), liverwort (*Hepatica*), wild ginger (*Asarum*), lungwort (*Pulmonaria*) and woodruff (*Asperula*). The hardy ivy (*Hedera*) which creeps and climbs even in very deep shade also makes excellent ground cover. It is suitable for flat surfaces as well as slopes and underneath trees, which it climbs just as it does walls and fences.

Various low-growing rockery plants which like warmth will soon form bright green, silvery grey or reddish growths. These include the undemanding stonecrop (*Sedum*), candytuft (*Iberis*), rock cress (*Arabis*), snow-in-summer (*Cerastium*), the rapidly spreading bugle (*Ajuga*) and some decorative grasses, such as fescue (*Festuca*) and sedge (*Carex*).

The lawn can also be replaced by growths of some heathers, such as heath (*Erica*) and heather (*Calluna*). Their numerous varieties create a natural impression especially in wooded areas of a garden.

Ferns make a suitable green feature in shady corners. Most popular are polypody (*Polypodium*), ostrich feather (*Matteucia*), hard ferns (*Blechnum*), hart's-tongue (*Phyllitis*) and spleenwort *(Asplenium).*

Of the woody species most suitable for this purpose because of their low, creeping habit are modern cultivars, both evergreen and deciduous, of cotoneaster (*Cotoneaster*). In the autumn these furthermore adorn the garden with their beautiful red berries. A nice green cover can also be provided by low-growing rhododendrons (*Rhododendron*), spindle trees (*Euonymus*) with their interestingly shaped leaves, creeping junipers (*Juniperus*) and Mountain Pine (*Pinus mugo*).

The lawn is not only an important aesthetic feature of every garden but it also has many other functions: it is a place for recreation and relaxation, a reservoir of water and a means of improving the microclimate.

Ornamental trees and shrubs

Ornamental trees and shrubs are basic and invaluable elements in creating an attractive garden. They may be planted as solitary specimens, in groups, as dividing hedges or boundary hedges for screening purposes and, in the case of climbers, as a means of creating a natural link between house and garden. Ornamental trees and shrubs, as we see, are something modern landscape gardening simply cannot do without.

They may be divided, according to their artistic effect in the design of the garden, into: conifers and evergreen broadleaved trees and shrubs, deciduous trees and shrubs, and climbing woody plants.

Evergreen trees and shrubs

The most important characteristic of conifers and evergreen broadleaved trees and shrubs is that they retain their foliage and are green practically throughout the year. For this reason they are invaluable for concealing unattractive vistas and creating an intimate, 'permanent' environment. Conifers and evergreen broadleaved shrubs may also be clipped in straight lines as hedges, in various geometric shapes as topiary or as area dividers and so on.

Conifers in the garden

The various species and cultivated forms of conifers are either planted as solitary specimens in a lawn, in groups in sunny positions as well as partial or even full shade in the rock garden, on slopes or in informal or formal clipped hedges. Some are of erect, spreading or arching habit, others are prostrate, and still others creeping, ground-cover plants. All are ornamental because of their constant colour or the autumn coloration of their needles; some are prized for their shapely contours, and many also because of their attractive cones.

In most cases it is impossible to state unequivocally that this or that species or cultivar is suitable for a single given location in the garden, say in the rockery. Generally, the uses to which it may be put are many and that is why outstanding species and cultivars are mentioned in a number of different chapters in this book.

Characteristic of many conifers is the regularly-

This romantic corner near a pond is formed by a group of coniferous and broadleaved trees with the Weeping Willow (*Salix alba* 'Tristis') in front.

shaped crown. This is true in particular of spruces and firs, as well as of arborvitae, cypresses, some columnar junipers and many more that have far wider uses in the garden. For this reason they are well suited for planting beside buildings where they form a visual continuation of the building's architectural lines.

Conifers are also good as dominant features in the garden, for a dominant feature — among other things — is supposed to attract the attention of the viewer and thus serve as a focal point in the overall design. Conifers should be used for this purpose much more frequently than they have been in the past.

Evergreen broadleaved trees and shrubs

Evergreen broadleaved trees and shrubs are a widely used group of plants even though their cultivation is more demanding than that of deciduous trees and shrubs. They are very striking and for that reason are planted out either as solitary specimens or in groups with their own kind. Only thus will they have the desired impact.

If planted in combination with other woody plants they should not be placed with deciduous ones but

The deciduous *Rhododendron* species enliven group plantings of trees and shrubs. They are attractive by virtue of the rich splash of colours made by their blossoms in spring and by the variegated coloration of their leaves in autumn.

Cultivars of *Prunus serrulata* are commonly cultivated and favourite woody plants. Some of them produce the most beautiful blossoms in spring. They can be used for solitary planting or in front of taller dark trees which set off the beauty of their flowers.

rather with conifers. Tall evergreens are often planted beside buildings and some are also good as hedges. Many species are grown in the heath garden and low-growing, prostrate species are used as a ground cover in place of a lawn in shaded areas.

Deciduous broadleaved trees and shrubs

Deciduous trees and shrubs change according to the seasons and hence in some respects are more interesting than evergreens. There is not only the difference in their effect when in full leaf and when leafless during the winter months, but also in their varying appearance during the course of the entire year; among other things there are the seasonal effects of spring and autumn when their leaves change colour or they produce berries, flowers, or both. The combination of these properties makes it possible to

Groups of conifers are quite indispensable in park arrangements. A clever combination of species and their cultivars provides a wide range of variations. *Pinus mugo* (in the foreground) is a commonly used species that looks well with many other trees.

create many interesting and attractive garden layouts.

Unlike conifers, the selection of deciduous trees and shrubs is often made for the colour and fragrance of their foliage and/or their flowers. Flowering trees and shrubs are without doubt the most popular group of woody plants in the garden, with those that bear ornamental fruits running a close second. The latter produce very attractive and sometimes dramatic effects in autumn and winter.

Climbing woody plants

Climbers are a very interesting group of woody plants. In addition to the fact that some species possess certain of the aforementioned characteristics of evergreen or deciduous woody plants they have others that make them even more versatile. Because they practically always climb up or cling to some kind of support they are a form of garden vegetation that can be directly linked with the architecture of the garden. For that reason the requirements placed on their aesthetic relation to the given architecture are much greater than in the case of the preceding groups of woody plants.

When combining greenery with architecture it is often necessary to pay attention to particular details. For instance, does the colour of the foliage or flowers harmonize with the colour of the facade, and is the size of the leaves in proportion to the details of the object on which the plant is to climb? Equally important is the manner in which a given species climbs. If it requires support, this should not mar the desired overall aesthetic effect. Climbing roses, for example, must be provided with a firm support; best suited for twining plants are vertically placed wires or wood strips. Climbers with sucker-tipped rootlets or tendrils will climb and retain a firm hold without any support. When choosing climbers, therefore, it is

When planting trees, one must always take into consideration their size in adult age — to provide enough space for their full and healthy growth and sufficient light.

also necessary to know all of the specific requirements of the given species or cultivar.

Choosing conifers

When choosing the various species and cultivars of conifers we must take into consideration their appearance and size when fully grown, their habit of growth, colour and site requirements, and we must choose those compatible with the specific conditions of the garden and the space available.

Conifers are in the main light-loving plants. This means that for their successful growth and development they require ample light, space and an airy, open location.

The yews, which grow well in partial shade and even in full shade, are very adaptable. Shade is tolerated in youth by firs, spruces, and cryptomerias; and of the pines by *Pinus flexilis, P. koraiensis* and *P. peuce.* Cypresses prefer partial shade or a site not exposed to direct sunlight. Thujas (arborvitae) are relatively adaptable. Other conifers, cultivated in Europe, like a place in the sun; junipers are very intolerant of shade.

As to soil requirements, conifers exhibit marked differences. Least demanding are larches, junipers, pines (excepting species with needles in clusters of five) and cypresses. These do well in sandy-loamy soil, pines even in stony soil. Cypresses, junipers, larches, spruces and yews like lime. Junipers furthermore tolerate soil that tends to become dry. Cypresses, on the other hand, require adequate soil moisture. Spruces like relatively moist loamy-sandy soil. Firs are more demanding in terms of soil requirements than spruces. They do well in moderately moist, rich and rather deep loamy-sandy soils and generally do not tolerate a high water table. Other genera like a deep, rich, moderately moist soil. Only swamp cypresses thrive in swampy ground or even in shallow standing water.

As to hardiness, most conifers tolerate low temperatures. Firs, cedars, cryptomerias, spruces and the more sensitive species of various other genera should not be planted in frost pockets, where they might suffer harm.

Of the firs, the hardiest are *Abies balsamea, A. concolor, A. grandis* and *A. homolepis;* of the cypresses *Chamaecyparis nootkatensis* and *C. lawsoniana;* of the spruces *Picea abies, P. alba, P. asperata, P. omorika* and *P. pungens,* and of the pines *Pinus banksiana, P. cembra* and *P. peuce.*

Firs require a location sheltered from the wind. Cedars will not thrive in any but a truly sheltered site. Because variegated cultivars of conifers and of the thujas (*Thuja orientalis*) do not tolerate winter sunshine this, too, must be kept in mind when selecting a suitable place for them.

Conifers also differ in their tolerance of atmospheric pollution. Some species do relatively well in industrial regions, others do not. A smoky atmosphere is not tolerated at all, for instance, by most firs. Relatively the hardiest of the lot are *Abies concolor, A. grandis, A. koreana, A. nordmanniana, A. pro-*

English Holly (*Ilex aquifolium*) has glossy green, very tough leaves with a spiny margin. The white flowers are followed by coral-red fruits. It can be used for solitary planting as well as for groups of evergreen trees and shrubs.

cera and *A. veitchii.* Atmospheric pollution is not tolerated by most spruces, pines and cryptomerias. It is more or less tolerated by greyish species of cedars and cypresses, yews, thujas and, of the pines, Mountain Pine, Austrian Pine, Scots Pine and others.

Subject to grazing damage by animals are firs with relatively soft needles, cypresses (primarily when young), some species of junipers in youth (such as Chinese Juniper and Red Cedar) and the Common Juniper in spring when it puts out leaves. Animals also nibble at larches, and of the pines species with relatively soft needles, the Common Yew and the American Arborvitae. Fortunately, other conifers are generally left unmolested by animals.

Tall conifers
Veitch's Silver Fir (*Abies veitchii*). A slender, 15—25 m high tree, attaining a width of about 4 m. The needles are crowded round the twig, glossy dark

Corylus avellana 'Contorta' is a cultivar of Common Hazel with a retarded, irregular growth and with contorted branches. It looks best if planted as a specimen, being most attractive in winter and during flowering.

Parthenocissus tricuspidata 'Veitchii' is an attractive climber forming compact green curtains on vertical walls. The autumn coloration of the leaves ranges from green to purple.

This front garden has been planted exclusively with conifers. They make a handsome outline but present a rather gloomy outlook before the surrounding plants have come into flower. A few deciduous broadleaved trees would enliven the scene.

green above and silvery below. Its annual growth is about 70 cm in height and approximately 20 cm in width. It is suitable for planting as a solitary specimen, particularly in large gardens.

The Norway Spruce (*Picea abies*) is a familiar, 20—25 (30—50) m high tree with a narrow, pyramidal crown. The branches are arranged in regular whorls and spread horizontally. It is a vigorous tree, its annual growth being about 80 cm in height and 30 cm in width. It is suitable for planting in large gardens as a solitary specimen, as a windbreak, or as a clipped hedge.

The Serbian Spruce (*Picea omorika*) is a handsome tree with a remarkably slender crown, branching generously from ground level. It is one of the hardiest of conifers, absolutely frost-resistant, and it stands up very well to the polluted atmosphere of cities. It attains a height of 25—35 m, but is only 2—3 m wide at the base. The annual increment is about 50 cm in height and 15—20 cm in width. It is an excellent subject for planting singly in a large or medium large garden.

The Austrian Pine (*Pinus nigra* ssp. *nigra*) has a crown that is conical at first, later broadly ovate and 4—8 m wide. It generally attains a height of 20 (exceptionally 25) m. The average annual growth is about 70 cm in height and 35 cm in width. It is an attractive solitary specimen for the large garden and is particularly fond of dry, well-draining soil with a content of lime.

The European Larch (*Larix decidua*) is also a very tall tree reaching a height of 35 m. The crown is generally 4—6 m wide, the needles pale green to greyish-green, and it is the fastest-growing of all the larches. The annual growth is up to 80 cm in height and 50 cm in width. It requires a sunny location, ample space and deep, not unduly light but sufficiently well-drained soil.

The steel-blue cultivar of the Lawson Cypress, *Chamaecyparis lawsoniana* 'Alumii', is a nice, narrowly-conical, densely branched conifer, about 10 m

high and 2—3 m wide. The annual increment is about 30 cm in height and 10 cm in width. This undemanding tree is fond of a sunny location and is usually considered to be well resistant to frost. It is suitable particularly for planting as a solitary specimen and also as an interesting hedge.

The English Yew (*Taxus baccata*) tolerates even full shade, but also does well in sunlight. This 10—20 m high tree with 10—15 m wide, rounded crown, often remains only a shrub but lives to a ripe old age. It likes well-drained, preferably lime-rich soil and is suitable for planting as a solitary specimen or in group plantings under taller trees and as a freely-growing or clipped hedge. Its annual growth is 30 cm in height as well as in width.

The White Cedar (*Thuja occidentalis*) is a conifer of conical habit with short, horizontally spreading branches. It reaches a height of 10—15 m and

Abies concolor is one of the most resistant firs as regards atmospheric pollution. The pale green needles contrast wonderfully with the deep green or golden shades of other conifers.

a width of 3—4 m. Its annual growth is about 20—30 cm in height and 20—30 cm in width. It likes a sunny situation, is exceptionally hardy and particularly suitable for planting as a free-growing or clipped hedge.

The Colorado White Fir (*Abies concolor*) is a 20—30 m high tree of upright habit with an attractive conical crown branching from ground level and reaching a width of 3—4 m. The grey-green needles are sickle-shaped. Its annual growth is up to 50 cm in height and about 15 cm in width. It likes a sunny location, but is exceptionally resistant to cold as well as to atmospheric pollution. It requires nourishing, well-drained soil and is planted chiefly as a handsome solitary specimen, even in large cities.

Medium-tall conifers

Medium-tall and low-growing conifers play an important role in garden design. Low-growing conifers

are planted near paths, alongside the house or cottage, in the rockery, and wherever larger conifers cannot be put for one reason or another.

A fir that has become a great favourite in recent years is *Abies koreana*. This slow-growing conifer of dense pyramidal habit, which in later years is generally broader rather than tall, reaches a height of 2—4 (8) m and width of 2—3 (4) m. Every year it grows about 30 cm in height and 15—20 cm in width. It is very fertile, already bearing lovely purplish-violet cones up to 7 cm long even as a very young tree.

Chamaecyparis lawsoniana 'Ellwoodii', the handsome, finely-leaved cultivar of the Lawson Cypress, has grey-blue scale-like leaves and is of narrowly conical habit.When fully grown it is usually 2—3 m high and about 1 m wide. It grows slowly, the annual increment being about 20 cm in height and 5—10 cm in width. It has no special requirements and is good for solitary planting even in a small garden.

Chamaecyparis pisifera 'Plumosa Aurea' is a cultivated form of the Sawara Cypress of upright, broadly conical habit with striking golden-yellow leaves. It

This group of tall trees bordering a small lake is complemented by flowering perennials to form a completely natural composition.

A solitary tall spruce with sculptural branches planted in the front garden makes a harmonious whole with the chosen type of fence.

Cones are usually not formed before the tree has reached 30 or more years of age. Only a few species make an exception. The cones of firs are darker in colour and stand upright on the branches, whereas spruces bear pale brown cones which hang suspended from the tree.

reaches a height of 6—8 (10) m and a width of 2—3 (4) m. Its annual increment averages up to 25 cm in height and 15 cm in width. It has no special requirements but is particularly fond of a rather moist location and a well-drained sandy soil. The leaves, however, acquire their vivid coloration only in a sunny site. This conifer is suitable for planting as a solitary specimen or in hedges.

Juniperus communis 'Hibernica', a lovely cultivated form of the Common Juniper of narrowly columnar habit, is an excellent conifer for planting as a solitary specimen in a large as well as small garden. It generally attains a height of 3—4 m and a width of about 1 m. The annual increment is 15 cm in height and only 5 cm in width. The not very prickly, densely arranged, needle-like leaves are silvery blue-green. It likes a sunny situation and sandy, well-drained soil. Excellent for planting in an informal natural setting, in a larger rockery and its immediate vicinity as well as in the heath garden, it is best grown singly or in a small group.

Juniperus chinensis 'Pfitzeriana' is an ornamental juniper of exceptionally good growth with spreading, slightly pendulous branches, up to 2 m high and 4 m wide. It is planted primarily as a solitary specimen. The cultivar 'Pfitzeriana Aurea' has a broadly spreading habit and grey-green leaves that are golden-yellow when they first appear and turn to bronze in winter. It reaches a height of 2 (2.5) m and a width of 6—8 (10) m. The annual increment is only about 20 cm in height but up to 40 cm in width. It is a very hardy tree that is not damaged by frost and one of the loveliest of the junipers of spreading habit. It likes well-drained soils and sunny to slightly shaded locations and is suitable for planting as a solitary specimen or in groups with other conifers.

The well-known cultivated form of the White Spruce, *Picea glauca* 'Conica' of regular conical habit, reaches a height of 3 m and a width of 1 m after about 30 years. It has a very slow rate of growth, the annual increment being about 10 cm in height and 5 cm in width. It is noted for its dense, compact habit and delicate grass-green leaves. It is eminently suitable even for very small gardens, where it may be planted in the lawn or in the rockery. It prefers lightly shaded spots as it is prone to sunscorch.

A group of conifers forms a natural transition between the level of the house and the surrounding hilly terrain.

Chamaecyparis pisifera 'Filifera Aurea Nana' is a dwarf conifer with a beautiful golden-variegated coloration. It is planted in rockeries, in groups of low conifers or in heaths.

An example of a good combination of conifers in well contrasting shades of green.

Pinus mugo var. *pumilio*, a dwarf pine, looks best in rock gardens or in the front plane of groups of woody plants.

Columnar junipers are usually used for solitary planting or for small groups. They look best in the neighbourhood of pieces of architecture, in lawns and in heather gardens.

Picea glauca 'Conica' is a slow-growing cultivar of the White Spruce. It attains a height of 3—4 m at the most and is suitable for solitary planting as well as for groups, and for rockeries.

Pinus mugo var. *pumilio* is one of the favourite forms of the Mountain Pine. It is of moderate growth, semi-spherical in outline — more wide than tall, with a spread of up to 3 m but a height of only 1—1.5 m. Its annual increment is about 5 cm in height and 10 cm in width. It likes a sunny situation and can be planted effectively either as a solitary specimen or in groups.

Conifers with variegated leaves

Picea pungens 'Glauca', the silvery-blue cultivated form of the Colorado Spruce, is commonly called the silver spruce. Most often sold on the market are nicely coloured seedlings that generally reach a height of 10—20 m in Europe.

Of the firs, one with needles of an unusual blue colour is the cultivated variety of the Noble Fir, *Abies procera* 'Glauca', reaching a height of 20—30 m. Older grafted specimens bear cones up to 25 cm long regularly every year. The annual increments are generally 30 cm in height and 15 cm in width.

Junipers likewise boast a wide range of blue leaves. One is *Juniperus chinensis* 'Pfitzeriana', a cultivar of the Chinese Juniper which forms a large, broad but not very tall shrub. Another, of like habit, is 'Hetzii'. A third is *J. squamata* 'Meyeri', which, unlike the other two, is of compact habit, has bright greyish-blue leaves and a much slower rate of growth. This juniper should be trimmed regularly to remain attractive.

The prostrate cultivated variety of the Creeping Juniper, *J. horizontalis* 'Glauca', is an excellent woody plant with steel-blue leaves suitable as a ground cover and one that furthermore does well even in a partially shaded location. It reaches a height of only about 20—30 cm and when fully grown, covers an area of 2—3 m².

Yellow-leaved conifers include some extraordinarily attractive species and cultivars. One of these, for example, is the interesting cypress with drooping branchlets and golden-yellow leaves, *Chamaecyparis lawsoniana* 'Golden King'. In winter the leaves attain a brownish-yellow colour.

One of the loveliest yellow-leaved cypresses is *C. lawsoniana* 'Lane' which grows to a height of 5 m

239

Silvery and bluish-white cultivars of the Colorado Spruce (*Picea pungens*) find their place in any garden or park arrangement. However, they are not very suitable for purely natural sections, where their conspicuous colours make a disturbing effect.

and even more. Cultivated varieties of the Chinese Juniper such as *J. chinensis* 'Pfitzeriana Aurea', 'Old Gold', and 'Plumosa Aurea' have yellowish to vivid golden-yellow leaves.

Yews and thujas also include several with interesting yellow-variegated leaves; for example, the cultivated variety of the Common Yew, *Taxus baccata* 'Fastigiata Aurea' and of the American Arborvitae, *Thuja occidentalis* 'Rheingold'.

Conifers for the rockery and for containers

Conifers are a must in every rock garden and its immediate vicinity. Most suitable for the small rockery, mini-rockery in a container or a dry wall and as a ground cover in the immediate vicinity are, above all, the dwarf, low or creeping cultivars of various species.

Abies balsamea 'Nana' or 'Hudsonia' is a dwarf cultivar of the Balsam Fir of low, nest-like habit. It is slow-growing and reaches a height of 50—100 cm. The needles are short, dense, and glossy dark green.

A. concolor 'Glauca Compacta' is a rarer dwarf cultivar of a more compact, irregular habit with striking grey-blue needles. It is suitable for a large rockery and its immediate vicinity as well as a lawn in a smaller garden.

Chamaecyparis lawsoniana 'Fletcheri' is a cultivar of columnar to conical habit. Younger needles are paler, more greyish-green. Although it is generally included in lists of conifers suitable for the rock garden it must be pointed out that it grows to a height of 5 m or more and this should be kept in mind when deciding whether it is suitable or not.

C. l. 'Minima Glauca' is an attractive dwarf form with shell-like twigs. It grows to a height of 1 m and has short leaves of a dull blue-green. In the early stages of growth it is spherical in shape, with advancing age becoming more conical.

C. obtusa 'Crippsii' is a striking cultivar of slow, broadly-conical growth with pale sulphur-yellow to golden-yellow leaves. Only after many years does it reach a height of more than 3 m. It is one of the loveliest of the low-growing so-called 'gold' conifers. 'Filicoides' is a slow-growing cultivar of upright, sometimes also irregular shrub-like habit with twigs resembling the fronds of a fern and dark green leaves. It is ornamental and striking even as a young specimen. After about 25 years it reaches a height of slightly more than 2 m. 'Lycopodioides' has a compact habit and deep green leaves. It often forms a richly-branched pyramid resembling club-moss with its decorative twigs. It attains a height of 1.5—2 m and a width of more than 2 m. *C. o.* 'Nana Gracilis' reaches a height of 80—100 cm after many years of growth. The fresh green colour of the leaves and also the lovely shell-like twigs are its most attractive features.

C. pisifera 'Aurea Nana' is a dwarf cypress of conical habit with deep yellow leaves and very slow rate of growth particularly well suited for the small rock garden, mini-rockery in a trough, and the like.

C. p. 'Nana Aureovariegata' grows to a height of 50 cm, with short and delicate twigs arranged stepwise, downcurved at the ends and with curly tips.

A group of conifers, grasses and perennials is dominated by a trio of columnar junipers (*Juniperus communis* 'Hibernica').

The Mountain Pine (*Pinus mugo*) here forms a soft link between a natural-style rock garden and the wall of a house.

Chamaecyparis obtusa 'Nana Gracilis' reaches a height of 2 m in adult age. A slow grower, it is often planted in rock gardens and in large containers.

The leaves are very small and a dull yellow colour. This form is suitable for smaller rockeries. 'Filifera Nana' has string-like, drooping twigs arranged all round the branch and leaves coloured fresh green. The maximum height of this form is 1 m. 'Plumosa Compressa' is one of the smallest conifers for the rockery. It reaches a height of only about 30 cm and is noted for its lovely, cushion-like habit. The leaves are pale green to bluish.

Cryptomeria japonica is a hardy representative of the Japanese cryptomerias. It is a slow grower of shrub-like habit with an irregular outline and fleshy, bluish-green leaves that turn reddish-brown in winter. It grows to a height of more than 1 m. It is of interest chiefly as a collector's item and requires a sheltered site or a protective cover for the winter.

Juniperus chinensis 'Old Gold' resembles the cultivar 'Pfitzeriana Aurea', differing from the latter by its more compact habit and the bronze-gold of the leaves that remains unchanged even in winter. It grows to a height of 1 m and to similar width.

Dwarf cypresses usually have a rigidly geometrical habit. They are thus suitable for rock gardens, regular arrangements and for planting in the neighbourhood of buildings. It should not be forgotten that they need calcium in the soil.

J. communis 'Compressa' is an extremely slow-growing, fully dwarf cultivar of the Common Juniper, increasing only 2—5 mm in height a year. The twigs are set very close together and the leaves are delicate and coloured pale blue-green. This is an interesting and unusual specimen for the discriminating gardener, suitable also for a small rockery. In more rugged and unsheltered situations it requires a protective cover in winter. 'Depressa' is of flat, prostrate habit, reaching a height of 50—60 cm. It has rather broad, short leaves coloured yellowish or brownish-green and acquiring a bronze tinge in winter. This natural variety native to the mountains of North America is the best of the low carpeting conifers, forming a nice green ground cover on large areas exposed to the sun. 'Depressa Aurea' resembles the preceding variety but its leaves are a vivid golden-yellow until early summer, changing to pale yellow only later. 'Depressa Aureospicata' is suitable particularly for the rock garden. The leaves are a fresh yellow colour at the start of the growing period. 'Hibernica' is a familiar and popular juniper of up-

Pinus mugo var. *mughus* and *Juniperus communis* 'Depressa', two dwarf conifers, are planted among rock garden plants in a rockery.

right habit with blue-green leaves. It grows to a height of 4 m. 'Hornibrookii' is a creeping form spreading to a width of 2 m and attaining a height of 30—50 cm when adult. The branches rest on the ground with only slightly ascending tips coloured a glossy dark brown. The twigs are of unequal length, the leaves crowded, pale green with a silvery white band, slightly brownish in winter. This juniper forms a dense carpet and is thus a good subject for covering rocks in larger rock gardens, slopes and also larger expanses of ground.

J. horizontalis 'Douglasii', a lovely, creeping juniper only about 30 cm high, is especially prized for its slow growth. Only at a very advanced age does it attain a width of 2—3 m. The leaves are a steel blue, acquiring a light purplish tinge and coated with a bluish-green bloom in the autumn. This juniper is often planted in cemeteries.

J. squamata 'Meyeri' is a slow-growing cultivated form of the Creeping Juniper with branches ascending at the tips and striking, vivid blue-white leaves. It grows to a height of 2 m.

J. virginiana 'Globosa', or 'Nana Compacta', is a low shrub about 1 m high, very spherical in outline and densely branched. The leaves are greenish-grey above and green on the underside; in winter they are a pale purplish-green. 'Skyrocket', though it should not rightfully be classed with the low-growing junipers, for in time it reaches a height of 5 m or more, is worthy of note for its extremely slender, columnar habit: 2 m high specimens are only 30 cm wide. The twigs are crowded, set very close to each other, and the leaves are blue-grey. This juniper is particularly recommended for the heath garden and wherever it is desired to break the uniform line of conifers and other plants.

Two columnar junipers (*Juniperus communis* 'Hibernica') planted as a dominant feature by the main entrance to a house.

Picea abies 'Echiniformis' is a dwarf spruce of cushion-like habit with delicate, dense branches and pale yellow-green needles. It is a very attractive cultivar suitable for planting in the rockery or its immediate vicinity, as well as in the lawn. It grows to a height of 60 cm. 'Maxwellii' is of compact, flattened spherical habit, has pale green needles and grows to a height of 100 cm. 'Nidiformis' is a dwarf spruce of cushion-like habit with a nest-like depression in the centre; also very suitable for the rockery, for it is only 60—100 cm high. 'Pumila Glauca' is a spreading, flat, dwarf form that has dark green needles, up to 80 cm high.

The edges of this pond are thickly planted with carpeting perennials and woody plants, their colours offset by variously-shaped dwarf conifers.

Picea glauca 'Alberta Globe' attains a height of 3 m at the most. It is recommended for rockeries, for groups of low conifers and for planting in front of tall trees.

Pines are favourite subjects for all park and landscape arrangements. Stunted forms, such as that of the Mountain Pine, are suitable even for smaller gardens, rockeries and water margins in the 'natural' sections of gardens.

P. glauca 'Conica' is a lovely dwarf spruce of conical habit with soft, pale green needles. It is a very decorative, slow-growing cultivar eventually reaching a height of 2 m.

P. pungens 'Glauca Compacta' is a striking dwarf form of 'silver spruce' reaching a height of 1—1.5 m. It has short dense branches and lovely blue needles. Plants cultivated from cuttings have a very slow rate of growth and are of an extraordinarily compact habit. 'Glauca Globosa' is a lovely vivid blue dwarf spruce of flattened spherical habit, reaching a height of 1 m.

Pinus densiflora 'Umbraculifera' is a very slow-growing small tree, that usually has an irregular, broad, umbrella-shaped crown and horizontally spreading branches. The needles are soft and strikingly pale blue-green. This is a hardy cultivar, reaching a height of about 2 m in thirty years.

P. mugo — the Mountain Pine — is practically a shrub, often with prostrate branches, and is an extremely good specimen for planting in the informal

garden or in a large rockery. It reaches a height of 3—4 m. *P. m.* var. *pumilio* grows more in breadth than in height and is one of the most popular conifers for the rockery. It reaches a height of 1 m.

P. pumila 'Glauca' is a low, shrub-like pine resembling the familiar Mountain Pine but related to the Arolla Pine. It attains a height of 1—1.5 m and has striking, blue-green needles. It is a slow grower and has no special requirements, but likes rather moist situations. It is an excellent specimen for the rock garden as well as for slopes.

P. strobus 'Nana' is a dwarf form of the Weymouth Pine of dense, broad habit. It reaches a height of 1.5—2 m and has strikingly blue-green, relatively short needles. This undemanding and hardy pine is suitable for planting as a solitary specimen even in a small garden.

Taxus baccata 'Compacta' is a very slow-growing yew of compact oval or spherical habit with ascending branches and dark green needles. It is superbly suited for smaller rock gardens.

Yews are the only woody plants that tolerate full shade, and among the best conifers for clipping and shaping. They also serve as a good protection against pollution in the atmosphere. The picture shows *Taxus baccata* 'Repandens'.

Tree-forming hemlocks are planted solitarily or in groups. Their irregular habit makes them suitable for natural landscape arrangements as well as for regular planting. The picture shows *Tsuga canadensis.*

Cotoneaster multiflorus is suitable for both solitary and group plantings. It is an undemanding species, thriving in full sun as well as in semi-shade.

Even a small garden, if planted sensibly with decorative trees and shrubs, can result in an effective composition of greenery and architecture.

T. cuspidata 'Nana' is a dwarf yew of well-formed compact habit with fleshy, dark green needles. It attains a height of 1 m and width of 3 m.

Thuja occidentalis 'Rheingold' is a slow-growing thuja of spherical habit, with golden-orange leaves. It attains a height of about 1.5 m. 'Little Gem' is a dwarf cultivar of compact growth tending to be of broader rather than tall habit with deep green leaves. 'Recurva Nana' is of dense, broadly conical or spherical habit, up to 2 m high when fully grown. The leaves are green, turning brown in winter; the twigs curve at the tip.

T. orientalis 'Aurea Nana' is a weak-growing thuja of spherical habit with yellow-green leaves. It is suitable also for smaller rock gardens.

Requirements of ornamental broadleaved trees and shrubs

Broadleaved trees and shrubs differ widely in their requirements. Some species have no special requirements at all, for example Virginia Creeper, hawthorn, privet, honeysuckle, spiraea, raspberry, elder and snowberry, but on the other hand there are some that have very specific requirements, such as buddleia, heath, heather, rhododendron, and the like.

Broadleaved trees and shrubs include among their number ones that are fond of sunlight, ones that like partial shade and ones that will grow even in full shade. Sunlight is required by the deciduous barberries, dogwoods, cotinus, forsythia, genista, walnut, kalmias, peonies, poplars and roses. Shade is needed by the Virginia Creeper, box, ornamental quince, deutzia, St. John's-wort, privet, buckthorn and evergreen viburnums. Most woody plants will grow in sunlight as well as in a slightly shaded location.

As with light, so it is with soil requirements. In the case of many species of broadleaved trees and shrubs soil requirements are minimal. Birch, genista, currant, raspberry, elder, snowberry, elms, and the like grow in poor and even stony soils. Other species, such as hazel, privet and sumach are very adaptable. However, there are also species that are more demanding; these include oak, magnolias, mock orange, broom, witch-hazel, maples and buddleia.

A great many broadleaved trees and shrubs require soil containing lime, others tolerate lime in the soil and still others are intolerant of lime (in which case they are said to be 'calcifugous'). However, even among the many species of rhododendron, a genus that is calcifugous, *Rhododendron hirsutum* and *R. × praecox* are two that tolerate lime in the soil quite well and one could easily find many more such examples.

Broadleaved trees and shrubs are remarkable in terms of their adaptability to soil moisture. For example barberry, snowberry and many others tolerate both dry as well as moist situations. Alder tolerates without harm the utmost soil moisture and even occasional flooding; snowberry, on the other hand, tolerates extremely dry conditions.

Most broadleaved trees and shrubs find rainfall sufficient for their need. Only evergreen species need to be watered thoroughly before the onset of winter and, if it does not rain, also during the winter months when the temperature rises above the freezing point.

Broadleaved trees and shrubs are generally hardy and tolerate rather severe frosts. Those that are less hardy have good powers of regeneration so that when they are damaged by frost they soon make new growth. Some, such as catalpa, are damaged by frost in youth but become hardy when fully grown. Damage by frost, of course, depends on many factors,

Witch-hazel flowers, conspicuous and decorative, open before the leaves emerge. If covered with snow, the petals curl to form a small ball, opening again once the snow has melted.

Berberis julianae is a hardy evergreen barberry with small clusters of yellow flowers and black, bluish pruinose fruits.

particularly the weather conditions during the growth period, the amount of sunlight, the amount of nutrients in the soil, the ripening of the annual shoots, etc. Species more susceptible to frost should not be planted in frost pockets.

Another important characteristic of broadleaved trees and shrubs is their ability to tolerate the atmospheric pollution of industrial regions and cities. There are species that will not adapt well to such conditions, for example clematis, Japanese Maple, and the like, but these are in the minority. Most species are adaptable and some even tolerate such conditions extremely well — among these are the laburnum, box, mock orange, elder, snowberry and the elm.

Even grazing animals are no great problem in the case of broadleaved trees and shrubs. Some are nibbled by animals primarily in the early stages of growth; for example apple, False Acacia, some species of maple, caragana, catalpa, ornamental quince, broom, some cotoneasters, forsythia, rowan and some viburnums. Most species, however, are not nibbled by animals.

Choosing evergreen broadleaved trees and shrubs

Evergreen broadleaved trees and shrubs are very important ornamental woody plants widely used in both parks and gardens. Besides their attractive flowers and fresh, vivid and often variegated foliage and decorative fruits, they brighten the garden at a time when other plants are taking their winter rest.

Barberry (*Arctostaphylos uva-ursi*) is an evergreen subshrub about 40 cm high and of prostrate habit, with branchlets up to 50 cm long. The slender, slightly drooping branchlets are covered with small, dark green leathery leaves. The small white flowers, faintly tinged with pink, are arranged in racemes and appear in April and May. In the autumn the shrublets are adorned with spherical pea-size, glossy scarlet-red fruits. This medicinal plant, a protected species, thrives in soils similar to those favoured by rhododendrons, but sandier and more on the dry than moist side. Barberry is usually planted in rockeries and heath gardens together with other heath plants. However it is equally suited for planting on a slope in a sunny situation.

Bruckenthalia spiculifolia is a small 10—20 cm high plant, greatly resembling the heaths, with crowded, slender, upright branchlets and a wealth of tiny, bright pink, fragrant flowers arranged in dense 2—3 cm long spikes. The flowering period lasts from June to July and the plant's requirements are the same as those of heaths.

Cassiope tetragona is a subshrub up to 30 cm high but generally lower, of strictly upright habit with branchlets that are prostrate at first. The small leaves are arranged tile-wise in 4 rows. The drooping, white, bell-like flowers are borne singly in April and May. This species is suitable for planting in the rockery and heath garden alongside plants of neat habit.

Daboecia cantabrica, called 'Irish heather', is a pretty subshrub with prostrate branchlets which grows to a height of 25—30 (50) cm. It has small, glossy dark green leaves that are white-felted on the

Forsythias are among the first woody plants to flower in spring. They are planted either singly or in groups. The picture shows *Forsythia × intermedia.*

The Winter Jasmine (*Jasminum nudiflorum*) sometimes opens its flowers as early as December, but its usual time of flowering is in February—April, before the leaves appear.

Hamamelis mollis looks best if planted solitarily against a background of dark conifers.

Daphne mezereum is usually grown singly — in rockeries, heather gardens, groups of perennials and in lawns, or as an undergrowth to tall trees. Its conspicuous, intensely fragrant flowers open early in spring.

underside and flowers from June until September. The minute flowers, arranged in racemes up to 10 cm long, are jug-shaped and coloured purple. This plant is excellent in combination with heaths, heathers, rhododendrons, and other evergreen plants. Because it is native to the west European coastal regions from Spain to Ireland, it is relatively delicate for growing in central Europe where it requires a good protective cover in winter. If damaged by frost it generally puts out new growth from the base after being cut back in spring. There are several cultivated forms with flowers of pure white, pinkish-purple, dark carmine-red and salmon-pink.

Choosing deciduous broadleaved trees and shrubs

Because of their changing aspect during the course of the year, deciduous trees and shrubs create a different setting, make a totally different impact through the seasons.

Spring-flowering deciduous broadleaved trees and shrubs

Some woody plants such as Winter Jasmine, witch-hazel, some viburnums, mezereon and dogwoods flower in March — sometimes even earlier if the weather is favourable.

Winter Jasmine (*Jasminum nudiflorum*) is a plant of relatively vigorous growth with branches attaining a length of 3—5 m. It is a shrub of prostrate habit with angled, deep green shoots that flower before the leaves appear, sometimes as early as December, but more usually in February, March or April. It has no special requirements and will grow in any ordinary garden soil. It should be planted facing west or southwest, in a sheltered spot. It is best suited for planting in a large rock garden or by a summer-house, arbour, pillar or ornamental grille which will not be completely covered by its growth. Cut-off twigs are readily forced and the interesting yellow flowers, arranged in an attractive vase, are a welcome room decoration in winter.

Other hardy early-flowering shrubs are the witch-hazels, which thrive particularly in sunny to slightly shaded locations in nourishing soil with sufficient humus. They rapidly grow into attractive shrubs that can be planted either singly or in groups together with other ornamental woody plants. The effect produced by the yellow, orange or red flowers on the bare branches, often heightened by the whiteness of a snow cover on the ground, is very striking. The magnificent bright coloration of the leaves in autumn is another attractive feature. The Japanese Witch-hazel (*Hamamelis japonica*) grows to a height of 2.5—5 m. It is of bizarre habit and in autumn its leaves are coppery red. Of the winter-flowering witch-hazels it is the first to open its large, bright yellow flowers. The flowering period is from January until March, depending on the weather. The cultivar 'Ruby Glow' is without doubt a true gem among deciduous broadleaved trees and shrubs.

The Chinese Witch-hazel (*H. mollis*) is a shrub up to 4 m high with young shoots and underside of the leaves densely silvery pubescent. The leaves are large and ornamental, turning a striking yellow in the autumn. The very fragrant yellow flowers, larger than those of the other witch-hazels, appear as early as February. The red-flowering cultivars are particularly attractive.

Mezereon (*Daphne mezereum*) is another very early-flowering shrub with clusters of sweet-scented, pinkish-violet flowers appearing on the branches at the beginning of March, perhaps even sooner if the weather is favourable. Mezereon likes a place in the partial shade of taller trees and shrubs. It does well in a well-drained garden soil rich in humus. It grows to a height of 1 m and bears flowers before the leaves appear. The large-flowered cultivars with deep pinkish-violet or white flowers are best for planting in the gardens of central Europe. The poisonous scarlet red fruits mature in July; the fruits of the white-flowering cultivar are coloured yellow and remain on the shrubs until eaten by birds.

Viburnums brighten the garden not only during

the growing period but in winter as well. A very attractive feature of some viburnums that flower in winter and early spring is the delicate, pleasant scent of the flowers. One such is the Fragrant Viburnum (*Viburnum farreri* or *fragrans*), which grows to a height of 1—3 m and bears fragrant flowers before the first leaves appear, generally as early as March. The flowers are pinkish in bud but whitish when open. In mild winters the blossoms appear as early as November and open even in rain, snow and frost. Cut twigs are taken indoors and the blossoms thus forced fill the room with their pleasant fragrance.

The Cornelian Cherry (*Cornus mas*) flowers in spring bearing a wealth of yellow, star-like blossoms that provide an early feast for bees. This shrub reaches a height of 2—8 m, has olive-green branches and stiff, ovate leaves that appear after the flowers have faded. It thrives in sun as well as partial shade and is used primarily to form large, clipped hedges; it stands up very well to such pruning.

Summer-flowering deciduous broadleaved trees and shrubs

One of the most popular of the summer-flowering shrubs is the Butterfly Bush or Buddleia (*Buddleia davidii*), also commonly known as the lilac bush. It is a 2—3 m high shrub with angled branches and slightly drooping annual shoots up to 2 m long. These are covered with ovate-lanceolate leaves, dark green above and white-felted below, and bear a profusion of tiny flowers arranged in 25—50 cm long panicles that are often branched. Commonly encountered nowadays are several excellent cultivars, for instance 'Empire Blue' with pure blue flowers, 'Flaming Violet' with dark purple flowers, 'Purple Prince' with violet-red flowers, 'Royal Red' with purplish-red flowers, and 'White Bouquet' with fragrant white flowers. Buddleias flower from July until October, depending on the cultivar, their blossoms are moderately, sometimes quite strongly scented, and the clusters of flowers are extremely lovely. These shrubs thrive in any rather light and rich garden soil in a sunny, best of all slightly shaded location. However, they also do well on sunny slopes. They are planted chiefly as solitary specimens in places where the relatively long branches have room to spread freely.

Another favourite group are the garden hydrangeas. Species grown in central Europe are mostly shrubs with simple, usually serrate leaves and striking flowers arranged in terminal corymbs, or occasionally in panicles. They are prized chiefly for their summer flowering and also because they tolerate even shaded sites very well. Another reason is the exceptionally long time the flowers remain on the plant. Most species have flowerheads with large sterile flowers on the margin and small fertile flowers in the centre.

All hydrangeas like loose, well-drained, rich garden soil with a large amount of humus and a sunny or semi-shaded situation. The soil should always be adequately moist and should not contain any lime. It may be improved by adding peat, leaf mould or well-

Viburnum opulus 'Roseum' is a profusely flowering shrub with many different uses in the garden. It is quite undemanding and tolerates even full shade.

rotted compost, always together with a small amount of sand. In winter the soil above the roots should be covered with a layer of humus.

The most familiar and most widely cultivated species is *Hydrangea paniculata*. This is a plant of vigorous growth and has cone-shaped panicles of white, later pinkish flowers. Generally found in gardens is the cultivar 'Grandiflora' which has massive, up to 30 cm long inflorescences, composed predominantly of sterile flowers.

Tree Hollyhock (*Hibiscus syriacus*) and its cultivars are medium-high shrubs, mostly of upright habit, with grey-green shoots and leaves very like those of chrysanthemums. They grow to a height of 2—3 m and bear flowers even as young plants. They should be planted in a sunny, well-sheltered site with light, well-drained soil rich in humus. The soil above the roots should be covered with peat and in winter with fir branches. Only outstanding cultivars with large single, semi-double or double flowers are cultivated nowadays. Worth mentioning are for example 'Coelestis' with violet-blue flowers, 'Hamabo' with large pale pink flowers, 'Monstrosus' with large white flowers with a dark red centre, 'Rubis' with dark red

Kerria japonica 'Pleniflora', a richly and long-flowering shrub, attracts attention even in winter by the fresh green colour of its twigs. It is equally good for solitary and group planting.

Buddleia alternifolia is a magnificent shrub which looks best if grown solitarily on a slope or a terrace.

flowers, and 'Woodbridge' with large carmine-red flowers. Double cultivars include 'Duc de Brabant' with deep rose-red flowers, 'Lady Stanley' with white flowers having carmine patches, 'Speciosus' with white flowers and red patches, and 'Coeruleus Plenus' which has violet-blue flowers and a red central patch.

Hibiscuses are planted either as solitary specimens or in small groups. They bring to the garden the magnificent splendour of tropical blooms and their late flowering — from August till October, depending on the cultivar — makes them one of the most highly prized of the summer- and autumn-flowering woody plants.

Autumn-flowering deciduous broadleaved trees and shrubs

In autumn, in some species of deciduous broadleaved trees and shrubs the coloration of the leaves remains unchanged, in others the leaves acquire brilliant hues whose beauty is generally undimmed until the first frost. The vividness of their coloration depends both on the weather at this late time of year and on the intensity of the sun's radiation and temperature during the summer and early autumn. The location and soil conditions also play a role.

Besides brightening the garden with their colourful foliage in autumn some woody plants delight us with their flowers as well. These include the already mentioned Butterfly Bush and its cultivars, flowering from July till October; *Caryopteris* × *clandonensis* bearing a profusion of violet-blue blooms from September till October; *Clematis tangutica,* an exceptionally long-flowering climber bearing lovely yellow bell-shaped flowers from July to October, later usually together with the pretty silvery ovaries or the witch-hazel *Hamamelis virginiana,* bearing yellow flowers from September till November. Also, numerous cultivars of *Hibiscus syriacus,* with flowers in a wide range of colours appearing from July to October, and the woody species of St. John's wort, for instance *Hypericum patulum* 'Hidcote Gold', an extraordinarily long-flowering cultivar bearing a profusion of lovely yellow blooms from June till October.

Autumn brings with it also the lovely brightcoloured fruits of some broadleaved trees and shrubs (for example, barberry and cotoneaster) which, at this time of year, replace the slowly vanishing flowers.

Hydrangea macrophylla 'Bouquet Rose' is noted for its summer flowering. It is planted singly or in small groups.

Deciduous broadleaved trees and shrubs in winter

The beauty of many plant species does not end with the onset of winter nor even throughout the winter months. One will find many attractive features even in a snow-covered garden.

Besides evergreen broadleaved trees and shrubs, attractive features include all woody plants with colourful fruits (barberry, cotoneaster and buckthorn) that remain on the branches long into the winter; also, woody plants of bizarre habit such as the dwarf oaks and witch-hazels. Others have bark that is attractively coloured or distinctive — for example, *Pterocarya fraxinifolia*.

Broadleaved trees and shrubs for the rock garden

For the rock garden to look as natural as possible, it must fit happily into the general environment. A great aid in achieving this end is the use of deciduous broadleaved trees and shrubs planted directly in the rock garden, either singly or in groups. Suitable for this purpose are plants of the heath family as well as other woody plants such as the Japanese Maple (*Acer palmatum*), dwarf birches, broom (*Cytisus* and *Genista*), barberries and cotoneasters. Many rhododendrons also play an important role.

Other ornamental woody plants good for planting immediately beside the rock garden or a bit farther off include, for example, mahonias, some spiraeas, viburnums, daphnes, woody potentillas, shrubby hypericums and some roses.

Low-growing, deciduous woody plants suitable for this purpose include the Japanese Maple (*Acer palmatum*) and, above all, its cultivated forms — shrubs or small trees of a shapely habit and with lovely ornamental leaves, such as 'Atropurpureum', about 3—4 m high, with dark red leaves; 'Dissectum Garnet', 2 m high with deep purple leaves; and 'Dissectum Viridis', also about 2 m high with strikingly green leaves. All require a sheltered site in sunlight or partial shade and a light, acid soil.

Most maples change the colour of their leaves in the autumn, providing a sumptuous display of fiery crimson before they fall.

Weigela florida 'Variegata' has conspicuous yellow-bordered leaves. Because of this feature, both its place and combinations with other plants must be carefully considered.

Also frequently used are some barberries, such as *Berberis buxifolia* 'Nana', a spherical, evergreen shrub which forms a small compact mound with yellow flowers and purplish-blue berries, and *Berberis candidula,* an attractive dwarf shrub with yellow flowers and red fruits. These should be grown in sun or partial shade and may be trimmed.

Of the birches worthy of note is *Betula nana,* a small (up to 1 m), hardy shrub of semi-spherical habit, with densely crowded branches and small, decorative deep green leaves.

Japanese Quince (*Chaenomeles japonica*) is a shrub barely 1 m high with brick-red flowers up to 3 cm across that are produced in March and April. The ornamental, spherical fruits are about the size of a walnut and yellow in colour. This undemanding woody plant thrives in a sunny as well as partially shaded situation in any, even very light soil.

The selection of cotoneasters includes *Cotoneaster adpressus* — a low-growing species with prostrate branches, reddish flowers and red fruits; the familiar *C. horizontalis,* suitable particularly for larger rock gardens, with pinkish flowers and red fruits; and

Hippophae rhamnoides bears a profusion of orange-coloured fruits, rich in vitamin C. Male and female shrubs must be planted close to each other for the fruits to be produced.

C. dammeri 'Skogholm', a very hardy, wide-spreading shrub with prostrate branches, white flowers and red fruits. All cotoneasters are noteworthy mainly for their fruits. They generally require a sunny location but have no special soil requirements.

The brooms are important woody plants for brightening the rock garden. Noteworthy examples include *Cytisus decumbens,* a prostrate shrub with golden-yellow flowers; *Cytisus × kewensis,* a spreading, completely prostrate shrub with creamy flowers; and several cultivated forms of *C. scoparius* which have more brightly coloured and even bicoloured flowers.

Daphnes also include among their number shrubs noted for their lovely flowers, for example *Daphne cneorum,* a dwarf shrub with fragrant pink flowers, and *D. mezereum,* about 1 m high, with sweetly scented flowers clothing the bare branches before the leaves appear.

Woody plants suitable for the smaller rock garden include *Euonymus fortunei* 'Gracilis', a variegated dwarf cultivar; and *E. fortunei* 'Minimus', eminently well suited for scrambling over rocks in the rockery or as a green ground cover.

The hebes are also suitable shrubs for the rock garden. The three most familiar are *Hebe armstrongii,* a richly branched shrub that has tiny, golden-coppery leaves; *H. buchananii* with grey-blue leaves, and *H. pimeleoides* with oval, blue-green leaves. They grow in sun or partial shade in humus-rich soils with an admixture of sand.

Sunny as well as fully shaded spots in the rock

When in flower, *Cytisus × praecox* is one of the most beautiful shrubs, whether planted singly or in groups; here it is used to good effect at the back of a rock garden.

garden are suitable for planting the familiar evergreen Ivy (*Hedera helix*). In addition to the type species, a number of cultivated varieties are grown, such as 'Arborescens', of low upright habit; and 'Conglomerata' with shoots that are upright at first, later prostrate, and an ability to clamber even over rocks.

Plants that have become popular in recent years are the woody forms of St. John's wort, low-growing, evergreen semishrubs with golden-yellow flowers up to 8 cm across that are best suited to the larger rock garden. They are *Hypericum × moseranum,* which bears a profusion of flowers in late summer and early autumn, and *H. patulum* 'Hidcote' flowering from July to October.

When choosing woody plants for the rock garden one must not forget some of the species roses, such as *Rosa hugonis,* up to 2 m high with arching branches, tiny leaflets, and pale yellow blossoms appearing as early as mid-May. It is best planted at the back of a larger rock garden.

Broadleaved trees and shrubs for the heath garden

Numerous heath plants are also invaluable for the rockery and heath garden. Most important are the

Daphne mezereum is particularly suitable for small gardens, rockeries and heather gardens. It is attractive for its flowers as well as the fruits, which are, however, deadly poisonous.

Acer palmatum 'Dissectum Ornatum' is noted for its slow, compact growth. It is suitable for solitary planting and for rockeries and heather gardens.

heathers, heaths, rhododendrons and Mollis azaleas. Other species and cultivars that add variety to these parts of the garden include kalmia, daboecia, bruckenthalia, andromeda, ledum, *Empetrum nigrum,* gaultheria, pieris and *Vaccinium vitis-idaea.*

Rhododendrons — including the Mollis azaleas, heaths and heathers — number many species and cultivated varieties in a wide range of shapes and colours. They also flower at various times so that not only does the gardener have a wide selection but also the possibility of laying out a rockery and heath garden marked by an ingenious use of colour and graced with flowers throughout the year.

Besides the type species of Common Heather (*Calluna vulgaris*) which forms richly branched shrubs up to 50 cm high with tiny, scale-like leaves and pinkish-lilac flowers arranged in narrow erect racemes, most often encountered are the numerous cultivated varieties differing in shape, colour and period of flowering. If suitably selected, the various cultivars will bear flowers in succession from July until November. All do best in rather poor, sandy, acid soil — and they do not tolerate lime.

Heaths, like heathers, are basic plants of every heath garden, be it a separate heath garden or one

Brooms (*Cytisus*) should be planted with a view to their beauty in the flowering period. They are typical shrubs for heather and rock gardens and other similar places. The colour of their flowers ranges from pure white over various shades of yellow and violet to dark brown. Bicoloured forms also exist.

that is incorporated in a rockery. They are also excellent planted in front of groups of Japanese and taller Mollis azaleas and rhododendrons, and they provide a linking element between various woody evergreens. Often they serve as an excellent ground cover in place of grass. Another of their worthwhile features is that they provide food for bees.

Noteworthy cultivars include *C. vulgaris* 'Alba Plena', 25—50 cm high, bearing a profusion of double white flowers in September and October, and 'Alportii', up to 50 cm high, bearing bright carmine-red flowers in August and September. 'August Beauty' grows up to 40 cm high with a profusion of medium-early single white flowers; 'County Wicklow', of a low compact habit, bears double bright pink flowers in August and September. 'Cuprea' has an upright habit with striking golden-yellow foliage that turns reddish-brown in winter and pale violet flowers in August and September, and 'C. W. Nix' grows up to 50 cm high, with dark green leaves and cone-shaped racemes of dark violet-red flowers.

The selection of winter-flowering Heaths (*Erica carnea*) grown in gardens is very wide and includes many cultivars with white, pink as well as red flowers that appear in succession, often from as early as Christmas until April. In congenial conditions they spread and form fresh evergreen carpets and during

Because of its trailing to creeping habit, *Cytisus decumbens* can be used very effectively as a ground cover.

Shrubby potentillas are recommended for small groups in lawns close to paths, for hedges and for planting in front of taller trees or buildings.

Cotoneasters are decorative by their habit, leaves, flowers and their fruits, which differ in size, shape, colour and number in individual species and cultivars. They can be yellowish or various shades of red, and some forms with black fruits also exist.

the flowering period adorn the heath garden with a profusion of blooms. In general, they like a sunny position and are content with any ordinary garden soil with an admixture of peat and sand. They prefer being left undisturbed in the same place for a number of years. They are invaluable plants not only for the rockery and heath garden, but also for low slopes, in front of groups of woody evergreens, and as ground cover.

Of the many cultivars, mention should be made of *E. carnea* 'Alba' of a pretty compact habit bearing snow-white flowers in March and April; and 'Atrorubra', 15—20 cm high and one of the latest-flowering heaths bearing carmine-red flowers that retain their colour from the middle of March till early May. Also 'James Backhouse', up to 30 cm high with large deep pink flowers produced in April; 'King George', one of the first to flower, often as early as late autumn, with blossoms coloured pinkish-red. Others of note are 'Springwood', up to 20 cm high and one of the best of the white-flowering cultivars bearing a profusion of large single white flowers from February to April; 'Vivellii', a cultivar of compact habit with deep green foliage that turns bronze-brown in winter and lovely carmine-red flowers appearing in the early spring. Finally, we must mention 'Winter Beauty', an early-flowering cultivar of compact habit that, in congenial weather, occasionally produces its deep pink flowers as early as November, but usually from January to April.

Other plants suitable for the heath garden include *Andromeda polifolia, Bruckenthalia spiculifolia, Daboecia cantabrica* and *Gaultheria procumbens.*

Kalmias rank among the loveliest flowering woody evergreens, next to some azaleas and rhododendrons. They do best in peaty soils, but also thrive in loamy-sandy soils rich in humus. They require a partially shaded site, but in adequately moist and loose soil they will tolerate even a sunny position. They are planted either singly or in the company of other heath plants, mainly Mollis azaleas and rhododendrons. *Kalmia angustifolia* is a shrub of moderate growth, reaching 1 m in height and bearing fresh green foliage and numerous purplish-red flowers arranged in multiflowered clusters. The flowering period is from June to July. The cultivar 'Rubra', with dark red flowers in large clusters, is popular mainly for its lengthy flowering.

Broadleaved trees and shrubs for miniature rock gardens and containers

In the garden, containers with plants are usually placed near a bench, a pool, in the lawn, at the edge of a paved area, on a patio, alongside a flight of steps, and at the edge of a dry wall.

Of the broadleaved trees and shrubs suitable for small containers, worthy of note, for example, is *Berberis thunbergii* 'Atropurpurea Nana', the small, red-leaved cultivar of Thunberg's Barberry, which reaches a height of 40—50 cm, is of broadly conical habit, has strikingly coloured foliage, and bears a profusion of scarlet-red berries. It thrives in a sunny situation as well as in partial shade.

The dwarf birch, *Betula nana,* which grows to a height of about 50 cm in a container, is a pretty, shrub-like plant with very decorative small, round, deeply crenate leaves. It does well in a sunny as well as partially shaded position and in a rather moist as well as drier site.

Also excellently suited for planting in containers are many cotoneasters. For instance, there is *Cotoneaster adpressus,* a slow-growing species about 25 cm high, of dense, compact habit with prostrate to creeping branches. The small dark-green leaves turn scarlet-red in autumn. Also decorative are the reddish-white flowers borne in May and the vivid red fruits in autumn. It likes a sunny situation.

Another cotoneaster suitable for containers is

Cotinus coggygria is a highly decorative shrub bearing conspicuous panicles of flowers and particularly fruits. The fruits are covered in long reddish hairs serving as means of seed dispersal.

Acer palmatum 'Atropurpureum' is a handsome tree which attracts one's eye by the red colour of its leaves. It is particularly attractive in the autumn, when sun's rays create in its crown a mosaic of reddish and yellowish tones.

C. horizontalis, a low, flat shrub with widely spreading branches and tiny deciduous leaves that, in mild winters, remain nice and green on the shrub until spring. Also attractive are the coral-red fruits that remain long into the winter. This is an undemanding shrub that thrives in a sunny situation as well as in partial shade.

A great favourite in recent years is the cultivar *C. dammeri* 'Skogholm'. It is a dense, prostrate shrub of very vigorous growth with branches more than 1 m long forming an excellent ground cover and trailing over the sides of containers to cover them with green. Its leaves are elliptic, 2—3 cm long, and the berries scarlet-red.

Decorative elements for smaller containers, due to their habit of growth, attractive foliage and lovely flowers, are certain brooms (*Cytisus* and *Genista*), tree hollyhocks, St. John's worts, kolkwitzias, and, above all, Mollis and Japanese azaleas and low-growing rhododendrons.

Besides the woody plants already mentioned, a number of other deciduous as well as evergreen broadleaved trees and shrubs are suitable for planting in containers. For instance, there is forsythia, above all its modern large-flowered cultivars; *Buddleia davidii* and its cultivars; the witch-hazel *Hamamelis japonica;* Mollis azaleas — *Rhododendron japonicum (Azalea mollis), R. luteum* and others; Highbush Blueberry — *Vaccinium corymbosum* with its profusion of tasty berries, and also certain viburnums, such as *Viburnum* × *burkwoodii, V. carlcephalum* and *V. farreri.*

Climbing woody plants

In gardens, on fences and on the walls of houses our gaze is often captured by the lovely green foliage of various climbing plants, which, in autumn, create magnificent patterns in a host of lovely colours ranging from yellow and orange to glowing red.

Climbing woody plants need not cover the whole object but may be used only to frame. On the other hand, they may be planted densely, for example, to

Cotoneaster horizontalis is probably the best known member of this genus. The coral-red fruits decorate the shrubs in late summer and in the autumn. It can be used in large rockeries, on slopes and in front of buildings.

Spiraea × *vanhouttei* is a favourite shrub suitable for solitary as well as group planting, and even for hedges.

Early-flowering rhododendrons, such as the *Rhododendron japonicum* shown here, are generally very attractive due to the colour of their flowers, which range from pure yellow over pink and orange to a vivid red.

separate one section of the garden from another. Summer houses, pergolas and other architectural elements in the garden begin to fulfill their purpose only in combination with suitable climbing plants. Pretty-flowering species, cultivars and taller-growing climbers are used chiefly for covering fences, garden gates, and the fronts of houses.

Still widespread is the belief that walls covered with climbing plants are continually damp and that the plants furthermore harbour various insects. It has been proved, however, that climbing plants do not damage either walls or plaster, for the leafy green cover does not let water through even in a heavy downpour and the walls remain dry. The foundations of the building also tend to be dry rather than damp because excess moisture is taken up by the plants. The only thing that is a must in the case of deciduous species is the timely removal of clinging leaves to prevent the retention of moisture after a rainfall and also the removal of fallen leaves and spreading shoots from gutters and rainpipes.

Climbing plants cannot be expected to reveal themselves in their full beauty in the first years after planting. It often takes several years for the plants to make an attractive expanse. However, such a growth is persistent, hardy and very vigorous so that its aesthetic effect, once achieved, is long-lasting.

Before starting to plant climbers it is necessary to choose the most suitable species for the given purpose — whether we wish to cover the whole object or merely adorn a part of it. It is also necessary to take into account the site, soil and climatic requirements of the climbers as well as their growth characteristics. Also important is the way they are attached to the support. Some have holdfast or sucker-tipped rootlets, others climb by tendrils and the like.

Most climbing plants must be trained in the right direction at the beginning, or even tied in place if need be. They should be pruned only after they have grown beyond the bounds of the space allotted for them. Some species may also be planted at the top of a slope or on a high terrace, along which they can trail freely downwards.

An important requirement for growing climbing woody plants by a stone fence or against a wall facing south, particularly in the case of deep rooting species, is adequately deep and loose well-drained soil ensuring the run-off of excess water. If the roof of the house extends beyond the wall, thereby forming a sort of sheltered zone, the plants must be placed farther away from the wall so that they do not suffer from drought.

The least demanding climbers include, first and foremost, certain species of vine (*Vitis*). Others with no special requirements are climbers of the genus *Parthenocissus,* most familiar being the Virginia Creeper (*P. quinquefolia*). This does very well in a sunny as well as partially shaded position, is a source of food for bees, and provides a good shelter for songbirds. Because of its many good properties, it finds a wide range of uses. It should be planted 1.5—2 m apart. In the first year the plants should be watered thoroughly in dry weather. In later years they require practically no care at all. Another recommended species is the Boston Ivy (*P. tricuspidata*) which is self-clinging and has not only lovely deep green leaves but also presents a brilliant display of colour in the autumn sunlight. It thrives in

Parthenocissus tricuspidata 'Veitchii' thrives in full sun as well as in shade. It tolerates being cut back quite heavily and is a good subject for completely covering unattractive buildings.

any garden soil in a sunny or partially shaded situation and does well even in the polluted atmosphere of industrial cities.

Russian vine (*Polygonum*) is good wherever fast coverage of larger spaces is desired. Planting it by fences that require upkeep is not advised because, in a very short time, it will cover them with an impenetrable mass.

Another commonly grown climber is Perfoliate Honeysuckle (*Lonicera caprifolium*), also known as 'Rose of Jericho'. This is planted by fences, summer houses and gateways. The fresh green leaves are an ornamental feature until late autumn and as of May it is further adorned by striking, trumpet-shaped flowers, followed in the autumn by red berries. All species and cultivars of climbing honeysuckles require a loose, rich soil that is constantly slightly moist, and fertilized well beforehand. In summer, particularly during lengthier spells of dry weather, they require regular watering and a repeated application of fertilizer. Light, spring thinning every year and occasional cutting back keeps them in good condition.

Ivy (*Hedera*) is a climber that tolerates partial shade to full shade and of provided with adequate moisture will grow even in sun. In a suitable location it will last a great many years; specimens more than 400 years old are not unusual. The lovely foliage of this woody plant serves to cover trees and mellow old walls as well as modern buildings.

Roses are familiar and very popular climbers. They are suitable for framing house walls, fences, archways and even for covering slopes exposed to the sun. Some cultivars flower only once, others repeatedly, their blooms adorning the garden from June until autumn. They are generally persistent, hardy and extremely decorative woody plants. Besides the lovely blossoms, the foliage and even the thorns are also attractive. Because they also creep over the ground they may be used as a ground cover on slopes. Climbing roses are the result of intensive selective breeding. More recent cultivars, in which hybrid teas figure in their parentage, have lovely glossy leaves and larger blooms. Because they bear

Clematis is one of the best-loved climbers. Here, a large-flowered variety has been used to cover a staircase railings.

Pyracantha coccinea 'Lalandei' with its rich abundance and attractive colour of the fruits is particularly appealing against a light-coloured background.

flowers on the previous year's wood they must not be cut back too heavily in ensuing years after planting. Only dry, weak and diseased shoots should be removed in early spring. Climbing roses like an airy, sunny location and a well-drained, loamy-sandy soil, fertilized well beforehand. It is recommended to give them a dressing of good-quality compost every year and, after they have become well-rooted, to give them a repeated dressing of artificial fertilizer from spring until late July. Lime should also be added to the soil occasionally. The best time for planting climbing roses is in the autumn, from mid-October until the first frost, and in early spring.

Wisteria (*Wisteria*) is another magnificently flowering climber that has become extremely popular. It should be planted in spring in the warmest, sunny spot in the garden, in rather deep, rich soil with a drainage layer; the soil should have a slightly alkaline pH. In youth, wisteria has long, slender shoots and in later years rigid, knotted wood looking rather like twisted rope. The flowers are borne on the slender, lateral twigs, and this should be kept in mind when cutting back or pruning.

Clematises are true gems among climbers. Of the species clematis the one that is most widely grown is *Clematis vitalba,* suitable for covering large spaces in warm and sunny locations and growing even in poor soils. *Clematis × durandii* is a blue-flowering clematis whose blooms may even be put in a vase. *C. alpina* (*Atragene alpina*) creeps amid rocks, which it covers with its growth. Also noteworthy is the yellow-flowering *C. tangutica.* The well-formed, large-flowered clematises are the result of multiple crossings. Their number includes cultivars with magnificent blooms as much as 10—15 cm across. In the case of large-flowered clematis it is necessary to know what group they belong to for that determines how they should be pruned for vigorous growth and profusion of flowers. Clematises are not tender plants as a rule, and do best in light, rich, well-drained soil. A layer of well-rotted manure or com-

Virginia creeper *Parthenocissus quinquefolia* has an airy, light habit and beautifully coloured autumn foliage.

Lonicera tatarica 'Alba', a white-flowering honeysuckle, is used for hedges and as an understorey for taller trees.

post placed over the root area does them good. They should be planted in a sunny situation but with the roots shaded by a suitable mulch or by planting a perennial in front of the clematis so that it shades the root area.

Hedges

Hedges are one of the best means of creating an intimate setting in the garden. The type of hedge naturally depends on the kind of garden, whether it is located in the city, in a village and so on. It is always important to select a suitable species of woody plant, one that will be in harmony with the immediate environment and will also blend in well with the surrounding landscape.

Conifer hedges

Particularly good for making dense, impenetrable green walls are certain species and cultivated varieties of thuja, cypress, spruce, yew and juniper that can be shaped by clipping or allowed to grow freely, especially when there is sufficient space. English Yew makes an attractive clipped hedge 60—100 cm high or even higher. Yews in general are very hardy, not prone to disease or damage by pests and, with a little care, will reward the gardener with vigorous, healthy growth. The plants can be kept at the desired height of 60 cm up to 2—3 m by clipping. They like rather deep, well prepared soil containing lime and adequately moist during the growing season. Because of their excellent properties yews head the list of conifers suitable for hedges. They tolerate pruning of any kind and are content with a sunny site (as long as they have sufficient moisture) as well as one in partial or even full shade without losing any of their beauty.

Besides the type species many cultivated varieties

of English Yew will also make nice 1—2 m high hedges. One example is *Taxus baccata* 'Fastigiata', of slender columnar habit with short, thickly branched branchlets and dense, dark green needles. This handsome yew is particularly good for the smaller garden. *Taxus media* 'Hicksii' is another interesting cultivar suitable for hedges. It grows to a height of 2 m, is of slightly sparser, columnar habit and the needles are glossy dark green on the upper side.

Besides yews, some cypresses may also be used for this purpose, for example, the attractive cultivated forms of Lawson Cypress — *Chamaecyparis lawsoniana* 'Alumii', 'Ellwoodii', and 'Fletcheri'.

Broad hedges may be formed of *Juniperus chinensis* 'Pfitzeriana', an interesting cultivated variety of the Chinese Juniper. It is an exceptionally well-growing juniper that reaches a height of 2 m and a width of 4 m, with wide-spreading, slightly drooping branches and greyish-green needles. It has no special requirements; however, it is suitable only for large gardens.

The Norway Spruce, a tree of relatively symmetrical, broadly pyramidal habit reaching a height of 30—50 m in the wild, also tolerates pruning and thus can be used for broader and taller hedges. It is fond of rich soil containing lime; it should also be adequately moist but not permanently wet.

The most widely used conifers for hedges are the thujas. Most of them are extremely hardy and thrive even in rather poor soils as long as they are adequately moist. The American Arborvitae or White Cedar is a particularly rewarding species. Of the many cultivated forms the following cultivars are particularly noteworthy. *Thuja occidentalis* 'Columna', a tree of erect, narrowly columnar habit with short, dense, horizontally spreading branches. It reaches a height of 8—10 m and has dark green needles that remain the same colour even in winter. It likes well-drained soil that is not too dry and a place in the sun or in light partial shade. *T. o.* 'Holmstrup', or 'Holmstrupensis', is a recent cultivar of symmetrical, erect, conical habit and slower growth. Its densely crowded needles are a nice fresh green, acquiring a light bronze tinge only in rugged winters. It grows to a height of only 1—1.5 m, in exceptionally congenial conditions to 2—3 m. It is planted either as a handsome solitary specimen or to form a low hedge or a green screen. 'Malonyana' is an exceptionally good cultivar noted for its upright, narrow, columnar habit and growing to a height of 5—10 m. The densely crowded needles are an unchanging deep green. It is excellent for making symmetrical hedges and taller green screens. The cultivar 'Viridis' is also very good for taller hedges and green screens. It is of compact, pyramidal habit with glossy dark green leaves and is readily contoured by pruning. It tolerates regular trimming, is very hardy and has no special requirements. Another advantage of this thuja is that hedges of this cultivar are a lovely green in winter and very attractive. Unclipped plants reach a height of 8—15 m when fully grown, depending on the location.

Thuja plicata 'Zebrina' is the only representative of the Western Red Cedar more often encountered in the garden. It is a vigorously growing cultivar of broadly conical habit with slightly drooping tips to the zebra-patterned, creamy-yellow and green shoots. It reaches a height of 10 m and is planted as a solitary specimen or as a tall hedge.

Hedges of broadleaved trees and shrubs

When one speaks of hedges, the only kind that often springs to mind is the formal, regularly clipped hedge, either of conifers or of broadleaved trees or shrubs. However, hedges may also be informal — which they generally are nowadays — made up of freely growing, mostly flowering shrubs that are of the same height and which often form harmonious colour combinations as well. Often planted also are hedges composed of only a single species.

Hedges composed of evergreen broadleaved trees and shrubs have their advantages. Not only do they form an impenetrable wall throughout the year but their relatively symmetrical shape makes such a hedge seem as if it were clipped, and, last but not least, their dark green foliage forms a contrasting background for other plants.

Hedges composed of deciduous broadleaved trees and shrubs have an airy look and are invaluable in natural freely-landscaped schemes. If they are not clipped they usually take up more room than trimmed hedges or conifer hedges.

Taller woody plants should be planted along the boundary and in front of these should be placed irregularly spaced groups of lower-growing woody plants, thereby making the effect seem more natural.

Recommended for informal gardens with natural layouts are hedges of untrimmed, freely-growing woody plants, broadleaved as well as coniferous, whose habit, attractive foliage and often also lovely flowers are much more effective and likewise create an intimate setting on a patio, in a garden alcove, and the like.

Suitably selected shrubs that are properly planted and given the correct treatment will not entail much work on the part of the gardener but will still make every garden much more attractive. As a rule, however, they require somewhat more room than clipped hedges. The shrubs are generally pruned only once a year, after flowering. They should be planted 80—100 cm from the boundary and 60 cm apart, in the case of low hedges, and 80—150 cm apart in the case of medium-high hedges, depending on the size of the various species and cultivars. Hornbeam should be set out 2—3 plants to 1 m, privet 3—4 plants to 1 m.

Besides the usual care ornamental shrubs require the application of a compound fertilizer at least once a year, to promote better and more rapid growth. Nevertheless here, too, a well-rotted compost remains the cornerstone of successful feeding. Shrubs also benefit greatly from an occasional loosening of the soil in their vicinity and thorough watering during lengthier spells of dry weather.

Low hedges

Thriving ornamental shrubs with a profusion of flowers or attractive foliage suitable for hedges up to 40 cm high include certain evergreen barberries, such as *Berberis buxifolia* 'Nana', *B. candidula,* and *B. verrucandii. Berberis buxifolia* 'Nana' stands clipping exceptionally well, has no special requirements and thrives in rather dry, sandy soils and both in sunny situations and in partial shade. *Buxus sempervirens* 'Suffruticosa', the edging Box, a low compact

Ivy (*Hedera helix*) is a nice subject with which to cover walls and fences. Here it adorns a trunk of a dead tree, the crown of which has been removed.

cultivated form of the Common Box with glossy green foliage, is also very attractive. So are several cultivated forms of *Euonymus fortunei,* such as 'Variegatus' with its greyish-green, white-veined leaves often tinged with pink; the Chinese Honeysuckle (*Lonicera nitida*) with dense, glossy dark green leaves, and *Lonicera pileata,* also with glossy green leaves and small fragrant pale yellow flowers. The latter species, which thrives in sunny as well as partly shaded places, tends to be hardier than the Chinese Honeysuckle.

Medium-high hedges

One of the most rewarding evergreen broadleaved shrubs for formal as well as informal hedges up to 1 m tall is, without doubt, the familiar and popular Oregon Grape (*Mahonia aquifolium*). It looks nice and fresh throughout the year with its deep green foliage which, in the cultivated form 'Atropurpurea', turns magnificent shades of scarlet-red in the autumn. Also lovely are the small, golden-yellow flowers as well as the racemes of pruinose, blue-black berries that adorn the shrub in the autumn. Mahonias have no special requirements and thrive in any rather moist garden soil, but best of all in loamy to clayey soils containing lime. They prefer partial shade, but are just as attractive in a sunny site or in deeper shade. Young plants can be transplanted without trouble and take root readily. To keep the shrubs low, dense and thickly leaved cut them back shortly after flowering, or just before the onset of winter.

For hedges up to 1 m high, it is also possible to use certain barberries such as *Berberis gagnepainii* var. *lanceifolia* and *B. verruculosa*. All should be provided with a protective cover of fir branches in the winter months.

For hedges 1—2 m high, best suited of the boxes is *Buxus sempervirens* var. *arborescens*. This evergreen shrub with small leathery, glossy green leaves, was at one time widely used in garden landscaping in France. It is excellent for formal clipped hedges, as well as informal hedges. There are several cultivars with variously shaped or white-variegated as well as yellow-variegated leaves.

Also suitable for hedges, because they are hardy and stand dry conditions extremely well, are two cultivated forms of *Laurocerasus officinalis* — 'Schipkaensis' and, in particular, 'Zabeliana'.

Fine woody plants and very popular in recent years are the Firethorns — *Pyracantha coccinea.* These thorny shrubs with small, faintly glossy, deep green leaves and a profusion of white flowers arranged in corymbs, brighten the garden every autumn with a wealth of bright red or orange berries the size of peas and these remain on the shrubs a long time. Pyracanthas require good, well drained soil, preferably on the dry side, and a sunny situation. In time they form an impenetrable evergreen hedge, in sun as well as in the partial shade of taller woody plants. Freely-growing plants reach a height of 2—3 m but they may be kept to the desired height by clipping.

Tall hedges

For tall hedges, 2 m high or even higher, there is a wide selection of suitable species and cultivars of ornamental woody plants as well as various trees and shrubs commonly found in the wild. Widely used are maples, hornbeams, Cornelian Cherry, Red Dogwood, hazels, beeches, oaks, poplars and roses.

The evergreen privet *Ligustrum vulgare* 'Altrovirens' is equally suitable for low clipped hedges 1—2 m high and taller ones up to 4 m in height. This attractive, completely hardy, slightly slower-growing, healthy cultivar has deep green leaves that turn purplish-brown in the autumn and remain on the shrub practically until spring, even in severe winters.

The Oval-leaved Privet (*L. ovalifolium*) sheds its leaves only in uncongenial winters. The leaves are

The large-flowered clematis 'Nelly Moser', with its distinctively striped petals, is a profuse flowerer preferring slightly shaded situations.

A large-flowered clematis here provides welcome colour on a dividing wall between two gardens. This is a late-flowering cultivar which opens its blossoms just as the climbing roses have finished flowering.

dark green above and bluish-green below and the flowers, arranged in dense panicles up to 10 cm long, are creamy white. This privet stands shade as well as clipping extremely well and does best in sheltered situations. It has no special soil requirements and will make a hedge up to 5 m tall within a relatively short time.

Hedges of holly are less common. Most often found in gardens is the common English Holly (*Ilex aquifolium*), of loose shrubby or slender pyramidal habit. This species has very stiff, glossy green leaves with a toothed margin. It does equally well in a sunny location as in a shaded one. In Europe, however, holly is generally grown as a solitary subject, ornamental not only for its unusual foliage but often also for its profusion of striking, coral-red fruits.

General rules for planting ornamental trees and shrubs

The best time of the year to plant trees and shrubs is in the autumn. In congenial climatic conditions and in the case of more tender species, however, spring is a more suitable time. Common species of ornamental woody plants, especially screening shrubs, are planted without a root ball either in previously prepared, sufficiently deep holes or in trenches, with the topsoil being put on one side and the bottom soil on the other when these are being dug. In recent years woody plants are being increasingly sold as container-grown specimens. These have a perfect root ball and can therefore be planted out practically any time during the growing season. Only the hot summer months are not suitable as the newly set out plants will require greater care, shading, and the like.

Before planting, take care that the plant roots do not dry out. Never leave bare roots exposed to the sun, wind or frost. If they dry up nevertheless, immerse the plants in water for about 24 hours until they absorb a sufficient amount and any wrinkled bark straightens.

'Nelly Moser' is attractive even when the flowers start to fade and their colour becomes less intense.

Woody plants should be planted at the same depth as they were grown in the nursery. Exceptions are grafted shrubs, such as woody peonies, large-flowered clematises and the like, which should be planted at a slightly greater depth so that the grafted-on part puts out roots and is thus able to provide the plant with better nourishment. Deep planting is not conducive to the growth of shrubs with shallow roots, particularly if they are put in heavier soil.

Always plant trees and shrubs upright, taking care that the roots are not turned sideways or upward but spread well out. Cover the roots with a layer of topsoil, best of all enriched with good-quality compost, and then top that, if necessary, with the remaining underneath soil. Do not apply fertilizer to newly planted trees and shrubs; wait until they are well rooted. Give the newly set out plants a thorough watering and when the water has soaked into the soil fill any hollows that have formed with humus or lawn mowings to keep moisture in the soil. This is particularly important if you are not always on hand to water the plants during dry periods when they need watering. Plants will also benefit by more frequent loosening of the soil after planting; this also reduces the evaporation of water. If some species of woody plants need supporting with a stake, this must always be inserted in the excavated hole before the tree or shrub is planted.

If a woody plant is to be planted singly in the lawn make an adequately large 'bowl' — one that extends to the perimeter of the crown — immediately after planting. This enables easier and more thorough watering and later on application of fertilizers, and the grass will not deprive the plant of moisture or food. Enlarge the 'bowls' as the plants grow and keep them free of weeds. Separate the edge of the 'bowl' from the grass with a small furrow to prevent the grass from invading it.

Taxus baccata is a low-growing, tree-like yew with a spreading, irregular, mostly conical crown.

Spiraea × bumalda with its small, neat flowers is a low shrub highly suitable for clipped hedges.

The choice of species for a hedge must be made carefully, with a view to the character of the garden and its neighbourhood. In this case, *Ligustrum vulgare* was used for a clipped hedge.

It pays to turn beforehand the whole band of soil in which the shrubs for a hedge are to be planted, as their growth will be more regular later. The roots should be covered with a high-quality topsoil. Even spacing between the individual shrubs can be marked with a lath of the requisite length.

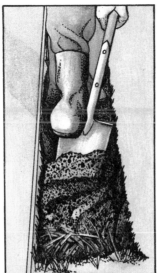 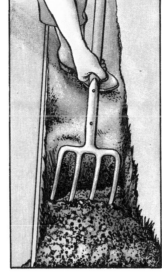 

Cutting of planted ornamental woody plants — if necessary — should be done immediately before or right after planting by up to two-thirds of their length. Shorter shoots should be cut back slightly more than the long ones; branches should never all be cut back to the same level. Before planting, remove damaged roots with a sharp knife. In the case of roses, trim only the roots before planting in autumn, otherwise they should be left unpruned until spring. At that time large-flowered roses should be cut back to within 2—3 buds of the base, climbers and shrub roses to within 3—8 buds of the base.

Planting conifers

Conifers should be planted between mid-August and the end of November; more tender species in spring — from March to mid-May. The best time for planting is on a cloudy day that is not too windy. The plants must have the root balls intact. Plant them in previously prepared holes of ample size with a layer of quality compost on the bottom. Place the tree or shrub in the centre of the hole, which must always be slightly wider and deeper than the root ball, and put some nourishing soil around and over the root ball, so that it settles well in between the roots. Then firm the soil by treading in the case of younger plants or by tamping with a stake in the case of larger specimens so that it is in close contact with the root ball and made really firm. Then make a shallow 'bowl' round the plant and water it thoroughly; allow the

water to drain into the soil and then water a second time. Afterwards, fill the 'bowl' with loose topsoil, but only after the water has soaked in completely.

Spray the seedlings overhead at regular intervals; during lengthier spells of dry weather and in the case of strong winds water them as required, preferably at less frequent intervals but thoroughly. Smaller plants may also be protected from drying out due to exposure to the sun by shading them with a screen of fir or similar branches. Older conifers should be watered often and thoroughly after planting and also sprayed several times daily.

Planting broadleaved trees and shrubs

Deciduous broadleaved trees and shrubs should be planted in the autumn, between mid-October and the first frost; or in spring, in March or April, depending

Various well-tried methods of trimming a hedge.

on the weather. Rarer sorts and evergreen broad-leaved trees and shrubs with perfect root balls may be planted out in congenial spring weather up to mid-May. The same applies to heath plants. As for container-grown specimens, they were discussed at the beginning of this chapter.

After planting the tree or shrub it should be watered. Broadleaved trees and shrubs are readily affected by moisture depletion and that is why it is important to remember that they need plenty of water in order to root well.

Care of trees and shrubs in later years

Pruning
The appearance of cultivated trees and shrubs depends on the care they are given in the ensuing years. Care consists of watering, feeding, removing dead flowers and inflorescences and maintaining the shape of the shrub so that it remains healthy and attractive.

Pruning and thinning
Many gardeners know little about pruning and by incorrect pruning or by not pruning at all they prevent the given plant from attaining its maximum beauty and producing the maximum of flowers.

Pruning and thinning are not nearly as complicated as it may seem at first glance. First of all, remove shoots damaged by frost and dry shoots in all woody plants without exception. Wait until spring, when new growth starts, to remove parts damaged by frost; then there will be no need to prune again later. In the case of cultivated forms also cleanly remove suckers growing from the base by cutting them out. In species that produce offshoots vigorously and have a tendency to become invasive and disrupt the surrounding arrangements, remove the offshoots together with the roots.

Woody plants that do not require pruning
Do not prune maples, evergreen barberries, ornamental quince, and even cotoneasters which will produce a profusion of flowers and fruits and show themselves in their full beauty only if left unpruned.

The privet *Ligustrum vulgare* is an ideal subject for both informal and clipped hedges.

The same applies to daphnes, witch-hazels, evergreen St. John's worts, holly, walnut, kalmias, rhododendrons, laburnum, magnolias, woody peonies, oaks, Smoke Tree, elms and evergreen viburnums.

Rejuvenation
From time to time, plants need to be rejuvenated or cut back — sometimes severely, at other times moderately; this means that old shoots are cut out leaving the same number of young shoots. Plants that are cut back in this manner include, for example, service-berry, deciduous barberries, hazels that have become thin at the base, hawthorns, poorly-flowering tree hollyhocks, kolkwitzias, privet, honeysuckle, Mock Orange, spiraeas, shrubby cinquefoil, currants, snowberry, lilacs, viburnums and weigelas. This is generally done during the non-growing period.

If you have in your garden a shrub or tree that is too dense or too tall, then it can be pruned and thinned more severely. Remove old branches and cut back by half the remaining branches. Severe cutting back is done successively over a period of two or

Mahonia aquifolium is a hardy shrub with beautifully shaped leaves which are tinged with red in winter. The yellow flowers arranged in racemes are followed by deep blue, strongly pruinose fruits in the autumn.

A low hedge separates the entrance to the house from the drive. The foot of the stairs is planted with climbing roses.

Pyracantha coccinea 'Kasan' is a cultivar of firethorn bearing large orange-reddish fruits. It has a sturdy, erect, richly branched habit.

three years. Woody plants that have been neglected for too long should be rejuvenated by cutting strong thick branches back hard or else by cutting out all old wood and leaving only the young shoots.

Broadleaved trees and shrubs growing in groups should be pruned in winter so that they do not smother each other and always have plenty of sun and air. Woody plants grown for the beauty of their coloured one-year shoots should be cut back hard every year so they will send up masses of new shoots. Woody plants with ornamental fruits or bark should be pruned only when winter draws to a close so that they can serve their ornamental purpose during the winter months.

Annual pruning

Woody plants that require annual pruning are divided into three groups, according to when they flower and on what growth they produce their blooms. The first group includes broadleaved trees and shrubs that bear flowers in spring on the previous year's wood. The second group contains those that bear flowers in summer on old wood and on the previous year's wood. The third group contains those that bear flowers in summer and autumn on growths formed in the current season.

Early-flowering plants of the first group should be trimmed in winter by cutting out all weakly and intersecting non-flowering branches and cutting back shoots that are unduly long. Winter pruning should be done between late October and mid-March; however, the first such pruning should not be performed until at least three years after planting. Prune shrubs near the base and in the centre, cutting as little as possible and with thought. This will maintain the shrub's natural shape and promote the formation of buds. The main pruning is done after flowering, usually in the second half of May, so that the plants have a chance, before autumn, to make new shoots that will then produce flowers the following year. Woody plants of this group include forsythia, some spiraeas, almond (*Prunus triloba*), plum (*Prunus cerasifera*), jasmine, brooms and some dogwoods.

Ornamental woody plants of the second group are pruned by cutting back strong shoots by as much as one-third so they will produce new lateral shoots. Typical plants of this group are ornamental apples in the first few years after planting, rowans, hawthorns, some barberries, currants and tamarisks.

Privet has all the necessary qualities of a good hedging shrub. It is undemanding, tolerates shade and clipping and is resistant to air pollution.

Ligustrum ovalifolium 'Aureum' used in a clipped hedge. Its light, vivid colour animates the whole garden.

The roots of woody plants must never be turned upwards as in (a), they should always be spread freely during planting (b).

Woody plants that flower in summer and autumn on the current season's wood, such as buddleia, caryopteris and so on, are cut back to the second to sixth bud from the ground, depending on the character of the plant and the thickness of the wood, and old and weakly stems are removed entirely.

Watering
Soils differ in their ability to absorb and retain moisture and other properties that affect the amount of moisture made available to plants. If, for example, the soil is not very permeable and rainwater penetrates only to a shallow depth it disrupts the structure of the top layer. And after it has evaporated, it causes caking and later cracking of the soil surface. Equally uncongenial is soil that is too permeable because then water passes through at a rapid rate leaving plant roots unquenched. Another of the gardener's main tasks, therefore, is to see to it that soil drainage is adequate for the plants' needs.

Drainage should be improved according to the

Preparation of soil around a newly planted tree. The peat or other suitable humus-rich material on the surface protects the soil from drying out.

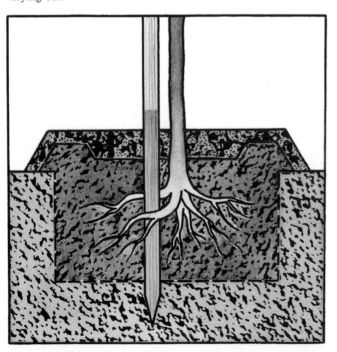

given type of soil and moisture should be provided additionally by watering. However this, too, must be done with care. Frequent watering that moistens only the surface layer is even harmful, as is abundant watering at too frequent intervals for then the soil becomes waterlogged and is depleted of oxygen that is just as vital to plant growth as moisture.

The rule of thumb is to water as much as is necessary to keep the plant roots moist. Plants should be watered in the morning or evening. It should be remembered that evergreens need moisture even in winter and they should be watered also at this time during dry spells if the temperature is above freezing point.

Feeding
Because of their great diversity, there can be no general rules for the feeding and fertilization of woody plants. However, it may be said that, by preparing the soil properly and enriching it with humus (by applying compost) the gardener can provide them with the necessary conditions for good growth. Artificial fertilizers should not be applied until the plants have become well rooted and then according to the requirements of the respective species. Keep in mind that the application of additional feed should cease by July at the latest so that the new annual shoots have time to ripen fully before the onset of winter.

Propagating ornamental trees and shrubs

Ornamental trees and shrubs may be propagated from seed or by vegetative means, from parts of the parent plant.

Raising from seed
Raising woody plants from seeds is the cheapest and most effective method if one desires to obtain a large number of plants. Such plants are hardier in rugged or changeable conditions than plants propagated by vegetative means. In most cases the fruits of woody plants are collected. For purposes of propagation, however, it is the physiological maturity of the seed that is important. The seed is mature when the embryo completes its development, which sometimes occurs before the fruits are fully ripe. Therefore, collecting the fruits at the right time and obtaining seeds that are viable is no simple matter. Some seeds do not tolerate being stored for long in a dry place because they dry out and this prolongs the germinating period. Other seeds germinate only after 2—3 years, either because of the properties of the seed coat or the concentration of growth inhibitors. Seeds must often undergo preparatory treatment such as stratification, immersion in tepid, hot and boiling water, mechanical rupturing of the seed coat, wrapping and the like, prior to sowing.

Thus treated, the seeds are sown in containers of various kinds that have been disinfected beforehand. The containers should be well drained, so place a good layer of crocks at the bottom of each and then fill them with good quality compost or a special growing medium. Keep the seeds in cool conditions in the same place for a certain period, or expose them to frost as appropriate, and afterwards place them in a greenhouse or in a frame. Tend the seedlings by loosening the soil, removing weeds, shading them and keeping them watered.

In winter they must be provided with protection against frost, and before planting the seedlings out they must be hardened off. Then they can be planted out in a nursery bed, in rows with appropriately wider spacing, according to kind.

Propagation by vegetative means

Woody plants may be propagated by vegetative means either directly or indirectly and in a number of ways. One of the direct and simplest methods is by **division** and reproduction by means of **root suckers.** This method can be used to propagate shrubs that continually form roots at the base of the stems or shoot out root suckers. The entire shrub is lifted from the soil and divided into sections by pulling it apart or cutting it with a sharp, clean knife. Sections with a poorly developed root system should be put in a nursery bed, stronger sections can be put out directly into their permanent site.

Rarely used is the method known as **stooling.** The shrub to be increased is covered with a mound of soil when the young annual shoots have reached the required height. Later the soil is piled up higher once or twice more so that several layers of new roots are formed. In the autumn or following spring the soil is removed and the young seedlings — newly rooted sideshoots — are cut away. The parent plant is then again covered with a small mound of soil for winter.

Another method of direct propagation is **layering,** during which the young shoot remains attached to the parent plant until it has become well rooted. Layering may be done in a number of ways. One is to lay one-year shoots in hollowed-out grooves in the

spring, peg them down, and then cover them with soil to encourage them to put out young shoots. This will yield a number of new plants in the autumn.

The simplest sort of layering, known as **arch layering,** is to take one-year, or very occasionally two-year shoots in early spring, bend them down, then curve them sharply upward, pressing the bend into soil and bringing the tip up so it rests against the edge of the groove. Cover the bent portion with soil and press it down firmly. Rooted layers are severed from the parent plant in the autumn, dug up, and planted out.

The most commonly used method of propagating woody plants is by **cuttings.** Deciduous broadleaved woody plants are propagated by spring and summer **softwood cuttings, hardwood cuttings** or **root cuttings.** Conifers are propagated by means of cuttings that are ripened but need not be hard.

More rapid rooting is promoted also by various growth stimulating preparations. Various types of propagators are used for the rooting of the cuttings — greenhouses, frames, foil propagators, etc. The cuttings are inserted directly into the substrate in the propagator or into a suitable medium in peat or plastic pots. The cuttings must be tended with great care and to master this method of propagation it is necessary to study detailed literature on the subject.

Besides direct propagation by vegetative means it is also possible to propagate plants by indirect means — by **grafting** and **budding.** This method is used in the case of those species and cultivars that cannot be propagated by other means or only with great difficulty. Grafting and budding involves uniting living parts of plants — the scion or bud of one plant being joined to the root system or stock of another. The various types of grafting include **whip** (whip or tongue) **grafting, rind-grafting, slit or notch grafting** and so on.

Ribes sanguineum is a sparse shrub suitable for solitary planting as well as groups. Here it is successfully combined with the yellow forsythias, but it also looks attractive with spring-flowering perennials or bulbs. It should be rejuvenated by cutting back old twigs from time to time.

Kalmias need not be shaped by clipping.

Habit, characteristics, and requirements of some ornamental conifers

Habit:
- ⌒ creeping and prostrate shrub
- ⌂ spherical or semi-spherical shrub
- ◊ elongate to ovate shrub
- ♀ tree with elongate and rounded crown
- ♇ tree with broad to semi-spherical crown
- ♁ tree with conical crown
- ⌇ climbing woody plant

Light requirements:
- ○ full sunlight
- ◑ partial shade
- ● full shade

The characteristics given for the individual species refer also to their cultivars, which are not listed in the table.

Species	Height in m	Habit	Growth	Colour of needles	Colour of fruits (cones)	Light requirements	Soil (requirements)	Soil moisture
Abies alba	20—50	♁	moderately rapid	dark green, green-yellow	green-brown	○ ◑	rather heavy, rather light	moderately moist
Abies concolor	1—30	⌂ ♁	rapid	grey-green, silver-blue	green-blue-brown	○	rather light, rather heavy	dry, moist
Abies nordmanniana	15—30	♁	rapid	dark green	red-brown	○ ◑	rather light, rather heavy	moderately moist, moist
Cedrus atlantica	0.5—40	⌂♁⌒	rapid	blue-green	brown	○ ◑	rather light, rather heavy	dry, moderately moist
Cryptomeria japonica	0.3—30	⌂ ♁	rapid	dark green, variegated	brown	○ ◑	rather light, rather heavy	moderately moist, moist
Chamaecyparis lawsoniana	0.5—40	⌂ ♁	moderately rapid	blue-green, variegated	blue-green-brown	○ ◑	rather light, rather heavy	dry, moist
Chamaecyparis nootkatensis	0.5—40	⌂ ♁	moderately rapid	dark green, variegated	blue-brown	○ ◑	rather light, rather heavy	moderately moist, moist
Chamaecyparis obtusa	0.5—15	⌂ ♁	slow	dark green, variegated	orange-brown	○ ◑	rather light, rather heavy	moderately moist, moist
Chamaecyparis pisifera	0.5—40	⌂ ♁	moderately rapid	green, variegated	brown	◑	rather light, rather heavy	moderately moist, wet
Ginkgo biloba	10—40	⌂ ♀	moderately rapid	green, yellow	yellow-green	○ ◑	rather light, rather heavy	dry, moderately moist
Juniperus chinensis	0.5—20	⌂ ♁	moderately rapid	green, variegated	brown	◑	rather light, rather heavy	moderately moist, moist
Juniperus communis	0.5—15	⌒ ◊ ♁	moderately rapid	green, blue-green, variegated	blue-white	○ ◑	rather light, rather heavy	dry, moderately moist
Juniperus horizontalis	0.3—0.5	⌒	moderately rapid	blue-green, variegated		○ ◑	rather light, rather heavy	dry, moist
Juniperus squamata	0.5—6	⌒ ◊	moderately rapid	blue-green	red-brown	○	rather light, rather heavy	dry, moderately moist
Juniperus virginiana	0.5—30	⌒ ⌂♁	moderately rapid	dark green, variegated	blue-grey	○ ◑	rather light, rather heavy	dry, wet
Larix decidua	2—30	◊ ♁	rapid	green	brown	○	rather light, rather heavy	dry, moist
Larix kaempferi	10—30	♁	rapid	blue-green	grey-brown	○	rather heavy	moderately moist, moist
Metasequoia glyptostroboides	15—35	♁	rapid	green	brown	○ ◑	rather light, rather heavy	moderately moist
Picea abies	0.2—40	⌒ ⌂ ♁	rapid	green, variegated	brown	○ ◑	rather light, rather heavy	moderately moist, moist
Picea glauca	4—15	♁ ◊	moderately rapid	blue-grey-green	green-brown	○ ◑	rather light, rather heavy	moderately moist
Picea orientalis	1—40	⌂♁	moderately rapid	green-yellow	violet-brown	○ ◑	rather light, rather heavy	moderately moist
Picea pungens	0.5—40	⌂♁	slow	blue-green-silver	brown	○ ◑	rather light, rather heavy	dry, moist
Pinus contorta	8—25	♀♁	moderately rapid	dark green	brown	○ ◑	rather light, rather heavy	dry, moderately moist
Pinus densiflora	1—20	⌂♀	moderately rapid	green, yellow-green	brown	○ ◑	rather light, rather heavy	moderately moist
Pinus mugo	0.5—3	⌂	moderately rapid	dark green	brown-grey	○	rather light, rather heavy	dry, moist
Pinus nigra	1—40	⌂♁	rapid	dark green	yellow-brown	○	rather light, rather heavy	dry, moderately moist
Pinus strobus	0.5—25	⌂♁	rapid	grey-green, green-yellow	brown	○ ◑	rather light, rather heavy	moderately moist, moist
Pinus silvestris	0.5—30	⌂♁	rapid	grey-green, variegated	brown	○	rather light, rather heavy	dry, wet
Pseudotsuga menziesii	0.5—60	⌂♁	rapid	grey-green, variegated	brown	○ ◑	rather light, rather heavy	dry, moist
Taxodium distichum	20—40	♁	moderately rapid	green	brown-grey	○ ◑	rather light, rather heavy	moderately moist, wet
Taxus baccata	0.4—20	⌂◊♁	moderately rapid	dark green, variegated	red	◑ ●	rather light, rather heavy	moderately moist, moist
Taxus cuspidata	0.3—20	⌂♁	slow	dark green, yellow-green	red	◑ ●	rather light, rather heavy	moderately moist, moist
Thuja occidentalis	0.2—20	⌂◊♁	moderately rapid	green, variegated	brown	○ ◑	rather light, rather heavy	dry, wet
Thuja orientalis	0.5—10	⌂♁	moderately rapid	green, variegated	brown-green	◑	rather light, rather heavy	moderately moist
Tsuga canadensis	0.5—30	⌂♁	moderately rapid	green-grey, variegated	brown	○ ◑	rather light, rather heavy	moderately moist, wet

Habit, characteristics and requirements of broadleaved trees and shrubs

Species	Height in m	Annual increment of type species — in height (cm)	Annual increment of type species — in width (cm)	Habit	Colour — Summer foliage	Colour — Autumn foliage	Colour — Flowers	Light	Soil	Soil moisture
Acer campestre	10—15	40	30		green	yellow	green	○ ◐	light, heavy	moderately moist, dry
Acer ginnala	5—7	25	20		green	orange-red	yellow-white	○ ◐	light, heavy	moderately moist, dry
Acer japonicum	2—4	15	10		green, variegated	red, yellow	purple	○ ◐	light, heavy	moderately moist
Acer negundo	15—25	50	40		yellow	yellow	yellow-green	○ ●	light, heavy	dry, moist
Acer palmatum	1—4	20	15		green, red	yellow-red	purple	○ ◐	light, heavy	moderately moist
Acer platanoides	20—30	75	50		green, red	yellow, red	green-yellow	○ ◐	light, heavy	moderately moist, dry
Acer pseudoplatanus	20—40	100	50		green	yellow	green-yellow	○ ◐	light, heavy	dry, moist
Acer saccharinum	30—40	75	50		green-white	yellow-red	green	○	light, heavy	dry, moist
Aesculus × carnea	10—20	25	20		dark green	yellow-brown	red-pink	○ ◐	light, heavy	moist
Aesculus hippocastanum	15—25	50	25		dark green	yellow-brown	white-yellow-red	○ ●	light, heavy	dry, moist
Aesculus parviflora	3—5	20	30		green	yellow	white	○ ◐	light, heavy	moist
Ailanthus altissima	15—25	50	25		green	green-yellow	white-yellow	○ ◐	light, heavy	dry, moist
Alnus glutinosa	15—30	50	20		dark green	green	green-brown	○	light, heavy	dry, wet
Amorpha fruticosa	3—4	25	15		green	green-yellow	blue-violet	○	light, heavy	moist
Aralia elata	2—6	25	15		green	green-yellow	white-yellow	○ ◐	light, heavy	dry, moist
Aristolochia durior	5—10	30	—		dark green	yellow-green	yellow-green	◐ ●	light, heavy	moist
Berberis julianae	1—2	15	15		green	green	yellow	◐	light, heavy	moderately moist, dry
Berberis thunbergii	1—1.5	15	15		green, red	yellow-red	yellow	○ ◐	light, heavy	moderately moist, dry
Berberis verruculosa	1.0—1.5	10	10		dark green	dark green	yellow	○ ◐	light, heavy	moderately moist, dry
Berberis vulgaris	2—3	15	15		green	yellow-green	yellow	○ ●	light, heavy	moderately moist, dry
Betula nana	1	5	5		green	green-yellow	green-brown	○	light	moist
Betula pubescens	15—20	30	15		green	yellow-green	green-brown	○	light	moist
Betula verrucosa	20—25	50	20		green	yellow	green-brown	○	light, heavy	moderately moist, dry
Buddleia davidii	3—4	40	10		dark green	green-yellow	pink, violet, white, red	○ ◐	light, heavy	moderately moist, dry
Buxus sempervirens	0.5—6	10	10		dark green	dark green	yellow-white	○ ●	light, heavy	moderately moist, dry
Calluna vulgaris	0.2—0.4	3	5		green, yellow	green, yellow	pink, red, white	○	light	moderately moist, dry
Calycanthus floridus	2—3	10	5		green	green-yellow	red-brown	○ ●	light, heavy	moderately moist, dry
Campsis radicans	5—10	40			green	yellow-green	orange-red	○	heavy	moderately moist
Carpinus betulus	10—20	30	20		green	yellow	green-yellow	○ ●	light, heavy	dry, moist
Castanea sativa	15—30	30	20		green	yellow	yellow-white	○ ●	light, heavy	dry, moist
Catalpa bignonioides	10—15	30	30		green	yellow	white	○ ◐	light, heavy	dry, wet
Ceanothus americanus	0.5—1	15	15		green	yellow-green	white	○ ◐	light, heavy	moderately moist, dry
Celastrus scandens	3—9	100			green	yellow-green	white-green	○ ◐	light, heavy	moderately moist, dry
Cercidiphyllum japonicum	5—10	30	15		green	yellow-red	yellow-white	○ ◐	light, heavy	moderately moist, moist
Chaenomeles japonica	1	10	10		green	green-yellow	red, pink	○ ●	light, heavy	moderately moist, dry
Chaenomeles speciosa	1—3	20	15		green	green-yellow	red, white	○ ●	light, heavy	moderately moist, dry
Chionanthus virginicus	2—3	15	10		green	yellow	white	○	heavy	moderately moist, moist
Clematis alpina	1—2	15			green	yellow-green	violet	○ ◐	heavy	moist
Clematis tangutica	1—3	20			green	green-yellow	yellow	○ ◐	heavy	moderately moist
Clematis viticella	3—4	20			green	green-yellow	pink-violet	○ ◐	heavy	moderately moist
Clematis × jackmanii	3—4	30			green	green-yellow	violet-purple	○ ◐	heavy	moist
Colutea arborescens	2—4	30	20		green	green-yellow	yellow	○	light, heavy	moderately moist, dry
Cornus alba	1—3	30	20		green, variegated	yellow, variegated	yellow-white	○ ●	light, heavy	moderately moist, moist
Cornus florida	1—5	20	10		green	violet-red	white, pink	○ ●	light, heavy	dry, moist
Cornus mas	2—8	25	20		green, yellow	yellow	yellow	○ ●	light, heavy	moderately moist, dry
Cornus sanguinea	2—4	20	20		green	green-yellow	white	○ ●	light, heavy	dry, wet
Cornus stolonifera	1—3	20	15		green-yellow	green-yellow	white	○ ●	light, heavy	moist
Corylus avellana	2—5	20	15		green, red	yellow-red	red, yellow	○ ●	light, heavy	dry, moist

267

Species	Height in m	Annual increment of type species		Habit	Colour			Requirements		
		in height (cm)	in width (cm)		Summer foliage	Autumn foliage	Flowers	Light	Soil	Soil moisture
Corylus maxima	2—5	15	15	⌂	green, red	yellow-red	yellow, red	○ ●	heavy	moderately moist
Cotinus coggygria	2—5	15	15	⌂	green, red	green-yellow-red	white-green	○	light, heavy	moderately moist, dry
Cotoneaster adpressus	0.25	3	10	⌐	green	green	red-white	○ ◐	light, heavy	moderately moist, dry
Cotoneaster dammeri	0.10	3	20	⌐	green	green	white	○ ◐	light, heavy	moderately moist
Cotoneaster horizontalis	0.50	10	15	⌐	green	red-orange	red-white	○ ◐	light, heavy	moderately moist, dry
Cotoneaster multiflorus	2—3	20	30	⌂	green	green-yellow	white	○	light, heavy	moderately moist
Cotoneaster salicifolius	2—4	30	30	Ⓤ	dark green	dark green	white	○ ◐	light, heavy	moderately moist
Crataegus monogyna	7—15	25	20	♀	green	green-yellow	white	○ ◐	light, heavy	moderately moist
Crataegus oxyacantha	4—6	25	20	♀	green	green-yellow	white, red	○ ●	light, heavy	moderately moist, dry
Cytisus scoparius	1—3	25	20	Ⓤ	green	green-yellow	yellow, white	○	light	moderately moist, dry
Daphne cneorum	0.20—0.30	5	5	Ⓤ ⌐	dark green	dark green	violet-red	○ ●	light, heavy	moderately moist
Daphne mezereum	1—1.5	10	15	⌂	green	yellow-green	violet-red	◐ ●	light, heavy	moist
Deutzia gracilis	1—1.5	5	10	Ⓤ	green	green-yellow	white	○	light, heavy	moderately moist
Deutzia scabra	1—3	20	10	Ⓤ	green	green-yellow	white	○	light, heavy	moderately moist, dry
Erica carnea	0.3	3	5	⌐	green, yellow	green, yellow	white, pink, red	○ ●	light, heavy	moderately moist, dry
Erica vagans	0.4	3	5	⌐	green	green	pink	○ ●	light, heavy	moderately moist, dry
Euonymus alatus	2—3	10	10	Ⓤ	green	red	green	○ ◐	light, heavy	moderately moist, dry
Euonymus europaeus	3—6	20	10	⌂♀	green	yellow-green	yellow-green	○ ●	light, heavy	moist
Euonymus fortunei	0.3	3	20	⌂	dark green, variegated	dark green, variegated	yellow-green	○ ●	light, heavy	moderately moist, moist
Exochorda racemosa	2—4	15	15	⌂	green	green-yellow	white	○ ●	light, heavy	moderately moist, dry
Fagus silvatica	20—40	50	40	♀	green, red	yellow, red	green-white	○ ●	light, heavy	moderately moist, dry
Forsythia × intermedia	2—4	30	20	Ⓤ	green	green-yellow	yellow	○ ●	light, heavy	moderately moist
Forsythia suspensa	1.5—3	20	30	⌂	green	green-violet-brown	yellow	○ ●	light, heavy	moderately moist
Fraxinus excelsior	20—40	30	15	♀	green	yellow-green	yellow-green	○ ●	light, heavy	moist
Fraxinus ornus	5—10	20	15	♀	green	yellow-green	white	○	light, heavy	moderately moist, dry
Genista tinctoria	0.5—1	10	20	Ⓤ	green	yellow-green	yellow	○	light, heavy	moderately moist, dry
Gleditsia triacanthos	15—25	30	20	♀	green	yellow	green	○	light, heavy	moderately moist, dry
Hamamelis japonica	2—3	15	20	⌂	green	yellow	yellow-purple	○ ●	light, heavy	moist
Hamamelis × intermedia	2—4	15	20	⌂	green	yellow	yellow, red, brown	○ ◐	light, heavy	moderately moist, moist
Hamamelis mollis	2—4	20	20	⌂	green	yellow	yellow	○ ●	light, heavy	moist
Hedera helix	5—20	10	15	⌐	dark green	dark green	green	○ ●	light, heavy	moist
Hibiscus syriacus	2—3	10	5	Ⓤ	green	green-yellow	white-pink, red-violet	○	light, heavy	moderately moist, moist
Hippophae rhamnoides	4—6	25	20	⌂	silver-grey	silver-grey	yellow	○	light, heavy	moderately moist, dry
Hydrangea arborescens	1—2.5	20	20	⌂	green	green-yellow	green-white	○ ◐	light, heavy	moderately moist, wet
Hydrangea paniculata	2—4	20	20	Ⓤ	green	green-yellow	white-pink	○ ◐	heavy	moderately moist
Hypericum calycinum	0.40	5	5	⌐	dark green	dark green	yellow	◐	light, heavy	moderately moist, dry
Hypericum patulum	0.5—1	20	5	⌂	green	green-yellow	yellow	◐	light, heavy	moderately moist
Ilex aquifolium	2—6	20	10	Ⓤ	dark green	dark green	white	◐ ●	light, heavy	moist
Jasminum nudiflorum	1.5—5	20	20	⌂	green	green-yellow	yellow	○ ◐	light, heavy	moderately moist, moist
Juglans nigra	25—40	50	20	♀	green	yellow-green	green-yellow	○	light, heavy	moderately moist
Kalmia angustifolia	1	5	5	⌂	dark green	dark green	purple	○ ◐	light	moist
Kalmia latifolia	1—3	10	5	⌂	dark green	dark green	pink	○ ◐	light	moist
Kerria japonica	1—2	15	15	⌂	green	green-yellow	yellow-orange	○ ●	light, heavy	moist, dry
Laburnum anagyroides	4—7	25	15	Ⓤ♀	green	green-yellow	yellow	○ ●	light, heavy	moderately moist, dry

268

| Species | Height in m | Annual increment of type species | | Habit | Colour | | | Requirements | | |
		in height (cm)	in width (cm)		Summer foliage	Autumn foliage	Flowers	Light	Soil	Soil moisture
Ligustrum obtusifolium	1.5—2	10	15	⌂	green	green-yellow	white	○ ◑	light, heavy	moderately moist, dry
Ligustrum vulgare	4—5	15	15	⌂	dark green	green-yellow	white	○ ●	light, heavy	dry, moist
Liriodendron tulipifera	20—30	30	15	♀	green	yellow	yellow-green	○ ◑	light, heavy	moderately moist
Lonicera caprifolium	4—7	50		ʒ	dark green	green-yellow	yellow-white	○ ◑	light, heavy	moist
Lonicera henryi	2—4	30		ʒ	green	green-yellow	yellow-red	◑ ●	light, heavy	moist
Lonicera maackii	2—5	30	30	⌂	green	green-yellow	white-yellow	○ ◑	light, heavy	moderately moist
Lonicera nitida	1.5	15	15	⌂	dark green	dark green	yellow-white	○ ◑	light, heavy	moist
Lonicera periclymenum	3—4	30		ʒ	green	green-yellow	yellow-white	○ ◑	light, heavy	dry, moist
Lonicera pileata	0.3	5	20	⌐	dark green	dark green	yellow-white	○ ◑	light, heavy	moist
Lonicera tatarica	2—3	30	20	⌂	green	green-yellow	red, pink	○ ●	light, heavy	moderately moist, dry
Lonicera xylosteum	2—3	30	30	⌀	green	green-yellow	yellow-white-red	○ ●	light, heavy	moderately moist
Lycium halimifolium	2—4	20	50	⌂	grey-green	green-yellow	purple-violet	○ ◑	light, heavy	moderately moist, dry
Magnolia kobus	2	20	15	⌂	green	green-yellow	white	○ ◑	light, heavy	moderately moist, dry
Magnolia × soulangiana	3—6	20	30	♀ ⌀	green	green-yellow	white-purple-pink	○ ◑	light, heavy	moderately moist
Mahonia aquifolium	0.5—1	10	5	⌐	green	green-red	yellow	○ ◑	light, heavy	dry, moist
Malus × atrosanguinea	5—10	30	30	♀	green	green-yellow	red-pink	○ ◑	light, heavy	moderately moist
Malus floribunda	5—10	30	30	♀	green	green-yellow	pink-red	○ ◑	light, heavy	moderately moist
Malus × scheideckeri	5—10	30	30	♀	green	green-yellow	pink-white	○ ◑	light, heavy	moderately moist
Paeonia suffruticosa	1—2	10	10	⌂	green	green-yellow	white, pink, red, violet	○	heavy	moderately moist, moist
Pachysandra terminalis	0.25	5		⌐	green	green	white	◑ ●	light, heavy	moderately moist, moist
Parrotia persica	4—10	20	30	♀ ⌀	green	yellow-red	yellow	○	light, heavy	moist, dry
Parthenocissus quinquefolia	8—12	50		ʒ	dark green	red	green	○ ●	light, heavy	moderately moist, dry
Parthenocissus tricuspidata	8—15	50		ʒ	dark green	orange-red	green-yellow	○ ●	light, heavy	moderately moist, dry
Philadelphus coronarius	1—3	30	30	⌂	green	green-yellow	white	○ ◑	light, heavy	moderately moist
Philadelphus × cymosus	2—4	40	30	⌂	green	green	white	○ ◑	light, heavy	moderately moist
Philadelphus inodorus	1—3	40	30	⌂	green	green-yellow	white	○ ◑	light, heavy	moderately moist
Philadelphus × lemoinei	1—2	15	15	⌀	green	green-yellow	white	○ ◑	light, heavy	moderately moist
Philadelphus pubescens	2—4	40	30	⌀	green	green-yellow	white	○ ●	light, heavy	moderately moist
Philadelphus × virginalis	2—4	20	20	⌂	green	green-yellow	white	○ ◑	light, heavy	moderately moist
Photinia villosa	3—5	20	20	⌀	green	orange-red	white	◑	light, heavy	moderately moist
Physocarpus opulifolius	2—3	30	30	⌂	green-yellow	green-yellow	white-red	○ ●	light, heavy	dry, moist
Platanus acerifolia	15—25	50	30	♀	green, variegated	yellow	green-white	○	light, heavy	moderately moist, dry
Populus alba	20—30	50	30	♀	green-grey	green-yellow	yellow-green	○	light, heavy	dry, moist
Populus balsamifera	20—30	100	50	♀	dark green	green-yellow	yellow-green	○	light, heavy	moist
Populus × berolinensis	20—35	80	50	⚲	dark green	green-yellow	yellow-green	○	light, heavy	dry, moist
Populus × canadensis	20—30	100	50	♀ ⚮	green	green-yellow	yellow-green	○	light, heavy	moderately moist, moist
Populus × canescens	20—30	100	50	♀	green	green-yellow	yellow-green	○	light, heavy	dry, moist
Populus nigra	25—30	100	15	♀	green	yellow-green	yellow-green	○	light, heavy	dry, moist
Populus simonii	10—20	50	10	♀	green	yellow-green	yellow-green	○	light, heavy	moist
Populus tremula	15—25	100	50	♀	green-yellow	green-yellow	yellow-green	○ ◑	light, heavy	dry, wet
Prunus avium	10—15	20	20	⚲	green	red-yellow	white	○ ◑	light, heavy	moderately moist, dry
Prunus cerasifera	4—8	30	10	⚮	green, red	green-yellow-red	white	○ ◑	light, heavy	moderately moist, dry
Prunus laurocerasus	1—2	10	15	⌂	dark green	dark green	white	◑ ●	light, heavy	dry, moist
Prunus mahaleb	6—10	30	20	⚮	green	green-yellow	white	○ ●	light, heavy	moderately moist, dry
Prunus padus	4—15	50	40	⌂ ⚮	dark green	red-yellow	white	○ ●	light, heavy	moist
Prunus sargentii	8—20	30	30	♀	green-red	yellow-green	pink	○ ◑	light, heavy	moderately moist

269

Species	Height in m	Annual increment of type species		Habit	Colour			Requirements		
		in height (cm)	in width (cm)		Summer foliage	Autumn foliage	Flowers	Light	Soil	Soil moisture
Prunus serotina	10—25	50	25	♀	dark green	yellow-green	white	○ ●	light, heavy	moderately moist, dry
Prunus serrulata	5—8	30	5	♀	dark green	yellow-green	pink, white	○ ◑	light, heavy	moderately moist
Prunus spinosa	2—4	20	20	⌂	green	yellow-green	white	○ ◑	light, heavy	moderately moist, dry
Prunus × subhirtella	4—6	20	15	♀	green	yellow-green	white-pink	○ ◑	light, heavy	moderately moist
Prunus triloba	1—2	10	10	⌂ ♀	green	yellow-green	pink	○ ◑	light, heavy	moderately moist
Prunus virginiana	6—10	30	30	⌂ ♀	green	yellow-green	white	○ ●	light, heavy	moist
Ptelea trifoliata	2—6	20	25	⌂	green	yellow-green	green	○ ○	light, heavy	moderately moist, dry
Pterocarya fraxinifolia	15—20	50	30	♀	green	yellow	brown-green	○ ◑	light, heavy	moderately moist, moist
Pyracantha coccinea	1.5—3	10	20	⌂	dark green	dark green	white	○ ◑	light, heavy	moderately moist
Quercus cerris	15—35	30	20	♀	dark green	yellow-brown	green-brown	○	light, heavy	moderately moist, dry
Quercus palustris	20—30	30	50	♀	green	red	green-brown	○	light, heavy	moist, wet
Quercus petraea	25—40	30	20	♀	green	yellow-brown	green-brown	○ ◑	light, heavy	dry, moist
Quercus robur	20—45	30	20	♀	green, yellow	yellow-brown	green-brown	○ ◑	light, heavy	moist
Rhamnus catharticus	2—6	20	20	⌂ ♀	green	yellow-green	yellow-green	○ ●	light, heavy	dry, moist
Rhamnus frangula	2—4	20	20	⌂	dark green	yellow-green	yellow-green	○ ●	light, heavy	moist
Rhododendron flavum	1—4	10	15	⌂	green	orange-red	yellow	◑ ●	light, heavy	moderately moist, moist
Rhododendron hybridum	1—3	15	15	⌂	dark green	dark green	pink, white-pink, red-violet	◑ ●	light, heavy	moderately moist, moist
Rhododendron japonicum	1—2	10	10	⌂	green	yellow-green	orange, red, pink	◑ ●	light, heavy	moderately moist, moist
Rhododendron × praecox	0.5—1.5	20	15	⌂	dark green	dark green	violet-pink	◑ ●	light, heavy	moderately moist, moist
Rhodotypos scandens	1—2	20	20	⌂	green	yellow-green	white	○ ◑	light, heavy	moderately moist, dry
Rhus typhina	3—4	30	40	⌂ ♀	green	orange-red-yellow	green	○	light, heavy	moderately moist, dry
Ribes alpinum	1—2	10	10	⌂	green	green-yellow	yellow-green	○ ●	light, heavy	moderately moist, dry
Ribes aureum	2—3	20	20	⌂	green	red-yellow	yellow	○ ●	light, heavy	dry, moist
Robinia hispida	1—8	20	30	⌂ ♀	green	yellow-green	pink	○	light, heavy	moderately moist, dry
Robinia pseudoacacia	15—20	40	25	♀	green	yellow	white	○	light, heavy	moderately moist, dry
Rosa arvensis	0.5	10	15	⌒	green	yellow-green	white	○ ◑	light, heavy	moderately moist, dry
Rosa canina	1—3	40	50	⌂	green	yellow-green	pink, white	○	light, heavy	moderately moist, dry
Rosa glauca	1—3	40	50	⌂	grey-blue-green	yellow-brown	pink	○	light, heavy	moderately moist, dry
Rosa multiflora	1—4	60	60	⌒	green	yellow-green	white, pink	○	light, heavy	moderately moist, dry
Rosa omeiensis	1—3	50	50	⌂	dark green	yellow-green	white	○	light, heavy	moderately moist
Rosa pimpinellifolia	0.8	10	15	⌒	dark green	yellow-green	white, pink	○	light, heavy	moderately moist, dry
Rosa × rehderiana (*polyantha*)	0.6	10	10	⌂	dark green	yellow-green	white, pink, red	○	light, heavy	moderately moist, dry
Rosa rubiginosa	2—3	50	50	⌂	dark green	green-yellow	pink	○	light, heavy	moderately moist, dry
Rosa rugosa	1—2	30	30	⌂	dark green	yellow-green	white-pink, red-violet	○	light, heavy	moderately moist, dry
Salix alba	15—25	50	50	♀	grey-green	yellow-green	green-yellow	○	light, heavy	dry, wet
Salix caprea	4—7	50	50	⌂ ♀	green-grey	green-yellow	yellow	○ ●	light, heavy	moderately moist, dry
Salix fragilis	10—30	50	50	♀	green	yellow-green	green-yellow	○	light, heavy	moist, wet
Salix purpurea	1—3	50	50	⌂	green	yellow-green	green-yellow	○	light, heavy	moderately moist, dry
Salix repens	0.5—1	15	20	⌒	grey-green	yellow-green	yellow-green	○	light, heavy	moist
Salix viminalis	2—10	70	50	♀	grey-green	yellow-green	yellow-green	○	light, heavy	moderately moist, wet
Sambucus nigra	3—8	50	40	⌂ ♀	green, yellow	green-yellow	yellow-white	○ ●	light, heavy	moist
Sambucus racemosa	1—4	50	40	⌂	green	yellow-green	yellow-white	○ ●	light, heavy	moderately moist, dry
Sorbus aria	6—10	40	30	♀ ⌂	green-grey	green-yellow-brown	white	○ ◑	light, heavy	moderately moist, dry
Sorbus aucuparia	10—15	50	30	♀	green-yellow	yellow-green	white	○ ●	light, heavy	moderately moist, dry

Species	Height in m	Annual increment of type species in height (cm)	in width (cm)	Habit	Summer foliage	Autumn foliage	Flowers	Light	Soil	Soil moisture
Sorbus intermedia	4—10	30	20	⌂ ♀	green-grey	yellow-green	white	○ ◐	light, heavy	moderately moist, dry
Spiraea × bumalda	0.5—1	10	10	⌂	green	yellow-green	pink, violet-red	○ ◐	light, heavy	moderately moist, dry
Spiraea douglasii	0.5—1	10	10	⌂	green	yellow-green	pink-violet	○ ◐	light, heavy	dry, moist
Spiraea menziesii	1—1.5	15	15	⌂	green	yellow-green	pink-violet	○ ◐	light, heavy	dry, moist
Spiraea nipponica	1—3	20	20	⌂	blue-green	yellow-green	white	○ ◐	light, heavy	dry, moist
Spiraea prunifolia	1—1.5	20	20	⌂	green	orange-yellow	white	○ ◐	light, heavy	moderately moist
Spiraea salicifolia	1—1.5	20	20	⌂	green	yellow-green	pink-violet	○ ●	light, heavy	moist, wet
Spiraea thunbergii	1—1.5	10	10	⌂	green	red-yellow	white	○ ◐	light, heavy	moderately moist, dry
Spiraea × vanhouttei	1—2	20	15	⌂	green	yellow-green	white	○ ◐	light, heavy	moderately moist
Staphylea colchica	2—4	10	10	⌂	green	yellow-green	white	○	light, heavy	moderately moist
Staphylea pinnata	3—6	10	10	⌂	green	yellow-green	white-green	○	light, heavy	moderately moist
Symphoricarpos albus	1—2	20	20	⌂	dark green	yellow-green	red-white	○ ●	light, heavy	moderately moist, dry
Symphoricarpos × chenaultii	1—1.5	30	30	⌂	dark green	yellow-green	pink	○ ◐	light, heavy	moderately moist, dry
Symphoricarpos orbiculatus	1.5—2	30	30	⌂	dark green	yellow-green	pink-red	○ ◐	light, heavy	moderately moist, dry
Syringa × chinensis	3—4	20	15	⌂	green	yellow-green	violet-pink	○ ◐	light, heavy	moderately moist, dry
Syringa × persica	1.5—2	30	30	⌂	green	yellow-green	purple-violet	○ ◐	light, heavy	moderately moist
Syringa reflexa	3—4	40	30	⌂	dark green	yellow-green	pink-white	○ ◐	light, heavy	moderately moist
Syringa vulgaris	3—7	30	20	⌂ ♀	green	yellow-green	white, pink, violet	○ ●	light, heavy	moderately moist, dry
Tamarix odessana	2	30	30	⌂	green-grey	yellow-green	pink	○ ◐	light, heavy	dry, moist
Tamarix pentandra	2—5	30	30	⌂	blue-green	yellow-green	pink	○	light, heavy	dry, moist
Teucrium chamaedrys	0.25	5	5	⌐	green	green	purple	○	light, heavy	moderately moist, dry
Tilia cordata	20—30	40	40	♀	green	yellow-green	yellow-white	○ ●	light, heavy	dry, moist
Tilia × europaea	20—40	50	30	♀	green	yellow-green	yellow-white	○ ◐	light, heavy	moderately moist, dry
Tilia platyphylla	20—40	50	40	♀	green	yellow-green	yellow-white	○ ●	light, heavy	moist
Tilia tomentosa	20—30	50	40	♀	silver-grey-green	yellow	yellow-white	○	light, heavy	moderately moist, dry
Ulmus carpinifolia	25—40	40	30	♀	green	yellow-green	brown-yellow	○ ●	light, heavy	dry, moist
Ulmus glabra	25—40	40	30	♀	green	yellow-green	brown-yellow	○ ◐	light, heavy	moderately moist, moist
Ulmus laevis	20—30	40	30	♀	green	yellow-green	brown-yellow	○ ◐	light, heavy	moderately moist
Viburnum × burkwoodii	1—2	20	25	⌂	green	green	pink-white	○ ◐	light, heavy	moderately moist
Viburnum × carlcephalum	1—2	20	25	⌂	grey-green	purple-green	white-red	○ ◐	light, heavy	moderately moist
Viburnum carlesii	1—1.5	10	15	⌂	grey-green	purple-green	white-pink	○ ◐	light, heavy	moderately moist
Viburnum farreri	1—3	20	15	⌂	green-red	green-yellow	pink-white	○ ◐	light, heavy	moderately moist
Viburnum lantana	1—2	30	30	⌂	grey-green	violet-red-green	white	○ ●	light, heavy	dry, moist
Viburnum opulus	2—4	30	30	⌂	green	yellow-green	white	○ ●	light, heavy	moderately moist, moist
Viburnum plicatum	2—3	20	15	⌂	dark green	violet-brown	white	◐ ●	light, heavy	moderately moist
Viburnum × pragense	2—3	25	20	⌂	dark green	dark green	white	◐ ●	light, heavy	moderately moist, moist
Viburnum rhytidophyllum	2—4	30	30	⌂	green	green	white	○ ◐	light, heavy	moderately moist, moist
Viburnum utile	1—2	15	15	⌂	dark green	dark green	white	○ ◐	light, heavy	moderately moist, moist
Vinca minor	0.15	5		⌐	dark green	dark green	blue-violet	◐ ●	light, heavy	moderately moist, dry
Vitis coignetiae	4—10	50		⌐	green	red	yellow-green	○ ●	light, heavy	moderately moist, dry
Vitis riparia	6—10	50		⌐	green	yellow-green	yellow-green	○ ◐	light, heavy	moderately moist
Weigela hybrids	1—2	40	40	⌂	green, variegated	yellow-green	white-pink-red	○ ◐	light, heavy	moderately moist
Wisteria floribunda	4—8	30		⌐	green	yellow-green	violet-blue	○	light, heavy	moderately moist, dry
Wisteria sinensis	8—10	50		⌐	green	yellow-green	violet-blue	○	light, heavy	moderately moist, dry

Roses

In the wild, roses grow as shrubs of various height. If they grow singly among low-growing plants they are small shrubs in terms of height but have broadly spreading branches so that they take up a large space. If they grow at the edge of a forest or among taller plants the shrubs are taller, sparser, and have longer branches. The shrub grows towards the light. If a rose grows among other trees and shrubs then its branches are very long, sparsely covered with leaves, and bearing only few, if any, blooms. The shoots weave in and out in the undergrowth trying to make their way to the top, to sunlight, where they again produce flowers in profusion. If wild roses, known as species roses, are planted in a site which provides the same conditions as those found in their natural environment then they will retain their original shape and aspect even in the garden. Though we find many species roses in gardens, chiefly grown there are the cultivated garden roses.

Description of the plant

The basic natural form of the rose is a shrub. The root system of wild, species roses (also of those used as rootstock for cultivated garden varieties) consists of a main taproot and branch roots growing from the main root. In plants propagated by vegetative means (that is, by cuttings, sideshoots, etc.) the root system does not have a main root but consists only of a number of branch roots. Some wild species, including *R. canina, R. laxa* and *R. multiflora,* which are used as rootstock, have on their roots latent buds which produce non-flowering shoots called 'suckers'. If roses are not tended properly these shoots, growing on their own rootstock, may reach a considerable size, outgrow the grafted-on cultivar and suppress it so that the plant then has the shape and flowers the colour and size of the original wild species — the rootstock.

In wild roses, the part of the shrub visible above ground consists of single shoots growing from the bottom buds on the root neck. In garden (grafted) roses, the shoots grow from the grafted-on part of the garden cultivar. Shoots are of varied age, thickness and length. Wild roses growing in their natural environment or planted out in the garden have much more three-year and older wood than do garden varieties. The shoots form the framework of the shrub, which bears a profusion of blossoms if it consists mostly of two-year and above all one-year shoots. It is from the buds on these shoots that the flowering annual shoots grow. Correct feeding, care and watering are required if the shrub is to develop every year strong and healthy shoots that will ripen sufficiently by winter. By correct pruning — the nature of which depends on the properties of the given species or cultivar, the age of the shrub and the shrub's condition — the annual shoots are cut back to a given number

The hybrid tea 'Whisky' reaches a height of 60 cm, has bronze-yellow double flowers and a very agreeable scent.

Climbing roses used for a hedge. Two colours have been used, but they were planted at a sufficient distance so that they form two large, distinctly coloured but complementary patches.

Even though roses usually look better if surrounded by a lawn, here the rose bush — thanks to the richness of its flowers — has retained its dominant position among a dense growth of border perennials.

of buds, thereby determining the number of blooms that will appear in spring.

The leaves of roses are odd-pinnate with a varying number of leaflets, usually 5—7 in species roses of European origin and 5—9 in their hybrids.

Stipules are a very important means of identifying the species. For example those of *R. multiflora* are fringed and broad, those of *R. wichuraiana* fringed and narrow, those of *R. chinensis* faintly toothed, those of the *Cinnamomeae* group very broad with rolled edge, and those of *R. rugosa* large and broad.

Thorns are the sharply pointed outermost layers of cells on the stalk. In the evolutionarily oldest species, e.g. *R. spinosissima* and *R. rugosa,* they are straight and erect — dagger-like, whereas in later, younger species the thorns are curved — hooked. Some garden roses have straight as well as curved thorns, for example, species of the *Gallicanae* section. *R. alpina* has no thorns or only very few.

The thorns of garden roses vary in shape, size and in density. Roses with small, dense thorns are less suitable for cutting because of the difficulty of the latter's removal.

Thorns are not only a means of identifying species and cultivars but also serve a practical purpose. They protect the plants from being nibbled by animals, and in the case of climbers they help in holding on to the support.

The most important organ of the rose is the flower. It has many characteristics that serve as a means of identifying the species. These include, for example, the neck of the flower, the petals, bracts, stamens, and style.

An important criterion for the classification of roses into groups is the number of petals — according to which flowers may be described as 'single', 'semi-double', 'double' or 'full-petalled'.

The shape, firmness and size of the petals determine the shape of the flower, which is extremely variable, ranging from flat, through spherical, to slender and cylindrical.

As to colour, blooms encompass a wide scale, ranging from pure white, through to yellow, pink and deepest red, as well as bi-coloured, multi-coloured and even striped petals. Garden cultivars have more colourful blooms than the species roses.

The flowering period of roses also varies greatly. Most species roses flower in the first half of summer. Some shrub roses such as *R. gallica, R. centifolia, R. muscosa* and *R. damascena* flower later, some even until the frost — for example, *R. rugosa.* Remontant roses flower in June and a second time at the end of August. Multiflowered roses (polyanthas and polyantha hybrids) bloom later than large-flowered (hybrid tea) roses. They flower until the first frost and the number of blooms depends on the cultivar and on the spring pruning.

The fruits of the rose are the hips, which are also an important means of identifying the species.

Biological properties of roses

An important property of roses is their hardiness, their resistance to low temperatures and damage by frost. Even though floribunda and hybrid tea cultivars are earthed up and often also provided with a cover for the winter in our gardens, still it is necessary to keep hardiness in mind when selecting cultivars for planting in less congenial locations and soils. Rose species and cultivars are divided according to their hardiness into the following several groups:

Group 1: Very tender, even the woody above-ground parts are readily damaged by frost.

The deep red of this lovely rose makes it a true gem in any garden.

Climbing roses have a wide range of uses. If trained up a stake one can even make a good subject for solitary planting.

The floribunda 'Geisha Girl' has relatively small, salmon-pink flowers and deep green leaves.

Shrub roses planted at the back of a rock garden. The generous splash of red contrasts wonderfully with the crisp white of the house walls beyond.

Group 2: Tender — the less ripened parts of the shoots as well as the ripe parts excepting the lowest 1—2 buds can be damaged by frost, sometimes also the main stem may be slightly damaged.

Group 3: The unripened parts of the shoots can be damaged by frost, ripe parts only half their length.

Group 4: Hardy — unripened parts of the shoots can be damaged by frost, ripe parts are damaged slightly, only a quarter of their length.

Group 5: Very hardy — only the tips of the shoots are likely to be damaged by frost.

Group 6: Absolutely hardy — no damage by frost.

Another important property of roses is stability of colour, a property that increases the value of the blooms of the given cultivar. Resistance to strong sunlight is also important in choosing a cultivar, particularly for extreme conditions.

Of equal importance is resistance to mildew and black spot. In evaluating resistance to these diseases, the degree of attack is rated according to a five-point scale from 1 to 5; the lowest number denoting great resistance, the highest number great susceptibility to attack by fungus diseases.

Also important is the rapidity and vigour of growth. Some cultivars make little growth (these should be spaced more closely), others make a lot of growth and therefore should be spaced farther apart.

Classification of roses

The study of form enables first and foremost the precise identification of botanical species and their separation into sections. The characteristics of highly-bred cultivated varieties have not been determined exactly and to classify the present-day range of roses strictly according to botanical characteristics is practically impossible.

Botanical and various other systems of classification are of importance chiefly for nurserymen, growers and breeders; for the average gardener and rose lover they are somewhat esoteric. Best suited for the purpose of the amateur grower is the practical classification of roses according to their use in the garden and park:

1. **Large-flowered and multiflowered bedding roses**
a) hybrid teas and Pernetianas
b) remontant roses and Bourbon roses
c) polyanthas and polyantha hybrids
d) floribunda and floribunda-grandiflora roses

2. **Ramblers and climbing roses**
a) *R. wichuraiana* hybrids
b) *R. multiflora* hybrids
c) Lambert's roses
d) climbing teas
e) other hybrids

3. **Shrub roses**
a) species roses
b) cultivated garden hybrids of *R. rugosa, R. gallica, R. lutea* and other hybrids.

Of the above groups most commonly grown in gardens are the large-flowered hybrid teas and remontant roses and the multiflowered polyanthas, polyantha hybrids, floribundas, floribunda grandiflora roses, climbers and, less frequently, also shrub roses. In addition to these there are further subgroups — Garnet's roses, miniature roses, and the like. For easy identification, the group to which it belongs is given in the description of each cultivar.

Soil and climatic conditions

The site, the climate, and the nature of the site as regards exposure (north, south, east, west), the amount

Large-flowered hybrid teas should be planted close to a house or a sitting-out area so that their beauty and fragrance can be admired in close-up.

'Peer Gynt' is a tall hybrid tea with golden-yellow flowers and deep green leaves that reaches a height of 60 cm.

and incidence of sunlight, the type of soil, the amount of moisture — all these factors must be carefully considered when establishing a nursery for growing roses or when laying out a large rose garden. Few people, however, are able to choose a place for a home garden that fulfills the requirements for growing roses. So they must opt for the opposite course — to adapt the given conditions accordingly; all but the climate, of course, which cannot be changed. Even though roses are warmth-loving plants there is no need to abandon the thought of growing them simply because the garden is located at a high altitude, in a rather rugged climate, or in a low-lying frost pocket.

Climate

The former concern as to the tenderness of roses is long a thing of the past, due in great part to the new, hardier and more resistant cultivars. It is only natural, of course, that growing roses in less congenial climates requires greater effort. The gardener must keep in mind the possibility of late spring frosts and the onset of winter being earlier, and he must also devote attention to the overwintering of the plants.

Soil

Roses grow well in soil that is deep, sandy-loamy, sufficiently light, not too dry and well-aerated, absorbing water well but not too quick-draining so that the roots and micro-organisms in the soil are continually supplied with the moisture and air they need. This is encouraged by providing the soil with plenty of humus.

Roses do not tolerate soils that are too heavy, clayey, compacted, waterlogged, muddy and cold, stony, or very shallow. Nor will they thrive in soils that are too acid or in sandy soils with insufficient humus

from which all nutrients are rapidly leached and washed down to the lower layers.

Heavy soils can be improved by adding peat, compost and other substrates. The aim is to improve their drainage and air content. Sand or sandy soil is also added — about 5—10 kg for every square metre. Ashes, best of all wood ash or even the fly ash from power stations, are an effective means of making the soil lighter. Recommended is the addition of well-rotted poultry or rabbit manure, which should not be dug in too deeply in heavier soils. Very acid soils are improved by adding powdered slaked lime or compost mixed heavily with lime, occasionally also by adding slightly alkaline or neutral soil.

Light, sandy soils are too quick-draining and loose and so must be improved by adding substrates that retain moisture and lower the air content in the soil. When digging heavier soil into light soil that tends to become dry it is not necessary to dig as deeply as in the foregoing instance because in time, the fine particles will be washed down to the bottom layer by rainfall or watering.

The main thing is to add well-rotted farmyard manure, good compost with peat, crumbled turf with clay, and the like. In the case of light soils, manure and other organic fertilizers must be added more frequently because they decompose more quickly in such soils. If it is necessary to lower the soil acidity ground limestone is recommended, for lime powder would increase the heat generating capacity of light soils to the detriment of the roses.

Waterlogged sites can sometimes be satisfactorily drained by means of trenches or drainage pipes. In the case of shallow soil on a rock substrate there is no solution other than to work in a thick layer of fertile arable soil so that the surface of the rose beds is at least 60 cm above the solid foundation.

The heads of standard roses are pruned into a spherical shape. The individual shrubs should be sufficiently spaced so that the heads are allowed to develop fully. Standards can be complemented with shrub roses.

There are a number of ways in which to train climbing roses. The easiest method is without supports, by binding the canes of two neighbouring shrubs to form low bows. Another simple way is to train them up pillars or slender pyramids. A construction made of metal tubes is more expensive but durable.

Roses do best in slightly acid soils, the optimum pH being between 6.0 and 6.5.

Many roses are grafted (budded) on to *R. canina* rootstock, which roots relatively deep down. This must be kept in mind when considering the water conditions. A high underground water level causes yellowing of the leaves and promotes black rust. In such a case it is necessary to drain the site. Roses welcome occasional thorough watering, particularly during dry spells, but do not tolerate a high water table. The permissible level of underground water is a maximum of 100 cm.

In gardens where normal sandy or loamy soil has been continually cultivated for years the soil will not need great preparation. However, it must be kept in mind that roses should not be planted in soil where unsuitable forecrops have been grown, particularly crops of the rose family; this includes also practically all fruit trees which, more than any other plants, deplete the soil of the nutrients required by roses.

Light and heat

All roses require as much light as possible, but it is not desirable that they be exposed to direct sunlight the whole day as this causes the blooms to fade rapidly and if planted alongside the south face of a house they suffer from sunscorch and drought. Cultivated roses develop best at temperatures between 15—20° C. As soon as the temperature rises above 25° C the colours of the blooms fade and the petals of dark varieties are literally scorched. In beds where roses are spaced far apart they furthermore suffer from rapid heating of the soil; but this may be limited by mulching.

For these reasons, when choosing a site for planting roses — particularly large-flowered hybrid teas — it is best to select a location where they will be slightly shaded for at least part of the day, especially during the heat of midday. On sloping land the best

A lawn makes the best connecting element between rose beds and other parts of the garden. It not only makes it possible to admire the beauty of the roses at any distance but also provides the best microclimate for them.

Climbing roses can be used to make an attractive dividing wall between two different parts of a garden.

The climber 'Danse des Sylphes' has pelargonium-red, semi-double flowers. It reaches 3 m in height and flowers repeatedly.

sites are those that slope southwest or west. A welcome service is provided by the moving shade of tall trees, as long as the roses are not shaded for a long time. Roses will not grow in full shade, alongside the north face of houses, or on a steep north-facing slope. In such places, they are more susceptible to diseases and attack by pests and their wood does not ripen, so that they are readily damaged by frost. Nor should roses be planted in the close vicinity of trees, particularly ones with roots that greatly deplete the soil of nutrients and moisture, for example birches, maples, elms and ash trees. Quite out of the question is a location beneath the crown of a tree or within the area of the crown's periphery. In the garden, roses should not be planted close to strawberries, lettuce and other vegetables, and fruit-bearing shrubs. It is not just a matter of aesthetics; the nearness of the vegetables and fruit-bearing plants would stand in the way of spraying the roses with protective agents at the necessary times and the roses would suffer as a result. Roses are also unhappy in situations such as at the corners of buildings and between the walls of adjoining houses where they suffer from constant draughts, nor are they happy in enclosed situations such as walled courtyards or gardens surrounded by a high wall. Ample ventilation is important for the good growth of roses and this should not be hampered even by thicker plantings of other shrubs nearby. Freely circulating air among roses that are not spaced too closely together is also a factor in preventing the incidence of fungus diseases and attack by animal pests.

Planting

Preparing the soil

Beds for planting roses in the autumn should be made ready by the end of summer at the latest. Sandy or loamy garden soils need to be dug only to a depth of one spade blade. Of the industrial fertilizers a slow-acting phosphate fertilizer may be incorporated into the bottom soil. It is also good to add substances rich in humus, such as compost or well-rotted manure.

To keep the prepared soil loose and moist, cover it with a thin layer of peat or lawn mowings. As the precise depth at which roses are planted has a marked influence on the development of the plants in the ensuing years it is not advisable to put out roses in freshly dug soil that later settles, because the plants may then find themselves too high in the soil and hence in danger of being damaged by frosts.

Spacing

Also of importance is the planting distance, which depends on the type of rose and cultivar, particularly on its vigour. Cultivars that are less vigorous and make little growth should be spaced 30—40 cm apart. More vigorous cultivars should be spaced 50 cm or more apart.

Planting roses too close together promotes the spread of fungus diseases, causes the plants to grow tall and the bottom leaves to drop. Planting them too far apart is not good either, for the soil between the roses is then fertile ground for weeds; it is also unduly heated and dried out by the sun.

Standard roses should be spaced at least 100 cm apart and enough room must be allowed for bending the stem down for winter protection.

A specific group unto itself as regards planting distance is the climbing roses. Their spacing depends on the vigour of the cultivar and also on the use for which they are intended. The minimum distance is 120 cm, but it may be 2—3 m, depending on the circumstances. The correct distance for shrub roses similarly depends on the growth they make, for some are slender and will be content with the minimum of space whereas others are of broadly spreading habit, up to several metres across. When planting this type of rose it is necessary to learn its requirements beforehand so as to avoid needless mistakes.

Shrub roses look gorgeous in a natural garden and can be planted singly or in small groups.

When to plant roses

Roses may be planted at any time from October to April, as long as the soil is not frozen. When planted in the autumn, the roses have time to make fine roots before the first frost and then in spring they will have a head start. The disadvantage of autumn planting is that the roses are exposed to the effects of frost. As for spring planting, it is not recommended to plant roses in spring into heavy soil that has been wet for a long time, becoming very consolidated and difficult to loosen after the roses have been planted. Extremely warm weather immediately after spring planting is also a hazard. In the case of standard roses, on the other hand, spring is the time recommended for planting in view of the difficulty of over-wintering such roses. Spring planting is also recommended in districts located at high altitudes and subject to early frosts.

Methods of planting

Roses are best planted after the well prepared soil has had time to settle. They must not, of course, be planted in wet sticky soil, in which case there is increased danger that the roots will rot. Temperatures below freezing point are also unsuitable.

The roses to be planted should never be left lying on the ground exposed to the sun, and the roots also should be protected against the effect of a drying wind. If the plants appear to be even slightly dry immerse the whole bush in water before planting.

If the roses are planted in the autumn, remove any damaged branches and the tips of broken shoots. Unripened shoots may also be removed, leaving only 3—5 of the strongest. Pruning these shoots to only a few buds from the base is then done in spring.

If the roses are planted in spring, remove unnecessary shoots before planting and cut back those remaining to 2—3 buds from the base, depending on how strong the shoots are. If the plants are in good condition and have strong shoots you may leave more buds at the base, but if the shoots are very thin leave only one bud. Also remove damaged roots and shorten the others by about one-half.

Roses should never be planted by the edge of the bed but at least 25 cm from the edge. After carefully pegging out the correct spacing dig holes 40 cm wide and 40 cm deep. At the bottom of the hole put some compost well mixed with the planting soil. Do not, under any circumstances, use manure or industrial fertilizer. Only slow-acting bonemeal should be used. Do not begin applying additional feed until the year after planting.

When planting, the roots must not be bent by force. Spread them out freely in the hole with their ends pointing downwards and hold the bush so that the point of union of the rootstock and scion is about 5 cm below the natural soil level. Fill two thirds of the hole with soil, press it down carefully, so it is worked in around and in contact with the roots; then water the plant. Thorough watering is a must particularly in spring. When the water has soaked in (not before) fill up the hole with soil and hill it up to a height of at least 20 cm. Before the first

'Gloria Dei' is a lush-growing, slightly spreading rose that reaches a height of 80 cm. The leaves are large and coloured a glossy dark green. It has a perpetual flowering and can be recommended for both solitary and group plantings.

frost, add a little more soil to this mound to make it bigger. In spring, the hilled soil will protect the plant from the effects of the sun and drying winds. To make this protection even more effective, the plant may be shaded with fir branches. In dry weather, water the roses every 5—6 days. Three weeks after a spring planting, carefully remove the hilled soil; if possible, do this on a cloudy day when there is no danger of a great drop in temperature during the night.

At the beginning of April, remove their protective cover and cut back in a like manner roses that have been planted in the autumn. Take care that the union of the scion and rootstock remains 5 cm below the natural soil level because this is the most sensitive part of the plant, above which a new shoot will be produced in spring. Species roses should be planted at the same depth as in the nursery.

Climbing roses should be planted somewhat deeper so that the union of the rootstock and scion is 10 cm below the soil level. This will promote the growth of shoots with roots of their own. These roses should also be earthed up after planting. If climbers are planted by a wall, never plant them closer than 50 cm; bring them to the wall by inserting them in the ground at a slight slant. If planted up directly against the wall they would suffer from drought.

Standard roses must be staked because the weak stem by itself would not be able to bear the weight of the crown. Drive the stake into the hole before planting. It should be sufficiently firm and should reach into the crown so that the latter does not break off, even in a strong wind. The rose should be tied to the stake at the crown with a single 'figure eight' bind that will not slide down either the stem or the stake. When planting, it is necessary to keep winter protection in mind. The standard should be planted at a slant, at an angle of about 30° from the stake towards the side to which it will always be laid, namely over the stump of old growth at the base. If it were bent in the opposite direction, away from the stump,

279

it might readily break. Bending of the stem is also facilitated by planting the rose at a shallower depth, a factor that will be appreciated when removing sterile suckers growing from the roots.

When planting standard roses in late spring in warm dry weather, covering the soil with moist peat will be of great benefit — as will packing round the stem moistened moss or some other substance that will retain moisture a long time. The crown may be shielded against too much exposure to the sun by shading it with paper.

Pruning roses

Important for roses is pruning in spring to rejuvenate them, as cultivated roses do not make new growth continually from the root neck on their own as do wild roses.

Because roses do not heal their wounds as some fruit-bearing trees and shrubs do by means of an exudate — instead, the wood and rind round the cut merely dries up — the cut must be made 5—8 mm above a healthy bud so it does not dry out. The secateurs must truly cut the stem, not crush it, so they must be very sharp. The cut should slope away from the bud so that rainfall does not hit the bud, but is deflected from it. Just as the cut should not be too close to the bud, so it should not leave too much stem above the bud. Otherwise, this stump soon dies, turns black and becomes a point of infection by fungus diseases.

The principal pruning of roses is done only in spring, after overwintering. Winter frosts often do

When planting roses grafted on the root neck, always take care that the place of grafting is covered with soil as in b); a,c) are wrong.

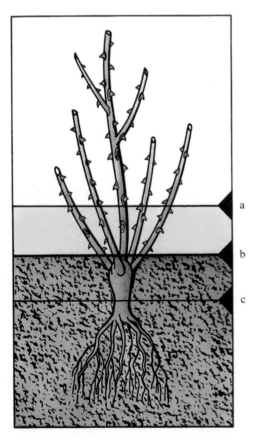

When planting climbing roses, the size of the given cultivar must be taken into account. It is a pity to have to cut off healthy canes of prospering roses later on just because you planted them too close to each other. The minimum distance is 120 cm, and in some cases even 200—300 cm.

not damage roses nearly as much as sudden changes of temperature in early spring. That is why the protective winter cover should not be removed until there is no longer any danger of night frosts.

The purpose of spring pruning is:
1. To concentrate the growth so that the plant is shapely and to limit its growth in undesired directions.
2. To attain the loveliest possible, large, long-stemmed blooms or a greater profusion of small flowers on a larger number of shoots.
3. To prolong the life of the whole rose bush by continually renewing the vigour of old stems and promoting the growth of young, healthy shoots.

The best time for spring pruning is before the buds begin to sprout but after all danger of severe frosts is past. This is usually in late March or early April. Timely spring pruning hastens flowering; late pruning delays flowering. Too early spring pruning — before the last frosts — may, of course, also be the cause of later flowering.

The pruning of all types of roses starts with the removal of all old, frozen dead wood. In a bush with little growth and few shoots, leave even the weaker shoots, cutting them back, say, only to one bud from the base so they will become stronger. In bushes with good growth, cut out weak shoots as well as shoots growing inward towards the centre. The thinning and opening-up of the bush in this manner is followed by the pruning proper. This is different not only for each of the various groups of roses but according to whether the object is to obtain a profusely flowering bush with blooms for cutting, or whether you wish to rejuvenate the whole bush.

How to prune the different groups of roses

Large-flowered roses in beds are pruned to within about 3—6 buds of the base of each shoot, depending on the thickness of the shoot. Weak shoots are pruned more severely, strong shoots are cut back less. If you want to obtain flowers for cutting, the shoots should be shortened more, to 3—4 buds of the base. This will yield fewer but strong, long stems with lovely flowers.

In the case of hybrid teas and floribundas grown singly as specimen roses, limit pruning to the removal

280

The multiflowered floribundas are excellent for mass planting where you intend to create a one-colour effect. They can be recommended, for instance, for borders along paths and drives.

of weaker shoots and adequate shortening of healthy shoots in order to obtain a shapely bush. If, later, they begin to flower less satisfactorily this may be remedied by heavier pruning.

Multiflowered roses (polyanthas and polyantha hybrids) are generally planted in masses, to form large expanses of colour, and thus all are usually pruned to the same height. Stating the most suitable number of buds to leave on the stem is very difficult because the various cultivars differ markedly in height. Whether to prune to 3, 6 or 8 buds of the base will depend on the cultivated variety and on the condition of the plant.

Roses of the Garnet's subgroup, if grown in beds, should always be pruned to 2—3 buds of the base; in other words, to only about 10 cm above soil level. It is when pruning climbing roses that inexperienced growers make the most mistakes. Sometimes, they even thing that young shoots growing from the base are wild growths and therefore must be removed. However, these shoots are the most important indication of the healthy growth of a climbing rose, by means of which the plant rejuvenates itself. As a rule climbers do not flower the first year, but this is no reason for severe pruning. Young shoots should be left intact; they should not be pruned even in spring because only in the following year will they produce short branchlets bearing flowers. The principal aim in pruning climbing roses is to promote the expedient growth of new shoots that will again produce flowers. It is better to try to make the buds of young shoots grow by bending them to a slanting or horizontal position.

In the case of single-flowering climbing roses, spring pruning is restricted to removing only the thin ends of the shoots which have been damaged by frost. The main pruning is done after flowering, at which time old growth — more than four years old — is cut out at soil level. After providing the plant with a generous application of feed, it can be expected to make vigorous new, strong young growths.

Remontant cultivars of climbing roses have a tendency to become bare at the bottom. For this reason, remove one or two old stems above a healthy bud close to ground level. If you want very long shoots, cut the growth off above the point where it forks, always leaving the younger shoot. This will yield single leading shoots that will readily make good new growth, after which only the thin ends of the lateral shoots need be shortened.

Shrub roses generally require no pruning, merely trimming, so it is only necessary to thin them out and shorten the ends of exceedingly weak or dry shoots.

Species roses are not pruned, except for the removal of dry and unhealthy branches. These roses are loveliest if they are given ample space and are allowed to grow freely.

Miniature roses should be shortened to half the height of the cultivated variety. Dead parts must be cut out with care.

Standard roses are pruned along similar lines to bush roses. It is recommended to prune severely rather than lightly in order to keep the size and weight of the crown within bounds. Take care to make it shapely.

Weeping standards are pruned according to some of the rules pertaining to the care of climbing roses. When pruning, leave young shoots until they are 3—4 years old and remove only older wood. Branches damaged by frost or otherwise should also be removed and the growth in the crown should be thinned out to prevent it becoming too crowded.

Care of roses

Roses require a loose soil, free of weeds, so that air and heat can penetrate easily. Shallow digging and frequent careful hoeing will maintain an open soil and preclude the need for much feeding and watering. It is important to break up any surface crust right away, particularly when the soil has dried after a rainfall. Loosening the top layer reduces the loss of moisture from the deeper layers. Deeper digging, however, may damage the roots. That is why soil cultivation should be only to a shallow depth (say, about 10 cm). Do not tread among the roses unnecessarily, particularly when the surface of the soil is moist. When this is unavoidable, the soil should be loosened immediately after it has been trodden on.

Standards must always be given a supporting stake and this should be long enough to reach into the crown. The surface of the stake can be treated with white varnish.

Unicoloured roses have their petals equally coloured on their upper and under side. The colour intensity decreases as the rose fades.

Mulching

Mulching is very beneficial for roses. The surface of the rose bed is covered by a layer of organic material such as leaves, lawn mowings, peat or old, well-rotted farmyard manure. This reduces the need for hoeing the soil for a longer time and also makes it unnecessary to water as frequently. Mulching promotes the favourable physical and chemical properties of the soil, improving the conditions for the activity of soil micro-organisms. In spring, right after pruning and fixing the beds, spread a layer of mulch about 8 cm thick between the roses before they start making growth. Otherwise, you might break off a great many buds. Mulching benefits the roses, promotes their growth, and at the same time acts as an

Infertile suckers sprouting from the stock should be removed in time. Cut them as close to the root as possible, digging back the soil as necessary, then replacing and firming it down.

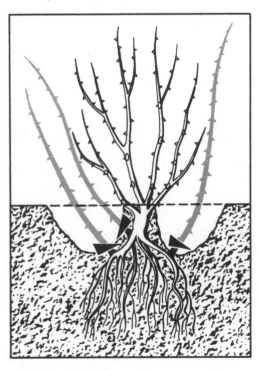

excellent weed barrier. However, it does detract from the attractive appearance of the bed, particularly in the ornamental part of the garden. That is why it is best to use material that can later be worked shallowly into the soil.

Pinching out

Timely pinching out helps to keep the growth of extremely vigorous shoots within bounds. Sometimes only a single, topmost bud — beneath the cut where a shoot has been pruned — starts into growth, thereupon developing into an excessively long stem ('shooting out' so to speak). This is not attractive in a bed and is particularly unattractive on a standard rose. If it happens in May, a very early flower may appear at the end of such a shoot. However, it is better to do without the bloom and pinch out the young shoot leaving about three or four buds which will give growth to shoots suitable for making a shapely crown. The rose will then also produce more flowers, although somewhat later.

Sometimes, a shoot is terminated only by a leaf without any bud, so that it cannot produce a flower. If such a 'blind shoot' is otherwise healthy, cut it back to the first leaf with a live bud. A shoot capable of bearing a flower will then grow from this.

If not properly planted and tended, roses often produce suckers (sterile shoots) from the rootstock. Compared with the garden variety, their leaves differ in size, colour (they are a paler green), and number of leaflets. There is also a marked difference in the shape and number of the thorns. Usually, these suckers can be removed for good only by scraping the soil away and cutting off the sucker at the point of origin on the rootstock. Sometimes, however, tearing off the sucker will suffice. Cutting it off at ground level, as some growers do, merely encourages an even more vigorous growth.

Summer pruning

Summer pruning involves shortening individual shoots whose growth is too vigorous, particularly in the case of hybrid tea bushes and the crowns of standard roses. But the main and very important purpose of summer pruning is to encourage the formation of further new flowers. The number of flowers produced by a rose bush during the summer depends on the properties of the given cultivar. Some cultivars flower less freely, others more profusely, but whether the bush bears the maximum number of flowers the cultivar is capable of producing will depend on the grower. Good general care, soil properties, watering, feeding, the weather, and preventive measures taken against pests and diseases all have a say in the matter. However, even if all these conditions were fulfilled the grower would be hard put to get three or even four healthy flowers (or flower trusses) on a single shoot without having carried out proper summer pruning.

Removing faded blossoms after the petals have fallen and just simply pinching off the flower stalk as is usually done in the case of daffodils, tulips, peonies, and the like, is a fundamental mistake with roses. The new shoot with the next flower will grow out too high up in the weak part of the original shoot and will be drawn-out and spindly.

When removing faded flowers it is advisable to observe the rules of correct summer pruning:

1. Remove faded flowers before the petals have fallen entirely, that is, as soon as the blooms have lost their beauty.

2. In the case of large-flowered roses (hybrid teas) cut off the faded bloom together with the part of the stem below the bloom with incomplete leaves and with at least one complete leaf that is, with five leaflets. Make the cut 5—8 mm above the nearest healthy bud; before doing so, however, check to see that the shoot is strong enough at this point to carry a new upright stalk and flower. So that the new shoots do not grow inwards, towards the centre of the bush (particularly in the crowns of standard roses), try to make the cut so that the topmost remaining bud points outwards, as in spring pruning. In the case of short shoots with few leaves also take care not to weaken them unduly by reducing the leaf surface area too much.

In September and later in the autumn, there is no point in shortening shoots with faded flowers by two leaves, because the forced shoot would no longer have any hope of producing a good blossom before the winter. At this time, be sparing of the rose so that the wood can ripen well and be more resistant to frost. This is also the reason why roses should not be cut with long stems for the purpose of room decoration in the autumn.

In the case of multiflowered roses, polyanthas and floribundas, cut off the whole flower cluster above the first leaf after all the blossoms have faded. Nowadays, some bedding roses of the multiflowered group are bred to shed the petals and stalks after the flowers have faded. This is a valuable asset of cultivated varieties for large plantings, particularly in white and other light-coloured roses whose petals turn dark and mar the appearance of a rose bed. In the case of climbers, which bear flowers in clusters like polyanthas, cut off the entire faded flower trusses in the same manner as for multiflowered roses. Timely removal of faded flowers is especially important in more frequently blooming climbing roses as so doing promotes more profuse repeat flowering. In summer, when the roses are in full leaf, it can be a very laborious task. However, growers should remove flowers shortly after they have faded, even in the case of single-flowering varieties, so their strength is not sapped by the formation of fruits and

The hybrid tea 'Dr. A. J. Verhage' forms a strong, compact shrub attaining a height of 60—70 cm. The flowers are amber-yellow with a slight bronze shade.

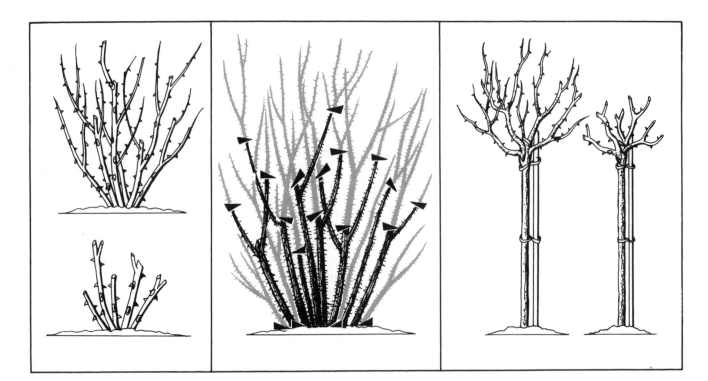

so they will form more flower buds for the following year.

Do not cut off the faded flowers of species roses and certain closely related cultivated varieties of shrub roses whose hips are a decorative feature in the garden late into the autumn.

Feeding

Feeding is very important in the cultivation of roses. This means providing them with a generous dressing of fertilizer.

Generally used for this purpose are industrial compound fertilizers, which contain a number of different nutrients in a given proportion.

Also important for correct feeding is the pH value of the soil, which should be between 6.0 and 6.5. The pH value may change over the years, becoming unsuitable for roses. Greater acidity slows the release of phosphorus in the soil. The plant is unable to obtain it from the soil and the grower must add lime or fertilizers that do not increase soil acidity. In alkaline soils, that is soils with a pH of more than 7.0, iron compounds change into forms that are rendered unavailable to plants and the plants suffer.

Roses are particularly sensitive to the concentration of salt in the soil and therefore it is better to go easy with artificial fertilizers, particularly in heavier soils where salts leach out slowly.

If plants are to be able to fully utilize all the nutrients added to the soil by the application of artificial fertilizers, the presence of sufficient humus is a must. Humus prevents the nutrients from being washed down to the deeper layers and at the same time increases the soil's ability to retain moisture, thereby helping the plants to survive critical periods of drought and frost. The main source of humus is farmyard manure but peat and compost in this context are also useful.

Farmyard manure should be worked into the top

Pruning roses. Bush roses are trimmed only moderately in the autumn (top left). The main cutting back is done in spring, when weak canes should be removed and the remaining ones shortened to 2—8 buds, according to the vigour of growth of individual varieties. In shrub roses (centre), which flower only once in a season, old canes and weak laterals are discarded in spring. Remaining canes are shortened.

soil layer. In lighter soils, up to 8 kg per a square metre should be used; in heavier soils, only about half that. Best of all is cattle dung; horse manure may burn the plants and should thus be used with care and only if well-rotted.

The roots of roses should never come in contact with fresh farmyard manure, particularly young transplanted seedlings for which such a supplement would mean certain death. For this reason, farmyard manure should be incorporated into the soil a sufficiently long time before planting. Bone and horn meal are likewise suitable fertilizers. So are poultry droppings, especially when applied in liquid form (a greatly diluted infusion of fermented droppings).

Climbing roses can be trained as an archway, above the entrance to a garden.

Peat is an excellent source of humus because it breaks down slowly. Roses root better in soils to which peat has been added.

Compost may be applied to roses at any time, mainly however in early spring before removing the protective winter cover. Good compost, rotted manure or peat should be spread over the ground in a layer 5 cm thick and then worked into the top layer of the soil. Where roses are earthed up for the winter, this material may be put in the formed hollows in winter. This will prevent the soil between the plants from freezing and when the hilled soil is spread out in the spring the fertilizer is readily worked into the ground.

Roses should not be fed the first season after planting. Begin adding some feed the second year and after that feed roses regularly every year. The feed should be applied in time, so the roses can make use of it in the period when they need nourishment most. There are two such periods: one in spring when the roses begin to grow, forming shoots, leaves and flower buds, and need more nitrogen; the second, after the first flowers have faded when the roses need potassium and phosphorus to form a second crop of bloom. The various proprietary fertilizers contain various proportions of the required nutrients, so it is recommended that you rotate their use.

Programme of feeding

To sum up the preceding points, feeding should be as follows:

1. Very early in spring. As soon as the weather permits, before uncovering the roses, apply 60—80 g of compound fertilizer per square metre. Spread the fertilizer evenly over the whole area. When the soil earthed up around the roses is spread, the fertilizer will be at a shallow depth below the surface level.

2. At about mid-May, when the roses begin to form buds, after a rainfall or after watering, apply a solu-

Rosa sericea var. *pteracantha* is one of the original rose species still cultivated.

tion of quick-acting compound fertilizer — 30 g of fertilizer per 10 litres of water. Apply three litres of the solution to every rose bush.

3. In late June. Repeat the application of liquid fertilizer in the same manner, but only after the soil has been well moistened.

4. In late October or early November, scatter fertilizer on the ground — 30 g of potassium fertilizer without chlorine and 30 g of phosphate fertilizer for every square metre. Before doing so, however, mound the soil up round the base of the bushes for the winter.

It is not always possible to adhere to a set programme of feeding. The given programme applies to normal weather, average type of soil, and light to medium-heavy garden soils. For light, quick-draining soils it is recommended to add the June application of liquid feed earlier, in mid-June, and give an additional feed of quick-acting liquid fertilizer no later than the first ten days in July. The same holds for very wet rainy weather, when nutrients tend to be washed out rapidly and in excessive amounts.

In a dry year, do not feed as much as in a year with a greater amount of rainfall, and be particularly careful with the application of nitrogen. If there is not enough moisture, part of the fertilizers applied in spring sometimes remain unutilized in the soil. If this happens, the plant begins to absorb nutrients only after the soil has been thoroughly moistened by late summer and autumn rains, its growing period extends well into the winter and there is then a great danger of damage by frost.

The physical condition of the soil is always extremely important. Roots cannot form in strongly compacting and very clayey soils and the applied fertilizers are of no use. They accumulate in the soil and prevent the circulation of air. The only help here is to add peat, humus, coarse sand and any other ma-

In climbing roses, old wood is removed during spring pruning. Six strongest canes at the most can be left, and these should be shortened to promote branching.

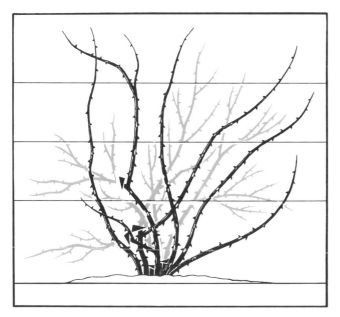

285

terial that loosens the soil, makes it more crumbly and prevents it from compacting.

Feeding the leaves benefits all roses; but for young, weakened bushes that have not yet had time to form an adequate root system, and sometimes also for older roses when newly transplanted, it can be a true lifesaver. Such plants have slightly yellowed, small, matt leaves and weak flower stalks. A liquid solution of compound fertilizer should be applied once a week or even oftener.

Now available are special preparations for foliar feeding which contain all the basic nutrients and some trace elements, as well as an ingredient that promotes the absorption of nutrients by the plant's conductive tissues. They may be watered into the soil but are intended primarily for nourishment of the plants otherwise than via the roots, for example, when a fault occurs in nourishment via the roots due to an excess or deficiency of some element in the soil. Spray the leaves and flowers with the solution (diluted strictly according to the manufacturer's instructions) three or four times at intervals of 10—14 days. Avoid adding more nourishment for good measure, as this would actually harm the plants.

Watering

Roses require a great deal of water. The appropriate amount is usually given as 700—800 mm of precipitation. The need for water differs in the various stages of growth. The greatest amount is needed during the period of intensive growth in spring, when the plant starts producing shoots and leaves and, again, after the first flowering, which is followed by further growth.

Greater need of water during periods of intensive growth goes hand in hand with increased application of feed. Without sufficient water and adequate nourishment the plant produces only weak shoots and stunted flowers on very short stalks. Only rarely does rainfall suffice to provide the necessary moisture and, as a rule, it is necessary to water the roses thoroughly so the moisture soaks right down into the soil. Watering merely the surface, even if it is done every day, is of no use whatsoever.

Rose beds are usually geometrically shaped to complement the architecture of the house.

The fullness of the flower is an important distinguishing feature in roses. According to the number of petals, roses are divided into single, semi-double, double, full and very full. Hybrid teas have very full flowers with more than 40 petals in 8 rows.

Keep watering in mind when you are loosening the soil and provide the bed with slightly raised edges so that the water will not run off but will soak in where it is needed. Do not water roses in hot sunshine. Use water that has been allowed to stand a while and a watering can with an open-ended spout (without a rose). Pour the water directly into the shallow depression that has been hollowed out round the base of the plant. Do not spray water on to the leaves.

Spraying with a hose usually provides the soil with less water than one thinks. However, if you must use a hose then at least avoid watering in scorching hot sun and see to it that the leaves always have time to dry before the evening. Leaves that remain wet overnight are more susceptible to fungus diseases.

In late summer and autumn excessive amounts of water do not benefit roses but, on the contrary, may even be harmful. Too much water in the autumn encourages the plant to go on growing, the shoots do not ripen in time and thus may be readily damaged by frost. For this reason, watering of roses is usually stopped at the beginning of September, rainfall then being sufficient for their needs. However, if the autumn weather is unduly dry, then the roses should be watered as required so they have sufficient moisture in their roots when freezing weather sets in. Frozen soil does not allow water to penetrate and the plants would then die as a result of drought. Generous watering before the onset of winter frosts is most important. Often one thinks roses have been killed by frost during the winter when, in actual fact, they have been destroyed by the dry conditions beneath the frozen top layer of the soil.

The danger is further increased by warm, sunny days in February and March, when large quantities of water are evaporated from the top parts of the plants and from the surface of the soil and when the sap rises prematurely from the roots while the surface layer of the soil remains frozen. That is why, in dry autumn weather, roses should be given plenty of water before preparing them for winter.

Winter protection

A very important procedure in the cultivation of roses is protection against frost. This begins with the choice of location and selection of cultivated varieties. Plants overwinter better if they are well developed, properly nourished in good humus-rich soil containing potassium and phosphorus, and unweakened by disease and/or pests. Roses with unripened shoots that continue growth until the onset of freezing weather are greatly endangered in winter and often killed by frost. Avoid any action that stands in the way of ripening of the wood and encourages the plant's continual growth even late into autumn. The gravest mistakes in this connection are: premature taking up of young (nursery) plants, planting in shade or directly beneath the crowns of trees, late feeding, excessive application of nitrogen or its application in July and later, watering, hoeing and cutting flowers with long stems in late summer and autumn (in September and October).

Not until November, before earthing up the roses for the winter, should the soil be loosened. The plants should be given a thorough watering if the autumn has been dry.

The selection of hardy cultivars is particularly important when planting climbing roses, for which it is difficult to provide winter protection. In central Europe it is necessary to provide most cultivated roses with a winter cover. Exactly when this should be done cannot be predicted beforehand. Some years the autumn weather is nice and warm for a long time

and roses that have been covered prematurely might be damaged by overheating on sunny days. Hence, the individual grower must keep an eye on the local weather, take heed of forecasts and not let himself be caught unprepared by the onset of winter.

Temperatures a few degrees below freezing point will not harm roses and a slight frost even helps the plant shed its leaves. However, as soon as there is danger of the temperature dropping to minus 10° C or of freezing weather setting in permanently, it is necessary to provide the roses with winter protection without further delay, before the soil or other material to be used for covering the plants freezes.

The best protection for roses is to earth up loose loam around the base. In the case of bushes spaced far apart or planted in a single row, earthing up the soil around them will suffice. Filling the resulting hollows with farmyard manure will prevent the soil from freezing and when the soil is spread out and covers the manure in spring it will add humus and nutrients to the soil. However, manure must not come into direct contact with the wood of the roses.

Where roses are spaced close together and in several rows so that one cannot use soil already in the bed, then other material must be used. Generally, well-rotted compost mixed with earth is used. Matter that is still rotting — decomposing — will generate heat and make the shoots tender. Crumbled peat, which is sometimes used, retains a great deal of water and if it freezes in such a state then it may tear the rind of the lower parts of the shoots with its sharp icy edges. Chopped straw and similar material often becomes a nesting site for voles. At most, such material may be used if mixed with loam, whose weight will keep it from being swept away by the wind. If a greater amount of protective material will be needed it is recommended to have it close by where it will be needed in good time, that is bring it closer than a more distant compost heap. Arrange this material in mounds, in the vicinity, even on paths, so that it can quickly be put round the rose bushes with a spade in case of sudden need. It does not matter if the surface of the soil is already hard-

The outline of the house can be extended by pergolas and walls covered with climbing roses, which make a nice link with the neighbouring terrace.

The floribunda 'Lilli Marlene', a lush-growing bush, 50—60 cm tall, has semi-double, dark fiery red flowers. It is suitable for group planting.

The rose bushes shown here form a sufficiently dense wall to create an intimate sitting-out corner on the terrace.

The floribunda 'Allgold' has large, golden-yellow, semi-double flowers and reaches 40—60 cm in height.

ened by the first frost or if it is covered with a sprinkling of snow.

Bush roses are usually earthed up in mid-November, up to a height of about 20—30 cm. The earthed-up soil must be worked in and around the shoots so that there are no air spaces which could be penetrated by frost or where mould could form. In cooler districts, place a light cover of bracken or fir branches over the hilled soil. Exceptionally good protection is required by those roses planted in the autumn that have not yet become well established and are not well rooted.

The crowns of standard roses should be divested of leaves for the winter and the shoots shortened to remove the unripened tips, then tied together with string. Younger standards may be bent down without fear of them snapping, particularly if they have been planted slightly at a slant. They should be laid

with care, however, so as not to break them off at the root neck or at a spot where the stem may have been damaged. See to it that such a healed (scarred) spot is on the inside of the curving stem. With one hand, hold the stem near the root neck and with the other bend it down slowly, always to the side, across the stump of old, cut-off wood. Secure the stem to the ground at the crown with crossed pegs or a hook. If you want the stake to remain in good condition you can take it up for the winter and put a short peg in its place to mark the hole.

In light, quick-draining soils you can hollow out a hole for the crown, but in heavier soil it is better to lay it on the surface because water might otherwise accumulate in the hole. Work loam into all parts of the crown and earth it up to a height of about 20 cm above the crown, especially above the point of union with the stem. Wrap the stem in a protective covering and earth up the soil above the roots. This will protect the stem not only from damage by frost and fluctuating temperatures, but also from possible damage by grazing animals. In severe frosts, add an additional protective cover of evergreen branches.

In the case of older standard roses with thick stems that can no longer be bent and with large, heavy crowns, the task of protecting them for the winter is more difficult. Bending them carries with it the risk of breaking the plant and therefore it must be overwintered standing upright or by laying the stem on the ground. It is best if you have a helper when carrying out this task.

When laying the rose on the ground you may use the Minnesota method. First of all, remove some of the soil from the stem on the side to which it will be laid. One person then grasps the stem close to the

The hybrid tea 'Bettina' forms medium-tall (about 60 cm), slightly spreading shrubs. The leaves have a conspicuous metallic gloss and recurrent orange flowers. It needs abundant feeding for a good growth.

soil surface, pulls it and simultaneously lays it towards the side while the other inserts a spade from the opposite side, under the more distant third-part of the roots and pries this section slightly towards the surface with the spade. The actual bending is thus shifted down to the flexible roots below the root neck with, at the same time, the greater part of the roots remaining undisturbed in the soil. Some of the roots on the opposite, upturned side may be divested of some of their root hairs during the process of lifting but this minor sacrifice will prevent the possible breaking of the stem. It will also save the whole rose from being damaged by frost due to insufficient protection in the upright position. The stem, laid on the ground together with the crown, should be secured with pegs as in the preceding instance and the exposed roots — stem as well as crown — should be covered thoroughly with loam. A healthy rose that is undamaged by frost will soon make plenty of new roots after being righted in the soil in spring.

If you wish to protect erect standards that cannot be bent by wrapping them for the winter, then you must use a light, dry and coarsely-woven material. Never use impermeable foil or impregnated paper, beneath which the temperature would increase markedly in sunny weather and the ensuing drop in temperature at night would thereby damage the rose even more. The best protection against frost, as well as against breaking by the wind or the weight of snow, is to insert three sticks into the ground at a slant to form a tripod with the rose inside, at the centre. Tie the branches of the crown together, fill straw or hay in and around all parts and secure it firmly with wire. Remember always to wrap the stem as well, that is, with sackcloth or burlap.

The hybrid tea 'Peter Frankenfeld' bears large, deep carmine-red, fragrant flowers. It is a vigorously growing, hardy shrub with dark green leaves.

The hybrid tea 'Mister Lincoln' has conspicuously large, deep red, strongly fragrant flowers borne on robust stalks. It forms stout, hardy shrubs.

The picture shows three stages of development of a rose, with only the flower in front fully open. As soon as the flower starts to fade, before the petals have started to fall, it should be cut off with a part of the stem to at least the first complete leaf.

Climbing roses are relatively resistant to frost and some of the newly cultivated ones, for example of the repeatedly flowering *Rosa kordesii* group whose ancestors include the very hardy *R. rugosa,* are almost totally frost-resistant. Climbing roses that are mutations of hybrid teas and floribundas, however, retain their sensitivity to frost. An excellent but laborious means of protecting climbers is to take down the branches from the support, lay them on the ground and cover them with soil. Usually, however, this is virtually out of the question. So, generally, climbing roses are protected only with sackcloth, burlap, paper or fir branches spread and secured over the roses on walls and pergolas. It is particularly important to shade the plants from the sun in winter and in early spring. It is often difficult to remove all the leaves from climbing roses and as these may

The colour of the rose flowers makes a nice contrast to the white of the walls.

The floribunda 'Europeana' has full, very fragrant flowers arranged in fiery blood-red trusses. The spreading bushes attain 50—60 cm in height.

harbour the spores of diseases and eggs of pests over the winter it is recommended to spray or sprinkle the whole plant as well as the surface of the soil. This is best of all done with a sulphur preparation. If the roses are on a wall take care not to use a preparation that would stain it yellow!

Earthed-up loam effectively protects mainly the union of the scion and rootstock as well as the base of the shoots, just as for bedding roses. A climber that is sometimes damaged by frost to the ground in a severe winter is not yet lost. The bottom buds that have been protected by earthing up will make profuse growth and by summer will have produced vigorous shoots.

Protection for shrub roses, particularly low-grow-

Standard roses must be well protected from frost. This should be borne in mind as early as when planting them; they should be planted at a slight slant to facilitate their being bent towards the ground. The cane is then pinned with hooks (see inset picture) and the head is covered with soil and the cane protected by evergreen twigs.

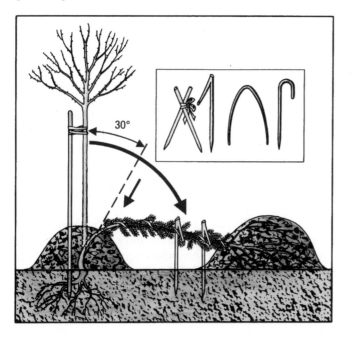

ing and ever-blooming cultivars, is provided in the same way as for bedding roses, by earthing up. Longer shoots may be screened by the provision of some form of protective material.

Some shrub roses and most species roses generally survive the winter quite well. At most, the surface of the soil may be covered with a layer of forest litter, chopped straw, and the like. Roses grown in containers and tubs on the balcony should be put in a cool cellar for the winter.

The winter cover should be removed gradually as of the beginning of April; always do this on a cloudy day, never in sun.

It is very difficult to protect the new, delicate shoots of roses that have had the winter cover removed from being damaged by late spring frosts. Covering them may break them off. If the shoots are affected by frost, the important thing is to prevent them from thawing out rapidly in the heat of the morning sun that usually follows a night frost.

If a night frost in April or May does not drop below − 5° C there is still hope of saving the young shoots, if their thawing is slowed. This is done by misting them with a fine spray of water, starting at sunrise. The light coating of ice formed by the water will not harm the plants, but a drop in temperature below − 5° C will destroy the first shoots completely. If they are killed by frost, new growth will be made by the bush − if it has been planted at the right depth and if the buds close to the root neck are protected by soil. New growth can be encouraged by timely cutting back of the frozen shoots. Early renewed growth is also encouraged by the application of a weak solution of quick-acting compound fertilizer and by watering.

Nowadays, roses are grown even in cold mountain regions and their overwintering in such extremely difficult conditions requires quite exceptional measures. Snow remains lying on the ground there throughout the winter, so there is no need to fear a temporary warm spell in winter with the ground exposed to freezing temperatures bare of snow,

The floribunda 'Irish Beauty' reaches some 50 cm of height and bears large, semi-double flowers, coloured salmon-red with a golden tinge.

Roses have all the good qualities for which they are indispensable in every garden. They are long-lasting, undemanding, need no special care, are hardy, tolerate any climatic conditions and come in a wide range of colours and scents.

a great danger for roses otherwise. In mountain districts, on the contrary, there is more than enough, even too much snow. The bottom, compressed layers turn to ice and the weight of the mass readily crushes the bushes cared for in the normal way. Years of experience in the Swiss Alps have shown that at altitudes of 1200—1900 m above sea level, roses overwinter well even without a special protective cover. Before the onset of winter, that is, as early as about 10 October, they must be cut back according to the condition of the roses — as a rule this means very hard, sometimes practically to the union of the scion and rootstock, to prevent the bush from breaking under the weight of snow.

Detrimental factors

Roses are harmed by uncongenial environmental conditions, by pests, by fungus, bacterial and virus diseases and by weeds.

Uncongenial environmental conditions are a deficiency or overabundance of nutrients, damage by

A rose must not be restricted in growth or forced into the background by other plants. It should always form the dominant of the scene.

frost, wind, drought, too much water, and the like. The effect of some of these may be offset or lessened by taking the appropriate measures in time, that is by correct feeding, watering, pruning and general care.

Roses damaged by frost are continually behind in their development, their leaves are smaller and a paler green to yellow. Sometimes this happens only to part of the bush, perhaps to one of the shoots, in which case it is best to cut it out in time so that the remainder grows well. Greater damage by frost cannot be treated. Such a bush wastes away — rarely does it revive sufficiently to overcome the damage.

Control of pests and diseases

The first thing to remember is that well tended plants are more resistant to attack by pests and diseases. Therefore, see to it that they have a well balanced diet, are watered in time and as needed, that the soil is kept in good condition by regular hoeing, the beds are kept clean by removing fallen leaves and weeding and so on. Also remove plants that show signs of a virus disease; otherwise the disease may spread.

Climbing roses can be a wonderful decoration near the entrance to a house.

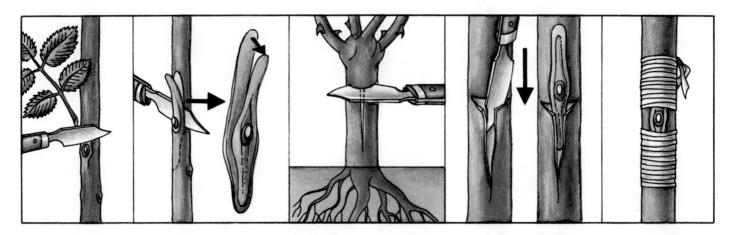

Rapid and effective protection is made possible by the suitable and timely use of chemical preparations.

The best time for spraying is in the late afternoon, when the sun is not so hot and there is no need to fear that the plants will be scorched. On cloudy days, plants can be sprayed at any time when there is no wind. The solution should be sprayed in a fine mist and the leaves should not be sprayed directly from close up. Carefully observe the instructions on the label for diluting the preparation, for a stronger concentration might greatly damage the plants. Signs of burning in a plant caused by such spraying become evident soon after — the tips and edges of the leaves where the solution has accumulated begin to dry up. It is necessary to alternate the preparations, particularly the finer organic agents.

The assortment of chemical preparations available on the market changes continually as new ones are being introduced; these are usually better, being less dangerous to man and bees and at the same time more effective against pests.

When using these preparations, of course, it is necessary to take care not only to avoid damaging the plants but also to avoid harming oneself. Therefore, carefully read and observe the manufacturer's instructions and use protective glasses and gloves. Finally, spray so that any stray breeze will carry the spray away from you — never toward you.

Propagation of roses

Roses can be increased from seed and by means of offshoots or cuttings. Another, and the most commonly employed method for the large-scale propagation of the majority of garden varieties is budding — the uniting of a bud of the garden variety with the root neck of the stock.

Countless kinds of rootstock, obtained from the selected seeds of various species and types of roses, are used. The choice of stock can increase the hardiness of the rose to changes in temperature, influence the flowering and successful development of the rose in various conditions. Commonly used as rootstock, for example, is *Rosa canina* 'Pollmeriana'.

The stock is grown from the seed. The seedlings are pricked out when they have three true leaves. Their further successful growth is ensured by hoeing, weeding, feeding, watering and preventive care against fungus diseases.

Budding of roses is done in their full strength, that is, in the second half of July. All leaf blades must be removed from around budstick. Then a very sharp knife is used to cut out a 3.5-cm shield-shaped piece of stem including the bud and a small part of wood. Carefully remove the wood, taking care not to damage the bud. The piece of bark with the bud is then inserted into a T-shaped incision in the rootstock, close above the ground and tied in place with raffia, leaving the bud itself uncovered, as shown.

The seedlings should be transplanted in early spring, so they can grow sufficiently strong before budding. Before transplanting the seedlings, trim the top parts as well as the roots.

Roses can be propagated either by the budding of a latent bud or an active bud. Budding of a latent bud is more common and is done between the end of June and end of August. The success of budding depends also on the quality of the bud (best of all are ones taken from the middle of a ripened annual shoot, after flowering). Insert the bud into a T-shaped incision on the root neck of the rootstock and cut the top part of the shield of rind (the small piece of stem taken with the bud) so it corresponds to the slanting cut on the rootstock. Then press it in and bind it firmly in place with raffia or plastic foil. If raffia is used it must be treated against possible infestation. After budding pile up soil round the root neck of the rootstock. Loosen the bind as soon as you see that the bud has taken. If the bud does not 'take' then the procedure may be repeated.

In spring, prune the roostock above the point of budding by making a slightly sloping cut away from the bud, so that water runs off in that direction (away from the bud), otherwise the bud might rot. When a shoot emerges, pinch off the end so it will fork.

Roses are also propagated by cuttings prepared from semi-ripened growth in June or July and by hardwood cuttings in winter. Herbaceous or softwood cuttings are used with success in propagating miniature roses.

Some species roses may be propagated by means of root cuttings (*R. rugosa*), root runners (*R. hugonis*), division or layering.

Select list of roses

Key to abbreviations used:

BLf — bush with long-lasting
    flowers
S — shrub rose
HT — hybrid tea

Cl — climbing rose
Pol — polyantha
F — floribunda
FGr — large-flowered floribunda

Colour	Type	Flowers	Habit	Height in cm	Other characteristics
Red					
Alain	Pol	bright carmine-red, faintly double, in umbels	upright, bushy	50—80	faintly fragrant
Ave Maria	HT	salmon-red, well-formed	bushy	50—60	pleasantly fragrant
Bad Füssing	F	glowing red, always in umbels	very bushy	50	hardy (resistant to cold)
Berlin	BLf	orange-scarlet, centre golden, in large umbels	upright	150	flowers until the frost
Blaze Superior	Cl	bright scarlet, semi-double, large clusters	very vigorous climber	250—300	recurrent bloom
Duftwolke	HT	coral-red becoming geranium-red, large bud	very vigorous, upright	70—90	very fragrant
Erotika	HT	velvety dark red, slender bud	very vigorous, upright	70—90	very fragrant
Europeana	F	bright crimson, double, in umbels	spreading, bushy	50—80	very fragrant
Gruss an Bayern	Pol	blood-red, faintly double	markedly upright	50—80	fragrance of wild roses
Lady Rose	HT	bright salmon, flowers very large	very bushy	70	pleasantly fragrant
Lilli Marlene	F	velvety crimson, double, in umbels	spreading, bushy	50—80	flowers large, slow-fading
Paprika	Pol	brick-red, faintly double	vigorous, upright	50—80	hardy (resistant to cold)
Prominent	F	red-orange, double	markedly upright	80	excellent garden rose and good for cutting
Pink					
Coral Dawn	Cl	rose-pink, double, persistent	vigorous climber	250—300	fragrant
Elysium	F	light salmon	very erect, bushy	60	marvellous fragrance
Esmeralda	HT	deep rose-pink	branched	80—90	very fragrant
Michèle Meilland	HT	bright pink shaded lilac, long bud	vigorous	70—90	fragrant
New Dawn	Cl	blush-pink, double	strong	250—300	fragrant
Pariser Charme	HT	clear pink, double	spreading, bushy	50—80	very fragrant
Rosenfee	F	clear pink with silvery gloss	speading, bushy	40—50	lovely bedding rose
The Queen Elizabeth Rose	FGr	carmine-rose and dawn-pink, double	very vigorous, upright, bushy	over 80	tolerates partial shade
Yellow					
Allgold	F	bright buttercup-yellow, double, in umbels	spreading, bushy	40—50	glossy green foliage
Gloria Dei	HT	golden-yellow edged rose-pink	very vigorous, tall	100	hardy (resistant to cold)
Goldstern	Cl	golden-yellow, double	vigorous, bushy	220—300	deep green foliage
Hugonis	S	yellow, simple, solitary	vigorous, upright, bushy	200—250	single flowering
King's Ransom	HT	clear golden-yellow, ovoid bud	vigorous, upright	70—90	very fragrant
Norris Pratt	F	bright yellow, double, in umbels	spreading, bushy	30—50	colour constant
Westerland	BLf	yellow and orange, semi-double, in umbels	vigorous, spreading, bushy	150—200	very fragrant
White					
Edelweiss	F	creamy-white, faintly double, in umbels	spreading, bushy	40—50	holds in all kinds of weather
Pascali	HT	creamy-white, bud long	vigorous, upright, bushy	100—150	recurrent bloom
Virgo	HT	pure white	very vigorous	60—80	very abundant bloom, moderately to very fragrant
Lavender shades					
Mainzer Fastnacht	HT	lilac, bud long, pointed	very vigorous	70—90	very fragrant
Shocking Blue	F	magenta-lilac, double	broad, bushy	50—80	profuse bloom, long flowering
Silver Star	HT	lavender, bud long	vigorous, bushy	70—90	very fragrant

Perennials

Perennials live for a variable number of years, unlike annuals and biennials, so they flower and produce seeds a number of times during their life span.

Usually, only their underground parts with buds in readiness for the next growing season survive uncongenial periods. In some species, however, particularly those of cushion-like habit, the green aerial parts also live over from season to season. The underground organs, which may be roots, rhizomes, tubers or bulbs, are often organs of storage not only of food but also of water. The uncongenial conditions a plant must survive need not be only periods of insufficient warmth (winter), but may also include periods of drought (summer in continental regions) and periods of an insufficient supply of light (as, for instance, may be the case in a broadleaved forest when it is in full leaf).

The term 'perennial' as understood by the gardener does not correspond exactly to the botanical definition. The gardener is generally not interested in species that are not ornamental, for him plants that do not survive the winter in open ground are not perennials, even though from the botanist's viewpoint they are. Sometimes the gardener does not include in this group even those species that are commonly transplanted every year purely for growing reasons. On the other hand, classed by gardeners as perennials, once again for purely practical reasons, are certain small subshrubs (*Dryas, Thymus, Helianthemum, Lavandula* and the like). The gardener's term 'ornamental perennials' is hence rather inaccurate from the scientific, botanical viewpoint.

Importance of site

A plant that requires moist soil can grow in any region that has an abundant rainfall, whereas in drier regions it can grow only on the edge of stretches of water that do not dry out. If they are to be grown elsewhere they must be watered by other means (as in the case of *Ligularia*). A plant that requires moist soil and moist air can grow only in regions with abundant rainfall, by the sea or at higher elevations. Elsewhere it will do poorly, even though it is watered (*Gentiana farreri, Astilbe*). In order for it to thrive it would also be necessary to moisturize the air by misting. Even this is done in practice; for exam-

ple, for rock garden plants of alpine origin. A plant that requires moist soil, moist air and warmth can grow only in rather warm maritime regions such as the south of England, Portugal and central Japan. Since it is difficult to provide suitable conditions for such plants, they do well only in the greenhouse (*Lilium auratum* is one example).

Contrariwise there are plants that require dry soil (*Gypsophila*) and rot in damp locations or in regions with abundant rainfall. If these are to survive in the garden they must be planted in an elevated bed with good drainage and, if necessary, covered with glass or foil during the period when they need dry conditions or, if this is not feasible, should be moved to a dry environment (xerophilous rock garden plants to a glasshouse and bulbs to a heated storage room).

If the plant requires not only dry soil but dry air as well it cannot be grown in regions with more abundant rainfall. *Iris pumila,* for example, will not last long in western Europe.

Of course, it is not only the annual rainfall and average annual temperature of the place of origin that

Phlox paniculata 'Starfire' is one of the taller cultivars of phlox. It can be grown in full sun at submontane regions, where the atmospheric moisture is higher, but it needs slight semi-shade if cultivated in the lowlands in drier conditions. The soil should be nourishing and sufficiently moist.

A group of tall grasses combined with the loosestrife *Lysimachia punctata* form a natural link between the lawn and a low wall which is partly covered by vegetation.

are important; much also depends on their distribution. The environmental conditions in a district with overcast summers and damp, cold winters are different from those in a region with dry sumer, heavy rainfall in autumn and freezing weather in winter, even though the total annual rainfall is the same.

Types of climate
The characteristic climate of regions from which most of the perennials grown in the garden have their origin may be roughly divided into the following five different types.
1. **Mild and moist climate** with overcast summer and snowstorms or freezing weather with snow cover in winter (as in southern Scandinavia, northern Germany, the Netherlands, Belgium, northern Japan, the Atlantic coast from the Canadian border to Washington DC, and the Pacific coast of Canada).
2. **Mild and rather dry climate** with sunshine in summer, temperatures rising even above 30° C and 2—3 week, occasionally even lengthier, periods without rain; winters in which temperatures drop even to below −20° C, light snow cover, and often freezing weather without any snow cover (e.g. Hungary, Romania, the vine-growing regions of central Europe and the Great Lakes region in the USA).
3. **Rather warm and dry climate** with hot dry summers (without rainfall even for several weeks) and with winds and freezing weather in winter (as in the Ukraine, southern Siberia, central USA).
4. **Rather warm and damp climate** with warm summers with frequent rain and rainy winters with only occasional mild freezing spells (as in the south of England, Atlantic coast of France and northern Spain, southern slopes of the Alps, the Pacific coast of the USA excepting California, central Japan).
5. **Subarctic climate** with very late spring, short cool summers and long winters with snow and severe frosts (as in central and northern Norway and Sweden, Finland, northern Scotland, high mountain regions of central Europe, the greater part of Siberia, Alaska and the greater part of Canada).

Temperature, soil and atmospheric moisture are not the only environmental factors. Equally important are light and shade, type of soil (loamy, sandy, humusy; shallow, deep; rich, poor; acid, calcareous). All these factors in various combinations give rise to diverse habitats — different environments. In each habitat one will always find only certain plant species or groups of species — plant communities. Sometimes the same species may be found in like habitats throughout the northern hemisphere (*Caltha palustris* alongside streams, *Saxifraga oppositifolia* in cold and damp districts in very shallow soils, *Convallaria majalis* in partial shade in rich, humusy soils). At other times, species are limited to only a certain geographical district.

If planted in a like situation in another geographical district, however, they generally adapt readily. It is thus possible to plant *Caltha palustris* and *Iris kaempferi* of eastern Asia together with *Mimulus luteus,* which is native to North America, because all three species grow in muddy meadows. However, *Caltha palustris* cannot be planted together with *Achillea millefolium,* even though they may be found growing fifty paces apart in the wild, because each requires entirely different conditions: the one wetland and the other a sunny hillside or hedgerow.

The origin of perennials must therefore be judged not according to the continent where they occur but according to the environment in which they grow.

Selecting perennials for the garden

Plants are adaptable to a certain degree and you can also provide for some of their needs by preparing the site accordingly, so that a single garden may contain plants from different habitats and some may even be grown in the same bed. This, however, requires a great deal of work, knowledge and individual care and the plants will not last long, making it necessary to dig up the bed and put in new plants again after a few years.

This group of perennial plants, forming a nice composition with a small garden fountain, provides a good example of the effective use of water in the garden.

Informal perennial beds have become a common feature of modern gardens. Here, a well-matched group is formed by *Chrysanthemum maximum, Coreopsis verticillata* and *Phlox paniculata* 'Septemberglut'.

Perennials are a good complement to groups of woody plants. Equally suitable are low-growing or carpeting species and ornamental grasses, as well as many fern species.

If, on the other hand, you select only those species whose requirements can be met by the conditions of your garden, then the plants will be strong and healthy and will need much less care.

If you want to have other species then, at least, put plants with the same requirements in one bed. For example, plants that grow in lush meadows, be they native to Europe, Asia or America, should be put in a well-fertilized, low-placed bed, sited even below the level of the surrouding terrain, into which rainwater will run down and where the soil remains continually fresh and loose. Together with such plants you may also put those that grow by the waterside or in acidic mountain meadows, because these will not find it hard to adapt.

Plants that grow in dry meadows and steppes should be put out (in central Europe) on south-facing slopes, in rather light soil or soil provided with good drainage, because many of these species do not tolerate soil moisture. You can combine these with plants that grow in shallow soil if they like sunshine, also with mountain species that grow in foothill districts where there is sufficient water only when the snow melts and where otherwise conditions are mostly rather dry.

If your garden faces north, is shaded, damp and cold, in addition to the woodland species that find such conditions congenial you can also grow some waterside plants or species that grow in foothills with frequent rainfall, as long as they flower readily even in shade.

There is a wide selection of plants to choose from for every garden and every location but the choice must be made with due care, for the correct selection of species determines to a great extent the success of the outcome.

Cultivated varieties

What was said about plant species applies in great measure also to plant cultivars, particularly those that are the result of selective breeding without hybridization with another species. These cultivars generally require the same climate as the type species but they do not tolerate extremes and are more demanding in terms of nourishment and, as a rule, water as well. However, much depends on the climatic conditions of the place where they were developed. If these conditions are very different from those where you live then it may happen that the cultivar will do less well in your garden than the type species.

Particularly striking is the influence of origin in the case of cultivars obtained by crossing several species with different site requirements. You must be prepared, for example, for the cultivars of Californian or Japanese provenance possibly failing to thrive in your garden. However, hybridization (the crossing of species) is a good means of obtaining thriving plants if it is difficult to grow the type species. Thus, for example, *Dryas* × *suendermannii* grows relatively better than *Dryas drummondii* and *Dryas octopetala*, which it has practically superseded in our gardens. The same is true of the garden forms of *Gentiana acaulis* and *Iris pumila* hybrids.

Use of perennials

Perennials are the latest group of plants to be put out in the garden. Even though some species have been known for centuries, they were grown for cutting rather than as an integral part of the garden design (ox-eye daisies, peonies, lilies, chrysanthemums). Most of the commonly grown species of perennials, however, did not appear on the pages of garden catalogues until the end of the 19th century, when perennials began to be used as an element in their own right.

In England, perennials were first used in gardens as companion plants or substitutes for annuals and

Two types of garden

In substance, there are two types of garden schemes. The first stresses the fact that the garden is the artificial creation of man — the architect. He views it as a room or open-air receiving hall which, instead of being furnished with objects of wood and fabric, is furnished with objects of cut stone and living plants. Suitable for this type of garden are plants that rapidly attain the desired shape and keep it for as long as possible. Best for such a garden is a bed of polyantha roses, begonias or salvias in a lawn. Perennials are not at all suitable for growing in a lawn.

The second type of scheme respects nature and its aim is to mirror nature. Within the small space at his disposal the gardener wishes to have all that he admires in nature — diversity of shape and colour as well as pleasing patterns and blendings, changes during the day as well as from season to season. Their

Lysimachia punctata can be recommended particularly for larger gardens. It is undemanding and almost indestructible, and suitable for semi-shaded to shaded places. It looks excellent if planted close to water. Here it is combined with the day-lily *Hemerocallis fulva*.

A group of woody plants and perennials here offsets the attractively flowering annual *Salvia splendens* and enclose a large sculpture-like boulder at the edge of a lawn.

roses that flower poorly in the damp English climate. They were planted in long, regular borders, as was also the custom with roses and annuals. All maritime countries with a similar climate soon followed suit. However, perennials are of an entirely different nature. That is also the reason why in countries with a warm and sunny summer which suits roses and annuals, the use of perennials did not become widespread until gardeners worked out how to make the most of their typical characteristics.

wealth of species and varieties makes perennials a must in a garden of this kind.

In practice, of course, one does not come across just these two distinct types of gardens, but with all manner of inbetween types. Nevertheless, these principles should be kept in mind when deciding whether to plant perennials and, if so, what kind.

The most difficult to design a layout for is also the most common: a small, regularly-shaped plot on level ground dominated by a house that also has a regular groundplan. In such a place, where geometric shapes predominate, it is not possible to create the

298

Perennials have a large variety of uses. They can be planted singly, combined with woody plants, biennials, annuals or bulbs and tubers, in beds as well as in various containers.

Stachys byzantina (S. lanata) is suitable for covering large spaces in dry, sunny situations. In such conditions its furry leaves remain fresh and attractively coloured from spring to autumn.

illusion of natural surroundings. One must opt rather for stylization.

Divide the garden up as little as possible and when doing so use simple geometrical shapes but in an asymmetrical pattern. In particular, the most important elements such as the main path leading to the house, the area round the entrance, a sitting-out place, the principal tree or group of woody plants, a pool, must be arranged asymmetrically. This arrangement, however, must create the impression of utmost usefulness.

For a garden of this kind, it is possible to choose a flower layout of both types — depending on what

the gardener prefers. Under no circumstances, however, should the two types be combined. If you want both types of layout in one and the same garden then they can be used only if kept in quite separate areas, each out of view of the other one.

From spring till autumn

Perennials brighten the garden with flowers throughout the growing season including, as they do, species that flower in early spring (*Helleborus, Eranthis*), species that flower until late in the autumn (*Aster, Chrysanthemum*) and species that are decorative

Hemerocallis hybrida 'Burning Daylight' is one of the lower cultivars. Attaining 60 cm in height, it has a nice, shapely growth and its deep orange flowers with a soft brown-red tinge decorate the bed from June to July.

Spring-flowering perennials, framed by a group of woody plants and accented by the fresh greenery of the lawn, decorate a sitting-out corner close to a house. Particularly nice is the yellow *Alyssum saxatile* 'Compactum' and the red and pink flowers of *Phlox subulata*.

A hedge forming a background to a group of tall perennials — the blue delphiniums match with the red-flowering *Phlox paniculata* and the white lilies. Ornamental grasses and *Limonium latifolium* supplement the group.

Campanula glomerata, with dark blue-purple flowers, and *Lysimachia punctata* with flowers coloured golden-yellow, are two undemanding perennials suitable for all types of garden soil.

even in winter (grasses and evergreen species such as *Iberis, Sempervivum, Sedum*).

A well-planted and tended bed will last five years and often even longer without transplanting. Its aspect will change continually during the course of the year, making it a living calendar of the seasons. Perennials may be planted also in shaded or otherwise less congenial positions. If necessary, it is possible to make a grouping of perennials that do not need watering, except in a definitely dry year.

As a rule, however, a single species of perennial flowers lasts for only 3—4 weeks. Therefore, if you want to have flowers the whole growing season you must plant at least seven species that will flower in succession. This means that for every clump in full bloom there should always be 1—2 clumps that are beginning or finishing flowering and 4—5 clumps without flowers, that is, with flowers completely spent or just beginning to put out buds. This proportion may be improved somewhat if you use species with recurrent bloom. Many perennials have orna-

mental foliage (for instance, *Astilbe, Hemerocallis, Pulmonaria*) so that they are decorative even when not in bloom. However, it must be kept in mind that a group of perennials never bears such a profusion of flowers and never forms such a compact expanse as do roses or carpeting plants.

Much, therefore, depends on the correct selection of species and cultivars and on their correct grouping. In tending the plants, it is also necessary to keep in mind the requirements of the individual species and provide for their separate needs. During the first year after planting perennials require particular care.

Rules for siting perennials

If, for aesthetic and practical reasons, you decide to have perennials in your garden you are then faced

A mixed group of conifers, grasses and perennials, dominated by a large flowering tuft of *Sedum telephium* 'Herbstfreude' decorates the rear view of a house.

with having to decide on the shape and size of the bed and where to site it. The beds should be wide enough to hold at least three or, better still, four rows of perennials. As to outline, angled beds are preferable to rectangular shapes or simple curves. Long straight beds, if there must be such, should be interrupted by clumps of species of irregular, spreading habit.

Perennials should be placed either in a spot where the individual plants can be observed close up and in detail, for example, next to a sitting-out area, or so that the layout can be perceived in its entirety; in other words, where it can be viewed through the living room window or from the patio.

Always remember to have several permanent elements that will form a framework for the whole grouping. In the case of smaller groups it is sufficient to have such a framework only at the back; larger groups must have such fixed points directly in the bed. As a rule, such stable elements are trees and shrubs. Evergreen species make the grouping decorative in winter, deciduous species add to the colour effect twofold — during the flowering period with their blossoms and in the autumn with their colourful foliage. The background framework may also be a house, a dense hedge or small garden building, and fixed points in a bed may be a group of small rocks or a garden sculpture.

Plants in a grouping of perennials should always be placed irregularly but this does not mean that their placing should be unplanned. If the bed is to create a pleasing effect it is necessary to observe certain rules in planning its layout.

Perhaps the most important rule is that the most striking element should never be placed in the centre but always slightly to the side, best of all to within about one-third of the length and one-third of the depth of the bed. On the opposite side, this dominant element must then be balanced by a similar but less dominant element. For example, when using the same species and cultivar put a group of 5—6 plants on one side and only 2—3 plants on the opposite side. Or when putting a vigorous, brightly coloured cultivar on one side place a smaller and more delicately coloured one on the opposite side. You may also use two species of like aspect but different size (such as *Aster novi-belgii* and *Aster dumosus*).

If the bed is wide, balance three similar elements, putting the most striking on one side, the lesser element on the opposite side and the least notable of the three at the front of the bed, slightly off centre. In this case, however, it is not enough to plant a different number of specimens or different cultivars in each of the three places; you must combine various different species (for example, *Heliopsis, Rudbeckia fulgida* and *Oenothera missouriensis*).

If the bed is long divide it into shorter sections: work out a suitable grouping for one section and then repeat this grouping in several different sections, like links in a chain. In such a section you can also put the elements behind one another in the following order: striking, less so, least so. These elements should not be put in a single line nor with the same spacing but should be positioned so as to exploit the whole width of the bed. The aim is to have the same, irregular grouping repeated regularly, thereby obtaining a rhythmic arrangement.

The most important, that is, the determining element of the grouping cannot be just any plant. It must be a tall species that will thrive in the given location, flower profusely and for a long period and be brightly coloured. When planning your bed, first of all decide where you will put these determinative plants.

Sedum spectabile 'Brillant' is an excellent houseleek with greygreen succulent leaves and an immense abundance of carminepink flowers arranged in umbels. It is a strong grower, is very hardy and can be recommended for solitary planting, for borders and for groups with ornamental woody plants.

Veronica spicata 'Blaubart', an undemanding perennial for sunny situations, looks best in larger groups, in rock gardens or in the company of other perennial species. It needs a normal, permeable soil.

Monarda didyma 'Cambridge Scarlet', a relatively tall, decorative and profusely flowering perennial, is suitable for mixed groups in informal gardens, for planting in front of ornamental shrubs and for cutting.

Primroses are among the most favourite and commonly grown perennials. The earliest species start flowering at the very beginning of spring while others decorate the garden with their rich variety of colourful flowers throughout the whole of spring.

Perennials are particularly important for planting in informal natural-style gardens. Low-growing species are used for covering the ground and taller, attractive ones are then planted, singly or in small groups, among them.

Semi-shaded places can be enlivened with carefully chosen perennials and woody plants that not only tolerate shade but even do better in it. These are predominantly species growing under tall broadleaved trees in the wild. Most of them open their flowers before the trees start into leaf.

Because dominant perennials naturally flower for only part of the year you must choose suitable plants to take their place, chiefly for the remaining weeks of summer and autumn. They may be species that are entirely different in aspect and colour and even non-flowering plants or ones with insignificant flowers, such as tall grasses. These plants are the next to be placed in the plan.

After these comes the selection and placing of the plants that are to round out the arrangement. They must flower at the same time as the dominant species or at the same time as the second group but must be lower and less prominent and their colours must blend well with the general colour scheme.

The remaining space in the bed is then filled with perennials that flower at a different time to the dominant and complementary species. Here, it is important to fill not only the space but above all the whole time period you want to have flowers and also to choose species that together will form pleasing colour combinations.

It is also necessary to keep in mind that many perennials that flower in spring or early summer have unattractive foliage or die back after the flowers have faded. It is better to place such species in the rear part of the bed and ones that keep their attractive foliage until the autumn in the front.

Last of all, put in plants that add variety to the scheme. These include first and foremost various bulbs. Put smaller bulbs, such as tulips, between autumn-flowering perennials. Variety can also be added to the bed by plants of striking habit, for example *Liatris, Platycodon, Eryngium* and grasses such as *Molinia* and *Pennisetum*.

The mixed border
The various species of perennials planted in a border, which in substance is a long narrow bed of regular outline, should be selected so they form a pleasing display, a harmonious blend of colour and size.

Instead of the conventional compact borders with plants staggered precisely according to height, nowadays emphasis is placed on looser, less structured arrangements. Taller species of attractive habit and foliage are now often placed in the front, that is, amid shorter species. Contrariwise, some profusely flowering shorter species are planted so that, in the form of rather large, irregular 'spills', they invade ground occupied by tall perennials. In the same way, certain species of solitary character when placed in a border create an individual effect with their pleasing shape and distinctive features. Also effective in such a border are perennials with less attractive flowers but with pleasing foliage or distinctive habit, such as ornamental grasses.

Such borders are a kind of stepping-stone to unstructured perennial groupings. They are particularly effective against a dark backing of shrubs or against the light backdrop of a wall or building.

Before laying out a border by a hedge it is necessary to make sure that the roots of the shrubs do not penetrate into the border for this would hamper the growth of the perennials. It is a good idea to sep-

Doronicum columnae is one of the most favourite early-flowering perennials. It is particularly suited for borders, mixed perennial groups and for planting in front of dark green conifers. The flowers are also excellent in a vase. It does best in slightly damp places shaded in summer by broadleaved trees.

Trollius × cultorum is a multipurpose plant suitable for informal gardens, for the margins of brooks and pools, for borders and perennial groups. Recently cultivated varieties with large flowers can be used for cutting.

arate the border from the hedge by inserting a strip of metal or fibreboard to a depth of at least 50 cm.

The low border

Borders are of different types according to the kind and the arrangement of the perennials planted there, namely low borders consisting chiefly of shorter species of perennials and tall borders comprised of taller species. The type generally used are one-sided borders that are to be viewed from one side only and are hence arranged accordingly. In some instances, however, it is possible to have a two-sided border planted to provide a pleasing view from both sides.

Borders consisting of shorter perennials have many uses in the garden. If, for example, dry walls are used in the garden to solve small height differences in the terrain these may be topped by low borders of flowering plants that serve as an ornamental

Papaver orientale is a gem among perennial groups and borders, thanks to its large, bright red flowers. If given a good, nourishing soil and a sunny situation it will remain for years without any special care. It is also good for solitary planting and for mixed groups together with irises (*Iris × barbata*), lupins, delphiniums and sages (*Salvia nemorosa*).

Delphiniums are among the most beautiful of the blue-flowering perennials. They are particularly attractive in well-kept gardens, planted either alone or as a dominant feature in mixed perennial groups. Their wonderfully coloured flowers also look good in a vase. It is recommended that you plant them in loose groups composed of several differently coloured varieties, but their combination with roses is excellent, too.

supplement, heightening their colourfulness. Low borders may also be used alongside paths, particularly paved ones, and beside regularly shaped sitting-out places and patios. Low borders are also sometimes laid out alongside a fence separating the garden from a public road if it is desired to create a feeling of spaciousness, this being welcomed particularly in the case of a rather narrow front garden.

In the low border are planted short, cushion-like or prostrate perennials and species no taller than 40—50 cm. These include many bulbs and tubers and some low-growing broadleaved and coniferous woody plants. Ornamental grasses, groups of which are a lovely addition to the low border, can similarly be used here.

Most short and prostrate perennials flower in spring so it is no problem to plan a border that will be a riot of colour at this time of the year. However, the task of providing for colourful hues in summer and autumn is more difficult. Nevertheless, there are species that flower even then and therefore these must not be overlooked.

Their number includes, for example, *Oenothera missouriensis, Silene schafta, Viola cornuta, Papaver nudicaule, Gaillardia grandiflora* 'Kobold', *Prunella, Nepeta × faassenii, Campanula poscharskyana, Dianthus, Lavandula, Veronica*, and others. For late summer and autumn, it is also possible to use various species of *Sedum, Calluna, Aster dumosus, Colchicum* and autumn crocus. One way or the other, of the spring species try to choose those that have attractive foliage, so they remain a decorative element even after their flowers have faded. Particularly good for this purpose are grasses, dwarf conifers and other evergreen shrubs.

Clusters of bulbs should be planted as far as possible among plants that begin growth late and have roots that are rather deep and not too invasive, for example *Oenothera missouriensis, Gypsophila repens, Brunnera, Incarvillea* and *Platycodon*. Bulbs fill spaces that otherwise would be empty of growth in spring, the perennials planted there growing up in their stead after the bulbs have finished flowering and have died back. Keep a note of what is planted so you do not accidentally dig them up.

In the low border always put several plants of the same species together to form a harmonious blend of colours. Short perennials are generally planted in groups of at least 3—5; bulbs should similarly be planted in groups of at least 7—10 of one species.

The principal low perennials for partial shade are the primulas, which flower from early spring until the beginning of summer. The first to bloom, often as early as March, is *Primula rosea*, followed by *P. vulgaris, P. denticulata*, and *P. elatior*. Those that

Ligularia × hessei is a robust, very decorative perennial for solitary planting. It is particularly effective in informal garden sections in the vicinity of water. Both its flowers and leaves are ornamental and it is therefore better not to form too large groups of this species. It can last for more than 10 years without transplanting if the soil is sufficiently moist and rich in humus.

bloom from June until the beginning of July include *P. japonica, P. bulleyana, P. × bullesiana* and others. And at the summer's peak, *P. florindae* brightens the scene with its yellow blossoms.

In summer, the main colour in the perennial border is provided by the various species and varieties of *Astilbe*.

Partially shaded locations are also suitable for *Anemone, Bergenia, Brunnera macrophylla, Hacquetia, Helleborus, Hepatica nobilis, Hosta, Polygonatum, Omphalodes, Pulmonaria* as well as the grasses *Luzula* and *Carex morrowii* and various ferns.

The tall border

Borders of taller perennials are generally placed in front of a backing of some kind or are used to separate the ornamental area of the garden from a less ornamental one.

Medium-tall and taller perennials generally flower in late spring, summer and autumn — unlike short perennials, which flower chiefly in very early spring and spring. The selection of earlier-flowering, medium-tall perennials is relatively limited; it includes mainly *Doronicum, Dicentra*, and *Trollius* and several other species. The colour provided by this sparse se-

Chrysanthemum maximum is a characteristic plant of country gardens. However, it is equally indispensable for modern-style gardens, being particularly attractive if grown close to plants with differently coloured flowers. Its flowering lasts from June to August, according to the variety.

Paeonia lactiflora is a beautiful, much-grown, hardy perennial bearing a profusion of flowers and decorative leaves. It can be recommended for both small and large gardens and the cut flowers last relatively long in the vase. Single-flowered varieties are nice in informal gardens and close by woody plants. Double-flowered plants are best for solitary planting in lawns.

lection is also very limited. Here, however, bulbs can come to our aid. The colour gap in spring can be filled by tulips, though these die back after flowering and cannot be left in place for several years. They are not perennials in the true meaning of the term but are worth making use of for their colourfulness. They should be planted out in groups of 15—20, in several places, and after they have finished flowering and died back should be lifted for storing and the resulting empty spaces filled in by annuals.

Empty spaces in perennial borders, however, may also be left by perennials that die back after flowering; for example, *Papaver orientale,* commonly plant-

Perennials are as important in front gardens as are some of the broadleaved and coniferous woody plants. However, the usually small size of such plots determines both the choice and quantity of plants that can be used. Crammed front gardens are not attractive, as dense greenery suppresses not only their architecture but also the beauty of the individual plants.

Acanthus spinosus is interesting for its leaves and attractive inflorescences. It is grown either singly in large rock and heather gardens or in large groups in informal gardens, particularly among ornamental grasses and other suitable perennials.

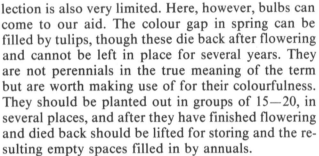

Achillea filipendulina 'Golden Plate' is a tall perennial that forms tufts of sparsely-leafed stems. Numerous small flowers are arranged in dense inflorescences, their deep yellow colour being most attractive against a background of dark conifers.

Front gardens that are in sun for a good part of the day offer more of the colourful beauty of flowers than the shaded ones. Besides the queens among flowers — roses — and many annuals, they can be brightened, particularly in spring, by various perennials, bulbs and tubers.

ed for its vivid colour. This problem may be resolved by putting in front of such species plants that begin growth later and do not reach full size or bear flowers until summer. Examples are *Rudbeckia, Heliopsis* and taller *Phlox paniculata.*

Rules for planting borders

Perennials suitable for the border may be roughly divided into three categories. The first includes taller, more vigorous perennials that are put out singly, as solitary specimens that capture the gaze of the observer and add interest to the arrangement. These may be flowering or foliage only plants and include *Ligularia, Eremurus, Dictamnus, Miscanthus* and *Yucca*.

The second group comprises species that are used for their profuse flowering and bright colours to form the main colour pattern in the layout of the border. They should be planted in larger groupings for massed colour and so that their colours blend to form a pleasing whole. Their number includes *Lupinus, Chrysanthemum, Paeonia, Doronicum, Heliopsis, Rudbeckia, Phlox paniculata, Solidago* and *Aster*. These profusely flowering species are then supplemented by fill-in perennials of the third group, according to personal choice.

When planting borders, correct spacing is most important. Gardeners often make the mistake of planting certain species too close together and when they are fully grown the plants are then too crowded and cannot show themselves in their full beauty. Correctly spaced plants should cover the allotted ground without any large gaps after the first growing season; however, they should not be too crowded.

In tall borders, there should be 3—4 plants to a square metre, sometimes even less, whereas in low borders the same space should be occupied by 9—12 plants. Low borders may be only 70—100 cm wide, whereas borders of taller perennials must be at least 1.2—2 m wide.

When planting the border you must naturally also place plants so that the colours of adjoining groups harmonize and form pleasing colour contrasts when in flower. For example, blue perennials can be combined with yellow, red perennials with white or yellow ones, and so on. When planning such layouts, also keep in mind that the various species must flower at the same time in order to obtain the desired effect. In addition to this, it is necessary that the soil and light requirements of the selected perennials be more or less the same. If you want to have a pleasing arrangement then you must know something about the characteristics and requirements of the plants. There are countless possible combinations and there is no specific blueprint, even though good examples will facilitate the gardener's task. No two gardens are

The tall *Phlox paniculata* is a favourite, undemanding perennial with beautifully coloured flowers.

307

Coreopsis grandiflora has a particularly long flowering period and its flowers also last long in a vase. It needs a sunny situation and a nourishing, slightly moist soil. It is recommended for borders and mixed perennial groups.

alike; each differs in some way — be it the location, exposure, soil conditions or light conditions. You will be aided in your choice by the list of perennials on pages 326—329 which includes helpful information such as the period of flowering, the colour of the flowers, the height of the plants and their most important requirements.

Perennials planted in borders generally require good soil. This is only natural when you consider that in the main they are selectively bred varieties of tall, vigorous species and their roots must provide

Phlox paniculata can be used in many different ways. Its tall stems and attractively coloured flowers make it a good solitary feature, but it looks equally well in large or small single-species or mixed groups. Even planting in rows is possible, or in carpets of low-growing perennials where they produce a contrasting effect.

for the nourishment of massive above-ground parts and a profusion of blooms. For this reason, not only is it necessary to prepare the site and improve the fertility of the soil before planting, it is also necessary to provide the plants with regular applications of fertilizer in the ensuing years.

Also important is the life-span of individual species. As a rule, it is the species with a shorter life-span that generally bear profuse and long-lasting flowers but they are soon finished and need to be replaced by new plants.

Informal, unstructured perennial groupings

Informal perennial groupings have much in common with the informal, unstructured type of border, but differ from the latter in that they do not have regular contours and include fewer cultivated varieties and more type species. This manner of using perennials in the garden corresponds to the informal arrangement of the larger garden, where the paths are not

Achillea ptarmica 'The Pearl' is a long-cultivated plant suitable for mixed perennial groups, where its white flowers act as a neutral, unifying element. The long-lasting flowers can be used for cutting.

laid out in straight lines but in irregular curves, making such informal groupings of flowers better suited to the general layout than the regular border.

The principal aspects of such a grouping are an irregular outline and manner of planting, consisting of a ground cover of prostrate and short perennials in which are placed groups of medium-tall and taller perennials for height — to create a pleasingly spatial arrangement. Such an arrangement has a light and airy effect. Perennials for this purpose must be selected with care in order to make the utmost use not only of the beauty of the flowers but also of the plant's entire habit.

In informal, unstructured perennial groupings, utmost use is made of species with attractive foliage that are decorative not only during the flowering period but at other times as well. Examples are *Stachys olympica, Acaena,* various species of *Sedum* and *Ajuga.* Wide use can also be made of bulbs, particularly of botanical tulips and narcissi, as well as most small bulbs that can serve to brighten the carpet of shallowly rooting prostrate plants and will not leave behind empty spaces when they die back.

Very important in informal perennial groupings are the ornamental grasses. The low-growing types, such as fescue, can be used to cover various irregularly-shaped spaces, together with the prostrate perennials. Medium-tall grasses, such as *Avena, Deschampsia, Pennisetum* and the like, can be planted in small groups amid the prostrate plants. Taller grasses such as *Miscanthus, Spartina* and *Cortaderia* are planted as solitary specimens, in the same manner as taller perennials.

The groupings may be augmented also by trees and shrubs (dwarf spruce, Mountain Pine, juniper, and of the broadleaved species, cotoneaster, shrubby potentilla, barberry, ornamental quince etc.).

Such groupings may be of any shape or size. Here, too, it is important to know something about the plants so as to combine species that go well together and will thrive in the given conditions.

In the garden, informal perennial groupings may be put in a great variety of places, in sunny positions as well as in shade. In the front garden, where there is little space, it is best to use shorter species and dwarf trees and shrubs. Such a grouping is very attractive if backed by a group of darker shrubs, either broadleaved or coniferous, which serve as a foil for the perennials, and a very pleasing effect is produced if the group of perennials is set off by a green expanse of lawn in front. Paths, best of all of natural stone, should be laid in gently curving lines near these groupings or straight through them. Another suitable location for informal flower groupings is by a sitting-out place, or beside a pool. Here the selection of species should correspond to the given site and should consist of ones that go well with the water. Last, but not least, such informal groupings may also be placed by the house.

Large groupings

In a way, large informal groupings with mass displays of flowers are analogous to the mixed border but are of irregular outline and, applying the design principles for the layout of informal perennial groupings, mainly those species of perennials that bear profuse and striking blooms are planted here. In these sections, a bright and varied display of colour is the main criterion. This can be employed only in a larger garden as such sections must be at least 2—3 m wide. The individual species should be in groups of at least 15—20 plants, to create the desired impact of a mass display of blooms. Also, such a large grouping should be set off by a large expanse of lawn which will underscore the colour arrangement of the flowers. Depending on the size of the

Chrysanthemum maximum is the leading representative of the so-called 'daisy-flowered' perennials. Modern varieties, bearing profusions of pure white single or double flowers, reach a height of 50—100 cm. Cut flowers last extremely well in a vase. It needs a well-fertilized, permeable soil and full sun for good growth.

floral grouping, there should be at least 8—10 m of lawn, and in the case of larger groupings preferably even more.

Mass groupings must also have a good height arrangement so that the separate species can all be seen; an interesting spatial layout will also add to the pleasing effect of the whole. Shorter species should naturally be placed at the front. Plants that are prostrate should not be used because their effect when viewed from a distance is negligible.

The plants mainly used in such a grouping are

profusely flowering species such as *Paeonia, Papaver orientale, Delphinium, Lupinus, Lychnis chalcedonica, Monarda didyma, Coreopsis verticillata, Helenium, Chrysanthemum maximum*, tall species of *Achillea, Phlox paniculata*, autumn species of *Aster, Solidago, Rudbeckia* and *Chrysanthemum × hortorum*. One thing about this selection, however, is that the main flowering period of these plants is from late spring until autumn, which leaves the early spring period devoid of bloom. Tulips are recommended for providing colour at this time of the year.

Perennials for cutting

The keeping qualities of cut flowers differ and depend on many circumstances. Important factors are: the stage of the flower's development, the weather at the time of cutting, the temperature and humidity in the place where the flowers are stored, and the freshness of the water in the container. Most important, however, is the plant species. Frequently, various species of the same genus behave differently. For example, *Rudbeckia nitida* and *R.* 'Gloriosa Daisy' have very long-lasting flowers which, under good conditions, will last 1—2 weeks, sometimes even longer; on the other hand, *Rudbeckia fulgida* will last no longer than 3—4 days.

Species with good keeping qualities, whose flowers will last at least 5—7 days in a vase, include for example *Achillea filipendulina, Chrysanthemum coccineum, C. maximum, C. indicum, Convallaria majalis, Doronicum, Erigeron × hybridus, Eryngium alpinum, Gaillardia aristata, Gypsophila paniculata, Heliopsis scabra, Liatris spicata, Linum, Limonium, Paeonia lactiflora* and *Scabiosa caucasica*.

Goldenrod (*Solidago*) is an indispensable feature of autumn borders. Modern taller varieties are usually planted at the back of mixed perennial beds and in front of deciduous woody species which change the colour of their leaves in the autumn.

Iris pallida 'Variegata', like most other irises, is usually grown in perennial beds and groups. This cultivar with ornamental leaves and pleasantly fragrant flowers can be used even for solitary planting. All irises prefer a sandy-humusy, non-acid soil and a sunny situation.

Other species will last 3—5 days in a vase under normal conditions. Some species with long racemose clusters are excellent for short-term decoration in a large vase. Examples are *Delphinium, Eremurus, Digitalis* and *Lupinus*.

Perennials that can be dried and used for winter decoration include *Achillea filipendulina, Eryngium, Gypsophila paniculata, Leontopodium alpinum, Physalis, Limonium tataricum, L. latifolium, Liatris spicata* and *Solidago*. The flowers of certain grasses can be dried and used for indoor decoration.

Specimen perennials

Solitary specimens are used in the garden to attract notice because of their important features. They are planted singly or in small groups, either by themselves in the lawn or as a part of a group of other plants but always so that they are somehow conspicuous. However, they need not always be plants of large size. For example, a small group of the grass *Helictotrichon sempervirens*, set off by a flat grouping of prostrate plants, has the effect of a solitary specimen. Specimen perennials have an important place in modern gardens with their informal perennial groupings.

Sites for solitary plants in the garden should be chosen so that such specimens underscore the general effect of the layout. Larger specimens, for example, are placed by the house entrance or by steps, on patios, by a sitting-out place, beside a pergola or freely in the lawn.

The selection of perennials affords and ample number of species suitable for use as solitary specimens. Larger specimens include *Aruncus dioicus, Astilboides tabularis, Crambe cordifolia, Eremurus robustus, Helianthus salicifolius, Heracleum laciniatum, Ligularia dentata, Macleaya cordata, Phytolacca americana, Rheum palmatum, Rodgersia aesculifolia, Rudbeckia nitida* and *Verbascum olympicum*.

Solitary specimens of medium height include *Acanthus longifolius, Achillea filipendulina, Aconitum fischeri, Centaurea macrocephala, Dictamnus albus, Echinops ritro, Hemerocallis hybrida, Kniphofia hybrida* and *Yucca filamentosa*.

Prime sites for garden perennials

Perennials can also be used with success in certain special sections of the garden which are brightened by their colour and/or fragrance or whose natural aspect is underscored by their presence.

First and foremost they are of value in the heath garden, where some perennials can be used to great advantage amid the irregular expanse of heaths and heathers. Examples are *Antennaria dioica, Aster linosyris, Carlina acaulis, Dianthus arenarius, D. deltoides, Filipendula hexapetala, Hieracium, Lotus*

Verbascum thapsus is, in fact, a biennial but it is often grown with perennials, particularly in country gardens and in informal garden arrangements. Up to 2 m tall, this plant bears an abundance of yellow flowers arranged in long racemes. Since time immemorial it has been cultivated as a medicinal plant.

The very decorative *Yucca filamentosa* is planted in large rock gardens, in borders, beds and singly in lawns, but group planting is also possible. The large, white bell-shaped flowers arranged in racemes open on tall woody stems and the narrow, sword-shaped leaves have a bluish tinge.

corniculatus, Thymus serpyllum and *Veronica prostrata*.

In dry, warm situations you can create very effective plantings among characteristic trees and shrubs, close to freely-placed rocks, by using groups of certain grasses along with clumps of *Acantholimon, Lavandula, Marrubium, Anthemis* and *Sedum*.

In the steppe garden, with layout analogous to that of the heath garden but incorporating steppe plants that generally require neutral soil, you can put grasses and also many other perennials. Grasses form the basis of the layout and can be supplemented by perennials such as *Yucca filamentosa, Lavandula, Pulsatilla grandis, Adonis, Iris, Eryngium, Echinops, Euphorbia polychroma, Aster linosyris, Filipendula hexapetala, Sedum spectabile, S. telephium* and *Inula ensifolia*.

Perennial edgings, used only in small measure in modern gardens, must fulfil certain important requirements. They must first and foremost be of compact habit and their sideways growth should not be too vigorous so it will not require too much effort to keep them within bounds. Furthermore, besides having decorative flowers they must also have attractive foliage and be of pleasing habit. Examples are *Armeria maritima, Euphorbia polychroma, Lavandula angustifolia* and *Veronica teucrium.*

A section that is becoming increasingly important and popular in the garden is the garden pool. The aquatic plants that are grown in the water have a special character of their own, one that differs from most other perennials. Therefore, if you wish to put out plants by the poolside you must select ones that are similar in kind, for example *Astilbe, Filipendula, Iris, Ligularia, Lysimachia, Rodgersia, Tradescantia, Hemerocallis hybrida* and *Kniphofia hybrida.*

Preparing the soil

If you have prepared a plan for placing perennials in your garden then mark out the various sites and prepare the soil before planting. Preparing the soil is important even for those perennials that are often listed as being undemanding. First and foremost, preparing the soil involves thorough loosening and weeding.

Iris intermedia 'Frithjof'. Irises from this group start flowering when the low-growing varieties have finished and before the beginning of the flowering period of the tall varieties of the *Iris × barbata* group. Besides late-flowering tulips, they are the first large-flowered spring perennials to be used for cutting.

Euphorbia polychroma is a veritable gem of every spring rock garden. It is equally suitable for growing in front of ornamental shrubs and, in autumn schemes, next to perennial asters. The leaves are the most ornamental feature of this plant; flowers are quite inconspicuous, except for the bright yellow perianths. The picture shows the fresh green *Euphorbia* leaves contrasting effectively with the white-felted, silvery-green leaves of *Stachys olympica.*

Loosening the soil

The soil where perennials are to be planted must first be thoroughly dug over. If it is covered with grass, then the layer of turves must first be removed. Turves may be dug in only if the perennials are to be planted at least one season later, to give turves buried in the soil time to break up and rot. Single digging to the depth of a spade — say 30 cm — is sufficient for most perennials. However, some require deep soil and for these deeper digging is advisable. For most short, prostrate perennials, on the other hand, a depth of 20 cm is sufficient.

Eliminating weeds

The most important task in preparing the soil for perennials is thorough weeding, one of the main prerequisites for success. Weeds that spread by means of underground rhizomes are a great nuisance — most often these are Couch Grass, Ground Elder, Mare's Tail, Creeping Thistle, Coltsfoot, Creeping Yellow Cress and Creeping Buttercup.

All have the same property — if a bit of the rhizome is left in the ground undisturbed, after a while the weed spreads just as vigorously as before.

Particularly troublesome are weeds that root and have rhizomes deeper than it is possible to dig. Examples are Coltsfoot, Creeping Thistle and Mare's Tail. Field Bindweed is also a great nuisance because, even though it does not have rhizomes, its roots reach so deep that they cannot be extracted mechanically. Perennial weeds of this category cannot be destroyed by digging and even the most careful removal of roots from the soil. On plots pervaded by these types of weeds it is best not to plant perennials at all. However, if you have no other choice the only possibility is to postpone the planting until the following year and devote one entire growing season to extermination of the perennial weeds. During this time, dig or fork over the soil frequently. If the

Tradescantia × andersoniana 'Zwanenburg Blue' bears throughout the summer profusions of flowers which open in the morning and close towards noon. It is suitable for large rockeries, borders and beds, in the company of medium-tall perennials. Individual varieties bear flowers of different shades, particularly nice being the sky-blue ones.

Aquatic and bog plants enrich the choice of cultivated garden flowers by a variety of shapes and colours. Many nice perennials typical of aquatic environments can be grown in the neighbourhood of water — such as the illustrated *Trollius*, which flowers in May and June.

weeds are not allowed to grow green parts the whole season, generally they will not survive. Only bindweed has such great vitality that it will survive even such intensive measures.

It is best to avoid chemical agents for destroying weeds, particularly agents that have lengthier residual effects. It is always better to rely on mechanical means and patience.

Soil that has been prepared a year before planting the perennials gives the gardener the chance of spotting weeds that were bypassed when digging and getting rid of them subsequently. If the plot is infested with perennial weeds usually they will not be eradicated by a single digging, be it ever so thorough. It is then difficult to get rid of such weeds once the perennials are growing and generally the bed or border becomes an untidy, weed-filled site.

Annual weeds are not such a nuisance, though they are often quite troublesome. Every soil contains the seeds of weeds that will germinate in congenial conditions. These are mainly Common Chickweed, Ragwort, Gallant Soldier and Annual Meadowgrass. These are kept in check by digging mainly during the growing season and best of all in dry weather. Soil that has been prepared a year beforehand is good for getting rid of annual weeds as well.

Improving the soil

Preparing the soil includes not only digging and eliminating weeds but also improving its properties. Here, however, there is no general rule. It is necessary to consider first and foremost the requirements of the species that are to be planted there. If the soil is good garden soil, that is, loose, well-draining, rich in humus and loamy-sandy, it will generally not need much attention because such soil is suitable for most perennial plants.

If the soil is a heavy, clay type that is not well-draining then it must be improved, primarily by the addition of humus to make it lighter and richer. Heavy soil should be dug to a good depth, at the same time incorporating peat, sand, ash and well-rotted compost. It is recommended that you then leave the dug soil in rough clods over the winter to provide maximum exposure to frost, sprinkling it with ashes during that time, then digging it again in spring and working it with an aerator or cutter. Sandy soil that is too light should be improved by the addition of peat, well-rotted compost or some heavier soil. Shallow, stony soil should be made deeper if possible, the stones removed, and peat, compost or woodland humus (leaf mould) added to improve its quality.

Knowing the soil requirements of the individual species of perennials is another prerequisite of success. It is not always necessary to improve the soil as some species will actually do better if it is not. In the case of such species, improving the soil will make them less attractive or shorten their life-span. For instance, the grass *Helictotrichon sempervirens* does very well in dry, sandy, rather poor soil. If fertilizer is added to the soil and it is provided with ample moisture it will grow vigorously the first year but will begin to decline in the ensuing years until it eventually dies.

Feeding

In ground where species that require rich nourishing soil are to be planted it will be necessary to incorporate plenty of organic matter and to apply additional feed in the ensuing years. Before planting never use fresh farmyard manure or artificial fertilizers that will burn the young, newly emerging roots. Instead, always use only good, well-rotted, nourishing compost. You may also use various slow-acting organic fertilizers such as horn and bone meal.

As soon as the plants are established (rooted) you can apply artificial fertilizers, best of all by spraying them with a liquid solution of compound fertilizer.

313

Some species, and even whole groups of perennials, have specific likes and dislikes with regard to soil acidity, and these requirements must also be respected if the plants are to be grown with success. This applies chiefly to the calcifugous or lime-hating species, for those that are happy in soils containing lime will generally thrive in neutral soil whereas calcifugous plants need an acid soil for good growth.

If the soil is alkaline it must be prepared accordingly if you want to grow calcifugous plants. Best of all, however, is to remove and replace it. Remove the soil in the given site to a depth of at least 25—30 cm and in its place put a mixture of peat, woodland humus, leaf mould and sand. Such a mixture is neutral or slightly acid but usually poor in nutrients, so an application of feed is required. For heath plants the mixture should contain a greater amount of sand.

If the soil is neutral, your task is easier. For heath

When bulbs have finished flowering, carpeting and clump-forming perennials take their turn. Their green mass covers the empty places and furthermore, they produce numerous flowers. The white-flowering *Arabis procurrens* and the yellow *Alyssum saxatile* 'Compactum' contrast beautifully with the nearby dark conifers.

plants incorporating sand and peat will suffice. For lime-loving plants, add pulverized limestone or even some old plaster.

For plants that like humus-rich soil add peat, leaf mould, frame soil, possibly also good compost. Peat is the most important material of all for improving the soil. It makes heavy soils lighter and improves the drainage, and in light soils it improves the moisture-retention properties. It is immensely water- and food-retentive and so peat is a very good admixture as well as substitute for compost when this is occasionally hard to come by.

Modern varieties of the columbine (*Aquilegia*) are robust, graceful plants bearing flowers in a wide range of colours. They reach a height of 60—80 cm and flower in May—June. They should be planted in small groups with other adequately tall perennials, best in borders or beds along paths so that the beauty of their flowers can be admired at a close distance. The flowers can be used for cutting but they will not last very long.

Papaver orientale is most appreciated for the conspicuous red colour of its flowers, which is otherwise quite rare in the garden before the roses start to bloom. Not only fiery red, but also scarlet, brick-red, salmon-red, pink, or even pure white varieties with a dark centre are available nowadays. They are all very decorative and deserve much interest.

Sedum spectabile 'Brillant' is an undemanding, modest succulent needing very little special care. It is decorative by its leaves as well as flowers, which open at the end of summer and the beginning of autumn.

Hosta undulata 'Medio-Variegata', a modest perennial suitable for semi-shaded and shaded situations, has handsome, undulated, white-variegated leaves and lilac-coloured, six-petalled, bell-shaped and slightly pendent flowers, arranged in racemes. They open in July and August. This hosta is planted either singly or in groups among woody plants in the neighbourhood of water and in borders.

Planting

Opinions as to when perennials should be planted differ widely. As a guide, one can use the general rule of thumb that spring-flowering species are planted in the autumn whereas species that flower in summer and autumn are planted in spring. This rule, however, is not immutable.

The advantage of spring planting is that at this time of the year the plants get more rainwater and their growth is more vigorous. As a rule, spring planting begins in early March and ends in mid-May. Autumn planting begins in mid-August and may continue until the beginning of November at the latest. Early autumn is best, as this gives the plants time to root properly before winter. Otherwise, particularly in freezing weather without a snow cover, they may be damaged by frost or, in the case of fluctuating temperatures during the winter, they may be lifted by frost and their roots damaged. If plants are put out later in the autumn it is advisable to provide them with a protective cover of fir or evergreen branches. In districts where the ground is regularly covered by snow, plants are well protected by this layer. In more rugged climatic conditions spring planting naturally begins later and the planting period is hence shorter. Autumn planting must also be terminated sooner.

Some species do not tolerate autumn planting in heavier soils at all. These include *Anchusa, Anemone japonica, Anthemis, Aster amellus, Chrysanthemum indicum, C. maximum, Kniphofia, Lupinus, Nepeta* and *Scabiosa.*

The spacing of perennials depends on the size of the plants and on how fast they spread. Larger plants such as *Paeonia, Hemerocallis* and *Rudbeckia nitida* should be planted 80—120 cm apart. Medi-um-sized perennials such as *Erigeron, Helenium* and *Delphinium* are generally spaced 50—60 cm apart. Smaller perennials, such as *Campanula persicifolia,* are planted 30—40 cm apart. Prostrate perennials that spread rapidly are planted 20—30 cm apart. Where it is desired to have a rapid ground cover of some such plants, for example, *Thymus, Sedum, Vinca minor,* small clumps of these should be spaced 10—15 cm apart.

If perennials cannot be planted immediately on arrival from the nursery, they must be heeled-in temporarily in the open ground in a shaded position and given some water. They may remain thus for several days, until you get around to planting them. If they cannot be heeled-in in open ground they can be placed in a cellar, sprinkled with water. However, they should not be kept in such a place for too long, generally no longer than 2—3 days.

Seedlings are planted with a garden trowel or small hoe. If they have long roots these should be shortened with a knife. If the roots are bare, without a root ball, the plants will root better if the roots are immersed in a thin paste of loam and water before planting. It is always good to put a handful of moist peat in the hole before inserting the plant. Put soil in the hole, firm it round the roots and then water the plant thoroughly with a hose or by pouring the water from the spout of a can.

As for the depth of planting, plants are generally inserted so that the sprouting shoots are approximately at the level of the soil surface. If planted too deep, some species will not flower, will become diseased or may even die. These include irises, peonies, Solomon's seals, and the like.

Dictamnus albus is an extremely persistent plant for dry soils containing calcium. It looks well in large rock gardens.

Beds containing perennials may be covered with mulch, best of all a layer of peat at least 5 cm thick. This will not only retain soil moisture but will also help to suppress the growth of weeds. Furthermore, there is no need to hurry with hoeing for the soil surface will not cake beneath the peat layer. The peat mulch will also do the plants good if it is later dug into the soil.

Care of perennials

In comparison with other groups of flowers, perennials require less work, but this does not mean they do not need any care at all. One advantage is that perennials need not be planted anew every year. Some species form such a thick mass that annual weeds are unable to grow there and die. These include certain species of cushion-like habit as well as taller species that form a dense mass.

The care required by perennials is not the same

Sanguisorba tenuifolia 'Wiesenknopf' is a graceful perennial bearing interesting flowers arranged in pendent spikes. The fresh green, lobed leaves are also very decorative. It is suitable for natural garden sections, for planting among shrubs and for borders. It prefers slightly shaded situations and grows to a height of up to 180 cm.

every year. The first year after planting, when the plants are not yet fully grown, they need greater care, more or less the same as for other flowers. In ensuing years, when perennials are fully grown, their care entails fewer tasks, depending on the type of plant. So-called 'bedding' perennials, those grown in beds and borders, or in other words cultivated forms, require greater care than some of the type species which are often grown in the more informal, unstructured sections of the garden.

During the first year, the important thing is to see to it that the plants become established and grow as rapidly as possible. They must therefore be watered more frequently (particularly if there is a spell of dry weather after planting). However, the soil must not become unduly wet; it is necessary to keep it evenly moist all the time. For those who are unable to water

Bearded irises (*Iris × barbata*) of the Elatior group are beautiful perennials suitable for borders, groups and mass planting. The colour scale of their flowers can hardly be matched by any other perennial. Indiviudal varieties differ in height and the time of flowering, opening successively from May to June. Good companions are other perennials that tolerate drier soils.

The unusually ornamental *Kniphofia uvaria* 'Nobilis' with tough evergreen leaves bears dense racemose inflorescences composed of tubular pendent flowers. It is recommended for perennial groups and for solitary planting and looks very nice if planted close to water. A native of South Africa, it needs dry conditions and a good cover in winter.

Paeonia officinalis. The original species used to be a common feature of country gardens, but modern cultivars are among the most beautiful perennials — the true queens of spring garden flora.

the plants regularly, mulching will solve this problem. Maintaining a constant soil moisture can also be facilitated by sprinklers. These have the advantage that the water is applied as a spray so that the soil surface does not become unduly wet and does not cake.

Before the plants become fully grown and start filling the space entirely, the soil between the plants should be hoed occasionally to loosen it. It has already been stressed how important it is to eliminate perennial weeds before planting. If such weeds remain in the soil they will greatly hamper future work. However, even if you have eliminated perennial weeds before planting, a great many of their seeds still remain in the ground and these soon germinate. Such germinating weeds are most readily destroyed by occasional hoeing. This, of course, should be done only in dry, rather warm weather when the undercut weed will dry rapidly.

Another task that should be kept in mind is additional feeding. However, that does not mean that all plants should be given additional feed, for each has different requirements. In general it may be said that cultivated varieties need more nourishment than the botanical species usually planted in the natural, informal sections of the garden.

If the soil is a good garden type, that is, in good biological condition, and if you occasionally spread compost between the plants then they will generally grow normally and bear flowers without any additional feed. Generous feeding is likely to lead to lush growth and fewer flowers of poor substance, and this is far from desirable.

However, on poor soils regular feeding of border perennials is a must. Best for this purpose are compound organic or organic-mineral fertilizers. On sandy soils containing a small amount of humus, care must be taken when using artificial fertilizers. Here it is always better and safer to use peat or other humusy manure in which the nutrients are humus-bound, released more slowly and made available to the plants in proper amounts. Also good are slow-acting organic manures such as horn and bone meal. Spread the peat or manure between the plants and dig it in to a shallow depth. A suitable dose is 30—50 grams per square metre.

Artificial fertilizers are best applied in liquid form with a watering can. Suitable for this purpose are certain of the compound fertilizers. Some plants, however, have tender foliage that is readily burned if the solution remains on the leaves. Therefore, when applying the solution, take care not to wet the leaves or, to be on the safe side, lightly spray them with water afterwards.

Botanical species of perennials need practically no additional feed. They are mostly not demanding in

317

Rudbeckia (Echinacea) purpurea, one of the summer-flowering perennials, grows to a height of 60—100 cm. Its firm stems bear relatively large, ray-like flowers with a black-brown disc at the centre. It is grown either individually or in groups with other tall perennials and will thrive in any garden soil.

Hemerocallis hybrida. Day lilies form a group of undemanding, hardy, beautifully flowering perennials with a number of uses. In the last 25 years their selection has been enriched by numerous valuable varieties noted for the size and rich colour of their flowers.

their food requirements and adding humus to the soil in the form of leaf mould, peat, forest litter or compost will generally be sufficient.

It is important and necessary to remove faded flowers during the growing season. Indeed, some species should be cut back to the ground after flowering. In the autumn, the top parts of all perennials, excepting evergreen species, should be cut back to ground level.

Flowers are removed for the following reasons:

1. Faded flowers are unattractive.
2. In the case of species that tend to seed themselves (*Aster amellus, Alyssum argenteum*) faded flowers are removed to prevent them seeding and growing where they are not wanted.
3. In some species timely removal of faded flowers will produce another crop of flowers (*Lupinus, Delphinium*).
4. Removal of faded flowers prevents seed formation and makes for stronger, more vigorous plants. Some biennials will even last another year and in some it is a vital necessity — *Lilium pumilum*, for example.

Species that have woody shoots, in other words shrubs that for practical reasons are included among perennials, will be of more compact habit and will produce more flowers if trimmed over hard on occasion, and in some instances this will even prolong their life-span, for example, *Calluna vulgaris, Erica carnea, Helianthemum, Hypericum, Iberis, Lavandula, Santolina, Teucrium* and *Thymus citriodorus.*

Perennials in winter

In the late autumn perennials should be cut back to the ground, mainly those in borders. This will facili-

tate access to the border, where it is advisable to hoe and open up the soil between the plants before winter. In large perennial groups you can leave the top parts of those species with flowers that are decorative even when faded. These include, for example, *Ligularia, Rudbeckia fulgida, Eryngium* and *Sedum spectabile.* Also leave uncut for the winter ornamental grasses, which are very attractive when covered with hoar-frost or snow. These should be cut back in spring before they start into growth again.

Perennials are referred to as hardy plants but some species may be greatly damaged by frost in winter, particularly in winters without a snow cover, which is the best form of protection. Do not forget that the term perennials includes a great many genera and species that have their origin in widely different parts of the world and that they do not always find the climatic conditions of central Europe congenial. That is why it is sometimes necessary to help them survive winters such as they are not accustomed to by their origin. Also, some plants that remain green in winter — particularly those with larger, broader leaves — are occasionally 'burned' by frost. Though this poses no threat to their survival it definitely detracts from their appearance. Examples are *Yucca filamentosa, Kniphofia* and *Iberis.*

The best protection for such plants is a cover of fir or spruce branches that will mainly protect them from the sun's rays.

Some perennials that are tender in central European conditions, such as *Anemone japonica,* some species of *Eremurus* and *Helianthus atrorubens,* welcome a protective cover of leaves or dry peat.

In spring, when there is no longer any danger of severe frosts, begin loosening and removing the covers. In the case of evergreen plants, never remove the cover all at once, because the plants could be readily damaged by the sun. Remove the covers only partially. Wait some time before removing them entirely and, to be on the safe side, always do so on a cloudy day. Leaving the plants covered for too long is also dangerous, particularly in the case of plants that begin growth early in spring.

Propagating perennials

Raising from seed

This is the most important method of propagating perennials. Uniform offspring (uniformity of size and colour) can be obtained usually only from the seeds of pure species, possibly also some varieties. Plants grown from the seeds of most cultivated varieties are not uniform. To be absolutely certain that the offspring of cultivated varieties will come true the best, indeed only, method of propagation is by vegetative means.

A must for success in raising pure species from seed are clean, well-ripened seeds, and knowledge of when and how to sow, the germinating properties of the seeds, etc.

Seeds are sown (sometimes preceded by dressing) in a greenhouse in winter. Earthenware dishes and

Eupatorium purpureum, a robust, up to 180 cm tall perennial with thick, unbranched stems bears narrow leaves and wine-red flowers. It is particularly valued for its late flowering and recommended for informal gardens, for aquatic arrangements and for planting next to woody plants. It needs deep soils and a sunny to semi-shaded situation, where it will thrive for many years.

Anemone sylvestris 'Grandiflora' resembles the Wood Anemone, but its cream-white flowers are larger. It is quite hardy and spreads very quickly, preferring calcium-rich soils and semi-shaded places though it will thrive even in full sun.

flowerpots in which the seed is to be sown must be washed thoroughly and possibly also flamed inside to destroy any traces of a fungus that might infect the plants. Boxes should be new or disinfected with a suitable preparation. Also used are plastic dishes which maintain an equal moisture and are readily cleaned. Always put coarse sand or crocks in the bottom of the containers to provide drainage.

A suitable sowing medium is a mixture of equal parts of old leaf mould, peat and river sand. This must be sterilized before sowing. Fill the containers with the sowing medium and press it down evenly and fairly firmly. How densely the seed is sown depends on its power of germination. Seeds with good germinating power are sown thinly and vice versa. After sowing the seeds sprinkle a fine covering of overfired sand over them. The thickness of this layer depends on the size of the seed; large seeds are covered with a thicker layer, fine seeds are not covered at all.

With some seeds, it is necessary to keep in mind their light requirements. Seeds that germinate better when exposed to light should be carefully sprinkled with sand only after they have germinated. Seeds that do not germinate readily should be covered not only with sand but also with a layer of sphagnum, which is better at keeping the medium evenly moist. Then attach a data label to each pot, giving the name of the plant, the date of sowing, and possibly also the origin of the seed.

Even though most seeds germinate well in a greenhouse it is advisable to place them outdoors at first — some species will germinate only after being

Gaillardia aristata 'Fackelschein' is an extremely long-flowering plant. It is recommended for flower borders, perennial groups and for cutting. The plants should be cut back at the end of summer in order to overwinter successfully and to produce a profusion of flowers in the following year.

Lychnis viscaria 'Plena', attractive for its wonderful colours, is suitable for flower borders, large rock gardens and margins. It forms a ground rosette of leaves from which emerge the sticky stems bearing double, fragrant, relatively large carmine-red flowers. Very harmonious colour compositions are achieved with some other perennials flowering at the same time, for example, *Veronica teucrium* 'Royal Blue', *Aster tongolensis* 'Wartburgstern' and *Cerastium tomentosum* var. *columnae.*

frozen. After 14—20 days (depending on the species and when they germinate) put them in the greenhouse at a temperature of about 10—12° C where the young seedlings are later pricked out.

In the spring, seeds of species that germinate readily may be sown in the open or in a cold frame.

After moving the containers with the seeds to the greenhouse it is most important to ensure that they do not dry out. The containers may be covered with plastic foil but must be checked daily for signs of fungus or signs that some species have already begun to germinate. They should be watered with great care, for otherwise any fine seeds may be readily washed out. Bottom watering has proved to be a good method. On sunny days the plants should be slightly shaded, but you must remember to remove the screen in time. Another thing you must not forget is to provide the plants with ample ventilation; this is very important for hardening them off.

As soon as they are large enough to handle, the young seedlings are pricked out into a medium which should be the same as the sowing medium, but may be slightly richer. The boxes containing the pricked-out seedlings should be watered carefully at first, shaded more and kept at a higher temperature. When the seedlings have become rooted, begin hardening them off gradually: give them less water, more time in the open air and shade them only in strong sunshine. In some plants it is necessary to pinch off the terminals (as is the case for *Dianthus, Iberis, Hypericum*) to promote branching. Loosen the soil in the boxes at regular 2—3 week intervals. A compound fertilizer may be applied in liquid form to well-rooted plants.

As soon as the plants in the box have grown to

such a size that their leaves touch or even overlap, prick them out again, with a wider spacing, into another box or into a frame, where they are then hardened off in preparation for putting out in the bed.

In March, April and May seeds may be sown straight in the open ground. Just as soon as the soil can be prepared in spring prepare the beds for sowing. The soil must be loose, well-drained, humus-rich, fertilized well beforehand and free of all perennial weeds. It can be improved as needed with humusy manure, peat, and the like. If the area where the seeds are to be sown is not too large then it is ad-

Ligularia × hessei is a stout, 150—180 cm high perennial with decorative leaves and flowers arranged in upright racemes. It is best planted singly or in small groups, particularly close to water.

visable to top the prepared soil with a layer of sterilized soil. This will prove worthwhile wherever the soil is invaded with weeds and where there are also many weed seeds in the soil.

Seeds are sown either broadcast or in drills. Sowing in drills makes weeding and, above all, loosening of the soil and hoeing easier after the plants have sprouted. Furthermore, plants from seeds sown in drills develop better because they have plenty of room on either side. Mark out the rows and draw out the drills for sowing with a wood strip or hoe. Larger seeds, such as those of *Lupinus* or *Lathyrus,* should be pressed in firmly before being sprinkled with a layer of sand.

Aster alpinus is a valuable perennial of many uses. A wide range of varieties with differently coloured flowers are available. It is grown in rock gardens in cracks between stones, in flowering walls and particularly at their top. It is also nice for borders, informal perennial groups and for cutting.

Beds sown with seeds should be given a cover of evergreen branches or suitably shaded in some other way to prevent the soil from drying out and birds from eating the seeds. If there is a long dry spell when the seeds begin to sprout, they must be watered; otherwise germination will be irregular and all the work entailed in the sowing will have been for nought. After the seeds have sprouted, remove the cover of evergreens and shade them only during lengthier dry spells and in sunshine. Hoe the soil round the young seedlings and remove weeds regularly. Seedlings that are too close together should be thinned so that the remaining seedlings have plenty of space in which to grow.

Most plants sown in the open ground are left in the seed bed for a whole year, the young plants being lifted up the following spring, sorted, and then planted in their flowering quarters.

It should be pointed out that raising plants from

Chrysanthemum × hortorum. Chrysanthemums are usually the last plants to flower in the autumn. They come in a wide range of colours and types — single, semi-double or double — opening successively until the first frosts.

when the basal shoots are well developed, and separate the individual shoots, putting them in pots and then in a frame to overwinter. Peat pots are very good for this purpose. To prevent them from freezing, cover the frames with glass and then with leaves or farmyard manure. In spring, harden off the plants gradually by progressively giving them more time in the open air. Then in May-June put them out in the bed where they are to flower.

Perennials that flower in the autumn (*Aster, Chrysanthemum, Helenium, Helianthus* and *Rudbeckia*) and ones that begin growth late in spring (*Astilbe, Hosta*), are best divided in spring. If you want to divide spring-flowering perennials in spring you must do so early, while the plants are still dormant.

Autumn is the season to divide perennials that are exceptionally hardy and are not unduly sensitive to frost or dampness. The plants should be divided early in the autumn so that they have time to become rooted before the frosts. In late autumn, if the weather permits, it is possible to divide only the hardiest perennials (*Astilbe, Paeonia* and *Phlox paniculata*) which, after being put in the ground, should be earthed up while still in rows.

Perennials that flower in spring and are not tender (*Aubrieta, Arabis, Cerastium, Convallaria, Helleborus, Doronicum, Sanguinaria, Soldanella*) can also be divided in the autumn.

Astilbe chinensis 'Finale'. Recent astilbe varieties are excellent subjects for semi-shaded localities. They are planted in borders, perennial beds and large single-species groups, but also in rock gardens and informal arrangements. Its large masses look particularly nice near water.

seed makes it possible to obtain a truly unlimited number of new plants. Another advantage of this method is that the seedlings are more vigorous than ones obtained by vegetative means.

Vegetative propagation

Vegetative propagation is a means of increasing plants from pieces of a parent plant of known characteristics and has the great advantage of yielding new plants with all the desirable characteristics of the parents.

Division

Division is the most widely used and simplest method of increasing perennials by vegetative propagation. For the gardener this is the best method of all, for it can be used to increase most perennials.

Species that start growth later in spring or die back during the year are best divided during the resting or dormant period.

With a spade, lift the plants that are to be divided from the bed and remove all of the soil. Then divide them into sections, best of all cutting them up with a sharp knife. The size of the sections often depends on the number of parent plants; larger sections root better.

To get the maximum number of plants by division lift the whole plant from the ground in the autumn,

The vividly coloured spring-flowering perennials offer a continuously changing picture, full of fresh grace. The dense carpets of the creeping *Phlox subulata* and the shrubby tufts of *Alyssum saxatile* are massed with flowers every year.

The success of dividing perennials in spring and summer, as well as in early autumn, depends in great measure on the weather. In dry, sunny and windy conditions it is necessary to divide the plants in an enclosed or at least covered place; otherwise their roots may dry out. Roots shortened to about the width of the palm of the hand should be immersed in a thin paste of soil and water before planting. The aerial parts of the plants should be cut back to about one-half or one-third of their length.

In congenial conditions — that is in cool, damp weather — the parent plants may be divided where the new plants are to grow and the prepared plant sections may be inserted in the ground without prior wetting. The percentage of those that do not take is much lesser under such conditions. Most successful is propagation during the dormant period, particularly in the early spring. At this time of the year the soil is usually sufficiently moist, which is one of the most important conditions for successful rooting. There is also no need to shorten the top parts and this is just as important as some species do not stand up well to cutting back.

Propagation by cuttings

Perennials are propagated by cuttings if you wish to obtain a greater number of plants of a given species or cultivar and if there is only a small number of parent plants available. Perennials are also naturally propagated by cuttings if another method of vegetative propagation is uncertain or not possible.

Perennials are propagated by soft, herbaceous cuttings after they have started growth, when the new shoots reach a length of 10—15 cm. Results are best at this time. In practice, such cuttings are taken from April until late August. Propagation by autumn cuttings is usually not as successful; their rooting is irregular and sometimes the cuttings do not become rooted until the following year.

It is important that the cuttings be taken from healthy plants, best of all from terminal shoots. The cuttings should be shortened to about 4—6 cm, and the bottom leaves cut off with the leaf stalks close to the stem. Upper leaves should be reduced by one-third to one-half, depending on their size. The foliage of small-leaved perennials is not reduced. The use of growth stimulators, a common practice in propagating conifers as well as certain broadleaved woody plants by cuttings, has not yet been sufficiently tried and tested for perennials.

The prepared cuttings are put directly in the propagating bed or, best of all, in boxes that are then placed in a frame. The rooting medium is a mixture of peat and sand in varying proportions, generally about one part sand to one part peat. Plastic materials that lighten the soil and, because of their great moisture retention capacity, improve the moisture conditions of the medium are also very good.

When taking cuttings, particularly if taking

Omphalodes verna is a modest, shade-loving perennial with grace-ful forget-me-not-like flowers. A good ground-coverer, it can be used to enliven shaded rock gardens and other shaded spots.

Phlox paniculata 'Frührosa'. Tall phloxes are among the most attractive of the summer-flowering perennials.

a greater number, it is necessary to make sure they do not wilt before being inserted. After insertion water the cuttings properly. Further care consists of maintaining maximum humidity and optimum temperature. The cuttings should be misted 2—4 times a day with a fine rose, as needed. In strong sunshine, especially in summer, they should be provided with shade until evening. At night, especially in spring when there are great differences between daytime and nighttime temperatures, the frames should be covered with straw matting.

As soon as the cuttings begin to root, misting must be gradually reduced. And after they have rooted, the plants should be watered only when the substrate begins to get dry. They should be given less shade and progressively more exposed to the open air.

Propagation by rosette cuttings

Rosette cuttings are actually soft, herbaceous cuttings with the leaves arranged in a rosette. These rosettes are separated from the parent plants by cutting or pulling them off. The dying leaves on the underside of the rosette are removed before planting. In some cases, it is recommended that you make a slight nick in the stem beneath the rosette, as it then roots better. It is important that the rosettes, which have a relatively short stem, should be in firm contact with the soil. Cuttings are taken in the autumn and winter and they tend to root best if they are placed in a deep frame.

Propagation by leaf cuttings

Some perennials are also propagated by leaf cuttings. Suitable for this purpose are well-developed, healthy leaves which are inserted together with part of the stalk in a mixture of sand and peat. Besides sterilizing (steaming) the peat, it is also advisable to

rid all containers of possible traces of fungi and bacteria — scrub them, then sterilize them in steam.

Leaves are inserted in a number of different ways. Sometimes they are merely laid flat on the surface of the rooting medium and pressed down, as is the case for *Cardamine*. The leaves of other perennials (*Ramonda, Haberlea, Sedum spectabile*) are inserted into prepared drills, about 1 cm deep, and pressed in lightly. Large and absolutely healthy leaves of *Ramonda* and *Haberlea* may be cut into 2 parts, crosswise — then the stalk of the lower part of the leaf is inserted in the rooting medium and the top part of the leaf is inserted in a drill.

Propagation by stolons

This method is used to propagate species that produce self-rooting, trailing branches or stolons. Plants that spread in this manner often crowd their neighbours but, from the practical viewpoint, this property of some perennials is a welcome one for the gardener.

Propagation by this method is done in spring or early autumn. To do so, scrape away the soil from the root system of the parent plant and cut off, tear off, or sever with a spade the stolons growing from the base of the plant along with the roots. Strong stolons may be inserted directly in the bed where they are to grow. In this case they must be watered in afterward or else immersed in a thin paste of soil mixed with water before insertion (e. g. *Chrysanthemum maximum, Rudbeckia*). Weak ones should be inserted singly in a box or frame where, at a temperature of 10—12° C, they usually root rapidly.

Layering

Layering is quite a common method of propagation. Gardeners use this simple, though slow, method to propagate choice perennials that root with difficulty (such as *Acantholimon*).

After flowering, peg the shoots down so they touch the ground, making several fine nicks on the underside at the point where they are expected to put out roots. Then sprinkle sandy soil, in some cases a mixture of sand and peat, over the prepared plant. When the layered shoots have rooted separate them from the parent plant and put them in a pot or directly in the bed where they are to grow to maturity.

Propagation by root cuttings

This method is becoming increasingly popular because it makes it possible to obtain a large number of plants, particularly in the winter months. In the autumn, before the first frost, lift the parent plant from the soil, taking care to damage the root system as little as possible. Then cut off healthy, undamaged roots with a sharp knife, tie them together in a bundle, label them and heel them in, in a frost-proof place. The actual cuttings are made later — in January. Cut the roots into pieces 4—5 cm long and insert these into boxes of sandy soil, about 0.5—1 cm apart, or lay them flat on the surface and cover them with 1—1.5 cm of sandy soil. Some species (*Anchusa azurea, Papaver orientale, Verbascum*) should never be laid on the surface because they sprout on the upper side of the cut surface. They must be inserted in drills, with the tops of the cuttings above the level of the soil in the box. To ensure that the cuttings will be planted the right way up make the cut at the base end slanting and the cut at the top straight across.

Adventitious buds will sprout in about 20—40 days at a temperature of 10—12° C. Put the rooted cuttings in pots and in the autumn put them out in open ground in their permanent site. Root cuttings of *Phlox paniculata, Papaver orientale* and *Paeonia officinalis* can be put out directly in open ground and provided with shade if necessary.

Bergenia cordifolia, a modest and hardy evergreen perennial, bears large leathery leaves. Being decorative throughout the year, it looks good in borders, perennial groups and beds, in front of woody plants, at the edges of water and in rock gardens.

Propagation by rhizome cuttings

This method is less widely practised. It can be used to increase only certain perennials, namely species with a thick, branched rhizome and well-developed top parts (*Bergenia, Peltiphyllum, Rodgersia* and, of the ferns, for example *Adiantum pedatum, Blechnum penna-marina* and *Polypodium vulgare*). The manner and the time it is done is much the same as in propagation by root cuttings. Cuttings about 4—5 cm long are inserted in boxes and covered with 2—3 cm of sandy sterilized soil. At a temperature of 8—12° C, the cuttings will begin growth in 40—60 days. Some 4—6 weeks after they have made growth the cuttings should be potted on. Then, in early autumn, they are planted out in the flowering bed.

Propagation by grafting

Propagation of perennials by grafting is not a very common method. It is used only to increase double cultivated varieties of *Gypsophila*. Used as stock are the roots of *Gypsophila paniculata,* which are lifted from the nursery bed in the autumn and sorted. Roots about the thickness of a pencil are suitable. In late autumn, put the parent plants in the greenhouse in light. The best scions are ones that are half-ripened and have one pair of leaves. Unripened scions are not suitable because they rot readily. Grafting is carried out between January and April by any of the known methods.

Put the grafted plants in pots, or better yet in boxes, with the graft beneath the soil surface. The growing medium should be thoroughly moistened so that it will not be necessary to water the freshly grafted plants. In 3—5 days, when it is evident that the grafts have taken, they can be misted a bit more profusely. After 4—6 weeks, move the grafted plants in their pots to a frame where they should be hardened off gradually. In May or June, put them out in well prepared soil in their permanent site.

Gypsophila paniculata is a favourite and almost omnipresent perennial. Its tiny but abundant flowers are a good complement for cut flowers in a vase. It is, however, equally suitable for perennial groups, among other tall species. The fluffy panicles of white flowers decorate the garden from July to September.

Select list of perennials

Species, variety	Height in cm	Colour of flowers	Flowering period	Requirements		Uses
				Soil	Light	
Acanthus longifolius	80—100	purplish-pink	VI	rather heavy to medium heavy	○	in large rockeries, singly
Achillea millefolium 'Kelwayi'	50	dark red	VI—IX	sandy-loamy, Ca	○	in borders, beds, smaller and larger groups, larger rockeries, for cutting
Achillea ptarmica 'Schneeball'	60	white	VI—IX	sandy-loamy, Ca	○	in borders, beds, for cutting
Actaea alba	80	whitish	V—VI	sandy-loamy, humus-rich	◑ ●	beneath and in front of woody plants, in larger groups
Adonis vernalis	20—30	bright yellow	IV—V	loamy-sandy, well-drained, Ca	○	in rockeries, the heath garden, steppe sections
Anchusa azurea 'Dropmore'	100	gentian-blue	VI—IX	sandy-loamy	○	in beds
Anemone hupehensis 'Praecox'	40	pinkish-red	VIII—IX	sandy-loamy, humus-rich	◑	in beds, informal sections, for cutting
Anemone hupehensis 'Septembercharm'	60	pink	VIII—IX	sandy-loamy, humus-rich	◑	in beds, informal sections, for cutting
Anemone japonica cultivars	60—80	varied	VIII—X	sandy-loamy, humus-rich	◑	in perennial beds, informal sections, for cutting
Anemone vitifolia 'Robustissima'	100	pink	VIII—X	sandy-loamy, humus-rich	◑	group planting in informal sections, for cutting
Antennaria dioica	5—15	whitish-pink	V—VI	sandy	○	in rockeries, heath gardens, as substitute for lawn
Anthericum liliago	50	white	V—VI	rather poor, loamy-sandy, Ca	○	in rockeries, borders, beds, informal sections
Aquilegia caerulea 'Crimson Star'	60	white and red	V—VI	sandy-loamy, humus-rich	○ ◑	in beds, borders, in front of woody plants, for cutting
Aquilegia caerulea 'Mc Kana'	60	varied	V—VI	sandy-loamy, humus-rich	○ ◑	in beds, borders, in front of woody plants, for cutting
Aruncus dioicus	120	white	VII—VIII	sandy-loamy, humus-rich	○ ◑ ●	singly, in beds, by waterside in informal sections, for cutting
Asclepias tuberosa	50	orange-yellow	VII—VIII	sandy-loamy, humus-rich	○	in beds, informal sections, for cutting
Asphodelus albus	100	white	V—VI	sandy-loamy	○	singly, in rockeries, beds, informal sections
Aster amellus cultivars	40—60	varied	VII—IX	sandy-loamy, Ca	○	in beds, larger and smaller groups, for cutting
Aster dumosus cultivars	25—50	varied	IX—X	sandy-loamy	○	in beds, as edging, in rockeries
Aster novae-angliae cultivars	80—150	varied	IX—X	sandy-loamy	○	singly, in beds, groups
Aster novi-belgii cultivars	60—130	varied	IX—X	sandy-loamy	○	singly, in beds, groups, for cutting
Astilbe arendsii cultivars	60—100	varied	VII—IX	sandy-loamy, humus-rich	○ ◑	in beds, groups, as undergrowth, by the waterside, for cutting
Astilbe japonica cultivars	50—70	varied	VI—VII	sandy-loamy, humus-rich	◑	in beds, for cutting
Astilbe simplicifolia cultivars	40—50	varied	VII—VIII	sandy-loamy, humus-rich	◑	in beds, informal sections, for cutting
Bergenia hybrids	30—50	pink	IV—V	sandy-loamy	○ ◑	in rockeries, beds, groups, informal sections
Brunnera macrophylla	30—50	blue	IV—V	loamy-sandy	◑	as undergrowth, among other perennials
Calamintha grandiflora	50	pink	VI—VIII	sandy-loamy, humus-rich	○	in rockeries, beds, informal sections, for cutting
Campanula glomerata 'Joan Elliott'	40	deep violet	VII—VIII	sandy-loamy	○ ◑	in beds, for cutting
Campanula lactiflora 'Prichard'	60	amethyst-blue	VII—VIII	sandy-loamy, humus-rich	○ ◑	in beds
Campanula persicifolia 'Grandiflora Caerulea'	100	bright blue	VII—VIII	sandy-loamy	○ ◑	in beds, for cutting
Cardamine trifolia	20—30	white	IV—V	sandy-loamy, humus-rich	◑ ●	in woodland sections, shaded rockeries
Centaurea macrocephala	80—110	deep yellow	VII	rather deep, loamy-sandy	○	in groups, large rockeries, informal sections
Centaurea montana	40—50	blue	V—VI	loamy-sandy	○	in groups, large rockeries, informal sections

Species, variety	Height in cm	Colour of flowers	Flowering period	Requirements		Uses
				Soil	Light	
Chrysanthemum coccineum	50—90	varied	V—VI	sandy-loamy	○	in beds, groups, for cutting
Chrysanthemum × hortorum	40—80	varied	VIII—X	sandy-loamy, Ca	○	in beds, groups, for cutting
Chrysanthemum leucanthemum 'Maistern'	60	white	V—VI	sandy-loamy	○	in beds, groups, for cutting
Chrysanthemum maximum cultivars	60—100	white	VII—IX	sandy-loamy	○	in beds, groups, for cutting
Cimicifuga racemosa	180	white	VII—VIII	sandy-loamy, humus-rich	◐ ●	singly, in beds, in front of and among woody plants
Clematis integrifolia	60	blue-violet	VII—VIII	sandy-loamy, humus-rich	○ ◐	in groups, rockeries, among woody plants
Convallaria majalis	10—20	white	V—VI	sandy-loamy	○ ◐	as undergrowth in woodland sections, for cutting
Coreopsis grandiflora 'Badengold'	80	golden-yellow	VI—IX	sandy-loamy	○	in larger and smaller groups, beds, for cutting
Coreopsis lanceolata 'Goldfink'	25	golden-yellow	VI—IX	sandy-loamy	○	in rockeries, groups
Coreopsis verticillata 'Grandiflora'	60	yellow	VI—IX	sandy-loamy	○	in larger groups, beds
Delphinium hybrids	80—200	varied	VI—XII IX—X	sandy-loamy	○	singly, in beds, groups, beneath woody plants, for cutting
Dianthus plumarius cultivars	20—30	white, pink, red	V—VI	sandy-loamy, Ca	○	in beds, as edging, for cutting
Dicentra spectabilis	80	pink and white	V—VI	sandy-loamy, humus-rich	○ ◐	singly, in beds, for cutting
Dictamnus albus	40	golden-yellow	IV—V	sandy-loamy, Ca	○ ◐	singly, in beds, informal sections
Digitalis purpurea	80—120	light purple	V—VI	loamy-sandy	○ ◐	in mixed borders, informal sections
Doronicum orientale	40	golden-yellow	IV—V	sandy-loamy	○ ◐	in groups, beds, for cutting
Echinacea purpurea 'Odin'	60	burgundy-red	VII—IX	sandy-loamy	○	in groups, beds, for cutting
Eremurus robustus	150—220	white	VI—VII	medium-heavy, well-drained	○	singly, together with dark woody plants
Erigeron cultivars	60—70	varied	VI—VIII	sandy-loamy	○	in groups, beds, for cutting
Eryngium alpinum 'Opal'	80	silvery-white	VII—VIII	sandy	○	in beds, informal sections, for cutting
Eryngium planum 'Blauer Zwerg'	50	deep blue	VI—IX	sandy	○	in beds, informal sections, for cutting
Euphorbia polychroma	30—50	greenish	V—VI	loamy-sandy, well-drained, Ca	○ ◐	singly, in larger rockeries, informal perennial sections
Filipendula vulgaris	30—50	cream-white	VI—VII	well-drained, loamy-sandy, Ca	○ ◐	in steppe sections, heath gardens
Filipendula ulmaria	100—150	cream-white	VI—VII	loamy-sandy	○ ◐	in informal sections, on the banks of streams and beside small lakes
Gaillardia cultivars	20—70	red	VII—IX	sandy-loamy	○	in groups, beds, for cutting
Geranium platypetalum	50	blue-violet	VII—VIII	sandy, humus-rich	○ ◐	in groups among woody plants
Geum 'Princess Juliana'	50	orange-yellow	VI—VIII	sandy-loamy	○ ◐	in smaller and larger groups, beds, for cutting
Gypsophila paniculata cultivars	100—120	white pink	VII—VIII	rather dry, sandy, Ca	○	singly, in beds, in smaller and larger groups, for cutting
Helenium cultivars	80—180	varied	VII—IX	sandy-loamy	○	in groups, beds, for cutting
Helianthus salicifolius	250	yellow	IX—X	sandy-loamy	○	singly, by artificial pools
Heliopsis helianthoides 'Sonnenschild'	120	dark yellow	VII—IX	sandy-loamy	○	in beds, smaller and larger groups, for cutting
Helleborus niger	30	white	XII and II—III	loamy-sandy, well-drained	◐	in rockeries, informal sections, for cutting
Helleborus abchasicus	30—40	dull purple	III—IV	loamy-sandy, well-drained	◐	in informal sections
Hemerocallis hybrids	50—120	varied	VI—VIII	sandy-loamy, rather moist	○ ◐	in beds, smaller and larger groups, by artificial pools, for cutting
Heracleum lanatum	120—250	white	VI—VII	loamy-sandy	○ ◐	singly, in informal sections
Hosta sieboldii (albomarginata)	60	lilac	VII—VIII	sandy-loamy	◐ ●	as edging, in beds, groups, by pools

327

Species, variety	Height in cm	Colour of flowers	Flowering period	Requirements		Uses
				Soil	Light	
Incarvillea delavayi	50—60	pink	VI—VII	loamy-sandy, well-drained, Ca	○	in borders, informal perennial groups, rockeries
Inula × hybrida 'Golden Beauty'	60	golden-yellow	VI—VII	sandy-loamy	○ ◑	in smaller and larger groups, informal sections
Iris germanica- Barbata-Elatior-Group	80—130	varied	V—VI	sandy-loamy, humus-rich	○	in beds, groups, by artificial pools, for cutting
Iris germanica Barbata-Media Group	30—40	varied	V	sandy-loamy	○	in beds, groups, by artificial pools, for cutting
Iris germanica Barbata-Nana Group	15—30	varied	IV	sandy-loamy, humus-rich	○	in rockeries, as edging, in groups, beds
Iris kaempferi cultivars	80	varied	V—VII	sandy-loamy, marshy	○ ◑	alongside pools, in groups, borders, for cutting
Iris sibirica cultivars	80	varied	VI	sandy-loamy, rather moist	○	alongside pools, in groups, borders, beds, for cutting
Kniphofia hybrids	50—120	varied	VII—IX	sandy-loamy	○	alongside pools, in groups, borders, beds, for cutting
Lathyrus latifolius	up to 200	pinkish-red, white	VII—IX	sandy-loamy	○ ◑	for covering fences, in beds, for cutting
Leontopodium alpinum	15—20	whitish	VI—VII	poor, sandy, Ca	○	in rockeries
Liatris spicata	80	white, violet	VII—X	sandy-loamy	○	singly, in beds, informal sections, for cutting
Limonium latifolium	60	lilac	VII—VIII	rather poor, sandy	○	in rockeries, beds, informal sections, for cutting
Lupinus polyphyllus hybrids	80—120	varied	V—VII	sandy-loamy	○	in groups, beds, for cutting
Lychnis chalcedonica	100	scarlet	VI—VII	sandy-loamy	○	in groups, beds
Lysimachia punctata	80	golden-yellow	VI—VIII	sandy-loamy	○ ◑	in smaller and larger groups, informal sections, by artificial pools, in front of woody plants
Malva moschata	60	pink	VI—IX	sandy-loamy	○ ◑	in groups, in front of and beneath woody plants, in informal sections, for cutting
Monarda hybrids	100—150	varied	VII—IX	sandy-loamy	○ ◑	in smaller and larger groups, borders, in front of woody plants, for cutting
Oenothera tetragona	30—50	golden-yellow	VI—VIII	loamy-sandy, rather poor	○	in mixed borders, informal groups
Oenothera missouriensis	20	sulphur-yellow	VI—X	loamy-sandy, rather poor	○	in large rockeries, informal perennial groups
Omphalodes verna	10—15	sky-blue	III—IV	loamy-sandy, humus-rich, Ca	◑	in woodland sections
Paeonia lactiflora	60—100	varied	V—VI	sandy-loamy	○	singly, in groups, beds, borders, for cutting
Papaver nudicaule	20—40	yellow to orange	VI—VIII	loamy-sandy	○ ◑	in rockeries, carpeting plantings
Papaver orientale	50—120	varied	V—VII	sandy-loamy	○	in smaller and larger groups, borders, beds, for cutting
Penstemon barbatus hybrids	80—100	red	VI—IX	sandy-loamy, humus-rich	○	in beds, borders, for cutting
Phlox paniculata hybrids	50—120	varied	VI—IX	sandy-loamy	○ ◑	in smaller and larger groups, beds, borders, for cutting
Physalis alkekengi var. *franchetii*	40	whitish	VIII—IX	sandy-loamy	○ ◑	in groups, informal sections, for cutting
Platycodon grandiflorus	30—60	deep blue	VII—VIII	sandy-loamy, well-drained	○ ◑	in rockeries, groups, beds, borders, informal sections
Polygonum amplexicaule 'Atropurpureum'	100	pinkish-red	VIII—X	sandy-loamy, rather moist	○ ◑	singly, in larger groups, informal sections, for cutting
Potentilla hybrids	40	varied	VI—VIII	sandy-loamy	○	in larger groups, beds, in front of woody plants, for cutting
Primula elatior hybrids	25—30	varied	IV—V	humus-rich, well-drained	◑ ●	in rockeries, groups, borders, in front of woody plants
Prunella grandiflora	15—25	violet	VI—VIII	loamy-sandy	◑	in rockeries, informal perennial sections
Pulmonaria angustifolia	20—30	carmine-red	IV—V	loamy-sandy	◑	in informal groups, spring-flowering sections together with bulbs
Ranunculus acris 'Multiplex'	60	golden-yellow	V—VI	sandy, humus-rich	○ ◑	in smaller and larger groups, borders, for cutting

Species, variety	Height in cm	Colour of flowers	Flowering period	Requirements Soil	Light	Uses
Rheum palmatum	200	yellowish	V—VI	deep, loamy-sandy	○ ◑	singly, in informal sections
Rudbeckia fulgida 'Goldsturm'	60	golden-yellow	VIII—X	sandy-loamy	○	in smaller and larger groups, beds, borders
Rudbeckia laciniata 'Goldquelle'	80	golden-yellow	IX—X	sandy-loamy	○	in smaller and larger groups, beds, borders, for cutting
Rudbeckia nitida 'Herbstsonne'	200	deep yellow	VII—IX	sandy-loamy	○	in mixed groups, informal sections
Salvia nemorosa 'Ostfriesland'	50	dark violet	VII—X	sandy-loamy, Ca	○	in larger groups, beds, informal sections
Scabiosa caucasica cultivars	80	varied	VI—IX	sandy-loamy, Ca	○	in larger and smaller groups, beds, borders, for cutting
Sedum spectabile 'Carmen'	40	carmine-pink	VIII—IX	sandy-loamy, even rather poor	○	singly, in beds, borders, for cutting
Sedum telephium 'Herbstfreude'	50	brownish-red	IX—X	sandy-loamy, even rather poor	○	in beds, borders, in front of and among woody plants
Solidago hybrids	60—80	golden-yellow	VII—IX	sandy-loamy	○	in beds, groups, autumn-flowering borders, for cutting
Stachys byzantina 'Silver Carpet'	30	does not flower	—	sandy-loamy, Ca	○	silvery grey ground cover
Stachys grandiflora 'Superba'	40	purplish-pink	VII—VIII	sandy-loamy, Ca	○ ◑	in mass plantings, groups, in front of and beneath woody plants
Stachys olympica	15—25	dark pink	VI—VII	loamy-sandy	○	as undergrowth for striking plants
Telekia speciosa	180	yellow	VI—VII	sandy-loamy	○ ◑	singly, in front of and beneath woody plants, in informal sections
Thalictrum aquilegifolium	100	lilac to purple	VI—VII	sandy-loamy	○ ◑	in groups, in front of and beneath woody plants, in informal sections, for cutting
Thalictrum dipterocarpum	120	purplish-lilac	VII—IX	sandy, humus-rich	◑	in groups, in front of and beneath woody plants, in informal sections, for cutting
Thalictrum minus 'Adiantifolium'	40	yellowish	VI—VIII	sandy-loamy	○ ◑	in groups, beneath and in front of woody plants, in informal sections, for cutting
Tradescantia andersoniana cultivars	40—50	varied	VI—VIII	sandy-loamy	○ ◑	in groups, beds, borders, by artificial pools, in informal sections
Trollius chinensis 'Golden Queen'	100	golden-yellow	VI—VII	nourishing, humus-rich, rather moist	○ ◑	in borders, informal sections, alongside pools, for cutting
Trollius hybrids 'Orange-globe'	90	orange-yellow	V—VI	nourishing, humus-rich, rather moist	○ ◑	in borders, informal sections, by water, for cutting
Veratrum nigrum	100	black-red	VII—VIII	sandy-loamy, and low-moor peat	○ ◑	singly, in groups, among woody plants, in informal sections
Verbascum hybrids 'Golden Bush'	50	yellow	VI—IX	sandy-loamy, even rather poor	○	singly, in groups, informal sections
Verbascum hybrids 'Pink Domino'	100	pink	VI—VIII	sandy-loamy, even rather poor	○	singly, in groups, informal sections
Veronica incana	30—40	dark blue	VI—VII	loamy-sandy	○	in the heath garden, xerophytic sections
Veronica spicata	20—30	lilac-blue	VII—VIII	loamy-sandy	○	in borders, informal groups
Veronica austriaca	30—40	blue	V—VI	loamy-sandy, Ca	○	in borders, informal groups, rockeries
Viola cornuta cultivars	10—25	varied	V—IX	loamy-sandy, loose	○ ◑	in mixed borders, mass plantings
Viola odorata cultivars	10—15	varied	III—IV IX—X	loamy-sandy, loose	○ ◑	as undergrowth, for cutting
Yucca filamentosa 'Elegantissima'	140	white	VII—VIII	sandy-loamy, humus-rich, Ca	○	singly, in rockeries, groups, borders, informal sections, for cutting
Yucca glauca	200	greenish-white	VII—VIII	sandy-loamy, humus-rich, Ca	○	singly, in rockeries, groups, borders, informal sections, for cutting

Annuals and biennials

Annuals are plants which, in terms of gardening, can only be used for one season, during which they germinate, develop, flower, bear fruit, seed and die. In our climatic conditions their growing period lasts a maximum of ten months. This group also includes plants introduced from warmer regions where they are perennial but in our conditions they are not able to withstand the winter temperatures. Finally, there are also species which have a life span of several years but their maximum effect is restricted to the first year of their life, so that they are grown as annuals and, in some cases, as biennials.

Biennials resemble annuals in their life cycle. To develop fully they need cold winter weather. At the end of the first growing season they germinate and mature, then they rest through the winter and at the beginning of the season they flower and form seeds. Their life cycle lasts about twelve months but, unlike that of annuals, spans two calendar years.

Origins of annuals

Ecologically, annuals are representatives of all continents and various plant families. The majority of annuals originate in dry regions, the deserts and semi-deserts of southern Europe, South America, Asia, southern Africa and Australia. They have therefore developed in areas with extreme climatic conditions, a typically short and irregular season of spring rains followed by long, hot and dry summers. Their vegetative cycle evolved so that they are capable of germinating and developing during the short season of spring rains, flowering at the beginning of summer and finally ripening before the hot drought arrives. The seeds of many annuals have a relatively long viability, lasting between 3—5 years, and all for a specific purpose. The rainy seasons do not arrive at regular intervals but, despite this, such seeds survive safely in the soil, even over three years of drought.

Annuals originating from such dry desert and semi-desert regions soon get used to the different conditions in the garden but they also retain their genetic characteristics, which are reflected in their need for reasonable amounts of sun and water at the beginning of their development.

Tagetes erecta 'Clinton' attains a height of 60—80 cm, the flowering period lasting from June to September. It thrives in full sun and in slight semi-shade and needs a humus-rich, permeable soil.

Chrysanthemum carinatum 'Polaris' has a compact, regular habit and flowers profusely. One plant can produce as many as 70 flowers.

China Asters are grown mostly for cutting, their planting in beds is less common. They are divided according to the type of their flowers; the picture shows one of the so-called 'quills'.

Zinnias are favoured for their long flowering, which starts at the beginning of June and lasts until the onset of the first frosts. *Zinnia angustifolia* 'Persian Carpet' is a multicoloured cultivar preferring sunny situations and a permeable soil. Sufficient watering is necessary at the beginning of the plant's development.

Venidium fastuosum 'Orange' is an interesting annual, native to Africa. Its flowers are heliotropic, that is, they turn towards the sun. Cut flowers last 5—7 days in a vase. It is planted either singly or in groups and does better in dry, sunny weather, being intolerant of prolonged rain.

Use of annuals

Annuals for cutting

Annuals have a wide range of uses. They include species suitable for planting out as well as species which are grown to supply cut flowers and some fulfil both requirements.

Fresh cut flowers of annuals make an important contribution in enriching the range of flowers traditionally accompanying any important event in life and they are also an indispensable element in the decoration of our homes.

If annuals are grown in the garden the ones most suitable for display in vases will be species with long firm stalks and impressive blooms.

Small flowers with shorter stalks are used in small vases as a table decoration. These include Daisy (*Bellis perennis*), pansy (*Viola* × *wittrockiana* hybrids), toadflax (*Linaria*), Love-in-a-mist (*Nigella damascena*), Nasturtium (*Tropaeolum majus*) and French Marigold (*Tagetes patula*). For large display vases Sunflower (*Helianthus annuus*), Hollyhock (*Althaea rosea*) and Vervain (*Verbena bonariensis*) are recommended.

However, none of the mentioned species is cultivated in the garden simply to provide cut flowers because they are also essential to any flower bed arrangement. The most appropriate garden species are those which continue to flower throughout the summer. Such plants are equally attractive in the flower bed and in a vase. If their blooms are carefully cut the plants do not lose their beauty but, on the contrary, benefit by continual regeneration. Such plants include zinnia (*Zinnia*), coneflower (*Rudbeckia*), Summer Marguerite (*Chrysanthemum carinatum*) and snapdragon (*Antirrhinum*).

In order to enjoy the freshness of cut flowers as long as possible, it is best to cut them in the afternoon, during the period of greatest heat or even early in the evening when stalks placed in water start to absorb it immediately. Flowers should not be cut during rainfall because if this is done they often develop unsightly blotches.

The flowers should be cut in the most appropriate phase of their growth. Some are best cut when they are merely green buds — poppy (*Papaver*) — or just as the plant has become erect. Pot Marigolds, cornflowers and Summer Marguerites are cut as soon as the coloured tips of the corolla start to show above the calyx. In contrast, snapdragons and mignonettes need to have at least one-third of their flowers in the inflorescence open while Sweet Peas (*Lathyrus odoratus*) and Stock (*Matthiola incana*) must be half

Lathyrus odoratus is one of the annual species excellent for covering fences, pergolas etc. The cultivar 'Spencer' forms a dense fragrant wall, lasting from June to August. It needs a nourishing soil and abundant watering in the growing period and should be sown in a different place every year.

open. Satin Flower (*Godetia grandiflora*), Clarkia (*Clarkia elegans*) and bellflowers (*Campanula*) are also cut when in bud and Clove Carnations (*Dianthus caryophyllus*) are cut when half open. From among the species of the genus *Helianthus,* with the exception of those already mentioned, the Pincushion Flower (*Scabiosa atropurpurea*), Cosmea (*Cosmos sulphureus*), Mexican Sunflower (*Tithonia rotundifolia*) and dahlias (*Dahlia*) are cut when their flowers have colour but are still closed. Cape Daisy (*Venidium fastuosum*) is cut at a very early stage, before its yellow tubular disk florets open. China Asters (*Callistephus chinensis*) must have at least half of their flower head well developed, while zinnias and marigolds should have the greater part of it developed. Rudbeckia must have a fully ripened inflorescence with a conical central disc.

Fresh flowers are much easier to arrange than fading ones. If the flowers are slightly wilting, dip them whole in water in a large container and they will regain their freshness. After this, damaged leaves and stems should be removed and only then should the remainder be arranged in a vase.

Apart from cut flowers, house interiors can be embellished with some types of annuals cultivated in flowerpots. The seedlings of such plants are grown outside and, if necessary, their growth can be speeded up in a frame. As soon as they develop buds and start to flower they can be put in flowerpots and brought inside. Some of the nicest species include low-growing marigolds, low varieties of asters, *Chrysanthemum parthenium* cultivars and, of course, begonias, which of the listed plants are the least demanding in terms of light but the main flowering period is relatively short.

Particularly suitable for forcing in flowerpots are the low, compact cultivars of Stock. They have a pleasant scent and dense inflorescence reminiscent of hyacinths. The seeds are sown in December or January; the seedlings are pricked out twice, first into small and then into larger flowerpots with a diameter of 10 cm. The plants will root at a temperature of about 12° C and in a warm well-lit greenhouse will produce flowers in about four-and-a-half months from the point of sowing.

Annuals contain several species the flowers of which have everlasting calyces or several rows of papery bracts which, when dried, do not lose their shape nor usually their colour. They are collectively known as 'everlasting' flowers and include the following species: Monstrosum (*Helichrysum bracteatum*), which is a typical everlasting flower; its flowers resemble another everlasting species, the Sunray (*Helipterum roseum*); popular Sea Lavender (*Limonium sinuatum* and *L. bonduellei*), the small white *Ammobium alatum* and the bright carmine red *Gomphrena globosa*.

Everlasting flowers are cultivated mostly for winter flower arrangements. The flowers are cut when they are almost open, but before the bracts reveal the yellow disc of the flower head (Sea Lavender when the whole cluster opens out into a white or yellow flower). Tied in small bunches they are left to dry

Marigolds (*Tagetes*) are typical representatives of the summer-flowering annuals. They tolerate both dry and rainy weather and have a wide range of uses. Dwarf cultivars are best for margins and borders, the tall ones are usually used in mixed beds. All marigolds are very suitable for growing in boxes and other containers. Cut flowers will last some 8—15 days in a vase.

suspended with their inflorescences pointing down in a well aired, preferably dark place.

It is possible to dry many other inflorescences appropriate to a range of decorative containers, such as baskets, ceramic and earthenware vessels or even to be used as framed wall hangings. The delicate colouring of the Sea Lavender *Limonium suworowii* can be accentuated by a dark conifer. The dainty blades of decorative grasses, including Switch Grass (*Agrostis nebulosa*) provide a background for the compact dense inflorescences of coloured sea lavenders, while the black cones of *Rudbeckia* complement the yellow berries of *Lonas inodora*. Love-in-a-mist supplies winter flower arrangements with its striped follicles, poppy (*Papaver somniferum*) provides pods, the Pincushion Flower, brownish cones. If the ar-

Limonium sinuatum is mostly used for dried flower arrangements but live cut flowers are also very decorative. For drying, cut whole flowering stems, bind them into bunches and leave them to dry in a dark, airy room.

Lunaria annua is particularly decorative for its fruits — very ornamental, conspicuous flat seed pods which are wonderful subjects for winter decoration. The plants are grown as annuals or biennials, two-year-old specimens being more robust and bearing more fruits. It is an undemanding species which can be grown with success in semi-shade.

rangement is short of some colour this can be found among the most popular straw flowers. Pure white is supplied by the tiny flowers of Sand Flower, deep pink by the cultivar 'Roseum' of the attractive *Helipterum roseum*. The typical everlasting flower, *Helichrysum bracteatum,* has — apart from its white, yellow and pink cultivars — also a variety with vivid, glossy brownish red and dark carmine-red inflorescences which are perfectly complemented by the soft light grey, pubescent ears of Hare's Tail Grass (*Lagurus ovatus*) or Feathertop (*Pennisetum villosum*). Bullrushes, commonly used in tall vases on landings and in large rooms, can be replaced by the

Annuals offer an almost unlimited variety of uses, depending only on the gardener's taste. For instance, petunias can be planted in annual beds or they can be used for enlivening perennial groups.

interesting, thin but tough branches of vervain or the dry, long-stalked inflorescences of larkspur (*Delphinium consolida* and *D. ajacis*). For this purpose it is best to dry out the plant before it can open out.

The above is only a random selection of plants which can improve home interiors in winter. However, when compared with live flowers, even the most striking colours of dried flowers are subdued. As a result, a lot of creativity is needed to display their shape and texture successfully.

Annuals in flower beds

Annuals are a relatively popular component of many gardens, despite the labour-intensive care they require. This is because the garden provides active relaxation and, as it can be easily modified, it gives the gardener a chance to test his imagination. Annual flower beds usually give a more formal impression than flower beds planted with perennials. This can be put to good use in beds close by buildings. The colour of the flowers is all important. By choosing one or a limited number of suitable colours, it is possible to achieve a harmonious relationship between the house and its immediate environment.

The choice of suitable species is determined by the biological requirements of the plants and the size of the flower bed. Small flower beds are not normally planted with robust bushy annuals and similarly, large spaces are not appropriate for small, compact species. The smaller the flower bed the better the planning of its smallest detail must be, as well as its upkeep, since every plant in it is important. As the small flower beds are usually viewed from a close distance, the plants used for them can have inflorescences of varied colours. According to the variety of colour, they are planted either individually or used to complement some species of a single colour.

Winter flower arrangements are becoming more and more popular in our homes. *Helichrysum bracteatum* is one of the most favourite plants for this purpose, as its coloured bracts retain their colour even when dry. It can be used either individually or in combinations with other plants, as shown in the picture.

Small areas, especially if surrounded by, or bordered by, paving stones, can be planted with individual specimens of Livingstone Daisy (*Dorotheanthus bellidiformis*), Sun Plant (*Portulaca grandiflora*) or Phlox (*Phlox drummondii* 'Cuspidata'). The yellow-brown mixture of zinnias can be accentuated by the blue colour of Sage (*Salvia farinacea*) or Floss Flower (*Ageratum houstonianum*). Both of the latter plants are well suited for mixing with Treasure Flowers (*Gazania rigens*) with their dominant yellow and white colours. Of all the annuals which are directly sown in the flower bed the most appropriate is the Californian Poppy (*Eschscholtzia californica*). Of the spring-flowering biennials, a vivid mixture of pansies is very popular for it contains almost all colours.

Apart from the variegated cultivars of one species, mixtures of several annual species, varied in colour and shape, are often planted together. Such flower beds have the one indisputable advantage that if early species are mixed with late-flowering ones, there is a continuous supply of flowers throughout the growing season. An obvious precondition of success is the choice of suitable colours and shapes to achieve a continuously flowering and well balanced mixture. Apart from the low-growing, typical flower bed species, you can also plant species which are suitable for cutting.

The flower bed is most effective, however, if composed of several larger groups of single colour species. These should be chosen so that the colours complement each other and also stand out against a light background of masonry or the dark background of green shrubs. A stretch of green lawn always provides the best framework for such a colourful display of plants.

The layout of individual annual beds can vary enormously. This is because the character of annuals suits both regular geometric arrangements and irregular compositions. Rigid ornamental layouts have ceased to be popular and are rarely seen in gardens. On the other hand, irregularly shaped arrangements are very much in vogue.

The technique of preparing layouts is not very easy. The ground plan can easily be sketched on a piece of paper, but is much more difficult to execute in reality. It is therefore easier to achieve asymmetry by the irregular organization of symmetrical areas or by differentiating the height of the plants. This method is appropriate for all long-flowering annuals and their combinations that have already been mentioned. Another less usual but still very pleasing arrangement is achieved by using one low-growing species as a base for the whole surface area which is then interspaced with groups of one or two taller-growing annuals, perhaps even two differently coloured cultivars of the same species.

Some tall-growing annuals can also be used singly in the lawn, such as *Rudbeckia hirta*, *Tagetes erecta*, *Tithonia rotundifolia*, *Amaranthus caudatus*, *Cleome spinosa* and *Ricinus communis*. Those that can be placed close to the house near the door, the porch or along the patio include *Ricinus communis*, *Kochia scoparia* and *Althaea rosea*.

Eschscholtzia californica has a number of uses in the garden. It can be grown in rock gardens, dry walls, in beds, mixed groups or singly. It is also suitable for cutting.

The type of layout and the choice of plants is determined by the character of the house. The area surrounding a modern family house should be different from the surroundings of a typical country cottage. Natural surroundings are best planted with less decorative species not very different from the original natural forms, but the area around conspicuous modern architecture can be planted with the striking cultivated varieties of double-flowered decorative Stock, large-flowered marigolds, begonias and *Petunia* hybrids. More natural arrangements might be made up of most directly sown annuals in flower beds and also of *Salvia horminum*, *Gazania rigens*, *Verbena erinoides*, *V. canadensis* and *Ursinia anaethoides*.

Annuals in rockeries and dry walls

Rockeries and walls form a very popular component of gardens. Rockeries are planted with stocky and reclining or creeping species of coniferous and deciduous woody species and perennial rock garden plants. They can be embellished by the blossoms of

Portulaca grandiflora is only 10—15 cm high, but an attractive annual recommended for large as well as small groups in beds, for rockeries, dry walls, boxes and flat earthenware containers. The plants are put out at the end of May in sunny places. They need a light, sandy soil, being intolerant of heavy soils, rainy weather and shaded situations.

Hollyhock (*Althaea rosea*) grows to a height of as much as 250 cm. The height depends on the variety, the nutrients in the soil, and on the location. It needs deep soils, full sun and sufficient moisture. It looks best in cottage gardens, close to wooden fences and stone walls.

small bulbs and also by suitable annuals which add colour to the rockery or dry wall in the summer.

Depending on the size of the rockery, annuals can be planted singly or in small groups. First of all they can be used to fill in empty spaces which appear when the spring bulbs die back. Annuals flower considerably longer than perennials, most of them from the time of planting out until the first frosts, sometimes even longer. For example, Sweet Alyssum (*Lobularia maritima*) flowers continually from May until autumn and its cushions are most striking in the autumn, especially after the mild autumn frosts when there is no longer any sign of the flowers produced by the majority of creeping perennials. The yellow-flowering Creeping Zinnia (*Sanvitalia procumbens*), the Vervain (*Verbena × hybrida*), available in many variously coloured cultivars, and the Sun Plant (*Portulaca grandiflora*) with its large blossoms that glisten in the sunshine like precious stones, all bloom throughout the summer. Perhaps even more

handsome is the Livingstone Daisy (*Dorotheanthus bellidiformis*) which flowers only until August but once its radiant star-shaped flowers have embellished your garden, you will probably plant them again in the following seasons.

Vivid colour is added to rockeries by the low-growing cultivars of Snapdragon (*Antirrhinum majus* 'Pumilum'), while the carmine red Campion (*Silene pendula*) is attractive for its reddish follicles even when it has finished flowering. Blue colour is provided by the Swan River Daisy (*Brachycome iberidi-*

Tall cultivars of *Matthiola incana* are grown in beds, low, compact ones can be used for pots and containers. It is an excellent flower for cutting.

Zinnias (*Zinnia elegans*) look best in groups, either of a single colour or in a mixture of colours. The beauty of the bed will not be spoiled if you cut a few flowers here and there. Only fully opened ones should be cut, and they will last some 6—10 days in a vase.

Pelargoniums in combination with annuals have been used for this raised bed. The final effect is very colourful.

after the spring-
bling alpines in

surroundings can be planted with all the above mentioned species and also with more decorative plants, such as *Petunia* × *hybrida* or low-growing cultivars of *Matthiola incana*.

All the above-mentioned species require a well-drained soil, which in rockeries is usually guaranteed. They also require an alkaline soil, and finally a maximum of light and sun. Therefore, they should not be grown in shaded rockeries or in some specialized rockeries (e.g. in heath sections) where conditions are unsuitable for annuals.

Annuals in boxes and bowls

In window-boxes and bowls kept on balconies, annuals have no rivals because only they can tolerate a limited depth and volume of the soil. Similarly, their life cycle in this context reflects our requirements. In the autumn, window-boxes are usually removed, because if they have been planted in summer with geraniums or tuberous begonias they need protecting from both winter dryness and frost. On the other hand, annuals are given care from spring onwards when a new system of window-box decoration may be considered.

Boxes can be planted by the following methods:
1. Compact, low-growing but upright annuals which grow above the top of the box.
2. Plants which are decumbent or creeping in habit and which hang over the edge of the box.
3. Climbing plants.

If the box does not face north and if it is not in the shade, the first type of box, which in fact is a parallel to a flower bed, can be planted with compact, low-growing annuals. According to the size of the box, and in particular its width, one or several species can be used. If the boxes are required to be in flower over a longer period of time, early species can be combined with late-flowering ones. Very effective are low-growing cultivars of Stock, which flower from mid-June. When they stop flowering they can be replaced with begonias (*Begonia* × *tuberhybrida*) in full bloom. Another possible solution is that the

flowers. The
diminutive,
erfly Flower
are covered

tivated seed-
directly sown
gold (*Dimor-*
luebell (*Pha-*
nd July, and
californica),
ually it is suf-
the rockery
le, the plants
years.
the natural

338

Petunias need a heavier, nourishing soil and a sunny, sheltered situation. They will flower all summer long and should therefore be given a regular supply of feed once a week. The picture shows one of the uses of this annual plant. The wooden tub is overflowing with colourful flowers throughout the summer.

plants can be interspaced with seedlings of compact, low-growing Michaelmas Daisies which guarantee a continuous flowering season.

If the boxes need not be removed in winter they can be planted with pansies in early spring. If the seeds are sown in the autumn they must be protected from freezing by a covering of coniferous branches but, unfortunately, this does not give sufficient protection during severe frosts.

The second type of display involving flowers hanging over the edge of the boxes is best represented by petunias which are perhaps the most popular window-box flowers. They flower throughout the summer, producing a large quantity of bright variegated colours and they can best withstand extreme conditions in the open sun, surviving even some drying out of the soil.

Another rewarding plant for window-boxes is Nasturtium, although all species of cushion-forming annuals are suitable.

Species of the third type, the climbing plants, are best suited for patios and balconies. They can be trained along the railings or a light-weight support can be constructed for them so that they form a kind of green flowering wall. These climbing annuals, such as the Morning Glory (*Ipomoea purpurea*), Scarlet Runner (*Phaseolus coccineus*) or Sweet Peas can also be planted along wire fences or trellises, where they are always a welcome decoration.

Window-boxes and balconies facing north have a very limited choice of plants. The only species tolerating such conditions are tuberous begonias, Balsam (*Impatiens balsamina*) and low-growing Sweet Peas (*Lathyrus odoratus*).

Besides boxes, various types of stone and earthenware bowls can be planted with annuals. They can

Petunia × hybrida is one of the most favourite annuals for window-boxes and other containers. White-flowered cultivars underline the beauty of the composition and form an attractive contrast with the dark background.

Tropaeolum majus attains a length of up to 2 m. It is grown in beds, trained along railings, balustrades, arbours and pergolas or it can be used to form green curtains. Cut flowers can last up to 10 days in water.

The possibilities of uses of various plant species for the decoration of a roofed terrace are documented by this photograph. Annuals play an important part here.

Public spaces can be enlivened throughout the summer by large concrete containers planted with a rich variety of annual plants.

Pennisetum villosum is most beautiful at the end of summer, when it forms ornamental feathery spikes. It can be used for solitary planting and as a complement in groups. It needs an airy, permeable soil and a lot of sun for good growth.

also be placed on balconies and patios, in atrium-type gardens, in front of the house entrance or even on a well-kept lawn. Apart from the annuals that have been described, sufficiently large and deep containers are excellent for Love Lies Bleeding (*Amaranthus caudatus*), French Marigolds (*Tagetes erecta*) and the white Tobacco Plant (*Nicotiana alata*), particularly striking in the evening. These containers are best arranged so that the centre of the container is planted with a taller upright plant which is then surrounded by lower species overhanging the edges.

Care of the flowers in boxes and bowls is more intensive than that for plants in open flower beds. First

Hordeum jubatum planted in groups attracts one's eye by the delicate play of colours, particularly if it is stirred by the wind. It is also used for cutting, for fresh as well as well as dry arrangements. It needs a nourishing soil and a sunny situation.

of all, it is important to water them frequently and abundantly as the containers, in particular boxes suspended on walls, dry up very easily and very quickly. During the growing season, the plants should be fed several times with compound garden fertilizer. This is best supplied in liquid form, as used for potted plants. It must not be forgotten that the volume of soil, and therefore its nutritional value, is limited in boxes and although it is only used during one growing season, its regular enrichment will be appreciated by the plants. The latest date for effective feeding is the end of August.

Annual decorative grasses

Annual decorative grasses, particularly attractive at the time of flowering, can be successfully used in annual plantings. They remain decorative over a relatively long period of time since some grasses flower in succession and furthermore they retain their inflorescences in the ripened form after flowering.

Grasses are added to flower beds for their refining and relieving effect which is due to their indistinct, often neutral colour and their attractive habit. They are best placed in large, irregularly-shaped flower beds. Very effective and unusual is a combination of large groups of Feathertop (*Pennisetum villosum*) and Vervain (*Verbena bonariensis* or *V. erinoides*) or Barley (*Hordeum jubatum*). Of the other grasses, Cloud Grass (*Agrostis nebulosa*), Hare's Tail Grass (*Lagurus ovatus*), Switch Grass (*Panicum capillare*), Quaking Grass (*Briza maxima*) and *Lamarckia aurea* are also suitable. All of these grasses not only decorate the garden where, apart from their use in annual beds, they are also welcome additions to steppe-type sections, but they also yield excellent material for bouquets and flower arrangements — both when green and when dried.

Lagurus ovatus is most decorative in flower beds in large or small groups, but also in borders. Dried inflorescences retain their decorative character until spring.

The care of annual grasses is very simple and similar to that of annuals. They can be sown directly in flower beds or they can be pre-cultivated in nurseries.

Annuals with decorative leaves and fruits

Annuals with decorative leaves and fruits form the last specific group of annual plants. Of the low-growing species the genera *Alternanthera, Echeveria, Pilea* and *Iresine* can be ranged in this group. The Summer Cypress (*Kochia scoparia*) and Cosmea (*Cosmos bipinnatus*), which also has decorative flowers, are other good examples. Some species are decorative for their leaves even before they start flowering (for example, *Matricaria maritima*). Others

Kochia scoparia is a good short-term substitution for a hedge and it also makes an excellent background for variegated annuals. Solitary plants are also nice. It has no special requirements on soil and location.

Euphorbia marginata, up to 80 cm tall, has decorative, white-streaked leaves and bracts. It is used in flower beds among low, dark-flowering annuals. Singly planted individuals are also decorative. It should be grown in a light sandy soil in dry places and in full sun.

have interesting supporting bracts when in flower, such as in *Verbena bonariensis*. Some are attractive for the size of their exotic leaves (*Ricinus communis*). The dark red Mountain Spinach (*Atriplex hortensis*), which is 2 m tall, is cultivated as a solitary plant. Flame Needle (*Coleus × hybridus*), with its colourful leaves, makes a striking spectacle; while Senecio (*Senecio bicolor*) has a conspicuous silvery colour.

The fruit of some annuals, fresh or dried, can be used for indoor decoration. The seed-heads of large poppies, the sack-like seed pods of Love-in-a-mist, the faded inflorescences of the Pincushion Flower

A large bowl planted with flowering annuals is a nice summer decoration for a lawn. *Senecio bicolor* with its silvery leaves forms a fine contrast to the colourful pelargoniums.

Dimorphotheca sinuata 'Tetra Goliath' is grown in beds, singly or in groups; it is also used in rock gardens and dry walls. It is, however, attractive only on sunny days, when its flowers are open.

and the papery bracts of Honesty provide a great variety of shapes for beautiful flower arrangements.

Sowing, planting and care

The cultivation of annuals is quite time-consuming, because they have to be sown, pre-cultivated and transplanted every year. However, all of this can be done without expensive equipment and the seed — which is the most important component — is also reasonably priced. Cultivated seedlings gain in value with the necessary care and attention.

Direct sowing in the flower bed

Most annuals are propagated from seed. The simplest and most advantagenous method is to sow the seeds directly where the plants are to flower. This method is used with species that have a high reproduction rate. The cost of their seeds is therefore minimal and they do not require pre-cultivation. Some of them, in fact, do not tolerate transplanting at all, particularly those with a tap root. The seed is sown in pinches at recommended distances in a well prepared and carefully raked flower bed. The seedlings are then thinned out leaving just 2—3 plants to a cluster. The depth of sowing is determined by the size of seeds. Since they are usually very small they are sown in shallow drills, carefully covered with a very thin layer of soil and lightly pressed in, making sure that the soil is kept damp. Very delicate seeds are not covered at all but simply pressed down.

The time of sowing depends on the requirements of individual species, the temperature of the soil and the time when the plants are required to flower. Species which can withstand May frosts can be sown in the first half of April; more sensitive species, such as Nasturtium, in May so that they start to grow in the second half of the month. Some species can even overwinter in the bed and benefit from being sown in the autumn; the sowing should be done as late as possible so that the plants do not start growing before the winter.

The flowering season can be extended by sowing some species at regular monthly intervals, from early spring to the beginning of summer. In real terms this means sowing in the beginning of April, May and June. This method can usefully extend the flowering of species which otherwise have a short life-span.

The direct sowing method still remains to be adopted on a more extensive scale. It is ideal for gardens which can be looked after only at weekends and where caring for seedlings is problematic. Annuals which can be sown directly include both the low-growing species and those suitable for cutting. These include the popular and undemanding Pot Marigold (*Calendula officinalis*), the Cornflower (*Centaurea moschata* and *C. imperialis*), the delicate Baby's Breath (*Gypsophila elegans*), Marguerite (*Chrysanthemum carinatum*) and Larkspur (*Delphinium consolida*).

Another way of directly sowing annuals is in combination with pre-cultivated seedlings, to form a full ground cover. For example, in the middle of April, Stock can be transplanted to the flower bed and the Californian Poppy sown among the seedlings at the same time. The Stock is then removed at the beginning of July when it has finished flowering but the Californian Poppy will go on flowering until autumn when it can be replaced by biennials. This method can be adopted for flower beds planted with attractive but short-lived plants.

Ursinia anethoides is one of the earliest flowering annuals. The flowers open at the end of June and last about a month. The short flowering time is the only shortcoming of this nice plant, which is suitable for various types of planting as well as for cutting.

Dianthus chinensis and its many cultivars are excellent for flower beds where a rich variety of colours is required.

Pre-cultivation of seedlings

Species that have sensitive, slow-growing seedlings must be pre-cultivated in a protected and warm place in a greenhouse, frame or even in the house, on a window-sill, and then transplanted at the appropriate time. Seed-boxes, bowls and flower pots used for sowing must be clean. Delicate and sensitive species, such as begonia or lobelia, are best sown in new or at least sterilized containers. The soil for sowing should be sterilized, finely sieved and light. The actual time of sowing depends on the species. The seeds should be sown thinly and lightly covered with river sand. They are then pricked out into peat pots when they develop their first pair of true leaves. Seedlings grown in this way have a well developed root system by the time they are transplanted and will root well in their permanent place.

If the seedlings are too small and the box is filled with a thick growth, they need to be pricked out twice. The first time they are transplanted at greater distances so that they can continue to develop. Only when the seedlings are bigger and stronger can they be placed individually in seed-pots. The majority of species germinate and develop best at a temperature of about 18° C. The seedlings need plenty of light; otherwise they tend to grow in the direction of the light, become thin and tender, and susceptible to various diseases — the most frequent of which is the so-called damping off which causes a collapse of the small seedlings. Watering should be adequate enough to prevent the soil from drying out but it must not be too wet either.

The time of sowing — and the time needed for pre-cultivation — varies according to how long it takes the seeds to germinate and to develop into plants. Begonias are sown very early in January be-

cause their development is very long and only mature plants can be put out. Verbena is sown in February because it needs up to a fortnight to germinate and start to grow. Neither species should be put out before mid-May, because they will not survive even the slightest frost. On the other hand, French Marigolds, which are similarly sensitive and are transplanted at the same time, need only 5 weeks from the time of sowing to develop into flowering plants.

The seedlings of Stock are prepared for planting out as early as the middle of April, because if they are transplanted later they form poorer inflorescences. The seed should thus be sown in February.

While in January and February seeds can be sown only in the greenhouse, from mid-March they can be sown in warm frames either in drills or broadcast, that is, scattered over the soil. Again care must be taken to sow as thinly as possible. If the seedlings have enough space to develop they can be transplanted to the flower bed without being pricked out. Such plants, however, must be given greater attention because they will be weaker. They must be hardened off before being put out, by gradually increasing the ventilation — which helps them to get used to the outside temperature. Not even hardy plants can be transferred from the greenhouse without being hardened off first, as the greenhouse temperature does not drop below 10° C while the temperature in the garden especially at night can fluctuate around 0° C.

Biennials are sown from May to July in cold frames or in a very carefully prepared seed-bed. They are covered with a 1-cm layer of soil, which helps to retain the moisture around the seeds. At this time, the light and warmth is usually more than sufficient, so that the plants sometimes need to be shaded. In hot weather, germinating seeds and seedlings need to be given extra care and watered with a fine spray twice a day — that is, early in the morning and again in the early evening.

Convolvulus tricolor, about 30 cm in height, has a widely spreading habit (up to 80 cm across). The tips of the stems are decumbent.

Transplanting

The time for planting annuals is not dependent on so many specific factors as when sowing. In this respect annuals can be divided into two groups. The first contains species which, when young, are not harmed by low and near to zero temperatures which occur regularly in the middle of May. These can be planted in the flower bed from mid-April. The second group is formed by species whose seedlings cannot stand even mild ground frosts and therefore cannot be transplanted before the end of May.

The time for planting out may also be controlled by other circumstances. Sometimes it is necessary to wait until the flower bed becomes empty, if spring planting has been late and it is just at its best flowering stage or if the flowering period has been prolonged by staggered planting.

The bed where the annuals are to be planted needs to be well hoed because, in addition to water, plants also need a well aerated soil. The seedlings have to be planted at such a depth as to allow the root system to be completely submerged in the soil or even deeper if the seedlings are susceptible to being pulled out. The distance between the individual seedlings is determined by the size of the mature plant, which must be considered beforehand.

Biennials are planted out from the end of August to the end of September. The plants need to be well rooted before the winter arrives and therefore they need to be watered several times as required. They can be protected from frost, especially if there is no snow, by coniferous branches.

Care during the growing period

This includes particularly generous watering until the plants start to flower. During hot summer months it is better to water early in the morning or in the evening, because some species do not like cold water in contact with their plant tissue as it might kill them.

If, after a good watering or downpour, the surface of the flower bed becomes covered with a crust, this has to be broken up so that the air can get to the roots. During summer the soil should also be kept free of weeds.

Mineral substances, particularly phosphorus and potassium, should be added to the plants, best in the form of compound fertilizers. The first dose — the recommended quantity is dependent on the composition of the fertilizer — is worked into the soil about 14 days before sowing or planting. After thinning out or transplanting, the level of nutrients is restored by adding about half the first dose. Of organic fertilizers only old, well rotted compost can be used, because it improves the structure of the soil, especially of heavy, clay ones. Fertilizing with farmyard manure only suits certain species, in particular those of the cabbage family; it is not beneficial for the majority of annuals and some do not tolerate it at all. Most annuals like calcium and prefer a neutral soil.

Annuals can be grown in the same place for several consecutive years. The exception are Sweet Peas, since if they are sown in the same location as in the previous year they will sprout with difficulty and grow very slowly.

Annuals in an unfenced plot may be chewed by hares and wild rabbits. These, however, do not damage all species to the same degree. Above all, they will damage carnations, summer cypresses, marigolds, gazanias and vervains. If the annuals are therefore to be seen flowering, they must be protected by some form of fence.

In some species, it is possible to influence the length of flowering and in some cases determine the number of flowers by regularly removing the faded ones. A plant which is not weakened by developing

Phlox drummondii 'Cuspidata' reaches a height of 25 cm. It can either be combined with other low species or planted singly and is also suitable for rock gardens and dry walls. An undemanding plant, it will tolerate prolonged drought rather than long spells of rainy weather.

Antirrhinum majus, an attractive annual, comes in a wide range of multicoloured varieties. Taller forms are very good for cutting. The flowering season lasts from the second half of June to mid-August.

Zinnia flowers can be obtained in all colour shades except blue. *Zinnia elegans* is divided into several forms which differ in the shape of their flowers: dahlia-flowered (see the picture), cactus-flowered, miniature-flowered and 'scabiosaeflora'.

seeds produces larger flowers or in an effort to reproduce itself develops new buds.

Propagation

Vegetative reproduction

Vegetative reproduction of annuals is rarely used. In the past it was commonly used for cushion-forming plants with not only decorative leaves but also flowers. This method of reproduction used to guarantee the absolute similarity of plants, which is an important quality in an ornamental carpet cover. Nowadays, improved cultivars are available with seedlings that are so well balanced that vegetative reproduction is done almost entirely by green cuttings and is used only for species with decorative leaves in the early phase of growth before flowering.

In summer, the mother plants are chosen and at the beginning of August green cuttings are taken and inserted into boxes or peat pots filled with fine, light soil consisting of 2 parts compost and 1 part sand. The boxes are placed in a frame, partly shaded and kept as damp and ventilated as required. When the cuttings take root, the shading is gradually reduced and the young plants are hardened off by increasing ventilation until the windows and shading mats can be removed altogether. The rooted plants are put in the greenhouse at the end of September. The closer they are to the glass the better, as this stops the plants growing too tall. During the winter, they should be watered sparsely. In February, they can be transplanted to a warm frame where they will quickly form buds. Cuttings can be taken from stalks until mid-March, every cutting being left with 2—3 pairs of mature leaves. These are planted in a mixture of peat and sand in a warm frame. Rooting is promoted by higher temperatures (about 25°C) and a greater humidity. The cuttings are covered with glass and shaded with paper. The small, rooted cuttings are potted or planted directly in a warm frame in a sandy substrate. Afterwards they are cared for in the same way as seedlings, which involves adequate shading, watering, ventilation and hardening off before transplanting.

Reproduction of annuals from seed

Seeds of annuals are cheap, accessible and easy to obtain from specialized seed shops. They sell clean seed, guaranteed to germinate, well packed and accompanied by brief growing instructions. If you intend to acquire seeds of a species or a cultivar, determine beforehand whether the species in question is self-pollinating or not.

Self-pollinating plants, that is those which pollinate themselves predominantly by their own pollen, provide seeds which grow into plants with the same appearance as the parent plant. Species which are not self-pollinating need pollen from other plants for fertilization. The male plant, however, may belong to a different cultivar, growing perhaps in the neighbouring garden, and their offspring will then differ considerably in appearance from the female plant. If seeds are therefore required from a cultivar which is not self-pollinating, it is necessary to have only this cultivar in the garden and its neighbourhood or else the female plant must be isolated.

345

Select list of annuals and biennials

Species	Height in cm	Time of sowing	Time of transplanting	Distance in cm	Colour of flowers	Time of flowering	Light	Soil
Abronia umbellata	15—20	II—III	V	30—40	violet-pink	VII—VII	○	light
Adlumia fungosa	400	VIII	V	50	red-white	VII—IX	◑	light, heavy
Adonis aestivalis	30—50	III—IV		15	red, yellow	VI—VII	○	light, heavy
Adonis annua	10—30	III—IV IX		15	red	VI—VII	○	light, heavy
Ageratum houstonianum	25—35	I—II	V	20—30	violet-blue	VI—X	○	light
Agrostis nebulosa	30—50	IV	V	30		VII—VIII	○ ◑	light, heavy
Althaea rosea hybrids	100—200	VI	IX	80	red, pink, white, yellow	VII—IX	○ ◑	heavy
Alonsoa acutifolia	30—40	III	V	30—40	red	VII—VIII	○	light, heavy
Althaea ficifolia	100—120	V—VI	VIII	50	yellow	VII—IX	○	heavy
Amaranthus caudatus cultivars	60—100	IV—V	V	50	red, green-white	VII—IX	○	light, heavy
Amaranthus tricolor	80—100	III	V	50—60	green-white	VII—IX	○	light, heavy
Ammobium alatum	40—50	III—IV	V	40	white	VII—XI	○	light, heavy
Anagallis linifolia	20	I—II	V	30	blue	VI—X	○	heavy
Anchusa capensis cultivars	40—50	III	V	20—30	blue-red-white, blue	VII—VIII	○	light
Antirrhinum majus cultivars	30—60	II—III	IV—V	30	white, pink, red, yellow	VI—IX	○	light, heavy
Arctotis breviscapa	10—15	III	V	15	yellow-orange	VI—XI	○	light
Arctotis grandis	60—100	III—IV	V	40	white-blue-violet	VI—IX	○	light
Arctotis venusta	50—70	III	V	40	blue-violet-white-yellow	VI—XI	○	light
Argemone grandiflora	80—100	III	V	40—50	white-yellow	VII—IX	○	light
Artemisia gmelinii	100—200	III—IV	V	40—60	white-violet	VII—VIII	○	light, heavy
Asperula orientalis	5—10	IV		20	blue	VII—VIII	○	light, heavy
Atriplex hortensis	70—130	IV		40	yellow	VIII—IX	○	light
Begonia × semperflorens cultivars	10—40	I	V—VI	20—30	white, pink, red	V—XI	○	light, heavy
Bellis perennis cultivars	10—15	VI—VII	IX	20—30	white,, pink, red	IV—VII	○	light, heavy
Brachycome iberidifolia cultivars	25—30	III—IV	V	30	blue, pink, white	VII—IX	○	light, heavy
Briza maxima	40—50	IV		20	green	VI—VIII	○ ◑	light, heavy
Bromus briziformis	40—50	IV		20	green	VI—VIII	○	light, heavy
Browallia grandiflora	40—50	III	V	20—40	white, blue	VI—VIII	○	light
Calendula officinalis cultivars	30—50	IV		40	yellow, orange	VI—IX	○	light, heavy
Callistephus chinensis cultivars	25—80	III—IV	V	30—40	white, pink, red, yellow, violet	VII—XI	○	light, heavy
Campanula medium cultivars	60—1000	IV	IX	50	white, pink, violet, blue	VI—VII	○ ◑	light, heavy
Celosia argentea cultivars	20—100	III	V—VI	20—30	red, yellow, violet, pink, red-yellow	VII—VIII	○	light, heavy
Centaurea americana cultivars	100—200	III—IV	V	40	violet, pink, red, white	VII—VIII	○	light, heavy
Centaurea cyanus cultivars	20—50	III—IV	V	30	blue, white, pink, red	VII—VIII	○	light, heavy
Centaurea imperialis	90—100	IV		40	white, violet, red	VI—X	○	light, heavy
Centaurea moschata cultivars	60—90	IV		40	yellow, white	VII—X	○	light, heavy
Cheiranthus cheiri cultivars	25—50	VI	IX	30	brown-yellow, red-yellow, red-brown, yellow-orange	V—VI	○	light, heavy
Chloris virgata	50—60	IV		30	green	VII—VIII	○	light
Chrysanthemum carinatum cultivars	40—60	IV	V	40	white-yellow, red-yellow, red, orange-red	VII—IX	○	light, heavy
Chrysanthemum parthenium cultivars	20—30	II—III	IV—V	20—30	white, yellow	VII—VIII	○	light, heavy
Chrysanthemum segetum cultivars	30—60	IV		40	yellow	VII—IX	○	light, heavy
Cineraria maritima	40—50	III	V	20—30	yellow	VI—VIII	○	light
Clarkia elegans cultivars	60	IV	V	40	white, purple, lilac, orange	VI—IX	○	light
Clarkia unguiculata cultivars	50—60	IV	V	40	white, pink, red	VI—VIII	○	light, heavy
Cleome spinosa	100—150	III	V	50	white-violet, red-pink	VI—IX	○	light, heavy
Cobaea scandens	200—300	II—IV	V	20	violet, red	VII—X	○ ◑	light, heavy
Coleus Blumei hybrids	50—100	II—III	V	30	blue-white	VI—VIII	○	light, heavy
Collinsia heterophylla cultivars	25—30	III—IV		15	violet-white, pink-violet, violet, pink, white	V—VI	◑	light, heavy
Convolvulus tricolor cultivars	20—30	IV		50	blue, white, white-pink-blue, red, white-blue-green	VI—X	○	light, heavy
Coreopsis basalis cultivars	25—60	III—IV	V	40	yellow-brown	VII—IX	○	light, heavy

346

Species	Height in cm	Time of sowing	Time of transplanting	Distance in cm	Colour of flowers	Time of flowering	Light	Soil
Cosmos bipinnatus cultivars	100—150	IV	V	40—50	white, pink, red, red-violet	VIII—X	○	light, heavy
Cosmos hybrids	100—150	IV	V	40	red-pink, orange-white, pink, white	VIII-X	○	light, heavy
Cosmos sulphureus	40	IV	V	40—50	orange, yellow	VII—IX	○	light
Crepis rubra	25—35				pink with a darker centre	V—VIII	○	light, heavy
Cucurbita pepo	300 (length of tendrils)	IV	V	80	yellow	VII	○ ◐	light
Cynoglossum amabile	40	IV		40	blue	VI—VIII	○	light
Dahlia hybrids	45—200	III—IV	V	40	white, pink, red, yellow, orange	VII—XI	○	light, heavy
Delphinium consolida cultivars	30—100	IV X—XI		20	white, red, blue, pink-violet, blue-violet	VI—XI	○	light, heavy
Dianthus caryophyllus cultivars	40—70	II	V	30	white, pink, red, violet	VI—IX	○	light, heavy
Dianthus chinensis cultivars	15—40	III	IV	30	white, pink, red	VI—IX	○	light, heavy
Didiscus caeruleus	30—40	III	V	30	blue	VII—IX	○	light, heavy
Digitalis ferruginea	100—150	VI		40—50	yellow, yellow-brown, yellow-red	VI—VIII	○	light, heavy
Digitalis lanata	80—100	VI		40—50	white, white-yellow	VI—VIII	○	light, heavy
Digitalis purpurea	60—100	VI		40—50	white, yellow, pink, red	VII—VIII	○ ◐	light, heavy
Dimorphotheca sinuata cultivars	20—40	IV		30	white, yellow, orange, orange-brown	VI—VIII	○	light, heavy
Dorotheanthus bellidiformis	8—10	III—IV	V	20—25	white, yellow, pink, red, violet	VI—VIII	○	light
Dracocephalum moldavica	30—50	III	V	25	white, blue	VII—VIII	○ ◐	light, heavy
Eccremocarpus scaber cultivars	400—500	III	V	75	orange, red, yellow, pink	VI—XI	○	light, heavy
Echium plantagineum cultivars	30—50	IV		20—30	violet-red, white, blue	VII—VIII	○	light, heavy
Eschscholtzia californica cultivars	30—60	IV		30	orange, red, yellow	VI—IX	○	light, heavy
Euphorbia marginata	60—80	III	V	40	green-yellow	VII—VIII	○	light, heavy
Gaillardia pulchella	30—50	III	V	40	yellow-red	VI—XI	○	light, heavy
Gamolepis tagetes	15—25	III	V	15	yellow	VI—VII	○	light, heavy
Gaura lindheimeri	50—120	III	VI	60	white, red-white	VII—XI	○	light, heavy
Gazania longiscapa	15—20	III	V	25—30	yellow-brown-white	VI—VIII	○	light, heavy
Gazania rigens	15—25	III	V	30	yellow-brown-white	VI—VIII	○	light, heavy
Gilia capitata cultivars	50—80	IX—X	V	30	blue, white	VII	○	light, heavy
Gilia tricolor cultivars	20—40	IX—X	V	25	white, pink, red-brown, violet	VII	○	light, heavy
Godetia grandiflora	25—40	III—IV	V	30	white, pink, red, orange, with a dark or yellow centre	VI—VIII	○	light, heavy
Gypsophila elegans cultivars	30—50	III—IV		40	white, pink	VIII—XI	○	light, heavy
Gypsophila muralis	5—15	IV		30	pink, white	VIII—XI	○	light, heavy
Helianthus agrophyllus	100—150	IV	V	40—70	yellow	VII—X	○	light, heavy
Helianthus annuus cultivars	100—200	IV	V	40—70	yellow, brown-red	VII—X	○	light, heavy
Helichrysum bracteatum cultivars	30—80	III—IV	V	40	white, pink, red, red-violet, brown	VII—X	○	light, heavy
Helipterum roseum cultivars	30—50	III—IV	V	30	white, pink, with a yellow or black centre	VII—IX	○	light, heavy
Hibiscus trionum	30—60	III—IV	V	30—80	yellow, with purple patches	VII—IX	○	light, heavy
Hordeum jubatum	60—80	IV—V		20—30	green-white	VII—VIII	○	light, heavy
Humulus scandens	200—400	II—III	V	100	green	VII—VIII	○ ◐	light, heavy
Iberis amara	20—30	III—IV	IV	30	white	VI—VIII	○	light, heavy
Iberis umbellata cultivars	15—40	III—IV	IV	30	violet, red, white, pink	VI—VIII	○	light, heavy
Impatiens balsamina cultivars	20—60	III	V	20	white, pink, red, violet	VII—VIII	○ ◐	light, heavy
Impatiens walleriana cultivars	25—40	IV	V	20—30	red, pink	VII—VIII	○ ◐	light, heavy
Ipomoea tricolor cultivars	200—300	IV	V	30—40	white, blue, red, red-white, blue-white	VI—IX	○	light, heavy
Kochia scoparia 'Trichophylla'	80—100	III—IV	V	50			○	light, heavy
Lagurus ovatus	30—40	IV		20—30		V—VI	○	light, heavy
Lamarckia aurea	20—30	IV		10	green-yellow	VIII	○	light
Lathyrus odoratus cultivars	100—150	III—IV	IV—V	10	white, pink, red, violet	VI—IX	○	light, heavy
Lavatera trimestris cultivars	60—100	IV		50	pink, white	VII—IX	○ ◐	light, heavy

Species	Height in cm	Time of sowing	Time of transplanting	Distance in cm	Colour of flowers	Time of flowering	Light	Soil
Limnanthes douglasii	10—15	IV	V	15—20	yellow-white	VI—VII	○	light, heavy
Limonium bonduellei	40—50	III	V	40	yellow	VII—X	○	light, heavy
Limonium sinuatum cultivars	50—80	III	V	40	blue, white, pink	VII—X	○	light, heavy
Limonium suworowii	50—70	III	V	30	pink-red	VII—X	○	light, heavy
Linaria heterophylla	20—40	IV—V		15—20	yellow, with an orange-yellow-red band	VII—VIII	○	light
Linaria incarnata	20—40	IV		20	violet	VII—VIII	○	light
Linaria reticulata cultivars	40—60	IV—V		20	red, red-yellow	VII—VIII	○	light
Linum grandiflorum cultivars	20—40	IV		30	red, green	VII—XI	○	light, heavy
Lobelia erinus cultivars	10—20	II—III	V	20	white, blue, violet, pink	VII—IX	○	light, heavy
Lobularia maritima cultivars	10—40	III—IV	V	30	white, violet	VI—XI	○	light, heavy
Lonas annua	20—35	III—IV	V	40	yellow	VII	○	light, heavy
Lunaria annua	80—100	IV—VI	IX	30	scarlet red	V—VI	○ ◑	light, heavy
Lupinus — annual hybrids	50—150	IV		20—40	white, pink, yellow, red	VII—X	○	light, heavy
Lupinus hartwegii	50—75	IV		30	white, violet-pink, violet	VII—X	○	light
Lupinus luteus	30—80	IV		20—40	yellow	VII—IX	○	light, heavy
Malope trifida	80—100	IV		50	white, pink, red	VII—IX	○	light, heavy
Malva verticillata	150—200	IV		60—80	white-green-red	VIII—XI	○	light, heavy
Matricaria maritima	30—40	III—IV	V	30	white	VI—VIII	○	light, heavy
Matricaria perforata	20—50	III	V	25—30	white	VI—VIII	○ ◑	light, heavy
Matthiola incana cultivars	20—60	II—III	IV	20—30	yellow, white, pink, red-violet	V—VII	○	light, heavy
Meconopsis sinuata	40—50	IV	V	30	blue	VII—VIII	◑	light, heavy
Mesembryanthemum cristallinum	6—8	IV	V	10	white, yellow, pink	VII—VIII	○	light, heavy
Mimulus hybrids	30—70	IV	V	30	pink-white, red, pink	V—VIII	○ ◑	light, heavy
Mimulus luteus cultivars	20—60	III—IV	V	30	brown-yellow, yellow, yellow-red	V—VIII	◑	light, heavy
Mirabilis jalapa	30—100	IV—V	V	50	white, yellow, red, white-yellow, yellow-red	VII—X	○	light, heavy
Myosotis alpestris cultivars	20—35	VI	IX	20—30	white, pink, blue	IV—IX	○ ◑	light
Myosotis hybrids	20—35	VI	IX	20—30	blue, white	IV—IX	○ ◑	light
Myosotis sylvatica cultivars	15—30	V—VI	IX	30	blue, pink, white	IV—V	○ ◑	light
Nemesia strumosa cultivars	25—35	III—IV	V	20	white, yellow, orange, blue	VII—VIII	○	light, heavy
Nemesia versicolor	35—50	III	V	15—20	white, red, blue, violet	VII—VIII	○	light, heavy
Nicotiana alata cultivars	80—150	III—IV	V	50	green-white, white, pink	VII—XI	○	light, heavy
Nierenbergia hippomanica	10—15	III	V	20	violet	VII—IX	◑	light
Nierenbergia repens	15—20	III	V	20	white, yellow-white	VII—IX	◑	light
Nigella damascena cultivars	30—50	IV		30	blue, white	VI—VIII	○	light, heavy
Oenothera drummondii	50—60	III	V	25—40	yellow	VII—VIII	○	light, heavy
Oenothera rosea	10—20	III	V	20	pink-white	VII—VIII	○	light, heavy
Oenothera speciosa	30—70	III	V	25—40	white	VII—VIII	○	light, heavy
Oxalis corniculata	8—10	III—IV	V	5—10	yellow	VI	○ ◑	light
Oxalis rosea cultivars	10—15	III—IV	V	10	pink-red, white	VI	○	light, heavy
Panicum capillare	60—70	IV		40	yellow-green	VII—X	○	light
Papaver glaucum	40—50	IV		20—30	red, with a black centre	VI—VIII	○	light, heavy
Papaver rhoeas cultivars	30—60	IV		20	white, pink, red	V—X	○	light, heavy
Papaver somniferum cultivars	50—90	IV		20	white, red, pink	VI—VIII	○	light, heavy
Pennisetum setaceum	50—70	IV		40	green	VIII—X	○	light, heavy
Penstomon hybrids	30—80	I—II	IV	40	pink, red, blue, violet	VI—X	○	light, heavy
Perilla frutescens	50—100	III	V	40—50	green-yellow	VIII—IX	○	light, heavy
Petunia hybrids	25—50	II—III	V	20—30	white, pink, red, violet	VI—IX	○	light, heavy
Phacelia campanularia cultivars	15—30	IV		20—30	blue, white	VI—VII	○	light
Phacelia minor cultivars	30—50	IV		20—30	blue, violet, white	VI—VIII	○	light
Phlox drummondii cultivars	20—50	II—III	IV	20—30	red, pink, yellow, white	VI—IX	○	light, heavy
Polygonum orientale cultivars	40—150	IV	V	40	pink, white, yellow	VII—X	○ ◑	heavy
Portulaca grandiflora cultivars	4—6	III	V	30	white, pink, yellow, red	VI—X	○	light
Quamoclit coccinea cultivars	300—500	III	V	50	orange-yellow, yellow-red, yellow	VI—IX	○	light
Reseda odorata cultivars	15—40	IV		30	red, white, yellow	VI—VII	○ ◑	light, heavy
Ricinus communis	300	III—IV	V	50—80	green	VII	○	light, heavy

348

Species	Height in cm	Time of sowing	Time of transplant-ing	Distance in cm	Colour of flowers	Time of flowering	Light	Soil
Rudbeckia hirta cultivars	30—50	III—IV	V	40	yellow, with a dark centre	VIII—IX	O	light, heavy
Salpiglossis sinuata cultivars	40—100	III—IV	V	30	yellow-white, yellow, violet-pink	VII—X	O	light, heavy
Salvia farinacea	60—80	II	V	40	blue	VI—IX	O	light, heavy
Salvia patens cultivars	50—60	II	V	40	blue, white	VIII—X	O	light
Salvia splendens cultivars	20—40	II	V	30	red, white, pink	V—XI	O	light
Salvia viridis cultivars	30—60	II	V	50	white, violet, red	VI—VIII	O	light
Sanvitalia procumbens	10—15	III	V	30	yellow, with a black-purple centre	VI—VII	O	light, heavy
Saponaria calabrica cultivars	10—20	III	V	10	pink-red, red, white	VI—VII	O	light, heavy
Satureja hortensis	10—20	IV		10	white-violet	VI—VIII	O	light, heavy
Saxifraga cymbalaria	15—20	IV		10	yellow	VII—VIII	◐	light, heavy
Scabiosa atropurpurea cultivars	50—90	III—IV	V	30	white, red, pink, blue	VI—XI	O	light, heavy
Schizanthus pinnatus cultivars	30—45	III	V	20—30	violet, white, pink	VI—VIII	O	light
Sedum caeruleum	6—10	III	V	5—10 m	blue, white	VIII—X	O	light, heavy
Silene armeria cultivars	30—50	III	V	30—40	red, white, pink	V—IX	O	light, heavy
Silene coeli-rosa cultivars	20—50	III—IV	IV—V	30	white, violet, red	V—IX	O	light, heavy
Silene pendula cultivars	15—25	III—IV	V	30	pink, red, violet, white	V—IX	O	light, heavy
Tagetes Erecta-hybrids	30—100	IV—V	V	40	yellow, yellow-brown, yellow-orange	VI—XI	O	light, heavy
Tagetes Patula hybrids	40—60	IV—V	V	30	yellow, brown, yellow-orange	VI—XI	O	light, heavy
Tithonia rotundifolia	100—120	IV	V	50	red-yellow	VII—XI	O	light, heavy
Tropaeolum majus cultivars	15—30	IV—V	V	50	yellow, orange, red	VI—XI	O ◐	light, heavy
Ursinia anethoides	20—30	IV	V	30	orange	VI—VII	O	light
Venidium fastuosum	60—80	IV	V	60	orange	VI—VII	O	heavy
Verbena canadensis	25—40	II—III	V	30	violet-pink	VI—X	O	light, heavy
Verbena hybrids	30—40	II—III	V	30—40	red, blue, pink, white	VI—VIII	O	light, heavy
Verbena rigida	25—40	II—III	V	30	violet-blue	VI—VIII	O	light, heavy
Viola Wittrockiana hybrids	10—20	VII	XI	30	white, red, brown, yellow, blue	I—XII	O	light, heavy
Xerathemum annuum cultivars	40—60	III—IV	V	40	pink, violet-pink	VII—XI	O	light, heavy
Zinnia angustifolia cultivars	30—40	III—IV	V	30	yellow, orange-yellow, red	VII—XI	O	heavy
Zinnia elegans cultivars	30—60	IV	V	30—40	white, yellow, pink, red, violet	VII—XI	O	heavy

Bulbs and tubers

Plants that have bulbs and tubers are perennials, their main characteristic being the formation of an underground storage organ which is the basis of life of the same or a substitute plant in the following vegetative period. The one-year vegetative cycle is typical of this group, during which the plant forms its aerial organs, flowers, usually seeds, and accumulates nutritional substances in the underground storage organ for further vegetation. Each vegetative period is concluded with a dormant period, the beginning of each cycle being at the same time the end of the previous one. The course of the growing cycle in different genera and species does not keep to the same timetable, but it always lasts one year. The whole cycle takes place over a period of twelve months, though the beginnings and ends may not correspond to the beginning and end of the calendar year. According to the calendar, almost all plants of this group would have to be considered as biennials, as their vegetative cycle most nearly approaches the group of flowering biennials, such as pansies, daisies and forget-me-nots. Basically, biennials are also annual plants, whose vegetative cycle covers part of two calendar years.

The beginning of the vegetation of the various genera of bulbous and tuberous plants varies, being dependent on the advent of favourable climatic conditions that trigger off the beginning of the life cycle. However, no new vegetative cycle can begin until after the completion of the last one. This fact must be taken into account when cultivating these plants in the garden, and especially not forgotten when forcing flowers. The beginning of the growing cycle of bulbs, corms and tubers is not usually the same as the time when the aerial parts of the plant are formed. Indeed, this may be considered a major characteristic feature of this group of plants. Whereas in the majority of perennials the new growing period starts with physiological and biological changes in the parts of the plant that are above ground, in bulbs and tubers considerable changes occur first in the underground storage organs, from which the aerial parts only grow later.

In generative reproduction, only in the first year of their lives do bulbs behave like most other plants. Their life cycle starts with the germination of the seed and the formation of the first vegetative organs. Soon afterwards comes the foundation and development of the underground storage organ (the bulb or tuber), the main organ of these plants. The moment the bulb comes into being, the plants start to differ from others and become, not only biologically but morphologically, true members of their group.

Bulbs and tubers are cultivated in gardens for two reasons; partly for decoration (the ornamental part of the garden), and partly for cutting (the useful part of the garden). Some plants are more suitable for planting out of doors, others are more effective cut, and displayed in vases. An example of flowers that are much more decorative and lasting in vases than in flowerbeds is gladioli.

Flowers planted in the ornamental part of the garden should beautify it for as long as possible, so it is not suitable to use them as cut flowers. This applies especially to tulips, lilies, daffodils, snowdrops, snowflakes and fritillaries.

One of the most important and special qualities of many species of bulbs is that the flowers can easily be brought on or forced, even in the most critical

Low-growing tulip species are favourite rock garden plants. *Tulipa eichleri,* although its flowers are large and conspicuous, looks better in display planting.

Narcissi are used either in perennial beds or in groups, by themselves or with other spring-flowering bulbs. Here, an irregular bed of *Narcissus* 'Urania' is planted in a slight semi-shade.

winter months or early spring. Owing to lack of light in the winter, most other plants cease flowering, so it is mostly flowers from bulbs that herald the approaching spring into our parks and gardens.

Use of bulbous and tuberous plants

The following are the most usual ways of using these plants:
For decorative planting in gardens.
For planting out of doors for cutting.
For cultivation in pots indoors.
For bringing on and forcing.

Decorative planting in gardens
In gardens, bulbs and tubers are often planted in combination with other decorative plants. However, their location and arrangement is not always correct and often does not provide the best aesthetic effect. In principle, an ornamental garden should represent a natural formation concentrated in a small area. A garden is really a bit of live nature near our homes and so, here too, nature should be respected. The aesthetically most effective and most perfect rock gardens, mountain meadows, flowering walls and water and swamp gardens were formed according to nature's own laws. These natural formations not only satisfy man's aesthetic needs, but correspond to those of the plants, which is why — in a natural state — one never finds plants next to each other that do not go well together. Nor does one find plants growing in regular rows. A row of fading tulips combined with an equally straight front row of yellowing snowdrops, backed by roses hardly yet coming into leaf, will never produce the right effect. It is quite wrong to suppose that simply by supplementing this spring flowerbed with further rows of gladioli, marigolds and other attractive flowers, even orchids, a satisfactory effect can be achieved.

Even the most ordinary nettle naturally grows in loose groups, never attempting to form a rigid row.

The colour of tulip flowers asserts itself only in display plantings. The cultivar 'Maytime' of the Lilium-flowered group is suitable for beds as well as for cutting.

Yet, despite the fact that it is an unwelcome weed, such a cluster of nettles is extremely decorative from the moment they sprout in the early spring, when they are in flower and later when the faded stems are wrapped in crystals of hoarfrost. So, if you are using aesthetically valuable ornamental plants, do take a page out of nature's book and try to create in your garden charming harmonies of colour and form that do not disturb the surroundings but rather improve and add expression to them.

Group planting of bulbs alone
Group planting, either in regular or irregular forma-

Varieties of *Gladiolus hybridus* are grown exclusively for cutting. The flowering stem is cut off with no more than two stem leaves.

352

tions, should be the basis of a garden. Plants of one species forming groups are not only pleasing to the eye — they also provide expedient conditions for their own existence. They do *not* compete with one another in height, they take water and nourishment evenly from the soil, on hot days they shade each other's roots, in heavy rains or strong winds they support one another, so that they need less care from the gardener. Just by being together they form an appropriate microclimate; without the aid of man even within a very small area they create a natural home. This applies to bulbs and tubers even more than it does to other groups of flowers.

All bulbs and most tubers always grow in groups in the wild. In the course of years a mass of junior plants originate through the vegetative reproduction of the mother plant's storage organ, and these form a more or less dense growth of plants of the same species. In the case of small plants with an almost negligible leaf surface area, new plants grown from seed add their number to those produced vegetatively. Few bulbs have seeds equipped with wings or other apparatus aiding dispersal. When the seed pod bursts the bare seeds simply roll away somewhere close to the mother plant and start to grow. The large or more vigorously reproduced bulbs do have seeds with floats, and the wind carries these away to some more distant place, where they found a new colony.

In some lilies, which need a lot of light, the stalk of the mother plant travels some distance from the bulb before sprouting, so that the new bulbs that grow on it will have the living space they need. By this inborn behaviour the lily provides new plants with sufficient light and food for their existence. The differing behaviour of various species of bulbs is no

Fritillaria imperialis 'Lutea Maxima' is best suited for solitary planting. It can be left permanently in the ground. The bulb has a characteristic smell; it contains a poisonous alkaloid which can also be found in the aerial parts of the plant.

game of chance or carelessness on nature's part, but the result of thousands of years of development and it should be respected, even in garden cultivation.

Bulbs and tubers can be planted in gardens either in small, independent groups in the lawn, or combined with perennials. Even though many of them (crocuses, tulips and daffodils etc.) look very decorative as part of the lawn, scattered freely in the grass, this method cannot be recommended. In ornamental gardens the lawns have to be cared for and, espec-

Leucojum vernum, a favourite, undemanding spring bulb, is a good subject for rock gardens. It is also planted in groves under tall trees or in similar shaded places. The flowers can be used for cutting.

Gladiolus hybridus 'Black Jack' bears about 20 red flowers, arranged spirally along the stem.

Galanthus nivalis does best in semi-shade. It is intolerant of drying out of the soil during its vegetative rest and should therefore be planted under woody plants or mixed with perennials which provide shade in the summer months.

Cultivars of *Dahlia pinnata* are divided into groups according to the shape of their flowers. This picture shows a bed of multicoloured cactus-flowered varieties.

ially, cut often. But the bulbs need a long time to complete their vegetative cycle and form new storage organs. Any damage to their leaves before this time has elapsed will decrease their ability to flower the following year. Nor, in grass, can the plants be given the care they need, such as hoeing and fertilizing.

It is more recommendable from an aesthetic point of view and that of cultivation that the individual groups of bulbs should consist of only one species, and also if they are varied in shape and spacing. When early-flowering bulbs complete their cycle, their places can be taken by annuals, tuberous begonias, geraniums and so on.

Bulbs look very attractive, too, at the edges of wide paved paths or close by unbordered crazy paving. If the traffic on these paths permits, some of the stones at the edge can be taken out and the resultant square or oblong shapes planted with bulbs. When they are over they can be replaced with annuals or with the original stones. Even with this method, regularity or repetition should be avoided. The groups may be planted in place of one, two or more stones or, if the path is wide enough, flowering oases can be

formed between the paving stones. However, this method can only be used where the path leads through a grassy area.

In all these monoculture plantings, taller, early-flowering bulbs can be combined with biennials (pansies, forget-me-nots, daisies) that decorate these small beds before the bulbs sprout and especially after they have faded. For planting under tall bulbs, there is another bulb that can be used — the Grape Hyacinth (*Muscari armeniacum*). This plant, that grows up in the autumn if planted in time and covers the earth with its beautifully shaped clusters of leaves, is not appreciated as it should be. Its intensively blue racemes lasting 4—5 weeks can brighten the beds through April and May, and successfully replace pansies or forget-me-nots, which often do not winter well.

Combined planting of bulbs and perennials

Another way of using bulbs and tubers in the garden is to combine them with other ornamental plants, in the first place perennials. This offers almost unlim-

Crocosmia masonorum is used in perennial beds and is also grown for cutting. If the tubers are left in the ground in winter they should be protected from frost and dampness. They can be left in the same spot for a maximum of three years.

A yellow-flowered dahlia of the pompom group.

The genus *Crocus* includes some 80 original species. The modern large-flowered varieties originated predominantly from two species — *C. vernus* and *C. chrysanthus*. The picture shows *C. vernus* 'Queen of the Blues'.

ited possibilities. Besides the frequently used spring bulbs, which decorate all rock gardens and perennial beds, there are many very interesting and undemanding summer-flowering varieties that are very effective. To achieve success in combining flowers, however, one must have a good knowledge of their appearance, height, colour, flowering time and demands. By placing the individual cultivars correctly in the bed, unpleasant surprises can be avoided.

Even so, the use of bulbs and tubers among perennials can bring about some problems. At the time when spring bulbs should be dug up, most perennials are at the peak of their growing period and their root systems should not be disturbed by digging up bulbs. There are two possible solutions: either the bulbs can be left to their fate, and you can trust to what the following year will produce, or only those species and cultivars are planted that do not require to be dug up every year. Plants that should be dug up in the summer include tulips, hyacinths and, on account of voles, crocuses. These plants should be afforded at least the most important conditions for survival on the site during their dormant period. All crocuses need is protection against voles. Tulips and particularly hyacinths are subject to various fungus and bacterial diseases in the soil during their dormant period. The spread of these diseases is promoted by warmth and soil moisture. It is thus advisable not to water more than necessary places where bulbs remain in the soil, or to protect these places with cushions of shallow-rooting, creeping perennials such as *Thymus, Aubrieta* and *Cotula.* These low perennials prevent the earth from getting too hot and wet during the summer, and no ugly empty places appear in the beds when the bulbs have died back.

Bulbs that will not survive the winter out of doors must be dug up every year and planted again in the spring. These include *Ranunculus asiaticus* and *Ixia speciosa,* which complete their vegetative cycle in the summer and may sprout again in the autumn. If left in the ground over the winter they will die.

Feeding is another problem that arises if perennials are grown together with bulbs and tubers. Plants with underground storage organs require

Colchicum × hybridum 'Waterlily' is a beautiful double-flowered cultivar of Meadow Saffron. It is recommended for rock gardens, bed margins or lawns and can be put in the front of shrubs or in other similar places where its large leaves, produced in spring, will not spoil the setting.

Multiflowered varieties of *Crocus chrysanthus* can be used singly for miniature gardens made in containers. They must be removed after flowering, however, as their leaves might otherwise shade the remaining plants.

large quantities of nutrients, especially nitrogen, which is unsuitable for perennials, as it makes them grow too fast and decreases their flowering capacity. So here, too, some compromise has to be reached.

In view of the fact that bulbs can never be given optimum conditions in perennial beds, it has to be taken into account that, sooner or later, some of them will disappear and have to be replaced. But this sad fact also applies to many of the more sensitive perennials.

When planting bulbs among perennials they should again be placed in groups. Scattered individually among perennials they are never so effective as when there are several irregular groups. The number of plants in each depends on the robustness of the species and the character and size of the bed. There should be a minimum of three plants of one species or variety to a group, even with the most attractive

plants such as *Eremurus, Fritillaria, Allium* etc. The decorative effect of groups is considerable.

Combined planting of bulbs and decorative grasses
This is an interesting combination, forming so-called 'wild' areas in the garden. Not only does it make for texture and colour contrasts that can be achieved through correct placing of the plants, but also it is a natural combination of two groups that geographically belong together, as many bulb species grow in the wild along with grasses.

Bulbs in rock gardens
A very frequent way of planting small bulbs that do not make too great demands on their environment is to put them in rock gardens or dry walls. They are usually planted where carpeting perennials grow in summer. They look beautiful like that in the spring and enliven the rock garden at a time when rock plants are not yet sprouting.

Muscari armeniacum is one of the least demanding of bulbs. It thrives both in full sun and semi-shade and can be put out from August till the first frosts. The plants need no special care and can be left in the same spot for several years. The picture shows the cultivar 'Heavenly Blue'.

Eremurus stenophyllus var. *bungei* bears flowers which range in colour from yellow to orange-red. The inflorescence reaches a height of 120—150 cm. Its combination with *Allium giganteum* is particularly attractive.

Allium moly is used in single-species groups, best in large masses, or in perennial beds. The decorative inflorescence can be dried and used in winter floral arrangements.

Spring bulbs are favourite subjects for rock gardens. They should be planted in groups and the individual groups tastefully combined, either with other bulbs or with suitable perennials.

Low-growing species of the following genera of bulbs are suitable for rock gardens: *Allium, Chionodoxa, Crocus, Cyclamen, Erythronium, Galanthus, Incarvillea, Iris, Ixiolirion, Leucojum, Muscari, Narcissus, Ornithogalum, Platycodon* and *Tulipa.*

As in planting all bulbs, the aesthetic effect must be kept in mind in the rock garden too, and the needs of the individual species have to be respected.

Bulbs and tubers for cutting

Besides vegetables, those flowers you grow specifically for cutting can be cultivated in the kitchen garden. In the case of bulbs, this part of the garden can be used to bring the small, non-flowering storage organs to flowering size. Also, as some species in the ornamental part are almost bound to die off or weaken, a reserve can be formed in the kitchen garden to supplement them.

The following species and genera of bulbs and tubers are suitable for cutting: *Acidanthera, Allium, Anemone coronaria, Camassia, Crocosmia, Dahlia, Endymion, Eremurus stenophyllus* var. *bungei, Fritillaria meleagris, Gladiolus, Hyacinthus, Hymenocallis, Iris, Ixiolirion, Leucojum, Liatris, Lilium, Muscari, Narcissus,* and all the taller varieties of *Tulipa,* with the exception of botanical tulips.

Of course, only fully-grown plants with well-developed storage organs are suitable for cutting because only these plants are able to produce good quality flowers and, when cut correctly, form a substitute storage organ.

The flowers should be cut in the early morning, when they are fresh and sufficiently supplied with water. All flowers of bulbs and tubers, with the exception of dahlias and anemones, should always be cut when the buds are fully developed and coloured, but before the flower opens. They should come into flower in the vase. Cutting them at a later stage

Chionodoxa luciliae is an undemanding and tolerant plant, good for rockeries and the borders of perennial beds. It can also be planted in masses under sparse shrubs and trees and thrives in full sun as well as in semi-shade.

Anemone blanda is one of the earliest and most beautiful tuberous plants to be used in a rockery. The tubers are not quite hardy and therefore should be covered for the winter with dry leaves or other suitable material. This must be removed before the plants start to emerge.

Lilium auratum is a very beautiful lily belonging to the Oriental hybrids. It is excellent for cutting; cut the stems before the first bud has opened. A sufficient number of leaves must be left on the plant for the nourishment of the bulb; stop watering the plant at the end of the growing period to allow the bulb to mature adequately.

The cactus-flowered varieties of *Dahlia pinnata* are best suited for solitary planting. Cut flowers are highly decorative in the vase; one-flower stems without lateral buds last the longest.

means missing the most beautiful phase, the opening of the flower, and needlessly shortens the time they will last in a vase. The colour of flowers that blossom in water is rather lighter, but there is nothing wrong in that. The transport and manipulation of flowers in bud is easier and the flowers are not needlessly crushed and damaged. When arranging the spring-flowering species such as tulips and daffodils, it must be reckoned that, in the vase, both flower and stem will be prolonged by about a third of their original duration.

In the case of dahlias and anemones it is better to cut them when just fully out, but not going over. In cutting plants with a single stalk (tulips, lilies, gladioli etc.) care should be taken to ensure that at least the basic part of the leaf remains on the plant, as this is essential for the development of the reserve storage organ. If you do not wish to cultivate new bulbs the stalk can be cut down to the ground. If, however, new bulbs for future planting are wanted, the leaf surface should not be damaged. The development of the underground organs of bulbs reaches its height when the flowers fade and every leaf that is cut off decreases the size and quality of the bulb, and so of the flower the following year.

Cultivation in pots

Nowadays portable mini-gardens are becoming ever more popular. Earthenware or other pots of various sizes are planted with slow-growing shrubs, low perennials or rock garden plants. These miniature gardens are an interesting decoration not only in public places but also on balconies, terraces, verandas, paved courtyards and so on. The bottom of the pot should be covered with drainage material (bits of brick or broken flowerpots) and then filled with suitable soil. A thin layer of sphagnum moss should be placed between the drainage material and the soil, as this ensures the regular transfer of water from the drainage layer into the soil, so the plants do not have to be watered so often.

To bring variety to such mini-gardens, small spring-flowering bulbs can be used. They are planted in the ordinary way and at the usual time among the other plants. They should not be too near the sides of the pot or trough, so that the roots do not suffer from fluctuating temperatures during the winter. The plants should be placed in small groups or individually, and should not be fertilized. When they have finished flowering they should be removed, so that their growing leaves do not overshadow other plants in the miniature garden.

Forcing bulbs and tubers

Only healthy and large bulbs or tubers can be used for forcing and bringing on. Before planting the bulbs should be stored at temperatures up to 20° C.

Hyacinthus orientalis 'Delft Blue'. Small groups of hyacinths are planted in rock gardens or in perennial beds, combined with other spring-flowering bulbs. Large groups can be planted in lawns to great effect.

The genus *Narcissus* includes 40 original species. Mostly grown today, however, are cultivars originated by multiple crossing. They are divided into groups according to the shape of their flowers. The picture shows a member of the Daffodil group (with a trumpet centre).

Allium karataviense, decorative mostly for its ornamental leaves and dry inflorescences, is planted in rock gardens, in the front of perennial beds and in containers. The bulbs do not tolerate much dampness during the resting period.

Crocosmia × *crocosmiiflora* is noted for its long flowering, which lasts from July to the first frosts. The inflorescence is composed of 15—20 trumpet-shaped flowers.

They should be brought on in proportionately large pots or troughs, from which the plants are transferred to ornamental bowls before they flower. Anemones (*Anemone coronaria*) and daffodils or narcissi need pots at least 20 cm deep, but soil layers 5—8 cm deep are sufficient for the roots of other species. There is no point in using big pots or bowls for a single plant, nor does it look nice. Much more decorative is a group of 3—10 plants of one species or cultivar. For combinations of several species, plants brought on in troughs should be used, planted out according to their stage of development, as they must all flower at the same time. If some fade earlier it spoils the whole effect.

When bringing on bulbs at home, it is best to aim at their flowering in February or March, not earlier; otherwise, expert treatment is necessary. During the process there is no need to give extra feed to the bulbs, as they get what they need from their own

Eranthis hyemalis is particularly attractive at the end of winter and the beginning of spring, when its flowers emerge. They are not even deterred by snow and frost, and are good subjects for miniature rock gardens. Forcing of this species is also possible.

Crocus vernus 'Pickwick' produces 2—4 flowers from each bulb, which needs no cover in winter. Sufficient watering is necessary in the growing period.

supplies. The only exception are anemones, which should be treated with a fertilizer for indoor plants at regular 10—14 day intervals from the time the leaves start sprouting till the individual plant has finished flowering. Anemones and winter aconites (*Eranthis*) should be placed in full light as soon as the leaves start sprouting. Other species have to reach a height of 5—10 cm in darkness.

The soil for bringing on bulbs should be light, loose and contain a sufficient amount of sand. It should not be left to become too wet, so perfect drainage is a must. Most species are planted at the beginning of October (the depth of planting is given in the table on p. 361). In order to take root well the plants need an appropriate amount of moisture and, in most cases, a temperature of 2—8° C. At both lower and higher temperatures the bulbs and tubers do not root well and the flowering is poor. The plants are left to take root in a special rooting base (a heaped-up, well drained and heated garden frame) or in a damp cellar. After planting, they must be well watered. The pot or trough is then placed in the cellar, sprinkled with sawdust or peat so that the soil does not dry, though it is recommended that you should check the moisture every now and then. This is not necessary if they are in a frame. The bulbs must be protected from being eaten by voles and from frost. In the frame, the flowerpots are thus covered with up-turned flowerpots of the same size, with at least 15—20 cm of soil heaped up over them. When the surface of the soil freezes over, the frame should be covered with leaves or sawdust.

Only well rooted plants with developed buds are transferred indoors for the actual forcing (with the

exception of anemones and winter aconites). This takes place at various temperatures (see table), but always in the full light. The forcing period depends on the genus and species and many other factors. The table gives a rough guide to the number of days the plants need in which to form flowers. Throughout this time the plants should be well watered, but only narcissi need watering twice a day. The prescribed temperatures must be observed during rooting and especially during forcing (these are also given in the table). It is especially dangerous to exceed the given temperatures, as this leads to the buds drying, the flowers becoming papery, or even not forming at all (crocuses). Forced plants only last well in cool rooms.

Forced bulbs and tubers are not suitable for further forcing but, with the exception of tulips, they can be planted out in the garden. After flowering they are usually left in their pots till the end of the growing period and then planted out at the proper time. At the end of the cultivation period in pots the plants must be fertilized regularly.

Cultivation in the garden

Environmental requirements of bulbs and tubers

Most bulbs and tubers need a sunny situation but will tolerate a slight semi-shade. Permanently shaded places are unsuitable for any of them. The plants will bloom earlier in an open, sunny place, but the flowers last a little longer in semi-shade. However, the development of the plant and the new underground storage organ is always better in sunny places, as is the general health of the plant. The following species and genera can be planted in semi-shade: anemone (*Anemone blanda*), tuberous begonias (*Begonia × tuberhybrida*), cyclamen (*Cyclamen*), *Chionodoxa*, winter aconite (*Eranthis*), dog's tooth violet (*Erythronium*), the Chequered Fritillary (*Fritillaria meleagris*), snowdrop (*Galanthus*), snowflake (*Leucojum*), some lilies, the Squill (*Scilla sibirica*) and others. Indeed, some of these even call for a shaded place, as they otherwise suffer from sunscorch.

Bulbs and tubers can be grown successfully in almost all garden soils, but they do best in sandy-loamy, well-drained, neutral or slightly alkaline

Begonia × tuberhybrida of the Gigantea group needs a semi-shaded situation and a light, permeable soil with an acid pH. It is intolerant of drying out, even for a short time.

Bulbs and tubers suitable for forcing

Genus/species	Temperature during rooting (in °C)	Layer of soil over bulb (in cm)	Time of rooting (in weeks)	Temperature during forcing (in °C)	Period of forcing (in days)
Anemone blanda	10 or more	2	till sprouting	8—10	20—30
Anemone coronaria	10 or more	5	till sprouting	8—10	30—40
Crocus	4—8	4—5	8—10	8—9	15—20
Eranthis	4—8	2	12	8—10	15—20
Galanthus	4—8	1	12—14	12—15	15—20
Hyacinthella	4—8	1	12	10—12	20—25
Hyacinthus	4—8	0	10—12	20—22	20—25
Chionodoxa	4—8	1	10—12	12—15	20—25
Iris reticulata	4—8	4	12—14	8—9	20—30
Leucojum	4—8	1	12—14	12—15	20—30
Muscari armeniacum	4—8	1	12	10—12	20—30
Narcissus	4—8	2	12	14—16	25—35
Scilla	4—8	1	10—12	12—15	25—30
Tulipa	4—8	0	9—12	16—18	25—30

soils, supplied with humus and nutrients. They do not like heavy, wet soils or really dry, sandy or gravelly situations where the plants develop poorly and suffer from a permanent lack of moisture. Unrotted organic waste should never be worked into soil intended for the cultivation of bulbs and tubers, with the exception of alkalized peat, which is the only sterile substrate of organic origin. It is totally wrong to plant bulbs in a bed fertilized with fresh manure from any domestic animal.

Preparation of the soil, feeding and principles of correct planting
The bed for bulbs and tubers must be well, deeply dug, in the case of autumn planting at least 10—14 days in advance. For large bulbs the minimum depth is 20—25 cm, that is the entire length of the spade.

This is because the root system mostly extends below the storage organ, and the ground is prepared in the first place for the roots. During digging, all weeds should be removed, special care being taken to eradicate perennial weeds. The soil is prepared well before planting to allow the upper layers to settle, so that the correct depth for planting can be determined accurately. For spring planting, the ground should be prepared before the start of winter and the clods left to freeze. Heavy soils can be lightened by the addition of sawdust, sand, ashes, roughly alkalized peat or artificial lightening substrate. Drying light soil can be adjusted by the addition of well rotted compost mixed with heavy soil. For the basic feeding before planting, combined fertilizers can be used that contain the three basic elements: phosphorus, potassium and nitrogen. For species with a short

Erythronium dens-canis has not only attractive flowers but also very ornamental leaves. It prefers permeable soils, rich in humus, and sufficiently damp situations in semi-shade or light shade. It suffers from wet conditions in winter.

Iris reticulata is an attractive early-flowering bulb suitable for rock gardens, dry walls, perennial beds and for planting in lawns. Its bulbs are quite frost-resistant but they do not tolerate wet conditions during the resting period. The picture shows two cultivars — the violet 'J. S. Dijt' and blue 'Joyce'.

growing period, 100 g of compound fertilizer per square metre is recommended. For species with a long growing period, such as gladioli and lilies, that will be given a further dose before the period ends, 50 g is enough before planting. The fertilizer is added to the soil one to two weeks before planting. It is important to spread the fertilizer evenly and mix it into the whole layer of soil over the newly planted bulbs. During vegetation it will gradually be washed down to the roots. For some more sensitive outdoor species such as *Erythronium*, *Cyclamen* and *Begonia*, it is recommended to use only repeated watering with a fertilizer solution during vegetation.

Before the actual planting, the ground should be lightly raked over, care being taken not to stamp the earth down, so as not to sabotage the beneficial results of digging. In small beds the work can be done from the path; in big ones a broad board will diffuse the body weight and avoid tamping the earth down in one place.

The depth and time of planting depend on the species but, roughly, it can be said that, with the exception of a few species, the depth of planting should be about three times the height of the bulb. Depth of planting means the height of the layer of soil above the bulb or tuber, so it is measured from its top, not from the bottom of the hole or trench. Small bulbs should therefore be planted more shallowly than large ones, even of the same species. In heavy clay soils this depth can be 2—3 cm less; in very light ones 2—3 cm more. Also, in freshly dug beds where the soil has not had time to settle before planting, the bulbs should be planted some 2—4 cm deeper.

The distance between the plants depends on the species and on the purpose of planting. In decorative beds they should be planted in irregular groups, not in rows. In beds of flowers intended for cutting and for the cultivation of small bulbs, regular rows are more convenient.

Bulbs and tubers can be planted in holes or shallow trenches, or at the bottom of a bed that has been hollowed out to the required depth. The last method is probably the best, but it is the most time-consuming. After being hollowed out, the bed is again dug over at the bottom, the bulbs gently pressed in and the soil carefully replaced. This method enables the bulbs to be planted evenly at the same depth and it is particularly suitable for small groups. In the usual way of planting with a trowel, the plants are often not sufficiently or evenly deep, which means they develop irregularly, are of different heights and do not bloom at the same time. When planting in trenches equal depth can be easily maintained.

The growing tips of the bulbs or tubers must always point straight upwards when planted. Bulbs planted upside down always sprout later and irregularly and grow into weak plants; some cannot grow at all and die (*Anemone coronaria*). So, when planting, the bulb or tuber should be gently pressed in and then covered with soil, care being taken that the tall bulbs especially do not fall on their sides. After planting, the soil is lightly raked over and watered thoroughly; not so little that the water does not reach the bulbs, not so hastily that the top layer of soil becomes muddy. If it does, a hard crust will form on the surface when the earth dries, which is difficult for the plant to pierce and may have an unfavourable effect on the health of the underground organs. In dry weather, watering should be repeated as needed. Field mice should be kept in check during rooting time, as these are a great danger to some species. In combating them, a cat is much more reliable than even the most efficient vermin poison.

Care during vegetation

As soon as the plants start sprouting, the surface of the bed should be loosened and weeded. The loosen-

The genus *Lilium* includes some 90 species occurring in the temperate and subtropical zones of the Northern Hemisphere. Lilies were among the first ornamental flowers cultivated by man. Their bulbs can be left in the ground for several years but they need an annual supply of fertilizers. The picture shows a pink-flowering cultivar belonging to the group of Trumpet-flowered lilies.

A lily cultivar of the Trumpet-flowered group.

Colchicum bornmuelleri needs deep humus-rich, medium heavy soils containing sufficient accessible nutrients. Older specimens flower more profusely than newly planted ones. The plants must be given fertilizers every year.

Hyacinthus orientalis 'Bismarck' is a very demanding and sensitive plant. Maximum care must be paid to the preparation and cultivation of the soil before planting, and a supply of compost is also recommended. The surface of the soil must be kept loose during active growth.

ing is particularly necessary if a saltpetre fertilizer has been used, as this promotes muddy soil and subsequent crust formation.

During vegetation, the soil surface should be regularly dug over, weeded and watered. Watering should be done in the cool of the morning or, better still, in the early evening. If the plants are watered at high temperatures, especially in hot summers, their underground or aerial parts may be damaged. This applies particularly to hyacinths, tulips, begonias and some other sensitive plants. Rainwater or soft water is best slightly warmed, and is preferable to cold well water. Tap water, treated with chlorine, should stand several hours in the sun in an open vessel before watering, so that the excess active chlorine can escape. Particularly sensitive to chlorine are, for instance, hyacinths.

After watering, and also after heavy rain, the surface of the earth should be dug over to break the crust. Failure to do this leads to an excess formation of steam in the soil, which may destroy the plants altogether, especially in the final phases of vegetation. The young supply organs, which are still relatively soft and mostly unprotected, are most sensitive to infection at this stage. Decreased transpiration of the plants at the end of vegetation, and thus a lesser uptake of water from the earth, increases the excess moisture formed, and high temperatures in the warm, wet soil during the day provide an ideal environment for the spread of all pathogenic fungi and bacteria. It often happens that when digging up the bulbs of quite healthy plants the remains are found of recently healthy storage organs, quite rotten or severely damaged. So, the watering of all bulbs and tubers should cease about a month before the natural end of the growing period. At this time, the supply

organs do grow bigger to some extent, but mainly their root hairs mature, and for this they do not require much water from the soil. The bulbs are preparing for their dormant period.

All processes grouped together under the word 'rotting' are caused by the activities of pathogenic fungi or bacteria that infect parts of the plant and destroy them. In many cases, the gardener can prevent infection by proper care and cultivation, which

Recommended depths for planting bulbs and tubers (measures are given in cm). On the left, from top: *Lilium giganteum*, *Scilla*, *Crocus*, *Eranthis*, *Hyacinthus*, *Lilium candidum*, *Lilium regale* and *Lilium tigrinum*. On the right, from top: *Anemone*, *Ranunculus*, *Muscari*, *Galanthus*, *Leucojum*, *Lilium umbellatum*, *Tulipa*, *Lilium tenuifolium*, *Fritillaria imperialis*.

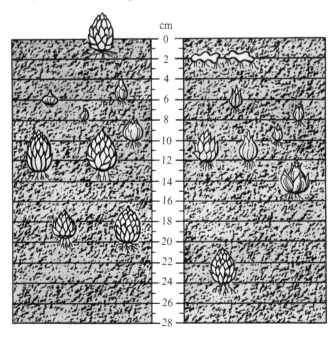

is the basis of optimum soil activity. In healthy, biologically active soil, harmful organisms do not multiply sufficiently to damage cultivated plants seriously. However, man can often upset the natural biological balance in the soil by wrong cultivation, and so allow the spread of pathogenic micro-organisms. Cultivation of the soil should be carried out according to its state and the requirements of the plants.

Garden soil is not usually sufficiently supplied with nutrients necessary for the development of bulbs and tubers. Gardens with plenty of humus and well cultivated soil have a better supply of available nutrients than extensively maintained gardens. Light, sandy soils usually have a smaller supply of nourishment than clay or loamy soils. Bulbs and tubers consume large quantities of nitrogen, potassium and phosphorus during their vegetation, so these must be added to all types of soil in the form of industrial fertilizers.

Besides the basic fertilizing before planting, bulbs and tubers require supplementary feeding with nitrogen or combined fertilizers during vegetation, when they are forming their new supply organs.

Spring-planted species mostly require fertilizing twice — about a month after sprouting and again at flowering time. Species having a short growing period such as *Anemone coronaria, Ranunculus* etc. should not be fertilized twice, though they do sprout in the spring. Dahlias should never be fertilized during vegetation, as they flower poorly if there is too much nitrogen in the soil.

Hardy bulbs that remain in one place for several years must be given their annual supply of feed every year. This is done by putting down a compound fertilizer in the autumn. Spring fertilization with nitrogen is the same as for annuals. Immediately after fertilization the plants must be well watered, so that the fertilizer is quickly dissolved and

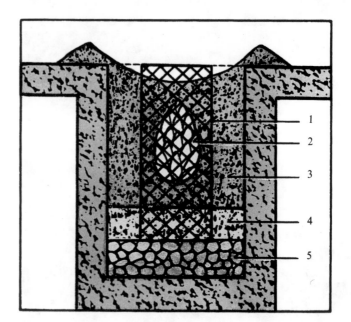

Planting lilies. Put a layer of gravel or a similar drainage material at the bottom of the hole (5), then a layer of sand (4). Then add a layer of high-quality soil (3) in which the bulb is laid at a proper depth and the hole is filled up with the rest of the soil. To protect the bulb from voles, it is advisable to plant it within a small cage made of wire (1).

reaches the roots. Watering is repeated once or twice over a period of 14—20 days after fertilization, to prevent a temporary increase in the concentration of mineral substances in the layer of earth over the roots as, particularly with the use of saltpetre, this might burn the underground part of the stalks. Watering must always be thorough, but should not exceed the absorbency capacity of the soil.

The faded flowers of plants grown in the ornamental part of the garden should be removed immediately after flowering, as if the seeds are left to form the development of the vegetative storage organs is

Lilium candidum does best in full sun. It is put out as early as the beginning of August and does best in a south-facing spot. The soil should be enriched with a well-rotted compost mixed with leaf mould or with peat and river sand.

A yellow-flowered cultivar of *Dahlia pinnata*, belonging to the singles group.

'Tartan', a dahlia of the decorative group.

The Waterlily Tulip, *Tulipa kaufmanniana*, is one of the early-flowering tulips, used for planting in rock gardens and lawns.

suppressed severely. The flowers are removed by breaking them off directly below the petals or by taking off the flowering stem under the lowest flower. Take care not to damage the assimilation organs when doing this.

Care for the plants' health

As soon as the aerial parts start to sprout, all the plants should be examined to see if they are healthy and any diseased ones should be removed, so that they do not infect the healthy ones. This should be done repeatedly throughout the whole growing period. Signs of fungus diseases appear at the beginning of the vegetative cycle, whereas those of others, mostly bacterial and virus diseases, are manifested later. Plants showing signs of any infectious disease must always be removed, regardless of the season or the growing phase of the plant. This applies especially to virus diseases of tulips and gladioli, which can only be diagnosed when the flowers are out.

Besides this negative selection, the plants should be sprayed preventively with chemical preparations. Although the use of chemicals in the garden is complicated, some plants do need spraying three or four times a year. Plenty of chemicals used for protecting plants are not poisons; for instance, fungicides can safely be used if the minimum of hygienic measures is observed. Unfortunately, there are not as yet suitable preparations for spraying against bacterial diseases. The worst problems arise in the use of insecticides to destroy sucking or biting insects that damage the plants.

As yet, there is no all-purpose chemical spray that cures everything. The various available preparations cure specific diseases. However, in all cases the hygiene instructions of the producer as well as instructions regarding concentration, method of application etc. should always be observed.

Bulbs and tubers in winter

With the fading of the aerial parts of the plants, bulbs and tubers pass into their dormant phase. The following principles should be observed in garden cultivation:

Storage organs of species sensitive to frost such as *Acidanthera, Anemone coronaria, Begonia × tuberhybrida, Canna, Crocosmia, Dahlia, Freesia, Galtonia, Gladiolus, Hymenocallis, Iris × hollandica, Ixia, Oxalis, Ranunculus* and *Tigridia* should be dug up every year. The same applies for plants requiring summer storage, such as hyacinths, garden tulips, sensitive species of botanical tulips, and even crocuses.

Other genera and species, including botanical tulips such as *Tulipa kaufmanniana, T. eichleri, T. urumiensis, T. tarda, T. biflora, T. turkestanica* and *T. praestans,* can be left on the same site for several years.

Narcissi, lilies and autumn crocuses should be dug up after 3—4 years, when the plants start to multiply rapidly and their growth becomes too dense.

Bulbs and tubers should be dug up before the aerial parts die down completely. The storage organs must be lifted out with care and the stalks or leaves taken off directly above them. This is essential to maintain the bulb in good health. The only exception is dahlias, where only the dry leaves are removed and all the old stalks are cut down to a height of about 10 cm.

After all the remnants of soil have been removed, the bulbs and tubers are placed in thin layers in crates and stored in a dry, well-ventilated room. The crates should be raised on legs, so that currents of air can pass under them. Only species that are dug up in the autumn can be dried in direct sunlight, but they must be protected against evening dew and cold.

As soon as they are dry, which is usually after about a month, the bulbs should be cleaned, the

Tulipa kaufmanniana 'Heart's Delight'.

dried remains of old storage organs taken off, and stored. Lily bulbs, with the exception of *Lilium candidum,* are not dried.

The state of health of the supply organs should be carefully checked during digging up and cleaning and throughout the storage period. All diseased bulbs and tubers must be removed at once, or they will infect the others and may cause a mass spread of fungus and bacterial diseases.

If the storage room has no ventilation to take off the damp air, the temperature must be kept low, never more than 20° C, especially in the early phases of drying.

Preventive disinfection of all the bulbs and tubers with a suitable disinfectant, as soon as they are dug up, is the best way to restrict the spread of fungus diseases. Before this is done the storage organs must be washed to rid them of all remains of the soil. This is best done by putting them in a net and dunking this in a bowl of water, then rinsing them with clean water. When they have been disinfected, the bulbs are left to dry slightly, and only then are they laid in the storage room.

Throughout this cleansing of the bulbs and tubers it should be remembered that they are living organisms that are undergoing internal changes even during this apparently dormant period, the course of which depends on the storage conditions and the care of the gardener. All bulbs and tubers must be well protected from frost.

Reproduction

Bulbs and tubers reproduce both by vegetative and generative means. Indeed, vegetative reproduction is a basic method of natural reproduction for members of this group, unlike most other plants. The cultivated varieties of many species can only be reproduced vegetatively.

Generative reproduction
In the garden, reproduction from seed is only suitable for botanical species. It is true that in large-scale nursery gardens plants in which vegetative reproduction is not very productive are usually produced from seed (anemones, begonias, cyclamens, freesias etc.), but the offspring obtained in this way are not uniform in their characteristics, so this method cannot be recommended for the cultivation of garden varieties.

The seeds of botanical species should be sown in a garden frame or a seed bed. The soil in the seed bed must be lighter and better prepared than in an ordinary bed. The seeds of most species should be sown 1—2 cm deep; those of hardy species must be sown in the autumn, as they are unable to germinate without being touched by frost. Sensitive species should be sown in spring. Special care must be given to plants in the seed beds, where they should be left to develop for 2—3 years. The soil should not be fertilized before sowing or during the first season. After this, however, the young plants should be given some feed in the autumn and spring, the same as for adult plants. In the case of most species, only small bulbs are formed during the first 2—3 years. These must be transplanted two or three times and then cultivated for a further 1—3 years. At each transplanting the bulb is planted deeper, to ensure the right warmth and moisture conditions. Of course, the seedlings of non-hardy species must be dug up every year before winter.

Vegetative reproduction
Vegetative reproduction is the basic method for the natural reproduction of bulbs, corms and tubers.

Annuals produce not only a substitute bulb every year, but also a larger or smaller number of small bulbs (tulips, irises, fritillaries). These vary in size, but some are always capable of flowering. Species with bulbs lasting for several years produce much fewer small bulbs which must always be cultivated for at least a year to reach the flowering size. In this group, the small bulbs are only produced by very large mother bulbs. In practice, an artificial method

Tulips, particularly the Darwin hybrids, are excellent for display planting in large groups.

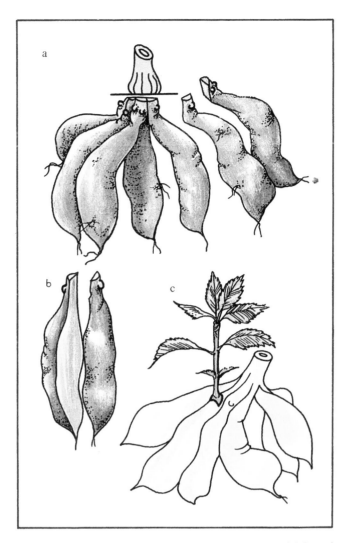

Propagation of dahlias: a) by division of clumps, b) by division of tubers, c) from cuttings.

Small storage organs and young plants of all bulbs and tubers are cultivated in the same way as is the case for adult plants, but more care must be devoted to them. The storage organs large enough to be cultivated should always be planted more carefully than fully grown bulbs, which are better able to stand up to possible negligence.

Bulbs and tubers in pots

Some genera and varieties that come from tropical and subtropical regions are not suitable for outdoor cultivation in European conditions. Many of them, however, can be successfully cultivated in pots, indoors. The most suitable for this are the following genera and species: *Agapanthus, Amaryllis, Amorphophallus, Calladium, Cyclamen persicum, Eucharia, Gloriosa, Haemanthus, Hippeastrum, Scilla violacea, Vallota* and *Zantedeschia*.

When cultivating bulbs in pots, like other indoor plants, it should not be forgotten that they still undergo the regular alternations of vegetative and dormant periods. If they are not given their rest at the appropriate time, by restricting or \completely ceasing watering, lowering temperatures etc., they will not complete their vegetative cycle and usually will stop flowering. During the growing period, on the other hand, these plants require increased amounts of water and feed, which should be supplied by regular watering and fertilizing. Most of them can be grown on the balcony in the summer, or put in a sheltered place in the garden in their pots. The dormant period can be triggered off artificially in most species by simply reducing the supply of water. Species that go through their dormant period without leaves should be watered again only when the new leaves or flowers appear. After the end of the dormant period it is best to transplant the plants into fresh soil every year.

Meadow Saffrons are very decorative plants, much valued for their autumn flowering. *Colchicum byzantinum* var. *cilicicum* bears deep pink flowers.

of vegetative reproduction is used for some bulbs. This consists of wounding the base of the bulb (hyacinths, squills), or detaching the scales of the mother bulb (lilies, fritillaries). Small bulbs develop after a certain time, under favourable climatic conditions, on the cut surfaces or on the separated scales, and these then have to be cultivated for a further 2—4 years to reach flowering size.

Corms either form a certain number of small corms that are capable of flowering every year (autumn crocus, crocus, montbretia), or, besides the one substitute corm, a large number of small vegetative reproductive organs, called offsets or spawn (gladioli, acidantheras, ixiolirions). These offsets are mostly not capable of producing flowers the following year, and have to be cultivated further.

Tubers seldom produce small tubers, and only if the plant grows to a maximum size. Mostly, however, they do not produce new storage organs but the mother tuber simply divides into two or more substitute tubers (dahlias, anemones, eremuruses). Therefore, in the case of most tubers, only the generative method of reproduction is used, or some artificial method of vegetative reproduction, such as making cuttings of young stalks (dahlias, begonias, cannas).

Select list of bulbs and tubers

Species	Height of plant (in cm)	Colour of flower	Flowering time	Requirements Soil	Light	Depth of planting (in cm)
Acidanthera bicolor var. *murielae*	80—100	white with reddish-brown spot	VIII—X	nourishing, loose	○ ◑	6—8
Allium aflatunense	80—100	light violet	V	light, loose	○	12—14
Allium caeruleum	50—60	azure blue	VI—VII	light, loose	○	6—8
Allium karataviense	15—20	white with pink	IV—V	no special demands	○ ◑	12—14
Allium moly	20—25	yellow	V—VI	no special demands	○ ◑	6—8
Allium oreophilum	15—20	pink-red	VI—VII	sandy-loamy	○	6—8
Anemone apennina	15—20	sky blue	IV—V	dry, permeable	○ ◑	5—7
Anemone blanda	10—15	blue	III—IV	moist, warm	○ ◑	5—7
Anemone coronaria	20—25	variable	V—VI	light, humus-rich	○	5—6
Begonia × tuberhybrida	15—40	white, yellow, orange, red	VI—X	light, humus-rich, permeable, acid	◑	2—3
Bletilla striata	20—50	carmine-pink	VI—VII	humus-rich, Ca	○ ◑	7—10
Bulbocodium vernum	10—15	mauve, purple	II—III	sandy, humus-rich, moist	○ ◑	8—10
Camassia quamash	40—50	steel blue	V—VI	sandy, humus-rich permeable	○	10—12
Canna indica	40—150	yellow, pink, red	VII—X	nourishing, loamy-sandy, permeable	○	5
Chionodoxa luciliae	10—15	blue, white centre	III—IV	light, humus-rich	◑	5—8
Colchicum autumnale	10—15	mauve	IX—X	humus-rich, moist	○	10—15
Colchicum bornmuelleri	12—15	mauve	VIII—IX	sandy-loamy	○ ◑	10—15
Crocosmia × crocosmiiflora	60—80	orange-red	VII—IX	nourishing, permeable	○	5—8
Crocus chrysanthus	10—12	yellow	III	light, humus-rich	○	6—8
Crocus kotschyanus	10—15	mauve	IX—X	light, humus-rich	○	6—8
Crocus cultivars	10—15	variable	III—IV	light, permeable	○	6—10
Cyclamen purpurascens	10—12	purple, pink	VIII—IX	light, humus-rich	◑	2—3
Dahlia hybrids	25—200	various	VI—X	medium, heavy, Ca	○	8—10
Eranthis hyemalis	6—10	yellow	II—III	light, humus-rich	◑ ○	5—7
Eremurus stenophyllus	60—80	dark yellow	VI	sandy-loamy	○	15—20
Erythronium dens-canis	15—20	white, pink	III—IV	loose, humus-rich	◑	5—6
Freesia hybrids	60—80	white, pink, yellow, carmine, purple	VII—VIII	light, permeable	○	5
Fritillaria imperialis	80—100	yellow-red, orange	IV—V	loose, permeable, nourishing	○	15—20
Fritillaria meleagris	20—40	wine-red	IV—V	loose, permeable	○	6—8
Galanthus nivalis	15—20	white	III	loose, permeable, nourishing	○ ◑	6—10
Galtonia candicans	80—100	white	VII—IX	light, permeable, nourishing	○	6—10
Gladiolus hybrids	80—100	variable	VII—IX	light to medium heavy, permeable	○	8—10
Hyacinthus orientalis cultivars	15—30	variable	IV—V	permeable, loamy-sandy	○	10—15
Hymenocallis narcissiflora	60—100	cream-white	VI—VII	light, humus-rich	○	10
Ipheion uniflorum	10—20	pale violet, blue	IV—V	no special demands	○ ◑	8
Iris hollandica hybrids	40—50	white, blue, violet, yellow	VI—VII	permeable, humus-rich	○	10—12
Ixia speciosa	15—30	pink, carmine	VI—VII	light, permeable, nourishing	○ ◑	8—10
Leucojum vernum	25—30	white	III—IV	permeable, moist	◑	5—8
Liatris spicata	60—100	pink	VII	loamy-sandy	○	6—8
Lilium candidum	100—140	white	VI—VII	loamy, permeable, Ca	○	2—3
Lilium martagon	60—180	pink with dark spots	VI—VII	permeable, humus-rich, Ca	◑	10—12
Lilium pumilum	30—60	scarlet-red	VI	loamy, permeable	○	6—7

Species	Height of plant (in cm)	Colour of flower	Flowering time	Requirements Soil	Light	Depth of planting (in cm)
Lilium regale	80—140	cream-white, chestnut-red outside	VII	sandy, humus-rich, tolerates Ca	○ ◑	10—12
Lilium speciosum	80—140	pink with purple spotted turbans	VIII	sandy, humus-rich	◑	10
Muscari armeniacum	15—25	cobalt-blue	IV—V	no special demands	○ ◑ ●	8—10
Muscari botryoides	10—20	blue	IV—V	no special demands	○ ◑ ●	8—10
Muscari comosum	20—45	amethyst-blue	V—VI	sandy, humus-rich	○	6—8
Narcissus cyclamineus	15	yellow	III—IV	permeable, damp	◑	8—10
Narcissus poeticus	40	white with red	IV	loamy, permeable	◑	10—12
Narcissus triandrus var. *albus*	18	white	IV—V	loamy, permeable	○	1
Narcissus cultivars	25—60	variable	III—V	permeable, loamy-sandy, nourishing	○ ◑	10—12
Ornithogalum umbellatum	10—30	white	IV—V	permeable, humus-rich	○ ◑	10
Oxalis adenophylla	8—10	violet-pink	V—VI	humus-rich, permeable	○ ◑	5
Puschkinia scilloides var. *libanotica*	15—20	pale blue	III—IV	loose, humus-rich	○ ◑	5—6
Ranunculus asiaticus	20—30	variable	V—VI	permeable, humus-rich	◑	3—4
Scilla hispanica	20—30	violet-blue	V—VI	light, garden-type	○ ◑	6—10
Scilla sibirica	10—20	bright blue	III—IV	nourishing, permeable, humus-rich	○ ◑	6—8
Sparaxis grandiflora	30—45	purple	IV—V	light, permeable	○	6—10
Sternbergia lutea	10—15	yellow	IX—X	sandy, stony, Ca	○ ◑	10—12
Tigridia pavonia	40—60	variable	VII—ÌX	permeable, nourishing	○	5—7
Tulipa eichleri	30	red	III—IV	loamy-sandy, permeable	○	10—12
Tulipa fosterana	15—35	scarlet-red	IV	loamy-sandy, permeable	○	10—12
Tulipa kaufmanniana	15—20	white, pale or dark yellow	III—IV	loamy-sandy, permeable	○	10—12
Tulipa tarda	10—15	yellow with white circle	IV—V	loamy-sandy, permeable	○	6—8
Tulipa cultivars	15—80	variable	III—V	permeable, nourishing	○	10—12

Rock plants

Within the category of rock plants there are species of varied height and with widely different characteristics. They grow for longer than two years and, with the exception of evergreen species, spend winter in a seemingly dormant state. In the autumn, at the onset of winter, their flowers fade and their aerial parts die back, only to start shooting again at the end of winter and during spring. Only their underground organs survive.

Many species of rock plants can be found growing in the wild and therefore people may be tempted to collect them and plant them in their gardens. Such behaviour is quite wrong, of course, because some species are protected by law and furthermore, plants transplanted in this way usually do not take. Such action is therefore a waste of both effort and plant.

Rockeries and dry walls

Rock plants can be grown in rockeries, on dry walls and in various types of containers. However, before deciding to grow rock plants in the garden, lessons can be learnt from seeing them growing in their natural habitat, in the mountains. Points to note are the natural appearance of the rocks, the rich vegetation with its numerous species, the mountain streams, meadows and the soil which make up the microclimate in which the plants grow naturally. Such information will prove invaluable when deciding whether to develop a rockery and what form it should take, though, of course, we are not suggesting that a trip to the mountains is an essential prerequisite. Books can teach you quite a lot, too.

If there is no suitable natural location available, a man-made rockery has to be appropriately separated from the rest of the garden, since it is to a certain extent an independent feature. It needs to be sited where there is a pleasing background and in a 'natural' setting.

The layout of the rockery is mainly determined by the character of the garden. A natural slope at a sufficient distance from the house can provide the location for an equally 'natural' rockery. It can be constructed from irregularly shaped and weathered stones to give it a natural character. Ideal is a slope

Alyssum saxatile is found in the wild growing on rocks in unbelievably small amounts of soil. This undemanding plant is indispensable for every rock garden or dry wall in full sun. It forms overhanging masses attracting one's eye by the optimistic yellow colour of its flowers.

facing east or north-east as this will meet the needs of even the most demanding rockery plants.

If the sloping terrain adjoins the house, the character of the rockery should correspond to the architecture of the building. Using large square or flat stones, it can be constructed in the shape of a sloping terrace.

Modern gardens on various levels which may be unsuitable for a full-scale rockery, can be harmoniously complemented by open-plan rockeries or rocky sections. Natural irregularities of the terrain are retained and interspaced by large, rounded boulders placed individually or in small groups. The slope prepared in this way can be planted with irregular clusters of perennials.

Level differences in the garden can be coped with by means of dry walls, built of natural stone, without the use of mortar. Gaps between the stones are filled with soil and planted with cushion-forming, profusely flowering species. The height of the wall

Water in all forms brings life to the rock garden, but a pool must be sited where it blends most naturally into the surroundings and the nearby vegetation should be chosen very sensitively to enhance this natural effect.

The sloping terrain near to this house has been used for building a rock garden of great charm. The type and size of the rocks and the whole character of the rockery must be in agreement with the style of the house, when the two are in such close juxtaposition.

should not exceed 50—60 cm. Larger differences in height are best dealt with by building two walls. Any steps are also made without mortar and cracks or gaps in them are planted with those plants which are not usually damaged when they are stepped on.

Growing rock plants in various types of containers is also very popular. They have the advantage that you can place them anywhere without them clashing with their surroundings.

Establishing a rock garden or a dry wall

A rock garden can be constructed at any altitude, regardless of the soil conditions because these can always be modified. The best location is in sun or in partial shade. Rockeries should never be sited in the shade of large trees.

When building a rockery, advantage can be taken

A dry wall can be a good solution for irregularities of the terrain. The chosen plants can be planted while the wall is being constructed or inserted afterwards, according to their size and character.

of both natural and artificial slopes adjoining a wall or a fence. Even a flat surface can be adjusted by digging out an irregularly shaped depression and using the soil to make a small mound nearby. However, care must be taken to make such landscaping appear natural. Finally, rock garden plants can also be grown on a flat terrain if this is accentuated by flat stones and even more bulky ones, set out individually or in groups. If carefully constructed, such a rockery can create an even more natural impression than one established on an artificial slope.

Stone

Apart from the plants, stone is the most important feature of the rock garden. In the construction of a rockery only one type of stone should be used, preferably one occurring commonly in the given region.

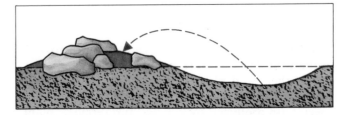

A low rock garden can be constructed in a flat terrain by simply transferring some soil from another part of the garden. The resulting hole in the ground there can be used to construct a pool.

The surface of the stone should be rough, weathered and preferably overgrown with lichen. Most effective for this purpose are limestone or sandstone. However, sometimes the use of stones bought from a quarry cannot be avoided. When using recently quarried material, great care must be taken if you are to achieve the desired results. Natural stone is also used for building dry walls. If the wall adjoins a house with a stone-made basement, then it should be built of the same type of material. Large stones are placed as the foundations, at a depth of some 20—30 cm and smaller ones are used to make up the upper layers.

The foundations

As soon as a suitable location is found, work can start by marking out a rough outline for the rockery, remembering that the original shape may well need to be modified to some extent later. Then, the surface area needs to be prepared. If this is not covered with turf it does not need to be dug. Grassy areas, however, have to be cleared by carefully removing all of the turf and the top soil. If the turf and soil is of good quality it can be used elsewhere. Then you need to provide a layer of drainage material, about 20 cm deep. This can be of gravel, pebbles, broken roof tiles or bricks. If large stones are going to be used in the rockery, it is a good idea to reinforce the foundations with pillars made of bricks, stones or concrete slabs, to bear the weight of the stones and prevent the rockery from being damaged by them later. This is especially important in rockeries built near fences.

The drainage layer is covered by a layer of fertile soil which can include any soil put aside earlier. This has to be sifted, and all remnants of weeds removed, before the soil is mixed with sand, crushed bricks or peat as required. At the top of the rockery the soil should be 10—15 cm deep and at the bottom a little deeper. Finally, the whole surface area of the rockery should be compacted.

The normal range of rock plants will thrive in the standard mixture of soil, sand and a little peat, which is used to cover the rockery before the stones are positioned. However, if certain demanding alpine species are to be grown, the soil mixture must be prepared accordingly and substituted for the standard mix in those areas where these particular alpines will be grown.

Building the rock garden

After the rockery has been prepared, the laying of the stones can begin. A natural slope can be exploited by making various 'pockets' to catch water during rain or when watering, and prevent soil from being washed away. At this point begins the truly creative work, calling for all your sensitivity to nature, developed tastes and cultural experience. Stones are sunk halfway to two-thirds into the soil to give as natural an appearance as possible, which means that their tips should never be pointing upwards. Position them with the tips buried in the soil and the flatter edge jutting up above the soil. The soil surrounding them is then firmed up so that no empty pockets are left. This will also serve to prevent further settling down of the rockery.

Finally, the completed rockery is swept clean and sprayed. Even at this stage it should present an aesthetically pleasing appearance. The rock garden should be as varied as possible, offering numerous protected corners, crevices, overhanging ledges and hollows facing various points of the compass. In this way conditions are created for planting a wide range of rock garden species with various requirements as to location. When building a rockery, it is also important to incorporate a system of paths and small

The size of the rock garden determines the choice of woody plants to be used. They underline the natural appeal of the rockery, enhancing its general effect.

A bowl planted with lewisias and placed in a lawn is particularly nice in the flowering season. At the end of summer, when lewisias must be protected from dampness, the bowl should be re-sited in a more sheltered place.

Evergreen and deciduous woody plants form a natural link between the rock garden and the surrounding vegetation. The conifers planted at the back of this rockery offset the colourful beauty of the flowering broadleaved shrubs.

steps to make it accessible and therefore easily maintained. The steps should also be safe to use.

Water in the rock garden should not be forgotten, as this provides a pleasant and refreshing feature. It improves the microclimatic conditions and allows for the addition of attractive plants that will only thrive in aquatic, muddy and wet conditions. Ideally, there should be a natural source of water running through the rockery in the form of a stream or small waterfall. However, it is always possible to build a smal artificial pond or pool in almost any rockery, if the natural element does not exist.

All this work is best done in the autumn. The rockery will then have chance to settle down before spring so that when the plants are planted, there will be no

Cracks in a dry wall can house quite a number of plants, for instance, various bellflowers. The picture shows a tuft of *Campanula carpatica* 'Alba'.

danger that the soil will sink further. If there is no alternative however, the rockery can be built in spring provided you do so well before the plants are put out, so that the soil between the stones has as much time as possible to settle down.

The dry wall can be built at any time but, as it is usually planted during the actual construction, the best time to do this work is in spring or autumn. Square-edged stones are placed so that they fit close to one another, like bricks, and the wall is constructed at a slight angle, so that the top layer of stones inclines about 10 cm closer to the slope than the foundations. Crevices between the stones are filled with the standard soil mixture appropriate for dry wall rockery plants. Thick- or long-rooted alpines are planted during the building of the wall, but mat-forming ones can be inserted afterwards. The plants must then be well watered.

Work to be done immediately before transplanting

Before the rockery is planted, a plan showing the position of the plants should be prepared. This involves choosing suitable types of rockery plants from a catalogue, drawing them into the plan and choosing suitable companions for them. Colour combinations, not only of the flowers but also of the leaves, should be well considered, as the rockery should remain interesting even when the plants are not flowering. Finally, it should be remembered that the rockery should always have several species in flower at any given period between spring and autumn.

Careful thought should be given as to which species it will be possible to cultivate successfully, given your present experience and knowledge. The addition of more demanding species should wait until you have sufficient experience.

Besides plants, it is also important to have all the requisite tools. These include garden trowels, a spoon with a long handle or possibly a ladle — for spooning out soil from larger pockets. A rounded small shovel will be useful for covering over such places

An informal rock garden, built with taste and appropriately planted, can be one of the most attractive features of a garden.

Steps made of stone are very natural-looking, particularly when they are bounded by a rockery, as here.

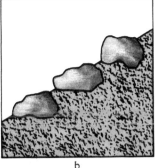

a
b

Neither large nor small rocks should be placed with their narrow end up (a); this looks very unnatural and small plants become quite lost among them. Well-placed rocks (b) are deeply buried in the soil with no more than one-third or a half of their true size showing; sharp edges are better hidden in the soil.

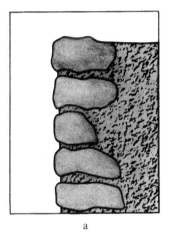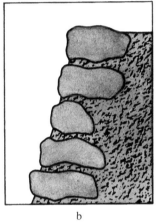

a
b

A properly built dry wall should not be upright (a) but slightly slanting backwards (b). The top rocks should not overlap the bottom ones otherwise rainwater will not be able to penetrate to the roots of plants growing in the wall.

Walls planted with suitable plants look much better than those in which the cracks have been filled completely with concrete or mortar. Instead, the individual rocks are connected with a well sieved, slightly sandy soil with an admixture of humus. The plants are then placed in cracks between the rocks. However, species with long, fleshy roots should be planted as the wall is being constructed.

Lower walls (30—40 cm) can be built directly on the ground but taller ones need good foundations. The first row of stones must be bedded some 30—40 cm deep; a bed of concrete ensures better stability. A dranaige layer of coarse gravel and sand behind the wall allows removal of surplus water.

with soil. Similarly, a peg for compacting the soil between the stones will come in useful, as will garden secateurs, pincers, a fine spray nozzle for the hose and a small watering can.

Seasons in the rock garden

The calendar division of the year into four seasons does not always coincide with the growing seasons. Favourable or adverse weather can influence the flowering of typical seasonal species and will often cause certain plants to burst forth even in the middle of winter or, at other times, cause them to flower much later than usual.

However, for a gardener — and in particular a rockery enthusiast — a traditional year in the rock garden has several timespans, of which the most important and the most impatiently awaited season is the beginning of spring with its abundance of plants in flower.

Early spring

Every year the awakening of nature has several distinct facets and is never repeated at exactly the same time, or in the same way even when weather conditions are similar. It is natural that the development of the weather determines the characteristics of the plants' environment when they are waking up. Sometimes, the rockery is covered by a layer of ice and snow, broken only here and there. However, the stones warm the soil in their immediate proximity, having absorbed the warmth of the early spring sun, and these shelter and encourage the first, and therefore the most precious, spring rockery plants.

Rock gardeners welcome the early spring charm of the most hardy perennials and woody plants, the exquisite flowers of the Christmas Rose, the richly budding heathers, the Mezereon or the interesting flowers of witch-hazels which can even withstand several degrees of frost. They seem to appreciate the durability and fresh charm of the flowers of the earliest bulbous and tuberous plants emerging in rock gardens and under sparsely planted trees and shrubs where the spring sun has already succeeded in penetrating.

Bulbous plants, particularly the low-growing ones, are quite indispensable in a rock garden. Taller species can be planted in irregular borders close by.

Adonis vernalis flowers in April, when the flowering plants are often surprised by a spell of unfavourable weather. However, as soon as the snow has melted, their beauty is restored. They do best in well-drained places and a calcium-rich medium. The soil in their vicinity should not be aerated too often.

A melodious trickle of water feeding a small pool in a rock garden evokes similar feelings to those we experience when strolling in the country. Furthermore, a pool makes it possible to enrich the rockery with other, aquatic plants.

These plants are usually of foreign origin and include cyclamens, winter aconites, snowdrops and some species of saffron. The hardy cyclamens (*Cyclamen*), which do best in a permeable soil with a high humus content and particularly in shade, are well suited to the decoration of the rock garden when used in combination with heathers or dwarf deciduous and coniferous trees.

Winter aconites (*Eranthis*) should be included in every rock garden. They can be planted in partial shade underneath ornamental shrubs. Their golden flowers and finely cut leaves decorate the garden from February until March.

The earliest plants of domestic origin are the well-known and ever popular snowdrops (*Galanthus*), the flowers of which appear very early in spring — even

The Christmas Rose (*Helleborus niger*) flowers from December to March. It likes semi-shade or even full shade and a sufficiently damp, humus-rich soil. It looks wonderful in rock gardens or in large perennial groups, and is a good subject for planting under ornamental shrubs. The flowers can be used for cutting.

Cyclamens are tuberous plants which flower either in spring — like the one shown here — or in the autumn, according to the species. They can be grown in the neighbourhood of heathers or next to dwarf conifers and ferns. They are also very nice when mixed with small bulbs or Christmas Roses and primroses.

flowers and a strong pleasant scent, which reveals its presence at some distance and which attracts bees on their first spring flights.

Winter Jasmine (*Jasminum nudiflorum*) is an interesting, prostrate shrub originating from China. Its flowers, slightly reminiscent of forsythia, are delicately scented. In a sheltered corner of the garden or a large rockery, it will open its flowers as early as January.

Stemless primroses (*Primula*), either botanical species with sulphur-yellow flowers or some of the attractively coloured hybrids, significantly enliven wooded areas and rock gardens in the early spring. First to appear are the small buds from within last year's dry tuft of leaves. These are gradually followed by outcrops of low-growing flowers in the middle of the leaf rosettes.

Galanthus nivalis is one of the earliest bulbs. It does well in full sun as well as semi-shade and prefers heavy, humus-rich and sufficiently damp soils. It can be planted in rock gardens or in groves.

in February. Some of the earliest-flowering rock garden plants and woody species start to form their buds in the autumn of the preceding year. These include hellebores with their beautiful, popular Christmas Rose (*Helleborus niger*). Some cultivars of the Christmas Rose start to flower before Christmas, others continue gradually through to April. It is remarkable that they are not harmed even by several degrees of frost. Spring-flowering heathers (*Erica*) similarly start to flower as soon as the snow has melted.

Heathers are often complemented by bushy Mezereon (*Daphne mezereum*), a beautiful ornamental shrub. It has a profusion of pink-red or white

The rock gardens of more experienced gardeners are often ornamented by the charming saxifrages, belonging to the *Porophyllum* and *Engleria* groups. Crocuses, such as *Crocus heuffelianus* and other botanical species often break the hard crust of the melting snow with their flowers.

Early bulbs are represented by some less common species such as spring meadow saffron (*Bulbocodium*), a plant of south European origin with attractive, lilac-pink and purple flowers reminiscent of autumn crocuses.

Hepaticas push their buds and flowers through the tangle of branches and last year's fallen leaves soon after the first warm rays of the sun fall on the cool ground. *Hepatica transsylvanica* (*H. angulosa*) opens its handsome blue flowers in March. It has several large-flowered cultivars which produce a profusion of pink and white flowers.

During early spring, the flowers of miniature bulb irises and dwarf narcissi can also be seen in gardens and rockeries. The Early Adonis (*Adonis amurensis*) blossoms in February and is followed by *A. vernalis*.

Early spring cleaning

Pleasant early spring days are often accompanied by favourable weather which encourages people to make a start on tidying up the rock garden. First of all, this involves loosening and removing the winter cover from flowering species to allow full enjoyment of their attractive colours.

Generally this does not harm most plants, including the numerous spring bulbs, even when changeable weather brings sleet, frost or more snow. Nevertheless, premature removal of all cover, particularly on a sunny day, can be very dangerous to some rock garden plants as they can be burnt by the sun or suffer damage from frost.

If the rockery is close by the house, tidying up can commence in warmer rainy weather. The coniferous loppings can be removed, accumulated fallen leaves raked away and the dry parts of plants cut off. It is still a good idea to keep coniferous loppings handy in case the frosts return. If the following days bring fresh falls of snow and a thick layer settles on the ground, there is no need to worry about the plants as the snow itself will protect them from frost.

Only when the weather has settled down can the covering be removed, including any plastic and glass roofing deemed necessary to protect plants intolerant of winter dampness. The plants are then tidied and made firm in the ground if they have been loosened by the frost.

Stones which have worked loose should be straightened and secured, perennial weeds should be removed and bushy plants trimmed by about a third. The soil between the plants should be loosened and replenished as required, if it has been washed out of hollows and crevices between the rocks. Some excessively pervasive plants should either be transplanted or their growth thinned out.

Early spring in the rock garden is not only a season of charming flowers but also a time when cleanliness, order and harmony is restored among the plants. This means that some of them will have to be transplanted to other, more suitable, places in order to match with one another not only by their colour and shape but also by their character, so that the individual sections of the rockery resemble various natural groupings as can be seen in the wild.

Helleborus × *hybridus* is a beautiful and undemanding, early-flowering perennial, decorative not only for its flowers but also for the evergreen leaves. The flowering period is from March to April. The picture shows a white-flowering variety.

Daphne cneorum 'Major' thrives in full sun or slight semi-shade. A mixture of sandy loam, humus and old plaster should be added to the soil.

Always bear in mind that night frost can cause a lot of damage to some rock plants, in particular those of alpine origin, such as Asiatic primroses, bleeding hearts (*Dicentra*) lilies (*Lilium*), astilbes (*Astilbe*) and many other perennials. Frost-damaged plants usually lose their leaves; it then takes a long time for them to recover and usually they do not flower in that year.

Spring

The rock garden is beautiful in every season but without doubt it is at its most attractive in spring, when it is literally flooded with drifts of radiant colours. At this time, usually from the end of March until mid-June, all plants commonly grown in gardens and rockeries blend together in perfect harmony.

Besides the numerous bulbs and tubers, the great variety of primroses (*Primula*) and other members of the Primulaceae family all contribute to the attractiveness of the rock garden.

Among the most charming of spring plants are a number of bellflowers, many of which continue to flower successively through the following seasons. However, not all the species and cultivars belong to the Campanulaceae family and, from the botanical point of view, their flowers are not true bells but only resemble them in shape.

The best known bell-shaped plants are the snowflakes (*Leucojum*) with their rounded, broad bell-shaped, white flowers with green-tipped petals. The delicate snowbells (*Soldanella*) flaunt their fringed, bell-shaped flowers from January, despite being surrounded by snow or ice-water from the melting snow.

After several warm, sunny days in March the large, bell-shaped flowers of pulsatillas (*Pulsatilla*) start to open, vigorously penetrating the layer of the preceding year's leaves and the blades of enveloping grasses.

As soon as spring finally arrives and the soil becomes warmer, plants with bell-shaped flowers start to bloom in large numbers. They are first represented by the dense ground cover of Lily-of-the-valley (*Convallaria majalis*) with its pure white flowers and strong pleasant scent which fills the air far around them.

Due regard must also be given to several early flowering bellflowers with their attractive blossoms. They are best planted in sunny locations, in crevices between stones in the rockery or in dry walls. These include *Campanula aucheri* with large violet flowers appearing from April to May; *C. tridentata* with single flowers coloured blue-violet outside and blue-white inside, and *C. bellidifolia* with flowers similar to *C. aucheri,* which open from April to June.

Work in spring

When the winter cover has been removed from the last delicate rockery species, when the ornamental

A heather section is often used to join a rockery with the rest of the garden.

grasses have been stripped of their old leaves almost to ground level and when persistent weeds have been taken out and soil added where necessary, the new planting can be started. First of all, it is essential to replace plants that have perished during winter. Secondly, the range of plants can be extended by adding species and cultivars which can be relied upon to bring beauty to individual sections of the rockery.

The rockery should be watered according to weather conditions, particularly during prolonged droughts. This is best done towards the evening or in the early morning, using a watering can with a fine nozzle or a mist spray. These protect flowers from damage and prevent the soil from being washed away from sloping areas and crevices. Some plants can be given a fertilizer, best administered in liquid form during watering.

Early spring is the main propagating season for many rock plants. This is done either by sowing seeds or by dividing strong plants. Cuttings are taken from early flowering varieties when they have finished blossoming or in the autumn, from the end of September to November. If the seeds are not needed, it is best to remove the faded flowers immediately after flowering to avoid unnecessary loss of strength.

As spring develops, aggressive weeds start to spread, particularly in newly established rockeries, and therefore in sunny weather the soil should be lightly loosened and the weeds eradicated. Places where small bulbs were flowering in early spring can be planted with cushion-forming, spreading but not too vigorous perennials or some annuals suitable for the rock garden.

The spring care of rock plants should also include a treatment to control pests and diseases which attack plants both above and below ground level. In some cases, the plant has actually to be taken out of the ground, examined, its roots treated and pests destroyed before it can be put back, in fresh soil.

Summer

Before rock gardens became popular, the beginning of summer used to be marked by a relatively poor selection of flowering plants — with the exception of traditional annuals and roses. Now modern perennial varieties, and in particular alpine plants, give the gardens their attractive and vivid colour range.

Besides perennial beds, it is particularly the rockery that provides a continually changing kaleidoscope of colours, full of individual character and living beauty. Indeed, summer vegetation is usually more vigorous and its colouring correspondingly more vivid.

This is the time of the year when whole areas in the rockery or the dry walls become overgrown with the chalk plant (*Gypsophila*), bearing a profusion of white and pink flowers. This includes the popular *Gypsophila paniculata* 'Bristol Fairy', a very valuable and profusely flowering perennial with double white flowers.

The sulphur-yellow flowers of the Evening Primrose (*Oenothera missouriensis*) brighten up rockeries in the early evening but they fade away in the morn-

Crocuses are favourite bulbous plants for a rockery. They are planted in groups which spread after some time to form whole colonies, and flower in early spring.

ing. Another evening primrose, *O. tetragona* 'Fireworks', is slightly taller and more erect, has red buds and its beautiful yellow flowers remain open throughout the day.

Summer also brings a rich profusion of the low and taller bellflowers. The most popular is the quickly-spreading *Campanula carpatica,* with its numerous cultivars. Of the smaller bellflowers, a popular rockery species is *Campanula cochleariifolia* (*C. pusilla*) with delicate pale blue, bell-shaped flowers. Its cultivars have white or dark blue flowers. Other bellflowers, particularly *C. garganica, C. portenschlagiana, C. poscharskyana* and their cultivars display their star-shaped flowers throughout the summer.

Summer-flowering gentians should also be men-

Adonis vernalis is a plant found on sunny steppe slopes in limestone regions. In the garden, it can be grown in rockeries or in borders along dry walls.

tioned, particularly *Gentiana septemfida* var. *lagodechiana* with its bright, pale blue flowers, which successively open in clusters on the tips of the stems between July and September. *G. farreri,* native to Tibet, blooms at the end of summer. It has narrow lance-shaped leaves and beautiful large flowers which are turquoise-blue inside and green with white stripes on the outside. It is a relatively rare rock plant suitable for experienced gardeners.

The tunic flowers (*Petrorhagia saxifraga* 'Pleniflora') are perfect, particularly in a dry wall. They produce an abundance of double pink flowers forming a dense veil above the foliage throughout the summer. The undemanding campion (*Silene schafta*) bears a delightful profusion of pink flowers in high and late summer.

This is also the flowering season of *Inula ensifolia,* a rewarding, drought-loving plant with ray-shaped yellow flowers. Another attractive plant of this sea-

Primroses are welcome not only for their early flowering but also for the wonderful colours of their flowers. Their uses are many. In rock gardens they should be grown in groups according to their height, colour and time of flowering. The picture shows a variety of *Primula elatior,* flowering from March to April. It prefers slight semi-shade and should be grown in a humus-rich soil.

Autumn

If the choice of species for the rockery has been made with thought, it should not be without flowers even in the autumn. Besides the popular meadow saffrons (*Colchicum*) large rock gardens are the appropriate setting for the large pink flowers of numerous cultivars of the Windflower (*Anemone japonica*). Truly undestructible is the robust *A. vitifolia* producing profusion of white flowers with a pinkish hue every year. It can grow to a height of 40—80 cm.

Primula denticulata (at the rear of the picture) has an interesting spherical inflorescence, borne in March—April on a 15—25 cm tall stem. It forms a graceful spring composition with the yellow-flowered *P. vulgaris.*

Adonis amurensis is native to Manchuria. It flowers earlier than *A. vernalis,* mostly at the same time as the Winter Aconite. It needs a semi-shaded situation. The plants die back relatively early, usually in June.

son is a low-growing cultivar of the Common Marjoram (*Origanum vulgare* 'Compactum') which has pink-violet flowers and a strong scent. This list of summer-flowering rock plants is by no means complete. Many species which flower in spring do so again at this time, especially if they were cut back immediately after their first flowering.

Work in summer

There is not so much to do in the rock garden in summer. Work is limited to weeding, watering as required, hoeing, the removal of dead flowers and dry parts of plants and regular protection against diseases and pests.

Another perennial which is worthy of attention is *Phygelius capensis,* native to South Africa. It flowers in the autumn and reaches some 70 cm in height. It is a sub-shrub with a profusion of coral-red trumpet-shaped flowers which appear continuously from the end of July.

Rock gardens can be enlivened in the middle of autumn by the Californian fuchsia (*Zauschneria*). It is native to California and has an abundance of scarlet-red, long-lasting flowers.

These plants, which mostly originate from countries with a warmer climate, should be given a protecting layer of humus-rich soil above their roots. They need to be especially protected during wet, changeable winters. Therefore, good drainage ensuring a prompt removal of surplus water is a must.

Autumn work

The time arrives when mild autumn frosts help to harden plants against worsening weather conditions and assist in ripening of the wood in woody species. It is therefore unwise to stimulate further growth of plants by artificial watering. Only those plants which are still expected to produce flowers need to be watered. Other perennials will benefit from the loosening of the soil around them and the removal of their seeds. Plants that threaten their neighbours by their excessive growth have to be cut back. However, severe pruning of some of the vigorous species such as

Soldanellas are recommended for slightly damp, humus-rich soils with an admixture of heath mould or peat and for situations facing away from the sun. *Soldanella carpatica* bears profusions of blue-purple flowers in April and May.

Pulsatillas should not be omitted from any rock garden. They have fine leaves and attractive flowers in a variety of hues. Also their feathery, silvery seed-heads are ornamental. They thrive in sunny situations in permeable, well-drained soils, rich in humus.

Bellflowers are favourite summer-flowering plants suitable for rock gardens. *Campanula poscharskyana*, a lush-growing, hardy species producing long shoots, reaches some 20 cm in height. It flowers in May—June and does well in full sun or semi-shade, preferring a loose, sandy-loamy soil.

Campanula cochleariifolia 'Alba' is an undemanding bellflower, tolerating both sunny and semi-shaded places. It likes stony, humus-rich situations with a sufficient content of calcium. The flowers open successively from June to August.

sun roses (*Helianthemum*) is not recommended as a hard winter could then destroy them. They should therefore be pruned only at the end of the winter.

In late autumn, all evergreen woody species have to be well watered. This applies to rhododendrons (*Rhododendron*) and to young conifers. Most rock garden plants, however, can be greatly damaged by damp conditions in their dormant season and thus have to be protected by sheets of glass or polythene.

Most rock garden plants can be transplanted at the beginning of autumn. Those pre-cultivated in containers can be put out any time during the autumn. Early autumn is the main planting season for bulbs and the majority of tubers. This work should be finished by the middle or, at the latest, the end of October. Another task to be remembered is the collection of seeds in plants that are reproduced from seed. Seeds that need freezing over before they can start to germinate should be sown at this time.

In favourable weather conditions, it is possible to remove the dying stems of tall perennials by cutting them at the base. However, this must not be done without thought. The foliage of plants which retain their green colour through the winter should be saved. This applies to irises (*Iris*), leopard's bane (*Doronicum*) and low-growing perennials forming evergreen cushions or carpets. This period is also unsuitable for the shortening of overgrown evergreen plants. The cut plants would be less resistant to bad weather, particularly to frosts without a covering of snow. Furthermore, the garden would be deprived of a rich flowering in the following year as some plants produce their new flowers on older wood. They are best trimmed after flowering, when the plants are still capable of replacing quickly the parts lost.

After such basic pruning, the soil should be lightly loosened between the plants. A small wooden peg will be sufficient for this in a rockery. Small weeds should also be removed but care must be taken not to damage the roots of the perennial plants and the

bulbs. Empty places around the plants can be scattered with a sieved compost. Equally beneficial is peat or a coarse leaf mould. Fallen leaves should always be removed from the rockery, as they are the source of many diseases. The exception to this rule are shady areas and corners planted with woodland species, where a covering of fallen leaves is beneficial to the plants. In such places the leaves can be weighed down by coniferous loppings in order to prevent them from being blown away by the wind.

You should never be in a hurry to provide winter covering for the rock garden. Plants need to mature and ripen well and the experience of the first frosts gives them a better resistance. In damp and warm weather the covering promulgates the growth of moulds and also provides a hideout for various pests, in particular mice.

Many perennials now cultivated in rock gardens originate in warmer countries and are thus seriously affected by enduring winter dampness and changes in the weather. The best protection is afforded by a sheet of glass or plastic resting on stones or another base. Bulbs are best protected by a layer of humus or dry leaves weighed down with coniferous branches.

Winter

In winter the garden may be covered with a layer of snow for a few days or so, but at other times it is more likely to experience a mild frost followed by rain and a thaw — both of which provide a source of moisture that is vital for all evergreen plants. On the other hand, a heavy frost without snow but accompanied by a strong flow of cold air is bad for the garden. This kind of weather is particularly harmful to all perennials that have been transplanted in the autumn and did not have time to root properly as well as to those that have not been left to ripen by watering and feeding them long into the autumn.

It can be said that nature, throughout the growing

The graceful *Silene schafta* is a favourite with many gardeners, for its large profusion of flowers and for the relatively late flowering, which takes place in August and September. This undemanding plant is well suited to rock gardens and dry walls and looks particularly good in the company of summer-flowering gentians.

Inula ensifolia, tolerant of hot sun, is a good subject for extremely sunny aspects in rock gardens or in group plantings. It forms dense, up to 30 cm high clumps, and its flowers open in July and August.

season — and especially during favourable weather in the autumn — prepares rock plants, perennials, shrubs and trees for the frosty days ahead. Many plants sheath their new buds in a scaly covering, others protect them by a double layer of easily-peeled tissue. The buds of Lily-of-the-valley and other plants which lose their leaves in winter are covered by scales and are usually hidden safely in the soil or submerged in a layer of leaves provided by neighbouring woody species. Grass-like plants hide from frost and wind underneath the dead stems and leaves and are usually effectively protected even in the middle of winter, if heavy frosts without snow do not occur.

One of the most important factors in the successful hibernation of plants is snow. A covering of snow during this period acts as an effective insulator but not as a source of moisture. It is self-evident, there-

Origanum vulgare 'Compactum', a low-growing variety of Wild Marjoram, can be grown in rock gardens, heather gardens or in perennial mass plantings. It spreads to form large carpets and will thrive even in very poor soils, but a sunny situation is a must. The flowers open from July to October.

fore, that it is important to water well all evergreen, deciduous and coniferous species not only before the onset of heavy frosts but — if it is possible — throughout the winter. Care should also be taken that the soil above the roots is sufficiently well covered to prevent excessive evaporation of water from the soil. Leaves and coniferous needles absorb a certain amount of moisture even during the heaviest of frosts. However, the longer the snow is frozen solid and made immobile, or is frozen quickly again after a thaw, the less likely it is to protect the roots of plants. Only a thick soft layer of fine snow is able to protect the soil from freezing at temperatures of up to $-15°$ C.

Work in winter
The rock garden should be covered with coniferous branches before the first snow and the arrival of hard frosts, which means during December in the lowlands and a little earlier in mountain regions. The advantage of this covering is the protection of plants but there is also a disadvantage, and that is the cutting off of the flow of air. If a thick layer of snow falls, however, its full weight does not rest directly on the plants, and air can still get through. Best for this purpose are freshly cut fir and spruce branches, as their needles remain on the branches for a long time as opposed to pine loppings which soon discard their needles and prove difficult to remove.

Fallen leaves do not provide useful material for covering a rockery as they settle down during the winter and form an air-tight layer, which promotes the growth of fungi and moulds. In addition, they provide a welcome home for mice, the greatest enemies of rock plants. The rockery need not be without the charm of flowers even in winter. Rock garden enthusiasts will detect the buds and flowers of hardy rock and woodland species even in the middle of winter hidden in piles of leaves, under the coniferous branches or in a sunny sheltered spot. The most impatient plants include hellebores, primroses, heathers, daphnes and jasmines, the flowers of which foretell the coming of spring.

Planting rock garden plants

Spots where rock garden plants are going to be planted must be thoroughly cleared of weeds which multiply vegetatively. Such preparatory work will save a lot of time in the future. In places with a relatively high water table or with an impermeable soil, a thorough drainage should be considered.

Most rock plants thrive in normal, rather poor, loamy-sandy soil. Some, however, require a special soil mixture, which involves the addition of sand, peat, garden soil, leaf mould, sphagnum moss and

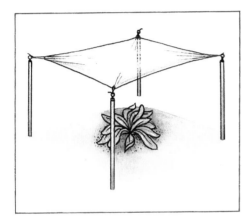

Many rock garden plants suffer from too much damp in winter. A good drainage of surplus water must therefore be provided when building a rockery. Very sensitive species will welcome a simple roof of glass or transparent foil to protect them in winter.

sometimes even small pebbles or limestone, added in the form of old plaster.

The rockery is planted in spring or in autumn, some time after its construction, to allow the soil to settle properly. In contrast, dry walls are mostly planted during their construction. Plants cultivated in pots or other containers can be transplanted at

Rhododendrons are a happy solution to the question of linking the rock garden with the surrounding garden. They are unrivalled in the garden when in flower.

Meadow Saffrons open their wonderful flowers when the summer-flowering plants have finished. They can be used in a rockery, but only where their rather unsightly leaves will not disturb the view in spring. They are relatively large (up to 25 cm long) and die back in June or July. The flowers emerge from August to October. They look best in group arrangements, planted in front of dwarf shrubs or among low ornamental grasses in sunny situations.

any time during the growing season, with the exception of the hot summer months. After planting out, the plants should be well watered and shaded in order to root properly.

When choosing the plants, take into account not only the suitability of the species for a given situation but also its flowering season, so that the rockery can flower continuously from spring until winter. The indispensable plants for every rock garden are evergreen and deciduous, broadleaved woody species, conifers and a selection of bulbs and tubers.

Basic care of rock plants

The rock garden should be kept clear of weeds throughout the year and supplied with sufficient

Leontopodium alpinum is one of the most favourite rock garden plants. It is grown in full sun in a poor, lime-rich soil with an admixture of sand. A good drainage for the removal of surplus water is a must if you want the plant to produce compact, healthy clumps.

Conifers should never be omitted when creating a rock garden. If combined with heaths and heathers, they can produce natural and very attractive compositions in which the colour of their leaves plays an important part.

A number of plants can be used to create a nice miniature rock garden. The picture suggests some of these, including the least demanding ones.

moisture. Also, systematic preventive measures for checking diseases and pests must be maintained throughout the whole growing season.

Rock plants should never be given industrial fertilizers. The most that should be done for older plants that have been in the same spot for a considerable length of time is to provide them with well-ripened compost or to replace the old soil with a similar suitable mixture.

Miniature rock gardens

Growing rock plants in various types of containers is an altogether different and specific method of cultivation, worthy of being discussed in some detail.

In a small area provided by one or more window-boxes or by large earthenware bowls or troughs, it is possible to concentrate a relatively wide assortment of rock plants, bulbs and other suitable subjects, including miniature woody species.

If there is any possibility of choice, the miniature rockery should be located so that it faces the east or west, as a southerly aspect is subjected to a strong sun, while a northerly one suffers from a lack of it. If

the container is to be placed on a window-sill it should be secured so that it cannot fall down and care must be taken not to spoil the house walls by surplus water when watering. If the container is made of wood, it should be given some waterproof insulation. Plastic or earthenware containers are suitable. Miniature rock gardens in containers can also be placed on the balcony, on a flat roof or outside in the garden, in the yard, on the patio, by the stairs, close to a garden seat, near a dividing wall or simply in any place where they can be admired. Apart from various bowls, troughs of stone or carved out of tree trunks can be used although, because of their weight, they are not suitable for balconies or flat roofs. Another material for miniature rock gardens is tufa, large pieces of which look wonderful when planted with suitable rock garden species. Bowls look best if placed on a pedestal and heavy troughs should be supported by stone or concrete blocks or wooden logs.

One of the most important requirements for the successful cultivation of most rock garden plants is good drainage, providing an immediate removal of surplus water. Adequate lighting and attention in

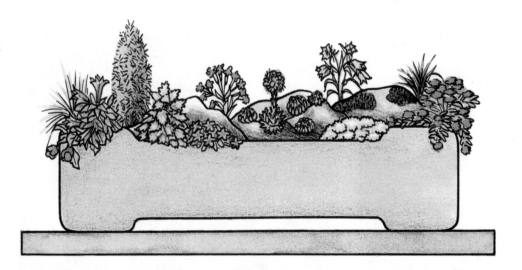

When choosing plants for a miniature rock garden in a sink, you should prefer not very vigorous, low-growing and undemanding species. Their beauty is enhanced by dwarf coniferous and broadleaf trees and broadleaf trees and shrubs, rock roses and numerous small bulbs and tubers.

A bowl planted with houseleeks can make a nice decoration for a terrace or balcony.

A miniature rock garden in a raised stone trough can be made into a focal point of the garden.

terms of regular watering and occasional misting are also important. Particular attention must be paid to the choice of suitable species. As a rule, too vigorous, tall or deeply rooting plants are unsuitable.

Good drainage is achieved by covering the bottom of the container with a soil mixture consisting of one-third topsoil (the soil from molehills in a nearby meadow would be particularly useful), one-third leaf mould and one-third well ripened compost with an admixture of river sand. According to the plant's specific requirements, 'pockets' can be made with the mixture enriched with lime for calcium-loving plants, while plants which do not like lime will need an addition of peat or moss. The addition of any fertilizer is not to be recommended, particularly during planting. The majority of rock plants are perfectly happy with the mineral content naturally present in

Tufa is an ideal sort of limestone which can be used for building a rockery or for adding a 'natural' touch to various other sections of the garden.

stones or light spots facing away from the direct sun but not shaded provide excellent habitats for some very rare rock plants. These are best planted close to tufts of modest ornamental grasses, which will provide a natural background.

The margins of bowls, troughs and boxes facing towards the sun usually suffer from permanent lack of water and should therefore be planted with drought-loving plants such as houseleeks (*Sempervivum*) and stonecrops (*Sedum*). Alternatively some drought- and warmth-loving annuals such as purslanes (*Portulaca*) or vervains (*Verbena*) can be used. Slightly shaded places can be planted with the spring- and summer-flowering miniature cyclamens (*Cyclamen*), snowballs (*Soldanella*), primroses (*Primula*), succulent or moss-like saxifrages (*Saxifraga*), wulfenias (*Wulfenia*), swertias (*Swertia*) and some small ferns.

The early spring colour in miniature rock gardens is provided by a rich assortment of small bulbs and tubers. These include snowdrops (*Galanthus*), bluebells (*Scilla*), snow glory (*Chionodoxa*), winter aconites (*Eranthis*), anemones (*Anemone*), miniature nar-

Saxifraga grisebachii attracts attention by its green leaves with a whitish pattern, arranged in a ground rosette that contrasts wonderfully with the purple-red flowers. It looks very good if planted in the cracks in a block of tufa.

Sedum spathulifolium 'Capa Blanca' does best in full sun and in a poor, sandy soil. It is intolerant of calcium and suffers if subjected to prolonged dampness. Under favourable conditions it will spread to form dense, colourful carpets to cover a rockery or a dry wall.

the finely sifted compost, added in appropriate amounts to the standard soil mixture. Such a compost can also be added in places where the rain or excessive watering has washed away the soil.

When building a miniature rock garden, the container should be filled with the soil up to its edge. It should then be watered and left for several days to settle. It is only at this point that the surface of the rock garden can be shaped, stones added and partially covered with soil. Very small stones by which the final touches to the 'landscape' are added should be placed only after the plants have been set out. If lime-loving rockery plants are particularly required, it is best to place them separately in plastic containers or other pots, to which lime can be added in the form of pieces of plaster.

The planting should be started with dwarf conifers and other dwarf woody species, which usually dominate the whole arrangement. The limited space available for their root systems naturally leads to a stunted growth and this ensures that the plants need not be pruned.

The choice of rock plants is mostly determined by the conditions of the habitat. Although preference should be given to small, undemanding plants, miniature gardens can provide ideal conditions for some of the true alpine gems. Narrow crevices between

388

Scilla hispanica grows to a height of 30 cm. Its flowers open in May and June and the plants can be grown in full sun or semi-shade. In a rock garden, it can be planted under shrubs and in front of conifers.

cissi (*Narcissus*) and some species and cultivars of botanical tulips (*Tulipa*).

If they are properly started and appropriately planted, miniature rock gardens do not require much care. They are satisfied if the soil is occasionally loosened, weeds removed, and plants in vertical crevices are secured by the addition of some sphagnum moss. Soil that has been washed out should be replaced; frequent spraying with a fine nozzle and thorough watering according to the needs of individual plants are a must. Bird droppings also play a certain role in providing nutrients for rock gardens, because, of course, birds like to settle on the stones. In winter, the plants should be protected with an adequate layer of coniferous branches.

Rock garden plants in the greenhouse

Rock garden enthusiasts who admire the beauty of rare rock plants, in particular those of alpine origin, find a greenhouse invaluable. They are attracted by the real challenge that the growing of such difficult rock plants presents.

English rock gardeners were the ones to pioneer this method of growing such demanding and sensitive alpine species. It was initiated by the necessity to control an unfavourable climate characterized by excessive dampness and a lack of sunshine in the summer months. For these reasons, they began to build very simple, unheated greenhouses. These were partly sunk into the ground, had large windows and were well ventilated, to meet the most important requirements for the successful cultivation of these plants, which are plenty of light and fresh air. After the success achieved in Great Britain, rock garden enthusiasts started to build similar constructions in other countries.

Even a very small greenhouse which can be heated in the winter meets a wide range of uses. It can be used not only to cultivate perfect specimens of plants otherwise usually affected by excessive dampness during an inclement growing season (such as lewisias), but it also offers protection from frost, particularly if there is no snow cover there to provide a shelter. The greenhouse can also be covered or shaded by a suitable material to delay growth and early budding and prevent the scorching of plants by midday sun.

The greenhouse is a simple construction with a saddle-shaped roof, which should be as high as possible to facilitate safe and comfortable movement. It should be aligned north to south and its foundation can be partly sunk into the ground.

Good ventilation is ensured by large windows and

A small greenhouse will allow you to grow even the most demanding alpine species with success.

heating can be provided in a number of ways. The side benches and tables used for the cultivation of rock plants should be as high and as wide as necessary for easy access. They are usually covered with pebbles, a layer of river sand and fine gravel. Flower pots, earthenware bowls and other suitable containers are then sunk into this drainage layer.

Gardeners can cultivate in such greenhouses most rock plants native to New Zealand with safety. Such places are also ideal for the growth of sensitive bulbs, including miniature narcissi, some cyclamens, saxifrages from the *Porophyllum* and *Engleria* groups and miniature rock jasmines (*Androsace*).

Many alpine species thrive much better in the greenhouse than in a rock garden, although they can often be seen in an alpine garden. These include the more delicate species of soldanellas, some orchids belonging to the *Pleione* and *Calypso* genera and primroses (*Primula petiolaris*). The young plants of some species of the genus *Hebe* grow much better in a protected greenhouse atmosphere, the same being true of *Pachystegia insignis*, *Helichrysum coraloides*, *H. microphyllum*, *H. selago*, *Cotula atrata*, *Rubus parvus* and members of the genera *Coprosma*, *Aciphylla* and *Raoulia*. Some recently cultivated primroses of American origin, e.g. *Primula × pubescens*, also give a better performance in a greenhouse than even in the most favourable position in a rock garden. Even lewisias will welcome being transferred to a greenhouse after flowering so that they do not have to endure excessive dampness in the rainy season.

The greenhouse also provides an excellent habitat for some other rare species, such as *Saxifraga grisebachii* from the *Engleria* group or *Saxifraga lilacina* from the *Porophyllum* group, along with other more sensitive species, hybrids and cultivars. At the same time, it must be pointed out that some species, particularly those of the *Porophyllum* group, lose some of their characteristics, especially their dwarf size, after having spent some time in a greenhouse. Their stems grow longer, and their foliage loses its compactness and becomes much thinner. This reality needs to be recognized and appropriate action taken.

It stands to reason that such rare rock garden species require care almost throughout the year.

Perfect ventilation is a must but draughts, which are harmful to the majority of these plants, must be avoided. Watering should be given according to the specific requirements of the individual species, so that every plant needs to be watered separately. Dur-

Lewisias belong to the alpine species. Their place in a rockery is in vertical cracks, best of all south-east or east-facing, and they can be also used in scree beds and dry walls. A good drainage is necessary in all these locations. The ideal soil mixture should include humus, rotted turves and sand. Surround the root necks with small pebbles to protect the plants from lingering dampness. At the end of August the plants should be given shelter against rain.

Androsace mucronifolia is another plant suitable for rock gardens and dry walls. It needs a sunny or semi-shaded situation and a sandy-loamy, humus-rich soil.

ing the main growing season, from spring onwards, most plants need more water than in summer or autumn. It is also a good idea to keep the concrete floor wet as this increases the humidity. In winter, watering is reduced to a minimum.

Pleione bulbocodioides is a ground orchid flowering from May to June. It needs a mixture of loamy soil, leaf mould, peat and sand, with an addition of crushed bricks and sphagnum moss. The best situation is a slight slope facing away from the sun. Good drainage should be provided, as well as appropriate watering from March throughout the whole growing season. One-fifth of the corm should be left showing above ground.

Characteristics and requirements of some important rock garden plants

Species	Appearance and characteristics		Time of flowering	Light conditions	Requirements		Other characteristics
	Height in cm	Colour of flowers (inflorescence)			Soil	Soil humidity	
Achillea millefolium	50—80	white, red, pink	VI—VIII	○	light or heavy	dry	melliferous, lime-loving
Achillea serbica	10—20	white	VI—VIII	○	light	dry	melliferous, lime-loving
Adonis amurensis	25	green-yellow	III—IV	◑	light	dry	drainage, lime-loving
Adonis vernalis	10—30	yellow	IV—V	○	light	dry	melliferous
Aethionema grandiflorum	10—25	pink	V—VI	○	light	dry	lime-loving
Ajuga reptans	10—30	blue	V—VI	◑ ●	light or heavy	dry to damp	lawn replacement, particularly resistant to pollution, evergreen
Alyssum argenteum	40—50	yellow	VI—VII	○	light	dry	melliferous, lime-loving
Alyssum montanum	10—15	yellow	V	○	light	dry	melliferous, lime-loving
Alyssum saxatile	20—30	yellow	IV—V	○	light	dry	melliferous, lime-loving
Anemone vitifolia	80—100	pink	VIII—X	◑	light	medium dry	lime-loving, drainage
Anthyllis montana	5—8	pink	VI—VIII	○	light	dry	lime-loving
Aquilegia discolor	10—15	blue-white	V—VI	○ ◑	light or heavy	medium damp	
Arabis caucasica	15—20	white	IV—V	○	light or heavy	dry to damp	sweet-scented, melliferous, lime-loving
Armeria juniperifolia	5—8	pink	V	○	light or heavy	dry	intolerant of lime, lawn replacement
Artemisia nitida	10—20	white	VII	○	light	dry to damp	decorative foliage, lime-loving
Asarum europaeum	8—10	brown-red	III—V	●	light or heavy	medium-damp to damp	decorative foliage, evergreen lawn replacement
Asperula nitida	3—5	pink	V—VI	○	light	dry	lime-loving
Aster alpinus hybrids	10—20	violet, blue, white, pink	V	○	light or heavy	dry	melliferous
Aster amellus	30—90	blue-violet	VIII—IX	○	light or heavy	dry to damp	melliferous
Aster dumosus hybrids	20—80	blue, pink, white	IX—X	○	light or heavy	dry to damp	
Aster tongolensis	30—50	blue-violet	VI	○	light or heavy	medium damp to damp	
Aubrieta × cultorum hybrids	5—10	blue, violet, pink, red	IV—V	○	light or heavy	dry	evergreen, melliferous
Bergenia cordifolia	30—40	pink-red	III—IV	○ ◑	light or heavy	dry to damp	decorative foliage, melliferous, evergreen, unusually resistant to pollution
Campanula bellidifolia	10—15	blue	IV—V	○ ◑	light	medium damp	
Campanula carpatica	20—40	blue, white	VII—VIII	○ ◑	light or heavy	dry to damp	melliferous, lime-loving
Campanula cochleariifolia	3—8	blue, white	VII—IX	○ ◑	light or heavy	dry to damp	melliferous, lime-loving
Campanula glomerata	20—50	blue-violet	VI—VII	○ ◑	light or heavy	dry to damp	melliferous
Campanula portenschlagiana	10—15	violet	VI—IX	○ ◑	light or heavy	medium damp to damp	melliferous
Campanula poscharskyana	10—25	blue	VI—IX	○ ◑	light or heavy	medium damp to damp	melliferous
Centaurea montana	30—60	blue-violet	VI	○	light or heavy	medium damp to damp	melliferous
Cerastium biebersteinii	20—30	white	V—VI	○	light or heavy	dry	extremely resistant to pollution
Cerastium tomentosum	10—15	white	V—VI	○	light or heavy	dry	extremely resistant to pollution
Ceratostigma plumbaginoides	20—30	blue	IX—X	○	light or heavy	dry to damp	

Species	Appearance and characteristics		Time of flowering	Light conditions	Requirements		Other characteristics
	Height in cm	Colour of flowers (inflorescence)			Soil	Soil humidity	
Chrysanthemum arcticum	30—40	white-pink	VII—IX	○ ◐	light or heavy	dry to damp	melliferous
Convallaria majalis	10—15	white	IV—V	◐ ●	light or heavy	medium damp to damp	scented
Corydalis lutea	20—40	yellow	VI—IX	◐ ●	light or heavy	dry to damp	
Cotula squalida	4—6	green	V—IX	○ ◐	light or heavy	dry to damp	decorative foliage, lawn replacement
Dianthus deltoides	10—15	red, pink	V—VI	○	light or heavy	dry	
Dianthus gratianopolitanus	10—20	pink, red	V—VI	○	heavy	dry to damp	scented, lime-loving
Dianthus plumarius hybrids	15—25	red, pink, violet, white	V—VI	○	light or heavy	dry to damp	scented, evergreen, lime-loving
Dodecatheon meadia	15—30	pink	V—VI	○ ◐	light or heavy	medium damp to damp	
Doronicum orientale 'Goldzwerg'	20	yellow	IV—V	○ ◐	light or heavy	medium damp	melliferous, lime-loving
Draba aizoides	5	yellow	III—IV	○	light	dry	lime-loving, evergreen
Draba sibirica	10—15	yellow	IV—V	○	light	dry	lime-loving, evergreen
Dracocephalum austriacum	30—40	blue-violet	VI—VII	○ ◐	light	dry to damp	lime-loving
Dryas octopetala	10	white	V	○ ◐	light or heavy	dry to damp	lime-loving, evergreen, lawn replacement
Erigeron aurantiacus	20—40	pink-red	VI—VII	○	heavy or light	dry to damp	
Erinus alpinus	5—10	white, pink, red	V—VII	○ ◐	heavy or light	dry	lime-loving
Eryngium alpinum	50—60	red-blue	VII—VIII	○	light or heavy	dry	
Euphorbia polychroma	30—60	yellow	V—VI	○	light or heavy	dry to damp	extremely resistant to pollution
Gentiana acaulis	5—10	blue	V	○ ◐	light	dry to damp	lime-loving
Gentiana asclepiadea	50—70	blue	VII—IX	◐	light or heavy	damp	
Gentiana farreri	10	blue-white	VIII—IX	○ ◐	light or heavy	medium damp	requires humus
Geranium cinereum	10—20	red	V—VIII	○ ◐	light	dry	lime-loving, extremely resistant to pollution
Geum coccineum	30—60	red	V—VI	○ ◐	heavy	medium damp to damp	
Geum montanum	30—40	yellow	V—VII	○	light or heavy	dry to damp	intolerant of lime
Globularia cordifolia	5—10	blue-violet	V—VI	○ ◐	light or heavy	dry	evergreen, lime-loving
Globularia punctata	10—30	blue	V—VI	○ ◐	light or heavy	dry	evergreen, lime-loving
Gypsophila repens	20—30	white, pink	V—VI	○	light	dry	lime-loving, melliferous
Helianthemum apenninum	20	pink	V—VII	○	light	dry	lime-loving
Helianthemum hybrids	10—20	white, green, red, brown	V—VII	○	light or heavy	dry	melliferous
Helleborus niger	15—20	white	II—III	◐ ●	heavy	dry to damp	melliferous, intolerant of pollution
Hepatica nobilis	10—15	blue, white, pink	III—IV	◐ ●	light or heavy	dry to damp	lawn replacement
Hepatica transsylvanica	10—15	blue	III—IV	◐ ●	light	medium damp	woodland areas, lawn replacement
Herniaria glabra	3	yellow-green	VI—X	◐ ●	light or heavy	dry to damp	evergreen, lawn replacement, intolerant of lime
Heuchera hybrids	30—60	red, pink, white	V—VI	○ ◐	light or heavy	dry to damp	lime-loving, extremely resistant to pollution
Horminum pyrenaicum	15—20	blue-violet	VI—VII	○ ◐	light or heavy	medium damp to damp	melliferous

393

Species	Appearance and characteristics		Time of flowering	Light conditions	Requirements		Other characteristics
	Height in cm	Colour of flowers (inflorescence)			Soil	Soil humidity	
Hosta lancifolia	15—30	white, violet	VII—VIII	◐ ●	heavy	medium damp to damp	around ponds, extremely resistant to pollution
Hosta plantaginea	30—60	white	VII—VIII	◐ ●	heavy	medium damp to damp	around ponds
Hosta sieboldiana	40—60	violet	VI—VII	◐ ●	heavy	medium damp to damp	around ponds, extremely resistant to pollution
Hypericum polyphyllum	10—20	yellow	V—VI	○	light or heavy	dry to damp	lime-loving
Iberis sempervirens hybrids	20—30	white	V—VI	○	light or heavy	dry to damp	lime-loving, melliferous
Incarvillea delavayi	50—100	pink	VI—VII	○	light or heavy	dry	
Incarvillea mairei var. *grandiflora*	20—30	pink	VI	○	light or heavy	dry	
Inula ensifolia	20—30	yellow	VII—VIII	○	light or heavy	dry	
Iris pumila hybrids	10—20	blue, violet, brown, yellow, white	IV	○	light and heavy	dry and damp	around ponds, melliferous plant, extremely resistant to pollution
Lavandula angustifolia	20—40	blue-lilac	VII—VIII	○	light or heavy	dry	melliferous, lime-loving
Leontopodium alpinum	5—20	white	VII—VIII	○	light	dry	lime-loving
Liatris spicata	50—100	violet-pink	VIII	○ ◐	light or heavy	medium damp	around ponds, melliferous
Limonium latifolium	30—60	blue	VII—VIII	○	light or heavy	dry	
Limonium tataricum	30—40	white	VII—VIII	○	light or heavy	dry	
Linum flavum	20—40	yellow	VI—VII	○	light or heavy	dry to damp	melliferous plant
Lithospermum purpureocaeruleum	10—25	red-blue-violet	V—VI	○ ◐	light or heavy	dry to damp	melliferous
Lysimachia nummularia	2—4	yellow	V—VII	○ ◐	light or heavy	medium damp to damp	lawn replacement, around ponds, melliferous
Marrubium velutinum	15—20	yellow	VI—VII	○	light or heavy	dry	
Mimulus luteus	30—50	yellow-red	VII—VIII	○ ◐	light or heavy	medium damp	intolerant of lime
Oenothera missouriensis	15—25	yellow	VI—X	○	light or heavy	dry to damp	melliferous, lime-loving, extremely resistant to pollution
Oenothera tetragona	50	green-yellow	VI—VIII	○	light or heavy	dry to medium damp	
Opuntia phaeacantha	20	yellow	VI—VII	○	light or heavy	dry	evergreen
Opuntia rhodantha	20	red	VI—VII	○	light or heavy	dry	evergreen
Origanum vulgare 'Compactum'	15	pink-violet	VII—X	○	light	dry	
Papaver nudicaule	20	white, yellow, pink, red	VI—VII	○	light or heavy	medium damp to damp	
Penstemon menziesii	15—25	violet	VI—IX	○	light or heavy	dry	intolerant of lime
Phlox divaricata	20—30	violet-blue	V	○	light or heavy	medium damp	evergreen
Phlox subulata hybrids	10—15	white, pink, red, blue-violet	IV—V	○	light or heavy	medium damp to damp	evergreen
Phyteuma scheuchzeri	10—25	blue	VI—VII	○	light	dry to damp	lime-loving
Primula denticulata	10—20	white, violet, pink-red	IV	○	heavy	medium damp to damp	

Species	Appearance and characteristics		Time of flowering	Light conditions	Requirements		Other characteristics
	Height in cm	Colour of flowers (inflorescence)			Soil	Soil humidity	
Primula japonica	20—50	white, red	V—VI	◐ ●	light or heavy	medium damp to damp	
Primula rosea	8—12	pink	IV	◐	light or heavy	medium damp to damp	melliferous
Primula vulgaris	5—12	red, pink-violet	III—IV	◐ ●	light or heavy	medium damp to damp	
Pulsatilla halleri	10—20	violet	IV—V	○	light	dry	lime-loving, decorative fruit, melliferous
Pulsatilla pratensis	20—25	violet	IV—V	○	light	dry	lime-loving, decorative fruit, melliferous
Pulsatilla vulgaris	10—20	violet, pink, red	IV—V	○	light	dry	lime-loving, decorative fruit, melliferous
Ranunculus gramineus	20—30	yellow	V—VI	○ ◐	light or heavy	dry to damp	
Salvia argentea	60—100	white	VII	○	light or heavy	dry to damp	extremely resistant to pollution
Saponaria ocymoides	10—20	pink-red	VI	○	light or heavy	dry	lime-loving
Satureja montana	20—25	white, blue	VIII	○	light or heavy	dry	lime-loving, melliferous
Saxifraga cespitosa	15—20	pink, red, yellow, white	V—VI	○	light or heavy	medium damp to damp	evergreen
Saxifraga cotyledon	40—70	white-pink	V—VI	○	light or heavy	medium damp to damp	intolerant of lime, evergreen
Saxifraga muscoides	5—10	red	V—VI	◐	light or heavy	medium damp to damp	evergreen
Saxifraga paniculata	10—25	white, yellow, pink, red	V—VI	○	light or heavy	medium damp to damp	evergreen
Saxifraga trifurcata	15—20	white	V—VI	○	light or heavy	dry to damp	lawn replacement
Sedum album	8—12	white, pink	VII	○	light or heavy	dry	extremely resistant to pollution, decorative foliage
Sedum sieboldii	10—15	red-pink	X	○	light or heavy	dry	extremely resistant to pollution, decorative foliage
Sedum spectabile	20—40	red	VIII—IX	○	light or heavy	dry	extremely resistant to pollution, decorative foliage
Sempervivum arachnoideum	5—10	pink	VII—VIII	○	light or heavy	dry	decorative foliage, evergreen
Silene acaulis	3—5	pink-red	VI—IX	○	light or heavy	average damp	lime-loving
Silene schafta	10—20	pink-red	VIII—IX	○ ◐	light or heavy	medium damp to damp	lime-loving
Soldanella carpatica	5—10	blue-violet	IV—V	◐	light	medium damp	requires humus
Soldanella montana	12—15	blue-violet	III—IV	◐	light	medium damp	requires humus
Thymus serpyllum	2—5	white, pink, red	VI—VIII	○	light or heavy	dry to damp	melliferous, lawn replacement
Viola cornuta	10—15	blue, white, yellow	V—IX	○ ◐	light or heavy	dry to damp	melliferous
Viola odorata	10—20	white, blue, yellow, red	III—IV	◐ ●	light or heavy	dry to damp	scented, melliferous

Heath garden

A heath garden is an attractive section that adds colour to the garden from spring until autumn and has a magic of its own even in winter. It is often incorporated into the rock garden, as a rule at the edge, where it provides a smooth transition between the rockery and the adjoining garden. The heath garden is also often located beneath taller woody plants that permit the penetration of sufficient light. Typical heath plants require acid, humus-rich, sandy soil. Most do not tolerate lime in the soil.

Plants for the heath garden

The chief plants that form the ground cover of the heath garden are the many species and cultivated varieties of heather (*Calluna*) and Heath (*Erica*).

Callunas are fond of sun. Even light, partial shade causes them to flower poorly and to become spindly and less compact. They do best in very sandy, poor, rather dry soils. Ericas tolerate partial as well as full shade but bear fewer flowers in a shaded location. Some maritime species of *Erica*, particularly *E. cinerea*, are less hardy in central Europe, where they require a protective cover for the winter. A winter cover is a must wherever there is danger of freezing weather without snow.

The variously coloured cultivated varieties of these basic heath garden plants make it possible for the gardener to plan all sorts of colour combinations. However, they should always be planted in drifts of the same colour. Mixing together plants of different colours creates a chaotic effect and when viewed from a distance the colours merge into an indeterminate grey. For smaller areas, choose shorter to dwarf cultivars.

The heath garden can be successfully supplemented with such companion plants as are found in the wild. Irregularly placed junipers (*Juniperus*) of columnar and spreading habit will look good, as will certain species of *Cotoneaster* with their attractively coloured fruits, and *Genista*. Brooms (*Cytisus*) brighten the heath garden with their profusion of flowers in spring and early summer.

Examples of some other woody plants that can also be incorporated in the heath garden are *Betula pendula* 'Youngii', a birch of weeping habit with branches drooping to the ground, that reaches a height of only 5—7 m, and the bushy, common English Holly (*Ilex aquifolium*), which does particularly well in places shaded by tall trees.

Other plants that must not be overlooked when deciding what else to choose to brighten the heath garden are the ornamental grasses, which form emerald-green or blue-grey carpets or rise above the surrounding growth to give the whole a very natural look. Also many rhododendrons, including the well known Mollis and Kurume azaleas, members of the genera *Andromeda, Daboecia, Bruckenthalia, Kalmia, Gaultheria, Ledum, Empetrum* and similar plants fully deserve the gardener's consideration when choosing what to put in the heath garden. Even perennials and rock plants of suitable appearance can be used (see the lists on pp. 326 and 392).

To link the heath garden with neighbouring parts of the garden, it is recommended that you use various woody plants. Also good for this purpose are a number of perennials, which make for a smooth transition and link up with the flowers in other parts of the garden. The only necessary proviso is that the selected perennials should be able to tolerate rather poor acid soil and need no special care. Otherwise, the soil where they are to be planted must be prepared to suit their needs.

Basic care

Once the heath plants have become established and have spread to form a continuous cover they will

A heather garden complemented by a choice of conifers is beautiful in all seasons.

Larger surfaces planted with a single species of heather are very attractive. Species with different coloured flowers and leaves can be combined.

Columnar junipers are excellent among heathers. They look very natural and underline the beauty of the lower, shrubby plants.

prevent the growth of weeds and thus dispense with the onerous task of weeding. The only thing to watch out for is that the plants do not become invasive and crowd out their neighbours, chiefly rock garden plants of lower growth. Older callunas should be clipped over occasionally in spring. This will renew their vigour and keep them compact. This, plus an occasional sprinkling of peat, is generally the only care required by heath garden plants.

The heath garden throughout the year

If you have devoted the proper attention to the choice of plants for the heath garden then you will be rewarded with a display of colour throughout the year. The first ericas generally flower as early as December, white blooms being succeeded by pink and red until April. As the seasons change, so does the colour pattern of the heath garden. The early spring beauty of the ericas is replaced by the lovely spring hues of rhododendrons and other woody plants, followed by the blooms of the summer heaths of the

Rhododendrons should not be omitted in a heather garden. Their species and cultivars vary in height and in the colour and opening time of their flowers.

Erica cinerea and *Erica vagans* group and in the autumn by those of *Calluna vulgaris* cultivars. Also brightening the scene in the autumn is the foliage of deciduous broadleaved trees and shrubs and the fruits of a number of woody plants.

Recommended plants

Calluna vulgaris — Common Heather or Ling
C. v. 'Alba Plena' — a 25—50 cm high cultivar of broad, upright habit, bearing a profusion of white double flowers in September and October.
C. v. 'Alportii' — an upright cultivar up to 50 cm high with bright crimson flowers borne in August and September.
C. v. 'County Wicklow' — a low-growing cultivar up to 20 cm high with double, bright pink flowers appearing in August and September.
C. v. 'Cuprea' — an interesting cultivar of upright habit with striking greenish-yellow foliage turning reddish-brown in winter. The flowers, simple and coloured pale violet, appear in August and September.
C. v. 'C. W. Nix' —a plant of attractive habit, up to 50 cm high, with dark green foliage and dark violet-red flowers arranged in conical racemes. The flowering period is in August and September.
C. v. 'Foxii' — this heather, only about 10 cm high, forms low, deep green cushions. The purplish-pink flowers are borne in moderate profusion in August and September.
C. v. 'H. E. Beale' — a very attractive, vigorous cultivar of upright habit, up to 50 cm high. In September and October it bears a profusion of double pink, white-centred flowers arranged in long racemes. The flowers are very long-lasting and excellent for cutting and keeping in a vase.
C. v. 'J. H. Hamilton' — reaches a height of 25 cm, is of rather broad compact habit, and in August and September bears double, salmon-pink flowers.
C. v. 'Mullion' — a lovely cultivated variety of compact cushion-like habit, richly branched, and bearing a profusion of dark pink flowers in August or September. It is only 20 cm high and eminently suited, particularly, for covering larger areas.
C. v. 'Tib' — a 25—30 cm high cultivar of upright habit, bearing double, deep pink flowers in profusion very early, from July to August.

Erica carnea — Winter-flowering Heath
E. c. 'Alba' — a 20—30 cm high variety of attractive compact habit bearing snow-white flowers from March to April.
E. c. 'Atrorubra' — a 15—20 cm high cultivar with dark green, faintly blue-tinged foliage and carmine red flowers appearing from mid-March till the beginning of May.
E. c. 'Aurea' — interesting cultivar with bright golden-yellow foliage in spring and early summer. It reaches a height of 15—20 cm and bears pink-red flowers in March and April.
E. c. 'James Backhouse' — reaches a height of 25 cm and has large pink flowers. The flowering period is from March till April.

A growth of heathers is a good idea for a front garden. They offer a variety of colours throughout the year and their combinations with conifers are particularly attractive.

E. c. 'King George' — an early red-flowering cultivar reaching a height of 15—20 cm. It is one of the first to flower.
E. c. 'Ruby Glow' — a 15—20 cm high cultivar with reddish-brown foliage and relatively large, deep dark red flowers from March to April.
E. c. 'Snow Queen' — a very early-flowering cultivar with large, pure white flowers located above the leaves, which are thereby practically entirely hidden

Rhododendrons are favourite shrubs, suitable for planting in the most exposed places in the garden. They can be grown either as solitary specimens or in groups.

Cultivars of *Calluna vulgaris* differ in the colour of their leaves and flowers, the profusion of flowering and, of course, in their habit and height. The pink-flowered *Calluna* is one of the medium-tall varieties which are suitable for rock gardens and for planting in containers.

Heathers are a good subject for planting under rhododendrons. This, however, is only a temporary solution before the rhododendrons grow too thick and the situation becomes too shaded for the heathers.

Heathers should always be grown in large masses. The picture shows a growth of *Erica carnea* 'Snow Queen', a white-flowering cultivar. Not even snow can spoil the beauty of its delicate flowers.

from view by the blooms. The flowering period is often from as early as January until March.

E. c. 'Vivellii' — a very precious cultivar of vigorous, compact habit, only 15 cm high, with magnificent carmine-red flowers and deep green foliage that turns bronze-brown in winter. The flowering period is generally from as early as January until March.

E. c. 'Winter Beauty' — a cultivated variety of low, dense, compact habit, reaching a height of only 15 cm. It is a very early-flowering variety and in congenial conditions bears its deep pink flowers as early as November. Otherwise, the flowering period is normally from January until March.

Erica vagans — Cornish Heath
E. v. 'Alba' — a summer-flowering variety of compact habit, 20—30 cm high, with a profusion of pure white flowers appearing in July and August.
E. v. 'Mrs. D. F. Maxwell' — an outstanding cultivar up to 35 cm high with carmine-red blooms arranged in compact racemes. The flowering period is in August and September.
E. v. 'St. Keverne' — a pretty heath up to 35 cm high, of compact, bushy habit, with pure salmon-pink flowers appearing from July until September.

Heaths of the *Erica vagans* group welcome a good cover in winter to protect them from snowless frosts. They also benefit from an application of dry peat in and around the plants, to half their height, topped by a light protective cover of evergreen branches for the winter.

In addition to the main heath plants, there are many other interesting species with attractive displays of flowers. Their number includes the following:

Andromeda polifolia, Bruckenthalia spiculifolia, Daboecia cantabrica, Gaultheria procumbens, Kalmia angustifolia 'Rubra', *Pernettya mucronata, Rhododendron impeditum, Rhododendron* × *praecox,* and rhododendrons of the Kurume group, also called 'Kurume azaleas'.

Kurume azaleas flower from as early as April but the main flowering period is May. Most often encountered are the following cultivars:
'Hatsugiri' — of sparse, densely compact habit, up to 50 cm high and about 1.5 m across, with small leaves and funnel-shaped, carmine flowers.
'Hinodegiri' — of looser, more broadly spreading habit, 50—60 cm high, with large, ruby-red flowers.
'Hinomayo' — of low, spreading habit, also reaching a height of 50—60 cm when fully grown, with a profusion of early, bright pink flowers.
'Kermesina' — a very hardy cultivar of compact, bushy habit with medium-large, early, vivid carmine-pink flowers.
'Orange Beauty' — 100—200 cm high, flowers up to 3 cm across and coloured salmon-pink tinged with orange when in full bloom.
'Sakata Red' ('Kurume Red') — with relatively large flowers coloured a beautiful red.
'Vuyk's Scarlet' — with bright scarlet flowers completely concealing the leaves. It is a later-flowering, hardy cultivar reaching a height of 80—100 cm.

Erica carnea belongs to the early-flowering heathers. The picture shows a happy combination of colours with the yellow-flowering Barberry at the back.

Bruckenthalia spiculifolia with its wonderful flowers opening from July to August is a good companion to heathers. Its requirements are similar to those of heathers; it need not be cut back but requires winter cover in extreme situations.

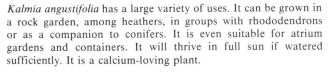

Kalmia angustifolia has a large variety of uses. It can be grown in a rock garden, among heathers, in groups with rhododendrons or as a companion to conifers. It is even suitable for atrium gardens and containers. It will thrive in full sun if watered sufficiently. It is a calcium-loving plant.

Red-flowering cultivars of rhododendrons are often combined with light-flowered ones.

Grasses and ferns in the garden

Grasses and ferns will be much appreciated by anyone who likes the unusual and has room for them in the garden — a casual, informal group of perennial plants typical of steppe regions. Such plants have their origin in regions with a warm and dry climate so they need a sunny location; they also require neutral soil. Grasses are an important component and give the area a distinctive character.

Ornamental perennial grasses are nowadays an indispensable item also in gardens with a well-tended lawn, informal or formal rock garden, dry wall or pool. Many are eminently suitable particularly close to a sitting-out corner by water, next to a bird bath, garden sculpture or large, randomly placed boulders. Taller grasses are excellent as solitary specimens, especially against a darker backdrop of conifers which sets off not only their shape but also the colour of the foliage. Medium-tall grasses can be put to good use in group plantings and in the rock garden, dry wall, or as a green ground cover in larger as well as smaller areas.

A wide selection of ornamental grasses is available now, and the many different species and varieties enhance the beauty of the garden the whole year long. Apart from the ones with fresh green and deep green leaves, other attractive grasses are those with yellow, green and white, reddish-brown, and above all lovely bluish and silvery foliage. Also, the spent inflorescences of some of the taller grasses are excellent for indoor arrangements in winter.

Grassy and steppe areas still have not been duly estimated by many gardeners. The picture shows one of the many possibilities for using ornamental grasses; the group of large cobbles being a nice complement.

Though some of the ornamental grasses are of exotic origin they are mostly hardy and stand the cold of central Europe quite well. Many like a dry and sunny position, others prefer a very moist situation. These conditions, along with their growth characteristics, predetermine the selection and use of the many different species and cultivars, not only in or near the lawn but also in the miniature rockery, in containers and in roof gardens.

For ornamental grasses to keep their natural habit, attractive appearance and, above all, the typical coloration of the leaves they must be planted according to their specific requirements — either in a sunny location or in partial shade, preferably always in rather poor soil, best of all a mixture of rotted turves and some river sand. All grasses make a good ground cover, prevent the soil from drying out, are firm and persistent, and spread readily.

Recommended ornamental perennial grasses

Alopecurus lanatus — This fox-tail grass is an interesting species with narrow, silvery-grey felted leaves and 10—15 cm long inflorescences. It is suitable only for sunny situation and requires well drained sandy soil with an admixture of peat.

Arrhenatherum elatius ssp. *bulbosum* 'Variegatum' — This oat-grass is 20—30 cm high, with narrow, silvery-white striped leaves. The flowering period is in July and August. It is suitable for a sunny situation as well as partial shade.

Ornamental grasses should not be neglected in a rock garden. As testified by this picture, tall species have an almost sculptural look.

Helictotrichon sempervirens has beautiful blue-grey leaves, similar to *Festuca glauca*. They make an attractive contrast with the growth of *Pennisetum japonicum* at left and the deep green *Pyracantha coccinea* in the background.

Cortaderia selloana is one of the most attractive grasses, particularly when in flower. It is usually planted singly, needs dry conditions in winter and is intolerant of low temperatures.

Helictotrichon sempervirens (*Avena candida*) — This wild oat is a rather tall, 50—80 cm high grass with erect blue-grey leaves and erect pale yellow spikes extending beyond the leaves. An attractive solitary specimen for sunny locations. It flowers from July to August.

Briza media — Common Quaking Grass. A handsome, rather short grass that forms turfy cushions, 30—40 cm high. It likes a sunny aspect but tolerates light partial shade. The flowering period is in May and June. The dry inflorescences are good for room decoration.

Carex montana — This is a densely tufted sedge with narrow leaves that turn brown in the autumn. It reaches a height of 20—30 cm, flowers in April and May, and does well in a sunny location as well as in partial shade.

Carex morrowii 'Variegata' — A handsome cultivar 30—50 cm high with narrow, glossy green leaves edged with white. It tolerates sun as well as partial shade and flowers in June and July.

Cortaderia selloana — Pampas Grass. An outstanding solitary grass 2—3 m high with grey-green, gracefully arching leaves. The huge inflorescences are excellent for indoor decoration. The flowering period is from August to October. It is recommended that this grass be planted only in spring, and in winter it must be provided with a protective covering.

Deschampsia caespitosa — Tufted Hair-grass. An attractive grass, 30—80 cm high, with deep green leaves and spreading green panicles which bear a great many spikelets. It does well in sun as well as semi-shade, flowering in June and July.

Elymus arenarius — Lyme Grass. A vigorous grass, 60—100 cm high, with steel-blue, faintly striped leaves and yellowish-brown spikelets. It is very decorative and grows well even in the driest sandy soils, where it spreads rapidly. The flowering period is in June and July.

Festuca cinerea (*F. glauca*) — An excellent short grass with blue-green foliage, invaluable in the rock garden and in plantings of shorter perennials. It makes nice, 15—20 cm high tufts and likes full sun but will tolerate light, partial shade. The flowering period is in June and July.

F. scoparia — A dwarf grass forming compact, deep green cushions only about 10—15 cm high and flowering in June and July.

Glyceria maxima 'Variegata' — Reed Sweet-grass or Reed-grass. A decorative grass with variegated leaves striped in pale yellow or white and turning red in the autumn. It is 50—60 cm high, undemanding, hardy, and thrives exceptionally well in muddy soil. It flowers in July and August.

Miscanthus sinensis — Porcupine Grass. A large grass, up to 150 cm high, with broad, light green leaves with a prominent midrib. It forms large dense tufts and in September or October bears very attractive panicles, generally with a pinkish hue. A handsome grass for open sites, particularly near water. In less congenial climates it requires a protective cover in winter.

Molinia arundinacea — A grass 60—80 cm, sometimes even more than 1 m high, with foliage that is particularly attractive in the autumn, when it turns a lovely golden-brown. It may be planted in a sunny location as well as in partial shade. The flowering period is from August to October, so the inflorescences are an ornamental feature in the garden over a long period.

Panicum clandestinum — An unusual grass slightly reminiscent of the bamboo in habit. It is 60—80 cm high, has short, broad leaves and attractive brownish inflorescences that are also good for cutting. It flowers from June to August and may be planted in a sunny location as well as in a slightly shaded one.

Pennisetum alopecuroides — An ornamental, very hardy grass with long, reddish-brown cylindrical spikes and narrow, grey-green leaves. It is particularly attractive planted as a solitary specimen or in less dense plantings of perennials. It is 50—100 cm high and flowers reliably in August and September even as a young plant. The dry inflorescences are excellent for room decoration in winter.

Hordeum jubatum is grown as an annual, planted singly or in groups composed of perennial grasses.

Phalaris arundinacea — Reed Canary-grass or Reed Grass. A vigorous grass with reed-like leaves and pale green or reddish spikes. This robust grass reaches a height of 150 cm and is exceptionally attractive when planted by a lake or pool. It requires

Miscanthus sinensis 'Gracillimus' is noted for its decorative leaves. It is planted in groups or singly, and can also make a nice complement of woody plants.

a sunny site, but will tolerate light partial shade, and likes a soil that is slightly moist. It flowers from July till August and is also good for indoor decoration.

Spartina pectinata 'Aureomarginata' — A handsome grass 100—150 cm high, with long, yellow-edged leaves curving almost to the ground and lovely pale brown inflorescences that can be used for room decoration. It likes sun, and flowers in August and September.

Shaded areas with ferns

Of the plants that are being increasingly used nowadays in the shaded areas of the garden, most important are the ferns. Their ornamental effect, often lasting the whole year, makes them worthy of more than just passing notice. In spring, it is their changing appearance as the fronds unfurl that makes them interesting. In summer, it is the beauty of their lacy foliage. In autumn, it is the golden tint of the dying leaves and in winter either the fresh green of the evergreen species or the splendour of the previous year's fronds coated with hoar-frost and glittering in the pale winter sunshine.

Though some ferns do quite well even in a sunny position, most cultivated species are used to brighten places that are partly shaded or in full shade. Many are noteworthy for their lovely habit or exceptionally beautiful foliage and can therefore be grown as attractive solitary specimens. Others are excellent in mixed or group plantings in rockeries, garden nooks, courtyards and other parts of the garden.

Ferns are known to be among the hardiest of perennials, ones that will grow in the shade of taller trees and shrubs. Most cultivated species of taller ferns not only grow well but are particularly attractive amid plantings of numerous shade-loving perennials such as *Asarum,* low-growing False Goat's Beard (*Astilbe*), Lily-of-the-valley (*Convallaria*), Windflower (*Anemone*), Hepatica, Barrenwort (*Epimedium*), Lungwort (*Pulmonaria*), Navelwort (*Omphalodes*), primrose (*Primula*), periwinkle (*Vinca*) and other woodland plants.

In more open woodland sections, ferns can also be teamed with carpets of small bulbs and tubers such as squill (*Scilla*), Glory of the Snow (*Chionodoxa*), Grape Hyacinth (*Muscari*), Snowdrop (*Galanthus),* Snowflake (*Leucojum*), crocus, and Winter Aconite (*Eranthis*), which brighten such places with a profusion of flowers in late winter and early spring.

Most ferns do best in loose, appropriately moist, humus-rich woodland soil. If you do not have such soil in your garden you can prepare the required mixture by adding peat, low-moor peat, leaf mould or heath mould and an appropriate amount of river sand. The soil may even be stony but it must always be well drained. Ferns generally are not particularly delicate but one thing they do not tolerate is losing their roots, primarily when they are being transplanted. Some species do not even tolerate the loss of their fronds during the growing period.

Pennisetum japonicum and *Helictotrichon sempervirens* are often planted together for the contrasting colours of their leaves. *P. japonicum* is particularly decorative at the end of summer for its inflorescences which remain on the plants long into the winter.

Ferns are suitable for shaded and semi-shaded situations, where they can be grown either singly or in groups.

Recommended ferns

The North American Maidenhair (*Adiantum pedatum*) is one of the favourite shade-loving ferns grown in central European gardens. It is a delicate fern with flat, fan-like foliage on thin stalks. The black, wiry leaf-stalks carry at a height of about 50—60 cm delicate, pale green, horizontally-spread, very ornamental leaves resembling those of rue. Maidenhair likes partial shade to full shade and is particularly effective planted together with low-growing False Goat's Beard (*Astilbe*), primrose (*Primula*), Slipper

A bird bath, besides being useful, is a highly decorative feature in the garden. Ferns are among the most suitable plants to surround it.

Orchid (*Cypripedium*), Windflower (*Anemone*) and autumn-flowering crocus. It likes slightly acid, appropriately moist, loose soil, rich in humus. In congenial situations it will flourish for years in the same place, in time covering a space of up to one square metre.

The evergreen Hard Fern (*Blechnum spicant*) is another very decorative plant that flourishes in slightly shaded places and moist peaty-sandy soil without lime. It requires more moisture than the other fern species. In young plants the fronds are arranged in rosettes; in older plants the fronds form dense tufts.

The Male Fern (*Dryopteris filix-mas*) is a familiar tall fern, reaching a height of 60—100 cm or more, with oblong fronds and alternate, pinnatipartite leaflets. The dark green fronds, which form a sort of funnel, reach a length of more than 1 m. This fern will grow even in rather poor soil but does not tolerate permanent dampness. It likes shady situations.

The Ostrich Fern (*Matteucia struthiopteris*) is particularly decorative in spring when its fronds unfurl to form a broad funnel. It grows to a height of 80 cm and likes an appropriately moist situation, either in a sunny spot or in partial shade. It will even tolerate a temporary drought. It spreads rapidly by underground shoots.

The Hart's Tongue Fern (*Phyllitis scolopendrium*) is an interesting fern with evergreen, tongue-like entire fronds attaining a length of up to 40 cm. It flourishes even in very shaded situations that are appropriately moist. It is most effective planted amid suitably arranged rocks, to which it will become close pressed.

The Adder's Fern (*Polypodium vulgare*) is a low-growing, evergreen fern with leathery, pinnate leaves. It reaches a height of only about 20 cm and can be planted in shady places wherever the soil does not contain lime.

Water in the garden

Water in various forms as well as aquatic and waterside or bog plants should be included in every garden. All sorts of ornamental basins, miniature lakes, ponds, pools, streams, fountains and bird baths are welcome features of small-scale garden architecture and the plants that grow there add variety and interest to the garden with the unusual beauty of their flowers, leaves and general shape. Furthermore, any water feature favourably affects the microclimate in its immediate vicinity.

Water has been traditionally used in large-scale garden schemes for centuries but it is only recently that scaled-down lakes, ponds and pools are being incorporated more often also into smaller gardens. This has brought with it an increased interest in aquatic and waterside plants than heighten the effect of such a feature.

Just as mountain streams and brooks with their crystal-clear water are a vital element for the plants growing along their banks, so, too, even a small rivulet in the rock garden, a 'waterfall' of several boulders, a tiny spring supplied with water from the mains or a little stream terminating in a miniature lake help to provide better conditions for plants for whom water or permanent moisture is a must. Besides this, water brings to every garden and rockery constant motion, birdsong and, above all, a little of the magic of the natural world.

Plants in and by water

Inasmuch as the conditions of aquatic and permanently as well as temporarily wet situations are very different from those of normal garden soil, it is obvious that only certain species of plants can be grown successfully in such places. These plants are divided into three main groups: bog plants, moisture-loving plants and aquatic plants.

Bog plants
Shallows, small bogs as well as the wet banks of small streams, lakes and pools are particularly good

It is quite easy to maintain a pool or pond with rich aquatic vegetation. Various subtropical or tropical species can be added in the summer. The picture shows *Eichhornia crassipes* in flower.

Not every gardener is lucky enough to have a brook running through his plot. The possibilities offered by such a situation are shown in the picture. Small waterfalls formed by large boulders and the tastefully chosen vegetation help to make the setting look completely natural.

places for siting the lovely bog plants. Most familiar of all is the Marsh Marigold (*Caltha palustris*) that flowers in April and May. It has 20—50 cm long stems with broad, kidney-shaped leaves and yolk-yellow, five-petalled blossoms. It should be planted in mud or with no more than 5 cm of water over the roots. Most often encountered in gardens is the magnificent double cultivar 'Multiplex', with golden-yellow flowers.

The Bog Arum (*Calla palustris*) is another of the group of shorter bog plants. It is 15—30 cm high, with heart-shaped leaves on long stalks, and generally grows in wet mud or in shallow water. The long stems are terminated by flowers like small arums with a white spade flushed green on the reverse, enclosing a short yellow-green spadix. The ripe fruits are coral-red berries, poisonous but very ornamental.

Bog Bean (*Menyanthes trifoliata*) is an interesting perennial reaching a height of 20—30 cm. The leaves are long-stalked and clover-like (ovoid and divided into three) and the flowers, borne in profusion in May and June, are white to pinkish and arranged in racemes. The water level should not be more than 30 cm above the roots.

Arrow-head (*Sagittaria sagittifolia*) is noteworthy for its unusual, decorative foliage. It grows to a height of 30—60 cm and the leaves are arrow-shaped and long-stalked. The white flowers, usually appearing in June and July, are arranged in loose

Caltha palustris occurs in the wild where there is sufficient moisture during its growing season. It should not be omitted in similar places in the garden.

whorls. The green globular fruits are also decorative. Arrow-head is suitable for growing in water 5—40 cm deep.

Many bog plants grow to a greater height. Flowering Rush (*Butomus umbellatus*) is usually 50—90 cm high and noteworthy for its stiff, iris-like leaves. The flowering stems are up to 1.5 m long and terminate in showy umbels of red-white, darkly striated flowers. It should be planted in water 10—20 cm deep.

Yellow Flag (*Iris pseudacorus*) is another familiar bog plant, reaching a height of 80—100 cm. It is a robust plant with deep green, sword-shaped leaves and bright yellow flowers opening in June. It likes mud but will grow even in ordinary, adequately moist garden soil and will also tolerate 5—30 cm of water over the roots.

Caltha palustris 'Alba' is a delightful white-flowered variety of Marsh Marigold. It is slightly smaller than the species and flowers earlier.

Sweet Flag (*Acorus calamus*) is an equally familiar bog plant, 60—120 cm high and with sword-shaped leaves with a prominent midrib. It grows from a thick, fleshy, aromatic rhizome with medicinal properties. The flowers, which are small, inconspicuous and yellowish-green, are borne in June and July. Sweet Flag grows in mud and in shallows with about 5 cm of water.

Common Water Plantain (*Alisma plantago-aquatica*) has long-stalked, broadly lanceolate leaves arranged in a rosette, from which rises a thick branching stem with white or pinkish flowers that appear in succession from June until September. This plant, which grows to a height of about 80 cm, is suitable for water about 20 cm deep.

Reedmace or Cat-tail (*Typha latifolia*) grows to a height of 150—200 cm, has long, upright, grey-green leaves and flowers in July and August. The 10—30 cm long, dark brown fertile spadices are very

Alisma plantago-aquatica grows in water 10—20 cm deep. It does best in full sun or semi-shade and its flowers open successively from July to September.

popular for indoor decoration. Because of its robust size this reedmace is suitable for planting only in larger ponds, with water about 50 cm deep. Often encountered in gardens is the very attractive species *Typha minima,* a low-growing, smaller reedmace reaching a height of only about 30—80 cm and bearing attractive, small poker-like heads of flowers in the autumn. It is eminently suitable for small ponds with water less than 20 cm deep as well as for planting by the waterside.

Of the ornamental grasses suitable for places that are permanently or temporarily wet as well as for pools with shallow water, particularly worthy of note is Manna Grass (*Glyceria aquatica*). Generally en-

Reedmaces are typical of ponds and pools. Because of its robust growth, *Typha latifolia* (shown here) is suitable for larger bodies of water. There exists, however, a smaller species — *Typha minima* — which is well suited even to very small gardens with miniature pools.

countered in gardens is the elegant cultivated variety 'Variegata' with variegated leaves striped in yellow and white. It grows to a height of about 80 cm and likes a sunny, warm and damp situation.

Moisture-loving plants

Alongside lakes and pools it is possible to grow in ordinary garden soil many interesting, attractively-flowering perennials whose aspect makes them suitable for such locations. To grow well, of course, they must be provided with plenty of water when necessary. Among the loveliest of all are the Japanese Clematis Irises (*Iris kaempferi*). Many outstanding cultivated varieties with pure white, pink, blue and dark violet flowers are grown in gardens, their unu-

Margins of garden ponds and pools should have plantings like those that can be found in similar places in the wild. Among the most favourite plants belonging to this category are irises.

sual, almost exotic beauty making them truly exciting waterside plants.

Other perennials for planting by the waterside include the *Sibirica* and grassy-leaved irises, various primroses (*Primula*), False Goat's Beard (*Astilbe*), Orchids (*Orchis*), Forget-me-nots (*Myosotis*), Sedge (*Carex*), tradescantias (*Tradescantia*), Meadow Rue (*Thalictrum*), Day Lily (*Hemerocallis*), Bugbane (*Cimicifuga*), Navelwort (*Omphalodes*), Meadow Sweet (*Filipendula*), and many other hardy perennials.

Aquatic plants

The most popular, typically aquatic plants are without doubt the water-lilies. The water-lilies (*Nymphaea*) represent a genus that has undergone much selective breeding and embraces countless species and cultivated varieties with simple, semi-double and double flowers ranging in colour from white through yellow, pink, and copper-red to purple. Their glossy

Forget-me-nots often cover the margins of bodies of water. *Myosotis palustris* is an exclusively bog plant which can be grown only along streams and pools; there exist, however, many other *Myosotis* species which are good for the neighbourhood of concrete-lined ponds where no water soaks through the soil. The picture shows a growth of *M. alpestris* interspersed with pink tulips.

green, orbicular to ellipsoid leaves of various sizes floating on the water are also ornamental. Water-lilies in general like warm, still water and a sunny situation. Some species tolerate cooler, and even gently flowing, water. The various species differ in their water depth requirements, ranging anywhere from 20 to 150 cm. These requirements are the determining factor when selecting varieties for your pool.

In time, water-lilies spread and their blossoms open in succession from June until September. To promote continual good flowering it is recom-

Nymphaea colorata is a greenhouse water-lily.

mended that you lift and divide the plants after about four years and change the soil.

Besides water-lilies, other plants that root in the bottom and require deeper water over the roots are also grown in pools. The leaves and flowers of these plants either rise above the water or float on the surface. Like water-lilies, they keep the water in the pool clean for they suppress the growth of algae.

The large leaves of the Pond Lily (*Nuphar lutea*) float on the water and the yellow flowers, borne singly, rise above the water surface. The flowering period is in June and July, but flowers are not produced for the first time until at least the third year after planting. The plants should be grown at a depth of 40—200 cm.

Water Hawthorn (*Aponogeton distachyus*) has floating leaves and fragrant, forked white flowers with jet-black anthers. It blooms in spring and again in the autumn. This plant is good for depths of 10—45 cm.

Some plants, however, do not root in the bottom but float on the surface, dropping to the bottom only

Nymphaea alba needs a relatively great water depth and is thus suitable only for larger ponds at least 80 cm deep. It flowers from June to August.

in the autumn to wait out the winter in the mud. They often spread at a rapid rate and their number must therefore be reduced by thinning every now and then. The floating aquatics include Frogbit (*Hydrocharis morsus-ranae*), the duckweed *Lemna trisulca* and Water Soldier (*Strationes aloides*)

Planting and care of the plants

To obtain the most natural effect, the pool or bog should be planted with plants of varying height. They should cover only one-third of the whole surface area for otherwise the effect of the water would be lost and the general impression would be that of a green carpet.

Aquatic and bog plants should be planted out in late spring and early summer; water-lilies from the beginning of June and, if they are pre-cultivated in containers, from as early as May. Bog plants grown-on in containers may be planted out from spring until September.

With all aquatic plants, it is necessary to plant them at the depth required for optimum growth. It is best to plant them in the pool when it is empty.

Various ponds and pools are a welcome component of any garden, enriching the choice of plants by many aquatic species. Water in the garden furthermore positively influences the microclimate. Water borders can be planted with many attractive bog and marginal plants, and the best idea for deeper floors are surely water-lilies. These are planted either into a shaft in the bottom of the pool filled with a nutritive soil or in containers placed on the floor of the pool. Water-lilies need a calm milieu and at least 6—8 hours of sunshine a day for good growth.

Water-lilies and other aquatic plants may be put either between several stones directly on the bottom of the pool or better yet in a firm container of 10—50-litre volume, depending on the size of the plant. The container may be of wood, metal, or plastic. Metal or plastic containers should have holes in the sides or bottom. Before putting the plant in, line the sides of the container with moss or dense nylon netting. When planting water-lilies you may put well-rotted cow manure round the sides of the container and then fill in the space round the plant with heavy loam mixed with horn meal. Water-lilies should be inserted so that the root neck remains above the level of the soil. Then cover the soil surface either with moss held in place with galvanized netting or similar material, or else with sand and fine gravel so the soil is not washed away by the water.

Water in the garden has a calming effect; and if it is planted with taste, it can become a delight to the eye.

Overwintering aquatic plants

One of the most important tasks in the care of water-lilies is proper overwintering. The safest method is to leave the water-lilies in water in the pool at a depth where the water does not freeze.

The success of overwintering depends on many factors — the course of the winter, the construction of the pool, proper winter shelter of the pool, the depth of the water, balanced chemical composition of the water, the manner in which the water-lilies are planted, their resistance to low temperatures, the plants' condition (age, health, degree of rooting), the content of nutrients in the substrate (good feeding with potassium increases resistance to cold). The most important factor, however, is the depth of the water above the rhizomes. You must take into account the thickness of the ice sheet and drop in water level and so the minimum ice-free depth is considered to be 30 cm.

If the water-lilies are planted in containers then they should be moved to the deeper part of the pool at the beginning of November. Also see to it that the chemical composition of the water is not disrupted unnecessarily; this means the timely removal of fallen leaves so there will be little or no rotting plant material beneath the ice.

In pools with a depth of 30—40 cm it is not safe to overwinter very delicate cultivated varieties and young or weak plants. These should be moved together with their containers to another, deeper pool.

Overwintering water-lilies without water, that is, in pools that have been emptied, is not nearly as safe. They are exposed to the danger of water penetration which will disrupt the insulation; to attack by rodents; to the unfavourable effects of drought and warmth when the rhizomes may dry up or else begin growth prematurely and, furthermore, all the aforesaid factors promote the growth of mould. Water-lilies overwintered in this manner must be provided with an adequate layer of insulating material (leaves, straw, grass, boards, and the like). Last of all the pool should be covered with foil.

If you have to overwinter water-lilies in indoor frost-free places the chief danger is that they might dry out. For this reason, the plants must be kept moist. You must also take care to keep rodents in check and to provide adequate ventilation to maintain a constant, rather low temperature and to prevent the spread of mould.

Other species of bottom-rooting aquatic plants are left *in situ* for, unlike water-lilies, they require practically no care at all.

Protection of pools in winter

Leave floating on the surface of the water some object that will yield to the pressure of ice (a block of

411

The choice of water-lilies is large both in terms of colour and in depth requirements. There even exist several red-flowered varieties.

wood, a closed tin, barrel, pieces of polystyrene, and the like). The darker the material, the better.

Bulrushes, reedmace, grasses and so on should not be removed from the pool in the autumn nor should they be cut back. On the contrary, it is desirable to have as many of these plants as possible in the pool in winter. If there are no such plants in the pool, put in the water a bundle of pressed straw or a bundle of plant stems tied together. The ice round these objects which jut above the surface thaws more rapidly and furthermore the air that is necessary for fish will have access to the water through the bundles. Even

smaller, shallower pools need not be emptied for the winter. Merely cover them with boards, mats, foil, polystyrene, dry plant remnants, and the like.

In exceptionally severe winters, when the ice is very thick, it is recommended that you slightly lower the level of the water beneath the layer of ice. The resulting layer of air between ice and water will then serve as thermal insulation.

Care of pools in summer

An aquatic garden with water-lilies and other plants does not require any particular care, even in summer. During the growing season such a garden does not have to be hoed, weeded, aerated, shaded, watered, fertilized, treated with chemical agents, etc. In addition, water-lilies cannot be completely destroyed by pests underwater. All that needs to be done is to add more water now and then and wash debris off the surface with a stream of water.

Practically the only great problem of garden pools is algae. These appear in summer and usually within a few days make the water cloudy and cover the surface with a green film. Because of the ornamental plants growing in the pool using chemical means of control is out of the question; the only possible means is biological control. Good helpers here are water snails that feed on the algae. Also, some species of aquatic plants eliminate algae. For these reasons a pool should contain one or more of the following plants: Hornwort (*Ceratophyllum*), Water Soldier (*Stratiotes aloides*), Curled Pondweed (*Potamogeton*), Duckweed (*Lemna*), Bulrush (*Scirpus*), and the like.

Water is a common feature in rock gardens. Even a very small pool or pond can enlieven the rockery and enrich the variety of vegetation by the addition of a number of aquatic and bog plants.

Select list of bog and aquatic plants

Species, cultivar	Height in cm	Water depth in cm	Flowering period	Colour of flowers	Light require- ments	Other characteristics
Acorus calamus	60—120	5—10	VI—VII	yellowish, later light brown	○ ◐	
Acorus calamus 'Variegatus'	60	10	VI—VII	yellowish, later light brown	○ ◐	variegated foliate
Alisma plantago-aquatica	70—80	20	VII—IX	white-pink	○ ◐	
Butomus umbellatus	80—100	30	VI—VIII	reddish-white		
Calla palustris	15—30	15	VI—VII	white		poisonous fruits
Caltha palustris 'Multiplex'	20—50	0—5	V—VI and IX—X	golden-yellow		double flowers
Carex grayi	80	up to 5	VII—VIII	—	○ ◐	exceptionally decorative ovaries
Glyceria maxima 'Variegata'	40—80	—	VII—VIII	—	○	leaves striped in white and yellow
Hippuris vulgaris	40	up to 30	VII—VIII	—	○ ◐	
Iris kaempferi	60—80	—	V—VII	varied	○	rather dry soil in winter
Iris pseudacorus	80—100	5—30	VI	yellow	○	
Juncus maritimus	30—100	up to 20	VII—VIII	—	○ ◐	dark brown fruits
Menyanthes trifoliata	30	up to 30	V—VI	white-red	○ ◐	leathery leaves
Nuphar lutea	—	40—200	VI—VIII	yellow	○ ◐	oval leaves float on the water
Nymphaea × hybr. 'Froebeli'	—	20—40	VI—IX	dark carmine	○	
Nymphaea × hybr. 'James Brydon'	—	40—80	VI—IX	pink-red	○	double flowers
Nymphaea × hybr. 'Marliacea Albida'	—	40—80	VI—IX	white	○	fragrant
Nymphaea × hybr. 'Marliacea Chromatella'	—	40—100	VI—IX	pale yellow	○	large leaves
Nymphaea odorata 'Sulphurea'	—	20—40	VI—IX	delicate sulphur-yellow	○	
Nymphaea pygmaea 'Alba'	—	5—15	VI—IX	white	○	dwarf water-lily
Pontederia cordata	60	up to 30	VII—VIII	flower spikes blue	○	
Sagittaria sagittifolia	30—60	5—40	VI—VII	white	○ ◐	ornamental globular fruits
Scirpus lacustris	100—150	20—100	VI—VIII	brown	○ ◐	blue-green foliage
Scirpus tabernaemontani 'Zebrinus'	80—120	10—20	VI—VIII	—	○ ◐	leaves horizontally barred in green and white
Typha latifolia	150—200	50	VII—VIII	dark brown spadices	○	
Typha minina	40	5—10	VI—IX	black-brown spadices	○	

Flowers without a garden

For many people who live in large cities, a garden close to home often remains an unfulfilled dream. Yet this need not be the case; it is still possible to brighten their environment and bring a little bit of nature within their reach. It may call for a little more ingenuity, but it can be done! Miniature gardens in the form of window-boxes, troughs, bowls, tubs and other containers placed on balconies, terraces, flat roofs, landings and close to house entrances can, and do beautify many of today's urban dwellings.

This type of gardening offers new possibilities for making use of numerous — even less well-known — plants. However, certain basic principles differing from the common practice of gardening must be taken into account.

The aesthetic relationship of the chosen flower decoration with the various architectural elements is very important. Even the colour of walls to a certain extent influences the choice of plants to be grown. Clearly, a different plant will be chosen to complement a turn-of-the-century stone building than will be selected for a concrete block of flats, or a modern family house with its own garden.

Window-boxes

Containers planted with flowers and placed on the window-sill become part of the building. You should therefore ensure that the shape and colour of the container and choice of the plants fit properly into the picture. For the same reason, the container itself must be carefully chosen. Even a fairly standard, rectangular container comes in various materials.

The length of the window-box or of several boxes placed in a row is limited by the width of the window. A single box, however, should not be more than 1 m long, as longer boxes are too heavy when filled with soil. The inner width of the box should be at least 15 cm, but better still 20—25 cm, and the depth about 14—20 cm.

Window- or balcony-boxes are made of various materials — wood, plastics, earthenware or concrete. Whichever material is used it should always be a

poor conductor of heat; otherwise the plants will suffer from overheating in summer, particularly on the sunward side of the container.

Wooden boxes can easily be made, even by a layman. They have many excellent qualities, can be fastened to the window-sill without too much effort and ensure good growing conditions for the plants. However, wood is not resistant to permanent dampness; it is a must that, every year, you treat the boxes with a preservative harmless to the plants. The outer paint should also be renewed from time to time, to keep the box weather-proof.

Containers made of plastics are used to an ever increasing extent. They are particularly welcome for their light weight and durability and come in a wide range of colours and sizes. Always check whether there are drainage holes at the bottom; if not already present these must be drilled out before you start filling the container.

The boxes must always be carefully and securely fastened to the window-sills. If a box is to be placed on a slanting sill, then several wedges must be positioned under it or a wooden lath fastened on the underside front edge of the container to make it sit level. To prevent the box from slipping off the sill, or being pushed off accidentally, it should be fastened to the window-frame by a pair of hooks.

Planting

Before filling the boxes with soil, the holes in the

Trailing pelargoniums (*Pelargonium peltatum*), here grown in uniform boxes, match the sunscreens shading the balconies and provide welcome splashes of bright colour against the stark modern architecture.

Bowls decorating the entrance to a house have been planted with tuberous begonias, petunias and other plants arranged in an asymmetrical composition.

415

Petunias are favourite window-box and balcony flowers. They can be used in a mixture of colours or in single-coloured groups. They should complement the colour of the house for best effect.

Ivy-leaved pelargoniums produce rich cascades of flowers during the summer. They tolerate full sun but can be placed in semi-shade also.

bottom must be covered with large crocks and the whole of the bottom should then be covered with a shallow layer of river sand for good drainage. Then fill up the boxes with the growing medium, to within 2 cm of the rim. Smaller plants can be inserted with the aid of a dibber; for larger ones, simply ease aside a sufficient depth of soil with your hands, set the plant in place, then carefully replace the soil round and over its roots, up to the existing soil mark. Firm in with your fingers, then water the plants with a fine rose on the watering can. After planting, continue to water regularly according to the plants' individual needs. The substrate should always be slightly damp. However, do not be over enthusiastic: overwatering is as detrimental as insufficient watering.

Plants grown in containers have a limited amount of growing medium and consequently the nutrients necessary for good growth are soon exhausted. It is therefore necessary to supply fertilizers to well-rooted plants during their growing period. Various compound feeds can be used for this purpose — they can be bought at every florist's or seedsman's shop. Feeding is done together with watering, once in 7—10 days, taking care to apply strictly according to the manufacturer's instructions and the needs of individual plant species.

Plants will also welcome an occasional loosening of the soil with a small peg, removal of dry leaves and regular clipping of stalks with faded flowers, as the formation of seeds exhausts the plants greatly and they will flower less profusely. On the plus side, however, flowers in window-boxes usually suffer less frequently from various pests and diseases than do indoor plants. Most cases of their ill health are due to wrong watering or to overfeeding. Most commonly found pests are various plant-lice, which thrive particularly well in a dry atmosphere.

Plants for balconies

A balcony can become the most pleasant spot in your home if only it is made use of properly and any plantings are designed as an integral part of the flat.

The rigid outlines of modern facades usually call for some optical 'softening', which can be best achieved by placing on the balconies and window-sills containers filled with suitable plants.

The furnishings of a balcony can be quite inexpensive and simple. Where there is a shortage of space, a collapsible table and a few wicker or canvas chairs will do. A small sunshade provides necessary shade in summer, and creates privacy.

The most beautiful decoration for balconies is flowers. However, always bear in mind the colour of the building's facade; the flowers used should be in either pleasantly contrasting or complementary colours. As for containers, these can be of various materials, shapes and sizes. Balcony boxes are usually suspended from the railings on solid iron hooks, either on the inner or outer side of the balcony. If possible, it is always better to think of this while the house is being built, as the construction of a supporting device may cause some difficulties later on. In taller buildings, however, it is advisable to place the boxes inside the balcony because this is safer and the plants will not suffer so much from being buffeted by wind.

Containers planted with flowers can also be placed on the floor of a balcony, along its walls. But as a considerable weight is involved, do check first that the balcony is able to bear such a load. The walls can be equipped with variously-shaped wooden trellis or frames, with a wire or nylon fibre stretched to form a support for perennial or annual climbing plants. Many of these produce an extraordinary abundance of beautiful flowers or fruits and most are relatively fast growers. A choice of annual non-climbing plants can be planted beside them.

Where balconies are equipped with iron bars for the purpose of safety, the containers can be suspended on the inner side of these railings. With a suitable choice of plant species, you can soon create a nice green 'curtain' to cover the bars and form a pleasant, shaded retreat.

For larger balconies, a construction of bamboo sticks, laths or light-metal tubes can be made. Hooks or holders fastened at irregular intervals will bear pots or boxes, preferably lightweight plastic ones, planted with a variety of flowers.

Roof gardens

Landscape gardeners agree that modern urban architecture has, to a great extent, limited the possibilities of gardening in cities. But, at the same time, it has initiated the introduction of new means of plant growing — in the form of transportable greenery on balconies and terraces or actually in small gardens on the flat roofs of buildings. These, however, should be planned before the house is built, if possible. Special care should be taken to provide sensible safety precautions, and a waterproof insulation.

Many-storey city buildings usually afford little space for a garden or a piece of public greenery as, sadly, the free spaces that remain after a block of flats has been built usually have to serve other purposes than those of beautifying our environment. That is why roof gardens are becoming more and

more popular today, providing a place for relaxation out in the open air, even in the centre of a city. Many large hotels, too, now offer their guests access to specially adapted roofs, laid out with luxuriant greenery and comfortable seating.

When planning to adapt a roof for the purposes of a garden, several basic preconditions must be considered. First of all, the load-bearing capacity of the roof must be checked, then perfect insulation. A slight inclination of the plane of the roof is also important, as a quick discharge of surplus water after watering and particularly after a heavy rain must be provided — otherwise, the water might leak into the rooms below.

It is also recommended that the newly constructed roof garden is equipped with an adequately high boundary wall, that is, some 60 cm higher than the level of the roof. This not only provides safety but also, to a certain extent, protects the plants from blustery wind, and the soil from drying out in summer and quick freezing in winter. The layer of soil should be some 30—40 cm thick.

If you intend to have a pool or some other small body of water in your roof garden then you must bear this in mind when starting to build, so that the pool as well as the inlet and outlet of water are properly incorporated into the construction of the roof. A very small, shallow pool, however, can be made simply by using one of the polythene pool liners widely available for making garden pools.

Plants for roof gardens
It must be borne in mind that the amount of soil from which the plants obtain water and nutrients is

Flowers in window- and balcony boxes can enliven a whole house. In this case, the colour of ivy-leaved pelargoniums was chosen to match the colour of the roof.

A mixture of zonal and ivy-leaved pelargoniums has been used here to decorate both the balcony and the terrace. They give a lively touch to the otherwise rather monotone architecture.

417

essentially limited in a roof garden and the choice of plants is limited accordingly. Nevertheless, there still exist a large number of plant species and their cultivars which can be successfully grown in such conditions. First of all, there are various bulbous and tuberous plants, perennials, rock garden plants, decorative grasses and deciduous as well as evergreen woody plants, including several conifers. Always remember, however, that the plants in a roof garden are permanently exposed to extreme conditions — sunscorch, wind and frost — and protection will have to be provided for them.

The basic element of each garden — a stretch of lawn, be it even the smallest one — should never be omitted. For this purpose, a layer of soil some 15 cm thick will suffice.

The best method of founding a nice 'lawn' in a roof garden is by turfing. Strips of turf must be clean and weedless and be positioned close to each other on a 10-cm layer of soil. Cracks between the individual strips should then be filled with a loose garden soil and the lawn lightly treaded down.

Lawns look nice framed with paving stones or concrete, or ceramic slabs arranged in various patterns. Also, large wooden offcuts of varying size can be used. They should be about 15 cm high, and well impregnated with a wood preservative before being positioned close to each other. Not only paths, but also larger areas intended for sitting-out places can be paved in this way.

Small patches of lawn can be brightened, particularly in spring, by a number of small bulbs. These are planted in the autumn to make small informal groups. The possible choice covers all garden and botanical crocuses, snowdrops, snowflakes, scillas, grape hyacinths and puschkinias; also narcissi, hyacinths and tulips, including early botanical species.

Nowadays, it is often recommended that you substitute for the lawn carpeting perennials whose aesthetic function is identical to that of the lawn.

A nice heath garden can also be created on a roof. What you need for this particular type of garden is a special soil mixture composed of compost, leaf mould, peat and river sand, with an admixture of bone meal and perlite. To provide good drainage, an adequate bottom layer of coarse sand must be used.

A heath garden should include not only heaths, heathers and related plants, but also conifers and other woody plants. Attention should also be paid to decorative grasses which, if chosen with taste, will enhance and underline the beauty of this section of the roof garden. Also, some rock garden plants are good choices for a heath garden.

A 25-cm layer of good garden soil should be sufficient for most species of low-growing, cushion-forming or creeping plants intended to provide the necessary green or multicolored patches in the roof garden. It stands to reason that even in such special conditions you should always pay heed to the resultant colour combinations, not only of flowers but also of foliage. Remember that a lesser number of species planted in larger groups makes a better effect.

Even a small terrace can be enlivened by a display of colourful beauty. *Phaseolus coccineus* covers the pergola, and the gaily coloured petunias evoke a cheerful and optimistic atmosphere.

Ivy-leaved pelargoniums are a good choice wherever their trailing habit can be made use of. They are excellent for window- and balcony boxes, where the red of their flowers stands out magnificently against white walls.

Greenery in containers

Plants in our homes, working places or in a garden greatly beautify our living environment. Modern urban architecture does not offer much space for creating such beauty spots, and landscape gardeners thus have to seek other solutions as to how to bring at least a little bit of nature closer. Container greenery is nowadays installed in large shopping centres, in spas and many other public places. Department stores, hotels, factories, hospitals and large administrative buildings make use of free spaces in front of their entrances, on flat roofs, in yards and on the pavements, placing there large containers planted with trees, shrubs or flowers, thus offering to their guests, customers and employees a pleasant resting place among greenery.

A transportable 'garden' for everybody

Movable greenery finds its place even in small or large gardens, in backyards, on balconies, terraces and flat roofs of garages and family houses.

A transportable 'garden' with an appropriate choice of plants properly planted and cared for will enliven places where rigidity and drabness of urban architecture has prevailed, places devoid of life or even polluted with garbage. Containers used for planting are made of various materials: ceramic, stone, concrete or asbestos bowls, troughs and vases, wooden boxes and plastic containers of many different shapes. Particularly nice are ornamental ceramic bowls planted with woody plants — deciduous as well as coniferous ones — and complemented with attractive perennials and long-lasting annuals. Their decorative effect can be almost permanent thanks to the evergreen quality of the woody plants and of some perennials which retain their foliage even through the period of vegetative rest.

When siting such containers in a garden try to choose quiet places — close to sitting-out areas, pools and bird-baths, the borders of lawns and paved areas, flights of steps, rims of dry walls and patios.

All containers should be of adequate dimensions, neither too small nor too large for the given spot. Also, the number of plants for a container must be carefully considered so that they can grow fully and properly later on. You should never combine too many different species as their individual beauty would be swamped and the effect diminished.

Choice of plants and their combinations

Besides 'classic' balcony and window-box flowers such as geraniums (*Pelargonium*), petunias (*Petunia*), tuberous begonias (*Begonia* × *tuberhybrida*), fuchsias (*Fuchsia*), nasturtiums (*Tropaeolum*) and other similar plants, particularly annuals, you can use a wide range of perennials. These can include rock garden plants and some woody species — both evergreen and deciduous broadleaved trees and shrubs, as well as conifers. By a good combination with some decorative grasses, bulbs and tubers, and ground-covering evergreen perennials to enliven the

A small balcony garden not only pleases its owners but decorates the exterior of the house. Window-sills which do not get direct sun can be decorated with tuberous begonias, and the balcony boxes are planted with petunias, fuchsias, marigolds or climbing nasturtiums. Suspended pots contain pelargoniums and fuchsias.

If the balcony is too small for the containers to be placed on the floor, pots or other containers can be suspended from the ceiling or walls.

lowermost part of the 'garden', an extraordinary all-the-year-round effect can be achieved.

Before starting to plant the 'mobile garden', one should remember that all tall-growing species must be omitted and the medium-tall ones, particularly woody plants, will need sufficiently large containers so that their future growth is not stunted. Although, of course, plants are sometimes grown in containers deliberately to control and check their size if space is really at a premium.

Broadleaved trees and shrubs

Good for this purpose are some cultivars of the Japanese Maple (*Acer japonicum*) with variously coloured and finely shaped leaves; also, the Mountain Currant (*Ribes alpinum*), the summer-flowering buddleias (*Buddleia*), heathers (*Calluna*) and heaths (*Erica*). Ornamental quinces (*Chaenomeles*) bear attractive flowers and decorative fruits, the hazel *Corylus avellana* 'Contorta', the Smoke Tree (*Cotinus coggygria*) with its beautifully coloured autumn foliage and decorative flowers and fruits. Other possibilities are the Golden Rain (*Laburnum*), the delicately flowering tamarisk (*Tamarix*), brooms (*Cytisus*) attracting one's eye by their rich profusion of flowers, deutzias (*Deutzia*), witch-hazels (*Hamamelis*), particularly interesting for their unusual time of flowering in winter and early spring, low-growing spiraeas (*Spiraea*) with red flowers opening in July and August. Not to be forgotten are some evergreen barberries (*Berberis*) or firethorns (*Pyracantha*) bearing large amounts of conspicuously coloured fruits, and many other shrubs.

Particularly suitable for planting in 'container gardens' are cotoneasters (*Cotoneaster*), best of all being the evergreen, pendent or spreading species, bearing a profusion of white flowers and red or orange decorative fruits which remain on the shrub long into the winter. They are exceptionally modest in their requirements, thriving in full sun as well as in semi-shade and — which is even more important — they perfectly tolerate the unfavourable conditions of large industrial cities.

Because of their decorative flowers, you should not omit the early-flowering forsythias (*Forsythia*) and the tree hollyhocks (*Hibiscus*), woody St John's worts (*Hypericum*), kolkwitzias (*Kolkwitzia*) and, last but not least, some rhododendrons (*Rhododendron*) and the beautifully flowering azaleas (*Rhododendron obtusum*). Also mentioned must be the queens among flowers — bush, botanical and climbing roses.

Among climbers can be recommended mainly the modest evergreen ivies (*Hedera*), which willingly cover not only sunny places, where they even produce flowers after seven years of cultivation, but also deeply shaded corners. Shrubby honeysuckles are delightful, emitting a sweet fragrance in the evening; for instance, the favourite Perfoliate Honeysuckle (*Lonicera caprifolium*) as well as some other, no less graceful species, the wonderful wisterias (*Wisteria*) and clematises (*Clematis*) valuable for the fresh greenery of their foliage and the colourful splendour of the flowers adorning various sections of gardens, balconies, terraces and roofs.

Climbing plants should never be combined with other plants but always planted by themselves, either singly or in groups — all individuals being of one and the same species. The only exception to the rule are some low-growing, carpeting perennials or woody plants which can be used for covering the ground. This method of planting is particularly advantageous for clematises, which welcome permanent shading of their roots from direct sun that otherwise overheats and dries up the top soil.

Conifers

Permanent enlivenment in many shades of green can be attained by using some conifers, particularly junipers (*Juniperus*) of spreading, shrubby or even columnar growth; also cypresses (*Chamaecyparis*), dwarf pines (*Pinus*), slow-growing yews (*Taxus*), low-growing varieties of firs (*Abies*) and spruces (*Picea*) with their nest-forming or very stunted, conical shapes. Also very beautiful and well suitable for this aim is the cedar (*Cedrus*) which, however, is more tender and needs a good cover for the winter.

Care of the plants

To assure a good and healthy growth of plants in container gardens, it is a must that the containers have one or, in the case of larger ones, several holes in the bottom to provide a regular drainage of surplus water. As for balcony boxes, the drainage holes are covered with large crocks so that they do not become clogged with soil. Then comes a layer of gravel or coarse sand and finally the growing medium — a mixture of sifted rotted turves, peat, well rotted compost and sand, so that the container is filled to within 2—3 cm of the rim. After having planted them up, water the plants carefully several times so that the soil becomes attached to the root balls.

A large bowl planted with an attractive mixture of annual plants.

A stone trough planted with pelargoniums and a large-flowered clematis which climbs a simple trellis placed on the wall. This is an unprententious but very effective decoration for a house entrance.

A front garden featuring only woody plants and a lawn can be given more colour by planting pelargoniums or a variegated mixture of annuals in window-boxes or other containers.

Plants in containers need no special care throughout the year. However, they will welcome occasional loosening of the soil with a wooden peg, removal of weeds and, in dry weather, sufficient watering accompanied by regular feeding in the growing period. Annual plants and bulbs and tubers can be added in due time.

To provide the best possible all-the-year-round ef-fect, remove dry leaves and stalks of annuals and perennials and cut off the dead flowers in woody plants so that they do not become exhausted by fruit-forming. Some woody plants benefit from occasional pruning or clipping that positively influences their shape and growth. Also, spent annuals must be lifted and discarded; these can be replaced by the seedlings of suitable biennials or by carpeting evergreen perennials.

Plants suitable for balconies, terraces and roof gardens

When choosing subjects for planting, it is always necessary to have an appropriately-sized container for each plant species or cultivar. Tiny, low-growing plants should never be planted in large boxes, bowls or troughs, as their fragile beauty is completely suppressed there. Similarly, too robust plants look incongruous if planted in small containers and will quickly exhaust the soil — and themselves.

Window-box and balcony plants for sunny aspects

Asparagus sprengeri — Asparagus. Its bright green fronds look particularly well among various flowering plants, such as petunias, pendent geraniums and fuchsias. It is quite modest in its requirements, thriving both in sun and semi-shade, and will tolerate even full shade for a short time.

Calceolaria integrifolia — Slipperwort. A profusely-flowering plant with attractive yellow flowers resembling tiny slippers. It is about 30 cm high and looks best if planted together with red-flowering geraniums or blue petunias. Slipperwort loves full sun but its flowers are easily damaged by wind and rain. It can survive for several years.

Campanula isophylla — Bellflower. Formerly a favourite and much cultivated house plant, 10—20 cm tall, with white or blue flowers. It needs a sunny situation but will tolerate even semi-shade for a short period of time. The plants should be cut back after flowering in order to promote further growth.

Dianthus suffruticosus — Tirolean Pink. A well-known pink with a compact, erect growth and a profusion of beautiful red flowers which open from spring to autumn. It needs a relatively high atmospheric moisture and protection against rain and direct sun. It thrives particularly well in an eastern or northern aspect.

Pelargonium zonale hybrids — Zonal Geranium. A favourite plant for window- or balcony-boxes offering a rich choice of low-growing and taller cultivars with single, semi-double and double fowers coloured white, pink, red, orange or purple. It flourishes in full sun as well as in semi-shade and has a long flowering period, usually from May to the first frosts.

Pelargonium peltatum hybrids — Ivy-leaved Geranium. Plants with a more or less trailing habit. A wide range of cultivars with single or double flowers coloured white, pink, red or purple can be obtained. Their uses and requirements are similar to those of *P. zonale.*

Petunia × *hybrida* — Petunia. The most commonly used balcony plant, with a semi-trailing to trailing habit. It comes in a number of cultivars, varying in height from 20 to 40 cm and in the type of flowers, which can be single, semi-double or double, large or small, and range in colour from white to pink or red, blue to purple. Cultivars with single flowers bear a greater profusion of blossoms. Petunias require full sun but suffer in overdry conditions as well as from long continuous rain. They should therefore be located under ledges, balconies and so on.

Plants suitable for semi-shaded places

Begonia × *tuberhybrida* — Tuberous Begonia. It comes in numerous cultivars with small as well as large single, semi-double and double flowers in a wide range of colours. The height ranges from 20 to 35 cm. Flowers open in May and last until the first frosts. Tuberous begonias thrive particularly well in semi-shaded and shaded places well protected from wind.

Fuchsia × *hybrida* — Fuchsia. You can choose from a wide range of hybrids with erect or trailing habit and variously shaped and coloured flowers. Even the flower buds are decorative. Fuchsias thrive in semi-shade and even in full shade for a short time. It is advisable to put fuchsias into containers still in their own individual pots as they require a frost-proof environment for the winter.

Fuchsia fulgens — Cluster-flowered Fuchsia. This species is noted for its profusion of long, trumpet-shaped, scarlet or pink flowers. It prefers semi-shade but will tolerate even full sun.

Flowering woody plants for balconies

Best for the decoration of balconies are container-grown plants, which are first cultivated as potted plants in cool rooms. Once they have formed a nice habit, they can be put out on a large balcony, a terrace or a roof garden.

The most commonly used are probably oleanders, but many other plants are equally well suited.

A hollowed-out birch trunk made into a tub and planted with a mixture of multicoloured annuals can decorate a paved path.

Abutilon — Indian Mallow. A shrub-forming woody plant native to South America, where it can reach a height of as much as 4 m. It has evergreen, palmately-lobed leaves and large, long-stalked, bell-shaped flowers growing from the leaf axils. Most commonly cultivated is *A.* × *hybrida,* a cross of several original species; it flowers almost throughout the year bearing orange, pink, red, yellow or white blossoms. Tree-like forms, grafted on more vigorously growing stocks, are also attractive. It will need winter protection.

Bougainvillea. A thorny climber that has ovoid-lanceolate leaves. Relatively small yellow flowers are subtended by conspicuously coloured bracts.

An autumn scheme planted in concrete containers. Besides flowers, a woody plant has also been used — *Rhus typhina* — ornamental for its reddish autumn coloration of the leaves.

422

Even a small bowl planted with ivy-leaved pelargoniums breaks the angularity of the staircase and house wall.

The original species have mostly pinkish-violet bracts, but recently many new cultivars have been introduced, with bracts of orange, pale pink or carmine-red.

Callistemon. An evergreen shrub native to Australia. Its longish-lanceolate, leathery leaves emit a strong scent. The cylindrical inflorescence, about 5—10 cm long, bears densely packed flowers with protruding slender stamens and yellow anthers. The flowers mostly start opening in spring and early summer. *C. citrinus* reaches 3 m in height in its native land. Its leaves smell strongly of lemon, when rubbed between the fingers. The cultivar 'Splendens' has carmine-red stamens.

The choice of containers used for planting depends just on your taste.

Datura — Thornapple. A deciduous shrub, up to 3 m tall, native to tropical America. *D. suaveolens* bears 30 cm long, white, sweet-scented flowers which open from August to October. *D. sanguinea* has its main flowering season from January to March, and the flowers are orange-red, scentless and can measure up to 20 cm.

Erythrina. This is another favourite subject for growing in containers. *E. crista-galli* is a shrub reaching a height of some 2 m and producing dense racemes of scarlet-red flowers, mostly in summer. When the leaves have fallen in the autumn the annual growth should be cut back up to the old wood; it will sprout anew profusely in spring.

Hibiscus. A woody plant attractive for its exotic-looking, large flowers. *H. rosa-sinensis* from south-eastern Asia, where it reaches some 3 m in height, is a sparsely branched shrub with ovoid-lanceolate leaves. The flowers, forming a wide tube (up to 15 cm across), have their protruding stamens fused with the style into one column. The original species have pinkish-red flowers. However, many new cultivars have been introduced and these produce single, semi-double or double flowers, coloured pink, red, orange, yellow, white or even bicoloured. Hibiscuses flower mostly from March to October, but greenhouse-grown specimens can be seen flowering almost throughout the year.

Lantana. An easily cultivated, container-grown plant suitable even for window-boxes. *L. camara* from Brasil grows to a height of up to 1 m, is sparsely branched and bears deciduous, wrinkled leaves. The inflorescence consists of tiny orange-red flowers which gradually change colour. Many cultivars exist with white, yellow, orange, pink-red, brownish-red, blue or lilac-violet flowers. They open successively from June to October.

Nerium — Oleander. An evergreen shrub with leathery, longish-lanceolate leaves. When cut, the shrub sheds a white mucous fluid. *N. oleander* grows wild along the rivers of southern Portugal. Its many-flowered inflorescences are composed of five-petalled, 3—5 cm wide flowers. The original species has pink flowers, but there are numerous cultivars with white, pink, orange, yellow, scarlet-red, purple or even two-coloured flowers, either single or double. They have a very pleasing fragrance.

Punica — Pomegranate. In subtropical regions the fruits of this plant are used to produce a refreshing juice. *P. granatum* is native to north Africa, but to-day it grows wild almost throughout the whole Mediterranean as far as the Himalayas. It is a thorny, deciduous shrub reaching a height of up to 5 m in the wild. It does not surpass 1.5 m in a container, however. The red flowers with fleshy sepals open from July to August. The fruits have a hard rind and pinkish-red, sour-sweet flesh.

Some problems may arise with the overwintering of such container-grown woody plants. Most need a constant temperature of several degrees above zero throughout the winter. Furthermore, a sufficient amount of light is a must, particularly in species bearing evergreen leaves. If there is no greenhouse at

Pelargonium zonale comes in a number of variously coloured varieties. They do not tolerate wind and permanent moisture and should be cut back several times to promote branching. For the winter, they should be placed in a light room with a temperature of 6—10° C. The root ball must never be allowed to dry out completely.

hand, use a covered veranda, a light hall, a staircase or a cool and sufficiently light cellar. Watering should never stop completely but simply be sufficiently reduced, as the plants go on transpiring even in winter. Persistent overwatering is detrimental, however, as the soil soon turns sour, the plant starts shedding its leaves and often dies.

Annuals and biennials for containers

Ageratum houstonianum — Floss Flower. The plants reach a height of 15—20 cm, forming compact tufts that flower from May until the first frosts. The flowers are either pale blue, dark blue, pink or white. Floss Flower is particularly attractive if combined with petunias, fuchsias or geraniums. It likes full sun but will tolerate semi-shade.

Amaranthus caudatus — Love Lies Bleeding. A 70 cm tall annual, particularly suitable for solitary planting in boxes and decorative containers, for the enlivening of annual flower beds, lawns or groups of decorative trees or shrubs. Most commonly grown are the red-flowered cultivars. The small flowers are arranged in long, pendent spikes. From May onwards, the seeds can be sown directly in the container where the plant is to grow. *A. caudatus* is a warmth- and sun-loving species that likes humus-rich soils containing calcium.

Antirrhinum majus — Snapdragon. A 15—25 cm high, densely branched plant in a wide range of colours from pure white to deep red. It flowers profusely from the beginning of June to the autumn. A warm and sunny site is preferred. In some cultivars, the central stem should be pinched out to promote branching.

Begonia × *semperflorens* — Begonia. Best for window-boxes are the low-growing cultivars producing a rich profusion of flowers from May until the first frosts. The flowers range in colour from white through to pink and to many shades of red; even the colour of the leaves differs according to the cultivar — they can be green or reddish-brown. Begonias like full sun but will tolerate slight semi-shade.

Callistephus chinensis — China Aster. Mostly low-growing (20—25 cm) cultivars are recommended for planting in window-boxes and similar containers. They bear numerous flowers in a good range of colours from the end of July till autumn. China asters need a rich soil and a sunny situation.

Celosia argentea var. *cristata* 'Nana' — Cockscomb. A conspicuous, about 30 cm tall plant, with an interesting inflorescence in the form of a cock's comb in red, yellow or white. It is a nice ornament for balconies from July to September, but needs a rich, nutritious substrate and full sun.

Chrysanthemum segetum. A 30—50 cm tall plant bearing a profusion of relatively large, golden-yellow flowers, often with a dark centre. The seeds are sown at the end of April, directly where the plants are to be grown. These chrysanthemums, which open their flowers from the beginning of July to late autumn, like full sun but will thrive even in semi-shade.

Cleome spinosa — Spider Plant. An interesting annual suitable for solitary planting in large containers. It often reaches a height of up to 1 m. Its widely branched stems bear large, multiflowered racemes of white, pink or carmine-red flowers, which open in succession. The flowering period lasts from mid-June till autumn. It prefers warm and sunny places.

Cosmos bipinnatus — Cosmea. This plant, 80—100 cm high, can be recommended only for large containers. The seeds can be sown from the end of April directly on the spot. The attractive, bright green leaves are finely dissected. The flowers, which range in colour from white and pink to dark red, can be enjoyed from July to late autumn, until they are destroyed by frost. Cosmea is good for warm, sunny places sheltered from wind.

Dorotheanthus bellidiformis — Livingstone Daisy. A graceful, low (up to 10 cm), cushion-forming annual bearing variegated flowers measuring 3 cm across from June to September. They are white, pink or purple in many different shades but open only when the sun shines. This species is recommended for low containers placed in full sun in warm, dry situations. The seeds can be sown during April directly on the spot, where they are to be grown on.

Dahlia variabilis — Dahlia. Best for window-boxes are low-growing cultivars of the Mignon group which reach no more than 50 cm in height. Pre-cultivated seedlings are planted into the containers at the end of May. They offer a rich variety of flowers in yellow, pink, salmon or dark red and open from July to October. Dahlias need a loose, nutritious soil, a sunny situation and abundant watering. They welcome occasional feeding during the growing period.

Eschscholtzia californica — Californian Poppy. A delicate annual with nice-looking, silvery grey-green, finely dissected leaves. It reaches some 20—30 cm in height and bears a profusion of yellow, orange, red, pink or white flowers which open from the second half of June until the autumn. It does best in dry, sandy soils in full sun.

Gazania rigens — Treasure Flower. A perennial in its homeland, it is treated as an annual in our conditions. The plants, about 20 cm tall, bear attractive ray-like flowers from June until October. They are coloured yellow-orange, orange-red, white or bronze. This is a relatively undemanding plant, preferring warm, sunny situations. The flowers open only in full sun.

Ivy-leaved pelargoniums flower in a number of shades from April to autumn. They are relatively fragile and should thus be placed in a position sheltered from the wind. Faded flowers must be removed continuously, to promote further flowering.

Heliotropium arborescens. This perennial, reminiscent of vanilla, can be cultivated as an annual. The height ranges between 20 and 60 cm, according to the cultivar. The blue-purple flowers, arranged in large corymbs, open from May to September. It can be recommended for group planting. Being intolerant of frost, it should be planted after mid-May in warm, sunny spots.

Iberis amara — Rocket Candytuft; *I. umbellata* — Candytuft. These two related species, reaching a height of up to 30 cm, produce a profusion of tiny white or purplish-pink flowers. The flowering period lasts from the beginning of June until the end of July. If the plants are cut back and fed in time they will soon sprout and flower again. The seeds can be sown directly where the plants are to grow. They are suitable for sunny and semi-shaded places.

Lobelia erinus — Lobelia. A pleasant looking, 8—15 cm high, richly flowering annual with a densely-branched habit. Several cultivars exist with

A large trough can be planted with a mixture of annual plants, including upright as well as trailing species.

Single-flowered fuchsias are usually more resistant to drought than the double varieties and can thus be grown even in full sun. They flower profusely from May to October.

beautiful blue or white flowers opening from the end of May until September. If cut back after the first flowering, they produce further flowers. The seedlings can be put out in the second half of May, best in sunny situations, but they will tolerate semi-shade as well. Lobelia is good both for window-boxes and smaller bowls. It looks best if combined with red geraniums or yellow slipperworts.

Lobularia maritima var. *benthamii* — Sweet Alyssum. A profusely flowering, low-growing plant with a semi-globular, compact habit about 12—15 cm high. The flowers can be white, pink or purple. Lobularia thrives in any soil, in a warm, sunny situation. The flowering period is from mid-May to the autumn. It can be rejuvenated by cutting back.

Mimulus luteus — Musk. This favourite rock- garden plant is grown as an annual in boxes or other containers, in windows or on balconies. It reaches a height of 20—30 cm and produces up to 5 cm long, yellow flowers which are not damaged by wind or rain. The flowering period lasts from the beginning of June until the end of summer. Musk favours damp, slightly shaded spots and is very sensitive to drying of the soil.

Penstemon hartwegii — Beard Tongue. A plant with a rigid, erect growth, 40—60 cm tall, bearing a rich profusion of bell-shaped flowers of various colours and arranged in long panicles. It should be planted in larger containers and tolerates full light but does better in places sheltered from midday sun. It flowers from end July until late autumn.

Iberis amara should be put out in early spring, as its flowering is confined to June and July. It is usually combined with other, mostly low, annuals.

Phlox drummondii — Annual Phlox. A conspicuous, 20—30 cm high annual with flowers in a wide range of colours, from red and purple to pink and white. Most suitable for window-boxes are the low-growing cultivars belonging to the group 'Nana Compacta', reaching no more than 15—20 cm in height. The flowers are arranged in compact inflorescences and open from July to October. Annual Phlox prefers well-fertilized soil and plenty of sun.

Portulaca grandiflora — Sun Plant. Only 5—15 cm high plants with fleshy, linear leaves and relatively large flowers in beautiful pastel colours. The flowers, which open only when the sun shines, last from June to September. Sun Plant does best in dry, sunny, warm conditions.

Salvia splendens — Scarlet Sage. A 30—40 cm tall plant with predominantly scarlet-red, long-lasting flowers arranged in whorls. It needs a nourishing substrate and full sun for good growth. The flowers occur in June and last till October. Scarlet Sage is

a good subject for window-boxes as well as for decorative containers.

Tagetes patula 'Nana' — French Marigold; *T. tenuifolia* 'Pumila'; *T. erecta* — African Marigold. The low-growing types (15—30 cm) can be grown in window-boxes; taller cultivars (40—80 cm) are better planted in bowls. They flower from July to October, bearing single or double blossoms, usually coloured yellow, orange or brown-red. This undemanding annual, tolerating even rainy weather, grows equally well in full sun and semi-shade. The plants can be transplanted even when in flower.

Verbena × *hybrida* — Vervain. A graceful, 15—30 cm high annual bearing a profusion of small, variously-coloured flowers opening from June to October. It will thrive in any soil in sunny, warm situations but is sensitive to too much damp. It can be planted in window-boxes as well as in various containers on a balcony.

Zinnia elegans, Z. haageana — Zinnia. Individual cultivars differ in height — they can be 15—30 cm, 35—50 cm or even up to 1 m tall. Particularly recommended for containers or balconies are low-growing, early cultivars that flower from July to September. The flowers, coming in a wide range of colours and shades, are very attractive. Zinnias can be put out in mid-May and do best in sunny places. They welcome regular watering during dry periods and an occasional loosening of the soil. Faded flowers should be removed in order to promote further flowering.

427

Early-flowering biennials

Bellis perennis — Meadow Daisy. A 10—15 cm tall biennial bearing single as well as double, pink or red flowers which open in early spring. It needs a sunny or slightly shaded situation and can be transplanted even during the flowering period.

Cheiranthus cheirii — Wallflower. Reaching a height of some 40 cm, this plant is suitable only for larger containers. The yellow, orange or red flowers, which appear from April to June, look especially well if combined with Forget-me-nots or with certain bulbous plants such as the Grape Hyacinth or tulips. The Wallflower prefers shaded places.

Dianthus barbatus — Sweet William. Only low-growing cultivars, reaching a height of 25 cm at the most, are suitable for decorating windows and balconies. The white, pink, red and purple flowers open as late as May but the flowering period lasts until August. Sweet William is a sun-loving plant but it will accept even a semi-shaded place.

Myosotis alpestris — Forget-me-not. The plants are some 15—30 cm high according to the cultivar. Their delicate flowers are mostly blue and they are used for early-spring and spring planting in window-boxes and containers, before the traditional window-box and balcony flowers can be put out. Forget-me-nots look particularly attractive among flowering bulbs, pansies or daisies. They welcome full sun but will thrive even in semi-shade.

Viola × *wittrockiana (Viola tricolor* var. *maxima)* — Viola, Pansy. This biennial plant reaches a height of 10—15 cm, the main flowering season being in March and April. There is a wide choice of cultivars, with variously coloured flowers.

The seedlings of biennials, pre-cultivated in a frame or in a greenhouse, or bought from a specialized shop, are planted into window-boxes or other containers in early autumn, so that they can root properly before the onset of winter; or at the beginning of spring, as soon as the weather allows.

Favourite early-flowering perennials

Helleborus niger — Christmas Rose. An undemanding 25—30 cm high plant with decorative evergreen leaves. It produces beautiful white flowers from December to March, favours semi-shade and does best in a sufficiently damp, humus-rich soil.

Primula denticulata — Primrose. A nice, 15—30 cm high plant bearing white, pink, carmine-red or dark purple flowers arranged in spherical inflorescences from March to April. It prefers loose, sufficiently damp soils and slightly shaded situations.

Primula elatior 'Grandiflora' — Oxlip. Flowering plants reach a height of 25—30 cm. The large flowers are stalked and come in a variety of colours. The main flowering period is in March and April.

Primula vulgaris (P. acaulis) — Common Primrose. Best for planting in containers are garden varieties reaching a height of no more than 10 cm and bearing

Phlox drummondii is surprisingly tolerant of dry situations. It comes in low-growing as well as tall varieties and in a wide range of brilliant colours.

Cheiranthus cheirii is one of the longest-cultivated garden plants. Its brilliantly coloured flowers emit a sweet fragrance. Usually grown as a biennial, it will nevertheless last for several years in a shaded situation.

a profusion of flowers in many different colours, including blue. The flowers open from March to April.

The perennials are planted during spring or autumn or, if pre-cultivated in pots, even during the whole growing season.

Low-growing rock plants for roof gardens

Acaena microphylla. An undemanding evergreen, 5—10 cm high plant, forming spreading cushions. It has brownish-green leaves and interesting spiny fruits with a ruby-red tint.

Ajuga reptans 'Multicolor' — Bugle. This creeping, 10—15 cm high perennial forms dense growths, particularly in damp situations. The leaves are brownish-red and the blue flowers open from May to June. Bugle tolerates both sun and semi-shade and can be used as a substitute for turf in shaded places.

Antennaria dioica 'Rubra' — Mountain Everlasting. A low-growing plant with silvery-grey leaves, it thrives even in very dry situations in full sun. When in flower, it reaches a height of up to 10 cm. The small pink flowers appear in May. It is an excellent substitute for turf.

Armeria maritima — Sea Pink. This evergreen plant with freshly green leaves forms 10—15 cm high cushions. It loves sun and produces a profusion of pink flowers in May—July.

Aubrieta × *cultorum* — Purple Rock Cress. Low-growing spreading plants form extensive, only 5—10 cm high cushions. There are a number of garden cultivars bearing large amounts of variously coloured flowers. All have their main flowering season in April and May. It is a sun-loving species.

Campanula garganica 'Erinus Major' — Bellflower. An attractive cultivar bearing beautiful blue-

429

Dianthus barbatus can be obtained in a wide range of differently coloured cultivars. It is grown as a biennial for cutting, likes calcium in the soil and should be covered in winter if there is no snow.

The perennial Helleborus niger has a number of uses. It is suitable for planting in many different places in the garden and can be even used in containers, for instance, as an underplanting to conifers.

Iberis sempervirens, an undemanding evergreen perennial, forms nice cushions which makes it suitable for large and miniature rock gardens as well as for various containers.

purple, star-shaped flowers. This relatively robust plant, flowering in July and August, will thrive in full sun as well as in semi-shade.

Dianthus deltoides 'Brillant' — Maiden Pink. A favourite plant, bearing glossy green leaves and brilliant dark red flowers from June until August. The plants reach a height of up to 15 cm, preferring sunny situations and a loose, porous soil.

Helianthemum apenninum 'Rubin' — Sun Rose. This commonly grown semi-shrub has a stunted, up to 20 cm high habit and produces numerous double, dark red flowers from June to August. It loves sunny situations and will welcome a cover of evergreen twigs for the winter.

Hypericum olympicum — St John's Wort. About 20 cm high plant with nice foliage and a profusion of large, shining, yellow flowers which appear from June to September. Full sun or slight semi-shade.

Iberis sempervirens 'Little Gem' — Candytuft. This evergreen, richly flowering cultivar, particularly suitable for sunny situations, has a low (up to 10 cm), shrubby habit and white flowers produced in April and May.

Nepeta × *faassenii* — Catmint. Quite undemanding, long-flowering, up to 15 cm high and of compact growth. It has grey-green leaves and pure blue flowers appearing from June to September, and prefers sunny situations.

Phlox subulata 'Atropurpurea' — Moss Pink. The plants spread into large, about 10 cm thick carpets. They are evergreen and can thus be used as a substitute for turf in small areas. Moss Pink likes warm, sunny places and this cultivar bears the darkest flowers of all red-flowering ones, in May and June.

Saponaria ocymoides — Soapwort. A sun-loving, widely spreading species, reaching a height of 10—20 cm. It forms sparse carpets studded in the flowering season — from May to July — by a profusion of small, carmine-red flowers.

Sedum spurium 'Album Superbum' — Stonecrop. A vigorously growing cultivar forming dense carpets. The leaves are deep green and the plants grow to 10—15 cm in height. This stonecrop flowers relatively sparsely in July and August.

Silene schafta. A commonly grown, 10—15 cm high plant, particularly attractive for its rich profusion of pink flowers, which appear in late summer — from August until September. A sun-loving species, it will thrive even in a slight shade.

Thymus serpyllum 'Splendens' — Wild Thyme. A handsome cultivar forming neat carpets, decorated from May to July by numerous shining red flowers. The plant is only 5 cm high, likes full sun

Lychnis viscaria is a good subject for borders, formal as well as outcrop rock gardens, and for flower beds. Most effective are combinations with some perennials, for example, Veronica austriaca 'Shirley Blue', Aster tongolensis 'Wartburgstern' and Cerastium columnae.

and can be used as a substitute for turf in sun-exposed situations. It can also be used for covering small bulbs after they have finished flowering.

Veronica austriaca 'Shirley Blue' — Speedwell. Up to 25 cm tall cultivar with conspicuous, sky-blue flowers arranged in pyramidal racemes. Flowers appear from May until July and the plant does well in full sun as well as in semi-shade.

Medium-high perennials

Aster amellus 'Dwarf King' — Michaelmas Daisy. It is interesting mostly for its late flowering. The plants reach a height of 30—40 cm and the brilliant purple flowers open from August until September. This cultivar needs a nourishing, open substrate and a covering of evergreen twigs for the winter.

Aster dumosus 'Böhm'. A 30—40 cm tall cultivar, bearing fresh green leaves and conspicuous blue-purple flowers with a yellow centre. The flowers open in September and October, at the same time as those of *Rudbeckia fulgida* 'Goldsturm', with which it forms good colour combinations. It is a sun-loving plant with no particular demands on the soil.

Coreopsis verticillata 'Golden Shower' — Tickseed. A 60 cm tall plant bearing a profusion of small, golden-yellow flowers throughout the summer — from July until September.

Doronicum orientale 'Goldzwerg' — Leopard's Bane. A commonly grown, early-flowering 25 cm tall perennial, from April to May bearing numbers of pale yellow composite flowers. It thrives in full sun as well as in semi-shade.

Liatris spicata 'Kobold' — Gay Feather. This interesting perennial with a grass-like habit has brilliant pink-purple flowers arranged in spikes which open from July until September. It reaches a height of 40 cm and loves sunny situations.

Doronicum caucasicum can be used in rock gardens or in mixed spring perennial groups.

The undemanding *Tradescantia virginiana* tolerates dry situations as well as damp sites. It can be recommended for planting next to water as its habit is somewhat similar to that of reeds. It is also suitable for borders and groups in sunny places.

Oenothera tetragona 'Fireworks'. A beautiful cultivar with an erect, up to 40 cm high habit. The flowering period is relatively long, lasting from June to August, the red flower buds opening into brilliant yellow flowers. It likes full sun and will grow in any garden soil.

Rudbeckia fulgida 'Goldsturm' — Coneflower. An excellent, extremely long-flowering perennial having large, yellow, composite flowers with a black centre. These open successively from August until October. The plants reach a height of 50—70 cm, are very hardy and thrive both in full sun and semi-shade.

Sedum spectabile 'Carmen' — Stonecrop. A characteristic, up to 40 cm high, fleshy-leaved plant which will do well even in the poorest soil in full sun. The leaves are grey-green and the deep carmine-red flowers open from August until September.

Solidago virgaurea 'Perkeo' — Golden Rod. This well-known, modest and hardy perennial measures up to 40 cm in height, with golden-yellow flowers arranged in a flat pyramidal inflorescence. It loves sunny situations and its flowering season lasts from June until August.

Stachys grandiflora 'Superba' — Lamb's Tongue. An interesting perennial measuring 40 cm at the most and bearing large numbers of scarlet-pink flowers, arranged in whorls. It is content with an ordinary garden soil and will grow in full sun equally well as in semi-shade. The flowering takes place from July until August.

Tradescantia × *andersoniana* 'Leonora' — Tradescantia. A modest and hardy perennial bearing throughout the whole summer a profusion of attractive flowers which open in the morning and close before noon. It will be satisfied with any garden soil, even a dry one, but sufficient light is a must. It grows to some 40—50 cm and has deep blue-purple flowers. Several other cultivars with white, pink, bright red and deep blue flowers are also grown. All are excellent for planting close to pools or other areas of water.

Veronica spicata 'Romilex Purple' — Speedwell. An undemanding, up to 40 cm high perennial bearing grey-green leaves and scarlet-purple flowers in slender spikes. The flowering season is from July until August. This plant likes full sun and will thrive in an ordinary garden soil.

Lychnis viscaria 'Plena' — Catchfly. A favourite, double-flowered cultivar producing a profusion of large, pale carmine-red flowers. It needs a good garden soil and should be planted in full sun or only slight semi-shade. It is about 40 cm tall, its flowers opening from May until June.

Containers in the autumn

In some years, the annuals planted in containers flower continuously until November, although their flowers become more scarce with the shortening days. Next year, however, the first night frost may destroy their beauty as early as in mid-September, in which case the plants will have to be replaced by hardier ones.

Of course, the choice of suitable species is rather limited in comparison with that for the spring and summer seasons. Some pre-cultivated perennials are a good solution in warmer situations, where the first frosts are not likely to occur before the year ends.

Best are the late-flowering varieties of low-growing, small-flowered chrysanthemums which open from September to November, producing mostly yellow, pink, bronze-red or white flowers. They can be transplanted even during their flowering. When the flowering is over, they should be put into pots and stored in a light, cool place for the winter.

Faded annuals can also be replaced by the low-growing asters with variegated flowers, particularly *Aster dumosus* — a 20—25 cm high species that has flowers in many hues of pink or brown-red.

Another recommended plant is *Erica gracilis,* particularly its early-flowering pink, salmon- or purple-red and cream-white cultivars. The species comes from South Africa and is thus sufficiently hardy; the plants should be moved indoors for the winter, to places that have an optimum temperature of 6—8° C. It also needs a high humidity, is intolerant of lime in the soil and tends to shed flowers and leaves when the root ball is left to dry out.

Of the succulent plants, best for window-boxes are the stonecrops. *Sedum spectabile* is an upright peren-

nial, 30—40 cm high. The fleshy stems with oval leaves bear clusters of small flowers which are green at first and turn pink-red later. The plant needs full sun and moderate watering. *S. sieboldii,* only some 15 cm high, produces red flowers in October.

Shaded situations can be decorated with hydrangeas; for example, *Hydrangea macrophylla,* which can flower until October. They are woody plants needing a cool overwintering, best in a greenhouse.

The Ivy (*Hedera helix*), usually grown as an indoor plant, can also be kept in boxes on the north-facing side of the house throughout the year. Another plant suitable for a northern aspect is the Periwinkle (*Vinca major*). Its trailing stems make an attractive cover for the fronts of unsightly containers.

Before being put out, all the above-mentioned plants need a proper pre-planting and sufficient time to root well in the containers. It is thus advisable to have two sets of similar containers so that when the flowers in the first set have finished, the other one is already prepared to take its place.

Containers in winter

Our climatic conditions usually do not permit the planting of window-boxes with plants in winter. Even during mild frosts the soil in the containers freezes to such an extent that the roots stop absorbing water and the plants die. It would be rather expensive risking failure with dwarf conifers. On the other hand, the containers need not be left vacant during winter.

They can be decorated with spruce, pine or fir twigs or other cut greenery. Also, some broadleaf twigs with attractively coloured fruits, for instance rowans (*Sorbus*), buckthorns (*Hippophae*), viburnums (*Viburnum*), hollies (*Ilex*), cotoneasters (*Cotoneaster* and botanical roses (*Rosa*) all look very nice. These are not only decorative, but also useful, as they serve as food for songbirds in times when other sources are scarce.

Various decorative grasses and some cushion-forming evergreen perennials can also be used for window-boxes in winter. The containers, however, should be fairly large and the planting should be done early, so that the plants manage to take root properly before winter sets in.

Of the plants used for autumn decoration, some stonecrops can be left outside even in winter; for example, *Sedum sieboldii* or *S. spectabile* will tolerate even quite hard frosts and happily survive to greet the following early spring and the beginning of a new gardening year.

Index

Numbers in *italics* refer to illustrations

Abies 420
  balsamea 235
    'Hudsonia' 240
    'Nana' 240
  concolor 235, *236*, 237
    'Glauca Compacta' 240
  grandis 235
  homolepis 235
  koreana 235, 237
  nordmanniana 235
  procera 235
    'Glauca' 293
  veitchii 235
absorption capacity 60
Abutilon 422
  × *hybrida* 422
Acaena 231, 309
  microphylla 429
Acantholimon 311, 325
Acanthus longifolius 311
  spinosus 306
Acer japonicum 420
Acer palmatum 249
  'Atropurpureum' 249, *253*
  'Dissectum Atropurpureum' *251*
  'Dissectum Garnet' 249
  'Dissectum Viridis' 249
Achillea 310
  filipendulina 310, 311
    'Golden Plate' *307*
  millefolium 296
  ptarmica 'The Pearl' 308
acidanthera 267
Acidanthera 357, 365
Aciphylla 391
aconite, winter 360, 377, 388, 404
Aconitum fischeri 311
Acorus calamus 408
Adder's Fern 405
Adianthum pedatum 325, 405
Adonis 311
  amurensis 378, *381*
Adonis, Early 378
Adonis vernalis *376*, 378, *380*
Agapanthus 367
Agaricus hortensis 222
Ageratum houstonianum 335, 424
Agrostis nebulosa 333, 340
Ajuga 231, 309
  reptans 'Multicolor' 429
Alisma plantago-aquatica 408, *408*
Allium 192, 356, 357
  ascalonium 197
  cepa 192
  fistulosum 197
  giganteum *356*
  karataviense 359
  moly *357*
  porrum 196
  sativum 196
    ssp. *ophioscorodon* 198
  schoenoprasum 199
almond 117, 263
Alopecurus lanatus 402
Alternanthera 341
Althaea rosea *39*, 332, 335, *336*
Alyssum argenteum 318
  saxatile *323*, *371*
    'Compactum' *299*, *314*
Alyssum, Sweet 336, 426
Amaranthus caudatus 335, 340, 424
Amaryllis 367
amelioration 74
Ammobium alatum 333
Amorphophallus 367
Anchusa 315
andromeda 251
Andromeda 397
  polifolia 252, 400

Androsace 391
  mucronifolia *391*
anemone 305, 358, 359, 360, 366, 367, 388
Anemone 388, 404, 405
  blanda *357*, 360
  coronaria 357, 359, 362, 364, 365
  japonica 315, 318, 381
  sylvestris 'Grandifolia' *319*
  vitifolia 381
Anethum graveolens 212
anise 213—14
annuals 331—45, 354
  for boxes 338—40
  for containers 424—9
  for cutting 332—4
  for drying 333—4
  for forcing 333
  for rockeries 335—6, 338
Antennaria dioica 311
  'Rubra' 429
Anthemis 311, 315
Anthriscus cerefolium 215
Antirrhinum 332
  majus *344*, 424
    'Pumilum' 336
aphids 100, *102*
Apium graveolens var. *dulce* 219
    var. *rapaceum* *201*
Aponogeton distachyus 410
apples 12, 61, *94*, 117, *118*, 119, *121*, 122, *132*, *133*,
  134, 136, 137—8
  ornamental 263
apricots 61, 117, 119—22, *141*, 141—2
aquatic plants 27, 60, 409—12, *410*
Aquilegia 314
Arabis 321, 322
  procurrens 314
Arborvitae, American 235, 240, 256
Arctostaphylos uva-ursi 245
Aristolochia durior *47*
Armeria maritima 312, 429
Armoracia rusticana 202
Aronia melanocarpa 160
Arrhenatherum elatius ssp. *bulbosum* 'Variegatum' 402
Arrow-head 407
Artemisia dracunculus 214
artichoke, globe 218, *218*, 219
  Jerusalem 222
Arum, Bog 407
Aruncus dioicus 311
Asarum 231, 404
Ash, Black Mountain 160
  Mountain 160, *160*
asparagus 74, 217—8
Asparagus 421
  officinalis 217
  sprengeri 420
Asperula 231
Asplenium 231
aster 333
Aster 299, 307, 310, 322
  alpinus *321*
  amellus 315, 318
    'Dwarf King' *432*
Aster, China *331*, 333, 424
Aster dumosus 301, 304, 433
  'Böhm' *432*
  linosyris 311
  novi-belgii 301
Astilbe 295, 300, 305, 312, 322, 379, 404, 405, 409
  chinensis 'Finale' *322*
Astilboides tabularis 311
Astragalus 311
Atragene alpina 255
Atriplex hortensis 209, 341
aubergine 192
Aubrieta 322, 355
  × *cultorum* 429
Avena 309

  candida 403
Azalea mollis 253
azaleas 420
  Japanese 251, 253
  Kurume 397, 400
  Mollis 251—3, 397

Baby's Breath 342
balm 216
Balsam 339
barbecue *50*, *51*, 52
barberry 161, 245, *245*, 249, 257, 258, 262, 263, 309,
  420
Barberry, Thunberg's 252
bark beetles 102
Barrenwort 404
basil 215
bean 169, *210*, 211
Bean, Bog 407
bean, broad 211
  French 211
  runner *210*, 211
Beard Tongue 426
beech 258
beet, white 203
beetroot 162, *203*, 203
begonia 333, 335, 339, 343
Begonia 362, 424
  × *semperflorens* 424
  × *tuberhybrida* 338, 360, *360*, 365, 419, 422
begonia, tuberous 354, 360, 363, 366, 367, 419, 422
bellflower 333, 379, 421, 429
Bellis perennis 332, 429
Berberis 420
  buxifolia 'Nana' 249, 257
  candidula 249, 257
  gagnepainii var. *lanceifolia* 258
  julianae *245*
  thunbergii 'Atropurpurea Nana' 252
  verrucandii 257
  verruculosa 258
  vulgaris 161
Bergenia 305, 325
  cordifolia *28*, *325*
Beta vulgaris var. *cicla* 209
    var. *conditiva* f. *rubra* 203
Betula nana 249, 252
  pendula 'Youngii' 397
bibionid fly larvae 98—9
biennials 343, 344, 351, 424—9
birch, dwarf 249, 252
bird bath *45*, *47*, 402, *405*, 407, 419
black leg 93, 94
blackberries 117, 122, *150*, 151, 152—3
Blechnum 231
  penna-marina 325
  spicant 405
bleeding heart 379
blocking 77
bluebell 388
Bluebell, Californian 338
blueberries 120, 160—1, *161*
Blueberry, Highbush 253
bog earth 65
bog plants 407—9, 410
bone meal 69, 284, 313, 317
borage 216
Borago officinalis 216
borders, low 304—5, *307*
  mixed 303
  tall 305—7
botrytis 97
Bougainvillea 422
Box, Common 258
Brachycome iberidifolia 336
Brassica napus var. *napobrassica* 204
  oleracea var. *acephala* 181
    var. *botrytis* 182

var. *capitata* 179
var. *gemmifera* 181
var. *gongylodes* 181
var. *italica* 183
var. *sabauda* 179
pekinensis 183
rapa var. *rapa* 203
brassicas 178
broccoli 183, *183*
Briza maxima 340
media 403
broadleaved trees and shrubs 244—5, 261—2
deciduous 234, 246—9
evergreen 233—4, 245—6
for containers 252, 253
for heath gardens 250—2
for rockeries 249—50, 252—3
broom 249, 250, *251*, 253, 263, 397, 420
bruckenthalia 251
Bruckenthalia 397
spiculifolia 245, 252, 400, *401*
Brunnera 305
macrophylla 305, 325
Brussels sprouts 181
buckthorn 433
budding 80, *129*, 131—2, 265, 292
Forkert's method 80, *81*
fruit trees 128
roses *292*
Buddleia 247, 264, 420
alternifolia 248
davidii 247, 253
'Empire Blue' 247
'Flaming Violet' 247
'Purple Prince' 247
'Royal Red' 247
'White Bouquet' 247
buds, adventitious 119
axillary 119, 125
dormant 119, 125
flower 119, 125
lateral 119
leaf 119, 125
reserve 119
terminal 119
bugbane 409
bugle 231, 429
Bulbocodium 378
bulbs and tubers 104, 303, 304, 306, 309, 351—67, *363*, 388, 418, 420
for cutting 357—8
for decorative planting 352—6
for forcing 352, 358—60
for pots 358
for rockeries 356—7
bullaces 120, 138
bulrush 412
burr, New Zealand 231
Butomus umbellatus 408
Butterfly Bush 247, 248
Flower 338
Buxus sempervirens 'Suffruticosa' 257
var. *arborescens* 258

cabbage *168*, 171, *178*, 179, *179*
Chinese 74, 169, 183—4, *184*
red 179, *179*
round-headed 179
Savoy 171, 179—81, *180*
Calceolaria integrifolia 421
Calendula officinalis 342
Calla palustris 407
Calladium 367
Callistemon 423
citrinus 'Splendens' 423
Callistephus chinensis 333, 424
Calluna 231, 304, 397, 420
vulgaris 251, 318, 399, *400*
'Alba Plena' 251, 399
'Alportii' 251, 399
'August Beauty' 251
'County Wicklow' 251, 399
'Cuprea' 251, 399
'C. W. Nix' 251, 399
'Foxii' 399
'H. E. Beale' 399
'J. H. Hamilton' 399
'Mullion' 399
'Tib' 399
callunas *see* heathers
Caltha palustris 296, 407, *408*
'Alba' *408*
'Multiplex' 407
Calypso 391
Camassia 357
Campanula 333
aucheri 379

bellidifolia 379
carpatica 380
'Alba' *374*
cochleariifolia 380
'Alba' *383*
garganica 380
'Erinus Major' 429
glomerata *300*
isophylla 421
persicifolia 315
portenschlagiana 380
poscharskyana 304, 380, *383*
pusilla 380
tridentata 379
campion 336, 381
Campsis radicans *23*, 38
Canary-grass, Reed 404
candytuft 231, 425, 430
Candytuft, Rocket 425
canna 367
Capsicum annuum 191
caraway 212—3
Cardamine 324
Carex 231, 409
montana 403
morrowii 305
'Variegata' *403*
Carlina acaulis 311
Carnation, Clove 333
carrot 169, *197*, 199—200
Carum carvi 212
caryopteris 264
Caryopteris × *clandonensis* 248
Cassiope tetragona 245
Catchfly 433
Catmint 430
Cat-tail 408
cattle dung 68
cauliflower 171, *182*, 182—3
cedar 420
Cedar, Red 235
Western Red 257
White 236, 256
Cedrus 420
celeriac *91*, 171, *200*, 201, *201*
celery 74, 219
Celosia argentea var. *cristata* 'Nana' 424
Centaurea imperialis 342
macrocephala 311
moschata 342
Cerastium 231, 322
Ceratophyllum 412
Chaenomeles 420
japonica 161, 249
chalk plant 380
Chamaecyparis 420
lawsoniana 235
'Alumii' 236, 256
'Elwoodii' 237, 256
'Fletcheri' 240, 256
'Golden King' 239
'Lane' 239
'Minima Glauca' 240
nootkatensis 235
obtusa 'Crippsii' 240
'Filicoides' 240
'Lyxopodioides' 240
'Nana Gracilis' 240, *241*
pisifera 'Aurea Nana' 240
'Filifera Aurea Nana' 238
'Filifera Nana' 241
'Nana Aureovariegata' 240
'Plumosa Aurea' 237
'Plumosa Compressa' 241
chard, Swiss *208*, 209
Cheiranthus cheirii 429, *429*
cherries 61, 117, 119, 120, 122, 134, *138*, *139*, 139—40
Morello 117, *117*, 119, 120, 122, 134, *140*, 140—2
Cherry, Cornelian 161, 247, 258
chervil 215
chicory *206*, 206—7
Chionodoxa 357, 360, 388, 404
luciliae *357*
chives *196*, 199
chokeberry 160
Chrysanthemum 299, 307, 322
carinatum 332, 342
'Polaris' *331*
coccineum 310
× *hortorum* 310, *322*
indicum 310, 315
maximum 296, *306*, *309*, 310, 315, 324
parthenium 333
segetum 424
Cichorium endivia var. *latifolium* 206
intybus var. *foliosum* 206
Cimicifuga 409
cinquefoil, shrubby 262

Citrullus lanatus 187
Clarkia 333
elegans 333
climate 58, 296
climbers *23*, 27, 28, 29, 234, 235, 253—6, 339, 420
clematis 255, *255*, *258*, *259*, 420, *421*
Clematis 420
alpina 255
× *durandii* 255
'Nelly Moser' *258*, *259*
tangutica 248, 255
vitalba 255
Cleome spinosa 335, 424
cloches 54, *54*, *60*, 176, *176*, 177, 185, 186, 191, *205*
Cloud Grass 340
coating the seeds 75, 170
cockchafers 98
Cockscomb 424
Colchicum 304, 381
bornmuelleri *363*
byzantinum var. *cilicicum* *367*
× *hybridum* 'Waterlily' *356*
Coleus × *hybridus* 341
colour combinations 24, 25, 307
columbine *314*
commercial substrates 65
compost 65, *67*, 68, *68*, 79, 82, 285, 313, 314, 317, 383, 386, 387—8
coneflower 332, 432
conifer bark 68—9
conifers 82, 233, 235—44, 261, *386*, 402, 418, 420
for containers 240—4
for rockeries 240—4
medium-tall 237—9
tall 235—7
with variegated leaves 239—40
Convallaria 322, 404
majalis 292, 310, 379
Convolvulus tricolor *343*
Coprosma 391
Coreopsis grandiflora 308
verticillata *296*, 310
'Golden Shover' 432
coriander *214*, 215
Coriandrum sativum 215
Cornflower 342
Cornus mas 161, 247
Cortaderia 309
selloana 403, *403*
Corylus avellana 146
'Contorta' *235*, 420
colurna *16*, 146
maxima 146
pontica 146
Cosmea 333, 341, 424
Cosmos bipinnatus 341, 424
sulphureus 333
Cotinus coggygria 253, 420
cotoneaster 231, 249, 250, 252, *252*, 262, 309, 397, 420, 433
Cotoneaster 231, 420, 433
adpressus 249, 252
dammeri 'Skogholm' 250, 253
horizontalis 249, 253, *253*
multiflorus 244
Cotula 231, 355
atrata 391
courgette 186
cress, rock 231
Crambe cordifolia 311
crane fly larvae 98
Crataegus oxyacantha 161
cress 207—8
Cress, Purple Rock 429
Crososmia 357, 365
crocosmiiflora 359
masonorum 354
crocus 367, *380*, 404
Crocus 357
crocus, autumn 304, 365, 367, 405
botanical 418
Crocus chrysanthus 356
heuffelianus 378
vernus 'Pickwick' 360
'Queen of the Blues' *355*
crop rotation 62, 168, 174
cross-pollination 119
Cryptomeria japonica 241
cucumber *91*, 169, 171, 176, 184—6, *185*, 186
Cucumis melo 186
sativus 184
Cucurbita maxima 186
pepo 186
Currant, Mountain 420
currants 61, 119, 122, 135, 147—51, *148*, *149*, 150, *150*, 151, 262—3
black 117, *147*, 148, 151
red 117, *147*, *148*, 149

white *147*
cuttings 265, 292
cutworms 98
cyclamen 360, 366, 377, *377*, 388, 391
Cyclamen 357, 360, 362, 377, 388
  persicum 367
Cydonia oblonga 160
Cynara scolymus 218
cypress 256, 420
  dwarf *241*
Cypress, Lawson 236, 256
  Summer 341, 344
Cypripedium 405
Cytisus 249, *251*, 397, 420
  decumbens 250, *251*
  × *kewensis* 250
  × *praecox* 250
  scoparius 250

Daboecia 251, 397
  cantabrica 245, 252, 400
daffodil 358, 359
dahlia 333, 356, 365, *365*, 367
Dahlia 333, 357, 365, 424
  pinnata *354, 358, 364*
  variabilis 424
Daisy 332
  Cape 333
  Livingstone 335, 336, 424
  Meadow 429
  Michaelmas 339, 432
  Swan River 335
damping off 93, 343
damsons *137*, 138
daphne 249, 250, 262, 385
Daphne cneorum 250
  'Major' *378*
  mezereum 246, *246*, 250, *251*, 377
Datura sanguinea 423
  suaveolens 423
Daucus carota ssp. *sativus* 199
decorative garden 17, 18, 29, 31
delphinium *300, 304*
Delphinium 310, 315, 318
  ajacis 334
  consolida 334, 342
Deschampsia 309
  caespitosa 403
Deutzia 420
Dianthus 304, 320
  arenarius 311
  barbatus 429, *430*
  caryophyllus 333
  chinensis *343*
  deltoides 311
    'Brillant' *430*
  suffruticosus 422
Dicentra 305, 379
Dictamnus 307
  albus 311, *315*
digging 63, 74
Digitalis 310
dill 169, *211*, 212, *212*
Dimorphotheca pluvialis 338
  sinuata 'Tetra Goliath' *342*
disbudding 79
diseases, bacterial 92—3, *93*
  fungus 93—7, *94, 95, 96, 97*
  Fusarium 94
  parasitic 89, 91—7
  physiological *89,* 89—91
  tumour 93
  Verticillium 94
  virus 91—2, *91, 92*
disinfection of seeds 75
dogwood 263
Dogwood, Red 258
Doronicum 305, 307, 310, 322, 383
  caucasicum *432*
  columnae *303*
  orientale 'Goldzwerg' *432*
Dorotheanthus bellidiformis 335, 336, 424
drainage 62, *70*, 74, 264, 382, 385, 386, 387
Dryas 295
  drummondii 297
  octopetala 297
  × *suendermannii* 297
Dryopteris filix-mas 405
duckweed 410, 412
dung water 68
dwarfs *119,* 120, *131*

earthing up 74, 80, 173, 218, 287, 290
earhworms 63—4, 98—9
Echeveria 314
Echinops 311
  ritro 311

eelworms 97—8
Eichhornia crassipes 407
elm 262
Elymus arenarius 403
Empetrum 397
  nigrum 251
endive 206—7
Endymion 357
Epimedium 404
Eranthis 299, 360, 377, 388, 404
  hyemalis *359*
eremurus 367
Eremurus 307, 310, 318, 356
  robustus 311
  stenophyllus var. *bungei* *353,* 357
Erica 231, 377, 397, 420
  carnea 251, 252, 318, 399—400, *401*
    'Alba' 252, 399
    'Atrorubra' 252, 399
    'Aurea' 399
    'James Backhouse' 252, 399
    'King George' 252, 399
    'Ruby Glow' 399
    'Snow Queen' 400
    'Springwood' 252
    'Vivellii' 252, 400
    'Winter Beauty' 252, 400
  cinerea 397, 399
  gracilis 433
  vagans 399—400
    'Alba' 400
    'Mrs. D. F. Maxwell' 400
    'St. Keverne' 400
ericas *see* heaths
Erigeron 315
  × *hybridus* 310
Eriosoma lanigerum 100
Eryngium 303, 310, 311, 318
  alpinum 310
Erysiphe polygoni 95
Erythrina crista-galli 423
Erythronium 357, 360, 362
  dens-canis 361
escaroles 206
Eschscholtzia californica 335, *335,* 338, 425
Eucharia 367
Euonymus 231
  fortunei 'Gracilis' 250
    'Minimus' 250
    'Variegatus' 258
Eupatorium purpureum *319*
Euphorbia marginata 341
  polychroma 311, 312, *312*
Everlasting, Mountain 429

Feathertop 334, 340
feeding annuals and biennials 344
  bulbs and tubers 355, 361—2, 364
  container-grown plants 416
  foliar 286
  fruit trees 124, 128, 131, 133
  lawns 229
  perennials 313—4, 317, 355
  roses 284—6
  vegetables 168—9, 172
  woody plants 264
fences *39, 40,* 41, 304
fennel 214—5
ferns 231, 388, 404—5, *405*
fertilizers, artificial 313, 317
  compound 71, 284, 285, 313, 317
  industrial 62, 70, 123—4, 284
  liquid 71, 285
  mineral 70—1, 317
  organic 68—71, 317
  single element 70—1
  slow-release 71
  trace element 71
fescue 231, 309
Festuca 231
  cinerea 403
  glauca 403
  scoparia 403
field mushroom 222—3
Filipendula 312, 409
  hexapetala 311
fir 420
Fir, Balsam 240
  Colorado White 237
  Noble 239
  Veitch's Silver 235
firethorn 258, 420
Flag, Sweet 408
  Yellow 408
Flame Needle 341
flea beetles *104*
Floss Flower 335, 424

Foeniculum vulgare 214
forcing bulbs and tubers 352, 358—60
  vegetables 174—7
Forget-me-not 409, 429
forsythia 253, 263, 420
Forsythia 420
  × *intermedia* *245*
fountains *44,* 46—7
frame earth 65
frames 53, *53,* 54, 76, 82, *166, 173,* 174, 175, 178, 205, *205*
freesia 366
Freesia 365
Fritillaria 356
  imperialis 'Lutea Maxima' *353*
  meleagris 357, 360
fritillary 366, 367
Fritillary, Chequered 360
Frogbit 410
front garden 20, 26, *306, 307,* 309, 399, *421*
fruit 83, 104, 117, 134—6
  dry 118
  fleshy 118
  stone- 118—9
  with pips 118—9
fruit trees 73—4, 117—134
  in walls and belts 120, 122, *130, 131,* 134
fuchsia 419, 421, 422, *426*
Fuchsia 419
Fuchsia, Californian 382
  Cluster-flowered 422
Fuchsia fulgens 422
  × *hybrida* 422

Gaillardia aristata 310
  'Fackelschein' *320*
  'Kobold' 304
Galanthus 357, 360, 377, 388, 404
  nivalis *354, 377*
Galtonia 365
garden accesories *85,* 86, *98*
  earths 64
  furniture 17, *51,* 52, *52*
  planning 13, *16—19,* 19—25, *21, 22, 26,* 29—31
gardening tools, basic *64,* 83, 86, 374—5
  care of 84, *84*
  specialized 83, *84,* 86, *122*
garlic *195,* 195—6, 171
gaultheria 251
Gaultheria 397
  procumbens 252, 400
Gay Feather 432
Gazania rigens 335, 425
Genista 249, 397
Gentiana acaulis 298
  farreri 295, 381
  septemfida var. *lagodechiana* 381
geometrids 101
geranium 4, 19, 354, 421
Geranium, Ivy-leaved 422
  Zonal 422
germination 75, 170
  tests 75
ginger, wild 231
gladioli 365, 367
Gladiolus 357, 365
  hybridus 352
    'Black Jack' *353*
Gloriosa 367
Glory of the Snow 404
Glyceria aquatica 408
  'Variegata' 409
  maxima 'Variegata' 403
Goat's Beard, False 404, 405, 409
Godetia grandiflora 333
Golden Rain 420
Golden Rod 432
goldenrod *310*
Gomphrena globosa 333
gooseberries 61, 117, 119, 122, 135, *148, 149,* 151—2
grafting 9—80, *81*
  fruit trees *128,* 131—3
  ornamental woody plants 265
  perennials 325
grapes 82, 117, *158, 159*
grasses, ornamental *300,* 303, 304, 309, 318, 356, *402,* 408—9, 418, 420
  annual 340—1
  perennial *402*—4
greengages *136*
greenhouses 54—5, *54, 55,* 73, 82, 174, 175—6, 320, *389,* 389—91
Gypsophila 295, 325, 380
  elegans 342
  paniculata 310, 325
    'Bristol Fairy' 27
  repens 305

Haberlea 324
Hacquetia 305
Haemanthus 367
Hair-grass, Tufted 403
Hamamelis 420
  japonica 246, 253
    'Ruby Glow' 246
  mollis 246, *246*
  virginiana 248
Hard Fern 231, 405
hardening off 78
Hare's Tail Grass 334, 340
Hart's Tongue Fern 231, 405
hawthorn 262, 263
Hawthorn, Common 161
  Water 410
Hazel, Common *235*
  Giant 146
  Old World 146
  Ponticus 146
  Turkish 146
hazel-nuts 117
hazels 122, *146*, 146—7, 258, 262
hearth *48, 50*, 52
Heath, Cornish 400
heath garden 397—400, 418
Heath, Winter-flowering 399
Heather, Common 251, 399
  Irish 245
heather mould 65
heathers 73, 231, 251, 311, 377, *379*, 385, 397, 418, 420
heaths 73, 231, 251, 252, 311, 397, 400, 418, 420
Hebe 391
  armstrongii 250
  buchananii 250
  pimeleoides 'Glauco-coerulea' 250
Hedera 231, 420
  helix 250, *257*, 433
    'Arborescens' 250
    'Conglomerata' 250
hedge trimmers 88
hedges 13, *14*, 27, 28, 40, *86*, 233, 256—9, *260, 261*, *262, 263*, 273, 303
Helenium 310, 315, 322
Helianthemum 295, 318, 383
  apenninum 'Rubin' *430*
Helianthus 322, 333
  annuus 332
  atrorubens 318
  salicifolius 311
  tuberosus 222
Helichrysum bracteatum 333, 334, *334*
  coraloides 391
  microphyllum 391
  selago 391
Helictotrichon sempervirens *44*, 310, 313, 403, *403, 405*
Heliopsis 301, 307
  scabra 310
Heliotropium arborescens 425
Helipterum roseum 333, 334
hellebore 385
Helleborus 299, 305, 322
  × *hybridus* *378*
  niger 377, *377*, 429, *430*
Hemerocallis *23*, 300, 315, 409
  fulva 298
  hybrida 311, 312, *318*
    'Burning Daylight' *299*
hemlock *243*
hepatica 404
Hepatica 231
  angulosa 378
  nobilis 305
  transsylvanica 378
Hibiscus 420
  rosa-sinensis 423
  syriacus 247, 248
    'Coelestis' 247
    'Coeruleus Plenus' 248
    'Duc de Brabant' 248
    'Hamabo' 247
    'Lady Stanley' 248
    'Monstrosus' 247
    'Rubis' 247
    'Speciosus' 248
    'Woodbridge' 247
Hieracium 311
Hippeastrum 367
Hippophae 433
  rhamnoides 249
Heracleum laciniatum 311
herbicides 173
hoeing 74
holly 259, 262, 433
Holy, English *235*, 259, 397
Hollyhock 332, *336*
  Tree 247, 253, 262, 420
Honesty 342

honeysuckle 262
Honeysuckle, Chinese 258
  Perfoliate 255, 420
hoof and horn meal 68, 284
Hordeum jubatum 340, 404
hornbeams 258
Hornwort 412
horseradish 202—3
Hosta 305, 322
  undulata 'Medio-Variegata' *315*
houseleek 387, 388
humus 63—4, 284, 313
hyacinth 355, 358, 363, 418
Hyacinth, Grape 354, 404, 418
Hyacinthus 357
  orientalis 'Bismarck' *363*
    'Delft Blue' *358*
hydrangea 247
Hydrangea macrophylla 433
    'Bouquet Rose' *248*
  paniculata 247
    'Grandiflora' 247
Hydrocharis morsus-ranae 410
hygrophytes 60
Hymenocallis 357, 365
Hypericum 318, 320, 420
  × *moseranum* 250
  olympicum 430
  patulum 'Hidcote' 250
    'Hidcote Gold' 248
hypericum, shrubby 249
hyssop 216
Hyssopus officinalis 216

Iberis 321, 300, 318, 320
  amara 425, 427
  sempervirens *430*
    'Little Gem' *430*
  umbellata 425
Ilex 433
  aquifolium *235*, 259, 397
Impatiens balsamina 339
Incarvillea 305, 357
Inula ensifolia 311, 381, *384*
Ipomoea purpurea 339
Iresine 341
Iris 311, 312, 357, 383
iris, bearded 316
Iris × *barbata* 316
  × *hollandica* 365
  × *intermedia* 'Frithjof' *312*
Iris, Japanese Clematis 409
Iris kaempferi 296, 409
  pallida 'Variegata' *310*
  pseudacorus 408
  pumila 295, 298
  reticulata *361*
irises 366, 378, 383, 409
irrigation, furrow 73
  subsurface 73
  trickle 73, *73*
ivy 231, 250, *257*, 420, 433
Ivy, Boston 254
Ixia 365
  speciosa 355
Ixiolirion 357, 367

jasmine, miniature rock 391
Jasmine, Winter *245*, 246, 377, 385
Jasminum nudiflorum *245*, 246, 377
Juglans regia 145
juniper 231, 309, 397, 420
Juniper, Chinese 235, 239, 240, 256
juniper, columnar *239, 240*, 242, *398*
Juniper, Common 235, 238, 241
  Creeping 239, 242
Juniperus 231, 397, 420
  chinensis 'Hetzii' 239
    'Old Gold' 240, 241
    'Pfitzeriana' 238, 239, 256
    'Pfitzeriana Aurea' 238, 240, 241
    'Plumosa Aurea' 240
  communis 'Compressa' 241
    'Depressa' 241, *241*
    'Depressa Aurea' 241
    'Depressa Aureospicata' 241
    'Hibernica' 238, *240*, 241, *242*
    'Hornbrookii' 242
  horizontalis 'Douglasii' 242
    'Glauca' 239
  squamata 'Meyeri' 239, 242
  virginiana 'Globosa' 242
    'Nana Compacta' 242
    'Skyrocket' 242

kale, curly *180*, 181
kalmia 251, 252, 262, *265*
Kalmia 397

angustifolia 252, *401*
  'Rubra' 252, 400
Kerria japonica 'Pleniflora' *248*
Kniphofia 315, 318
  hybrida 311, 312
  uvaria 'Nobilis' *316*
Kochia scoparia 335, 341, *341*
kohlrabi 169, *169*, 171, *181*, 181—2
kolkwitzia 253, 262, 420

laburnum 262, 420
Lactuca sativa var. *capitata* 204
  var. *secalina* 206
Lagurus ovatus 334, 340, *341*
Lamarckia aurea 340
Lamb's Tongue 432
Lantana camara 423
Larch, European 236
Larix decidua 236
larkspur 334, 342
Lathyrus 321
  odoratus 332, 339
    'Spencer' *332*
Laurocerasus officinalis 'Schipkaensis' 258
    'Zabeliana' 258
Lavandula 295, 304, 311, 318
  angustifolia 312
Lavender, Sea 333
lawn 16, *69*, 227—30, *227, 229, 231*, 277, 309, 353, 402, 418, 419
  mowers 84, *86, 88*
  substitutions 231
layering 81, 265
leaf mining moths 102
  mould 65, 313, 314, 383, 385, 387
  roller moths 101—2
  spot 94—5, *95*
Ledum 251, 397
leek 74, 169, 171, 192, *196*, 196—7
Lemna 412
  trisulca 410
Lens culinaris 211
lentil 211—2
Leontopodium alpinum 310, *385*
leopard's bane 383, 432
Lepidium sativum 207
lettuce *89, 91*, 171, 204—6, *204, 205*
  crisp cabbage *204*
  lamb's 207
  loose-leaved 206, *206*
Leucojum 357, 360, *379*, 404
  vernum 353
Levisticum officinale 215
lewisia *373, 391, 391*
Liatris 303, 357
  spicata 310
    'Kobold' 432
lighting 52
Ligularia 295, 307, 312, 318
  dentata 311
  × *hessei* 305, 320
Ligustrum ovalifolium 258
    'Aureum' *263*
  vulgare 260, 262
    'Altrovirens' 258
lilac 262
Lilium 357, 379
  auratum 295, *358*
  candidum 364, 366
  pumilum 318
lily *300*, 353, 360, *364*, 365, 367, 379
Lily, Day 298
Lily-of-the-valley 379, 384, 404
Lily, Pond 410
lily, trumpet-flowered *362*
Limonium 310
  bonduellei 333
  latifolium *300*, 310
  sinuatum 333, *333*
  suworowii 333
  tataricum 310
Linaria 332
Ling 399
Linum 310
liverwort 231
Lobelia 425
  erinus 425
Lobularia maritima 336
  var. *benthamii* 426
Lonas inodora 333
Lonicera caprifolium 255, 420
  nitida 258
  pileata 258
  tatarica 'Alba' *256*
loosening the soil 63, 74, 312, 317
Lotus corniculatus 311
lovage 213, 215

Love-in-a-mist 332, 333, 341
Love Lies Bleeding 340, 424
Lunaria annua *334*
lungwort 231, 404
Lupinus 307, 310, 315, 318, 321
Luzula 305
Lychnis chalcedonica 310
  viscaria *430*
  'Plena' *320*, 433
Lycopersicon esculentum 188
Lyme Grass 403
Lysimachia 312
  punctata *295, 298, 300*

Macleya cordata 311
magnolia 262
mahonia 258
Mahonia aquifolium *262*
  'Atropurpurea' 258
Maidenhair, North American 405
Majorana hortensis 212
Male Fern 405
Mallow, Indian 422
Manna Grass 408
manure 65, 68, 70, 284, 313, 317
manuring 124
  green 63, 69—70, 124
maple *249*, 258
Maple, Japanese 249, 420
Marguerite 342
  Summer 332
marigold 333, *333*, 335
Marigold, African 427
  Cape 338
  French 332, 340, 343, 427
  Marsh 407
  Pot 342
Marjoram, Common 212, 381, *211*
marrow 169, 186
  custard 186, *186*
  vegetable 186, *187*
Marrubium 311
Matricaria maritima 341
Matteucia 231
  struthiopteris 405
Matthiola incana 332, *336*, 338
Meadow Sweet 409
Medlar 160
Melissa officinalis 216
melon 169, 176
  honeydew 186—7, *187*
  water 187
Mentha × *piperita* 213
Menyanthes trifoliata 407
Mespilus germanica 160
Mezereon 246, 375
mildew, downy 96—7
  powdery 93, 95, *95*
millipedes 98, *100*
Mimulus luteus 426
mint 213
Miscanthus 307, 309
  sinensis 403
  'Gracillimus' *404*
mock orange 262
Molinia 303
  arundinacea 403
Monarda didyma 310
  'Cambridge Scarlet' *302*
Monstrosum 333
montbretia 367
Morning Glory 339
mosaic 91, *91*
moulds 93—4, 97, *97*
mulching 68, 78, 173, 282, 316, 317
Muscari 357, 404
  armeniacum 354, *356*
Musk 426
Myosotis 409
  alpestris *409*, 429

narcissi 309, 359, *359*, 360, 365, 378, 418
  miniature 389, 391
Narcissus *351*, 357, 389
nasturtium 332, 419
Navelwort 404, 409
needle litter 64
Nepeta 315
  × *faassenii* 430
  mussini 304
Nerium oleander 423
new growth 119, 125, 127, 128
Nicotiana alata 340
Nigella damascena 332
noctuid caterpillars 97—8
Nuphar lutea 410
nutrients 65—8, 71, 124

Nymphaea 409
  alba *410*
  colorata *410*

oak 258, 262
Ocimum basilicum 215
Oenothera tetragona 'Fireworks' 380, 432
  missouriensis 301, 304, 305, 380
Oleander 423
Omphalodes 305, 404, 409
  verna *324*
onion *96*, *167*, 169, *169*, 171, 172, *177*, *191*, 192—5, *194*
  pearl 198
  salad 198
  sets 193—5
  spring 198
  winter 197—8
Orache 209—10
orchid 391, 409
  slipper 405
Orchis 409
Oregon Grape 258
Origanum vulgare 'Compactum' 381, *384*
Ornithogalum 357
ostrich feather 231
Ostrich Fern 405
Ostwald's colour cycle *23*, 25
Oxalis 365
Oxlip 429
oyster fungus 223

Pachistegia insignis 391
Paeonia 307, 310, 315, 322
  lactiflora *306*, 310
  officinalis *317*
Pampas Grass 403
Panicum capillare 340
  clandestinum 403
pansy 332, 429
Papaver 332
  nudicaule 304
  orientale *304*, 306, 310, *314*
  somniferum 221, 333
parsley 169, *198*, 200
  Hamburg 200
parsnip 169, *198*, 200
Parthenocissus quinquefolia 254, *256*
  tricuspidata 254
  'Veitchii' *236*, *254*
Pastinaca sativa 200
paths 13, 33—8, *33*, *34*, *35*, *36*, *37*, *185*, 304, 309, 354
pea, garden 209, 210—11
peaches 61, 117, 119, 120—2, 132, 134, *140*, *141*, 142, *142*, 143, *143*, *144*, 143—5
pears 117, 119, 120, 122, *131*, 134, *134*, *135*, 137—8
Peas, Sweet 332, 339, 344
peat 64—5
Pelargonium *338*, 419
pelargonium, ivy-leaved *416*, *417*, *418*, *423*, *425*
Pelargonium peltatum *415*, 422
pelargonium, trailing *415*
Pelargonium zonale *38*, 422, *424*
Peltiphyllum 325
Pennisetum 303, 309
  alopecuroides 403
  japonicum 403, 405
  villosum 334, 340, *340*
Penstemon hartwegii 426
peppers 171, 191—2
  hot 192
  sweet *89*, *102*, *165*, *190*, *191*
perennial groupings 308—10
perennials 231, 295—325, 397, 353, 354—5, 356, 397, 418, 420, 432
  bedding 315—6
  carpeting 418
pergolas 27, 28, *47*, 50—1
periwinkle 231, 404, 433
Pernettya mucronata 400
Petrorhagia saxifraga 'Pleniflora' 318
Petroselinum crispum 200
petunia 335, *339*, *416*, *418*, 419, 421—2
Petunia × *hybrida* 338, *339*, 422
Phacelia campanularia 338
Phalaris arundinacea 404
Phaseolus coccineus 339, *418*
Phlox, Annual 427
Phlox drummondii 427, *429*
  'Cuspidata' 335, *344*
  paniculata 300, 307, *307*, *308*, 310, 322, 325
  'Frührosa' *324*
  'Septemberglut' *296*
  'Starfire' *295*
  subulata *299*, *323*
  'Atropurpurea' *430*
Phygelius capensis 382
Phyllitis 231

scolopendrium 405
Physalis 310
Phytolacca americana 311
Picea 420
  abies 235—6
    'Echiniformis' 242
    'Maxwellii' 242
    'Nidiformis' 242
    'Pumila Glauca' 242
  alba 235
  asperata 235
  glauca 'Alberta Globe' *243*
    'Conica' 238, *239*, 243
  omorika 235—6
  pungens 235, *240*
    'Glauca' 239
    'Glauca Compacta' 243
    'Glauca Globosa' 243
pieris 251
Pilea 341
Pimpinella anisum 213
pinching 78, 282, 320
Pincushion Flower 333, 341
Pine, Austrian 235—6
pine, dwarf *239*, 420
Pine, Mountain 231, 235, 239, *241*, 243, *243*, 309
  Scots 235
  Weymouth 243
Pink, Maiden 430
  Moss 430
  Sea 429
  Tirolean 422
Pinus 420
  banksiana 235
  cembra 235
  densiflora 'Umbraculifera' 243
  flexilis 235
  koraiensis 235
  mugo 234, *234*, *241*, 243
    var. *mughus* *241*
    var. *pumilio* 239, *239*, 243
  nigra ssp. *nigra* 236
  peuce 235
  pumila 'Glauca' 243
  strobus 'Nana' 243
Pisum sativum ssp. *hortense* 210
planting annuals 344
  bulbs and tubers 361—2
  fruit trees 121—3
  hedges *261*
  ornamental woody plants 76, 259—62, *264*
  out 76—7, *78*
  perennials 315
  roses 278—80, *280*
  vegetables 170—1
Platycodon 303, 305, 357
Pleione 391
  bulbocodioides *391*
Pleurotus ostreatus 222, 223
Plum, Cherry 80, 141
plum pox 92
plums 61, *92*, 117, 119—20, 135, *137*, 138—9, 263
  Mirabelle 138
  Reine Claude 117, 138
Polygonatum 305
Polygonum 255
Polypodium 231
  vulgare 325, 405
polypody 231
Pomegranate 423
Pondweed, Curled 412
pools *43*, *44*, 43—6, 309, *371*, *377*, 402, 407, *410*, 410—12, 417, 419
popcorn 220—1
poppy 221, 332—3
Poppy, Californian 335, 338, 342, 425
Porcupine Grass 403
Portulaca 388
  grandiflora 335, 336, *336*, 427
  oleracea ssp. *sativa* 215
Potamogeton 412
potato, early 220, 221—2
potentilla, shrubby 249, *252*, 309
pricking out 77, *79*
primrose *302*, 377, 379, 385, 388, 391, 404—5, 409, 429
Primrose, Asiatic 379
  Common 429
  Evening 380
Primula 377, 379, 388, 404, 405, 409
  acaulis 429
  bullesiana 305
  bulleyana 305
  denticulata 305, *381*, 429
  elatior 305, *381*
    'Grandiflora' 429
  florindae 305
  japonica 305

petiolaris 391
× *pubescens* 391
rosea 305
vulgaris 305, *381*, 429
privet 258, 259, *260*, 262, *262*, *263*
Privet, Oval-leaved 258
propagating annuals 345
  bulbs and tubers 366—7
  conifers 82
  ornamental woody plants 264—5
  perennials 319—25
  rock plants 380
  roses 292
propagation by cuttings 81—2, 265, 292, 323—4
  by division 80, 265, 292, 322—3
  by grafting 325
  by layering 265, 292, 324—5
  by leaf cuttings 324
  by rhizome cuttings 325
  by root cuttings 325
  by rosette cuttings 324
  by stolons 324
  by stooling 265
  by root suckers 80, 265
  vegetative 79—82
Prunella 304
pruning fruit trees 125—31, *125*, *126*, *127*
  ornamental woody plants 262—4
  rock plants 382—3
  roses 280—3, *282*, *284*, *285*
Prunus cerasifera 263
  serrulata 234
  triloba 263
Pterocarya fraxinifolia 249
Pulmonaria 231, 300, 305, 404
pulsatilla 379, *382*
Pulsatilla grandis 311
Punica granatum 423
purslane 215—6, *388*
Puschkinia 357, 418
Pyracantha 420
  coccinea 258, 403
  'Kasan' *263*
  'Lalandei' 255

Quaking Grass 340
  Common 403
quarter-standards *119*, 120—1
Quince 160
  Japanese 161, 249
quince, ornamental 262, 309, 420

radish, red 201—2, *202*
  white 169, 202, *203*
raking 74
Ramonda 324
Ranunculus 364, 365
  asiaticus 355
Raoulia 391
Raphanus sativus var. *major* 202
  var. *radicula* 201
raspberries 117, 122, *150, 151,* 152—3, 135
Reed Grass 404
Reed-grass 403
reedmace 408, 412
Rheum palmatum 311
  rhabarbarum 216
rhododendron 231, 249, 251, 252, 253, 262, 383, *385,
398, 399, 400, 401,* 420
Rhododendron 231, *233*, 383, 420
  hirsutum 244
  impeditum 400
  japonicum 253, *254*
  luteum 253
  obtusum 420
  × *praecox* 244, 400
rhubarb 216—7, *217*
Rhus typhina *422*
Ribes alpinum 420
  sanguineum 265
Ricinus communis 335, 341
rock gardens *15, 26,* 27, 240, 335—6, 338, 356—7, *357,
372*—3, *372, 373, 374, 375,* 402
  miniature 386—9, *386, 387,* 402
  plants 231, 371—91, *385,* 418, 420
rodents 103
Rodgersia 312
  aesculifolia 311
rolling 74
roof gardens 402, 417—8, 429
Rosa alpina 274
  canina 273, 277
  'Pollmeriana' 292
  centifolia 274
  chinensis 274
  damascena 274
  gallica 274, 275
  hugonis 250, 292

kordesii 289
laxa 273
lutea 275
multiflora 273, 274, 275
muscosa 274
rugosa 274, 275, 289, 292
sericea var. *pteracantha* 285
spinosissima 274
wichuraiana 274, 275
Rose, Christmas 375, 377, *377*, 429
  of Jericho 255
  Sun 383, 430
roses 74, 249—50, 258, 273—92, 279
  bedding 275, 283
  botanical 420, 433
  Bourbon 275
  bush 420
  climbing 234, 255, *273, 274,* 275, *278,* 278—9, *280,*
281, 283, *284,* 287, *287,* 289, *291,* 420
  climbing tea 275
  floribunda 274—5, *275,* 280, 283, *287, 288,* 290, *291*
  floribunda-grandiflora 275
  Garnet's 275, 281
  hybrid tea *273,* 273—5, *276,* 277, 280, 283, *283,* 288,
289
  Lambert's 275
  large-flowered 274, 275, 277, 280, 283
  miniature 275, 281, 292
  multiflowered 274, 275, 281, 283
  multiflowered floribunda *281*
  Pernetiana 275
  polyantha 274, 275, 281, 283
  polyantha hybrid 274, 275, 281
  rambler 275
  remontant 274, 275, 281
  shrub 274, 275, *275,* 278, *278,* 281, 284, 290
  species 274, 275, 281, 284, *285,* 292
  standard *277, 278, 279,* 281, *281,* 288, *290*
  weeping standard 281
rot, brown *94*
  dry 92
  root 94
  soft 92
rotation of crops 15
rotivator 83
rowan 263, 433
rowanberries 117, 160
Rubus parvus 391
Rudbeckia 307, 310, 322, 324, 332
  fulgida 301, 310, 318
  'Goldsturm' 432
  'Gloriosa Daisy' 310
  hirta 335
  nitida 310, 311, 315
  purpurea *318*
rue 216
Rue, Meadow 409
Rush, Flowering 408
rusts 93, 95—6
Ruta graveolens 216

saffron 377
  meadow *367, 378,* 381, *385*
sage 214, 335
Sage, Scarlet 427
Sagittaria sagittifolia 407
Salix alba 'Tristis' *233*
Salvia farinacea 335
  horminorum 335
  officinalis 214
  splendens *298,* 427
Sand Flower 334
Sanguinaria 322
Sanguisorba tenuifolia 'Wiesenknopf' *316*
Santolina 318
Sanvitalia procumbens 336
Saponaria ocymoides 430
Satin Flower 333
Satureja hortensis 215
savory 215
Saxifraga 388
  grisebachii *388,* 391
  lilacina 391
  oppositifolia 296
saxifrage 378, 388, 391
Scabiosa 315
  atropurpurea 333
  caucasica 310
Scarlet Runner 339
Schizanthus Wisetonensis-hybrids 338
scilla 418
Scilla 388, 404
  hispanica *389*
  sibirica 360
  violacea 367
Scirpus 412
scion 79, 132
scorzonera 169, *199,* 200—1

Scorzonera hispanica 200
seaweed 68—9
sedge 231, 409
Sedum 231, 300, 304, 309, 311, 315, 388
  sieboldii 433
  spathulifolium 'Capa Blanca' *388*
  spectabile 311, 318, 324, 433
  'Brillant' *301, 315*
  'Carmen' 432
  spurium 'Album Superbum' 430
  telephium 311
  'Herbstfreude' *300*
seedlings 79, 121, 320
self-pollination 119
Sempervivum 300, 388
Senecio bicolor 341, *341*
service-berry 262
shallots 197
Silene pendula 336
  schafta 304, 381, *384*, 430
sitting-out areas *14,* 38—40, *38, 39, 48, 49,* 304, 309,
402, 419
Slipperwort 421
slugs and snails 99, 100, *101*
Smoke Tree 262, 420
Snapdragon 332, 336, 424
snow glory 388
snowball 388
snowbell 379
snowberry 262
snowdrop 360, 377, 388, 404, 418
snowflake 360, 379, 404, 418
snow-in-summer 231
Soapwort 430
soil, exhausted 62
  fatigue 62
  improving 313
  in its old strength 62
  pests 92, 97—9
  pH 61, 64—5, 284
Solanum melongena 192
  tuberosum 221
Soldanella 322, 379, 388, 391
  carpatica *382*
Solidago 307, 310, *310*
  virgaurea 'Perkeo' 432
Sorbus 433
  aucuparia 160
  domestica 160
sowing *73, 74,* 75—6, *76, 77, 78,* 169—70, 175, *175,*
264
  annuals 342—3
  lawn 227—8, *228*
  perennials 319—21
  vegetables 169—70, 174—5
Spartina 309
  pectinata 'Aureomarginata' 404
Speedwell 432, 433
Spider Plant 424
spiders, red 100, *102*
Spinacea oleracea 208
spinach *168,* 169, *207,* 208—9
Spinach, Mountain 341
  New Zealand 209
spindle tree 231
spiraea 249, 262, 263, 420
Spiraea × *bumalda* 260
  × *vanhouttei* 253
spleenwort 231
spruce *238,* 420
Spruce, Colorado 239, *240*
spruce, dwarf 309
Spruce, Norway 236, 256
  Serbian 236
  White 238—9
squill 360, 404
Stachys grandiflora 'Superba' 432
  lanata 299
  olympica 309, *312*
staking *80,* 122—3, 279
standards, half- *119,* 120—1
  quarter- *119,* 120—1
  tall *119,* 121
steps *46,* 47—9, *374*
St John's wort 248, 250, 253, 262, 420, 430
Stock 332—3, 335, 338, 342, 343
stocks 79, 120, 121, 132, 292
storing bulbs and tubers 104
  fruit 83, 104
  vegetables 83, 104, 177—8
strawberries *73, 97, 100,* 117, 119, 120, *120,* 121, *153,
154,* 154—7, *155, 156, 157*
Stratiotes aloides 410, 412
Stropharia rugosoannulata 223
stonecrop 231, 388, 430, 432
subsoiling 63
Sun Plant 335, 336, 427
Sunflower 332

439

Mexican 333
Sunray 333
swede 204
Sweet William 429
sweetcorn *219*, 219—21
Sweet-grass, Reed 403
Swertia 388
Switch Grass 340

Tagetes 333
  erecta 335, 340, 427
    'Clinton' *331*
  patula 332
    'Nana' 427
    'Ruffled Red' *338*
  tenuifolia 'Pumila' 427
Tamarix 420
tarragon 214
Taxus 420
  baccata 236, *260*
    'Compacta' 243
    'Fastigiata' 256
    'Fastigiata Aurea' 240
    'Repandens' *243*
  cuspidata 'Nana' 243
  media 'Hicksii' 256
terracing *28*, 75
Tetragonia expansa 209
Teucrium 318
Thalictrum 409
Thornapple 423
thrips 101
thuja 256
Thuja occidentalis 237
  'Columna' 256
  'Ellwangeriana Rheingold' 244
  'Holmstrup' 257
  'Little Gem' 244
  'Malonyana' 257
  'Recurva Nana' 244
  'Rheingold' 240
  'Viridis' 257
  orientalis 'Aurea Nana' 244
  plicata 'Zebrina' 257
thyme 214
Thyme, Wild 430
Thymus 295, 315, 355
  citriodorus 318
  serpyllum 311
    'Splendens' 430
  vulgaris 214
Tickseed 432
Tigridia 365
Tithonia rotundifolia 333, 335
toadflax 332
Tobacco Plant 340
tomato *80*, 171, *188, 189*, 188—91
  bush 191
  cordon *168*, 191
trace elements 65, 67, 71
Tradescantia 312, 409, 432
  × *andersoniana* 'Leonora' 432
    'Zwannenburg Blue' *313*
  virginiana 432
Treasure Flower 335, 425
trenching 63, 74
Trollius 305, *313*
  × *cultorum 304*
  hybridus 312
Tropaeolum 419

majus 332, *339*
Tsuga canadensis 243
Tulip, Waterlily *365*
Tulipa 357, 389
  biflora 365
  eichleri 351, 365
  kaufmanniana 365, *365, 366*
    'Maytime' *352*
  praestans 365
  tarda 365
  turkestanica 365
  urumiensis 365
tulips 91, 303, 306, 309, 310, *351, 352*, 355, 358, 360, 363, 365, 366, 418
  botanical 389
  Darwin *366*
  Rembrandt's 91
tunic flower 381
turfing 228, *230*
turnip 203
  swedish 204
tying 79
Typha minima 408
  latifolia 408, *409*

Ursinia anethoides 335, *342*

Vaccinium corymbosum 160—1, 253
  vitis-idaea 251
Valerianella locusta 207
Vallota 367
vegetables 83, 124, 161—222
Venidium fastuosum 333
  'Orange' *332*
Verbascum olympicum 311
  thapsus 311
Verbena 388
  bonariensis 332, 341
  canadensis 335
  erinoides 335, 340
  × *hybrida* 336, 427
Veronica 304
  austriaca 'Shirley Blue' 432
  prostrata 311
  spicata 'Blaubart' *301*
    'Romilex Purple' 433
  teucrium 312
Verticillium albo-atrum 94
Vervain 332, 336, 340, 388, 427
Verbena hybrida 427
viburnum 249, 262, 433
Viburnum burckwoodii 253
  carlcephalum 253
  farreri 247, 253
  fragrans 247
  opulus 'Roseum' *247*
Vicia faba var. *major* 211
Vinca 231, 404
  major 433
  minor 315
vine, Russian 255
vines 74, 157—9, 254
Viola 429
  cornuta 304
  tricolor var. *maxima* 429
  × *wittrockiana* 332, 429
  Violet, Dog's Tooth 360
Virginia Creeper 244, 254
Vitis 254

Wallflower 429
walls, constructing 39—40
  dry *37*, 304, 335—6, 338, 356, *372*, 374, *374, 375*, 402, 419
walnuts 117, 119, 120, 121, 122, 135, *145*, 145—6, 262
water 21, 43—7, *44, 61*, 71—4, 373, 407—12
  hardness 72
water-lilies 409—12, *412*
Water Plantain, Common 408
  Soldier 410, 412
watering *71, 72*
  annuals 73
  bulbs and tubers 363—4
  container-grown plants 416, 424
  fruit trees 73, 123
  heaths and heathers 73
  lawn *230*
  ornamental woody plants 264
  perennials 73, 316, 317, 320
  rock plants 380, 387, 389
  roses 286—7
  seedlings 78
  vegetables 73, 172
weed control 113, 115, 172, 173, 313, 317
weeds *47*, 113—5, *113, 114, 115*, 312—3
  annual spring 114
  annual winter 114
  perennial 114—5
weigela 262
Weigela florida 'Variegata' *249*
white flies *103*
  grubs 97—8, *99*
Willow, Weeping *233*
Windflower 381, 404, 405
winter protection of aquatic plants 411—2
  of bulbs and tubers 365—6
  of container-grown woody plants 423—4
  of perennials 318—9
  of rock plants 383—4, *385*, 389, 397
  of roses 287—91
wireworms 97—8, *99*
witch-hazel *245*, 262, 420
Witch-hazel, Chinese 246
  Japanese 246
wisteria 255
Wisteria 255, 420
woodruff 231
woody plants, ornamental 231, 233—65, 304, 399, 418, 419—20, 422—4
  for containers 420
Wulfenia 388

xerophytes 60

yew *243, 256, 259*, 420
Yew, Common 235, 240
  English 236, 256
Yucca 307
  filamentosa 311, *311*, 318

Zantedeschia 367
Zauschneria 382
Zea mays var. *saccharata* 219
zinnia 332, 333, *336*, 345
Zinnia 332, 427
  angustifolia 'Persian Carpet' *332*
Zinnia, Creeping 336
Zinnia elegans 336, 345, 427
  haageana 427

440